The Routledge Companion to Management and Organizational History

The field of management and organizational history has reached a level of maturity that means an overview is long overdue.

Written by a team of globally renowned scholars, this comprehensive companion analyses management and organizational history, reflecting on the most influential periods and highlighting gaps for future research. From the impact of the Cold War to global warming, it examines the field from a wide array of perspectives from the humanities to the social sciences.

Covering the entire spectrum of the field, this volume provides an essential resource for researchers of business and management.

Patricia Genoe McLaren is an Associate Professor in the School of Business & Economics, Wilfrid Laurier University, Ontario, Canada.

Albert J. Mills is Professor of Management at Saint Mary's University, Canada and co-chair of the International Board for Critical Management Studies.

Terrance G. Weatherbee is Professor of Management at Acadia University, Canada.

Routledge Companions in Business, Management and Accounting

Routledge Companions in Business, Management and Accounting are prestige reference works providing an overview of a whole subject area or sub-discipline. These books survey the state of the discipline including emerging and cutting edge areas. Providing a comprehensive, up to date, definitive work of reference, Routledge Companions can be cited as an authoritative source on the subject.

A key aspect of these Routledge Companions is their international scope and relevance. Edited by an array of highly regarded scholars, these volumes also benefit from teams of contributors which reflect an international range of perspectives.

Individually, Routledge Companions in Business, Management and Accounting provide an impactful one-stop-shop resource for each theme covered. Collectively, they represent a comprehensive learning and research resource for researchers, postgraduate students and practitioners.

Published titles in this series include:

The Routledge Companion to Fair Value and Financial Reporting
Edited by Peter Walton

The Routledge Companion to Nonprofit Marketing
Edited by Adrian Sargeant & Walter Wymer Jr

The Routledge Companion to Accounting History
Edited by John Richard Edwards, Stephen P. Walker

The Routledge Companion to Creativity
Edited by Tudor Rickards, Mark A. Runco, Susan Moger

The Routledge Companion to Strategic Human Resource Management
Edited by John Storey, Patrick M. Wright, David Ulrich

The Routledge Companion to International Business Coaching
Edited by Michel Moral, Geoffrey Abbott

The Routledge Companion to Organizational Change
Edited by David M. Boje, Bernard Burnes and John Hassard

The Routledge Companion to Cost Management
Edited by Falconer Mitchell, Hanne Nørreklit and Morten Jakobsen

The Routledge Companion to Digital Consumption
Edited by Russell W. Belk and Rosa Llamas

The Routledge Companion to Identity and Consumption
Edited by Ayalla A. Ruvio and Russell W. Belk

The Routledge Companion to Public-Private Partnerships
Edited by Piet de Vries and Etienne B. Yehoue

The Routledge Companion to Accounting, Reporting and Regulation
Edited by Carien van Mourik and Peter Walton

The Routledge Companion to International Management Education
Edited by Denise Tsang, Hamid H. Kazeroony and Guy Ellis

The Routledge Companion to Accounting Communication
Edited by Lisa Jack, Jane Davison and Russell Craig

The Routledge Companion to Visual Organization
Edited by Emma Bell, Jonathan Schroeder and Samantha Warren

The Routledge Companion to Arts Marketing
Edited by Daragh O'Reilly, Ruth Rentschler and Theresa Kirchner

The Routledge Companion to Alternative Organization
Edited by Martin Parker, George Cheney, Valerie Fournier and Chris Land

The Routledge Companion to the Future of Marketing
Edited by Luiz Moutinho, Enrique Bigne and Ajay K. Manrai

The Routledge Companion to Accounting Education
Edited by Richard M. S. Wilson

The Routledge Companion to Business in Africa
Edited by Sonny Nwankwo and Kevin Ibeh

The Routledge Companion to Human Resource Development
Edited by Rob F. Poell, Tonette S. Rocco and Gene L. Roth

The Routledge Companion to Auditing
Edited by David Hay, W. Robert Knechel and Marleen Willekens

The Routledge Companion to Entrepreneurship
Edited by Ted Baker and Friederike Welter

The Routledge Companion to International Human Resource Management
Edited by David G. Collings, Geoffrey T. Wood and Paula Caligiuri

The Routledge Companion to Financial Services Marketing
Edited by Tina Harrison and Hooman Estelami

The Routledge Companion to International Entrepreneurship
Edited by Stephanie A. Fernhaber and Shameen Prashantham

The Routledge Companion to Non-Market Strategy
Edited by Thomas C. Lawton and Tazeeb S. Rajwani

The Routledge Companion to Cross-Cultural Management
Edited by Nigel Holden, Snejina and Susanne Tietze

The Routledge Companion to Financial Accounting Theory
Edited by Stewart Jones

The Routledge Companion to Ethics, Politics and Organizations
Edited by Alison Pullen and Carl Rhodes

The Routledge Companion to Management and Organizational History
Edited by Patricia Genoe McLaren, Albert J. Mills and Terrance G. Weatherbee

This book provides a much-needed critique of how we do management history and why. It offers a wide variety of perspectives on the subject, critiques existing methodologies and stimulates much-needed debate about historical purpose and practice. Scholars will argue over some of the views presented here for years to come; and that is a very good thing.

Morgen Witzel, *Fellow, Centre for Leadership Studies, University of Exeter, UK and author of* A History of Management Thought

The editors and authors fulfilled a difficult task: tracing an arc on this topic to represent the ongoing process of thinking "history" in management and organization studies, as well as the intimate connection of history with thinking in our field altogether. An extraordinary collection and "must read" for anyone in management and organizational studies.

Marta B. Calás, *Professor, University of Massachusetts Amherst, USA*

This much-needed volume provides a critical foundation for the new historical turn in management research and scholarship. The authors have assembled a series of writers who provide both a substantive review of organizational theory through a historical lens but also provide a programmatic roadmap for the field.

Rakesh Khurana, *Professor, Harvard Business School, USA*

The Routledge Companion to Management and Organizational History

Edited by Patricia Genoe McLaren, Albert J. Mills, and Terrance G. Weatherbee

Routledge
Taylor & Francis Group
LONDON AND NEW YORK

First published 2015
by Routledge
2 Park Square, Milton Park, Abingdon, Oxon OX14 4RN

and by Routledge
52 Vanderbilt Avenue, New York, NY 10017

First issued in paperback 2020

Routledge is an imprint of the Taylor & Francis Group, an informa business

British Library Cataloguing in Publication Data
A catalogue record for this book is available from the British Library

Library of Congress Cataloguing in Publication data
The Routledge companion to management and organizational history / edited by Patricia Genoe McLaren, Albert J. Mills, and Terrance G. Weatherbee.
pages cm. – (Routledge companions in business, management and accounting)
Includes bibliographical references and index.
1. Management–History. 2. Organizational behavior–History. I. McLaren, Patricia Genoe. II. Mills, Albert J., III. Weatherbee, Terrance G.
HD30.5.R683 2015
658–dc23
2014045587

ISBN 13: 978-0-367-65630-0 (pbk)
ISBN 13: 978-0-415-82371-5 (hbk)

Typeset in Bembo
by Out of House Publishing

To Murray Genoe, from whom I clearly inherited my fascination with both history and academia. In the early days of my history work you kept asking "but what about Canada?" Chapter 22 is for you Dad.

Patricia Genoe McLaren

To Deans David Wicks and Patricia Bradshaw, whose support and nurturing of the Sobey PhD (Management) has helped to make it history.

Albert J. Mills

To my Mother and Father, Fred and Yvonne Weatherbee, who in living their lives have always reminded me you are never too old or too busy to learn something new.

Terrance G. Weatherbee

Contents

Figures

Tables

Editors and contributors

Patricia Genoe McLaren is an Associate Professor and Area Coordinator of the Business Technology Management Program in the School of Business & Economics at Wilfrid Laurier University, Ontario, Canada. Her work focuses on the development of management theory and education, management theory in Canada, and technology and innovation in Canada, using critical hermeneutic analysis and critical discourse analysis. Patricia is a co-investigator on an SSHRC funded project focused on *Reassembling Canadian Management Knowledge* with a special interest in dispersion, equity, identity, and history, and is a founding member of the Sociology of Management Knowledge Network (sociologyofmanagementknowledge.com).

Albert J. Mills is Professor of Management and Director of the PhD program at the Sobey School of Business, Saint Mary's University, Canada. He is the author of 35 books and edited collections, including *ANTi-History: Theorizing the Past, History, and Historiography in Management and Organization Studies* (with G. Durepos), *Absent Aviators: Gender Issues in Aviation* (with D. Bridges and J. Neal-Smith), and the forthcoming *Oxford Handbook of Diversity in Organizations* (with R. Bendl, I. Bleijenbergh, and I. Henttonen) and *The Routledge Companion to Critical Management Studies* (with A. & P. Prasad and J. Helms Mills). He currently serves as an Associate Editor of *Organization*; *Qualitative Research in Organizations and Management*; *Gender, Work & Organization*; and the *International Journal of Work Innovation*. He is also on the editorial board *Management & Organizational History* and several other journals.

Terrance G. Weatherbee is Professor of Management in the F.C. Manning School of Business at Acadia University. The university is located in Wolfville, a small town in the Annapolis Valley region of Nova Scotia on the east coast of Canada. In geographic terms he is quite content as it is a very safe and pleasant place to raise his two young sons and because in between classes the campus affords him an excellent view of the bay. His research interest finds itself presently encamped at the intersection of management and organization studies and history. It is here where he is investigating the historiographic dimensions of the evolution of management thought and theory. His current focus is centered on investigating the processes, historical and otherwise, which influence how disciplinary histories are written and the relationship these have with the disciplinary canon as located in journals, texts, and textbooks.

David M. Boje is Professor and past Bill Daniels Ethics Fellow, a past endowed Bank of America Professor of Management, and present endowed Wells Fargo Professor of Management at New Mexico State University (NMSU) in Las Cruces. He has published over 200 journal articles and book chapters, and over 20 books. He has over 8,000 citations in Google scholar and over 4,000 citations since 2009. He is known for his 1991 *Administrative Science Quarterly* and 1995 *Academy* *of Management Journal* articles on the 'storytelling organization'. He is also founder of the *Tamara Journal for Critical Organization Inquiry*.

Charles Booth is Associate Professor at Bristol Business School, University of the West of England. He is one of the founding editors of the journal *Management & Organizational History*.

Shawn Carraher (PhD) is Oxford Journal Distinguished Research Professor and Visiting Clinical Professor at the University of Texas at Dallas where he serves as the coordinator for International Business. He has his PhD from the University of Oklahoma and studied Management History from Daniel A. Wren. He is the editor of the *Journal of Management*, the *Journal of Technology Management in China*, the *Academy of Strategic Management Journal*, the *Academy of Health Care Management*, the *International Journal of Family Business*, and the *Cambridge Case Studies Journal*. He is a past Division Chair of the Management History Division of the Academy of Management as well as the Technology & Innovation Management Division and past President of the South West Academy of Management and the Small Business Institute. He has also served as a board member for the Southern Management Association, the MidWest Academy of Management, the Careers Division of the Academy of Management, and six divisions of the US Association for Small Business & Entrepreneurship.

Stewart Clegg has had a career that started in Yorkshire but, apart from a short sojourn in Scotland in the early 1990s, has been spent mostly in Australia from where he now travels frequently to Europe, where he is a Visiting Professor at EMLYON, France; Nova School of Business and Economics in Lisbon, Portugal; and Strategic Research Advisor, Newcastle University Business School in the UK. Widely acknowledged as one of the most significant contemporary theorists of power relations he is also one of the most influential contributors to organization studies, in which his theoretical interests in power connect with many substantive issues, recently ranging across food, gossip, teams, death camps, bullying, suicide, the collapse of the Soviet Communist Party, and Frank Ghery's model making, amongst many other topics. He has published a great deal about many things, given the ubiquity of power relations, his particular interest.

Kristene E. Coller is a PhD candidate at the Sobey School of Business (Saint Mary's University) currently studying the neglect of Canadian management thought. In addition to pursuing a PhD at Saint Mary's University, she has been a lecturer for the University of Lethbridge at the Calgary, Alberta campus over the past five years. In addition to research interests in management history, she has also written on topics including health care, workplace health promotion, and the impostor syndrome.

Diego M. Coraiola is Professor of Management and Organizations at Positivo University, Brazil. He has done research on institutional change and organizational practices. His current research is focused on issues of collective memory, rhetorical history, and symbolism in organizations.

Stephanie Decker is Professor of Organization Studies and History at Aston Business School, UK. As a historian working at a business school, most of her work is concerned with the relation between organization theory and history. She is co-editor of *Business History*, the recipient of the Leverhulme Trust Research Fellowship 2014–15, and the principal organizer of a seminar series on organizational history funded by the Economic and Social Science Research Council (UK). Her most recent publication was 'Research Strategies for Organizational History' (*Academy of Management Review*, 2014, co-authored with Michael Rowlinson and John Hassard).

Gabrielle Durepos is an assistant professor at Mount Saint Vincent University in Halifax, Canada. Her co-authored book, *ANTi-History: Theorizing the Past, History, and Historiography in Management and Organization Studies*, seeks to address the call for an historic turn. She is a co-editor of both the *SAGE Encyclopaedia of Case Study Research,* as well as the *SAGE Major Work on Case Study Methods in Business Research.* Her recent publications appear in *Management & Organizational History, Journal of Management History, Critical Perspectives on International Business,* and *Organization.* She is a co-investigator on an SSHRC funded project focused on *Reassembling Canadian Management Knowledge* with a special interest in dispersion, equity, identity, and history. She is the past-president of the Atlantic Schools of Business Conference as well as the newsletter editor of the Critical Management Studies Division of the Academy of Management. She is currently engaged in an organizational history of a provincial museum complex in Canada.

Alex Faria obtained his doctorate in Business Administration from the University of Warwick. He is Associate Professor at the Brazilian School of Public and Business Administration, Getulio Vargas Foundation (EBAPE/FGV), Rio de Janeiro and a Researcher of the National Research Council in Brazil (CNPq). He chairs the Strategy & Marketing Research Group at EBAPE/FGV and has contributed in the fields of strategy, marketing, and international management as well as critical studies in management in Brazil and abroad.

Jason Foster is Academic Coordinator, Industrial Relations at Athabasca University in Alberta, Canada. His research interests include critical re-examinations of management and organizational history and the history of management education in North America. Other, more contemporary, areas of interest include migrant workers and union revitalization in the twenty-first century. His recent publications include numerous articles examining the Temporary Foreign Work Program, Canada's migrant labor program.

William M. Foster (PhD, University of Alberta) is an associate professor of Management at the Augustana Campus of the University of Alberta. His research interests include rhetorical history, social memory studies, and business ethics. His current research interests focus on the individual and how history and social memory contribute to the construction and change of personal subjectivity.

Ana Guedes obtained her doctorate in International Relations from the London School of Economics and Political Science, UK. She was Associate Professor at the Brazilian School of Public and Business Administration, Getulio Vargas Foundation (EBAPE/FGV), and former editor of Cadernos EBAPE.BR. Researcher of the National Research Council in Brazil (CNPq), she chairs the International Studies in Administration Research Group at PPGA/UNIGRANRIO and has published in the fields of international political economy, international business, and international management.

Jean Helms Mills is a professor of Management at the Sobey School of Business, Saint Mary's University, Canada. She is an associate editor of *Gender, Work and Organization* and serves on the editorial boards of several other journals. Her books include *Making Sense of Organizational Change* (Routledge, 2003), *Understanding Organizational Change* (Routledge, 2009), and the forthcoming *Routledge Companion to Critical Management Studies.*

Eduardo Ibarra-Colado was, at the time of his death, Professor at the Autonomous Metropolitan University (Cuajimalpa Campus). He will no doubt be most fondly remembered for his strident yet sparkling works of critique that tackled the neoliberal university and the epistemic domination of 'the rest' by North Atlantic theories of organization. Compelling and forthright in print, Eduardo was, in person, a man of compassion and warmth as well as being active in the organizational politics of his own institution. He was a contributing author and associate editor of *Organization*, contributed to the development of LAEMOS and, over the years, to the Critical Management Studies Community through both the CMS division at the Academy of Management and at Critical Management Studies Conferences. Above all he was in the full sense of the term *a scholar*: a man of tremendous learning, whose writing forms a unique archive in its own right, but whose political sensitivities were always with the lives of people.

Roy Jacques is an independent management theorist, teacher, coach, consultant, and former small business owner presently living in Phoenix, Arizona. He has taught at several American and New Zealand universities, most recently as Professor of Management and Business Strategy at Massey University, Auckland, New Zealand. His graduate degrees are from the University of Massachusetts, Amherst. He is a founding co-editor of the journal *Management & Organization Studies*. His widely-cited study of the origins of management practices, *Manufacturing the Employee: Management knowledge from the 19th to 21st centuries* (1996), has been pointed to as one of the artifacts signaling the so-called 'historic turn' in organization studies. This interest in the construction of identity has also led Dr Jacques to do considerable work on the construction of gender and dominance/marginality in general. He is a past Chair of the Gender & Diversity Division of the Academy of Management.

J. Logan Jones is a doctoral candidate from the University of Mississippi. He has an MBA from Arkansas State University. His research interests lie in the areas of management history, organizational behavior, and human resource management. He is an active member of several management organizations such as the Academy of Management and Southern Management Association. Professionally, he has worked in law enforcement as a police officer and is a veteran of the United States Army. In his personal life, his hobbies include reading, food, and spending time with his wife and family.

Alfred Kieser is Professor Emeritus of Organizational Behavior at Mannheim University, Germany. His present position is Professor of Management Theory and Vice President Research at Zeppelin University, Friedrichshafen, Germany. His research interests include the history of organization, organizational evolution, cross-cultural comparisons of organizations, management fashions, consulting, rigor vs. relevance, and organizational learning. He has published in *Administration Science Quarterly*, *Journal of Management Inquiry*, *Organization Science*, *Journal of Management Studies*, *Organization Studies*, *Organization*, and in German journals. He has published two textbooks on organization theory (in German), one is now in its 7th edition, the other in its 6th. He received honorary doctoral degrees from the Ludwig Maximilians University of Munich and from Corvinus University, Budapest, and is a member of the Heidelberg Academy of Sciences.

Matthias Kipping is Professor of Policy and Chair in Business History at the Schulich School of Business of York University in Toronto, Canada. He has degrees from the Sorbonne in Paris as well as Harvard's John F. Kennedy School of Government and a doctorate from the University of Munich in Germany. He held previous appointments at the University of Reading in the UK and Universitat Pompeu Fabra in Barcelona. His main research interest has been the international dissemination of management ideas and fashions, with a particular focus on the role of management consultants and management education. He has published widely on these topics in business history as well as management journals and edited volumes. He edited (together with Timothy Clark) *The Oxford Handbook of Management Consulting* and is currently finalizing a manuscript (with Lars Engwall and Behlül Üsdiken) entitled *Authorities on Management: Business Schools, Consultants, Media*. His most recent project studies the worldwide transformation of the financial services sector by management consultants since the 1960s.

Corinne McNally is a PhD candidate at the Sobey School of Business at Saint Mary's University in Halifax, Nova Scotia. In addition to Canadian management thought, her research interests include leadership in groups and teams and employee well-being.

Richard Marens is a professor of Management at the California State University, Sacramento. He earned both a JD and a PhD from the University of Washington and has published in a number of management and ethics journals as well as chapters in books. His research interests include: the emergence of labor unions as financial activists, employee ownership, the evolution of the construct of Corporate Social Responsibility within the context of American social and economic history, and the rise and decline of middle management.

Ali Mir is a professor of Management at William Paterson University. He has published on a range of topics including the changing nature of work in late capitalism, the international division of labor, knowledge transfer, postcolonialsm, secularism, radical poetry, and Indian cinema.

Raza Mir is a professor of Management in the College of Business at William Paterson University. His research mainly focuses on the transfer of knowledge across national boundaries in multinational corporations, and issues relating to power and resistance in organizations. He currently serves as the Chair of the Critical Management Studies Division of the Academy of Management.

Alun Munslow is Visiting Research Professor at St Mary's University, Twickenham, London, UK, Professor of History and Historical Theory at the University of Chichester, UK, and Emeritus Professor of History and Historical Theory, Staffordshire University, Stoke-on-Trent, UK. He is the author of *Discourse and Culture: The Creation of America, 1870–1920* (1992), *Our American Cousins: Henry Demarest Lloyd's Critiques of American Capitalism, 1881–1903* (1992), *Deconstructing History* (1997), *The Routledge Companion to Historical Studies* (2000), *The Nature of History Reader* (with Keith Jenkins) (2004), *Experiments in Rethinking History* (with Robert A. Rosenstone) (2004), *The New History* (2005), *Narrative and History* (2007), *Manifestos for Historians* (with Keith Jenkins and Sue Morgan) (2007), *The Future of History* (2010), *A History of History* (2012), and *Authoring the Past* (2012). He is (with Robert A. Rosenstone) the Founding and UK Editor of *Rethinking History: The Journal of Theory and Practice*.

Milorad M. Novecivic (PhD, University of Oklahoma) is an associate professor of Management at the University of Mississippi and the Past Chair of the Management History division of the Academy of Management. His research focuses on management history, management education, and international management. He has published more than 100 articles in various peer-reviewed journals including the *Leadership Quarterly*, *Organizational Behavior and Human Decision Processes*, *Academy of Management Learning and Education*, *Journal of Management History*, *Management & Organizational History*, *Human Resource Management*, *Journal of World Business*, *Business Horizons*, *Organizational Dynamics*, *Business Ethics: A European Review*, *Journal of Business Ethics*, *International Journal of Human Resource Management*, *Human Resource Management Review*, and *Journal of Vocational Behavior*.

Tuomo Peltonen is Professor of Management and Organization at Turku School of Economics, University of Turku, Finland. He received his PhD from Helsinki School of Economics. His research interests include philosophy, methodology and history of organizational behavior, as well as the study of internationalization, the societal role of business schools, organizational architecture, and workplace spirituality. He has edited a special issue of *Academy of Management Review* on critical approaches to international management and published several articles and book chapters in outlets such as *Higher Education, Ethnography, International Journal of Work Organisation and Emotion*, and *Journal of Organizational Change Management*. Dr Peltonen is currently on the Editorial Board of *the International Journal of Human Resource Management*.

Adam Rostis obtained his PhD from Saint Mary's University in Halifax, Nova Scotia. His management research interests include humanitarianism, genealogy, critical management, organizational behavior, disaster and crisis in organizations, and how individuals and organizations perceive, construct, utilize, interpret, and remember these concepts. His doctoral research involved the development of a genealogy of humanitarianism through a critical historical examination of the Red Cross and Doctors Without Borders. His work has been informed by his time as a delegate for the International Red Cross in Zimbabwe and as Senior Policy Advisor for the Government of Nova Scotia's Emergency Management Office. Over the long term, he hopes to develop a critical mass of researchers with similar interests while maintaining a connection with those who experience disaster and crisis in government, communities, and business. He is currently completing his MD at Dalhousie University in Halifax, Nova Scotia.

Michael Rowlinson is Professor of Management and Organizational History in the School of Business and Management, Queen Mary University of London. He has published widely on the relationship between history and organization theory in journals such as the *Academy of Management Review, Business History, Human Relations, Organization*, and *Organization Studies*. His research on corporate history concerns the representation of history by organizations, especially the dark side of their involvement in war, slavery, and racism. This has been published in journals such as *Critical Perspectives on Accounting, Journal of Organizational Change Management*, and *Labour History Review*. His current interests include the methodology of interpretive historical research in organization studies. He edited the journal *Management & Organizational History* from 2008 to 2013 and is now a Senior Editor for *Organization Studies* and a co-editor for the Special Topic Forum of the *Academy of Management Review* on 'History and Organization Theory'.

Rohny Saylors holds a PhD from New Mexico State University. He has been published in the journal *Organizational Research Methods*. His passion is the advancement of human creativity, hope, and authentic compassion through, and within, organizational scholarship. His research is focused on entrepreneurial storytelling processes and methods.

Bert Spector is an associate professor of International Business and Strategy at Northeastern University's D'Amore-McKim School of Business in Boston. He is a frequent contributor to *Management & Organizational History* and has also published articles on management history in *Enterprise and Society, Leadership*, and the *Journal of Management History*. He is currently completing a manuscript, *Leadership: Discourse and Meaning*, scheduled for a 2015 publication by Cambridge University Press.

Nidhi Srinivas obtained his doctorate in strategic management at McGill University in Montreal, Canada. He is an associate professor of nonprofit management at the New School in New York City. His research centers on critical theory and is concerned with generating a reflective and emancipatory praxis within and around organizations. He has published on 'indigenous' theories of management, the professional projects of management, and managerialism within civil society.

Roy Suddaby is the Winspear Chair of Management at the Peter B. Gustavson School of Business, University of Victoria, Canada. He is the outgoing editor of *Academy of Management Review*. His research focuses on profound change in organizations and society.

Scott Taylor is Reader in Leadership and Organization Studies at University of Birmingham in the English Midlands. He teaches leadership development and organizational behaviour there, and has recently been working on a co-edited leadership studies textbook with Brigid Carroll and Jackie Ford (Sage, 2015). His research is always qualitative and interpretive, often focuses on issues relating to the meaning of work, and has been published in a range of journals and edited collections. He has written about historical methodologies in *Management & Organizational History* and is currently analysing a mixture of archival and life history interview data about the marriage bar. In 2012 he was elected with Emma Bell to the Academy of Management Critical Management Studies division executive.

Amy Thurlow is an associate professor at Mount Saint Vincent University in Halifax, Canada where she teaches public relations and communication in the Department of Communication Studies. Her recent publications appear in *Qualitative Research in Organizations and Management*, *The Scandinavian Journal of Management*, *Journal of Change Management*, and the *Canadian Journal of Communication*. She is a co-investigator on an SSHRC funded project focused on *Reassembling Canadian Management Knowledge* with a special interest in dispersion, equity, identity, and history. She is a member of the National Education Council of the Canadian Public Relations Society and the International Commission on Public Relations Education.

Behlül Üsdiken is Professor of Management and Organization at Sabanci University, Istanbul, Turkey; previously, he was a professor at Bogazici University. He has contributed to numerous journals as well as a variety of edited collections. He has served as a co-editor of *Organization Studies* from 1996 to 2001 and a section editor of the *Journal of Management Inquiry* from 2007 to 2012. His current research focuses upon the role of history in organization studies, management education, and universities.

Acknowledgements

We gratefully acknowledge the commitment of all of our contributors to building this wonderful volume of work. We know that each of you took time out of your busy schedules to support the field of management and organizational history, and we are thrilled with the result. We'd also like to thank Sinead Waldron and Terry Clague at Routledge: Terry for coming to us with the idea in the first place, and Sinead for her support in getting us through the process.

Acknowledgement is given for permission to use the following copyright material from other sources:

Charles Booth and Michael Rowlinson, Management and organizational history: Prospects, *Management & Organizational History*, 1(1): 5–30, copyright © 2006 Taylor & Francis Ltd, all rights reserved. See www.tandfonline.com.

Eduardo Ibarra-Colado, Is there any future for critical management studies in Latin America? Moving from epistemic coloniality to 'trans-discipline', *Organization*, 15(6): 932–35, copyright © 2008. Reprinted by permission of SAGE.

Alfred Kieser, Why organization theory needs historical analyses – and how this should be performed, *Organization Science*, 5(4): 608–20, copyright © 1994 INFORMS. Reproduced with permission, http://www.informs.org.

Trish, Albert and Terry

Part I

The historic turn in management and organization studies: critical responses

1

Introduction

The historic turn in management and organizational studies: a companion reading

Terrance G. Weatherbee, Patricia Genoe McLaren, and Albert J. Mills

Whether the beginning of the 'historic turn' in management and organizational studies (MOS) is marked at 1994 (Kieser, 1994), 2004 (Clark & Rowlinson, 2004), or earlier (Zald, 1993) is more a matter of choice in the tropics of narrative emplotment (White, 1985, 1987) than any signal of the primacy of a particular event. However, the benefit of two decades of hindsight does permit us to say – and without worry of compromise – that in the intervening period we have seen a veritable explosion of interest in history-work undertaken in MOS. Engagements with history in MOS have since spread from few to many, from the margins to the mainstream and back again, and are now established throughout a wide range of conference activities and journals, and in a growing number of texts. All of this work stems from, and is constitutive of, a deep richness to be found in the debates surrounding the various approaches used to interrogate where and how history is to be used (or not) for the study of organizations (Rowlinson, Stager Jacques & Booth, 2009; Weatherbee *et al.*, 2012). From our own position within the turn we now assess this sub-field as having matured sufficiently to warrant a survey of its state. Our survey is designed to provide management scholars and students an opportunity to familiarize themselves with the leading-edge and emergent thinking of scholars working within the turn as they engage in discussion and debate which collectively focuses on the problems, challenges, and potentials associated with doing history-work in MOS.

While we are collectively embedded within the varied interests and efforts comprising the historic turn, the story of this particular project starts with one of us. In 2012 Routledge decided that it was time for a *Routledge Companion to Management and Organizational History*. Our editor contacted Patricia Genoe McLaren and invited her to edit the companion. Trish immediately contacted Albert (Mills), who jumped at the opportunity to be involved, and Albert recommended bringing Terrance (Weatherbee) on board as well. Albert quickly drafted the first version of the proposal for this volume he had been thinking about for years, and after input from Trish and Terry the proposal was sent to Routledge, where it was quickly accepted. With the publisher having successfully enrolled the editors, it became time to put into practice what we had been preaching to ourselves in the proposal.

In order to publish a quality work that would capture our belief in the importance of history to MOS and engage a broad and diverse group of scholars, our small network needed to grow substantially. We needed scholars whose work in MOS is emblematic of the 'historic turn' and whose thinking could further inform us as to the many potentials to be found across the wide span of approaches to theory, methods, and purposes for doing history-work. Fortunately, each of us knew several like-minded researchers, some personally and others only by their scholarly reputation, whom we hoped would be interested enough in the project that they would be willing to commit the time and effort to work with us and create this companion.

As in all complex endeavours some of these efforts at enrolment into the project were successful on the first attempt, some on the second, and some not at all. However, between the merits of the idea and the persistence of our appeals – and with due accord given to the roles and effects of contingency, happenstance, and the odd dose of luck (of both kinds) – over the span of a year the network took shape. While its formation was to wax and wane through a series of welcome 'yes's' and regretfully accepted and usually apologetic 'no's', we endeavoured to remain true to our original aims. We envisioned our text as a somewhat authoritative reference that would be considered relevant to a wide audience across a number of overlapping academic areas (e.g. general management, organizational behaviour, organizational theory, organizational communication, international management, sociology of organizations, and the sociology of work, as well as business history, historiography, and business research methods). Our companion would be inclusive of multiple paradigmatic perspectives representative of the wealth of effort(s) taken and under way in the area (e.g. positivist, Marxist, postructuralist postcolonial, etc.), reflecting the widest set of scholarly geographies possible (east, west, north, and south), and possessing a variety of ends, ways, and means in the doing of history-work (theoretical, methodological, historiographic).

While *we* believe that we have been faithful to our intent and remain hopeful that readers will agree with us, we also know that the true utility and value of the companion can only be found in its use. Value is located in the relationships to be established between the reader and the works of the individual contributors. Value is located within the interstitial spaces created by the act of assemblage of such a diverse array of work. Value is to be found in the questions raised and the reflexivity invoked in the space between each reader's historiographic position and those of each contribution or the collection as a whole. So rather than engaging in obligatory convention for texts of this form – that is, a summary introduction of the chapters or sections accompanied by an appropriately sagacious and instructive detailing of how the various contributions interrelate to form a coherent whole – we thought it would be of more interest to briefly present some of our own thoughts and reactions (surprises, lessons learned, reminders, etc.) to our reading(s).

In the first contribution we see a unique blend of citation analysis and biography, sourced through both academic (journal articles) and personal accounts (letters) as method. Milorad M. Novicevic, J. Logan Jones, and Shawn Carraher provide us with an intellectual portrait of Daniel Wren and his signature work *The Evolution of Management Thought* (Wren, 1972; Wren & Bedeian, 2009). While they rightfully acknowledge Wren's role as one of the first progenitors of a canonical history of MOS and showcase the significant contribution he has made, through their decentring they also reveal to us how orthodox representations of the past may constrain our efforts to understand our discipline and the management and organizational phenomenon. We see their post-foundational surfacing of the construction of the disciplinary frames used in the dominant canonical history creating a space to displace the orthodox and the freedom to revise our history under different terms.

A canonical text of a different kind is the 1994 *Organizational Science* piece by Alfred Kieser that we have reprinted as a testament to our belief in its value – namely its oft-cited call for the launch of the historic turn in MOS and its contribution to the growth of management and organizational history (MOH) as a field. To that end, it is an understatement to say that we were surprised by the retrospective that he contributed to this edited collection. In our reading of Kieser's retrospective we are vaguely reminded (albeit for very different reasons) of the work of historian Keith Jenkins who began by 're-thinking history' (1991) and ended by 'rejecting history' (Jenkins, 2009). Kieser presents not so much a walking away from history as a somewhat ironic lament on the evolving homogeny of explanation in organizational theorizing. The lament comes at the beginning, where he states, "a historical turn is still not identifiable [in organization theory] and likely never will." He goes on to suggest that perhaps his call for a historical turn was "naïve". While this may be read as a rejection of his earlier call for a historic turn in MOS, it seems to us that there is an underlying disappointment in the direction that MOS has taken that makes its scholars less likely to be attracted to (or enrolled by) the need for historical analyses. That, at least, is our translation. Other readers may take something else away. That is always the issue of textual analysis.

The second reprinted article – by Charles Booth and Michael Rowlinson (2006) – is, metaphorically as well as literally, our reproduction of another work that has been widely cited as canonical in the field of MOH (see the many chapters throughout this collection that cite it). If there are any surprises here it is that (a) it continues to be cited as a critical starting point for a renewed call for the historical turn – despite the fact that in an earlier article Peter Clark and Mick Rowlinson (2004) made a much more explicit call – and (b) the call for greater methodological and philosophical debates inadvertently served to freeze debates around what Clark and Rowlinson had earlier problematized as a 'historic turn'.

Mick undertakes a personal reflection in relation to the way the historic turn unfolded. It is one that emotively resonates with us and his accounting of the circumstances by which the title of the article he co-authored with Peter Clarke (2004) became constructed strikes us an instructive in several ways. The use of his(own)story emphasizes for us the importance of the humanness of knowledge of the past and of the process nature of the interactions that lead to its co-creation. It sensitizes us to the networked nature of knowledge work and disciplinary projects comprised of authors, editors, and reviewers. In an academic world wracked by the pressures of publishing, author order, and evaluation exercises, this is sometimes easy to forget, as quite often in our individual life projects we forget that ours is a collective discipline rather than an individual one. Mick's recounting also highlights the oftentimes contingent nature of this process, revealing a case of the power of words. Power that was located in what was the right phrase at the right time, that is, the 'historic turn' – an ironic expression that became a symbolic rallying cry (a claim which is easily substantiated with citations).

Richard Marens' somewhat subdued polemic on how Marx and the intellectual corpus derived from his work has been marginalized, written out, and largely ignored by business and management scholars served us with notice that there are many differences between the approaches to the construction of history. These differences have historicity, arising as they do from the practices underwritten by politics, ideology, and geography over time. We find it ironic, as does he, that while the Marxian traditions have extensively informed the discipline of history, they have failed to do so for MOS. We agree that this is an unusual circumstance given that the large body of work on business and capitalism from a Marxian perspective represents a wealth of knowledge that we have eschewed for political rather than empirical reasons.

We read Roy Jacques and Gabrielle Durepos' review of textbook histories and the emplotment used by textbook authors as a clarion call that there is still much to be accomplished within the overall arc of the historic turn. The simplistic narratives of the historical orthodoxies found in chapter 2 (when there is one!) of our general and introductory texts are counted as failures in both historical and pedagogical terms. In historical terms they are so partial in their construction that they collapse into bowdlerized stories of the past that have little to no educational purpose.

This is a point Terrance Weatherbee also takes up in his chapter where he argues that simply adding in or transforming the form(s) of history in textbooks, though necessary, is insufficient if we wish to rid ourselves of the pedagogical history deficit. The work of all three –Jacques & Durepos and Weatherbee – reminds us that much of our pedagogical responsibility suffers from being ahistorical. Despite over a decade and a half of collective observations we still cannot seem to get it right in our teaching. The intersection of history and management pedagogy as pointed out almost a decade ago (Stager Jacques, 2006) seems to us to be rich with still untapped potential. Perhaps there is something in Alfred Kieser's lament after all!

Alun Munslow's observation that we all use and construct histories in our day-to-day practices stresses for us that our sense of the past is constructed in many ways – in speech, in writing, and in our use of other sense-making tools such as spreadsheets and PowerPoint slides. His perspicacious view reveals for us that it is history, rather than the past, which inheres strongly with our lived experiences. The relationship between organizing, business, and the past is an intimate one actively expressed in history-work. This reminds us that those working in organizations reconstruct history anew each day and that the continuity of action seen within them is a constructed one – a sense of pastness constructed on the basis of interpretation and meaning when articulated as histories (not the past!).

Scott Taylor exposed for us how hermeneutic approaches have moved far beyond their truth-in-text purposes and now represent a neglected method of interpretation of the past. He positions critical hermeneutics as an approach and method that, while underutilized, has significant potential for understanding the creation of historical narratives in the present. Given the textual nature of much of history in MOS (not to discount text in the broader sense, but used here in the sense of the textual presentation of history in journals and books), his observations draw our attention to different ways of seeing the textual and understanding its production.

Gabrielle Durepos' project, while still nascent, we see as being ripe with fruitful potential. She maps a way out of the divisive and intellectually sticky trap represented by the modern–postmodern duality that has consumed much effort in MOS over the last decades. Her explication of the dynamics of each of these positions with regard to history not only serves as a map of the intellectual terrain for each, but it provides a peek over the horizon of the possible. We are intellectually attracted to a way of seeing history as process, practice, and enactment, and her carefully constructed notions of 'amodern' historical approaches resolve to some extent the tensions we see in the either/or nature of singular and relational or unitary and relative. We can see openings for investigating and understanding how we can approach the historical as co-participants in the history we produce.

Somewhat shockingly, and wholly naively for us, Adam Rostis' powerful argument for a second look at humanitarianism has overturned our taken-for-granted conceptualizations of what we see as the 'good' in the humanitarian impulse. His use of Foucauldian genealogy uncovers the logics and orderings of organized humanitarianism and positions them as a colonizing discourse, a discourse which privileges a managerial ethos of efficiency and which treats the individual in economic terms. Humanitarianism has now become for us a history-laden and potentially repressive instrument that, when engaged in the recovery from hazard and disaster in failed/failing states, operates in the absence of countervailing factors. So when working in concert with private enterprise, humanitarianism can privilege the economic under the guise of doing good. It has, for us, radically signalled the need for expanding our attention to the intersection of history and organizing beyond simply the economic affairs of just business.

David Boje and Rohny Saylors have rewritten the story of the end of history. Their chapter crafts for us another potential ending – an ending heralded by the destruction of humanity. A self-imposed ending and concluding narrative brought about through the actions of the capitalist project(s) writ in its largest sense. A project that has become so vast in its longue durée that it may yet lay waste to our planet as it has made humanity a, if not the, dominant geologic force upon it. Theirs is a manifesto which we see as urging us to move beyond the modern and into a posthumanist historical space. A reminder that we can rewrite and recraft histories that do not artificially separate out human-centred histories from non-human-centred ones and which can refocus our attention upon our own selves living in an historically based world.

Diego M. Coraiola, William M. Foster, and Roy Suddaby resituate for us the critique of an ahistorical MOS. Drawing upon the work of Alun Munslow they investigate and categorize the approach to history in their analysis of the work of New Institutional scholars. Their study reveals that reconstructionist and constructionist approaches to historical understanding dominate that work and that rather than ignoring history, history is very much present. However, they also observe that this use of history is neither acknowledged nor problematized, nor is the relationship between the past and history questioned. They reinforce that MOS is *a*historical and not *un*historical, a lesson which informs us that we must be cognizant that our own theoretical and methodological choices commit us to a particular worldview and our disciplinary work is also a form of history-work (Weatherbee & Durepos, 2010).

While we saw Boje and Saylor's work as vast in both scale and scope, Stephanie Decker shows us that the 'small' is just as important in history-work as well. She reveals how microhistorians and those engaged in institutional perspectives often interrogate the same subjects – just from different scales. Consequently, her call for a more historiographic turn rather than a historic turn reminds us that there are many intellectual and methodological resources available to us in the discipline of history, an untapped stock of insight for doing history-work in MOS.

Tuomo Peltonen has abruptly shifted our own understanding of a canonical figure in MOS. Similar to the decentring of Wren's work by Novicevic, Jones, and Carraher, Peltonen has succeeded in changing how we now interpret the contributions of Elton Mayo as Peltonen's work both displaces and renews Mayo and his contributions in historical terms. This draws our attention to the tripartite dangers of unitary historical representations: histories which portray persons as one-dimensional in historiographic terms, that are essentialist in their treatments of persons, and which write-out the effects of the socio-political upon ourselves as scholars in the world (Cooke, 1999).

Using Fordism as their analytic framework, Ali Mir and Raza Mir reinforce for us the benefits of taking a longer historical view of management as practice. Their highlighting of the historically cyclical nature of managerial practices within the broader domain of the evolution of capitalism surfaces the strains experienced by management practices when engaged in the perennial search for solutions. It suggests to us that the dynamism of management and organizations may be the result of unreflexive practices passed on from one 'generation' of management to the next. For us this signals the trap of reading capitalism as a homogeneous economic form and managerial practice as tradition.

In a similar vein, Albert J. Mills, Terrance Weatherbee, Jason Foster, and Jean Helms Mills provide a rebuke to the way(s) in which we have constructed our own disciplinary history. They reveal for us that while socio-political activities operating within the contexts of what we know as the New Deal and the Cold War worked in tension to set the disciplinary boundaries of MOS, their import is conventionally absented from our renderings of our own past. Indeed, and not unsurprisingly, we are very much sympathetic to the problematic which they highlight for us. Any selections of what to include in representations of the past are also choices of what to exclude. Once taken and rendered into history these choices may become the normative discourse which signals what is a permissive activity within a disciplinary domain. Thus, for us, the revisiting of our disciplinary history permits new insights, new questions to be asked, and new frames for interpreting where our discipline has been and is or could be going.

Bert Spector's analysis of over 500 articles in the *Harvard Business Review* during the first two decades of the Cold War serves as a poke in our collective (and parochial) scholarly eye. His study re-emphasizes for us that the phenomenon we study is as much the result of practice as it is of scholarly study. His observation that the polishing of the foundations of a uniquely American notion of Liberal Market Capitalism was developed as a counter-ideology expressed in the pages of the business press brings new insights into stark relief, not only the heretofore unknown element of our collective past, but also the interrelationship between the formation of ideology and history-work by management in organizations. His study also drew our attention to the inherently dialectical nature of management development in the Cold War and raised for us a question of what was the dialectic that followed and what is it now?

Amy Thurlow's use of critical discourse analysis in her historical investigation into the development of public relations (PR) draws for us some stark similarities and parallels between the professionalization of both PR and MOS as academic fields. Her work reveals that the development of PR was subject to many of the same processes which have been observed in the formation of MOS. For us in particular, her observations of the unitary and US-centric origin from which PR developed its historiography are particularly germane. These saw a process of development which totalized the theoretical dimensions in that academic field from an American standpoint. A standpoint from which non-American – in her case Canadian – scholars find themselves just now debating in historiographic terms.

This is a condition observed throughout many of the works in this companion, and in particular in the efforts of Patricia Genoe McLaren and Albert J. Mills in their exploration of Canadian management theory. Similar to the observations Thurlow has made concerning the default Americanization of the PR field, they argue that the history of MOS has never been Canadian either. This has, of course, a great deal of resonance for us, not just in terms of our professional interest in historiography and history-work in MOS, but also personally as situated Canadian scholars.

These concerns are also shared by Kristene E. Coller, Corinne McNally, and Albert J. Mills who surface a demonstrably Canadian contribution to management theory. Their study of the scholarly contributions and theoretical influence of Canadians working in New Institutional Theory reiterates for us that the conjunction of theory development with history as written in our journals and texts does tend to assume the universal. If the Americanization of Canadian management theory could be explained solely as a function of the geographic, cultural, and political proximities shared between Canada and the United States it would be far less worrisome to us as Canadians. However, for us as scholars the evidence which is accumulating to the contrary would seem to suggest otherwise.

Our third reprinted article is by Eduardo Ibarra-Colado. Originally, Eduardo had agreed to contribute a new piece written especially for this edited collection. Sadly his untimely death left us with an important intellectual void in the book. We wanted to bring his very different perspective and challenging voice to the debate because it held the promise of a rethink of – rather than an extension to – the historic turn by reminding/informing us of the embedded (Western) knowledge work contained within our attempts to make that historic turn happen. To retain his voice and the challenge he posed to us we chose to reprint one of his earlier works where he first develops this argument. As we wanted to do more than simply add this as a chapter we asked several like-minded scholars and friends – Nidhi Srinivas, Ana Guedes, and Alex Faria – to reflect on the contributions made by Eduardo Ibarra-Colado. Eduardo's contributions problematizes our understanding of the practices of management knowledge in terms of research and education across national and cultural boundaries; especially when embedded in the knowledges of the so-called Other and the spaces in between. In their tribute to Eduardo as colleague, mentor, and friend, they reproblematize for us his project on epistemic coloniality and question a good part of the (Western/Northern) history project on which we are all embarked

Beyond the richly detailed and highly informative discussions concerning where the historic turn has been and where it is going found in the contributions of William M. Foster and Roy Suddaby and Matthias Kipping and Behlül Üsdiken, our own reading of the collective contributions to this companion has allowed us to sketch for ourselves a 'historical' arc of history-work in MOS. We find a trajectory which has seen movement(s) away from our singular and common-sense notions of the past – notions founded on a pragmatic realism where history was conceived as unitary and universal. We see movement towards multiple forms of history and history-work to arrive at relational amodern forms of co-construction. The in-between has, and still is, composed of a variety of theoretical and methodological choice. In this respect we see 'fragmentation' as richness and choice as freedom from the orthodox. If we are to grow our knowledge of that which we study, we need to continue to revisit what we know and how we have come to know it.

Finally, in closing this introduction, we would like to make especial mention of three individuals: Alun Munslow, Stewart Clegg, and Eduardo Ibarra-Colado. Alun Munslow very kindly responded to an unsolicited email from someone he had never met; one which asked him if he would be interested in bringing his unique perspective to a companion text to be published in a discipline that was not his own. Alun's theorizing in his own discipline is of world renown, and as many of us have drawn inspiration from his work we were more than pleased when he graciously accepted. To Alun, our most grateful thanks. As many of you know, Stewart Clegg is an éminence grise in MOS, and his stature and reputation keep him extremely busy as teacher, mentor, and scholar. With many persons and projects around the world seeking his attention and asking of his time, we were very pleased he agreed to provide our closing commentary. We are also appreciative that he has indeed held our individual and collective intellectual feet to the fires of critical observation. Thank you. Finally, and most sadly, we would like to remember Eduardo Ibarra-Colado who wished to contribute anew to our discussion and debate. You are missed.

References

Booth, C. and Rowlinson, M. (2006) Management and organizational history: Prospects, *Management & Organizational History,* 1(1): 5–30.

Clark, P. and Rowlinson, M. (2004) The treatment of history in organisation studies: Towards an 'historic turn?' *Business History*, 46(3): 331–52.

Cooke, B. (1999) Writing the left out of management theory: The historiography of the management of change, *Organization*, 6(1): 81–105.

Jenkins, K. (1991) *Re-Thinking History.* London and New York: Routledge.

Jenkins, K. (2009) *At the Limits of History: Essays on Theory and Practice.* London and New York: Routledge.

Kieser, A. (1994) Why organization theory needs historical analyses – and how this should be performed, *Organization Science*, 5(4): 608–20.

Rowlinson, M., Stager Jacques, R., and Booth, C. (2009) Critical management and organziational history, in M. Alvesson, T. Bridgman, and H. Wilmott (eds), *The Oxford Handbook of Critical Management Studies* (pp. 286–303). New York: Oxford University Press.

Stager Jacques, R. (2006) History, historiography and organization studies: The challenge and the potential, *Management and Organizational History*, 1(1): 31–49.

Weatherbee, T. and Durepos, G. (2010) Dar'Wren'ian evolution in management: Implications of the ethics of epistemology for the scholar. Paper presented at the Academy of Management, Montreal, Quebec, 8–9 August.

Weatherbee, T., Durepos, G., Mills, A. J., and Helms Mills, J. (2012) Theorizing the past: Critical engagements, *Management & Organizational History*, 7(3): 193–202.

White, H. (1985) *Tropics of Discourse. Essays in Cultural Criticism*. Baltimore: Johns Hopkins University Press.

White, H. (1987) *The Content of the Form: Narrative Discourse and Historical Representation*. Baltimore: Johns Hopkins University Press.

Wren, D. (1972) *The Evolution of Management Thought*. New York: Ronald Press Co.

Wren, D. and Bedeian, A. (2009) *The Evolution of Management Thought* (6th edn.). Hoboken, NJ: John Wiley.

Zald, M. N. (1993) Organization studies as a scientific and humanistic enterprise: Toward a reconceptualization of the foundations of the field, *Organization Science*, 4(4): 513–28.

2

Decentering Wren's *Evolution of Management Thought*

Milorad M. Novecivic, J. Logan Jones, and Shawn Carraher

> Today is not like yesterday, nor will tomorrow be like today; yet today is a synergism of all our yesterdays, and tomorrow will be the same. There are many lessons in history for management scholars, and the most important one is the past as prologue.
>
> *(Wren, 1994)*

Introduction

Throughout the twentieth century, management history had been viewed as a domain of inquiry with the capacity to produce a "unique and valuable form of knowledge" (Carson & Carson, 1998: 29). However, this historical knowledge was not recognized as a significant part of the foundational knowledge in management and organization domains. But in the twenty-first century, the scholarly significance of examining the history of management thought has been recognized (Booth & Rowlinson, 2006). Specifically, the focus on history has generated a 'historic turn' in management and organizational studies which is slowly gaining legitimacy in management and organizational scholarship (Rowlinson, 2013; Buchelli & Wadhwani, 2014). The proponents of this turn have called for a more critical approach to the history of management thought. This approach challenges the received view that the only proper way of conducting management history research is by investigating, synthesizing, and interpreting the evidence from the past in an objectivist and universalist manner (Mills & Mills, 2013).

This 'historic turn' has been championed by a number of distinguished British and Canadian researchers (Durepos & Mills, 2012a). However, the prominent US management historians have retained the traditional approach to historical research (van Fleet, 2008). The traditional approach involves: (1) chronological studies proposing periodization in the evolution of management thought; (2) studies aimed at ensuring that management's knowledge base does not contain any myths or misinterpretation from the past; (3) studies uncovering examples from the past to serve as benchmarks for the future; and (4) studies aimed at reevaluating the past against our current knowledge base to identify management fads and fashions (Kieser, 1994; Carson & Carson, 1998; Gephart, 1996; Smith, 2007). The outstanding proponents of the traditional approach in the US have been Daniel Wren, Arthur Bedeian, and Charles Wrege (Gottschalk, 1956; Lamond, 2005; Thomson, 2001; Wrege, Greenwood & Hata, 1999; Novicevic *et al.*, 2008).

These three outstanding US management historians have taken different, yet complementary paths to solidifying the foundations of knowledge in management history. By emphasizing the importance of dispelling myths embedded in the foundations of knowledge in the field of management history, Bedeian and Wrege have espoused that it is the primary obligation of management historians to focus on uncovering these myths and integrating their corrections into the practice of management education. In contrast to them, Daniel Wren developed a framework of narrating the presumably undisputed foundations of the history of management thought. His framework has been recognized by management historians across the world as exemplary primarily due to his most influential book, *The Evolution of Management Thought*, which has become a prominent locus in management history education (Gibson, Hodgetts, and Blackwell, 1999). Through nearly fifty years of active life in academia, Dan Wren has been "committed to teaching, promoting, and researching historical evolution of management" based on the foundations canonized in his book (Abraham *et al.*, 2009).

We use decentered theory (Bevir, 2003; Donovan, 2007) to examine the beliefs, practices, and meanings underlying Daniel Wren's book *The Evolution of Management Thought*. We focus our theoretical frame, which allows for an alternative conceptualization of history, to unpack the philosophical foundations of this exemplary book and decenter it as the received canon of the history of management thought from the management historians and researchers. The primary illustration of our decentered approach is related to the concept and practice of Taylorism.

We selected Taylorism for our illustration because it seems to be the conceptual gravity point of Wren's book, as both the symbol of modernity in management practice and the invented tradition of management thought (Nyland & Bruce, 2014). In particular, Taylorism has been both recognized as the legitimate object of theorizing (Wagner-Tsukamoto, 2008) and denied as a myth (Wrege & Greenwood, 1991). But Wren's book has unambiguously sustained its legacy both as a practical means to achieving harmony in management–labor relations and as a source of mental revolution that legitimized management as a discipline.

To present our decentered examination of Wren's history of management thought we have organized this chapter in the following manner. First, we provide an overview of Wren's life and intellectual contributions. Second, we decenter Wren's analytical framework to deconstruct his claims of historical knowledge about management thought. Third, we unpack the philosophical foundations of Wren's approach to the history of management thought. In conclusion, we outline the implications of our findings for alternate conceptualizations of the history of management thought.

Our decentering of Wren's conceptualization of management's past focuses on interpreting beliefs and meanings shared by Wren, other management historians, and great management thinkers who have been involved in articulating the traditional history of management thought. Taking a decentered theoretical perspective (Donovan, 2007) which is grounded in a specific postfoundational philosophical view (Bevir, 2013a), we uncover the meanings and beliefs of Wren and other management historians and thinkers and interpret their expressed claims. We selected a postfoundational philosophical approach, which falls within the anti-structuralist paradigm, as a source of the guiding logic for our attempts to answer what we know about the history of management thought. Our anti-structuralist paradigmatic approach is different from the poststructuralist approach that Durepos & Mills (2012b) have applied in an exemplary manner to management and organizational history (for a comprehensive overview and comparison of the anti-structuralist and poststructuralist paradigms, see Hassard & Cox, 2013).

We use specifically Bevir's (2013a) hermeneutic/phenomenological postfoundational version of the anti-structuralist approach, which suggests that individual management thinkers and historians socially construct characteristics of management and organizational phenomena and narrate management history based on the traditional webs of belief that they inherited. Bevir's version would suggest that they weigh their current beliefs against the inherited traditional ones that are reflected in the historical narratives. Only when contradictions between the individual current and the shared traditional beliefs become salient, does a dilemma emerge as to whether the traditional beliefs and narratives should be revised and modified. When this dilemma is recognized by a significant number of management historians, polarized views will emerge. These polarized views will likely suggest different ways of how the history of management thought should be narrated and how management's past should be theorized (Bevir, 2000a, 2000b).

Bevir's hermeneutic/phenomenological variation of postfoundational philosophy, which we use for grounding our decentered approach to interpreting Wren's book, rejects positivist factual truth-claims comprising the presumed historical conceptual foundation of management knowledge. This philosophical approach suggests that individual management historians and thinkers construct and reconstruct management concepts based on the beliefs inherited from traditions of interpreting the history of management thought. We examine how this conceptual construction and reconstruction is reflected in Wren's framework and used in his narration of the history of management thought. As we assume that Wren's framework reflects the traditional webs of beliefs about management history, we use it as the object of tracing the genealogical paths of management concepts espoused by management thinkers and historians. With this tracing, we attempt to uncover alternative ways to conceptualize the history of management thought and thus modify traditions of interpreting it.

The main purpose of our decentering of Wren's seminal history of management thought is to reveal how he navigates the historical maze of management traditions that are shaped by management thinkers and historians. We recognize that the main contribution of Wren's book is his development of the framework containing institutional, political, economic, and cultural dimensions that are instrumental to explicating the history of management thought. This framework rests on the assumption of epistemological universalism and its foundationalist principles of obtainable, objective, historical knowledge about management thought. In this chapter, we decenter Wren's foundationalist view of the history of management thought embodied in his framework. Our goal is to open paths to alternative conceptualizations of the history of management thought. In the following section, we examine how Wren's life experiences and his educational background have influenced his traditionalist understanding of management concepts and his foundationalist view of the evolution of management thought.

Wren's life-story and intellectual contributions

The life-story and intellectual contributions of Daniel Wren have been chronicled comprehensively in two separate articles published in the *Journal of Management History*: 'Becoming an outstanding management historian in the USA' (Abraham *et al.*, 2009) and 'Management history gurus of the 1990s' (Gibson, Hodgetts & Herrera, 1999). Therefore, our synthesis of Wren's life, education, and contributions is primarily grounded in those two articles. In addition we use the letters supporting Wren's nomination for the Academy of Management's awards.

Daniel Wren was born in Columbia, Missouri on January 8, 1932. He earned a Bachelor of Science degree in Industrial and Personnel Management from the University of Missouri in 1954. He spent the next four years in military service in the United States Air Force as a squadron/wing personnel officer. Wren then worked in his family's retail grocery business and focused on earning his Master's degree in Management and Labor Relations at the University of Missouri. After receiving his Master's degree in 1960, he left the family business to work as a production supervisor at Hallmark Cards Corporation in Kansas City, Missouri.

Having been intellectually stimulated by his previous academic experiences, Wren left Hallmark after just one year to pursue a PhD at the University of Illinois. He eventually received his doctorate in management, having also taken a diverse set of courses in economics, marketing, social psychology, and labor economics. In Wren's first job at Florida State University, his research focus in the 1960s was not on studying management history but on studying general management. His main research objective was to target the elite academic journals such as the *Academy of Management Journal*. During this decade he co-authored a book, *Management: Process, Structure and Behavior*, published several high-quality articles, and served as the Editor of Florida State University Press.

The 1970s marked the beginning of Wren's lifelong passion for teaching and researching management history which was largely triggered by his pedagogical experience with teaching a History of Management introductory course at Florida State University (Abraham *et al.*, 2009). Based on the material used in his teaching of management history in 1972, Wren wrote and published the first edition of what would become his most acclaimed book in the field of management history, *The Evolution of Management Thought* (Abraham *et al.*, 2009). Wren attributed his capacity to write this seminal book of management history to his generalist management training, which he received while simultaneously working and earning his doctorate (Abraham *et al.*, 2009; Gibson, Hodgetts & Herrera, 1999). In other words, the broad nature of both his work experience and his education helped him examine and narrate the history of many different fields of management.

In 1973, Wren accepted an academic position at the University of Oklahoma (OU) in the Department of Management, where he would later became the Curator of the Harry W. Bass Business History Collection. With access to the collection's unique and valuable historical resources and his passion for researching management history, Wren's research output peaked at the OU. Over the next five years, he authored or co-authored multiple articles that were published in leading journals such as the *Academy of Management Journal*, *Journal of Management*, and *Academy of Management Review*. He also published new editions of his books, *Management, Process, Structure and Behavior* and *Evolution of Management Thought*. Throughout his early career at the OU, Wren was able to contribute high-quality research while concurrently serving in multiple positions such as Director of the Division of Management and Editorial Review Board member of *Academy of Management Journal* (1973–1975), *Journal of Business Research* (1973–1975), and *Academy of Management Review* (1975–1978).

In the early years of his career in Oklahoma, Wren was honored by being listed in *American Men and Women of Science* (Social and Behavioral Sciences, 1973). He received an Outstanding Service Award from the Southern Management Association (1975), and became a Fellow of the Academy of Management (1976). Since these early years, Wren has continued his research in the area of management history, focusing mostly on several management pioneers (e.g. Frederick Taylor, Henry Fayol, and Whitney Williams). He acquired the titles of the David Ross Boyd Professor of Management (1989) and the McCasland Foundation Professor of American Free Enterprise (1994). He published several books including multiple editions of *The Evolution of Management Thought*. He served as the Interim Dean and Fred E. Brown Chair (2005–2006). In 2007, Wren was named Dean Emeritus, in addition to Fred E. Brown Chair Emeritus, and the David Ross Boyd Professor Emeritus, at the Price College of Business at the University of Oklahoma.

Throughout the later stage of his career at the OU, Wren has been committed to service through affiliation with multiple professional organizations such as the Academy of Management, the Southern Management Association, the Business History Conference Association, and the Southwest Academy of Management. Dan Wren is a Past President of the Southern Management Association (1973–1974) and one of the two original members of the Management History division of the Academy of Management. He has also served on the Editorial Review Boards of the *Oklahoma Business Bulletin* (1986–present), *Journal of Management* (1986–1995), *Journal of Managerial Issues* (1989–1998), *Journal of Management History* (1994–present), and *Journal of Applied Management and Entrepreneurship* (2000–present).

Wren's lasting impact on the work of many reputable researchers in the areas of management and management history can be illustrated with the following exemplary testimonials. "He is a wonderful colleague offering support and encouragement to doctoral students and other professors as well" (M. R. Buckley, personal communication, January 8, 2002). Dan Wren is committed to both offering guidance to academics and building the next generation of management history researchers. In his career, he has served on over 55 doctoral committees and he has mentored many of the top scholars in the field including Arthur Bedeian (former President of the Academy of Management), Richard Hodgetts (winner of the Academy of Management Distinguished Scholar Award), and David Van Fleet (Fellow of the Academy of Management).

"These three recognized management scholars influenced by Dan Wren maintained strong interests in management history for decades and they have all published major works in the management history area" (M. Wortman, personal communication, January 9, 2003). Bill Wolf, former President of the Academy of Management, said that "the fact remains that in the advancement of knowledge we stand on each other's shoulders ... to me the significant reason for awarding people such as Dan is that by making such an award we are saying to our members that behavior such as his is of value to our society and should be emulated." He went on to say about Dan that he is "at the pinnacle in contributing to the history of contemporary management thought" (personal communication, January 31, 2002).

For his contribution, Wren has received numerous noteworthy awards, including those for his dedication to teaching, research, and service, such as Outstanding Professor (University of Oklahoma, 1980), Merrick Foundation Teaching Award (1982), AOM Distinguished Educator (1991), Founding Fellow of Southern Management Association (1995), Associates Leadership Award (University of Oklahoma, 1996), AOM Ronald G. Greenwood Award (1999), SWAM Outstanding Educator Award (2001), and Distinguished Scholarly Contribution Award (AOM Technology & Innovation Management Division, 2010). He was inducted into the Oklahoma Higher Education Heritage Society Hall of Fame in 2011. Wren was the first active AOM recipient of three different Academy-related awards including the Distinguished Educator of the Year Award given by the Academy of Management (1991), the Ronald G. Greenwood Award (1999), also from the Academy of Management (Division 1), the Outstanding Educator Award (2001) from the South-West Academy of Management, and the Distinguished Scholarly Contribution Award (2010) from the AOM TIM Division. W. Jack Duncan, past President of the Southern Management Association said:

> In 1986 when the Academy of Management celebrated its 50th anniversary and the Centennial of Management, it was my honor to be selected to serve as Chair of the Centennial and Anniversary Celebration Committee which was celebrated at the

Table 2.1 Daniel Wren's research and service (not all inclusive)

Year	*Service: Editor*	*Research books*	*Research articles: people*	*Research articles: concepts*
1966	FSU Press			CNV: Televising a Basic Management Course
1967	FSU Press			AMJ: Interface and Inter-Org. Coordination
1968	FSU Press	*Management: Process, Structure and Behavior*, 1st edn.		SBJ: Personnel Testing
1969	FSU Press			
1970	Bus. Perspectives			
1971	Bus. Perspectives			
1972	Bus. Perspectives	*Evolution of Management Thought*, 1st edn.		
1973	Bus. Perspectives		AMJ: Lillian Gilbreth	
1974	AOM, JBR			
1975	AOM, JBR			
1976	AMR	*Management: Process, Structure and Behavior*, 2nd edn.	SOB: Fritz Roethlisberger	JOM: Anything New in Management
1977	AMR			AMJ: Perceptions of Management Pioneers
1978	AMR			JOM: Managerial Experience of Management Professors
1979		*Evolution of Management Thought*, 2nd edn.		
1980			AMR: Walter Polakov	JOM: Theory/Applications in Management Pedagogy
1981				
1982				AHJ: History in Business School
1983				BHR: American Business Philanthropy and Higher Education
1984		*Management: Process, Structure and Behavior*, 3rd edn.		BH: History in Business Schools
1985				JHBS: Industrial Sociology
1986	JOM, JLA	*Papers Dedicated to the Development of Modern Management*		
1987	JOM, JLA	*Evolution of Management Thought*, 3rd edn.; *White Collar Hobo: The Travels of Whiting Williams*		JOM: Management History: Issues and Ideas for Teaching and Research
1988	JOM, JLA			
1989	JOM, JLA			
1990	JOM, JLA, JMI			

1991	JLA, JMI			
1992	JLA, JMI			JOBM: Pay for Performance from Antiquity
1993	JLA, JMI			JOMI: Managerial Experience in Management Professors
1994	JLA, JMI, JMH	*Evolution of Management Thought*, 4th edn.		JOM: Theory/Applications in Management Pedagogy (revisited)
1995	JLA, JMI, JMH		JMH: Henry Fayol	
1996	JMI, JMH			
1997	JMI, JMH	*Early Management Thought*		
1998	JMI, JMH	*Management Innovators: The People and Ideas That Have Shaped Modern Business*	PAM: Andrew Carnegie	
1999	JMH			JASIS: Faculty Perceptions of Electronic Journals
2000	JMH, JAME			BHR: J & W Archives
2001	JMH, JAME	*Biographical Dictionary of Management*	MD: Henri Fayol	OD: Most Influential Books of the 20th Century
2002	JMH, JAME	*Collegiate Education for Business Administration at the University of Oklahoma*	MD: Henri Fayol, Chester Barnard	
2003	JMH, JAME			
2004	JMH, JAME			IJSE: Taylorization of Lenin
2005	JMH, JAME	*Evolution of Management Thought*, 5th edn.		AMLE: Teaching History in Business Schools
2006	JMH, JAME			AHN: Accounting History in Business Schools
2007	JMH, JAME			AMLE: Theory/Application Balance in Management Pedagogy
2008	JMH, JAME			
2009	JMH, JAME	*Evolution of Management Thought*, 6th edn.	JMH: Joseph Scanlon	
2010	JMH, JAME			
2011	JMH, JAME		JMH: Fredrick Taylor	

> Chicago meeting that year. One of our charges was to publish a special 'proceedings'. The committee was unanimous in selecting Dan to edit this proceedings entitled *Papers Dedicated to the Development of Modern Management* … I think that management scholars generally agree that Dan Wren is the most distinguished management historian of the current generation. Most scholars, I believe, would consider Dan of equal status to business historians such as Alfred Chandler which makes him a member of a very elite group of individuals.
>
> *(Personal communication, January 31, 2003)*

To establish a chronological timeline sequence, illustrating the breadth and the depth of Wren's contributions, we have listed the titles, themes, and concepts permeating all Wren's published books and articles (see Table 2.1). Table 2.1 shows not only the years when all of the editions of Wren's book were published, but also the key management thinkers and management concepts that he examined in his published articles. For the inputs to this list we utilized Google Scholar, Scopus, and JSTOR, to assess certain quantitative indicators of the direct and indirect impact of Wren's work (e.g. number of citations, types of subject areas, subsequent referencing research). This use is based on previous research that has supported Google Scholar as an accepted resource for evaluating article impact (Harzing & Van Der Wal, 2009; Kousha & Thelwall, 2007; Levine-Clark & Gil, 2009). A search of 'D.A. Wren' as author in Google Scholar undeniably established as salient his most influential work, *The Evolution of Management Thought*. Wren's book, which followed Claude George's popular book published a decade earlier, differed from George's book in that it examined management history within an analytical framework that contained economic, institutional, political, and cultural dimensions and encompassed a chronological timeline of the consecutive time periods or eras in the evolution of management thought. In contrast, George focused only on the contributions of seminal individuals without developing a chronological framework (Gibson, Hodgetts & Herrera, 1999).

In the Preface to the sixth edition of the book, Wren and his co-author Arthur G. Bedeian justify their focus on the chronological framework of periodization by stating that their research is designed to place "people and ideas that comprise the management discipline's intellectual heritage within a chronological framework" (Wren & Bedeian, 2009: xxv). To formalize this focus, the authors divide the book into four 'eras' of management: (1) early management thought; (2) the scientific management era; (3) the social person era; and (4) the modern era. Their periodization of management history into eras was also intended to facilitate the book's use in management education because the material was presented in a chronological and meaningful manner using a valid analytical framework (Abraham *et al.*, 2009).

In an interview in 1996, Wren explained the origin of his idea to develop an analytical framework for *The Evolution of Management Thought*:

> The University of Missouri offered an elective in the history of management, taught by Professor Robert Grant Cook. I have always loved history and took this course which involved each of the class members selecting two people to research and give oral reports in class. I chose Fredrick Taylor and Charles de Freminville. If we finished our reports before the class ended Professor Cook would fill the remainder of the period by reading passages from Copley's life of Taylor. I thought that there must be a better way to teach such a fascinating subject as management history. That was the germ of the idea for what became *The Evolution of Management Thought*, but it had to wait until I finished my master's degree, worked for Hallmark Cards, finished my doctorate, and co-authored another book.
>
> *(Wren, 1996)*

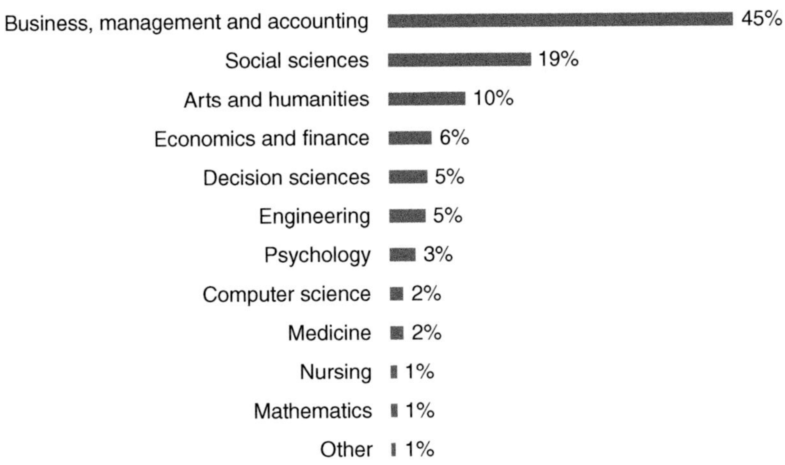

Figure 2.1 Academic disciplines influenced (Scopus as of October 15, 2013)

Table 2.2 Journal subject groupings (JSTOR as of October 15, 2013)

Journal groupings	*JSTOR publication category*	*Examples of journals in category*
Business	Business, management, accounting	*Academy of Management Journal* *Journal of Management* *Administrative Science Quarterly* *Management Decision* *Journal of Business Research*
Social sciences	Education, political science, psychology, sociology	*Journal of Applied Psychology* *Journal of Public Administration, Research & Theory* *Journal of Criminal Justice* *Innovative Higher Education*
Economics and finance	Economics, finance	*Economy and Society* *Journal of Economic Issues* *History of Political Economy* *Economic and Labour Relations Review*
Other	Other disciplines not listed	*Journal of Academic Librarianship* *International Journal of Technology Management* *Nonprofit and Voluntary Sector Quarterly* *Technology and Culture* *Journal of Health and Human Services Administration*

The Evolution of Management Thought has had a major impact across disciplines as it has been cited over a thousand times and is in its sixth edition. To capture the diverse impact of the book, we examined publications that have referenced *The Evolution of Management Thought* and grouped those journals utilizing Scopus analytics and JSTOR. Among the publications that have referenced his book the greatest percentage lies within business disciplines. However, as shown in Figure 2.1, there is evidence of the book's significant influence on other academic areas such

Table 2.3 Most cited publications referencing *The Evolution of Management Thought* (Google Scholar as of October 15, 2013)

Author(s)	*Title*	*Year*	*Type*	*Publisher*	*Citations*
Barley & Kunda	Design and devotion: Surges of rational and normative ideologies of control in managerial discourse	1992	Article	*Administrative Science Quarterly*	977
Weisbord	*Productive Workplaces: Organizing and Managing for Dignity, Meaning and Community*	1987	Book	Jossey-Bass	715
Griffin & Moorhead	*Organizational Behavior: Managing People and Organizations*	2011	Book	South-Western	689
Swanson & Holton	*Foundations of Human Resource Development*	2001	Book	Berrett-Koehler	595
Huczynski	*Management Gurus*	2006	Book	Routledge	569
Hunt	*Leadership: A New Synthesis*	1991	Book	Sage	562
Fournier & Grey	At the critical moment: Conditions and prospects for critical management studies	2000	Article	*Human Relations*	464

as social sciences and humanities. The specific groups of journal publications that contain references to Wren's book are shown in Table 2.2, following the grouping approach used by JSTOR. To illustrate the significant indirect impact of Wren's book, we identified the most cited publications that reference *The Evolution of Management Thought* as reported by Google Scholar; these results are shown in Table 2.3.

Our overview of Wren's life, education, and contributions points to his persistent focus on environment as the primary source of factors influencing our historical knowledge in the field of management. He believes that the evolution of management thought should be analyzed by grouping environmental factors into a framework that casts historical process in an analytical format that is also handy for effective teaching. In the following section, we decenter the beliefs, practices, and meanings underlying Daniel Wren's framework that is the backbone of his seminal book *The Evolution of Management Thought*.

Decentering Wren's history of management thought

We study Wren's history of management thought using Bevir's (2003) variation of decentered theory, which is grounded in the epistemological doctrine of hermeneutic/phenomenological postfoundationalism (Cederström & Spicer, 2014; Ginev, 2011). We examine Wren's book and articles about Wren in a decentered way with the intent of capturing the meanings that permeate them. In the examination, we use decentered theorizing as the lens for our interpretation of Wren's intentions and claims (i.e. 'speech acts') stemming from his beliefs about the history of management thought. In the development of this interpretation, we adopt Bevir's (2013a) assumption that we are constrained in our attempts at collecting sufficient evidence to develop meaningful interpretation of the history of management thought from the contemporary point of view (Bevir, 2003). Given this constraint, we can only develop an approximate interpretation of the way the evolution of management thought is explicated in Wren's book by comparing it iteratively to the interpretations of the beliefs about his book that are shared by outstanding management scholars and historians. This comparison is crucial to explicate in a decentered way Wren's meanings and beliefs about management's past (Bevir, 2013a, 2013b).

Our comparison indicates that Wren has had the capacity to change the webs of shared beliefs about management history that he inherited. In particular, we claim that Wren changed the way in which the history of management thought is now commonly viewed and taught by introducing the analytical framework of social, political, and economic factors that influenced historical change in management practices. We argue that in his book Wren depicts this historical change through the meanings that we uncover from his framework-based conceptualization and narration of the history of management thought.

Our decentered theorizing, however, introduces a destabilizing shift to Wren's framework-based way of interpreting the history of management thought. Specifically, we posit that traditional management historians like Wren may have developed their web of shared beliefs about the history of management thought not only objectively but also relationally through their socialization in their academic communities. The commitment to this web of beliefs in their academic communities may constrain the capacity of Wren and those sharing his views to change their inherited traditional beliefs. In other words, membership of management historians in traditional academic communities may constrain their individual capacity to reexamine their personal beliefs against the background of inherited webs of beliefs, and decide whether they need to modify the traditional beliefs. Our decentered perspective posits that management historians like Wren are situated agents who individually and collectively can change/modify the inherited traditional beliefs only when the community becomes polarized and contested views emerge. Our decentering efforts are focused on identifying these polarizing faults that may happen.

In our decentering of Wren's history of management thought, we focus on interpreting data as evidence of beliefs and desires that underlie Wren's claims (Håvard, 2014). Our data are thick descriptions of meanings found in Wren's book and the related articles. The data from the book represent rich evidence of Wren's beliefs, while the data from various articles and letters indicate the extent to which his beliefs are shared by the community of management historians. Our interpretation of data in decentered theorizing accentuates "the importance of learning about the intentionality of actors, that is, the beliefs, cultures, and traditions that inform actions and beliefs. The constructive relation of beliefs to actions encourages studies of beliefs and identities, and the actions and cultural practices to which they give rise" (Bevir, 2013b: 292). To insure quality interpretation, we focus on "thicker accounts of the divers webs of meaning that are embedded in human activity" (Bevir, 2013b: 292).

Our decentered theorizing is particularly focused on interpreting data that represent patterns of Wren's narration of the history of management thought with the purpose of revealing the underlying beliefs (meanings) embedded in these patterns. However, we recognize that the patterns cannot be captured as stable structures but can be only provisionally and temporarily described by pointing to how Wren tries to galvanize them as stable structures into his analytical frameworks that he presents as stable within specific time periods. As the decentered theory does not support the assumption of structural stability, our interpretation of data about Wren's developed framework calls for reframing that framework. Specifically, we call for decentering and recentering of Wren's frameworks through the "conditional connections between beliefs, actions, practice and their contexts" (Bevir, 2013b: 293) that weave the web of belief that is collectively shared among the thought leaders in the field of the history of management thought.

From a decentered perspective, Wren can be viewed as a 'primus inter pares' leader in the community of management historians sharing and shaping the webs of beliefs about the evolution of management thought (Abraham *et al.*, 2009). Decentered theory "emphasizes the meaningful and contextualized nature of actions and practices; methods that facilitate the recovery of webs of beliefs; and storytelling as a style of explanation ... it undermines a top-down approach to leadership" (Bevir, 2013b: 293). This privileges the focus on the collective leadership of management historians engaged in influencing readers' agency to adopt the follower role and accept the espoused history of management thought. This type of historians' influence allows the readers their autonomy to make their own choices about the way in which they can individually customize the narrative thus potentially opening alternative paths to conceptualizing the history of management thought.

Our decentered theorizing accentuates the need to develop a more eclectic approach to conceptualizing the history of management thought. This position is not only engendered by a different reading of Wren's book but also is supported by the unexplained fact why the titles of his book's editions use interchangeably the terms 'evolution' and 'history' of management thought. As a result of this conceptual instability, our interpretation of the data is likely to be unreliable as Wren's frameworks may be incomplete in terms of the meanings ascribed to them. Therefore, we suggest that decentering Wren's history of management thought implies initiating alternative narratives that would reframe Wren's frameworks and legitimize a plurality of approaches to conceptualizing the history of management thought (Bevir & Richards, 2009).

Our decentered theorizing of the history of management thought bridges the gaps between the espoused and alternative narratives by interpreting these gaps with the objective of discovering novel conceptualizations of the history of management thought or by viewing the established conceptualizations of Wren in innovative ways. We, as the proponents of decentered theory, posit that such innovations result from researchers interpreting diverse meanings that critical or traditional management historians like Wren, based on their inherited traditional beliefs, ascribe to these gaps that they observe (Donovan, 2007). To interpret using a decentered lens the different claims espoused by management historians, we need to infer the underlying individual and shared beliefs that explain their claims (Ooi, 2002). The most appropriate way is to interpret the alternative narratives that those researchers provide (Bevir & Richards, 2009). For example, a narrative alternative to Wren's history of management thought could be focused on interpreting latent dilemmas about the proper ways to explain how history of management thought is constructed (Bevir, 2000a, 2000b).

Overall, our application of decentered theory to Wren's history of management involves problematizing the meanings underlying Wren's traditional narration of the history of management thought. Our problematization does not deny, however, the fact that Wren is an exemplary traditional historian of management thought whose beliefs seem to be shared by the majority of the traditional community of US management scholars. We also do not deny the exemplary significance of this community, although it is resistant to endorsing alternative histories of management thought. But we posit that decentering his history of management thought may also have exemplary significance by opening alternative, non-traditional paths to conceptualizing organizational and management history. To illustrate this significance, we unpack the tradition of Wren's historical framework in the following section of this chapter.

Unpacking foundations of Wren's historical framework

We have labeled Wren as a foundationalist (DePaul, 2001; Hatchuel, 2009) in the philosophical sense because he implies that there is a foundational set of self-evident beliefs about past management practices which management historians share to establish the veracity of the acquired historical knowledge. The main assumption of his belief is that the world in which management practices have evolved over time is not socially constructed but real. Given this assumed reality, Wren claims that a management historian's mind can infer historical knowledge from the factual evidence collected about past management practices. The historical foundationalism that Wren implicitly adopts posits that real truth can be found in objective historical evidence collected from artifacts and original archived documents, as this evidence is foundational to building a truthful account of management's past. Committed to the assumption of the world's realism and the historian's objectivism, Wren ignores the possibility that a management historian may sometimes be biased to fit the collection of evidence to his or her espoused historiography, thus distorting the potential for the veracity of historical knowledge that is uncovered from such interpretation of evidence (Davis, 2011).

Based on the underlying foundationalist paradigm, Wren developed his analytical framework of historical processes, which gives primacy to the impact of the environmental factors on the evolution of management thought. He posits that historical processes related to management thought are influenced by economic, political, and socio-cultural factors that leave us historical evidence in the form of cultural relics that embody the traces of management's past. Wren prefers analyzing and synthesizing to deconstructing and questioning management's past when examining the collected evidence because he assumes that the evidence from the distant past has not been significantly distorted over time. In other words, he claims that his historiographical explanations can be developed from historical evidence because what we could know about management's past is preserved in the evidence that is selected for synthesis. In particular, Wren argues that through his synthesis of his selected historical evidence and interpretation of accumulated knowledge, management's past becomes the history of management thought as a prologue to management's present and future. Viewing management's past as a historical prologue in this way, Wren implies that management practices remain in the past while management thought persists as a residue of the past (Wren, 1994).

In his historical synthesis by grounding it in his foundationalist beliefs about objective knowledge foundations in management history, Wren assumes that our knowledge of management's past is objective and therefore does not require a rational ex post revision or justification. For example, he never justifies either his choice of historical evidence or his assumptions about the state of social equilibrium in management–labor relations that he presumes to be harmonious rather than conflicting. As a result, Wren's view of management history seems to evolve from the interplay between his reasoning based on the selected historical evidence and his assumptions about the equilibrium of management–labor relations which have likely been influenced by his ideology.

The allegiance to the doctrine of historical foundationalism might have led Wren to adopt the logic of 'developmental historicism' in explaining the evolution of management thought. This developmental logic becomes evident when Wren (1994: vii) specifically states: "Our knowledge about the development of management thought is constantly growing, although the knowledge related to the distant past grows more slowly. Some of our knowledge has not changed, some has been refined and extended, and recent developments are rarely, if ever, cast into a historical perspective." Wren integrates this historical developmental stance into his chronological framework to narrate an "unfolding story about the lives and the times of those who were our intellectual predecessors" (Wren, 1994: viii). Getting this genealogical narrative right about past management activities is crucial to Wren because "our problems today are basically the same; only the proposed solutions have changed as we have learned more, as we have sharpened our diagnostic tools, and as our values have changed." The main assumption underlying Wren's narrative is a systems view that "management is an open-ended activity in that what is done and thought is affected by the prevailing economic, social, and political values and institutions" Wren (1994: viii).

As a developmental historicist who believes that "management theory is a product of past historical forces", Wren (1994: viii) argues that the task of a historian of management thought is to outline the "paths of the past that have led to the present and provide a prologue to the future"; he assumes that the accomplishment of this task requires performing appropriately a comprehensive analysis of the impact of social, political, and economic forces that influenced that path of development.

Wren views management as not only an "activity central to all organized efforts" but also as a "conceptual function that must mold resources into a proper alignment with the economic, social, and political facets of its environment". As management thought is the "mirror reflection of the management activity", it brings "form to function and philosophy to practice" Wren (1994: 442). Management thought is thus an "existing body of knowledge about the activity of management, its functions, purpose, and scope, assuming that management has open-system characteristics in that managers affect their environment and in turn are affected by it" (Wren, 1994: 3–5). In the following section, we recenter the framework underlying Wren's systems view of management and the history of its thought, which is the backbone of his seminal book.

Recentering Wren's framework

Wren's framework for studying the history of management thought accentuates the relevance of environmental conditions for the development of knowledge about past management practices. In the development of his analytical framework, Wren focused on the historical process tracing how management practices became the source of management knowledge. Wren posits that this knowledge can be conceptualized as management thought articulated in the contributions of great management thinkers. In other words, great management thinkers narrate how management-as-practice evolves as a path to accumulating management knowledge; Wren weaves coherence into their narration by describing how management knowledge was gained and became historicized as management thought in a meaningful way. In his view, the evolution of management thought can be traced by examining and unpacking its historical embodiment in the practices of management. Wren suggests that this process of the evolution of management thought can be (re)constructed and narrated in retrospect as a prologue. In other words, Wren implies that the history of management thought evolves as if "driven from behind" (Rheinberger, 2010: 39) but is narrated as a prologue.

Wren's emphasis on retrospective reconstruction of the history of management thought reveals his intellectual commitment to the philosophy of foundationalism. However, this emphasis will likely be revised by the increasing number of postfoundationalist management historians who believe that management knowledge rests on an unstable platform rather than on a firm foundation of truth-claims about management's past. They will contest Wren's foundationalist way of historicizing management practice as a firmly-founded developmental process of acquiring management knowledge rather than as a historical product of possessing it. To paraphrase

Lakatos, they will likely propose a stance of viewing the history of management thought as an epilogue rather than as a prologue.

The outstanding foundationalist management historians will probably in turn contest post-foundationalist alternatives, supporting Wren in his claims that the history of management thought could be viewed as 'normal history'. Although they understand that it is difficult to talk about a Kuhnian paradigmatic consensus in historiography, the metaphor of normal history is handy for foundationalists. It is handy because it is broad enough to include both Wrege and Greenwood's (1991) view of Taylorism as a myth and Nyland and Heenan's (2005) view of Taylorism as a progressive, yet controlling management practice. In other words, this holographic view of management as both metaphoric thought and controlling practice allows for the tradition of Taylorism to be viewed both in functional terms as it actually happened and in metaphorical terms as it is actually remembered. By implying that his history of management thought can be conceptualized as normal history, Wren and his followers try to avoid the view of Taylorism either as the 'tradition of limited duration' (Kuhn's paradigm) or as a passing fad or fashion.

Our decentered theorizing of Wren's history of management thought seems to be compatible with the exemplification theory of history (Van den Akker, 2012: 236). The main assumption of this theory is that the past acquires its meanings through historical narrative and thus becomes history. The proponents of the exemplification theory of history argue that an account of the past is not historical if it incorporates the description of the events that could have been made only at the time when these events actually occurred. The account becomes historical only when it is made in retrospect, that is, when some later inputs are included into the description of the events. For example, Wren's account of Taylorism as scientific management is not historical but his account of Taylorism as systematic management and mental revolution is historical because it exemplifies a general thesis about Taylorism once it was historically explained.

Wren's conceptualization of exemplification, however, is different from Van den Akker's (2012) conceptualization of exemplification because Wren, as a foundationalist, believes that inferences from historical evidence and interpretation of the past are interdependent, while Van den Akker, as a postfoundationalist believes that they are independent. Wren's assumption of interdependence implies that his management historian's hindsight view and the view of those who lived in Taylor's time and left their accounts are both relevant for the historical understanding of Taylorism. The implication for an alternative conceptualization of the history of management thought is that it should be argued that Taylor lived with his prescriptions for management practices only in the past, while the history of Taylorism lives on today. This means that as a figure of the past, Taylor can be viewed as the originator of conceptualization of management, and therefore mattered practically only in the past, while Taylorism exemplifies the mental revolution of his legacy that matters symbolically in the present.

Wren's exemplification of Taylorism as a mental revolution could be supported by integrating the concept of exemplification into a theory of the 'sense-generation' of history (Rusen, 2012), which posits that "the past receives a meaning and importance by means of tradition" (Rusen, 2012: 47). In terms of the tradition of management thought and practice, Taylorism is often referred to as this tradition's origin which provides a sense of identity and legitimacy to the community of management scholars. By professing that management scholars should study the past as prologue to the future, Wren implies that Taylorism should be viewed as a tradition in the history of management thought that "binds past and future into a synthesis of duration" (Rusen 2012: 48). Therefore, from Wren's perspective of historical sense-generation, the tradition of Taylorism is not a construction of the past but rather a source of meanings for the history of management thought. In other words, he is attaching a historic meaning to Taylorism by interpreting it as an exemplary event that engendered the tradition of efficiency through a systematic approach in the history of management practice articulated as management thought.

Some critical scholars who are proponents of alternative ways of conceptualizing management history (e.g. Durepos & Mills, 2012b) may, however, view as problematic Wren's exemplification of Taylorism as the tradition of efficiency. First, these critics may claim that tradition and efficiency are two contradictory aspects of Taylorism that are not conducive to integration. Second, they may also argue that it is difficult to talk about Taylorism as a tradition across the board because of its varying success (and failure) in different cultures across the world. Third, the critics may state that ideologies that profess that management–labor relations are in a disequilibrium reflecting persistent social conflict, would likely oppose the view of Taylorism as tradition. Finally, critics may claim that Taylor triggered a break away from the traditional form of management and engendered a new tradition of Taylorism in management. These critiques will likely raise the question whether Wren's orthodoxy of foundationalism in the history of management should perhaps be dismantled to allow for interpretations based on postfoundational philosophy.

Discussion

Historical theory is traditionally viewed as an analytical framework conducive to developing and communicating historical knowledge (Partner & Foot, 2013). Foundationalist theorizing is based on the traditional assumption of building and integrating knowledge based on valuable factual evidence about the past, while postfoundationalist theorists posit that social construction is an alternative way of conceptualizing history (Mills & Mills, 2013). Being a foundationalist, Wren believes that management historians should uncover historical facts and present them in a reasonable, coherent manner following the logic of objectivism. His fundamental belief is that management thought originates from objective facts uncovered from archived sources, not from problematizing the ways in which the past constructed from archived documents should be understood and theorized.

Wren is a foundationalist as he assumes that historical knowledge is rooted in the management historian's objective observations embodied in the employed historical method that provides certainty to this knowledge. In other words, Wren does not believe in ontological dissonance between the past and history (Durepos and Mills, 2012b), but rather that management's past can be reconstructed and retold in an objective manner based on available historical evidence that is analyzed by applying appropriate historical methods. In this way, Wren subscribes to the foundationalist Rankean historicist approach to history. Moreover, Wren takes a developmental approach to the history of management thought and practice focusing on what he believed likely really happened, which contrasts with a more radical approach taken by Wrege and Bedeian who focus on what is espoused to have happened but they do not believe that it did happen. Both of these approaches share the assumption that historical knowledge grows from uncovering new archival evidence and interpreting it impartially. However, in his interpretation Wren puts a distinct emphasis on synthesis that reflects on how the past and the present are linked as a prologue to the future, rather than disconnected as espoused by Bedeian's and Wrege's interpretations of punctuated instances in the evolution of management thought.

Wren avoids making sweeping historical generalizations by focusing on historical contingencies within the eras of developmental stages in the history of management thought.

In his conceptualization of historical processes, Wren circumvents any possible association with Marxist scholars who ascribe structural properties to historical processes. Rather, Wren focuses on the relationship between history and psychology by implicitly adopting Collingwood's (1956: 2) position that the "fact demanding attention is neither the past by itself, as it is for the historian, nor the historian's thought about it, as it is for the psychologist, but the two things in their mutual relation". Wren's blending of history and psychology is grounded in the assumption that "only the thought-side of the past can be actualized in the present" (van der Dussen, 2012: 49) as a prologue to the future. In this way, Wren implies that it is management thought that gives historical quality to management practices.

In summary, Wren's foundationalist view of management history rests on the assumption of (1) the relevance of the individual agencies of great management thinkers, and (2) the legitimacy of a socially shared web of beliefs narrated by the community of management historians. Our postfoundationalist view of management history posits that individual management historians have had the capacity to change traditions of management thought and that they can capture the change process in a narrative form. In both foundational and postfoundational views, management thoughts can be shaped and reshaped in a thought-and-rethought manner in ways that "differ from ideas in that they do not need an owner to the contents of whose consciousness they belong" (van der Dussen, 2012: 52). Therefore, we can make a decentered inference that in six editions of his book Wren has been rethinking management thoughts without attempting to historicize management ideas and write an intellectual history of management.

Conclusion

Daniel Wren, along with Arthur Bedeian and Charles Wrege, is one of the American intellectual 'forefathers' of the history of management thought. Our decentering of his foundationalist view is aimed at safeguarding against the reification of Wren's book as a received canon of historical management knowledge. Specifically, our decentered examination of Wren's *Evolution of Management Thought* posits that this book should be viewed as a historical platform, rather than as a foundation of historical knowledge that is firmly grounding the history of management thought. The platform view suggests a focus on framing the history of management thought in a pluralist way as a discipline that offers opportunities for historical learning and reassembling management's past, rather than merely canonizing discourses within the disciplinary community of management historians.

We argue that decentered theory allows particularly for the development of multiple historical interpretations of management thought about specific historic phenomena (e.g. Taylorism). We recognize that these interpretations may overlap. We also recognize that they can be combined in a synthesis that may or may not be verified by the disciplinary community. But these interpretations will problemitize Wren's *Evolution of Management Thought* as a canon accepted by the international community of management scholars in the form of 'normal history', even if this acceptance is only contingent. Moreover, the decentered interpretations may engender alternative conceptualizations of history that legitimize multiple 'histories', rather than a single history of management thought. The emphasis on multiple 'histories' will likely "open to us other ways of thinking about the present" and have a "decentering effect as it offers epistemological challenges to whatever are the orthodox categories of current historiography" (Scott, 2011: 205).

References

Abraham, D. R., Gibson, M. C., Novicevic, M. M., and Robinson, R. K. (2009) Becoming an outstanding management historian in the USA: biographical research of Wren's and Bedeian's pathways, *Journal of Management History*, 15(1): 9–19.

Barley, S. R. and Kunda, G. (1992) Design and devotion: Surges of rational and normative ideologies of control in managerial discourse, *Administrative Science Quarterly*, 37(3): 363–99.

Bevir, M. (2000a) Historical explanation, folk psychology, and narrative, *Philosophical Explorations*, 3(2): 152–68.

Bevir, M. (2000b) On tradition, *Humanitas*, 13(2): 28–53.

Bevir, M. (2003) A decentred theory of governance, in H. Bang (ed.), *Governance as Social and Political Communication* (pp. 200–21). Manchester: Manchester University Press.

Bevir, M. (2007) The subject and historical theory distinction, *Scandinavian Journal of Social Theory*, 8: 25–42.

Bevir, M. (2011) Histories of analytic political philosophy, *History of European Ideas*, 37: 243–8.

Bevir, M. (2012a) Post-analytic historicism, *Journal of the History of Ideas*, 73: 657–65.

Bevir, M. (2012b) In defence of historicism, *Journal of the Philosophy of History*, 6: 111–14.

Bevir, M. (2013a) *Theory of Governance*. Berkeley, CA: University of California Press.

Bevir, M. (2013b) Cultural change in a professional sports team: Shaping environment contexts regulating power – a commentary, *International Journal of Sports Sciences and Coaching*, 8: 291–5.

Bevir, M. and Richards, D. (2009) Decentering policy networks: Lessons and prospects, *Public Administration*, 87: 132–41.

Booth, C. and Rowlinson, M. (2006) Management and organizational history: Prospects, *Management and Organizational History*, 1(1): 5–30.

Bucheli, M. and Wadhwani, R. D. (eds) (2014) *Organizations in Time: History, Theory, Methods*. Oxford: Oxford University Press.

Carson, P. P. and Carson, K. D. (1998) Theoretically grounding management history as a relevant and valuable form of knowledge, *Journal of Management History*, 4(1): 29–42.

Cederström, C. and Spicer, A. (2014) Discourse of the real kind: A post-foundational approach to organizational discourse analysis, *Organization*, 21(2): 178–205.

Collingwood, R. G. (1956). *The Idea of History*. London: Oxford University Press.

Davis, N. Z. (2011) Decentering history: Local stories and cultural crossings in a global world, *History and Theory*, 50(2): 188–202.

DePaul, M. (2001) *Resurrecting Old-Fashioned Foundationalism*. Lanham, MD, Rowman & Littlefield.

Donovan, C. (2007) Decentered theory, in M. Bevir (ed.), *Encyclopedia of Governance* (pp. 194–5). Thousand Oaks, CA: Sage.

Durepos, G. and Mills, A. J. (2012a) Actor-network theory, ANTi-history and critical organizational historiography, *Organization*, 19(6): 703–21.

Durepos, G. and Mills, A. J. (2012b) *ANTi-history: Theorizing the Past, History, and Historiography in Management and Organization Studies*. Charlotte, NC: Information Age Publishing.

Fournier, V. and Grey, C. (2000) At the critical moment: Conditions and prospects for critical management studies, *Human Relations*, 53(1): 7–32.

Gephart, R. P. (1996) Postmodernism and the future history of management: Comments on history as science, *Journal of Management History*, 2(3): 90–6.

Gibson, J. W., Hodgetts, R. M., and Blackwell, C. W. (1999) The role of management history in the management curriculum: 1997, *Journal of Management History*, 5: 277–85.

Gibson, J. W., Hodgetts, R. M., and Herrera, J. M. (1999) Management history gurus of the 1990s, *Journal of Management History*, 5: 380–97.

Ginev, D. (2011) Searching for a (post)foundational approach to philosophy of science: Part I, *Journal for General Philosophy of Science*, 32(1): 27–37.

Gottschaulk, L. (1956) *Understanding History: A Primer of Historical Method*. New York: Knopf.

Griffin, R. W. and Moorhead, G. (2011) *Organizational Behavior: Managing People and Organizations*. Mason, OH: South-Western.

Harzing, A. and Van Der Wal, R. (2009) A Google Scholar h-index for journals: An alternative metric to measure journal impact in economics and business, *Journal of the American Society for Information and Technology*, 60(1): 41–6.

Hassard, J. and Cox, J.W. (2013) Can sociological paradigms still inform organizational analysis? A paradigm model for post-paradigm times, *Organization Studies*, 34(11): 1701–28.

Hatchuel, A. (2009) A foundationalist perspective for management research: A European trend and experience, *Management Decision*, 47(9): 1458–75.

Håvard, A. (2014) Abduction, deduction and induction: Can these concepts be used for an understanding of methodological processes in interpretative case studies?, *International Journal of Qualitative Studies in Education*, 27(3): 289–307.

Huczynski, A. (2006) *Management Gurus*. New York: Routledge.

Hunt, J. G. (1991) *Leadership: A New Synthesis*. Newbury Park, CA: Sage.

Kieser, A. (1994) Why organization theory needs historical analyses – and how this should be performed, *Organization Science*, 5(4): 608–20.

Kousha, K. and Thelwall, M. (2007) Google Scholar citations and Google Web/URL citations: A multi-discipline exploratory analysis, *Journal of the American Society for Information Science and Technology*, 58(7): 1055–65.

Lamond, D. (2005) On the value of management history: Absorbing the past to understand the present and inform the future, *Management Decision*, 43(10): 1273–81.

Levine-Clark, M. and Gil, E. (2009) A comparative citation analysis of web science, Scopus and Google Scholar, *Journal of Business and Finance Librarianship*, 14(1): 32–46.

Mills, A. J. and Mills, J. H. (2013) CMS: A satirical critique of three narrative histories, *Organization*, 20(1): 117–29.

Novicevic, M., Harvey, M., Buckley, M., and Adams, G. (2008) Historicism in narrative reviews of strategic management research, *Journal of Management History*, 14(4): 334–47.

Nyland, C. and Bruce, K. (2014) Taylorism, the International Labour Organization, and the genesis and diffusion of codetermination, *Organization Studies*, 35(8): 1149–69.

Nyland, C. and Heenan, T. (2005) Mary van Kleeck, Taylorism and the control of management knowledge, *Management Decision*, 43(10): 1358–74.

Ooi, C. (2002) Persuasive histories: Decentering, re-centering and the emotional crafting of the past, *Journal of Organizational Change Management*, 15(6): 606–21.

Partner, N. and Foot, S. (eds) (2013) *The Sage Handbook of Historical Theory*. Thousand Oaks, CA: Sage.

Rheinberger, H. (2010) *On Historicizing Epistemology: An Essay*. Palo Alto, CA: Stanford University Press.

Rowlinson, M. (2013) Management and organizational history: The continuing historic turn, *Management & Organizational History*, 8: 327–8.

Rusen, J. (2012) Tradition: A principle of historical sense-generation and its logic and effect in historical culture, *History and Theory*, 51(4): 45–59.

Scott, J. W. (2011) Storytelling, *History and Theory*, 50(2): 203–9.

Smith, G. E. (2007) Management history and historical context: Potential benefits of its inclusion in the management curriculum, *Academy of Management Learning & Education*, 6(4): 522–33.

Swanson, R. A. and Holton, E. F. (2001) *Foundations of Human Resource Development*. San Francisco: Berrett-Koehler.

Thomson, A. (2001) The case for management history, *Accounting, Business & Financial History*, 11(2): 99–115.

Van den Akker, C. (2012) The exemplification theory of history: Narrativist philosophy and the autonomy of history, *Journal of the Philosophy of History*, 6(2): 236–57.

van der Dussen, J. (2012) *History as a Science: The Philosophy of R. G. Collingwood*. Dordrecht: Springer.

Van Fleet, D. D. (2008) Doing management history: One editor's views, *Journal of Management History*, 14: 237–47.

Wagner-Tsukamoto, S. (2008) Scientific management revisited: Did Taylorism fail because of a too positive image of human nature?, *Journal of Management History*, 14(4): 348–72.

Weisbord, M. R. (1987) *Productive Workplaces: Organizing and Managing for Dignity, Meaning and Community*. San Francisco: Jossey-Bass.

Wrege, C. D. and Greenwood, R. G. (1991) *Frederick W. Taylor, The Father of Scientific Management: Myth and Reality*, Chicago: Irwin Professional.

Wrege, C. D., Greenwood, R. A., and Hata, S. (1999) What we do not know about management history: Some categories of research and methods to uncover management history mysteries, *Journal of Management History*, 5(7): 414–24.

Wren, D. A. (1987) Management history: Issues and ideas for teaching and research, *Journal of Management*, 13(2): 339–50.
Wren, D. A. (1994 [1972]) *The Evolution of Management Thought*. New York: John Wiley.
Wren, D. A. (1996) Personal interview, October.
Wren, D. and Bedeian, A. (2009) *The Evolution of Management Thought* (6th edn.). Hoboken, NJ: John Wiley.

3

Why organization theory needs historical analyses – and how this should be performed

Alfred Kieser

Possible contributions of historical studies to organization theory

One of the forefathers of sociology and organization theory, Max Weber, was as much a historian as a sociologist. He was convinced that in order to understand contemporary institutions one has to know how they had developed in history. For him, history and sociology were inseparable disciplines. When he took over his last chair in Munich, he dryly commented: "I now happen to be a sociologist according to my appointment papers" (Burke 1992, p. 11).

Many sociologists of organization of the following two or three generations still took history very seriously. However, with the elapse of time interest in the history of organizations vanished, and nowadays, excursions of organization researchers into history have become extremely rare.

An explanation of this rejection of the past in modern organization theory would first of all have to take the process of the professionalization of sociology into consideration. In order to create an identity that was independent of other disciplines, especially history, sociology developed a preference for specific methods such as experiments or interviews (Burke 1992, p. 13) that, in conjunction with statistical analyses, offered the prospect of a precise methodology analogous to that of science.

Organization theory followed this trend away from history with one important exception, namely labor process theory. This exception has to do with Karl Marx, another forefather of sociology. According to Marx – and labor process theory closely follows him there – a given society always has to be interpreted as an epoch in a development *process* that owes its specific dynamics to class conflicts (Marx 1964). Defining this process on the level of organizations as being determined by changing combinations of tools, machinery, skills, work practices and organization, proponents of labor process theory raise key questions: who, and in whose interests, initiated changes, and who, in the end, gained control of the pace and direction of work? Organizational changes are analysed as struggles over "contested terrain," as the title of one study indicates (Edwards 1979); other, now classic, examples in this tradition are Clawson (1980), Goldman and Van Houten (1979), Braverman (1974), Marglin (1974), Stone (1974), Friedman (1977); for an overview see Goldman (1983). However, this approach, regardless of the many insightful interpretations of the history of organization it produced, did very little to restore the value of history in sociology or organization theory in general. Published in journals like *Critical Society*, *Review of Radical Political Economics*, or *Radical America*, it was broadly isolated from mainstream organization theory whose proponents, if they took notice of these writings at all, felt challenged to disprove the assertions of this theory – as we will see shortly in an example – rather than being animated to rediscover the potential of historical analyses in general.

At least four good reasons can be identified why historical analyses should generally be revitalized within organization research:

(1) Structures of and behavior in present organizations reflect culture-specific historical developments. Differences between organizations in different cultures can, therefore, only be explained completely if the historical dimension is included in the comparison.

A convincing example of a study in which this was done is one by Lutz (1976). Comparing matched pairs of work organizations in France and Germany he found remarkable differences. While in one German machine tool company one supervisor in production and maintenance, on the average, had to control 22 workers, his French colleague supervised only 11 workers; while the German company had 3 hierarchical levels to coordinate 452 workers, the French company needed 8 levels to control 406 workers. In the German paper company 37 persons worked in indirect functions, in the French company this number was 104. The differences in the other pairs were in the same direction and of similar magnitude. Another finding was that in French organizations more emphasis was placed on bureaucratic coordination of production, while coordination through face-to-face communication is more intensively applied in German organizations.

These differences are, to a large extent, due to differences in qualification systems. The French system places emphasis on general education, while in the German system professional qualification through apprenticeships plays a prominent role. Consequently, in a German plant we find a relatively high percentage of workers and supervisors who have completed professional training as *Facharbeiter* and are, therefore, capable of solving a lot of technical problems on their own initiative, while in France more detailed plans, more staff personnel in order to produce these plans, and also a taller hierarchy in order to control production processes are necessary.

But why are qualification systems in France and Germany different? The causes have to be tracked down far back in history: When the Industrial Revolution took off on the continent, France had a more developed educational system available than Germany. This meant that the early German factory owners could not expect to find qualified workers, foremen, and staff personnel in sufficient numbers on the labor market; they had to qualify their personnel themselves. They solved this task by adopting the apprenticeship system of the guilds that, at this time, were still in existence on a much larger scale than in France. Taking this course, German factory owners felt very backward compared to their French colleagues. They would have preferred state-run schools to do the training of supervisors and key workers, as was the case in France. Retrospectively, however, the apprenticeship system of qualification, that was not the outcome of a great strategy but forced by necessity, was a decisive factor in establishing the late starter Germany as one of the leading economic powers around the turn of the century.

Hofstede (1980, 1991) holds that cultural differences between organizational structures reflect differences in value systems. These value systems can also be identified in the theories that are developed and favored in these different cultures (Hofstede 1994). For instance, German organization theory stresses the importance of bureaucratic rules while French organization theory places emphasis on hierarchy. Thus, values shape organizational structures as well as organization theories that legitimize these structures. But how is it that values are different across cultures? A satisfactory answer can only be found in history.

The need to explain differences in organizations by tracing them back to historical developments is even more obvious when organizations of Western cultures are compared with those of more distant ones. For example, contrary to Western norms, it is not considered good management practice in Japan to define jobs and responsibilities *for individuals.* It is not the individual but the group which is held responsible for task fulfillment. Written job descriptions are unknown in Japanese companies. Some researchers even go so far to claim that the relationship of Japanese organization members to their organizations is of a different *type* than that in the West (Deutschmann 1989). In Western organizations the member–organization relationship is characterized by "partial inclusion" (Pfeffer and Salancik 1978, p. 31), meaning that "it is recognized that while the organization has the right to coordinate and control some behaviors related to organizational tasks, the individual retains control over other behaviors." In Japanese organizations a far-reaching identification of members with the organization is required and secured through specific recruiting procedures and in-house training (Ishida 1986; Clark 1979). The explanation for these differences has to be sought in history. "The Japanese company, in just the same way as the American or British, is the product of a particular history" (Clark 1979, p. 4). Consequently, a reconstruction of the specific paths that the development of organizations took in different cultures increases the understanding of these differences. In the Japanese case, for instance, it is important to identify the "merchant house" of the Tokugawa period with its justification provided by Samurai ethics and Confucianism as a forerunner of the keiretsu. The far stronger group orientation of Japanese people has to do with an absence of ideas and movements like the Renaissance, the Reformation or liberalism that in Western cultures were crucial for the emergence of individualism. Industrialization in Japan, in contrast, was predominantly legitimized through collectivistic Samurai values (Yoshino 1968). Sociology, and organization theory in particular, has to acknowledge that "present forms have their particular nature *by virtue* of their past" (Manicas 1987, p. 274).

(2) The identification of actual organizational problems and of their appropriate remedies is often not free of ideology. By confronting current "fashionable" trends in organization theory and practice with similar developments in the past, we can identify and possibly overcome prejudices that characterize the presentation of these trends.

The concept of organizational culture can serve as an example to illustrate this potential contribution of historical analyses. Organizational culture is commonly characterized as a modern and efficient instrument for coordination. A look into history shows that mechanisms that are discussed in present concepts of organizational culture have also been applied in former times, often in circumstances and for purposes that we would not like to reintroduce. For instance, with regard to the use of rituals, myths, and symbols the medieval guilds far outperformed companies that are known for their strong organizational cultures like Hewlett Packard or IBM (Kieser 1989). The guild's core symbol, the chest in which documents such as seals, privileges, the constitution of the guild, and register of members were kept, was a cultic shrine like the altar of a church, that is closely resembled. Dances and plays were performed during the numerous guild festivities, allegorically portraying the beginnings of the guild as well as highlighting important phases of its development. Extensive initiation rituals took place for the admission of apprentices and promotions from apprentice to journeyman and journeyman to master. This intensive use of rituals, symbols, and myths ensured that the many and detailed strict rules of the guild that concerned its economic, religious, social, military, jurisdictional, and political functions escaped criticism and that alternative modes of behavior did not occur to the members. Myths and rituals are beyond question. They are handed down from generation to generation and contain profound truths that remain beyond doubt. Consequently, the replacement of "organizational culture" by formalized procedures, and of a value-based attachment of members by a utilitarian one can be interpreted as important steps in the process of rationalization.

Another critical aspect of organizational culture becomes evident when it is confronted with the human relations movement (Ebers 1988). Similar to the organization culture approach, the human relations movement legitimized itself by pointing to the limited efficacy of technocratic and bureaucratic control mechanisms; it also nourished expections that behavior that is guided by common values and norms would be more effective than one that is enforced on the basis of formal procedures. Both movements promised management a more efficient and, at the same time, a more flexible and less conflict-prone control of organizational members than traditional management approaches could provide.

Today we know that the human relations movement was highly ideological; its concepts remained vague, and, therefore, it did not change much of the reality of organizations, but predominantly the way in which management talked about this reality. As one of its proponents put it:

> We generated a lot of new words but these words did not seem to produce anything very concrete, certainly not any visible, tangible products like machines. For all our huffing and puffing there was nothing to show. We did not even produce any sentences or propositions in a scientific sense to verify.
>
> *(Roethlisberger 1968, pp. 308–9)*

With regard to the use of symbols, rituals, and myths in order to control the thinking of organizational members, the Nazis were virtuosos. They not only celebrated *Reichsparteitage*, they also designed a concept for a *Betriebsgemeinschaft* that included many elements of organizational culture concepts, like the stylization of *Führers* or heroes and ceremonies (Krell 1988). A management book on socializing young employees into the company that was published in 1944 dedicated a whole chapter to "The Ceremony" in which it was pointed out that

> the ceremony is a means to directly mold the person's mind ... The monotony of a workday, the functional, the rational is not the whole, not the higher value for which one can totally sacrifice oneself. A ceremony makes symbolically comprehensible what is beyond all that ... The ceremony makes people see the great unity.
>
> *(Schlieper 1944, p. 218)*

Of course, all these examples are different in several respects from present concepts of organizational culture. However, they offer critical access to these: The study of medieval guilds informs us that organizational culture can jeopardize the mobility of organizational members as well as the adaptability of organizations, and that the pushing back of symbols, myths, and ceremonies has to do with the process of rationalization or disenchantment. The parallels to the *Betriebsgemeinschaft* of the Third Reich and to the human relations movement tell us that organizational culture is, in essence, management by ideology, and that we should be alert to the kind of value system or ideology on which the organizational culture is built. The case of the human relations movement reminds us that popular but vague approaches sooner or later, in order to avoid their own dissolution, have to produce more concrete concepts for research and practice.

(3) Historical analyses teach us to interpret existing organizational structures not as determined by laws but as the result of decisions in past choice opportunities, some of which were made

intentionally and others more implicitly. Choice opportunities that had not been used to the advantage of the actors involved possibly present themselves again or can be restored in some way or other. Historical analyses can prepare us to better identify and to make better use of choice opportunities.

The book *The Second Industrial Divide* by Piore and Sabel (1984) is a fine example of a study that demonstrates how choice opportunities were overlooked in the past and that, by interpreting the historical development as deterministic, we are in danger of overlooking alternatives for organizational design available at present. According to Piore and Sabel, the introduction of centralized mass production was generally hailed as a logical step toward progress. However, as we will see in more detail later, historical analyses reveal that putting-out systems survived as an efficient alternative to mass production in some national industries and are enjoying a renaissance in some parts of the world. Historical analyses thus help to break seeming invariances, to take up one of Galtung's (1977, p. 88) phrases. Of course, this point is not independent of the latter insofar as ideologies are often mobilized to make certain choices appear inescapable.

(4) By confronting theories of organizational change with historical developments, these theories can be subjected to a more radical test than they have to pass when merely being confronted with data on short-run changes.

For instance, organization ecology explains the evolution of organizational populations on the basis of three mechanisms (Hannan and Freeman 1989); variation, i.e., the generation of new organizational practices that occurs predominantly when new organizations are founded and when new technologies are developed; selection, i.e., the filtering out of unfit members of an organizational population which occurs, e.g., through the bankruptcy of companies; and retention, i.e., the preservation of organizational knowledge, e.g., in documents and files. Organization ecology rests on the assumption that these evolutionary mechanisms do not change over time. When confronted with longterm developments, it becomes obvious that this assumption does not hold. Thus, the guild masters of the Middle Ages were prohibited from innovating. Later, in early modern times, we find so-called project makers who were paid by the rulers to experiment with new products and new processes. However, their approaches were still "pre-rational," as is indicated by their attempts to produce gold out of lead. Nowadays, researchers apply proven theories in the R & D departments of companies to systematically produce new product and process variations. They apply various evaluation procedures and tests to emulate external selection processes as realistically as possible internally before they implement innovations on a broader scale. Organizations have learned to handle a growing number of innovations and to adapt these innovations to environmental selection criteria before exposing them to the environment. Evolution mechanisms are themselves subjected to evolution (Kieser 1989). Evolution of evolution mechanisms has not come to a standstill; it continues in modem organizations, and should, therefore, be considered in evolutionary approaches to organizations.

On the use of organization theory in historical analyses

Cooperation between sociologists and historians, if considered at all, is not free of tensions. Sociologists, and among them sociologists of organization, favor grand theories and do not want to bother too much about historical details that disconform these theories, while historians fundamentally distrust grand theories. Historians stress the uniqueness of organizations, while organization theorists stress the general dimensions of organizations. These differences in approach and methods have had the consequence that each group tends to see the other one in terms of a rather negative stereotype. Many historians perceive sociologists as people who state the obvious in an abstract jargon, lack any sense of differences in culture or time, squeeze phenomena into rigid categories and, to top it all, declare these activities as "scientific." Sociologists, for their part, see historians as myopic fact-collectors without a method, the vagueness of their data matched only by their incapacity to analyse them (Burke 1992, p. 3). As MacRae (1957, p. 302), a Scottish historian, has put it: "Sociology is history with the hard work left out. History is sociology with the brains left out." Despite the existence of a few bilinguals, sociologists and historians continue to speak different languages. Therefore, their dialogue, as the French historian Fernand Braudel has coined it, is usually a "dialogue of the deaf" (quoted after Burke 1992, p. 3).

In the following we will discuss how these tensions between historians and organization theorists can be overcome. At first, a certain strategy for applying organization theory to historical analyses will be exemplified by reporting how the development of early putting-out systems in Germany has been explained by labor process theory and new institutional economists. As we will see, both approaches leave many important questions unanswered and many phenomena unexplained. This debate will lead to a discussion of alternative strategies for applying organization theory to historical studies of organizations.

Early putting-out systems in Germany

The first putting-out systems in Germany came into being as a consequence of the division of work that had evolved between guilds during the Middle Ages (Jahn 1941). For instance, in textile production, spinning, weaving, finishing, and dyeing had been established as separate crafts. This division of work caused severe coordination problems between guilds, and in such a situation a central coordinator is likely to emerge. In most cases, this role was taken over by craftsmen who stood at the end or at the beginning of the production process, connecting it with markets. This central coordinator then soon became the putter-outer for other craftsmen. This kind of putting-out system – a network connecting guilds – can be found from the thirteenth century on.

In the sixteenth century another kind of putting-out system evolved: long-distance merchants contracted with guilds (Aubin and Kunze 1940). These contracts normally specified that the guild had to deliver certain products (textiles in most cases) in quantities that almost completely exhausted its production capacity. The merchants paid an advance in money in order to enable the guild masters to buy raw material and to sustain their living between delivery dates. Their contracts with guilds allowed the merchants to secure large quantities of goods in specified qualities without being forced to maintain a large administrative staff. The guilds coordinated the production and guaranteed the contracted delivery dates as well as the quality of the products. This form of putting-out proved advantageous for both sides. The guilds grew and gained a standard of living that was higher than that of comparable guilds that remained outside this system. The merchants were able to enlarge their international sales network.

The Thirty Years War weakened the influence of town guilds that had succeeded in forestalling commercial production in rural craft shops or in the homes of peasants. Now the merchants increasingly recruited producers in the countryside where labor was cheaper and duties were lower. It was also possible to organize production in a more flexible way outside the guilds that had severe problems in changing their production in order to meet changing tastes. Putting-out systems that relied on rural outworkers could become very complex and very large. For instance, in the year 1707 a handful of putter-outers in Wuppertal gave work to more than 30,000 producers (Kisch 1981).

A putting-out system was not an organization. It rather was a complex network of contracts of manufacture. The producers were formally independent, though often highly dependent economically. Putting-out networks comprised employees of the putter-outer ("foggers"), supervisors and carriers (sub-putter-outers), sub-sub-putter-outers, and producers who often employed workers in addition to their wives and children. The producers worked in their own shops, in shops jointly owned by a number of them, in shops of a putter-outer or a sub-putter-outer or of a third person to whom the producer had to pay rent. Working in a shop of a putter-outer did not mean necessarily that the producer became a salaried worker instead of a self-employed outworker. In many cases, the producer could still determine working time and pace of work; the contract referred to the products, not to the workforce of the producer, and the money paid was not a wage but still a price for products delivered.

In spite of this complexity in relationships coordination was a relatively simple task. Subcontracting in conjunction with economic pressure made it easier: As soon as the number of producers tended to become unmanageable, the putter-outer simply engaged sub-putter-outers who dealt on their own account with a number of producers. Instead of dealing with a large number of producers, the putter-outer then had only to deal with a much lower number of sub-putter-outers. Normally, this strategy did not increase costs since the sub-putter-outer could be obligated to deliver for the prices that the putter-outer had been paying to the producers. The sub-putter-outers made their profit by increasing pressure on the producers. Of course, this mechanism only worked as long as there was excessive supply of labor.

Putting-out systems contributed considerably to the development of the German economy: around the year 1800, 50 percent of the work force was employed outside craft production, and 85 percent of them were producers in putting-out systems (Henning 1974).

Most putter-outers maintained some central production. In the nineteenth century, they increasingly shifted work from outworkers to these centralized shops, for the following reasons (Kisch 1981): (1) Consumers demanded better quality that could only be achieved under more intensive control of central production. (2) Adaptation of products to changing demands could be achieved faster in central production; special production methods could better be kept secret in centralized production. (3) Technical progress, especially machines driven by water or steam power, required centralization of production. Factories that were founded in the course of the Industrial Revolution were highly centralized organizations right from the beginning. They replaced the bulk of putting-out systems during the second part of the nineteenth century.

Putting-out interpreted by labor process theory

Marglin (1974) argues that neither of the two decisive steps in depriving the worker of control of product and process, namely (1) the development of the minute division of labor that characterized the putting-out system and (2) the development of the centralized organization that characterizes the factory system, took place primarily for reasons of technical superiority. He holds that rather than providing more output for the same inputs, these innovations in work organization were introduced so that the capitalist could secure himself a larger share of the pie at the expense of the worker. Thus, according to Marglin, the division of work in the putting-out system came into existence, not as the result of a search for a technologically superior organization of work, but for an organization that guaranteed to the entrepreneur an essential role in the production process, as integrator of the separate efforts of his workers into a marketable product. And, likewise, the origin and success of the factory did not lie in technological superiority, but in the substitution of the capitalist's for the worker's control of the work process and the quantity of output.

Marglin's proof of these hypotheses relies more on reasoning than on collecting historical evidence. For instance, referring to needle manufacturing in the cottage industry he maintains that

> it appears to have been technologically possible to obtain the economics of reducing set-up time *without* specialization. A workman, with his wife and children, could have proceeded from task to task, first drawing out enough wire for hundreds or thousands of pins, then straightening it, then cutting it, and so on with each successive operation, thus realizing the advantages of dividing the overall production process into separate tasks.
>
> *(Marglin 1974, p. 70)*

This argumentation is questionable insofar as costs of equipment and training in different skills are neglected.

The putter-outer, who, according to Marglin, was technologically superfluous, brought himself into play on the principle "divide and conquer":

> The putter-outer's peculiar contribution to production was handsomely rewarded not because of any genuine scarcity of the ability to integrate separate functions; rather the scarcity was artifically created to preserve the capitalist's role.
>
> *(Marglin 1974, p. 70)*

This argumentation is not in line with historical facts: in the first putting-out systems, the guild masters of the first or last production phase necessarily had to take over the role of mediators between production and markets. They did not have to divide since production in guilds was already highly specialized. Putting-out was a consequence of a division of work that had already developed rather than its cause. The merchants who contracted with guilds also did not divide anything; instead they produced access to the world markets that the guild members were unable to organize themselves. That some of these mediators took advantage of their position is another story.

In a similar vein, Marglin argues that the replacement of the putting-out system by the factory can primarily be explained by the capitalist's striving for more control over the worker. According to Marglin, the agglomeration of workers into factories was a natural outgrowth of the putting-out system, a result of its internal contradictions. The success of the factory had little or nothing to do with the technological superiority of large-scale machinery:

> The key to the success of the factory, as well as its inspiration, was the substitution of capitalists' for workers' control of the production process; discipline and supervision could indeed reduce costs *without* being technologically superior.
>
> *(Marglin 1974, p. 84)*

Without doubt, in some instances, cottage workers did develop tendencies to slow down the working pace as soon as they had achieved a certain standard of living. However, there is ample evidence that in the majority of eases centralization of production was triggered by the need to fill the capacity of large-scale machinery.

> The new … machines … were incompatible with cottage or house shops because they were power-driven, look a lot of room while growing bigger from one generation to the

> next, and cost more money than a modest clothier could afford. Their capacity, moreover, exceeded the needs of the usual Yorkshire unit.
>
> *(Landes 1986, p. 606)*

The path of technological development toward centralized production was, to a large extent, dictated by the cost of power engines. As far as the exploitation of workers is concerned, the putting-out system seems to have been much more effective than the factory. The capitalists who had a preference for this model had to compromise since they could not find a technology for decentralized production that was equally efficient (Landes 1986).

Putting-out interpreted by new institutional economists

According to Williamson, capitalists did not prefer hierarchies over putting-out systems because they were superior in exploiting workers but because they were more efficient. The proof for this hypothesis is provided in Table 3.1 (Williamson 1985, p. 226) in which these two organizational modes are rated against a number of efficiency criteria. For the following criteria hierarchies are judged a "good mode" (denoted by 1) and putting-out systems a "poor mode" (denoted by 0): transportation expense, buffer inventories, interface leakage (embezzlement), contracting (with maintenance specialists), local responsiveness (process improvements at individual stations) and system responsiveness. Only for work intensity and local innovation is the rating in favor of the putting-out system.

Jones (1982), a historian, sharply attacked this concept by raising the following points: (1) Williamson neglects that putting-out and factories operated in different sets of labor markets. (2) Ranking on the basis of unweighted efficiency indicators is too crude a measure to do justice to the different degrees in which efficiencies or inefficiencies occurred in historical reality. (3) The scores are not assigned correctly: (a) transportation costs were small and, in most cases, had to be borne by the producers; (b) heavier stocks of work in process which had to be maintained by putter-outers were compensated for by smaller stock of finished goods and by higher flexibility in adjusting to fluctuations in demand; (c) contracting attributes were relatively unimportant because there were few trades in which outworkers employed techniques or machinery that required specialists. Jones also questions whether system responsiveness of the factory was really superior to that of putting-out (see also Brocklehurst 1989). He concludes that the "triumph of the factory system was *not* the result of any organizational superiority; nor was it the product of advantages gained through specialization and the division of labor. It was due mainly to the fact that factories incorporated machines that economized on inputs, especially labour" (Jones 1982, p. 136).

In a certain way, Williamson's model in which capitalists are treated as agents and workers as opportunists can be interpreted as a reversal of Marglin's model in which the workers are seen as the true agents and the capitalists as opportunists (Willman 1983; Brocklehurst 1989). In Marglin's approach, a small number of intermediaries purchase goods from a big number of producers who have very limited access to markets. Information is heavily impacted in favour of the intermediaries, who opportunistically exploit this advantage. For Williamson, the information impactedness is in favor of the producers who own the production equipment and the production know-how. They behave opportunistically by embezzling material and by avoiding investments for process, product or organizational innovations.

Neither Marglin nor Williamson take much care to present historical evidence on the motives of the actors involved.

Table 3.1 Simple efficiency properties of the putting-out and factory systems

	Product flow attributes			*Assignment attributes*			*Incentive attributes*					
Mode	Transportation Expenses	Buffer Inventories	Interface Leakages	Station	Leadership	Contracting	Works Intensity	Equipment Utilization	Lock Shock Responsiveness	Local Innovation	System Responsiveness	Score
Putting-out system	0	0	0	1	1	0	1	1	0	1	0	5
Factory system	1	1	1	1	1	1	0	1	1	0	1	9

The decline of putting-out interpreted by Piore and Sabel

Piore and Sabel (1984) introduce an additional factor in order to explain why putting-out systems were replaced by factories: the power of a vision – namely that of centralized mass production – that convinced powerful actors. Piore and Sabel (1984, p. 44) maintain that centralized, mechanized mass production became a paradigm which created

> the preconditions for a new orthodoxy. This new orthodoxy is exemplified in model machines and factories whose producers and owners never tire of advertising them, and its structuring principles are propagated in technical schools by textbook and example. At best half aware that their imagination has been circumscribed by convention, technologists pushed down the new path; they ignored the hints of alternative possibilities that are constantly unearthed by their experience with markets and machines – so long as the economy they are building meets the (frequently lax) test of international competition.

In this way

> mass production won out in the realm of ideas as it won out in the realm of practice ... Industrialization became synonymous with mass production, and the mass-production paradigm became self-evident truth.
>
> *(Piore and Sabel 1984, pp. 47–48)*

The power of this paradigm, according to Piore and Sabel, stamped out putting-out systems in many industries in which they could have remained a viable alternative.

The re-emergence of putting-out

Nevertheless, putting-out has survived in a few areas and is obviously even passing through a renaissance. High quality knitware production in Modena represents an outstanding example (Lazerson 1990, 1993; Best 1990, Ch. 7, sketches the history of this example). To a large extent, this production is organized by manufacturers who subcontract to artisans and homeworkers, i.e., small, legally independent firms whose main work force is often the family, production tasks like weaving, pre-pressing, embroidery, assembly, button-making, or finishing while maintaining direct control of the design of the first prototypes and the final marketing and distribution of the garments. Empirical analyses show that this kind of production is more profitable for these products than a centralized one (Bursi 1989), a finding that is at variance with Williamson's analysis. (Recently, Transaction Cost Economics has been successfully applied to this case (Mariotti and Cainarca 1986), providing that this approach is highly adaptable, or, as critics would say, that it provides a flexible language game for ex-post explanations.)

The factors that can be made accountable for this phenomenon are manifold (Lazerson 1993): (1) Because of unpredictable shifts in consumer tastes, knitware production is characterized by short production runs that preclude large economies of scale. (2) Possibilities for automation are limited for many phases of this production so that small firms can use the same technologies as large ones. (3) Since artisans and homeworkers, to a large extent, rely on employment of family members, they are less affected by high labor payroll taxes. (4) This workforce is also more willing than hired labor to work overtime, for less pay. (5) Though wages for artisanal and industrial employees are about equal, legislation provides the artisan employer with a number of privileges: he or she has to pay less for overtime, weekend and night work; reimbursement for workers absent for illness is only from the fourth day on while industrial workers get their wages from the first day on; and also dismissal is easier for workers employed in artisan firms. (6) Close supervision of work through the owners who work alongside their employees leads to higher productivity than in large firms. (7) The state, regional and municipal authorities offer to artisans, among other advantages, low interest loans for investment and grants for technologically advanced machinery, cafeterias, industrial parks and quasi-public consortia to aid marketing of the products. (8) Local authorities, trade unions, and voluntary associations of artisans cooperate in order to enforce tax, labor and environmental laws and to counter the destructive forms of competition that are symbolized in sweat shops. (9) Voluntary associations of artisans also develop vocational curricula and programs to link producers with subcontractors and wholesalers. (10) The risks of asset specificity that, according to Williamson (1985, p. 211), are likely to develop in putting-out production, are offset by long term contractual relationships between artisans and manufacturers. Because of these stable relationships and the enormous geographical concentration information on cost structures prices is readily available. All parties develop an interest in establishing and maintaining codes of fair conduct. Multiple customers offer another protection against the risks of asset specificity. Manufacturers often seek to divide their orders among several artisans and to mediate new customers to them in order to protect their supplier network from strong fluctuations in orders. (11) Costs of buffer inventories are lower than in centralized production since artisanal production is speedier, reducing the time for which work is in process, and since artisans temporarily store the unfinished products. (12) Transportation costs are not more than 0.6 to 3 percent of total production costs. (13) The long-term and close collaboration between manufacturers and artisans proves conducive for incremental but steady innovations in process, product. and organization (Brusco 1982). Thus, "none of the issues posited by Williamson and other new institutional economists has emerged as significant within the Modena knitware district" (Lazerson 1993, p. 219).

Applying theory to history

The studies by Marglin and Williamson on the development of putting-out systems represent a strategy that is quite common in historical sociology (Skocpol 1984); general models, i.e., models that are conceptualized independently of the phenomena which are to be explained, are applied as explanatory frames to historical data. Though this strategy is in line with what has been established as good social research practice, when it is pursued in explanation of historical events, a high degree of arbitrariness seems unavoidable. It is probably always possible to select historical facts that fit any general model, but one can never be sure that the researcher is not leaving out important facts that contradict it. It is also very unlikely that any two researchers would select the same historical data and interpret these data in the same way in order to prove the model. Therefore, charges of tailoring historical facts to fit a preconceived theory are near at hand (Goldthorpe 1991; Bryant *et al.* 1994). This strategy is also especially susceptible to ideologies.

A contrasting strategy is one in which theoretical concepts are used as "ideal types" to establish the particular features of historical cases. The investigator is not "proving" his model by historical "facts." He or she is aware that each model can only suggest certain motives or forces as influential in certain historical processes. He or she tries to find out, in what respects the historical case deviates from the "ideal type" (Kocka 1972). Instead of or in addition to comparing historical cases with ideal types, comparisons between structurally similar historical cases can be made. According to Bendix (1977, pp. 16–17) comparisons

> increase the visibility of one structure by contrasting it with another. Thus European feudalism can be more sharply defined by comparison, say, with Japanese feudalism, (and) the

significance of the Church in Western civilization can be seen more clearly by contrast with civilizations in which a comparable clerical orientation did not develop.

When, in the first section of this paper, we confronted the concept of organizational culture with similar earlier approaches, we also followed this strategy.

Applying this strategy to our example of putting-out systems, labor process theory and new institutional economics could be used to formulate themes and questions that guide the analysis of preindustrialization putting-out systems. And comparisons of these putting-out systems with the modern ones in the Modena textile industry could then be used to find out by which mechanisms the latter overcome problems which had not been solved in the former. In this strategy, comparisons are used to highlight the features particular to each historical context. The aim is to clarify particularities through contrasts. Explanations of this sort rely on the reader to understand more or less intuitively the specific forms of logic that produce the differences in the contrasted cases. Their advantage is that they can convey the impression of richness to a much higher extent than approaches that aim to apply models. Their disadvantage is, according to Skocpol (1984, p. 372), that "they are likely to display inconsistent causal assertions and missed opportunities for exploring causal regularities."

In a third major strategy the investigators assume that causal regularities may be found in history. In order to identify those regularities, the researcher tries out alternative hypotheses. These may be derived from several, even contradictory theories. Ideas from distinct theories may also be combined to formulate new hypotheses that seem appropriate to explain the historical cases in question. Historical events always have multiple causes, general models tend to concentrate on only a few. Or hypotheses are generated inductively from similarities between cases that are discovered in comparative historical investigations (Chandler 1984). In contrast to the first strategy, the analysis is not guided by a preconceived general model. The theory is rather modified and generated in a constant dialogue with the historical data (Kocka 1972). The researcher is not trying to prove any existing model; instead he or she is committed to generating causal schemes that are able to explain historical developments.

In this endeavour, the researchers should avoid "the dogma of universality," i.e., the conviction that no hypothesis is worth exploring unless it can be stated as a universally applicable law. They have to be content to work with explanatory generalizations that are assumed to be "relative to a certain context or contexts" (Beer 1964, pp. 6, 9; Kocka 1972).

In this strategy, comparisons between cases are made to find new historical generalizations. Similar cases, e.g., putting-out systems in preindustrialized Germany and Italy today, can be juxtaposed in an attempt to identify causal configurations that combine to account for outcomes of interest. For example, social embeddedness seems to be a factor which was also present in some German preindustrialization putting-out systems (Schmoller 1891). Nevertheless, these putting-out systems also disappeared. Comparing Italian putting-out systems and these historical cases could lead to the identification of factors, that, in spite of their social embeddedness, can endanger the existence of putting-out systems.

This "inductive strategy" that has been propagated by historians and by proponents of historical sociology, most prominently perhaps by Skocpol (1984), has been accused by sociologists of reflecting "the bias inherent in the nonsystematic nature of the sample from which they [its arguments, A.K.] were drawn" and as "empiricistic." A further point of critique is that in inductively generated theories "causal mechanisms are either absent, implicit or used in an ad hoc manner" and, therefore, "sociologists who seek consistent, testable causal explanation for historical events are ill-advised to proceed in this fashion" (Kiser and Hechter, 1991, pp. 13–16). This critique overlooks the fact that all general propositions have been generated inductively. It also neglects that it is not possible to clearly distinguish hypotheses that contain causal mechanisms from those that do not (Stegmuller 1983).

Another problem is that historical events always have multiple causes (Haussman 1991). Thus, the capitalists' striving for more control over the workforce, their motivation to increase efficiency, the ideology of mass production and several other factors can be regarded as causes that all contributed to the decline of early putting-out systems. Causes of historical events need not be mutually exclusive, as Williamson argues; they can be complementary. If several factors have been identified as possible causes for a historical event, then the researcher has to clarify whether single causes alone would have been sufficient to bring about its occurrence. Events can be over-determined, i.e., they can have several causes each of which alone would have been sufficient for it to occur. In this case it is not possible to rank causes. If none of the causes alone suffices to explain the historical event, the causes have to be regarded as *complementary*. In this case it is also unnecessary and futile to try to find out which explanation is the more adequate or the more important one. The identification of possible causes as real ones and their classification as sufficient or complementary ones is the task of a critical examination of historical sources.

If this characterization of historical explanations is accepted, the "inductive strategy" appears in a more favorable light. Its main concern is not to overlook possible causes. The emphasis is on critical examination of historical sources. Theory building may be biased through the "unsystematic nature of the sample" but, on the other hand, a theory-induced bias in selecting and interpreting historical sources is minimized.

From "horizontal multiplicity" of causes that we have discussed so far, a "vertical multiplicity" has to be distinguished (Acham 1974, p. 211): Conditions that have been identified as causes for specific historical events are themselves caused by conditions. The more "deep" causes, i.e., causes that influenced a number of "horizontal causes," a theory comprises, the more general and the more informative it is. General models like the ones by Marglin and Williamson claim to have identified "deep causes." However, explanations of this sort are also more susceptable to critique, since they necessarily contain assumptions on cause–event chains that are ill-specified and, therefore, not scrutinizable on the basis of historical data. Those researchers who prefer general, "deep" models should take care that the assumptions that link causes with the events that they wish to explain are specified in such a way that they can be confronted with historical sources.

Concluding this essay, it seems appropriate to point out that historical analyses within organization theory, even if performed in accordance to the third strategy, are not free of weaknesses. Since the historical material is inexhaustible, a selection cannot be avoided. This selection as well as the interpretation of events is always in danger of reflecting the ideologies of the researcher. It is no accident that Cohen and March (1986, p. 215) advocate the rule "interpret history" as a most powerful one in attempts to manipulate decision makers in organizations. This tactic takes advantage of the fact that "the belief in the relevance of history, or the legitimacy of history as a basis for action, is fairly strong," and that, at the same time, decision-makers strive to be consistent and have no time to check the appropriateness of the interpretation. As in any other theoretical approach, the results of historical analyses have to be subjected to a critical discourse. Another shortcoming of historical analyses is that recipes cannot be derived from them for the design of today's organizations. History does not repeat itself. Therefore, historical analyses can only serve to reflect on existing organizational designs and to criticize existing organizations theories. Historical analyses do not replace existing organization theory; they enrich our understanding of present-day organizations by reconstructing the human acts which created them in the course of history and by urging organization theories to stand the test of a confrontation with historical developments.

Acknowledgements

This article is based on an invited speech for the EGOS Colloqium, July 6–8, Paris. It profited a lot from the lively discussion that followed the presentation. I am also indebted to three anonymous reviewers.

References

Acham, K. (1974), *Analytische Geschichtsphilosophie, Eine kritische Einführung*, Freiburg, Germany: Karl Alber.

Aubin, G. and A. Kunze (1940), *Leinenerzeugung und Leinenabsatz im östlichen Mitteldeutschland*, Stuttgart, Germany: Kohlhammer.

Beer, S. (1964), "Causal Explanation and Imaginative Re-enactment," *History and Theory*, 3, 6–29.

Bendix, R. (1977), *Nation-Building and Citizenship*, Berkeley, CA: University of California Press.

Best, M. (1990), *The New Competition: Institutions of Industrial Restructuring*, Cambridge, MA: Polity Press.

Braverman, H. (1974), *Labor and Monopoly Capital: The Degradation of Work in the Twentieth Century*, New York: Monthly Review Press.

Brocklehurst, M. (1989), "Homeworking and the New Technology: The Reality and the Rhetoric," *Personnel Review*, 18, 2, 3–70.

Brusco, S. (1982), "The Emilian Model Productive Decentralization and Social Integration," *Cambridge Journal of Economics*, 6, 167–184.

Bryant, J. M., N. Hart, N. Monzelis, M. Mann and J. H. Goldthorpe (1994), "The Use of History in Sociology: A Debate," *British Journal of Sociology*, 45, 1–78.

Burke, P. (1992), *History and Social Theory*, Cambridge: Polity Press.

Bursi, T. (1989), *Piccola e Media Impresa e Politiche di Adamento: Il Distretto della Maglieria Carpigiana*, Milan. Italy: Franco Angeli.

Chandler, A. D. (1984), "Comparative Business History," in D. C. Coleman and P. Mathias (Eds.), *Enterprise and History. Essays in Honor of Charles Wilson*, Cambridge, MA: Cambridge University Press, 3–51.

Clark, R. (1979), *The Japanese Company*, New Haven, CT: Yale University Press.

Clawson, D. (1980), *Bureauracy and the Labor Process. The Transformation of U.S. Industry, 1860–1920*, New York: Monthly Review.

Cohen, M. D. and J. G. March (1986), *Leadership and Ambiguity*, 2nd ed., Boston, MA: Harvard Business School Press.

Deutschmann, C. (1989), "Der 'Clan' als Unternehmensmodell der Zukunft?," *Leviathan*, 17, 85–107.

Ebers, M. (1988), "Der Aufstieg des Themas Organisationskultur in problem- und disziplingeschichtlicher Perspektive," in E. Dülfer (Ed.). *Organisationskultur: Phänomen – Philosophie – Technologie*, Stuttgart, Germany: Poeschel, 23–48.

Edwards, R. C. (1979), *Contested Terrain: The Transformation of the Work Place in the Twentieth Century*, New York: Basic.

Friedman. A. (1977), *Industry and Labour: Class Struggle at Work and Monopoly Capital*, London: Macmillan.

Galtung, J. (1977), *Methodology and Ideology: Essays in Methodology, Vol. I*, Copenhagen. Denmark: Christian Ejlers.

Goldman, P. (1983), "The Labor Process and the Sociology of Organizations," in S. B. Bacharach (Ed.), *Research in the Sociology of Organizations*, Vol. 2, Greenwich, CT: JAI Press, 49–81.

Goldman, P. and D. R. Van Houten (1979), "Bureaucracy and Domination: Managerial Strategy in Turn-of-the-century American Industry," in D. Dunkerley and G. Salaman (Eds.), *The International Yearbook of Organization Studies*, London: Routledge & Kegan Paul, 108–141.

Goldthorpe, J. H. (1991), "The Use of History in Sociology: Reflections on Some Recent Tendencies," *British Journal of Sociology*, 42, 211–230.

Hannan, M. T. and J. Freeman (1989), *Organizational Ecology*, Cambridge, MA: Harvard University Press.

Haussmann, Th. (1991), *Erklären und Verstehen: Zur Theorie und Pragmatik der Geschichtswissenschaft*, Frankfurt, Germany: Suhrkamp.

Henning. F.-W. (1974), *Das vorindustrielle Deutschland 800–1800*, Paderborn. Germany: Schoningh.

Hofstede, G. (1980), *Culture's Consequences: International Differences in Work-Related Values*, Beverly Hills, CA: Sage.

Hofstede, G. (1991), *Chultures and Organizations: Software of the Mind*, London: McGraw-Hill.

Hofstede, G. (1994), "Management Scientists Are Human," *Management Science*, 40, 4–13.

Ishida, H. (1986), *Educational Credentials, Class and the Labor Market, a Comparative Study of Social Mobility in Japan and the United States*, PhD Thesis, Harvard University, Cambridge, MA.

Jahn. G. (1941), "Der Verlag als Unternehmungsform und Betriebssystem im ostmitteldeutschen Leinengewerbe des 16. und 17. Jahrhunderts," *Vierteljahreschrift für Wirtschafts- und Sozialgeschichte*, 34, 158–180.

Jones, S. R. H. (1982), "The Organization of Work: A Historical Dimension," *Journal of Economic Behavior and Organization*, 3, 117–137.

Kieser, A. (1989). "Organizational, Institutional, and Societal Evolution: Medieval Craft Guilds and the Genesis of Formal Organizations," *Administrative Science Quarterly*, 34, 540–564.

Kisch, H. (1981), *Die hausindustriellen Textilgewerbe am Niederrhein vor der industriellen Revolution*, Gottingen, Germany: Vandenhoek & Ruprecht.

Kiser, E. and M. Hechter (1991), "The Role of General Theory in Comparative-historical Sociology," *American Journal of Sociology*, 97, 1–30.

Kocka, J. (1972), "Theorieprobleme der Sozial- und Wirtschaftsgeschichte," in H.-U. Wehler. (Ed.), *Geschichte und Soziohgie*, Koln, Germany: Kiepenheuer & Wilsch, 305–330.

Krell, G. (1988), "Organisationskultur – Renaissance der Betriebsgemeinschaft?," in E. Dülfer (Ed.), *Organisationskultur: Phänomen – Philosophie – Technologie*, Stuttgart, Germany: Poeschel, 113–128.

Landes, D. L. (1986), "What Do Bosses Really Do?" *The Journal of Economic History*, 46, 585–625.

Lazerson, M. H. (1990), "Subcontracting in the Modena Knitwear Industry," in F. Pyke, G. Becatlini and W. Sengenberger (Eds.), *Industrial Districts and Inter-firm Co-operation in Italy*, International Institute for Labour Studies, 108–133.

Lazerson, M. H. (1993), "Factory or Putting-out? Knitting Networks in Modena," in G. Grabherr (Ed.), *The Embedded Firm: On the Socioeconomics of Industrial Networks*, London: Routledge, 203–226.

Lutz, B. (1976). "Bildungssystem und Beschäfigungsstruktur in Deutschland und Frankrejch – zum Einfluß des Bildungssystems auf die Gestaltung betrieblicher Arbeitskräftestrukturen," in Institut für Sozialforschung (Ed.), *Betrieb – Arbeitsmarkt – Qualifikation I.* Frankfurt, Ciermany: Campus, 83–151.

MacRae, D. G. (1957). "Some Sociological Prospects," in *Transactions of the Third World Congress of Sociology*, Vol. 8, London: International Sociological Association, 297–305.

Manicas, P. (1987), *A History and Philosophy of the Social Sciences*, Oxford, England: Basil Blackwell.

Marglin, St. A. (1974), "What Do Bosses Do? The Origins and Functions of Hierarchy in Capitalist Production," *Review of Radical Political Economics*, 6, 60–112.

Mariotti, S. and G. C. Cainarca (1986), "The Evolution of Transaction Governance in the Textile Clothing Industry," *Journal of Economic Behavior and Organization*, 7, 351–374.

Marx, K. (1964), *The Economic and Philosophical Manuscripts of 1844*, New York: International.

Pfeffer, J. and G. Salancik (1978), *The External Control of Organizations: A Resource Dependence Perspective*, New York: Harper & Row.

Piore, M. J. and Ch. F. Sabel (1984), *The Second Industrial Divide: Possibilities for Prosperity*, New York: Basic Books.

Roethlisberger. F. J. (1968), *Man-in-Organization*, Cambridge, MA: Cambridge University Press.

Schlieper, F. (1944), *Die Grundformen wirtschaftsberuflicher Jugenderziehung*, Berlin, Germany: Rudolf Müller.

Schmoller, G. (1891), "Die geschichtliche Entwicklung der Unternehmung. Part VI: Recht und Verbande der Hausindustrie," *Jahrbuch für Gesetzgebung, Verwaltung und Volkswirtschaft*, 15, 1, 1–37.

Skocpol, Th. (1984), "Emerging Agendas and Recurrent Strategies in Historical Sociology," in Th. Skocpol (Ed.), *Vision and Method in Historical Sociology*, Cambridge, MA: Cambridge University Press, 356–391.

Stegmüller, W. (1983), *Probleme und Resultate der Wissenschaftstheorie und analytischen Philosophie*, Berlin, Germany: Springer.

Stone, K. (1974). "The Origins of the Labor Process in the Steel Industry," *Review of Radical Political Economics*, 6 (Summer), 61–97.

Williamson, O. E. (1985), *The Economic Institutions of Capitalism*, New York: Free Press.

Willman, P. (1983), "The Organisational Failures Framework and Industrial Sociology," in A. Francis, J. Turk and P. Willman (Eds.), *Power, Efficiency and Institutions*, London: Heinemann, 117–135.

Yoshino, M.Y. (1968), *Japan's Managerial System: Tradition and Innovation*, Cambridge, MA: MIT Press.

4

Twenty years after

Why organization theory needs historical analyses

Alfred Kieser

It was most kind of the editors of *The Routledge Companion to Management and Organizational History* to ask me to write a comment on my perception of the impact of my essay on the need for historical analyses in organization studies. The answer given in 2004, after the first half of the 20 year interval, is still valid:

> Such an historic turn would entail questioning the scientistic rhetoric of organization studies, an approach to the past as process and context, and not merely as a variable, and an engagement with historiographical debates, especially regarding the epistemological status of narrative. However, we maintain that both the voluntaristic narratives of Heathrow Organization Theory and the scientistic analytic schemas of organization studies are resistant to an historic turn.
>
> *(Clark and Rowlinson, 2004: 346)*

A historical turn is still not identifiable and probably never will be.

In 1994, I had identified four reasons for engaging in historical analyses: (1) "Structures of and behaviour in present organizations reflect culture-specific historical developments. Differences between organizations in different cultures can … only be explained completely if the historical dimension is included in the comparison." (2) "The identification of actual organizational problems and of their appropriate remedies is often not free of ideology. By confronting current 'fashionable' trends in organization theory and practice with similar developments in the past, we can identify and possibly overcome prejudices that characterize the presentation of these trends." (3) "Historical analyses teach us to interpret existing organizational structures not as determined by laws but as the result of decisions in past choice opportunities." (4) "By confronting theories of organizational change with historical developments, these theories can be subjected to a more radical test than they have to pass when merely being confronted with data on short-run changes."

My impression today is that I greatly overrated the possibilities of historical analyses within organization studies. Ad 1: It seems that studies that compare organizations across different national cultures have died out. In the development toward internationally dominant standardized production and ERP systems, only little room seems to be left for preservation of cultural idiosyncrasies (Pil & Fujimoto, 2007). It seems that this topic no longer finds interested researchers. Ad 2: Entrepreneurship is an example of an actual problem which, seen from some researchers' perspective, is studied to some extent on the basis of ideological approaches (Armstrong, 2001; Brandl & Bullinger, 2009; Drakopoulou Dodd & Anderson, 2007). Those who get criticized do not respond to those who criticize their underlying ideology because, for them, it is science, not ideology. Tautological reasoning caused by ideology can serve as a shield against the critique of being ideological (van Knippenberg & Sitkin, 2013). If science is entrapped in ideology, historical studies are unable to mediate because those who are doing them are perceived as ideological by those who are getting criticized. Ad 3: In principle, it still seems a good approach to study organizations that decided against the current dominant fashion – and survived. For example, it could be possible to find a couple of banks in industrialized countries that did not grant bonuses to employees and still were successful. Unfortunately, banks of this sort do not exist. Ad 4: I must confess that, 20 years ago, I was naïve to assume that the quality of theories could be assessed by the quality of the results that they produce. However, the only test is the relation of peers who like certain results to those who do not.

Looking back, I conclude that the problems that I listed 20 years ago as challenges for historical analyses seem to have disappeared. Nevertheless, if organization studies did not make a historical turn, a very lively discourse on the use of historical studies in organizational analyses developed in a historically oriented sub-community on the basis of witty articles, foundations of scholarly journals, and editions of prudent handbooks.

References

Armstrong, P. (2001) Science, enterprise and profit: Ideology in the knowledge-driven economy, *Economy & Society*, 30(4): 524–52.

Brandl, J. and Bullinger, B. (2009) Reflections on the societal conditions for the pervasiveness of entrepreneurial behavior in Western societies, *Journal of Management Inquiry*, 18(2): 159–73.

Clark, P. and Rowlinson, M. (2004) The treatment of history in organisation studies: Towards an 'historic turn?' *Business History*, 46(3): 331–52.

Drakopoulou Dodd, S. and Anderson, A. (2007) Mumpsimus and the mything of the individualistic entrepreneur, *International Small Business Journal*, 25(4): 341–60.

Pil, F. and Fujimoto, T. (2007) Lean and reflective production: The dynamic nature of production models, *International Journal of Production Research*, 45(16): 3741–61.

van Knippenberg, D. and Sitkin, S. (2013) A critical assessment of charismatic–transformational leadership research: Back to the drawing board? *Academy of Management Annals*, 7(1): 1–60.

5

Management and organizational history

Prospects

Charles Booth and Michael Rowlinson

Our purpose in this article is to discuss the prospects as we see them for the new journal *Management & Organizational History*. The paper is set out in the form of a 10-point agenda with proposals for future directions in management and organizational history. Our intention is to stimulate debate, not to define boundaries or exclude other possibilities.

1. The 'historic turn' in organization theory

Our starting point is the 'historic turn' that is arguably taking place in management and organization theory (Clark and Rowlinson 2004), akin to that which has transformed other branches of the social sciences and humanities (Down 2001, 394–96; McDonald 1996). There have been repeated calls for a more historical approach to the study of management and organizations from leading organization theorists such as Mayer Zald (1993, 2002), Alfred Kieser (1994), Gibson Burrell (1997) and Stewart Clegg (2001). Zald (2002, 381) contends that the approach to problems in business school social science is 'universalist and presentist'. In 'the search for general and abstracted laws', he maintains, 'social science cut itself off from history'. Universalism leads to a view that contemporary organization theory applies to organizational phenomena in all societies at all times. Presentism results in research being reported as if it occurred in a decontextualized, extended present. Presentism contradicts universalism to the extent that the present is often assumed to be a period of unprecedented change, heralding the dawning of a new age. But this is usually done without proper consideration of possible historical precedents. It is largely a rhetorical device for privileging an unbounded, extended present, and it is a claim that has been made for at least as long as either of us can remember.

Universalism and presentism can be seen as the Flintstones and the Simpsons approaches to history. The Flintstones cartoon was 'set in a town called Bedrock, in the Stone Age era, but with a society identical to that of the United States in the mid-20th century' (Wikipedia 2005). The cartoon series revelled in its anachronisms, as when the characters appeared in a Christmas special, even though they must have lived long before Christ was born. The 'Flintstones method' assumes that any society, from the prehistoric to the present, faces the same organizational problems as our own (Steel 1999). As Jacques (1996, 14) observes, universalism means that 'management is presented as a continuous thread running through civilization', and even the Bible is cited by universalist organization theorists as addressing issues of organization. Universalism often 'emphasizes continuity over change' (Down 2001, 402). It proceeds from the saying, 'there is nothing new under the sun' (Moore and Lewis 1999, 2, 269; cited in Down 2001, 402), which, as Milton Friedman pointed out, is just as much a half-truth as the saying 'history never repeats itself' (1966, 25). Universalism can serve as a useful counter to claims for discontinuity between the present and the past. But Simon Down (2001, 402) argues that to describe ancient Greek enterprises as multinational enterprises (e.g. Moore and Lewis 1999), from the perspective of contemporary international business studies, and using 'the language of corporate capitalism' is to imply 'that most, if not all, economic organizations are forms of capitalism'. According to Down (2001, 403–4), the claim that multinational enterprises existed in antiquity, in a form amenable to analysis using concepts from Michael Porter (1990), is indefensible. It can only be made by assuming that market rationality has always existed, ignoring broader intellectual history and the historiography of the ancient world. Of course, we need, similarly, to be wary of Marxist inspired critiques of universal market rationality because Marxism makes the competing assumption of a universal class struggle.

Although it may be untenable to suggest that the ancient Phoenicians developed multinational enterprises, a convincing case can be made that there are historical precedents for developments in contemporary capitalism. For example, most economic historians are now agreed that globalization in the late 20th century is not unprecedented, and that the first period of globalization occurred between 1896 and 1914 (Eichengreen 1996). According to a leading economic historian:

> the most impressive episode of international economic integration which the world has seen to date was not the second half of the 20th century, but the years between 1870 and the Great War. The nineteenth century, and in particular the late nineteenth century, was the period that saw the largest decline ever in international barriers to trade and factor mobility.
>
> *(O'Rourke 2002, 65)*

The economy was even more globalized than the late 20th century in part because there was mobility of both capital and labour, whereas in the current period the mobility of labour is more restricted. The first age of globalization was undone by the First World War, a war that was seen as impossible by many commentators at the time due to the extent of global integration (Ferguson 1998a). Where historians disagree is over the role of imperialism in the first age of globalization.

The Simpsons is set in Springfield, which is 'a classic postmodern pastiche. The series systematically conceals the State in which Springfield is located', although many elements of it remind viewers of a typical, large American metropolitan area (Miani 2004, 17). Springfield is fictionalized in the same way that an organization is often fictionalized in organization studies; it 'may not exist, and yet everything that is said about it may be true', in the sense that 'it may be credible in the light of other texts' (Czarniawska 1999, 38). Bart Simpson never grows up, and no matter how many episodes he appears in, he always appears in the present. The Simpsons method presents fictionalized organizations in a non-dated, extended present. The historic turn problematizes universalism and presentism. It raises the question of the extent to which organizations, and organizational research, need to be historicized, that is, located in a specific historical context. For example, was the multinational enterprise born in ancient Greece? Or is it a form of organization that is specific to a globalized, capitalist economy? In which case, were the forms of foreign direct investment during the first age of globalization comparable to those of the late 20th century? And in terms of the present, how generalizable across time and space are the findings of an ethnographer from a fictionalized and supposedly typical organization?

Calls for more historical awareness are often aligned with critical management studies. Zald (2002, 381) contends that business schools have been 'cut off from humanistic thinking' and, according to Burrell, business school faculty have been allowed to escape from 'any real sensitivity to the issues raised by the humanities', including history (1997, 528). From a similar Foucauldian perspective Jacques claims that 'an historical perspective' can 'provide a critically reflective vision of the good society' (1996, viii, 190). So the historic turn also involves more critical and ethical reflection. Rewriting race (Nkomo 1992), gender (Aaltio-Marjosola, Mills, and Helms Mills 2002; Mills 2002, 2006; Thomas, Mills, and Helms Mills 2004), and sexuality (Mills 1997) into organization theory should also entail historical contextualization. For example, Anshuman Prasad 'seeks to theorize workplace diversity within the wider context of the (continuing?) history and experience of Euro-American imperialism and colonialism', and draws on postcolonial theory (Prasad 1997, 286).

As to how management and organization theory can respond to the calls for more engagement with history, Behlül Üsdiken and Alfred Kieser (2004) have identified three positions, which they label *supplementarist*, *integrationist*, and *reorientationist*. The *supplementarist* position adheres to the view of organization theory as social scientistic, and merely adds history as another contextual variable, alongside other variables such as national cultures. The *integrationist* position, which Kieser (1994) himself prefers, seeks to enrich organization theory by developing links with the humanities, including history, literary theory and philosophy, without completely abandoning a social scientistic orientation. The *reorientationist* agenda, which is very much our own (Clark and Rowlinson 2004), involves a thoroughgoing critique of existing theories of organization for their ahistorical orientation. There is scope for more debate about the extent to which history should merely supplement existing theories of organization, or be integrated with them, or whether a proper 'historic turn' requires a reorientation of organization theory along the lines of the reorientation called for from critical management studies or gender studies.

2. Historical methods and styles of writing

The historic turn in management and organization theory raises questions about methods and appropriate styles of writing for more historically oriented research. Management and organization theorists are often wary of both documentary historical research and narrative accounts of organizations (e.g. Barrett and Srivastava 1991; Strati 2000; Martin 2002). On the other hand, while business historians generally keep to documentary research and chronological narratives of individual organizations, they rarely engage with the epistemological questions concerning sources and historical narratives raised by organization theorists. This means that when management and organization theorists venture into historical research they have to tackle questions concerning historical methods, the status of sources and styles of writing (Rowlinson 2004). Here we mention just a few examples of the challenges raised by such writing. Pettigrew's (1985) longitudinal study of ICI's corporate strategy is highly regarded by business historians (e.g. Coleman 1987; Warren and Tweedale 2002, 212). But as Pettigrew admits, the combination of 'retrospective and real-time analysis of social and organizational processes' presents particular advantages and disadvantages (Pettigrew 1985, 40), and these are different to those usually encountered by business historians. Pettigrew's data consist of company documents, i.e. conventional historical data, as well as retrospective data from long semi-structured interviews. His main sources, however, were real-time observations and interviews conducted during his long stay in the organization. This combination led Pettigrew to a presentation of findings that repeatedly traverses the same period of time and departs from conventional chronological business history (Clark and Rowlinson 2002). Alongside Pettigrew's research, the strategic choice perspective (Child 1972) licensed several forays into business archives by organization theorists. These studies (e.g. Whipp and Clark 1986; Smith, Child and Rowlinson, 1990) incorporate the tension between action and structure in 'analytically structured narratives' (Clark 2000, 113). They are self-consciously situated 'on the bridge between narrative and analytic schemas' (Whipp and Clark 1986, 18). In other words they attempt to strike a balance between atheoretical, common-sense, empirical historical accounts of what actually happened, and overtheorized, sociological or economic accounts which explain the structural or economic necessity underlying events that have already been recounted by historians. Whipp and Clark (1986) are also notable as an example of organizational researchers who managed to secure possession of a large portion of historical records from a then extant company in order to carry out an historical case study without corporate sponsorship. Their study of innovations in work organization at Rover up until the early 1980s grants anonymity through pseudonyms for interviewees who gave retrospective accounts of events. These retrospective accounts are combined with liberal citation from company documents, including the directors' minutes, in order to construct a detailed narrative of the company's recent history. This allows for a historicized account of Rover, countering more universalist structural accounts of work organization derived from labour process theory (Braverman 1974). Whipp and Clark also demonstrate that anonymity for interviewees does not require the complete fictionalization of an organization, abstracted from time and place and as if existing in an extended present. Burrell's (1997) excursion in *Pandemonium* represents more of a challenge to both historical research and organization theory. Burrell eschews the aura of realism and objectivity that is normally found in historical writing, avoiding anything resembling a conventional chronological narrative. Instead he presents organization theory with an invitation to an odd and occasionally disturbing set of historiographical debates, from witchcraft to the Holocaust.

Historians, and especially business historians, are not usually expected to produce a methodological justification for their work. The copious notes detailing the location of sources in the archive are usually seen as sufficient methodological justification in their own right. On the other hand, for social science research in general, and for qualitative researchers in organization studies in particular, it is expected that there will be a detailed methodological justification of the research conducted. But while contributors to management and organization theory journals are expected to provide a detailed account of their methodology, they are usually discouraged from listing archival sources in endnotes. We would therefore expect the historic turn to lead to greater reflection on the historical methods appropriate for studying organizations. We also believe that if experiments in historical styles of writing using multiple methods are to be encouraged, then both methodological essays and detailed empirical, historical, archive-based research with copious notes listing documentary sources need to be accommodated. We aim to promote both historically informed writing in organization theory and historical research informed by organization theory.

3. The philosophy of history and historical theorists

If there is to be methodological reflection and experimentation in historical writing, then this will involve further engagement with the philosophy of history and historical theorists such as Hayden White (1973, 1987), Michel Foucault (1970, 1972), Paul Ricoeur (1984), David Carr (1986) and Deirdre McCloskey (1994). Carr's defence of narrative as the essence of human existence and consciousness in time stands at odds with the views of White or Foucault, that narrative is an imposition on the part of the historian as narrator. This impositionalist view of narrative in history is generally accepted within organization theory, as it is more broadly, so much so that Carr

(1998) describes it as the received wisdom. This is largely because, amongst the historical theorists we have mentioned above, it is Foucault who has attracted most attention in organization theory (Carter, McKinlay and Rowlinson 2002). The interest in Foucault has inspired historical research on organizations from management and organization theorists (e.g. Jacques 1996), as well as accounting researchers (Hoskin and Macve 1988) and sociologists (Savage 1998). McKinlay (2002), who is an accomplished historian as well as a management academic, demonstrates how a Foucauldian conceptualization of a phenomenon such as the modern career can lead to a researcher entering an archive with a completely different approach to a conventional business historian. McKinlay focuses on the cartoons he found in the margins of a bank ledger from the early 20th century. Foucault's *Discipline and Punish* (1977) was also the inspiration for Hassard, an organization theorist venturing into the archive of the Lancaster Monitorial Schools (Hassard and Rowlinson 2002). However, it seems to have gone unnoticed in management and organization theory that the impositionalist perspective is not completely accepted within the philosophy of history. Even as an impositionalist, White provides a licence for narrative historical writing, while Ricoeur appears to advocate narrative writing on the grounds that it is the only way to reconstruct the past in which people constructed their lives as narratives with plots.

In addition to Foucault, there has been increasing attention in management and organization theory to social theorists with a historical dimension. For example, Burrell (1997) relies heavily on Zygmunt Bauman's (1989) analysis of the Holocaust. Kieser (1998) and Newton (2001) have championed the work of Norbert Elias (1994). du Gay has also reclaimed Max Weber as a historical theorist, countering the ahistorical image of Weber that is found in organizational behaviour textbooks, where he is presented as 'the purveyor of a view of human history as a process of unrelenting rationalization' (du Gay 2000, 73). In other words, du Gay has contested the view of Weber's theorizing as universalist. The theoretical and philosophical status of narrative in history has relevance for narrative and storytelling in organizational ethnography. Boje (2001) in particular makes extensive reference to philosophers of history such as Deirdre McCloskey, Paul Ricoeur and Hayden White in his discussion of narrative. Newton (2004) maintains that if we accept McCloskey's point that history 'is a story we tell', and that 'continuity and discontinuity are narrative devices, to be chosen for their storytelling virtues' (McCloskey 1990, 22), then we are not compelled to choose between polarized positions that emphasize continuity or discontinuity.

4. Corporate culture and social memory

Business historians (e.g. Dellheim 1986) realized early on that the corporate culture boom of the 1980s could 'help the practice of business history' (Lipartito 1995, 5), and draw it to 'the centre of the study of management' (Westall 1996, 21; Rowlinson and Procter 1999). The more practitioner-oriented corporate culture literature attaches particular importance to history. According to Deal and Kennedy, for example, 'Good companies ... understand that it is from history that the symbolic glue congeals to hold a group of people together' (2000, 4). Collins and Porras (1996) famously argue that 'visionary companies' are 'built to last'. They maintain that vision and longevity are linked. In the knowledge management field, Brown and Duguid's (2000) attention to narrative as a means of transferring knowledge in organizations is deeply informed by history. Kransdorff (1998, 158), a corporate historian, argues that if the precepts of knowledge management are accepted, then corporate history is 'the most efficient and portable repository' of organizational memory. This is supported by Weick's wry contention that every manager is a historian, and 'any decision maker is only as good as his or her memory' (1995, 184–85). On the other hand, it can be argued that corporate cultures are 'invented traditions'

(Rowlinson and Hassard 1993), analogous to the traditions invented by nations (Hobsbawm and Ranger 1983). Gabriel (2000, 170–77) suggests that although 'organizational nostalgia' is a pervasive phenomenon, the mythologized past that it celebrates is 'generally idealized' and bears little relation to 'documented history'.

History also features in the field of organizational memory. According to Walsh and Ungson's basic definition, 'organizational memory refers to stored information from an organization's history that can be brought to bear on present decisions' (Walsh and Ungson 1991, : 61). However, Nissley and Casey (2002, S37) have argued that Walsh and Ungson present a 'repository image' of organizational memory. This reflects Walsh and Ungson's managerialist preoccupation with the usefulness of information retrieved from memory (Olivera 2000). The repository image is also prevalent in the emerging research programme on organizational forgetting (Martin de Holan and Phillips 2003a; Martin de Holan and Phillips 2003b; Martin de Holan and Phillips 2004; and Martin de Holan, Phillips, and Lawrence 2004), which explicitly connects memory, forgetting, and organizational learning.

Following on from Casey's (1997) previous work on collective memory in organizations, Nissley and Casey contest 'the static repository model of organizational memory' as a store for 'objectified truth', arguing instead that organizational memory is politicized (Nissley and Casey 2002, S44). They use the example of corporate museums to illustrate the way in which organizations can choose to 'selectively remember or forget', and that 'what is remembered or what is forgotten shapes an organization's identity and image' (Nissley and Casey 2002, S44). Whereas the organizational memory literature is predominantly psychological in its orientation, Nissley and Casey refer to the sociology of memory 'as a socially constructed process (collective memory)' (Nissley and Casey 2002, S38–40). Similarly, in a study of corporate war memorials, Gough argues that the repository model often strips 'memory' of 'any historical context, or, indeed, of much meaning: other, that is, than in a normative way that suggests organizations might lose something of possible future use to them if they do not maintain an archival memory' (Gough 2004, 444).

Casey (1997) hints at the connection between organizations and the 'politics of memory', which entails the recognition that as 'a cultural construction', memory is 'subject to the influence of powerful organizational actors who interpret and construe history in the service of their present interests' (Glynn 1997, 149). This is developed in Nissley and Casey's (2002) analysis of corporate museums and organizational memory. In a similar vein, but without an explicit connection to the politics of memory, is Hegele and Kieser's (2001) analysis of texts through which Jack Welch's legend has been constructed, and Rowlinson's (2002) essay on Cadbury World, which highlights the way in which corporate representations of heritage ignore controversial episodes in a company's history (see Satre 2005). Casey's work (1997; see Nissley and Casey 2002) also raises the prospect of an engagement with the growing field of social memory studies derived from Halbwachs (1950/1980; see Misztal 2003). Booth *et al.* (2005) make the connection between social memory and organizational symbolism, arguing that the symbolic life of an organization includes the symbolism of the past and the practices whereby the past is remembered. We feel that there is great potential to link the concepts of organizational culture and identity with social and collective memory studies.

5. Organizational history

Given the historic turn, the increasing reflection on appropriate styles of writing about organizations historically, the increasing attention to philosophers of history in organization studies, and the potential connections between organizational culture and collective memory, we feel that it is now possible to speak of 'organizational history' as a distinctive field, as proposed by Carroll (2002). According to Carroll, organizational history draws upon concepts from organization theory and the wider social sciences and humanities. Carroll's special issue of the *Journal of Organizational Change Management* on 'the strategic use of the past and future in organizations' includes ethnographic examinations of the meaning of an organization's past to its members in the present (Parker 2002), studies of the organizational processes behind official corporate histories (Taylor and Freer 2002), and the reasons for such histories being undertaken in the first place (Ooi 2002). We would count Boje's (1995) innovative dramaturgical analogy for analysing Disney's corporate culture as an indicative example of a distinctive approach to organizational history. By historicizing organization itself, Kieser's (1989, 1998) accounts of the genesis of formal organizations, and the evolution of rational organizational design in 18th-century German associations has opened a field of debate over 'the historical context in which organizing has developed' (Newton 2004, 1380). Organizational history also encompasses the historicization of subjectivity. Newton's historicization of stress counters the popular 'idea of Stone Age man suffering in the modern-day office', in which stress is attributed to the failure of our natural animal instincts to keep up with technological and social developments (Newton 1995, 22, 136–40). More broadly, Jacques (1996) has traced the hidden history of management knowledge, while Shenhav (1995, 1999) provides a cultural and political account of the evolution of rationality in management thought, identifying the role of engineers in particular. Townley (2002) historicizes the all-pervasive advocacy of abstract management concepts as the solution to all contemporary problems, locating its foundations in modernity itself. In addition to Shenhav (1995, 1999), Abrahamson (1997), Barley and Kunda (1992) and Guillén (1994), have conducted bibliometric research that provides periodizations for managerial and organizational discourse. These methodologically rigorous studies extend the influential historiographical surveys by authors such as Bendix (1956), Clegg and Dunkerley (1980) and Perrow (1986), which we would identify as contributions to the development of organizational history as a distinct field. In the closing pages of his classic, *Complex Organizations* (1986), Perrow invited readers to join him in the 'task of rewriting the history of bureaucracy'. Twenty years on we would say that the field of organizational history is tackling that task.

6. Business history and theory

Business history is already an established field in its own right, with its own well-regarded, long-standing journals, namely *Business History* and *Business History Review*. Narrowly defined, business history consists of 'the systematic study of individual firms on the basis of their business records' (Tosh 1991, 95). According to Chandler (1988, 302) the 'discipline's traditional sources' consist of 'letters, memoranda, periodicals and general accounts'. A distinction can be made between corporate, or company, history, which represents narrative accounts of individual businesses, often commissioned by companies themselves, and business history, which explores themes in the history of business organizations as institutions (Jones 1999). However, at the same time as the historic turn has been underway in organization studies, a consensus has emerged among business historians that they need to engage with the theoretical concerns from related fields if they are to refute the familiar criticism that they are '"inveterate empiricists", obsessed with setting the record straight, telling the story as it really was' (Hannah 1984, 219). This engagement is also part of an effort by business historians to realize the potential of their work 'to inform contemporary managerial decision-making, [and] influence public opinion' (Jones 1999, 14). Another reason for business historians to seek a more theoretical orientation is that they are under increasing pressure to find a home in business schools (Rowlinson 2001). Conferences of business historians in the USA (Scranton and Horowitz 1997) and UK (Slaven 2000) have specifically addressed the relation between business history and theory. Many business historians limit their engagement with theory to economics, on the grounds that various developments in the theory of the firm, especially the resource-based view, mean that economics now has 'more to offer business historians' (Casson and Rose 1997; Lamoreaux, Raff and Temin 1997). But others are more critical of economics and its inability to deal with process in history (e.g. Jones 1997). Prominent business historians such as Yates (1997) and Kipping (2003) have looked to other academic disciplines, principally historical and organizational sociology, and sociological concepts such as structuration, as an alternative to economic 'efficiency' theories of organization.

It is clear from Amatori and Jones's important survey of the field, *Business History Around the World* (2003), that Alfred Chandler (1962, 1977, 1990) remains the essential reference point for business historians. In following the work of Chandler, business history has tended to focus on entrepreneurship, corporate structures, competitive advantage and technological innovation (Wilson 1995). Hausman (2003) explores the influence of Chandler in US business history, focusing on the tension between Chandlerian business history and cultural studies. He suggests that even as business history becomes increasingly contested by '"cultural criticism" – business historians continue to define themselves in accordance with, in defiance of, but always in relation to Chandler's paradigm' (Hausman 2003, 97). Galambos (2003) traces the conservative political origins of business history and the increasing hostility towards it from the paradigm of neoclassical economics. According to Galambos, although Chandler is credited with moving business history away from political controversy, there could be little doubt about Chandler's benign view of big business. While Amatori and Jones praise Chandler for 'taking business history beyond the lurches of ideological disputes' (2003, 3), Galambos warns against the danger of consensus. He points out that under Chandler's influence 'the Harvard business school was and still is a powerfully consensus-oriented institution', which 'encouraged elaboration, not dissent' (2003, 18). In his own work on innovation, Galambos claims to have built on Chandler, while also looking 'beyond the firm to its political context, power relations, and links to the professions' (2003, 24). Galambos highlights alternatives to the Chandler-inspired 'conservative historical synthesis', from sociology and political science, as well as from the versions of postmodernism that hold sway in the history profession, which increasingly focuses on class, gender and race. He foresees fruitful 'turmoil in business history' (Galambos 2003, 29). Lazonick (2003) calls for the integration of business history with economic theory, even though he is critical of neoclassical economics and draws upon Penrose (1959), as well as Chandler, to make a strong case that economists should take more account of 'historical reality'. In common with most other contributors to Amatori and Jones's collection, Lazonick assumes that if theory and history are to be integrated, then business history should be integrated with economic theory, albeit in a modified form. He takes it for granted that business historians require the 'analytical tools' that only economists can supply. Thus Kipping (2003) admits that he is being provocative in criticizing business historians for their preoccupation with economic performance at the expense of understanding historical decision-making processes. Kipping attributes this preoccupation to the influence of mainstream economic theories and the 'dominant discourse' of economic efficiency derived from Chandler. Chandler himself gives short shrift to those who 'write business history as cultural history' (2003, 405), just as he previously dismissed 'psychological history' which focused on 'historical myths, symbols, images, and the like' (Chandler 1988, 302; quoting Higham and Gilbert 1965). He maintains that there are new opportunities for business historians to produce economic history as history again, as opposed to economic history as economics.

As more business historians question the Chandlerian consensus and the deference to economic theory that prevails in mainstream business history, we expect that there will be much greater engagement between business history and organizational history. A version of business history that is consciously informed by sociology and cultural studies may be virtually indistinguishable from organizational history, apart from its style and attention to sources.

7. Business ethics in history

Conventional business history has tended to neglect questions of meaning and ethics (Tweedale 1999, 93). However, historians contend that if the current business school preoccupation with ethics and corporate social responsibility is to be more than a passing fad, then it needs to be informed by history (Marens 1998; Marens and Wicks 1999; Warren and Tweedale 2002; Litvin 2003). What is more, companies are increasingly being held to account for their past ethical conduct. Probably the most extreme example of this is the pressure on German companies to account for their conduct during the Nazi era. It is notable that in their efforts to counter or pre-empt Holocaust-related lawsuits or public relations disasters, companies have commissioned historians who are expert in Holocaust history, rather than business historians, to lead 'independent critical reviews' of their records during the Nazi era (Pinto-Duschinsky 1998; Feldman 1999). A recent example is Bertelsmann, the German publishing company. In 1998 Bertelsmann was in the process of taking over Random House, the American publisher. Bertelsmann's then chairman made much of the company's history, claiming that in 1944 it had become 'one of the few non-Jewish media companies closed down by the Nazi regime', due to its continued publication of books that were banned by the Third Reich. But this company legend was challenged and proved to be false. Far from opposing the Nazi regime, Bertelsmann had published literature with anti-semitic content. In response, Middelhoff contacted Saul Friendländer, the renowned historian of Nazi anti-semitism, and asked him to direct an *Independent Historical Commission for Investigating the History of the Bertelsmann Firm during the Third Reich* (IHC) (Friedländer *et al.* 2002). Friedländer was joined by Norbert Frei, a social and political historian, Trutz Rendtorrf, a theologian, and Reinhard Wittmann, a specialist in the history of literature and the book trade (Friedländer *et al.* 2002). The IHC's final report, *Bertelsmann im Dritten Reich* [Bertelsmann in the Third Reich] (Friedländer *et al.* 2002), was presented in October 2002.

Non-German companies have also had their histories re-examined, although unlike the German companies, such accounts have not usually been commissioned by the companies concerned. Recent examples include Edwin Black's *IBM and the Holocaust* (2002) and Lowell J. Satre's *Chocolate on Trial* (2005), which tells the story of Cadbury's response to its discovery in 1901 that it had been purchasing cocoa beans from plantations in Portuguese colonies that used slave labour. The dilemmas that the company faced in the early 20th century resonate with contemporary issues of business ethics, corporate social responsibility and globalization. The darker side of corporate history, and how companies respond to revelations of their unsavoury past, raises interesting questions about the meaning and ethics of past business behaviour, and whether it can be studied for insights into contemporary dilemmas. On the one hand there is the obvious danger of judging past behaviour by today's standards, but there is also the risk that by historicizing past behaviour and explaining it in context, past wrongs are thereby excused, allowing organizations to celebrate a glorious past regardless of their involvement in war, racism, slavery and repression, or a disregard for human health and welfare.

8. Metanarratives of corporate capitalism

Chandler's monumental work, *The Visible Hand* (1977), while open to criticism (e.g. du Boff and Herman 1980; Roy 1990), has stood as virtually the only empirically researched historical metanarrative of the American industrial corporation, while his study of the USA, Britain, and Germany in *Scale and Scope* (1990) set the standard for comparative business history. But Chandler's interpretation has been challenged by several competing metanarratives of American capitalism, such as those of Fligstein (1990), Roy (1997) and Prechel (2000). In addition, the applicability of the American corporate model in Europe has been questioned (Djelic 1998; Kipping and Bjarnar 1998), as has Chandler's critique of family firms in the UK and other national contexts (Cassis 1997). Fligstein's (1990) work is rooted in the new institutionalism of organization theory, whereas Roy (1997) and Prechel (2000) are examples of the new economic sociology, the former with an institutionalist orientation, the latter with a more Marxian hue. Each offers multiple methods, from cross-sectional surveys of quantitative data sampled at regular historical intervals, through to detailed narrative case studies. These competing metanarratives of American capitalism reflect longstanding historiographical concerns with the viability of the industrial corporation in advanced capitalist economies, and the power that such corporations wield, which resonate with contemporary debates concerning globalization (e.g. Kaysen 1996; Marens 2003).

Chandler has consistently neglected the management of labour, and the role of labour itself in the modern corporation (McCraw 1988, 20). This lacuna in business history has been addressed by the work of Jacoby (1997, 2004a) on the USA, Gospel (1992) on the UK, as well as comparative studies by Jacoby (2004b), amongst others. Scranton's (1997) work raises the question of whether American capitalism could have taken alternative paths. The theme of historical contingency is picked up by Perrow (2002), in his masterful historiographical synthesis on the origins of American corporate capitalism, as well the 'historical alternatives' school outlined by Zeitlin (2003). The historical alternatives approach denies 'the existence of a unilinear logic of material progress' (Zeitlin 2003: 63). It also encourages an appreciation of narrative, since it is through narrative that historical agents 'constitute their identities and interests' (2003, 65). History matters because the contingencies of history facilitate alternatives, and contingency calls for narrative. There is also room for the 'dark side' of power: exploitation and conflict.

Faced with mounting criticism of the traditional Chandlerian viewpoint, business historians such as Toms and Wilson (2003) have suggested extensions to it, for example, to accommodate current concerns with corporate governance and accountability to external stakeholders. However, it should be noted that there has also been robust defense of the Chandlerian paradigm. Whittington and Mayer's (2000) landmark study stands in the tradition of the original Harvard studies that followed Chandler's *Strategy and Structure* (1962), such as Channon's (1973) study of British firms. They surveyed 'the domestically owned members of the Top 100 industrial companies by sales' in France, Germany and the United Kingdom (Whittington and Mayer 2000, 15), choosing two comparison points a decade apart, in 1983 and 1993. From their study they make strong political claims for the historical importance of the multidivisional corporation, and it is worth quoting them at length:

> We should recall the sense of shock and anxiety experienced by Americans and American-trained scholars as they contemplated the Europe of the 1950s and 1960s. Europe was a dark continent, historically the home of undemocratic fascism, then still threatened by undemocratic communism. While Soviet Europe seemed to be mustering huge economies of scale, industry in Western Europe was fragmented by history and borders. Western European business elites were untrained, stagnant, and incestuous; they had already shown themselves compliant in the face of military occupation and dictatorship ... The multidivisional, as it challenged the hierarchies of centralized functional organizations, and as it opened up the opaque complexities of holding companies, was part of a democratic as well

> as economic project. The transparency, meritocracy, and accountability of the multidivisional might have been limited – they were – but on the whole the new structure was much better than what went before. It was Europe's good fortune that democratic and economic interests coincided even to this extent.
>
> *(2000, 218–19)*

Whittington and Mayer (2000) characterize the debate between Chandlerian business history, which advocates the near universal superiority of the professionally managed capitalist corporation, and institutionalist defenders of alternative organizational forms, as a reflection of 'a wider contest between positivist universalism and contextualist relativism within the management sciences' (2000, 11). They accept that 'context matters', but their question is, 'how much?' (2000, 33). According to Andrew Pettigrew (2001, S66), Whittington and Mayer's systematic empirical work demonstrates that 'modernist forms of science variously labelled as "normal science", "positivism", or "rigorous research" are still alive and well' in management research. And we see it as significant that their research is resolutely historical, albeit 'history with purpose' (Whittington and Mayer 2000, 3). Even though they claim adherence to the Chandlerian view, Whittington and Mayer's bold claims reconnect business history with broader historiographical questions concerning the relationship between business and politics in Europe (Kobrak and Hansen 2004).

9. Management history and management education

Management history and business history overlap, especially in the study of management practices, such as scientific management (Nelson 1980), or corporate governance (Marens 2002), or particular management functions, such as labour management (Gospel 1992), marketing (Laird 1998; Witkowski 1998, 1999), or accounting (Kaplan and Johnson 1991; Toms 2002), and the role of management consultants (McKenna 2001, 2006) and management education (Locke 1989; Amdam 1996; Bjarnar, Amdam and Gammelsæter 2001) in diffusing management practices. However, the history of management thought constitutes a well-established and conceptually distinct field. Much of the research on the history of management thought is focused on F.W. Taylor and the influence of scientific management. Wrege and Greenwood's (1991) account is the most comprehensive and authoritative to date. Over the course of many years Wrege and his co-researchers have demolished many of the myths surrounding Taylor (Wrege and Perroni 1974; Wrege and Hodgetts 2000). In his popular biography of Taylor, Kanigel (1997, 571) duly acknowledges the work of Charles D. Wrege, his students and associates, and in particular his late colleague, Ronald G. Greenwood. Taylor's contribution to management thought has been continually contested. Nelson (1980), for example, contends that Taylor's technical achievements outweighed his contributions to management thinking. As a counter to Braverman's (1974) influential Marxist demonization of Taylor, Chris Nyland and his coresearchers (1996, 1998; Bruce and Nyland 2001) have drawn attention to the progressive elements in Taylorism and scientific management, and the close links between some Taylorists and organized labour. Monin *et al.* (2003) have used techniques derived from literary criticism to deconstruct Taylorist texts. Lois Kurowski has recently drawn attention to the significance of Taylor's views on race (Kurowski 2002) and religion (Kurowski and Rowlinson 2003) that have previously been overlooked.

Beyond Taylorism, the history of management thought has seen a series of important revisions. Mary Parker Follett is now acknowledged as an important management thinker whose contribution to management thought was hitherto overlooked due to her being a woman (Tonn 2003), opening the way for further research into the contributions of thinkers that have previously been overlooked. Hoopes (2003) provides a comprehensive critique of the influence of management thinkers in American society. Bill Cooke (1999) has argued that the leftist background of major figures such as Kurt Lewin has been written out of organization studies. Fiona Wilson (2003) has reconsidered management thinkers from a gender perspective, and Dallas Cullen (1994, 1997; Cullen and Gotell 2002) has provided a feminist critique of Maslow and motivation theory. Gantman (2005) combines a history of management thought with a telling critique of managerial ideology derived from critical management studies.

What brings business historians and management historians together is a concern to promote the study of history within business and management education. A case can be made that neither management practitioners nor management and organization studies academics know very much about business history, or the history of management and management thought. Chandler *et al.* (1986) made the case that history matters for practising managers. McCraw (in Chandler *et al.* 1986, 86) suggests that history can debunk an organization's myths. Nevertheless, and seemingly without contradicting McCraw, Tedlow claims that history can help managers by 'getting things, events, and facts into shared memory' (in Chandler *et al.* 1986, 82), and business historians remain convinced that 'good history is good business' (Ryant 1988, 563). But whether or not history is a valuable 'resource' for managers in business (Üsdiken and Kieser 2004, 329 note 11), that does not necessarily justify a place for history in business and management education. Debate on this issue has recently been prompted by David Van Fleet and Daniel Wren's (2005) article tracing the apparent decline of history teaching in American business schools during the last 20 years. In response Yates (2005) contends that MBA students probably need business history, as promoted by Harvard Business School's highly successful history course, whereas PhDs may need more management history. Bedeian (2004) criticizes the widespread 'historical illiteracy' amongst management researchers, and makes the case for studying the history of the management discipline in doctoral programs. In a long and considered review, Down (2001) takes on the argument that 'business managers simply do not have the time to think about the past'. Down's view is that business executives and management educators do not need to be historians, 'or even to learn history', but that since everyone involved in organizational activities bases their interpretations and decision-making on an analysis of past events, however recent, it is worth reflecting how such *historical* interpretations are constructed (Down 2001, 406). In other words, Down is arguing for an understanding of history as a process, rather than an accumulation of historical facts, and he warns against the use of historical case studies that are tailor-made for business students, which he describes as 'kitsch, or light' histories (2001, 407). In a similar vein Brady (1997) argues that 'the study of history can benefit the modern manager' by debunking erroneous business ideologies, such as free market economics.

Textbooks are one vehicle for promoting history within business schools, since even business school faculty who are committed to history can hardly be expected to teach history courses without the resources that are now expected by students. Wren's (2005) textbook is now well established for the history of management thought. McCraw's (1998) edited book derives from the Harvard business history course, and Wilson (1995) has provided an overview of British business history that can be used for teaching. Jeremy (1998) has produced a more conventional textbook for studying business history. However, each of these is predicated on the assumption that history should be taught as a separate course, rather than integrated into the main business school courses such as organization theory, marketing, strategy and human resource management. Keith Grint (2001), for example, draws on narratives of leaders in history, some of whom, such as Florence Nightingale, are hardly business leaders, in order to question conventional scientific leadership research.

If history is to be brought into the business school curriculum, then we should consider how it came to be excluded in the first place. Arguably, if there is a historic turn taking place in management and organization theory, then there was an earlier 'historic break', whereby history and narrative case studies were excluded. It is worth noting that John Child began his career as a leading organization theorist with a major study of the history of management thought in Britain (1964, 1969). Derek Pugh and David Hickson were both major contributors to the Aston Studies. Their *Writers on Organizations* series (Pugh and Hickson 2000) now constitutes a small library on the history management thinkers. Pugh has been a keen supporter of the Management History Research Group that promotes the study of management thought, and the inclusion of history in the business school curriculum in the UK.

10. Public history

There is increasing public interest in history. This is reflected in the rise of public historians, such as Simon Schama, who presented a highly successful televised history of Britain (Schama 2001). History departments at leading universities are keener than ever to recruit faculty members with a high public profile. The work of several public historians, such as Schama, is predicated upon a conscious, and to some extent ironic, return to narrative and storytelling licensed by theorists such as Hayden White. The theoretical ramifications of a return to narrative in history resonate with the increased attention to narrative and storytelling in organization theory (e.g. Weick 1995; Gabriel 2000; Boje 2001), but organization theorists have tended to use literary theory to interrogate texts in their own discipline (e.g. Czarniawska 1999), instead of improving their writing for a wider readership, as postmodernist historians have done (Evans 1997). Developments in history have implications for business schools. For example, one of the leading conservative public historians, Andrew Roberts, presented a television series on leadership based on historical lessons from Hitler and Churchill (Roberts 2003). If, as Grint (2001) claims, history can provide an understanding of leadership as an art rather than a science, then historians such as Roberts are likely to impinge upon the claims of business school faculty in relation to leadership and other fields. Management and organization theorists may dismiss this as pop history or Heathrow Organization Theory (Burrell 1997). But John Ramsden (2002, 584–6), a historian who has examined the memorialization of Churchill, is not so dismissive of the business books that use Churchill as a model of leadership. Public historians have occasionally turned their attention to business matters. David Halberstam's (1986) historical study of Ford and Nissan was a timely comparison of American and Japanese corporate cultures. In addition to his more popular work, Niall Ferguson is also the author of a major commissioned history of the Rothschild bank (1998b) that implicitly challenges conventional business school models (Rowlinson 2000). We wonder whether there is scope for considering the genres of public history and their relevance for management and organization theory.

One flourishing genre of public history is that of counterfactual history, which asks 'what if?' or 'what might have been?' (Cowley 2002). 'What if?'™ has been so successful that it is registered as a trademark of American Historical Publications, Inc. (Roberts 2005). This proliferation followed the success of Ferguson's (1998a) theoretically informed work on counterfactual history. Initially counterfactuals concerned perennial questions: What if Germany had invaded Britain during the Second World War? (Roberts 1998). What if Lincoln had not freed the slaves? (Wicker 2002). What ifs have become the preserve of conservative historians, and often tend to imagine how much better history would have been if some radical event had been avoided, or, less frequently, how much worse it might have been if a more progressive turn had been taken (Žižek 2005). Counterfactuals have been set up as a liberal or conservative challenge to the historical determinism that Marxists allegedly adhere to. However, as Kieser (1994) has pointed out, a more historical approach could also temper the determinism that prevails in the predominant theories of organization, and counterfactuals might be one way to counter such determinism (Booth 2003).

Summary and conclusions

As befits a new venture, we will finish with an optimistic overview of the prospects for management and organizational history. There is an historic turn underway in management and organization theory. Insofar as this turn leads to a historical reorientation, rather than merely a supplement or integration of history into management and organization theory, it is aligned with the reorientation from critical management and gender studies. As part of the historic turn there is scope for reflection on the appropriate methods and styles of writing for historically oriented studies of organizations. Management and organization theorists are taking more interest in the philosophy of history and historical theorists, such as White, Foucault and Ricoeur. While the initial concentration on Foucault reinforced the suspicion of management and organization theorists towards narrative, a greater understanding of White, Ricoeur and McCloskey is likely to lead to greater appreciation of well-crafted historical narratives. The connection of organizational culture and identity with history and social memory studies is one particular theme that we expect to see developing within the now identifiable field of organizational history. The field also encompasses the historicization of management and organizational phenomena. In parallel with the historic turn in management and organization theory, business history has become more open to an engagement with theory from sociology and cultural studies, even if many business historians remain in thrall to economics. The current concern with business ethics and corporate social responsibility needs to be more historically informed, and conversely historical research needs to pay more attention to the meaning and ethics of past business behaviour, as is illustrated by the treatment of history by many German companies that have only recently come to terms with their record during the Nazi era. The proliferation of metanarratives of corporate capitalism has challenged the Chandlerian paradigm, which opens up space for a much broader historiographical debate about the role of the modern corporation, not only in relation to economic growth, but also in relation to equality and democracy in an era of globalization. The study of management history continues to provide provocative revisions in the history of management thought. Lively historiographical debates in both business history and management history are likely to find an audience in business schools. Finally, there is enormous public interest in history, especially well-told historical narratives. This provides an impetus for business schools to respond to history, for example, by looking to historical insights into the art of leadership rather than dry science.

References

Aaltio-Marjosola, I., A.J. Mills, and J. Helms Mills, eds. 2002. Special Issue of *Culture and Organization* on 'Exploring Gendered Organizational Cultures', 8(2).

Abrahamson, E. 1997. The emergence and prevalence of employee management rhetorics: The effects of long waves, labor unions, and turnover, 1875 to 1992. *Academy of Management Journal* 40: 491–533.

Amatori, F. and G. Jones, eds. 2003. *Business history around the world*. Cambridge: Cambridge University Press.

Amdam, R.P., ed. 1996. *Management education and competitiveness: Europe, Japan and the US*. London: Routledge.

Barley, S.R. and G. Kunda. 1992. Design and devotion: Surges of rational and normative ideologies of control in managerial discourse. *Administrative Science Quarterly* 37: 363–99.

Barrett, F.J. and S. Srivastava. 1991. History as a mode of inquiry in organizational life: A role for human cosmogony. *Human Relations* 44: 231–54.

Bauman, Z. 1989. *Modernity and the holocaust*. Cambridge: Polity.

Bedeian, A.G. 2004. The gift of professional maturity. *Academy of Management Learning and Education* 3: 92–8.

Bendix, R. 1956. *Work and authority in industry: Ideologies of management in the course of industrialization.* New York: John Wiley.

Bjarnar, O., R.P. Amdam, and H. Gammelsæter. 2001. Management qualification and dissemination of knowledge in regional innovation systems: The case of Norway 1930s–1990s. *Journal of Industrial History* 4: 75–93.

Black, E. 2002. *IBM and the Holocaust: The strategic alliance between Nazi Germany and America's most powerful corporation.* New York: Crown.

Boje, D.M. 1995. Stories of the story telling organization: A postmodern analysis of Disney as 'Tamara-land'. *Academy of Management Journal* 38: 997–1035.

Boje, D.M. 2001. *Narrative methods for organizational and communication research.* London: SAGE.

Booth, C. 2003. Does history matter in strategy? Historiographical possibilities and path dependence. *Management Decision* 41: 96–104.

Booth, C., P. Clark, A. Delahaye, S. Procter, and M. Rowlinson. 2005. La memoria social en las organizaciones. Los métodos que las organizaciones usan para recorder el pasado. *Revista Empresa y Humanismo IX*, 2: 95–130.

Brady, F.N. 1997. Finding a history for management. *Journal of Management Inquiry* 6: 160–67.

Braverman, H. 1974. *Labor and monopoly capital: The degradation of labor in the twentieth century.* New York: Monthly Review Press.

Brown, J.S. and P. Duguid. 2000. *The social life of information.* Boston, MA: Harvard Business School Press.

Bruce, K. and C. Nyland. 2001. Scientific management, institutionalism, and business stabilization: 1903–1923. *Journal of Economic Issues* 35: 955–78.

Burrell, G. 1997. *Pandemonium: Towards a retro-organization theory.* London: SAGE.

Carr, D. 1986. *Time, narrative and history.* Bloomington, IN: Indiana University Press.

Carr, D. 1998. Narrative and the real world: An argument for continuity. In *History and theory: Contemporary readings*, ed. B. Fay, P. Pomper, and R.T. Vann, 137–52. Malden, MA: Blackwell.

Carroll, C.E., ed. 2002. The strategic use of the past and future in organizational change. *Journal of Organizational Change Management*, Special Issue, 15(6).

Carter, C., A. McKinlay, and M. Rowlinson. 2002. Introduction: Foucault, management and history. *Organization* 9: 516–18.

Casey, A. 1997. Collective memory in organizations. In *Advances in Strategic Management 14: Organizational Learning and Strategic Management*, ed. J. Walsh and A. Huff, 111–51. Greenwich, CT: JAI Press.

Cassis, Y. 1997. *Big business: The European experience in the twentieth century.* Oxford: Oxford University Press.

Casson, M. and M.B. Rose. 1997. Institutions and the evolution of modern business: Introduction. *Business History* 39: 1–8.

Chandler, A.D. 1962. *Strategy and structure: Chapters in the history of the industrial enterprise.* Cambridge, MA: MIT Press.

Chandler, A.D. 1977. *The visible hand: The managerial revolution in American business.* Cambridge, MA: Belknap Press.

Chandler, A.D. 1988. Business history as institutional history. In *The essential Alfred Chandler: Essays toward a historical theory of big business*, ed. T.K McCraw, 301–6. Cambridge, MA: Harvard Business School Press.

Chandler, A.D. 1990. *Scale and scope: The dynamics of industrial capitalism.* Cambridge, MA: Belknap Press.

Chandler, A.D. 2003. The opportunities for business history at the beginning of the twenty-first century. In *Business history around the world*, ed. F. Amatori and G. Jones, 394–405. Cambridge: Cambridge University Press.

Chandler, A.D., T.K. McCraw, R.S. McDonald, R.S. Tedlow, and R.H.K. Vietor. 1986. Why history matters to managers. *Harvard Business Review* Jan-Feb: 81–8.

Channon, D.F. 1973. *The strategy and structure of British enterprise.* Boston, MA: Harvard University Press.

Child, J. 1964. Quaker employers and industrial relations. *Sociological Review* 12: 293–315.

Child, J. 1969. *British management thought.* London: Allen and Unwin.

Child, J. 1972. Organizational structure, environment and performance: The role of strategic choice. *Sociology* 6: 1–22.

Clark, P. 2000. *Organizations in action: Competition between contexts.* London: Routledge.

Clark, P. and M. Rowlinson. 2002. Time and narrative history in organization theory: Charting historical narratives. Academy of Management Meeting, Organization and Management Theory Division, Denver, August.

Clark, P. and M. Rowlinson. 2004. The treatment of history in organization studies: Toward an 'historic turn?' *Business History* 46: 331–52.

Clegg, S. 2001. The bounds of rationality: Power/history/imagination. Keynote Address, Asia-Pacific Researchers in Organization Studies conference (APROS), Hong Kong.
Clegg, S. and D. Dunkerley. 1980. *Organization, class and control*. London: Routledge and Kegan Paul.
Coleman, D.C. 1987. The uses and abuses of business history. *Business History* 29: 141–56.
Collins, J.C. and J.I. Porras. 1996. *Built to last: Successful habits of visionary companies*. London: HarperCollins.
Cooke, B. 1999. Writing the left out of management theory: The historiography of the management of change. *Organization* 6: 81–105.
Cowley, R., ed. 2002. *More what if? Eminent historians imagine what might have been*. London: Macmillan.
Cullen, D. 1994. Feminism, management and self-actualization. *Gender, Work and Organization* 1: 127–37.
Cullen, D. 1997. Maslow, monkeys and motivation theory. *Organization* 4: 355–73.
Cullen, D. and L. Gotell. 2002. From orgasms to organizations: Maslow, women's sexuality and the gendered foundations of the need hierarchy. *Gender, Work and Organization* 9: 537–55.
Czarniawska, B. 1999. *Writing management: Organization theory as a literary genre*. Oxford: Oxford University Press.
Deal, T. and A. Kennedy. 2000. *The new corporate cultures*. London: Texere.
Dellheim, C. 1986. Business in time: The historian and corporate culture. *Public Historian* 8: 9–22.
Djelic, M-L. 1998. *Exporting the American model: The post-war transformation of European business*. Oxford: Oxford University Press.
Down, S. 2001. The use of history in business and management learning, and some implications for management learning. *Management Learning* 32: 393–410.
du Boff, R.B. and E.S. Herman. 1980. Alfred Chandler's new business history: A review. *Politics and Society* 10: 87–110.
du Gay, P. 2000. *In praise of bureaucracy: Weber – organization – ethics*. London: SAGE.
Eichengreen, B. 1996. *Globalizing capital: A history of the international monetary system*. Princeton, NJ: Princeton University Press.
Elias, N. 1994. *The civilizing process*. 2 vols. Oxford: Blackwell.
Evans, R.J. 1997. *In defence of history*. London: Granta.
Feldman, G.D. 1999. The business history of the 'Third Reich' and the responsibilities of the historian: Gold, insurance, 'aryanization' and forced labor. University of California, Berkeley, Center for German and European Studies, Working Paper.
Ferguson, N. 1998a. *The pity of war*. London: Penguin.
Ferguson, N. 1998b. *The world's banker: The history of the house of Rothschild*. London: Weidenfeld and Nicolson.
Ferguson, N. 1998c. Virtual history: Towards a chaotic theory of the past. In *Virtual history: Alternatives and counterfactuals*, ed. N. Ferguson, 1–90. London: Papermac.
Fligstein, N. 1990. *The transformation of corporate control*. Cambridge, MA: Harvard University Press.
Foucault, M. 1970. *The order of things: An archaeology of the human sciences*. London: Tavistock.
Foucault, M. 1972. *The archaeology of knowledge*. London: Tavistock.
Foucault, M. 1977. *Discipline and punish: The birth of the prison*. Harmondsworth: Allen Lane.
Friedländer, S., N. Frei, T. Rendtorff, and R. Wittman. 2002. *Bertelsmann im Dritten Reich*. Munich: C. Bertelsmann Verlag.
Friedman, M. 1966. *Essays in positive economics*. Chicago, IL: Chicago University Press.
Gabriel, Y. 2000. *Storytelling in organizations*. Oxford: Oxford University Press.
Galambos, L. 2003. Identity and the boundaries of business history: An essay on consensus and creativity. In *Business history around the world*, ed. F. Amatori and G. Jones, 11–30. Cambridge: Cambridge University Press.
Gantman, E. 2005. *Capitalism, social privilege and managerial ideologies*. Aldershot: Ashgate.
Glynn, M.A. 1997. Commentary: Collective memory as fact and artifact: Cultural and political elements of memory in organizations. In *Advances in Strategic Management 14: Organizational Learning and Strategic Management*, ed. J. Walsh and A. Huff, 147–54. Greenwich, CT: JAI Press.
Gospel, H.F. 1992. *Markets, firms, and the management of labour in modern Britain*. Cambridge: Cambridge University Press.
Gough, P. 2004. Corporations and commemoration: First world war remembrance, Lloyds TSB and the National Memorial Arboretum. *International Journal of Heritage Studies* 10: 435–55.
Grint, K. 2001. *The arts of leadership*. Oxford: Oxford University Press.
Guillén, M. 1994. *Models of management: Work, authority and organization in a comparative perspective*. Chicago, IL: University of Chicago Press.

Halberstam, D. 1986. *The reckoning: A tale of two cultures as seen through two car companies*. London: Bloomsbury.
Halbwachs, M. [1950] 1980. *The collective memory*. New York: Harpert Colophon Books.
Hannah, L. 1984. Entrepreneurs and the social sciences. *Economica* 51: 219–34.
Hassard, J. and M. Rowlinson. 2002. Researching Foucault's research: Organization and control in Joseph Lancaster's monitorial schools. *Organization* 9: 615–40.
Hausman, W.J. 2003. Business history in the United States at the end of the twentieth century. In *Business history around the world*, ed. F. Amatori and G. Jones, 83–110. Cambridge: Cambridge University Press.
Hegele, C. and A. Kieser. 2001. Control the construction of your legend or someone else will: An analysis of texts on Jack Welch. *Journal of Management Inquiry* 10: 298–309.
Higham, J. and F. Gilbert 1965. *History: The Development of Historical Studies in the United States*. Englewood Cliffs, NJ: Prentice-Hall.
Hobsbawm, E. and T. Ranger, eds. 1983. *The invention of tradition*. Cambridge: Cambridge University Press.
Hoopes, J. 2003. *False prophets: The gurus who created modern management and why their ideas are bad for business today*. New York: Perseus.
Hoskin, K.W. and R.H. Macve. 1988. The genesis of accountability: The West Point connection. *Accounting, Organizations and Society* 13: 37–73.
Jacoby, S.M. 1997. *Modern manors: Welfare capitalism since the new deal*. Princeton, NJ: Princeton University Press.
Jacoby, S.M. 2004a. *Employing bureaucracy: Managers, unions, and the transformation of work in the 20th century*. Mahwah, NJ: Lawrence Erlbaum.
Jacoby, S.M. 2004b. *The embedded corporation: Corporate governance and employment relations in Japan and the United States*. Princeton, NJ: Princeton University Press.
Jacques, R. 1996. *Manufacturing the employee: Management knowledge for the 19th to 21st centuries*. London: SAGE.
Jeremy, D. 1998. *A business history of Britain: 1900–1990s*. Oxford: Oxford University Press.
Jones, G. 1999. Company history and business history in the 1990s. *European Yearbook of Business History* 2: 1–20.
Jones, S.R.H. 1997. Transaction costs and the theory of the firm. *Business History* 39: 9–25.
Kanigel, R. 1997. *The one best way: Frederick Winslow Taylor and the enigma of efficiency*. New York: Viking.
Kaplan, R.S. and H.T. Johnson. 1991. *Relevance lost: The rise and fall of management accounting*. Cambridge, MA: Harvard Business School Press.
Kaysen, C., ed. 1996. *The American corporation today: Examining the questions of power and efficiency at the century's end*. Oxford: Oxford University Press.
Kieser, A. 1989. Organizational, institutional and societal evolution: Medieval craft guilds and the genesis of formal organizations, *Administrative Science Quarterly* 34: 540–64.
Kieser, A. 1994. Why organization theory needs historical analyses and how this should be performed. *Organization Science* 5: 608–20.
Kieser, A. 1998. From freemasons to industrious patriots: Organizing and disciplining in 18th century Germany. *Organization Studies* 19: 47–71.
Kipping, M. 2003. Business-government relations: Beyond performance issues. In *Business history around the world*, ed. F. Amatori and G. Jones, 372–93. Cambridge: Cambridge University Press.
Kipping, M. and O. Bjarnar. 1998. *The Americanisation of European business*. London: Routledge.
Kobrak, C. and P.H. Hansen, eds. 2004. *European business, dictatorship, and political risk, 1920–1945*. (Berghahn Series in Business History and Political Economy, Vol. 1.) New York: Berghahn.
Kransdorff, A. 1998. *Corporate amnesia: Keeping know-how in the company*. London: Butterworth-Heinemann.
Kurowski, L.L. 2002. Cloaked culture and veiled diversity: Why early management theorists ignored workforce diversity. *Management Decision* 40: 183–91.
Kurowski, L. L. and M. Rowlinson. 2003. 'The gospel according to St. Frederick': The friendship and shared beliefs of Frederick W. Taylor and Scudder Klyce. In *Conference Proceedings of the 2003 National Meeting of the Academy of Management, Seattle, Washington*, ed. D.H. Nagao. (CD-ROM).
Laird, P.W. 1998. *Advertising progress: American business and the rise of consumer marketing*. Baltimore, MD: Johns Hopkins University Press.
Lamoreaux, N.R., M.G. Raff, and P. Temin. 1997. New economic approaches to the study of business history. *Business and Economic History* 26, 1: 57–79.
Lazonick, W. 2003. Understanding innovative enterprise: Toward the integration of economic theory and business history. In *Business history around the world*, ed. F. Amatori and G. Jones, 31–61. Cambridge: Cambridge University Press.
Lipartito, K. 1995. Culture and the practice of business history. *Business and Economic History* 24: 1–41.
Litvin, D.B. 2003. *Empires of profit: Commerce, conquest and corporate responsibility*. London: Texere.

Locke, R.R. 1989. *Management and higher education since 1940: The influence of America and Japan on West Germany, Great Britain, and France*. Cambridge: Cambridge University Press.
McCloskey, D.N. 1990. *The narrative of economic expertise*. Chicago, IL: University of Chicago Press.
McCloskey, D.N. 1994. *Knowledge and persuasion in economics*. Cambridge: Cambridge University Press.
McCraw, T.K. 1988. Introduction: The intellectual odyssey of Alfred D. Chandler, Jr. In *The essential Alfred Chandler: Essays toward a historical theory of big business*, ed. T.K McCraw, 1–21. Cambridge, MA.: Harvard Business School Press.
McCraw, T.K. 1998. *Creating modern capitalism: How entrepreneurs, companies and countries triumphed in three industrial revolutions*. Cambridge, MA: Harvard University Press.
McDonald, T.J., ed. 1996. *The historic turn in the human sciences*. Ann Arbor, MI: Michigan University Press.
McKenna, C. 2001. The world's newest profession: Management consulting in the twentieth century. *Enterprise and Society* 2: 673–9.
McKenna C. 2006. *The world's newest profession: Management consulting in the twentieth century*. Cambridge: Cambridge University Press.
McKinlay, A. 2002. 'Dead selves': The birth of the modern career. *Organization* 9: 595–614.
Marens, R.S. 1998. Ending corporate absolutism: A proposal for managerial citizenship within the corporation. Proceedings of the Annual Conference of the International Association for Business and Society.
Marens, R.S. 2002. Inventing corporate governance: The emergence of shareholder activism in the nineteen forties. *Journal of Business and Management* 8: 365–89.
Marens, R.S. 2003. Two, three, many Enrons: American financial hypertrophy and the end of economic hegemony. *Organization* 10: 588–93.
Marens, R.S. and A. Wicks. 1999. Getting real: Stakeholder theory and the general irrelevance of fiduciary duties owed to shareholders. *Business Ethics Quarterly* 9: 273–93.
Martin, J. 2002. *Organizational culture: Mapping the terrain*. Thousand Oaks, CA: SAGE.
Martin de Holan, P. and N. Phillips. 2003a. Organizational forgetting. In *Handbook of organizational learning*, ed. M. Easterby-Smith and M. Lyles, 393–409. London: SAGE.
Martin de Holan, P. and N. Phillips. 2003b. Organizational forgetting as strategy. *Strategic Organization* 2: 412–30.
Martin de Holan, P. and N. Phillips. 2004. Remembrance of things past? The dynamics of organizational forgetting. *Management Science* 50: 1603–13.
Martin de Holan, P., N. Phillips, and T. Lawrence. 2004. Managing organizational forgetting. *Sloan Management Review* 45: 45–51.
Miani, M. 2004. The Simpsons: Innovation and tradition in a postmodern TV Family, http://www.baskerville.it/PremioB/2004/Miani.pdf
Mills, A.J. 1997. Duelling discourses: Desexualization versus eroticism in the corporate framing of female sexuality in the British airline industry, 1945–1960. In *Managing the organizational melting pot: Dilemmas of workplace diversity*, ed. P. Prasad, A.J. Mills, M. Elmes, and A. Prasad, 171–98. Thousand Oaks, CA: SAGE.
Mills, A.J. 2002. Studying the gendering of organizational culture over time: Concerns, issues and strategies. *Gender, Work and Organization* 9: 286–307.
Mills, A.J. 2006. *Sex, strategy, and the stratosphere: Airlines and the gendering of organizations*. London: Palgrave.
Misztal, B.A. 2003, *Theories of social remembering*. Milton Keynes: Open University Press.
Monin, N., D. Barry, and D.J. Monin. 2003. Toggling with Taylor: A different approach to reading a management theory text. *Journal of Management Studies* 40: 377–401.
Moore, K. and D. Lewis. 1999. *Birth of the multinational: 2000 years of ancient history*. Copenhagen: Copenhagen Business School Press.
Nelson, D. 1980. *Frederick Taylor and the rise of scientific management*. Madison, WI: University of Wisconsin Press.
Newton, T. 1995. *'Managing' stress: Emotion and power at work*. London: SAGE.
Newton, T. 2001. Elias and organization: Preface. *Organization* 8: 459–65.
Newton, T. 2004. From freemasons to the employee: Organization, history and subjectivity. *Organization Studies* 25: 1363–87.
Nissley, N. and A. Casey. 2002. The politics of the exhibition: Viewing corporate museums through the paradigmatic lens of organizational memory. *British Journal of Management* 13: S35–S45.
Nkomo, S. 1992. The emperor has no clothes: Rewriting 'race in organizations'. *Academy of Management Review* 17: 487–513.
Nyland, C. 1996. Taylorism, John R. Commons and the Hoxie report. *Journal of Economic Issues* 30: 985–1016.
Nyland, C. 1998. Taylorism and the mutual-gains strategy. *Industrial Relations* 37: 519–42.
Olivera, F. 2000. Memory systems in organizations: An empirical investigation of mechanisms for knowledge collection, storage and access. *Journal of Management Studies* 37: 811–32.

Ooi, C-S. 2002. Persuasive histories: Decentering, recentering and the emotional crafting of the past. *Journal of Organizational Change Management* 15: 606–21.

O'Rourke, K.H. 2002. Europe and the causes of globalization, 1790 to 2000. In *Europe and globalisation*, ed. H. Kierzkowski, 64–86. Basingstoke: Palgrave Macmillan.

Parker, M. 2002. Contesting histories: Unity and division in a building society. *Journal of Organizational Change Management*, 15: 589–605.

Penrose, E.T. 1959. *The theory of the growth of the firm*. Oxford: Blackwell.

Perrow, C. 1986. *Complex organizations*, 3rd ed. New York: McGraw-Hill.

Perrow, C. 2002. *Organizing America: Wealth, power, and the origins of corporate capitalism*. Princeton, NJ: Princeton University Press.

Pettigrew, A.M. 1985. *The awakening giant: Continuity and change in Imperial Chemical Industries*. Oxford: Blackwell.

Pettigrew, A.M. 2001. Management research after modernism. *British Journal of Management*, 12: S61–S70.

Pinto-Duschinsky, M. 1998. Selling the past: The dangers of outside finance for historical research. *Times Literary Supplement*. 23 October.

Porter, M. 1990. *The competitive advantage of nations and their firms*. New York: The Free Press.

Prasad, A. 1997. The colonizing consciousness and representations of the other: A postcolonial critique of the discourse of oil. In *Managing the organizational melting pot: Dilemmas of workplace diversity*, ed. P. Prasad, A.J. Mills, M. Elmes, and A. Prasad, 285–311. Thousand Oaks, CA: SAGE.

Prechel, H. 2000. *Big business and the state: Historical transitions and corporate transformation, 1880s–1990s*. Albany, NY: State University of New York Press.

Procter, S., C. Booth, P. Clark, and M. Rowlinson. 2003. *The symbolism of corporate history*. Conference of the Association of Business Historians, Churchill College, Cambridge.

Pugh, D.S. and D.J. Hickson. 2000. *Great writers on organizations: The second omnibus edition*. Aldershot: Ashgate.

Ramsden, J. 2002. *Man of the century: Winston Churchill and his legend since 1945*. New York: Columbia University Press.

Ricoeur, P. 1984. *Time and narrative*. 3 vols. Chicago, IL: Chicago University Press.

Roberts, A. 1998. Hitler's England: What if Germany had invaded Britain in May 1940? In *Virtual history: Alternatives and counterfactuals*, ed. N. Ferguson, 281–320. London: Papermac.

Roberts, A., ed. 2003. *Hitler and Churchill: Secrets of leadership*. London: Weidenfeld and Nicholson.

Roberts, A., ed. 2005. *What might have been: Imaginary history from 12 leading historians*. London: Phoenix.

Rowlinson, M. 2000. Review of N. Ferguson, 1998. *The world's banker: The history of the house of Rothschild*. *Human Relations* 53: 573–86.

Rowlinson, M. 2001. Business history and organization theory. *Journal of Industrial History* 4: 1–23.

Rowlinson, M. 2002. Public history review essay: Cadbury World. *Labour History Review* 67: 101–19.

Rowlinson, M. 2004. Historical analysis of company documentation. In *Qualitative methods in organizational research*, ed. C. Cassell and G. Symon, 301–11. London: SAGE.

Rowlinson, M. and J. Hassard. 1993. The invention of corporate culture: A history of the histories of Cadbury. *Human Relations* 46: 299–326.

Rowlinson, M. and S. Procter. 1999. Organizational culture and business history. *Organization Studies* 20: 369–96.

Roy, W.G. 1990. Functional and historical logics in explaining the rise of the American industrial corporation. *Comparative Social Research* 12: 19–44.

Roy, W.G. 1997. *Socializing capital: The rise of the large industrial corporation in America*. Princeton, NJ: Princeton University Press.

Ryant, C. 1988. Oral history and business history. *Journal of American History* 75: 560–6.

Satre, L.J. 2005. *Chocolate on trial: Slavery, politics, and the ethics of business*. Athens, OH: Ohio University Press.

Savage, M. 1998. Discipline, surveillance and the 'career': Employment on the Great Western Railway 1833–1914. In *Foucault, management and organization theory*, ed. A. McKinlay and K. Starkey, 65–92. London: SAGE.

Schama, S. 2001. *A history of Britain: The British wars, 1603–1776*. London: BBC.

Scranton, P. 1997. *Endless novelty: Specialty production and American industrialization, 1865–1925*. Princeton, NJ: Princeton University Press.

Scranton, P. and R. Horowitz. 1997. 'The future for business history': An introduction. *Business and Economic History* 26: 1–4.

Shenhav, Y. 1995. From chaos to systems: The engineering foundation of organization theory, 1879–1932. *Administrative Science Quarterly* 40: 557–85.

Shenhav, Y. 1999. *Manufacturing rationality: The engineering foundations of the managerial revolution*. Oxford: Oxford University Press.
Slaven, T., ed. 2000. *Business history, theory and practice*. Glasgow: Centre for Business History in Scotland.
Smith, C., J. Child, and M. Rowlinson. 1990. *Reshaping work: The Cadbury experience*. Cambridge: Cambridge University Press.
Steel, M. 1999. History to make a future. *Socialist Worker* 13 November, Issue 1672.
Strati, A. 2000. *Theory and method in organization studies*. London: SAGE.
Taylor, B. and B. Freer. 2002. Containing the nuclear past: The politics of history and heritage at the Hanford Plutonium Works. *Journal of Organizational Change Management* 15: 563–88.
Thomas, R., A.J. Mills, and J. Helms Mills. 2004. *Identity politics at work: Resisting gender, gendering resistance*. London: Routledge.
Toms, J.S. 2002. The rise of modern accounting and the fall of the public company: The Lancashire Cotton Mills, 1870–1914. *Accounting, Organizations and Society* 27: 61–84.
Toms, J.S. and J.F. Wilson. 2003. Scale, scope and accountability: Towards a new paradigm of British business history. *Business History* 45: 1–23.
Tonn, J.C. 2003. *Mary P. Follett: Creating democracy, transforming management*. New Haven, CT: Yale University Press.
Tosh, J. 1991. *The pursuit of history*, 2nd ed. London: Longman.
Townley, B. 2002. Managing with modernity. *Organization* 9: 549–73.
Tweedale, G. 1999. Management strategies for health: J.W. Roberts and the Armley asbestos tragedy, 1920–1958. *Journal of Industrial History* 2: 72–95.
Üsdiken, B. and A. Kieser. 2004. Introduction: History in organization studies. *Business History* 46: 321–30.
Van Fleet, D.D. and D.A. Wren. 2005. Teaching history in business schools, 1982–2003. *Academy of Management Learning and Education* 4: 44–56.
Walsh, J.P. and G.R. Ungson. 1991. Organizational memory. *Academy of Management Review* 16: 57–91.
Warren, R. and G. Tweedale. 2002. Business ethics and business history: Neglected dimensions in management education. *British Journal of Management* 13: 209–19.
Weick, K. 1995. *Sensemaking in organizations*. London: SAGE.
Westall, O.M. 1996. British business history and the culture of business. In *Business history and business culture*, ed. A. Godley and O.M. Westall, 21–47. Manchester: Manchester University Press.
Whipp, R. and P. Clark 1986. *Innovation and the auto industry: Product, process and work organization*. London: Francis Pinter.
White, H. 1973. *Metahistory*. Baltimore, MD: John Hopkins University Press.
White, H. 1987. *The Content of the form: Narrative discourse and historical representation*. Baltimore, MD: John Hopkins University Press.
Whittington, R. and M. Mayer. 2000. *The European corporation: Strategy, structure, and social science*. Oxford: Oxford University Press.
Wicker, T. 2002. If Lincoln had not freed the slaves. In *More what if? Eminent historians imagine what might have been*, ed. R. Cowley, 152–64. London: Macmillan.
Wikipedia 2005. The Flintstones, http://en.wikipedia.org/wiki/The_Flintstones
Wilson, F. 2003. *Organizational behaviour and gender*. Aldershot: Ashgate.
Wilson, J.F. 1995. *British business history, 1720–1994*. Manchester: Manchester University Press.
Witkowski, T.H. 1998. The early American style: A history of marketing and consumer values. *Psychology and Marketing* 15: 125–43.
Witkowski, T.H. 1999. The early development of family purchasing roles in America, 1750–1840. *Journal of Macromarketing* 19: 104–14.
Wrege, C. D., and R.G. Greenwood. 1991. *Frederick W. Taylor: The father of scientific management*. Homewood, IL: Richard D. Irwin, Inc.
Wrege, C.D. and R.M. Hodgetts. 2000. Frederick W. Taylor's 1989 pig iron observations: Examining fact, fiction, and lessons for the new millennium. *Academy of Management Journal* 43: 1283–91.
Wrege, C.D. and A.G. Perroni. 1974. Taylor's pig-tale: A historical analysis of Frederick W. Taylor's pig-iron experiments. *Academy of Management Journal* 17: 6–22.
Wren, D.A. 2005. *The history of management thought*, 5th ed. Hoboken, NJ: Wiley.
Yates, J. 1997. Using Giddens' structuration theory to inform business history. *Business and Economic History* 26: 159–83.
Yates, J. 2005. Recent article on teaching history in business schools. Message to H-Business listserv, 24 March, http://www.h-net.org/~business/

Zald, M. 1993. Organization studies as a scientific and humanistic enterprise: Towards a reconceptualization of the foundations of the field. *Organization Science* 4: 513–28.

Zald, M. 2002. Spinning disciplines: Critical management studies in the context of the transformation of management education. *Organization* 9: 365–85.

Zeitlin, J. 2003. Productive alternatives: Flexibility, governance, and strategic choice in industrial history. In *Business history around the world*, ed. F. Amatori and G. Jones, 62–82. Cambridge: Cambridge University Press.

Žižek, S. 2005. What if we don't act now? Review of A. Roberts, ed. 2003. *Hitler and Churchill: Secrets of leadership*. London: Weidenfeld and Nicholson. *London Review of Books* 18 August: 23.

6

Revisiting the historic turn: a personal reflection

Michael Rowlinson

Having contributed to the historic turn in organization studies in various ways, not least by naming it as such so that it can be dated and commemorated, and helping to launch the journal *Management & Organizational History*, I would like to reflect on what the historic turn means to me. First of all I will set out a celebratory story of the historic turn and my part in it. Then I will offer a more personal contingent counter narrative of how the historic turn nearly didn't happen, or at least how my part in it was more tenuous than might appear because of the difficulties I had in getting historical papers accepted at conferences and in journals. Finally I will describe the context in which my own personal turn to history came about.

The success of the historic turn

The article on "The Treatment of History in Organisation Studies: Towards an 'Historic Turn?'" that I co-authored with Peter Clark (Clark & Rowlinson, 2004), was published in a special issue of *Business History* on "History in Organization Studies," edited by Behlül Üsdiken and Alfred Kieser (Üsdiken & Kieser, 2004). It was one of the five papers that Üsdiken and Kieser selected for the special issue from the European Group for Organization Studies subtheme, "Rediscovering History in Organizations," which they had organized for the 2001 colloquium in Lyon. According to the Taylor & Francis website for *Business History* the article was the second most highly cited output from the journal up to the end of August 2014 (with 35 citations in CrossRef after 39 citations for the most highly cited output; 124 citations in Google Scholar, Sept. 8, 2014). The Introduction to the Special Issue was the sixth most highly cited output from the journal (with 26 citations in CrossRef; 80 citations in Google Scholar, Sept. 8, 2014); although it must be conceded that by the standards of business and management journals in general, and organization studies in particular, *Business History* does not have a high impact factor. So the most highly cited articles in *Business History* hardly count as highly cited articles in organization studies or business and management more generally.

Apart from Üsdiken and Kieser's introduction to the special issue of *Business History* there are several other articles that we cited in our own article which could be seen as initiating an historic turn before us, such as: Mayer Zald's (1993) reconceptualization of organization studies as humanistic as well as a scientific enterprise (109 citations in Google Scholar); Alfred Kieser's (1994) manifesto for history in organization studies set out in the Crossroads section of *Organization Science* (271 citations in Google Scholar); as well as Roy Jacques' (1996) book *Manufacturing the Employee* (359 citations in Google Scholar). I fully acknowledge the importance of each of these in relation to our own thinking. In fact I wrote a methodological chapter on historical perspectives in organization studies for a book devoted to discussing the significance of *Manufacturing the Employee* (Rowlinson, 2004), as well as a critique of Foucauldian history in organization studies (Rowlinson & Carter, 2002) that focuses on Jacques' book, along with Gibson Burrell's *Pandemonium* (Burrell, 1997) and Stewart Clegg's (1989) *Frameworks of Power*. In general terms my critique of Jacques, Burrell, and Clegg was that they tended to overlook relevant historiographical debates, and even if they didn't treat history as a repository of facts they did tend to rely on particular historiographical interpretations that appealed to their own historical sensibilities.

By referring to a 'historic turn' we were trying to overcome what we saw, and to some extent still see, as the insularity of organization studies, by using a term that seemed to have growing acceptance in the wider social sciences. The historic or 'historical turn' has also been picked up approvingly in influential books such as Sewell's (2005: 358) *Logics of History*, where it is linked to Giddens' (1984) recognition of the need for a diachronic notion of 'structuration' as a process rather than a synchronic static concept of structure. As far as I can make out we were the first to pick up on the terminology of the historic turn in organization studies, and I still feel that it provides a yardstick for assessing just how historical the various research programs in organization studies have become. It also has the advantage that it refers to history and the historic turn in social science more generally, rather than suggesting that organization studies should engage in dialogue with the specific field of business history.

I should note that I had already addressed the question of whether business historians should engage with organization studies, and if so which theoretical approach might be most conducive to theoretically informed research in business history. This was in an article for the *Journal of Industrial History* (Rowlinson, 2001), a journal that has since closed but which had recently been set up with John Wilson as editor. Wilson encouraged me to submit the article to his journal after hearing a presentation I gave at the Management History Research Group. For me there is a parallel between advocating an historic turn in organization studies and an organizational turn in business history, which means encouraging business historians to turn away from the deference towards economics that they have retained, especially in the UK, from when they shared economic history departments.

In the same year, 2004, that our article was published in *Business History* I also coordinated a showcase symposium on "Management and Organizational History: The Future of the Past" at the Academy of Management Meeting in New Orleans, sponsored by the Management History Division, Organization and Management Theory Division, and the Critical Management Studies Interest Group. Although it was scheduled for the last session in the Academy's program the room was packed and there was a lively discussion of how to advance history within the Academy of Management. The symposium encouraged Charles Booth and I to press on with our conversation with Sage about the possibility of launching a new historical journal. The journal *Management & Organizational History* was launched in 2006 with Charles Booth as editor and myself, Roy Jacques, Lois Kurowski, and Richard Marens as co-editors. I took over as editor in 2009 and continued in that role until 2013, managing the move to Scholar One and the remarkably smooth transfer from Sage to Taylor & Francis under the Routledge imprint for 2013, alongside *Business History*.

All of this might sound rather like the kind of celebratory self-congratulatory narrative that you might expect from a rhetorical (Suddaby, Foster & Trank, 2010) corporate history (Delahaye *et al.*, 2009). It would be all too easy to carry on in this vein by highlighting the various historical special issues of leading journals such as the *Journal of Organizational Change Management* (van Baalen & Bogenrieder, 2009), *Journal of Management Studies* (O'Sullivan & Graham, 2010), and the Special Topic Forum for the *Academy of Management Review* (Godfrey *et al.*, forthcoming), and the increasing readiness of leading journals to accept historical articles, with John Hassard's (2012) article on the Hawthorne Studies winning the prize for the best article in the year from *Human Relations*. However, as with any such narrative it is possible to construct an alternative that emphasizes the contingency of events.

The accidental historic turn

I was clearing out my office recently and as I was looking through a filing cabinet deciding what to throw away I came across some old files that reminded me of how coincidental it was that we named the historic turn when we did. I found an earlier version of our paper, "Towards a Historical Critique of Organization Studies," that we'd submitted to the Management History Division for the 2000 Academy of Meeting in Toronto, which I believe was the first submission I ever made to the Academy of Management. But unfortunately with two reviewers ticking "Definitely reject" and a third "Weak but accept" there was no way I was going to Toronto. The reviewers' comments did not encourage me to think that my work would ever be well received by the Management History division:

> A very thorough critique of approaches/theories in organization studies and certainly a sound argument for the position that they are ahistorical. While the author(s) makes this point well, I have a concern that this will not be of widespread interest to Management History division listeners.
>
> Why do I have the feeling that all of these approaches are full of scholarly debate and short on evidence? This appears to be a battlefield of theorists that practitioners would find incomprehensible.

Another reviewer's *only* handwritten comment was:

> THIS IS WAY OUTSIDE MY AREA OF EXPERTISE, BUT MY SEMI-EDUCATED GUESS IS THAT IT'S <u>NOT</u> A VERY GOOD PAPER & SHOULD PROBABLY BE REJECTED.

Apart from the generic comment that, "The writing style could be simplified and the paragraphs shortened for ease of reading," there was little or nothing in the reviews that suggested how we could improve our paper.

I cannot say we were undeterred but nevertheless we decided that the EGOS 2001 stream might be more receptive to our ideas than the Management History division the year before. So we submitted a slightly modified version of the paper titled "The Treatment of History in Organization Studies." There was no subtitle and no mention at all of 'the historic turn,' not even a citation for McDonald's (1996) book *The Historic Turn in the Human Sciences*. I can remember a lot about EGOS in Lyon. Many of the main characters that I associate with the historic turn attended the stream, which was held in a sweltering room with no air conditioning. I visited Lyon again this year for a workshop on "Business History in Mutation: Methodological and Interpretative Issues." I was reminded of how nice it is to walk around Lyon at night and how many restaurants there are serving regional French food, which makes it difficult for vegetarians like me. I can't remember if it was Lyon or Montreal around 1990 and my girlfriend at the time rang a restaurant and asked, in very good French, if they had any vegetarian options, only to be told, "It's a French restaurant." What I don't remember is how our paper was received, but it must have gone reasonably well to be selected for the special issue of *Business History*.

On Wednesday, September 26, 2001 Behlül and Alfred emailed me and Peter to inform us that they had selected our paper for inclusion in their proposal for a special issue and asked us to send them an abstract for a revised version of the paper we'd presented in Lyon. It was in the abstract that we sent to Behlül in return on September 27, 2001 that we mentioned the historic turn for the first time, and although it still wasn't in the title, we did so in much bolder terms than in the final published version. The abstract began:

> In this paper we call for a 'historic turn' in organization studies along the lines of the turn towards history that has transformed other fields in the social sciences and humanities.

You might think that once our paper had acquired an explicit call for a historic turn its significance was immediately recognized, but the review process for *Business History* belies any such notion. Emails from 13 years ago are hard to find, but hard paper copies in the filing cabinet do not disappear so easily, and fortunately for some reason I printed out some of the email correspondence between Peter Clark and Alfred Kieser concerning the progress of our paper, which Peter Clark must have forwarded to me. I would like to reproduce some extracts from the emails (with permission from Peter Clark and Alfred Kieser). The first one was sent from Alfred Kieser to Peter Clark at 5 p.m. on Christmas Day 2001, which gives us an indication of Alfred's work ethic:

> *Subject Special Issue*
>
> *Dear Peter, dear Mick*
> *I've got a very bad conscience. However, isn't Xmas a time for achieving forgiveness?*
>
> *About three months ago you sent Behlül and me an email in which you asked for advice concerning your contribution to the Special Issue. As I said, I feel very bad, but these last three months were just crazy. I hope my advice is not arriving too late!*
>
> *These are the three options that you saw for a revision of your paper:*
>
> *"1. Remove the Burrell, Bauman, the Holocaust and bureaucracy section …"*
>
> …
>
> *I'm clearly in favour of option 1. In the present version of the paper, I find the section on 'Analytically Structured Narrative' difficult to understand …*
>
> *From Alfred Kieser*

Peter Clark, no slouch himself, responded to Alfred the next morning:

> *Subject RE: Special Issue*
> *Alfred, Boxing Day*
> *We will probably take option 1 as you suggest …*

Later the same day Alfred emailed Peter:

> *Dear Peter,*
> *Thanks for the reward. Four grand-children were fighting each other with terrible bawling. I enjoyed it for a while then I fled from them to my desk. Reading your paper and commenting on it was like finding a shelter from the storm.*
> *The problem with population ecology with regard to history is that this approach does not take evolution in the evolutionary mechanisms into consideration. A medieval craft shop was not allowed to innovate. Nowadays, innovations (variations) are systematically produced and preselected by market tests before they are launched.*
> *The problem with neo-institutionalism is that it does not explain how rationality myths come about and, eventually, disappear.*
> *Have a nice stay in cold Berlin!*
> *Best wishes,*
> *Alfred*

Then the papers were sent out for review and we heard back from Alfred Kieser on July 14, 2002:

> *Dear authors,*
> *We finally received the reviewers' comments to your paper on The Treatment of History in Organization Studies. They are attached. You can read them for yourself so that I don't have to reiterate them in detail.*
> …
> *If you do decide to rewrite your paper … I very much hope you do, the reviewers and I would appreciate if you could explain what you could – or couldn't do – in response to the reviewers's comments.*
> *Looking forward to receiving the revised manuscript by the end of August/beginning of September.*
> *Best wishes,*
> *Alfred*

This was a formidable invitation to revise and resubmit given the stance of the two reviewers. Reviewer 1 was most critical and two out of the five paragraphs from the review were particularly dismissive:

> [paragraph 2]
> *At this point, I begin to struggle with the author(s)' presentation that the views of organizational economics, organizational sociologists, organizational culturists represent theoretical frameworks for organization studies. None of these collections of people, I feel, have any touch with real organizations. Academics theorize and jargonize and stretch macro theoretical discussions, scarcely without reaching reality. Why is it so seldom that any of these people are called to consult with an on-going enterprise? Because, in my opinion, they have no credibility with practitioners.*
> [paragraph 4]
> *Can the author strip away the platitudes, the academic posturing, the glossy jargon, and get down to basics? Nowhere do I see words like authority, responsibility, communication, coordination, purpose, and other words or phrases that describe problems and situations which organizations and their managers grapple with every day.*

Reviewer 2 was more encouraging but felt that we were trying to do too much, which was particularly helpful in forcing us to drop our empirical illustration of an analytically structured narrative. Even so Reviewer 2 maintained that our criticism of most business historians as common sense empiricists was unfounded:

> *It nevertheless seems unlikely that the authors have a solid knowledge of the current research in business history, especially of the kind that is usually published in Business History. The explicit policy of this journal is to publish theory-informed articles (even if not all of those published would fulfil this requirement).*

As is often the case we felt that we needed to respond to the reviewers at length in order to convince the editors of both the journal and the special issue that we had taken the reviewers' comments seriously enough for them to include our article, even though I strongly suspect that Reviewer 1 was in favor of rejecting it. However, it was in response to Reviewer 2 that we added a subtitle for clarification, "Toward an historic turn." And we explained to Reviewer 2 that, "We feel that this adds greatly to the paper as a discussion piece and that labelling our purpose in this way makes it much clearer." The extent of our revisions, and our detailed response to the editors and reviewers, must have been sufficient for Alfred and Behlül to accept our paper, but even though it was not sent out for another round of reviews, it was not until April 2004 that we finally received the proofs for our article which was thankfully included in the Special Issue published in the July issue of *Business History* that year.

I have read too many letters, and even articles, from authors complaining about the comments from reviewers. So I can't complain about the comments from the *Business History* reviewers, which undoubtedly helped us to sharpen up what was a vast and sprawling paper that was weighed down with too many digressions and an attempt to provide an empirical illustration of the kind of history we were advocating. Perhaps most importantly it was the reviewers who prompted us to include the "historic turn" in our subtitle, albeit with an ironic question mark. But the comments were far more extensive than the single review I received for my first ever published article, also in *Business History* (Rowlinson, 1988). What this illustrates is that although there may well have been some general convergence towards an historic turn, it was by no means a foregone conclusion that our article naming it as such would be published when it was with that subtitle. The special issue of *Business History* undoubtedly would have gone ahead even if we had not managed to respond to the reviewers sufficiently for our article to be included. So I wonder how significant it was that the historic turn acquired the name at that particular time?

A personal turn to history

My personal turn to history started a long time before our *Business History* article, when I began my PhD at Aston University in 1983. My thesis (Rowlinson, 1987) was a history of labor management at Cadbury, the British cocoa and chocolate manufacturer, from 1879 to 1919. I undertook the archival research in the library at Bournville in South West Birmingham where the Cadbury factory was relocated in 1879 from central Birmingham. I mostly looked at the minutes of various meetings, such as the Bournville Works Councils, and in particular the Cadbury Board Minutes, which started from 1899. I should say that I had no training in archival research. My first degree was in Sociology, not History, and I haven't formally studied history since I was at school, aged around 14. I have no qualifications in history whatsoever.

Before I started the research for my PhD my supervisor suggested that I should talk to a historian who was interested in the history of labor management, so I went down to the London School of Economics to talk to Howard Gospel, who was later to be the external examiner for my thesis. When Gospel realized that I had no historical training and no experience of archival research he more or less tried to dissuade me from doing the thesis, suggesting that I might be better advised to write a general history of the labor process rather than try to tackle an actual archive, which he assured me would be more or less impenetrable for a novice like me. To some extent he was right, but what he said was also a challenge, and I spent four years buried in the Cadbury archive in effect learning how to do archival historical research on the job, which is almost certainly the best way even if it is time-consuming. Having finished the thesis I was then faced with the difficulty of getting articles published, and once my first article on scientific management at Cadbury had been published in *Business History* it was made fairly clear to me that if I wanted a career in reputable business schools I would have to publish in leading business and management journals, not specialist historical journals.

I managed to get two more articles from my thesis published in leading journals. The first article in *Human Relations* (Rowlinson & Hassard, 1993), co-authored with John Hassard, used the historical concept of invented tradition (Hobsbawm & Ranger, 1992) to explain how Cadbury's labor management institutions had come to be so closely identified with Quakerism. I think this anticipated the current interest in memory and history in organization studies. The second article in the *Journal of Management Studies* (Rowlinson, 1995) focused on divisionalization at Cadbury in the 1960s and it reminds me how important Chandler's (1962) *Strategy and Structure* was for me at that time.

Before I went for the interview for the scholarship to do my PhD at Aston my undergraduate dissertation supervisor, Theo Nichols, suggested that I read *Strategy and Structure*. This saved me because one of the interviewers had advised me to read Bernard Alford's (2013: first published in 1973) history of the Bristol tobacco company, W. D. & H. O. Wills, presumably because I was a student at Bristol University where Alford was a professor in the Economic History department – or at least I think he was even though I can't find any trace of the department on the internet, which gives some indication about the current state of economic history in the UK.

Bristol University boasts of its Wills Memorial Building, a mock gothic monstrosity that opened in 1925 and stands at the top of a steep hill in central Bristol, a reminder of the university's connection with the tobacco industry. It still houses the law department and when I was a student many of the wealthy lawyers congregated in the entrance hall for a lunchtime social event known as "Wills at One." As a lifelong socialist and non-smoker I have to say that reading a history of Wills held no attraction because of everything the word "Wills" conjured up for me, and even when I dipped into the book I couldn't make much sense of it. Fortunately that was more or less what the interviewers wanted to hear.

Remembering this I looked up Alford's book on Google Scholar and read the preface, which exemplifies the objectivism of business history that I've found increasingly annoying:

> This history was commissioned by the Firm in 1965. From the outset, *however*, Wills agreed that it should be an objective study; and this implied acceptance of the principle that the Firm's shortcomings and failures should be treated as openly and as fully as its successes. Indeed, this is the only worthwhile approach to business history …
>
> *(Alford, 2013: xii, emphasis added)*

The insertion of the word "however" makes it appear as if Wills' agreement that the study should be objective was somehow exceptional, as if other commissioned histories were not objective, or as if the reader might be surprised that Wills' would agree to "an objective study." But in almost every corporate history that I have ever looked at which was commissioned from an academic historian, the author makes a similar statement proclaiming objectivity (Delahaye *et al.*, 2009). As we argue out in our *Academy of Management Review* article:

> the ideological content of corporate history is contained in its objectivist form and founder-centered emplotment, which would be compromised by any hint of distortion or lack of independence. The content of the form of corporate history is inimical to explicit theoretical considerations of historical epistemology.
>
> *(Rowlinson, Hassard & Decker, 2014: 263)*

From the outset of my own turn to history, then, I think I sensed that not only is this *not* "the only worthwhile approach to business history," but that it is a largely pointless approach which underpins the unreflexive empiricism in business history.

I'd like to say something about the context in which I did my PhD. Aston was of course the home of the Aston Studies, which must rank as the most successful UK research program ever in organization studies, or even in business and management as a whole. Just about every organizational sociologist in the UK seemed to have passed through the Aston Studies at some point and it constituted an important network. Strange as it may seem I hadn't even heard of the Aston Studies when it came to finding a PhD scholarship, but it turned out that Theo Nichols had some link to the Aston Studies and knew John Child. In my undergraduate degree the emphasis was on economic or industrial sociology, with a largely Marxist orientation which was reflected in the influential Marxist primer that Theo Nichols (1980) had put together. This was probably the high point for Bravermania in undergraduate sociology and *Labor and Monopoly Capital* (Braverman, 1974) had already acquired the status of a sacred text. Some years later when I told Theo Nichols that for my first lecturing job I had to teach "Organizational Behavior" he said something like, "Oh yes, I managed to save you from all that when you were an undergraduate."

Whenever I talk about the historic turn it seems that someone, usually a distinguished professor, gets up in an agitated state and says that all of this talk of a historic turn overlooks the importance of history for the founders of strategy and organization theory, recounting a list of important figures that might include names such as Weber, Selznick, and Chandler. This is understandable and I usually nod in appreciation of this timely reminder that much of what we are saying has been said before much more eloquently, and we have to be wary of getting carried away with the idea that we have reinvented the wheel.

But having studied at Aston in the aftermath of the Aston Studies it is hardly likely that I would think that previous generations of organizational scholars had no interest in history. One of my PhD supervisors was John Child whose own academic career started with a history of *British Management Thought* (Child, 2012: first published in 1969), and his historical article on "Quaker Employers" (Child, 1964) framed my own postgraduate research on Cadbury. If strategic choice (Child, 1972) can be seen as a diachronic a qualification to the synchronic excess of structural contingency theory in the original Aston Studies, then the Work Organization Research Centre (WORC) that I joined at Aston in 1983 allowed for the realization of a more historical approach in each of its major case studies, with funding specifically earmarked for my historical research in the Cadbury case study (Smith, Child & Rowlinson, 1990). I think of the 'firm-in-sector' approach that Peter Clark (Whipp & Clark, 1986) developed with other members of WORC as a theoretical underpinning for the case studies as kind of nascent historical version of new institutionalism, although I don't think that link has ever been explicitly made.

Even if as a research program structural contingency can be criticized for its emphasis on cross-sectional correlations, as individuals central members of the Aston Studies are well known for their interest in history. Derek Pugh in particular has a longstanding interest in history, and his successive editions of *Organization Theory: Selected Classic Readings* (Pugh, 2007), along with *Writers on Organization* (Pugh & Hickson, 2007), constitute a standard reference for the history of management and organization theory.

The annual International Labour Process Conferences started in 1983 and for the first few years they alternated between UMIST (now part of Manchester Business School) and Aston. The first one I attended was probably in 1984. At the outset Labor Process Theory was more historically oriented, with historical case studies constituting part of its original corpus (Zimbalist, 1979; Nichols, 1980). I'm not sure when, how, or why Labor Process Theory became disconnected from history, but I have always envisaged Critical Management Studies as offering a possible reconnection (Rowlinson, Stager Jacques & Booth, 2009).

Conclusion

Our call for a 'historic turn' was in a sense ironic and retrospective. The rising research programs of organizational economics, new institutionalism, and organizational symbolism may have appeared, or claimed to be more historical than the neoclassical economic theory of the firm or structural contingency theory. But on closer inspection each of the newly dominant paradigms turned out to harbor ahistorical or even anti-historical tendencies. These tendencies have been played out and somewhat to my surprise the advocates of a more historical orientation, such as Roy Suddaby (Suddaby, Foster & Mills, 2014) and Howard Aldrich (Lippmann & Aldrich, 2014) appear to be in the ascendancy. Of course this ascendancy should not be exaggerated. Most researchers continue doing what they do largely untouched by various turns, and if we take the historical implications of ecological, evolutionary, and institutional theory seriously that is presumably what we would expect. Genuine paradigm shifts are likely to be rare, so referring to a 'turn' makes a much more modest and less contestable claim of a perceptible change than a paradigm shift.

It was seemingly coincidental that our call for a historic turn was published when it was as the subtitle was only added for clarification in response to a critical reviewer after several versions of the paper had already been presented, or in the case of the Academy of Management, rejected. But if it provides a convenient label for an emerging network of scholars then it has more than served its purpose. Now that this network is becoming more established it seems appropriate for us to create our own etiological myths, and it would be gratifying if our article continues to be seen as the origin of the historic turn to describe a more self-consciously historical orientation within organization studies. This confirms to me the point that we made in the *Academy of Management Review* (Rowlinson, Hassard, and Decker, 2014), borrowing from Ricoeur, that a "beginning consists in a constellation of dated [or even undated] events" (Ricoeur, 2004: 139), whereas the origin of an organization or a concept, or in this case a 'turn,' is "a mythic event that requires a single, readily identifiable date and, preferably, an identifiable founder." An historic turn is something we will only recognize in retrospect, historically, when we look back and try to identify a turning point.

References

Alford, B. W. E. (2013 [1973]) *WD & HO Wills and the Development of the UK Tobacco Industry: 1786–1965*. Abingdon: Routledge.

Braverman, H. (1974) *Labor and Monopoly Capital: The Degradation of Work in the Twentieth Century*. London: Monthly Review Press.

Burrell, G. (1997) *Pandemonium: Towards a Retro-Organization Theory*. London: Sage.

Chandler, A. D. J. (1962) *Strategy and Structure: Chapters in the History of Industrial Enterprise*. Cambridge MA: MIT Press.

Child, J. (1964) Quaker employers and industrial relations, *Sociological Review*, 12(3): 293–315.

Child, J. (1972) Organizational structure, environment and performance: The role of strategic choice, *Sociology*, 6(1): 1–22.

Child, J. (2012[1969]) *British Management Thought (Routledge Revivals): A Critical Analysis*. Abingdon: Routledge.
Clark, P. and Rowlinson, M. (2004) The treatment of history in organisation studies: Towards an 'historic turn'? *Business History*, 46(3): 331–52.
Clegg, S. (1989) *Frameworks of Power*. London: Sage.
Delahaye, A., Booth, C., Clark, P., Procter, S., and Rowlinson, M. (2009) The genre of corporate history, *Journal of Organizational Change Management*, 22(1): 27–48.
Giddens, A. (1984) *The Constitution of Society: Outline of the Theory of Structuration*. Cambridge: Polity Press.
Godfrey, P., Hassard, J., O'Connor, E., Rowlinson, M., and Ruef, M. (forthcoming) Special topic forum on history and organizational studies: Toward a creative synthesis, *Academy of Management Review*, http://aom.org/STF-2014/ – History_and_Organization_Studies:_Toward_a_Creative_Synthesis
Hassard, J. (2012) Rethinking the Hawthorne Studies: The Western Electric research in its social, political and historical context, *Human Relations*, 65(1): 1431–61.
Hobsbawm, E. and Ranger, T. (eds) (1992) *The Invention of Tradition*. Cambridge: Cambridge University Press.
Jacques, R. (1996) *Manufacturing the Employee: Management Knowlege from the 19th to 21st Centuries*. London: Sage.
Kieser, A. (1994) Crossroads: Why organization theory needs historical analyses – and how these should be performed, *Organization Science*, 5(4): 608–20.
Lippmann, S. and Aldrich, H. E. (2014) History and evolutionary theory, in M. Bucheli and R. D. Wadwhani (eds), *Organizations in Time: History, Theory, Methods* (pp. 124–46). New York: Oxford University Press.
McDonald, T. J. (ed.) (1996) *The Historic Turn in the Human Sciences*. Michigan: University of Michigan Press.
Nichols, T. (1980) *Capital and Labour: Studies in the Capitalist Labour Process*. London: Athlone Press in association with Fontana Paperbacks.
O'Sullivan, M. and Graham, M. B. W. (2010) Moving forward by looking backward: Business history and management studies, *Journal of Management Studies*, 47(5): 775–90.
Pugh, D. S. (2007) *Organization Theory: Selected Classic Readings* (5th edn). London: Penguin.
Pugh, D. S. and Hickson, D. J. (2007) *Writers on Organizations*. London: Penguin.
Ricoeur, P. (2004) *Memory, History, Forgetting*. Chicago: University of Chicago Press.
Rowlinson, M. (1987) Cadburys' new factory system: 1879–1919, PhD Thesis, Aston University, Birmingham.
Rowlinson, M. (1988) The early application of scientific management by Cadbury, *Business History*, 30(4): 377–95.
Rowlinson, M. (1995) Strategy, structure and culture: Cadbury, divisionalization and merger in the 1960s, *Journal of Management Studies*, 32(2): 121–40.
Rowlinson, M. (2001) Business history and organization theory, *Journal of Industrial History*, 4(1): 1–23.
Rowlinson, M. (2004) Historical perspectives in organization studies: Factual, narrative, and archaeo-genealogical, in D. E. Hodgson and C. Carter (eds), *Management Knowledge and the New Employee* (pp. 8–20). Burlington, VT: Ashgate.
Rowlinson, M. and Carter, C. (2002) Foucault and history in organization studies, *Organization*, 9(4): 527–47.
Rowlinson, M. and Hassard, J. (1993) The invention of corporate culture: A history of the histories of Cadbury, *Human Relations*, 46(3): 299–326.
Rowlinson, M., Hassard, J., and Decker, S. (2014) Research strategies for organizational history: A dialogue between historical theory and organization theory, *Academy of Management Review*, 39(3): 250–74.
Rowlinson, M., Stager Jacques, R., and Booth, C. (2009) Critical management and organizational history, in M. Alvesson, H. Willmott and T. Bridgman (eds), *The Oxford Handbook of Critical Management Studies* (pp. 286–303). Oxford: Oxford University Press.
Sewell, W. H. J. (2005) *Logics of History: Social Theory and Social Transformation*, Chicago, IL: University of Chicago Press.
Smith, C. J., Child, J., and Rowlinson, M. (1990) *Reshaping Work: The Cadbury Experience*. Cambridge: Cambridge University Press.
Suddaby, R., Foster, W. M., and Mills, A. J. (2014) Historical institutionalism, in M. Bucheli and R. D. Wadhwani (eds), *Organizations in Time: History, Theory, Methods* (pp. 100–23). Oxford: Oxford University Press.
Suddaby, R., Foster, W. M., and Trank, C. Q. (2010) Rhetorical history as a source of competitive advantage, in J. A. C. Baum and J. Lampel (eds), *Globalization of Strategy Research*, Vol. 27 (pp. 147–73). London: Emerald.
Üsdiken, B. and Kieser, A. (2004) Introduction: History in organisation studies, *Business History*, 46(3): 321–30.

van Baalen, P. and Bogenrieder, I. (2009) Historical approaches in organizational research, *Journal of Organizational Change Management*, 22(1): 4–7.

Whipp, R. and Clark, P. (1986) *Innovation and the Auto Industry*. London: Frances Pinter.

Zald, M. N. (1993) Organization studies as a scientific and humanistic enterprise: Toward a reconceptualization of the foundations of the field, *Organization Science*, 4(4): 513–28.

Zimbalist, A. S. (1979) *Case Studies on the Labor Process*. New York: Monthly Review Press.

Part II

Debates in management and organizational history

7

He who may not be mentioned: Marx, history, and American business schools

Richard Marens

> Men make their own history, but they do not make it as they please; they do not make it under self-selected circumstances, but under circumstances existing already, given and transmitted from the past.
>
> *Karl Marx (1852/1972: 595)*

"Critical management studies?"

That was Robert Brenner's 1999 email response to my invitation to speak to the Critical Management Studies Interest Group (later a division) at the Academy of Management meeting that was to be held that year in San Diego, a very pleasant place to visit and one not far from his home in Los Angeles. It was understandable that Brenner, probably the most prominent Marxist historian working at an American university, was puzzled to learn that critical theorists actually have an organized presence within business schools.Very little happens at such schools that would pique the interest of a professional historian of any orientation, although ironically, Sanford Jacoby, perhaps the only American management scholar likely to be read by a Marxist academic, shares a campus with Brenner. While business schools in the rest of the English-speaking world have proven a little more supportive of both history and critical scholarship than their American counterparts, what critical history is produced by business academics outside of the United States is more likely to embrace a Foucauldian rather than a Marxist perspective. Given the neglect of history on the part of business schools, plus the anathema they have placed on even acknowledging Marx, it would be surprising if someone like Brenner paid them any attention at all.

There are two reasons that history has earned so little legitimacy within business schools. First, it does not fit readily into their model of serious research embraced almost universally by American business schools, a model derived from experimental science that presumes the formulation and testing of parsimonious and timeless hypotheses. Decision-makers at such schools are generally oblivious to the reality that such 'field' sciences as geology, paleontology, astronomy, and many sub-fields of biology are actually 'historical' in their approach to research. Since they cannot conduct controlled experiments to answer a great number of research questions, these fields tend to aim at reconstructing the past of a particular phenomenon in order to explain its present and even predict its future. While this more open-ended approach might appear to an objective observer as more appropriate for a subject as complex and contingent as business practices and outcomes, it has its disadvantages. First, it does not look like 'science' to those who established the research standards of business schools, namely experimental psychologists and physics-envious micro-economists, along with their graduate students. Second, a more historical approach is dangerous precisely because it is not parsimonious. The richness of detail of historical studies threatens to uncover too many specific examples of incompetence, dumb luck, or even rapaciousness on the part of at least some business leaders, a result not likely to be welcomed by potential patrons of business school faculties. While even some academics complain of the fundamental irrelevance of so much published business school research (Teece, 2011), this literature is, at least, innocuous, unlikely to offend anyone important.

As a result, history is just not taken seriously in any American business school that lacks the intellectual self-confidence of a Harvard or MIT. Consequently no jobs are ever posted by business schools which list history as even a secondary specialty, and the Management History Division is consistently the smallest division of the Academy of Management, never obtaining more than about half the membership of even such marginal groups as Critical Management Studies and Spirituality in Management. Given these circumstances, it is hardly puzzling that Joseph Litterer (1963), for example, abandoned his dissertation work investigating the rise of the crucial nineteenth-century 'systematic' management movement once he joined the professoriate, reinventing himself as a mainstream organizational behaviorist. Moreover, those few academics housed in American business schools who have published history tend to embrace a 'great person' perspective, with Jacoby and JoAnne Yates, MIT's historian of information technology, providing the significant exceptions. Studies of successful entrepreneurs or influential management thinkers can at least be framed as a kind of case study, an acceptable form of scholarship, albeit one of relatively low prestige. To be fair, the best of this kind of work from the likes of Harvard's McCraw and Chandler goes beyond simple hagiography and touches upon broader historical trends, but there is little in even their work to challenge the self-image of American executives as heirs to a noble tradition. Since the 1970s, American top management has mobilized against any threat to its autonomy in the form of regulation, organized labor, or even excessive attention to their role in increasing inequality (Clawson, Nuesdatl & Weller, 1998; Malott, 1978). Neither these executives, nor the academics who seek their patronage, are likely to tolerate a body of work that might demonstrate, for example, that government procurement is often the key to corporate success, let alone the more specifically Marxist assertion that prevailing in class conflict through the use of violence against strikers or reducing employee pay has at some time or other proven profitable for many well-known businesses.

As result, any display of appreciation of a Marx-connected idea is simply too dangerous to consider using, even if the particular concept is actually far removed from Marx's own personal ambition to destroy capitalism. Schumpeter's theory of creative destruction, for example, appears frequently in the management literature, and the ABI/Inform database of business-related periodicals lists 1,178 articles that cite him. While Schumpeter was relatively conservative politically, he was quite open about explicitly acknowledging his intellectual debt to Marx (1942). Nonetheless, Karl Marx is mentioned only 59 times among these articles, a bit more than 5 percent of the total. Apparently, those business school professors who claim to address creative destruction are either too lazy or frightened to dig deeper into a construct that they seemingly rely upon so often.

For those sincerely interested in explaining either the structuring or functioning of business, this avoidance behavior is unfortunate, since, as Schumpeter understood, the manner in which Marx and his intellectual descendants approach history could contribute greatly to the understanding of business. Marxian historiography has had a major impact on the larger discipline of history, and, if given the opportunity, could similarly contribute to a better understanding of business in at least four different ways. First, Marxist historians pioneered a powerful method of embedding the agency of individuals within the constraints of the material and relational conditions under which they operate, thus avoiding either the extreme of overreliance on individual genius on one hand or the determinism of social or economic forces on the other. Second, the dialectical nature of a Marxian approach can endogenize the causes of change over time, reducing the need to depend upon fortuitous events or trends to explain change. Third, Marxist historians have highlighted a social reality that has played an indisputably central role in the evolution of management: the existence of class interests and the resulting conflicts that arise from these. Finally, because the substantive concern of many Marxist historians has been a detailed analysis of the origin and development of capitalism, they have accumulated a great deal of knowledge about the workings of business over time, and such pertinent data can only lead to further understanding to those with the courage to apply it. This chapter will consider each of these potential contributions of Marx-influenced historiography in turn, and these are followed by a fifth section that briefly considers how these four potential contributions can also work to enrich other theoretical perspectives.

Structure and agency: together again

There is a popular misconception that Marxian history is necessarily grounded in economic determinism and is methodologically shaped by a teleological presumption of progress. This criticism is not without validity with regard to at least some work within the Marxist tradition, including a portion of Marx's and Engel's own seminal writings. Engels himself was apologetic about this in private correspondence, excusing his and Marx's excessive reliance on economic explanations as a polemical response to historians who either relied on the activities of great men, or viewed the history of ideas emerging mysteriously from the brows of brilliant thinkers (Hollander, 2011). Over the last 60 years, however, this criticism has rarely fit academically trained historians who have been influenced by Marx. These academicians have generally attempted to balance structure and agency, and they have proven more successful doing so than either the economic determinists of the new institutionalist economic history and the historical accounts of successful entrepreneurs most famously associated with Alfred Chandler (1977).

Marxian history is imbued with what Kaye (1984) calls "possibilism," a concept similar to but somewhat more specific than path dependency. As suggested in the quote from Marx himself that begins this chapter, men and women do indeed act, but their choices are necessarily constrained by both the physical resources available to act with, and the social structures that they must act within. This insight applies, not only to tangible actions, but also to the development of 'consciousness,' the ways actors are likely to view and think about their world. If the production of physical objects is the base upon which the (super)structures of social interactions are built, it is not because this productive base is totally determinant of everything less concretely material, but because *what* a society produces and *how* it produces such material objects as food, clothing, shelter, and prestige goods both constrains and encourages possible choices for behavior, even when such choices are not directly connected to production. As Marx himself explained, "writers of history have so far paid little attention to the development of material production, which is the basis of all social life" (Marx, 1967a: 286). Since then, and especially after the Second World War, historians influenced by Marx have literally labored to correct that error.

The result of these efforts that Marxian historians – 'Marxian' in that they have been influenced by Marx but have not necessarily embraced all of his major concepts or political views – have led the way in making individual choices central to historical accounts, but within a context of the limitations and incentives generated by a social structure generated by the actions of previous actors. Thus, 'human agency' has a collective meaning for Marxian historians: it is the legacy generated by the aggregated behavior, not only of the leaders of organizations, but of the countless anonymous individuals who support, acquiesce, resist, or even outright oppose the political or organizational choices made by those same leaders, including the leaders of dissident organizations. The value of applying such a broad view of individual choice to business history should be clear: Businesses succeed or fail not only because of the decisions made by executives, or even the choices of executives *plus* politicians, labor leaders, and financial professionals, but also the way these decisions are perceived, supported, or rejected by their constituents or potential constituents: voters, workers, consumers, investors, etc.

One historical puzzle that Marxian history is especially equipped to address is the relatively sudden emergence of a significant number of large, geographically dispersed, publicly-traded corporations in the United States around the turn of the last century, a trend that cannot be entirely attributed to economies of scale (Roy, 1997). This is a highly relevant question for understanding contemporary corporations, since explaining why these giants emerged ought to shed light on why a once highly successful organizational form has undergone recent transformations after so many decades of stability (Edwards, 1975; Fligstein, 1990). A mainstream economic historian might approach the question by focusing on the ability of giant corporations to reduce transaction costs relative to competitors by avoiding market failures or hold-ups, while a historian of entrepreneurs would see his or her subjects as taking advantage of the market opportunities and organizational innovations generated by the building of railroads, not so much to dominate existing markets, but to establish new ones (Chandler, 1977). The first explanation suffers from excess abstraction, even circularity, since transaction costs are notoriously difficult to compare and often measured by the very outcomes they are intended to explain (Bryer, 2013). The latter cannot by itself explain either the timing or location of the simultaneous emergence of so much large-scale managerial entrepreneurship (Roy, 1997).

An explanation that mixes agency and structure in a Marxian (though not necessarily Marxist) manner could go something like this: Entrepreneurs could not vertically integrate or geographically extend their firms until a cadre of middle managers trained in standardized practices capable of coordinating the activities of the new corporate giants appeared, and these middle managers were themselves an offshoot of professionalized engineers trained in the new railroad and manufacturing steam-based technologies (Marens, 2005). Moreover, these same railroads were in large part both built to serve a growing class of commercial farmers and their suppliers, and they were simultaneously beneficiaries of the success of these same farmers (and suppliers), whose profits, deposited in local banks, eventually flowed into major financial centers (Ott, 2011). In a fuller article-length explanation, a scholar could extend this brief explanation of aggregated agency by examining its interaction with limiting and enabling structures imposed by government, finance, markets, and technology, for example how land grants to railroads and agricultural universities facilitated some of these trends.

The utility of combining agency and structure has been recognized by any number of important historians who were themselves anything but full-blown Marxists, much as a Weberian theorist of bureaucracy need not embrace all of Weber's other concepts or political views. A. H. M. Jones, at one time the world's leading authority on the economics of the classical world, was no Marxist, but he appreciated this structure-cum-agency approach sufficiently to work with historians who were then literally card-carrying communists in order to help them establish that highly influential journal of social and economic history, *Past and Present* (Hill, Hilton & Hobsbawm, 1983). Such relatively conservative figures as Schumpeter, Douglas North, and Ferdinand Braudel all explicitly acknowledge an intellectual debt to Marx when it came to explaining economic development. In North's words, "[i]n contrast to current neoclassical economists, Marx had an integrated perception of the totality of societal relations. Institutions, the state, and ideology are all part of his analysis. Marx makes clear that if our thinking is to go beyond surface manifestations of an economy, we must explore the integrated relationships of all its parts" (North, 1987: 58). Braudel, who explicitly framed his own economic history in opposition to much of Marxist theory, could still find inspiration from this passage from *Capital, sans* vitriol, for his own explanation of the growth of world commerce, an intellectual project of his that would produce several thousand published pages:

> Thus the villainies of the Venetian thieving system formed one of the secret bases of the capital-wealth of Holland to whom Venice in her decadence lent large sums of money. So was it with Holland and England. By the beginning of the 18th century ... Holland had ceased to be the nation preponderant in commerce and industry. One of its main lines of business, therefore, [became] the lending out of enormous amounts of capital, especially to its great rival England. [And the] same thing is going on to-day between England and the United States.
>
> *(Marx, 1967a: 754)*

Dialectical thinking

Another highly useful aspect of Marx-influenced historiography is the manner in which it relates historical events and trends dialectically, offering insight into how change generates further change in a coherent, sometimes predictable manner. One does not have to embrace the labor theory of value, for example, to understand that the giant corporations of the end of the nineteenth century not only successfully reduced the transaction costs of conducting business by internalizing markets, they then used the economic power they accumulated through these efforts to further increase their cost advantage by (a) endowing educational institutions to train the managerial staff they depended upon, (b) lobbying state government to expand the right to merge and acquire other firms, (c) supporting transportation systems that extended their reach, and (d) influencing local, state, and federal government officials to suppress individual legal and organized mass resistance on the part of their employees (Marens, 2013a; Roy, 1997). Triumph, as Marx himself would have put it, creates the 'seeds of its own contradiction,' dialectically leading to a new set of problems and obstacles.

The triumph of American corporate giants illustrates this principle as well. During the early twentieth century these firms succeeded in suppressing unionization, taking control of training, and reducing the legal rights of their white-collar employees. These managerial achievements, however, ultimately led to a new set of personnel-related problems. Having won control of the workplace, corporate management found itself responsible for maintaining a sufficient level of employee satisfaction to prevent slacking and turnover, while also establishing the social legitimacy of its employment practices to a skeptical public (Leiserson, 1929; Marens, 2013b). Turnover became a particularly serious problem precisely because firms could no longer rely on pre-trained artisans and professionals supported by unskilled laborers to rapidly fill jobs (Slichter, 1921; Stone, 1974). As a result, companies developed a set of benefits under the rubric of 'corporate welfare' and began training managers and supervisors in 'human relations' in order to limit turnover and improve morale. Furthermore, the success of top corporate management at reducing the bargaining power of employees contributed to a shortfall of demand that become one factor in triggering the 1930s depression that led to further changes. This particular example also exemplifies another potential contribution of historical work influenced by Marx: reestablishing class conflict as an important driver of history.

Talking class

It is because neither the connecting of agency to structure nor the dialectic of historical change is necessarily tied to any particular political stance that so many historians have embraced these to one degree or another. When one historian complained, "we are all Marxists now" since even mainstream historians had followed Marxists in de-emphasizing the actions of public figures (Himmelfarb, 1987: 34), what she actually meant was that 'all' historians had become 'Marxian' in their analytic methodologies. Full-blooded Marxists have remained a minority within the field of history, distinguishable for their placing class interests and the resulting class conflicts and ongoing struggles at the explanatory center of their work. It is my contention that business scholars have much to learn from this smaller group of historians as well, without necessarily following them in embracing class conflict as their central explicans of all major historical change.

For Marx and those who have followed him, the operational definition of class conflict goes beyond Weberian or pluralistic acknowledgments of the occasional importance of the clash of economic interests between social groups. Marx offered a more specific and dynamic perspective, emphasizing the fundamental role of the production and distribution of the surplus of a society in shaping one's class position and ultimate class interests. What Marx labels "the ruling class" is that group who exploits others by siphoning off the lion's share of this surplus, that portion of wealth that the direct producers are unable to claim for themselves. A number of important historians have fruitfully applied this Marxian definition to understand a particular phenomenon more deeply. To illustrate: the author of *The Making of the English Working Class* (Thompson, 1963: 9) begins his definition of class in the general Weberian manner – "Class happens when some men, as a result of common experience (inherited or shared) feel and articulate the identity of their interests as between themselves, and as against other men whose interests are different from (and usually opposed to) theirs" – but then adds, "the class experience is largely determined by the productive relations into which men are born – or enter involuntarily." Furthermore, as the author of *Class Struggle in the Ancient Greek World* explains, classes are able to aggregate in advancing their particular interests without necessarily relying on deliberately organized collective action – which is often not even logistically possible – simply because similarly situated individuals will be constrained and channeled in similar ways under similar sets of class relations (De Ste. Croix, 1981).

An example from business of how a Marxist view of class differs from a more pluralistic one can be found in the different understanding of the conflict between corporate executives and wealthy investors. A Weberian or pluralist might place them in different classes based on function, which would likely lead at times to some conflict based on a divergence of interests (e.g. Davis, 1994). By contrast, a Marxist would view such disputes as an intra-class conflict that is triggered by shifts within a more fundamental and ongoing struggle. It is not that Marxists would dismiss disputes between executives and shareholders as irrelevant or unimportant any more than they would regard the War of Roses as trivial. What a Marxist *would* assert is that a full understanding of the dynamics and timing of elite conflicts requires an analysis of deeper changes in central productive relationships. In the case of the War of the Roses, that would mean analyzing the changing relationship between peasants, lords, and royalty, and for investors vs. executives, it would involve understanding the changing interconnections between the exploitation of employees, the rise of new competition, and the failure of Keynesian amelioration (Arrighi, 1994; Brenner, 2002; Bryer, 2013; Sweezy, 1953).

A scholar need not become monocausal in outlook to understand the important role of class conflict in understanding many business-related phenomena. Returning to our example of the rise of large American corporations, one can easily observe class interests at work as even competitors united in pressing politicians, judges, police, and even the military to support them a century ago in their conflicts with labor, often quite violently. This response explained, in part, the origins of both much of the coordination of corporate involvement in politics and the parallel political retreat on the part of organized labor (Hattam, 1993). One can further find other less obvious examples of the causal role of class conflict in the dispute between the executives of the National Civic Federation and the owner-operators of the National Association of Manufacturers over corporate welfare, or the diverging reactions to a resurgent United Steel Workers on the part of 'big' and 'little' steel during the 1930s, a divergence largely predictable based on whether a steel company relied primarily on government orders or the weak consumer markets of the depression years.

Clearly, class conflict cannot explain every twist and turn in the history of business, but its potential application can be a good deal more subtle and indirect than violent conflicts with unions or disputes between a burgeoning corporate elite and a battered *petite bourgeoisie*. There is a literature that dates at least to Gramsci's (1985) depression-era prison notebooks that ties the rise of mass consumer markets and popular entertainment to such conflicts in a variety of relatively subtle ways, which, while sometimes excessively didactic, can help provide a deeper understanding of these crucial modern trends. Or, to return to a previous example, a complete understanding of the connection between the emerging commercial family farming and the development of the American railroads, one would need to examine both the 'old country' class conflicts that encouraged immigration to these farmsteads in the first place, as well as the causes of the brutal conflicts with Native Americans that made this homesteading possible.

Nor does identifying class conflict as a major source of historical change require an exclusive focus on the struggle between an industrial working class and the management of their employing firm. Even writing before the dramatic twentieth-century multiplication of professional and intermediate levels of managerial employees (Stone, 1974), Marx (1967b) late in his life noted the trend among the then emerging corporations to both separate share ownership from control and to more finely divide managerial authority. A Marxist historical analysis can be constructed, for example, to account for the evolution of the class conflict between software workers and top management as agents of stockholders. According to a case study by Vicki Smith (1990), a student of a Marxist sociologist who actually did study shop-floor resistance (Burawoy, 1979), top management at a financially troubled major bank sought to increase the rate of exploitation of their various middle-managerial subordinates. The information systems managers, however, were uniquely able to resist due to their subordinates' near monopoly of the skills and knowledge that were paradoxically relied upon by top management to intensify exploitation elsewhere. Since then, however, this bank, along with many other American firms, learned the lesson of this defeat by using outsourcing and immigration to undermine the countervailing power of their programmers (Hira & Hira, 2005). Yet, the narrative continues to unfold in a dialectical manner as the very success of this process has led to critics and would-be reformers emerging in India questioning whether outsourcing has really proven to benefit to the Indian nation, both its workers and its taxpayers (Nadeem, 2011).

While class analysis can hardly explain everything about business, it can illuminate behavior that might prove puzzling otherwise. Efforts to offer some form of universal health insurance provide a good example. As Marxist theorists have long argued, one vital function of government is to find ways to solve the collective problems of the politically dominant class when divergent personal or professional (but not class) interests make it impossible for individual members to arrive at a consensus (Milliband, 1983). From a pluralistic perspective it is hard to fathom why the leaders of those firms with expensive health insurance plans would not support a government-run and funded system, such as extending Medicare coverage to everyone. This would remove a major administrative headache while reducing a large and volatile expense that foreign or less generous competitors do not have to deal with.

Viewing the broader class interests of top executives can solve this puzzle. After the crisis-filled decade of the 1970s, corporate executives and major investors coalesced politically around a few commonly-held principles of political action that reflected shared class interests regardless of other areas of disagreement (Clawson, Neustadtl, and Weller, 1998). The first is that employees' bargaining power should never be increased, and a healthcare system no longer tied to one's employer would reduce worker dependency on one's employer. Second, all business leaders should oppose, or at least try to limit, any proposed government programs that legitimize the power of government to tax and regulate. Third, a tacit agreement evolved that a firm or industry would tend to avoid interfering with the important political goals of another, and private insurers opposed any extension of direct government insuring because of the business they would lose as a result. Some corporate executives might have preferred no healthcare plan at all, but given the pressure from below for government to do something to solve the healthcare problem, it would be difficult to imagine a proposal that does less to empower employees and government or interfere with profits than the one that passed. Politicians succeed in passing the new healthcare plan largely because any alternative would have been even more damaging to ruling-class interests.

Similarly, a historically based class analysis that understands this function of government to look out for collective ruling-class interest can solve the puzzle of high levels of American peace-time military procurement, much of it unjustifiable by any national security concerns, and apparently in conflict with both free-market ideology and the commercial interests of civilian-oriented firms whose potential customers have to pay the taxes or inflation necessary to maintain this military-industrial complex (Cypher, 2007; Melman, 1987). After the Second World War, when many business leaders, fearful of a return to depression conditions that followed government of limited economic involvement, supported some degree of Keynesian demand management, military spending was the ideal form of such expenditures, and even the Interstate Highway Act was framed as a defense initiative. On the other hand, military procurement appeared to provide both a floor on demand and a permanent subsidy for technological innovations that was applied to a dizzying variety of civilian products (Marens, 2013a). It also offered a stream of rents extracted from taxpayers that can be shared with the most organized and threatening of industrial workers without empowering the entire working class in the manner of a full-scale welfare state. Moreover, as military production both moved to Southern states and became increasingly automated, organized labor's share of Pentagon rents could be shaved accordingly, a decline that recently culminated with the end of defined-benefited pension plans at the Boeing Corporation, the country's second biggest defense contractor, a result of threatening to move to a more union-hostile location. To the extent that such spending was actually useful militarily, it could be aimed at nations or groups hostile to American business. Hence, despite the end of the Cold War and expressed concerns over federal budget deficits, military spending remains quite high, including expensive Cold War weaponry never designed to meet current threats (Murray, 2005).

Knowledge of capitalism

The applications of Marxian or Marxist historiography that I have discussed up to this point have been largely methodological: the relationship of agency to structure, the dialect nature of change, the significance of viewing class interests and class conflict as central causes of social, organizational, and economic change. But the example of military spending indicates yet another potential area in which studying this literature can contribute to the understanding of business; historians who have been inspired by Marx present a great deal of information about the topics they study precisely because they emulate Marx's own efforts to understand as much as he could about both the past and current dynamics of capitalism. One can learn a great deal about the history of business from Marx-influenced historical research without necessarily accepting the conclusions of a particular scholar or even the causal priorities he or she assigns to various factors. Eric Hobsbawm has been one of the most widely read historians in the English language during the post-war era, and he is also nearly unique even among Marxist historians in spending his entire adult life as a member of the Communist Party. Nonetheless, one would be hard pressed to find a trace of didacticism, economic determinism, or teleology in his most popular books, and even conservative historians have professed respect for the importance and thoroughness of his work on the industrial revolution in England (Ferguson, 2002).

Examples abound of scholars, inspired by Marx, who have made important contributions to our understanding of the history of business. One can learn a great deal about the circumstances surrounding the emergence of various accounting practices from the work of Bryer (2013) without necessarily endorsing his polemical argument regarding which of these practices constitute full-scale capitalism. Stone's (1974) seminal article not only chronicled a major defeat of craft labor within manufacturing, it offers an explanation for the subsequent rise of middle-class corporate occupations. Baran and Sweezy (1966) influentially explained the explosion of expenditures on the part of corporations on such seemingly non-productive services as advertising as resulting from a need to stabilize the political economy of the United States after a depression and a world war. Others have collected, organized, and theorized upon a great deal of information to explain the collapse of this very same stability over the last generation (Arrighi, 1994; Brenner, 2002; Lash & Urry, 1987; Pollin, 2003).

Moreover, Marxist historians have not only applied theory to their narratives, but have used historical work to extend theory's ability to explain the development of capitalism. Brenner (1976), for example, is far better known and influential for his theory of European capitalist development than his specialized research of the political behavior of seventeenth-century English merchants. Nor does such theorizing begin and end with understanding the origins of capitalism. Over the past century, Marxist theorists have tried to refine and extend Marx's own theory of capitalist development by creating models of cyclical or secular changes in the system (e.g. Hilferding, 1981). While such models involve a degree of abstraction, they are better grounded in reality than the naïve neoclassical assumptions of an essentialist background of free exchanges depended upon enforceable property rights within competitive markets. Some Marxists have argued that capitalism has moved historically through stages that depend to varying degrees on competition or monopoly, finance or military force, government stimulation or wage cutting. Others have suggested that there is an cyclical oscillation between such stages: relatively laissez-faire eras tend to generate destructive mismatches between supply and demand, which then leads to demands for greater government involvement in the economy, but then Keynesian policies set off inflation and inhibit private investment, which causes the pendulum to swing back toward laissez-faire (Jessop, 1997).

One relatively recent theory in particular combines both a secular and cyclical element, and it deserves the attention of business scholars since it successfully predicted both the financialization of the American economy and the rise of East Asian manufacturing. Arrighi (1994) argues that the capitalist world is characterized by century-long waves of dominance centered upon a single economic power: first Genoa, then Holland, England, the United States, and perhaps China in the near future. Each wave differs in a number of respects, such as the size of the dominant power, but each also repeats three stages in running its course: first a rising stage powered by commercial and/or industrial leadership followed by a second period of global political and cultural domination effectively paid for by this economic success, and ending with a generation of financial dominance aimed at extracting previously accumulated wealth, during which time the fading dominant power finances its successor's rise. This particular theory can explain a great deal of what we have observed both recently and historically.

The overall point here is a simple one, but one that is too often overlooked. Many Marxist historians are excellent scholars whose work provides a great deal of pertinent information regarding the evolution of business. Similarly many Marxist social scientists have used historical research to build useful models regarding how capitalism and those businesses that operate within it evolve over time. Such work provides a valuable resource in our own era of volatile change, and one that should not be disparaged because of fear or political differences.

Applying the principles to other theories

Business schools in particular apply a variety of organization theories in attempting to explain business organization and performance, and certainly, there is no particular reason to assume that any theory, including Marxism, can reasonably claim a monopoly on usefulness in explaining business behavior and outcomes. As Harris, Johnson, and Souder (2013) have argued, powerful models of human behavior often combine multiple theories, and Marxian historiography can add explanatory power to any number of models in conjunction with other theories. Both resource dependency and population ecology depend on environmental pressures and opportunities, for the former to bring certain expertise to the fore, in the latter case, to explain the birth and death rates of various organizational forms (Pfeffer & Salancik, 1978; Hannan & Freeman, 1977). Marxian historians internalize this social environment within their analyses, explaining *how* these metaphorical resources and toxins within the social environment that resource dependency and population ecology rely upon are not given but are actually socially constructed over time, often by the collective actions of various organizations that these other theories regard as essentially the dependent variable at the mercy of environmental forces.

There are other organizational theories that could use an assist from a Marxian perspective. For example, the choice in organizational learning between further *exploiting* the tried and true versus *exploring* new products and processes is affected by such factors as the cost of labor, the robustness of a consumer class that is willing to spend on new products, and the availability of government procurement or funding to cover the cost of experimentation, all trends that Marxian history deals with well. Institutional theory focuses on pressures toward continuity (DiMaggio and Powell, 1983), while Marxian historiography is the chronicling of change despite such pressures. Some organization theorists have noted this apparent complementarity and have suggested a fusion of the two approaches (Clemens & Cook, 1999; Seo & Creed, 2002). Stakeholder management (Evan & Freeman 1993) has failed to develop as a theory because it has not adequately addressed the central questions as to *who* can make a claim to stakeholdership and *how* these stakeholders formulate, express, and negotiate demands upon management. Marxist history can explain why one group or another is considered a legitimate stakeholder at one time or another, and how they pursue their interests, consciously or not, whether as aggregated individuals acting independently or as organized collectivity.

A Marxist historical perspective is especially suited to shed light on the rise of one particular stakeholder group: shareholders. On first glance, it is puzzling as to why economists should presume that shareholder well-being is the sole legitimate concern of top management (Jensen, 1989) since there is no basis for this view in legal history, nor even a venerable tradition within the managerial literature that executives should only consider what is best for shareholders (Sweezy, 1953; Heald, 1970). In fact, the nineteenth-century expansion of corporate rights and privileges could never have been sold politically had such a principle been expounded by its advocates (Roy, 1997). A scholar familiar with Marx-influenced historiography, however, would understand that it was only when American industrial primacy was seriously challenged in the 1970s that the perception was propagated that corporate employees, as the beneficiaries of supposed excessive compensation and job security, were a large cause of these difficulties, which arose, according to disgruntled investors and their academic allies, supposedly because executives neglected their duty to utilize employees only to advance the interest of shareholders (Arrighi, 1994; Brenner, 2002; Pollin, 2003; Roy, 1997). At this point, top management, many of them rising to the top because they publicly embraced this view of the corporation, intensified the exploitation of their workforce, treating their own companies with almost the same ruthlessness as a corporate raider (Useem, 1996). Professing to look after shareholders, even if such concern was sometimes honored in the breach (Partnoy, 2003), allowed top management to justify squeezing or replacing their employees for their own enrichment through stock options.

Conclusion: bringing in Marx

In this chapter, I have tried to argue that there is an enormous amount of intellectual value in Marxist historiography that would aid any scholar interested in using history to achieve a deeper and richer understanding of business practices and its structural evolution. Some possible contributions are methodological. Marxist historians have developed an especially powerful grasp of the relationship between agency and structure as well as a deep understanding of how social change leads to further change, often in paradoxical or 'contradictory' ways. The works of Marxist historians illuminate a path that treads between reliance on overly abstract theorization or the fortuitous appearance of important individuals, while also providing a dialectical model of change in which social forces act as both cause and effect, not merely unexplained exogenous trends that appear somewhat arbitrarily in the narrative.

Some of the other contributions of Marxist historiography are substantive. The very best work of Marxist historians and social scientists brings exactly the same benefits that come from studying the work of other great scholars: they provide the basis on which to conduct further scholarship. More specifically, business school academics need to overcome their fears and prejudices and be willing to consider the historical significance of class conflict, the main preoccupation of Marxist scholars. One does not have to agree with orthodox Marxists as to its absolute centrality to finally admit during an era of Occupy Wall Street and its various successors that conflict between classes is an important factor in understanding social relations and historical change. Such an admission does not require abandoning other theoretical approaches, since a Marxist perspective on class relations can complement other theories, not simply replace them. Embracing some aspects of Marx's legacy has the potential of significantly contributing to the explanatory powers of multi-theoretical models. It is past time to find out if this potential can be realized.

References

Arrighi, G. (1994) *The Long Twentieth Century: Money, Power, and the Origins of Our Times.* New York: Verso Books.

Baran, P.A. and Sweezy, P.M. (1966) *Monopoly Capitalism: An Essay on the American Economic and Social Order.* New York: Monthly Review Press.

Brenner, R. (1976) Agrarian class structure and economic development in pre-industrial Europe, *Past and Present*, 70: 30–75.

Brenner, R. (2002) *The Boom and the Bubble: The US in the World Economy.* New York: W.W. Norton.

Bryer, R. A. (2013) Americanism and financial accounting theory, part 2: The rise of the modern business enterprise, America's transition to capitalism, and the genesis of management accounting, *Critical Perspectives on Accounting*, 24(4–5): 273–318.
Burawoy, M. (1979) *Manufacturing Consent: Changes in the Labor Process under Monopoly Capitalism*. Chicago: University of Chicago Press.
Chandler, A. D. (1977) *The Visible Hand: The Managerial Revolution in American Business*. Cambridge, MA: Belknap Press.
Clawson, D., Neustadtl, A., and Weller, M. (1998) *Dollars and Votes: How Business Campaign Contributions Subvert Democracy*. Philadelphia: Temple University Press.
Clemens, E. S. and Cook, J. M. (1999) Politics and institutionalism: Explaining durability and change, *American Review of Sociology*, 25: 441–66.
Cypher, J. W. (2007) From military Keynesianism to global neoliberal militarism, *Monthly Review*, 59(2): 37–55.
Davis, G. F. (1994) Corporate elite and the politics of corporate control, in C. Predergast and J. D. Nottnerus (eds), *Current Perspectives in Sociology*, Supplement I. Greenwich, CT: JAI Press.
De Ste. Croix, G. E. M. (1981) *Class Struggle in the Ancient Greek World: From the Archaic Age to the Arab Conquests*. Ithaca, NY: Cornell University Press.
DiMaggio, P. J. and Powell, W. W. (1983) The iron cage revisited: Institutional isomorphism and collective rationality in organizational fields, *American Sociological Review*, 48(2): 147–60.
Edwards, R. E. (1975) Stages in corporate stability and the risk of corporate failure, *Journal of Economic History*, 35: 428–57.
Evan, W. and Freeman, R. (1993) A stakeholder theory of the modern corporation: Kantian capitalism, in T. Beauchamp and N. Bowie (eds), *Ethical Theory and Business* (pp. 75–93). Englewood Cliffs, NJ: Prentice-Hall.
Ferguson, N. (2002) A truly great historian, *The Guardian*, 1 October, http://www.theguardian.com/commentisfree/2012/oct/01/eric-hobsbawm-historian
Fligstein, N. (1990) *Transformation of Corporate Control*. Cambridge, MA: Harvard University Press.
Gramsci, A. (1985) *Selections from Cultural Writings*. Cambridge, MA: Harvard University Press.
Hannan, M.T. and Freeman, J. (1977) The population ecology of organizations, *American Journal of Sociology*, 82(5): 929–64.
Harris, J. D., Johnson, S. G., and Souder, D. (2013) Model-theoretic knowledge accumulation: The case of agency theory and incentive alignment, *Academy of Management Review*, 38(3): 442–54.
Hattam, V. (1993) *Labor Visions and State Power: The Origins of Business Unionism in the United States*. Princeton, NJ: Princeton University Press.
Heald, M. (1970) *The Social Responsibilities of Business: Company and Community, 1900–1960*. Cleveland: Case Western Reserve University Press.
Hilferding, R. (1981) *Finance Capital: A Study of the Latest Phase of Capitalist Development*. London: Routledge & Kegan Paul.
Hill, C., Hilton, R., and Hobsbawm, E. (1983) *Past and Present*: origins and early years, *Past and Present*, 100: 3–14.
Himmelfarb, G. (1987) *The New History and the Old*. Cambridge, MA: Harvard University Press.
Hira, R. and Hira, A. (2005) *Outsourcing America: What's Behind our National Crisis and How We Can Reclaim American Jobs*. New York: American Management Association.
Hollander, S. (2011) *Frederich Engels and Marxian Political Economy*. Cambridge: Cambridge University Press.
Jensen, M. C. (1989) Eclipse of the public corporation, *Harvard Business Review*, 67(5): 61–74.
Jessop, B. (1997) Survey article: The regulation approach, *Journal of Political Philosophy*, 5: 287–326.
Kaye, H. (1984) *British Marxist Historians*. Cambridge: Polity Press.
Lash, S. and Urry, J. (1987) *End of Organized Capitalism*. Madison, WI: University of Wisconsin Press.
Leiserson, W. M. (1929) Contributions of personnel management to improved labor relations, in *Wertheim Lectures on Industrial Relations: 1928*. Cambridge, MA: Harvard University Press.
Litterer, J. (1963) Systematic management: Design for organizational recoupling in American manufacturing firms, *Business History Review*, 37: 369–91.
Malott, R. H. (1978) Corporate support of education: Some strings attached, *Harvard Business Review*, 56(4): 133–38.
Marens, R. (2005) Getting it right the first time: Alfred Chandler, anthracite coal, and the origins of American management, *Management History/Management Decision*, 43: 433–49.

Marens, R. (2013a) Calling in a debt: Government's role in creating the capacity for 'explicit' corporate social responsibility, *Business and Society Review*, 118(2): 143–69.

Marens, R. (2013b) What comes around: the early 20th century American roots of legitimating corporate social responsibility, *Organization*, 20(3): 454–76.

Marx, K. (1967a) *Capital: A Critique of Political Economy*, Vol. 1. New York: International Publishers.

Marx, K. (1967b) *Capital: A Critique of Political Economy*, Vol. 3. New York: International Publishers.

Marx, K. (1972 [1852]) Eighteenth Brumaire of Louis Bonaparte, reprinted in R. C. Tucker (ed.), *Marx–Engels Reader*. New York: W.W. Norton.

Melman, S. (1987) *Profits without Production*. Philadelphia: University of Pennsylvania Press.

Milliband, R. (1983) *Class Power and State Power*. London: Verso.

Murray, S. (2005) Proposed defense cuts draw fire, *Wall Street Journal*, 1 February.

Nadeem, S. (2011) *Dead Ringers: How Outsourcing is Changing the way Indians Understand Themselves*. Princeton, NJ: Princeton University Press.

North, D. C. (1987) Is it worth making sense of Marx? *Inquiry*, 29: 57–63.

Ott, J. C. (2011) *When Wall Street Met Main Street*. Cambridge, MA: Harvard University Press.

Partnoy, F. (2003) *Infectious Greed: How Deceit and Risk Corrupted the Financial Markets*. New York: Henry Holt.

Pfeffer, J. and Salancik, G. R. (1978) *The External Control of Organizations: A Resource Dependence Perspective*. New York: Harper & Row.

Pollin, R. (2003) *Contours of Descent: US Economic Fractures and the Landscape of Global Austerity*. New York: Verso Press.

Roy, W. G. (1997) *Socializing Capital: The Rise of the Large Industrial Corporation in America*. Princeton, NJ: Princeton University Press.

Schumpeter, J. A. (1942) *Capitalism, Socialism, and Democracy*. New York: Harper & Brothers.

Seo, M. G. and Creed, W. E. D. (2002) Institutional contradictions, praxis, and institutional change: A dialectical perspective, *Academy of Management Review*, 27(2): 222–47.

Slichter, S. (1921) *Turnover of Factory Labor*. New York: Appleton.

Smith, V. (1990) *Managing in the Corporate Interest: Control and Resistance in an American Bank*. Berkeley, CA: University of California Press.

Stone, K. (1974) Origins of job structures in the steel industry, *Review of Radical Political Economics*, 6(2), 61–97.

Sweezy, P. (1953) *Present as History*. New York: Monthly Review Press.

Teece, D. J. (2011) Achieving integration of the business school curriculum using the dynamic capabilities framework, *Journal of Management Development*, 30: 499–516.

Thompson, E. P. (1963) *The Making of the English Working Class*. London: Gollancz.

Useem, M. (1996) *Investor Capitalism: How Money Managers are Changing the Face of Corporate America*. New York: Basic Books.

8

A history of management histories

Does the story of our past and the way we tell it matter?

Roy Jacques and Gabrielle Durepos

Introduction

At an Academy of Management symposium in 2005 (Gibson *et al.*, 2005), several participants who have been influential in either writing Organizational Behavior textbooks or writing about the history of management complained that what they termed 'chapter two' – the obligatory history chapter of these texts – was becoming shorter and shorter. Why might this be, since with every year that passes the field's past becomes more extensive? One answer might be that the management disciplines are a science and a science is judged on its current body of knowledge – its data-based findings and their fit with theory. The past is of casual interest only, the story of our errors, our progressively declining ignorance. If 'chapter two' is dying, that simply leaves more space for useful knowledge.

Another answer might be that perhaps it deserves to die because it says nothing of interest. It is not history per se that is irrelevant, it is the specific history found in 'chapter two'. Industrialization and the changes in authority in work organizations which accompanied it caused civil wars in Russia, Germany, Japan, England, and France. They nearly caused a second civil war in the United States two generations after a first war of industrialization that remains today more devastating to the country than both world wars and Viet Nam combined. Could the history of industrialization and the practices called management, which emerged from this crucible, possibly be this uninteresting?

This chapter queries and critiques the discursive construction and embedded values of the currently-dominant 'chapter two' histories of management, problematizing both their content and the way in which the content is ordered or emplotted (White, 1973, 1985). White's theory of emplotment addresses how facts and traces get ordered into a story form, thus how actual stories are carved out of mere chronicles of events. He shows that plot structure ('modes of emplotment') is actively chosen by historians and influences the explanatory power of the historical construction. We argue that the way in which the past of management knowledge is created, written, and emplotted powerfully shapes the conditions of possibility and emancipatory potential of our discipline in the present and future.

This chapter proceeds in three sections. First, we propose that management and organization studies fail to deal adequately with their disciplinary past. Not only are histories of management and organization studies few and far between, those that do exist share the discursive qualities of 'chapter two'. These are inadequate in that they are simplistic and detached from both the context in which the events took place and their context of production. Due to the latter, they ignore the ideological forces at work in their construction.

Drawing on this point, we aim to show in the second section of the chapter that most extant histories of management are outcomes of an ideology shaped by conditions specific to modernism (Ermarth, 1992; Jenkins, 1999), which constitute a rigid prescription for ordering – emplotting – the events (White, 1973; Jenkins, 1995) which currently make up the dominant history of management. Modernist histories, according to Jenkins (1997) are characterized as those that are realist, objectivist as well as self-referential. Management histories that adopt a modernist mode of emplotment to create a particular order and convey the past of our discipline lead to histories that have a scientistic slant and appear timeless, universal, linear, progressive, and value-neutral (Ermarth, 1992; Jenkins, 1999). These histories portray our current condition as an unquestioned and uncontested outcome of our past – and in doing so presume an essence of certainty or false necessity (Unger, 1986). This mode of emplotting the history of management has consequences for how we come to know our past and our present and conditions how we come to know our future. Thus in the third section of the chapter, we discuss the consequences of adopting a modernist mode of emplotment.

The shrinking 'chapter two' of management textbooks

Over a century and a half ago, Freeman Hunt, a notable business author of his time, thought it would be "no great task" to create what he called a "Handbook of Mercantile Practice" and from this to construct "a true theory of business" (Hunt, 1857: vi). Since that time, it has been more or less continually announced in millenarian fashion that knowledge in this area was on the verge of becoming a true science (Jacques, 1996). Nowhere is this truer than in 'chapter two', which inevitably describes the history of management knowledge as a crawl out of the primordial ooze. On the one hand, management has presumably always existed; Robbins (1990: 36), in one of the most popular textbooks in the field, finds the roots of management knowledge in Leviticus. On the other hand, Bowditch and Buono (2005: 7), in another durably popular text, simply find the entirety of humanity, "largely biased against the concept of managing organizations efficiently and effectively" – except, that is, for Americans in the twentieth and present centuries.

'Chapter two' positions invariably give the impression that we slogged along in darkness and ignorance for two million years, until the dawn of Scientific Management. Then, in three generations, we developed humanistic theories of organizing exemplified by the 'Hawthorne Effect' studies, progressed to a Weberian understanding of bureaucracy, moved from closed-system to open-system thinking, advanced yet further into more sophisticated contingency theory, and are now just putting the final touches on (this valediction is invariable) – a true science of organizing. Is our story simply one of steady progress, a natural evolution of technical expertise, or has the construction been a more active, more values-based process? Consider these examples from the 'chapter two' canon:

- *Henry Mintzberg's 'classic' study*: It has become mandatory to refer to this study of what managers 'really' do (Mintzberg, 1968, and successor publications) as a classic and it is so, in terms of canonization. It has been cited tens of thousands of times. What is the basis of the 'scientific' knowledge in this study? Observation included only an $n = 5$ convenience sample of five relatively homogeneous, male, Canadian CEOs known to the author through family connections, yet Mintzberg (1971) claims that this study describes managers universally, from first-line supervisors to top management and 'chapter two' has canonized this wild extrapolation as fact. At best, this might be considered a severe problem of external validity, at worst, mere propaganda.

- *The Hawthorne Studies: Management and the Worker* (Roethlisberger and Dickson, 1939) was published fully 12 years after the Hawthorne experiments concluded, yet one does not find the legendary 'Hawthorne Effect' referred to within its 615 pages. There is little doubt that the phenomena which have subsequently been given that name did occur, yet why did they occur and why are only a few pages of a voluminous, landmark study canonically taught in business schools? Gillespie (1993) chronicles the construction of the Hawthorne legend and its artificial constriction to the supposed 'Hawthorne Effect' and the alleged discovery of the 'informal organization' (which was already both known and discussed prior to that time as documented in Jacques, 1996).
- *Theories X and Y*: Everyone who has studied management knows that McGregor divided management styles into two styles, X and Y – the problem is that this is clearly NOT what he was trying to discuss. Writing in 1960, McGregor invites the reader to consider that over all of history, there have only been two fundamental changes in sources of authority and that a third – which we would now probably call the post-industrial – was then just dawning. "The purpose of this volume is not to entice management to choose sides over Theory X or Theory Y. It is … to urge management to examine its assumptions and make them explicit" (McGregor, 1960: 246). McGregor was characterizing management styles of the *past* as X and Y and explicitly encouraging the reader to speculate on what the future might hold *beyond* these modes of authority. This is stated explicitly in *The Human Side of Enterprise* (1960), whose canonical role in 'chapter two' functions to support a point quite contrary to that of the author. This is discussed in more detail in Jacques (1996) and Stager Jacques (2006).
- *Eustress/distress*: Any good student of management knows the inverted-U shaped model of stress, based on the Yerkes-Dodson Law, which incorporates the term 'eustress' introduced by endocrinologist Hans Selye. According to the 'chapter two' interpretation of this model, employees should be tuned like violin strings to have the optimum, not the minimum, of stress. This is quite convenient for managers, as it provides a 'scientific' rationale justifying stress in work groups without providing a metric for determining what is optimal. Once again, however, the original evidence seems to be a great distance from this construction. According to historical research done by Le Fevre, Matheny, and Kolt (2003), the 'chapter two' construction of the relationship of stress to performance is questionable for both construct validity and accurate reading of the original source materials:

  > Selye's concept of eustress or 'good stress'appears to be largely ignored in the literature, while the Yerkes Dodson Law is illustrated as a model for management practice. We suggest that the meaning assigned to the word stress has shifted from Selye's original formulation, and that this shift, in conjunction with the use of the Yerkes Dodson Law leads to inappropriate management of stress in organizations.
  >
  > *(Le Fevre, Matheny, and Kolt, 2003: 726)*

- *Group dynamics*: Organizational reality is a group reality and anyone who has attempted to direct a group knows that they have a quality that is more than the mere sum of the individual participants. This is significant because, in work settings, the individual is insignificant; work is done by groups. At the other end of the telescope, the structural view of the organization is hypothetical. 'Apple' does not go to China; a marketing group does or a manufacturing group … it is always a group. One might expect, then, that the teaching of management would centre on competency in managing groups, yet this topic is so peripheral as to be almost nonexistent in business teaching. "Most of the mistakes I made [dealing with groups as a new manager] … were made *after* completing my MBA!" (Jacques and Hobson, 2011: 30).

- A rigorous 'behavioral scientist' might criticize Bion's foundational *Experiences in Groups* (1961) as subjective and anecdotal, despite the fact that it also showed keen insight into the phenomenon of 'groupness'. However, even these supposed limitations would fit with the evolutionary narrative character of 'chapter two', because the study of groups very quickly took on the form of an experimental science (e.g. Cartwright and Zander, 1968). A decade later, however, small group research could already be discussed largely in the past tense: "What's happened to small group research?" (Lakin, 1979). In yet another decade, those in this tradition, still marginal, discuss attempting to "reclaim the relevance and vitality of small group analysis" (Gillette and McCollom, 1990: 2). Their story is barely a footnote in 'chapter two'. Scientific rigour, it would seem, has not prevented this potentially vital stream of inquiry from developing *rigor mortis*. If organization studies is a scientific discipline and if groups are central to the phenomena we must understand, this raises two questions: (1) How/why has the study of groups become so marginal when the group phenomenon is central to organizing itself? and (2) Why has scientific rigour been named as a *cause* of this marginalization, rather than an *antidote*, not by critics of this work, but by advocates (cf. Lakin, 1979: Introduction)? The natural evolution of technical knowledge does not seem an adequate answer.
- *Personality vs. organization*: "[W]e conclude that the needs of the healthy individual (in our culture) tend to be incongruent with the maximum expression of the demands of the formal organization" (Argyris, 1957: 229). The subtitle to this book is *The Conflict Between System and the Individual*. In the present-day canon, Argyris is justly remembered as a major figure in the development of management knowledge, but how is he remembered? As an Action Researcher, as a figure in Organizational Development, as a theorist of the knowledge organization – NOT as a figure discussing power and conflict. It seems his claim that organizations are toxic to our well-being has been gently erased from history.
- *Behaviorism*: In a discipline based on empirical findings, we might expect to find a great deal written on Behaviorism, since we demonstrably both produce and respond to operant conditioning stimuli every day in innumerable ways. Yet, Behaviorists, despite possessing a strong experimental tradition, receive short shrift in 'chapter two', being generally treated as extremists at best, sinister characters at worst. A reading of *Beyond Freedom and Dignity* (Skinner, 1971) shows quite a different picture. The author invites us to consider that our social world *already* shapes our actions through operant conditioning. He is not the harbinger of a dystopian future, but a messenger inviting us to reflect on how we might most effectively achieve the greatest good for the greatest number in the operant-conditioning *present*. Try to find an extended discussion of Behaviorism in a management text. You will be disappointed (cf. Stager Jacques, 2006 for elaboration). In a discipline nominally based on the value-free accumulation of testable fact, this outcome is anomalous.

These are not the only examples we could produce, but they are sufficient to indicate that something is going on in the way we tell our history that goes beyond merely the compiling of tested and valid findings. Our point is not so simplistic as to argue that the dominant mythology of management history is 'wrong' or to suggest that it could possibly be replaced by a story that is 'right'. Our goal is to demonstrate that every story we could possibly tell is contestable, to show that what we believe about our past is power-laden because it conditions the *questions* we will ask, the *answers* we will generate, and the *actions* we will take in the future.

A critique and contextualization of what is currently present in 'chapter two' is not sufficient without some discussion of what is absent, such as the Group Dynamics tradition mentioned above. After all, the "question of *what* the history of management has been is far less interesting than *why* we have told the story in certain ways ... and *what* such tales cause us to see – and not see" (Jacques, 1997: 1). Our work is inevitably shaped as much by what we omit as by what we include. In a review of Wren's *Early Management Thought*, Jacques (1997: 2, 4) states in part that:

> In short, what is generally missing from these selections is anything that might contravene expectations set by exposure to the mainstream folklore about the universality of management knowledge, its quasi-natural 'evolution' and its separation from questions of social power and privilege ... Industrialization has also been the site of emergence of modern feminism, unionism, and a radically transformed and redeployed professionalism. It produced the Salvation Army and the Settlement movement. Wesley, Penn, the Cadburys and the 'Protestant ethic' of capitalizing time provided both an ethical basis for and a moral mandate to capitalize the work of the individual (cf. Langton, 1984) while Social Darwinism, and Eugenics provided a context for the industrial 'discovery' of a new (and conveniently hierarchical) 'human nature'. Trusts, monopoly power and public outcry (cf. Tarbell 1902 and the other 'muckrakers' of the Progressive movement).

This selection from a much longer list of omissions strongly suggests that such omissions are not random; they have a pattern which produces the illusion that one has a comprehensive knowledge of a past that is much more complex and indeterminate than our neat impression of it suggests. It is quite easy for omissions to be passively misleading, precisely because they are *not* there for examination. For example, Jacques (1997: 3) also notes:

> [A] tendency to underrepresent female contributors in these selections as well. Admittedly, management writing in the time period represented was largely a boys' game, but Mary Marshall, who is represented, hardly constitutes the scope of women's contributions. Without effort, the examples of Katherine Blackford, Lillian Gilbreth, Jane Adams, Charlotte Perkins Gilman, Ida Tarbell and especially Mary Parker Follett come to mind. This is particularly important in a collection of source documents because one of the sustaining arguments of patriarchal history is that women cannot be included because women were not permitted to participate and their lack of participation is circularly legitimated by their non-inclusion.

Since a signature feature of omissions is that their absence leaves no trace, in order to see them one must do the legwork of studying, if not primary sources, at least varying interpretations. Hunt (1857), for example, could afford himself the luxury of writing simply about the pragmatics of doing business. This does not mean that the problem of getting a group of people to achieve a planned outcome was not as thorny a problem then as it is now. However, 'management' was not yet an object of discourse, so its absence does not leave a trace. Indeed, even the 1901 *I.C.S. Business Man's Handbook* (International Correspondence Schools) which purports to offer encyclopedic advice to the business 'man', does not index 'management' nor contain a single entry about managing people. So, does the story of management begin at the same point as the need to manage organizational outcomes? It appears not. The story detailed in the paragraphs that follow is also missing from the contemporary 'chapter two' of management textbooks.

The emergence of management

What is now called management emerges from several major forces related to American industrialization beginning in the 1870s and largely complete by 1920 (Jacques, 1996; Chandler, 1977). During this period, society was radically transformed from one of self-employed small business people to one of 'wage slaves for life' or, as we now habitually call them, 'employees'. During this period, stories of the development of management could not simply treat the problem as a practical question of getting the job done. First, such stories had to address the issue of *legitimation*.

Contrary to the bland impressions given by compilations such as Wren (2004) or Wren and Bedeian (2008), 'chapter two', management did not just happen. As worker groups organized, their unions did not initially fight merely for wages and hours; they fought over who would get to control the process of production, what we now refer to as 'management'. Factory ownership struggled to keep things moving with annual turnover that was generally well above 100 per cent. 'Welfare workers' sought to change the destitute conditions of the average worker. Jacques (1996: 59) describes this period as an American "Reign of Terror" when traditional meanings that had sustained communities from early colonial times became "unbundled from practices" with, for a time, no new order of things to replace them. Now, the problem was not merely a pragmatic one of getting work done; it required a legitimating narrative to hold society together.

Responding to this turmoil, early representatives of management expertise – Systematic Management, Scientific Management, the 'Management Movement' (Litterer, 1959/1985; Taylor, 1911; Blackford and Newcomb, 1914) – made light of the fact that they represented a new source of power in 'the works', a shift of control away from the foreman and in the direction of technical experts representing the employer. Among the large financial interests, which were producing the 'trusts' – businesses so large that Americans of a generation before could not have imagined them – the rallying cry was 'rationalization'. A central figure, financier J. P. Morgan, had been educated in Europe and had interests that went beyond mere wealth (although he found plenty of that). 'Morganization' of the steel, oil, and other industries was often portrayed by the public as rape, but the interests Morgan represented spoke of eliminating 'destructive competition' and 'rationalizing' essential resources (Jacques, 1996). Neither position is a complete truth, nor is either entirely fanciful.

Early proponents of Scientific Management minimized the degree to which they were marginalizing the foreman, the traditional source of power on the factory floor, and emphasized that if production were put on a scientific basis, the worker would have – not less authority – but greater pay and reduced physical effort. A predominant theme pervading the narrative of legitimation of this power shift is education. Workers are not hostile; they are ignorant. The foreman hates the Taylor system because he doesn't understand the best way to do the work, not because it turns him from a person of authority into a proletarian. The human being in the factory is not just a factory 'hand', but a 'resource' to 'develop' (Blackford and Newcomb, 1914).

Another theme in the narrative of legitimation is fairness. From the writings of Scientific Management, through the stories told by such notables as Carnegie (1920), Ford (1922), even Sloan of General Motors (1963), we find legitimation based on the technical determination of what is putatively the one, best way to deal with production processes, wages, and working conditions. This effectively silences the fight that was going on between labour and employers for authority within the factory. The appeal to a nonexistent and unachievable standard of objective truth paves over the very possibility of class, occupational or cultural differences with the promise of, "[P]rosperity for the employee coupled with prosperity for the employer" (Taylor, 1911: 72) as well as society as a whole, '[I]n the end the whole people receive the greater part of the benefit … increasing … the prosperity of the civilized world' (Taylor, 1911: 136).

As edifying as this story of management history may have been to some parties it was not the only story available. Other stories were told in disciplines outside the discourse of management, disciplines which were then and remain today largely unheard in the business school (see for example Wiebe, 1967; Hays, 1957; Prude, 1983; Andreano, 1962). From these stories we see a less benign transition from a peasant America to an industrial power, one in which the social fabric frayed so badly that it nearly tore violently apart as it had in 1861. For example, in the decade of the 1890s, the US National Guard, nominally a defence militia, was called out against labouring Americans over 500 times (Jacques, 1996). If there was indeed 'one best way', many seemed to disagree as to what it was.

Explicit narratives of legitimation are found in virtually all major texts through the 1920s. One sign that a new order was, by then, fairly well sedimented is the disappearance of these narratives. Barnard (1938) is a lengthy tome on the functions of management, yet it treats the 'executive' and the 'employee' as common-sense roles even though they had been emergent and controversial barely a generation prior. His discussion of the executive role is framed entirely as a technical problem. The need for a narrative of legitimation has disappeared. Even labour organizations were, by this time, largely resigned to fighting for wages and working conditions rather than seeking control of the production process.

Why are these stories of the past of our discipline not told? A partial answer is that the view chronicled in 'chapter two' is so deeply entrenched that it is impossible to imagine otherwise – it is not a 'view'; it is 'fact'. Although a great deal of evidence which would cause us to question this story is "hidden in plain sight" (Stager Jacques, 2004: 54), we fail to see it because of our 'common sense'.

Constructing 'chapter two': an outcome of a modernist mode of emplotment

After the Second World War, a new need for legitimation arose within management discourse. Prior to this time, business schools were uncommon, generally attached to elite schools and dedicated to training future business leaders, not managers in general. At the other end of the spectrum were the correspondence schools which tended to focus on subjects that could be taught effectively by mail such as entry-level accounting or drafting. Beginning in the 1950s, and supported by the boom in higher education that lasted for the next two decades, the American business school metastasized. The question of legitimacy was no longer whether managerial capitalism was a justifiable practice. With the general public, that battle was over. The new challenge was for the business school to convince managers, employers – and especially students – that it contained a body of knowledge, which would result in superior organizational and career performance.

This is the literal source of 'chapter two', the first canonical, textbook version of who we are and how we got here. At this point we find that theoretical tomes accepted as canonical follow the Barnardian example of ahistoricism. Likert (1967), McClelland (1961), Thompson (1967), and March and Simon (1958) are representative in this regard. One might even draw the conclusion from Simon's highly influential earlier work (1945) that management decisions are simply a computational, a cybernetic, problem. One can scrutinize these works without finding any evidence that managing is something other than a contemporary problem with a technical solution. History is no longer an integral aspect of developing a critical understanding of one's situation. The 'evolution' of management has been reduced to the status of creation-myth *à la* Midgeley (1985), mere prologue to the 'real' knowledge.

The textbook version of 'who we are and how we got here' chronicled in 'chapter two' not only tells a tale of the progressive rise of modern(ist) management. The textbook is itself an effect of the very knowledge that it documents. Both in content and form, it is an outcome of a condition of modernity, characterized by an unquestioned (and blind) belief in progress, linearity, objectivity, rationalization, and efficiency (Cooper and Burrell, 1988). The hallmarks of modernity are active in shaping, not only the content but also the order with which the events are emplotted into story form. White's (1973, 1985) notion of emplotment pertains to the specific manner historians or scholars structure the content and order the events into story form. It pertains to the plot structure adopted by the historian that gives the narrative a recognizable form. According to White (1985: 83), "histories gain part of their explanatory effect by their success in making stories out of mere chronicles". What this means is that the story assumes part of its meaning through the way in which the "sequence of events is fashioned into a narrative" (Jenkins, 1995: 159). The fashioning of events is an activity undertaken by those who write the stories of our past. Histories have no meaning independent of the storyteller's touch. Storytellers of the past give "form to the apparently formless, shape to the apparently shapeless" (Jenkins, 1999: 15). History has always been "and always will be necessarily configured, troped, emplotted, read, mythologized and ideologized in ways to suit ourselves" (Jenkins, 1999: 3). Thus, imposing a plot structure is neither good nor bad but inevitable (Jenkins, 1999; Kellner, 1997).

The implications of adopting a modernist mode of emplotment to tell the story of the past of management are multifaceted (Jenkins, 2003, 1999, 1997, 1995; Ermarth, 1992) and invariably structure 'chapter two'. The following list tabulates some key qualities which will likely be familiar to the student of mainstream management history:

- *Timeless and universal*: The notion of universalism in many senses can be understood as closely related to and somewhat responsible for that of timelessness. Universalism suggests that a body of knowledge is applicable to all societies regardless of geographical location and temporal period (Booth and Rowlinson, 2006) and is therefore timeless. Management knowledge would, then, not be thought of as culturally or temporally specific. Rindova (1994), for instance, unapologetically 'discovers' the twentieth-century Theories X, Y, and Z existing in ancient China. Moore and Lewis (1998) anachronistically describe twentieth-century Japanese/Korean *keiretsu* capitalism in ancient Phoenicia. This strains credibility. In whatever ways the Chinese and Phoenicians were organizing, it is doubtful they were deploying the twentieth-century methods which constitute *managing*. Historians are generally more cautious about such universalism: "[K]nowledge of the past is always embedded in particular cultural practices and cannot exist outside of them" (Rigney, 2007: 152); *our* history is not understood to exist, "except as defined locally" (Ermarth, 1992 as quoted in Jenkins, 1999: 174; Jenkins, 1995).
- *Evolutionary*: The all-pervasive metaphor of 'chapter two' management history is that of 'evolution'. Management knowledge was not developed by individuals with power-laden values, perceptions, interests, and beliefs. It simply evolved (Wren and Bedeian, 2008). Any undergraduate biology major knows that evolution does not have goals, purposes, or interests. It is a value-neutral, blind mechanism of selection that has the effect of adapting populations to their environments. If management has 'evolved', there is no room to question its foundations, its construction, its embedded values – these are simply responses to the dictates of 'the environment' and, as objective responses to an objective problem, they are beyond questioning except in the descriptive sense that one can ask, "how does it work?"
- *Linear and progressive*: Management histories chronicle events in a linear and progressive way in that a later (presumably more advanced) event is linked to and illustrated as the inevitable, progressive outcome of a previous event. This 'certaintist' manner (Ermarth, 1992; Jenkins, 1999) in which events are sewn together leads to a narrative that projects a false necessity

(Unger, 1986), making it impossible to imagine otherwise – despite the fact that at any given moment in the past, a multitude of options could or may have been pursued. In 'chapter two', this is most evident in the popular opinion that management knowledge merely emerged from the growing desire and ability of people to do work more efficiently and productively. Other social issues of the time are shut down in the histories; they are portrayed by their absence as irrelevant.

- *Value-neutral and disinterested*: To offer that management history is value-neutral and disinterested is to suggest that it is portrayed as divorced from the values and interests of its writer. The chronicler is merely an observer, detached from the text. Historians have long argued that authors of history are always involved in the historical moment of writing and therefore historicizing is never a neutral task (Kellner, 1997; Ermarth, 2007). Maintaining the belief that management knowledge does not act for or against any vested interest is a condition of credibility within the discipline. To suggest otherwise is to relocate oneself from the dominant circle of 'behavioural scientists' into the never-never of 'radical' theory – and nobody needs to listen to a radical because we know radicals are all crazy.
- *Power is absent*: It is quite staggering that, within the study of the social force which, more than any other, shapes present-day American life, it is inappropriate to use the term 'power' in American business studies. Presumably, business school students study with the intention of having the power to influence organizations and their careers, but to suggest the presence of power undermines the presumption of value-neutrality. Managers do not represent vested interests. They represent only efficiency and effectiveness.
- *The scientistic imminence of a True science*: It is now *de rigueur* to describe management knowledge as a science that is neatly nailing down the final corners of paradigmatic completion. That this claim has been made continuously at least from Hunt (1857) to the present day should make one wonder.
- *All (wo)men are NOT created equal*: The social norms and institutions of America from its founding until the late nineteenth century were based on the philosophical presumption (if not the social reality) that all people have more or less the same capabilities. This follows a strong tradition of British philosophy going back at least to Hobbes. In a world of small communities composed largely of peasant farmers and self-employed small businesspeople, this assumption was workable. In the factory, it was not. As soon as there was a business need for hierarchy and specialization, it was neatly 'discovered' that people differ from each other in a way that corresponds to the positions available in that hierarchy. Initially, this followed the then-pervasive eugenic thinking. As the discipline of psychology developed, it provided a framework for producing and reproducing specialization and hierarchy that was less overtly sexist, racist, ethnocentric, and classist.

Having structured discourse in the field according to these modernist values, who would care if 'chapter two' is disappearing? What matters is the steadily increasing efficacy, of our body of objective knowledge. One cannot question facts. We once were lost, but now are found; were blind but now we see. What could be the problem? Well, here is one:

For a generation, thought leaders in business have increasingly been talking about a revolution in the workplace, one centred on the increasing knowledge demands of work. Some would call this the post-industrial economy. The Fordist factory hums along, but primarily in fast food and other service work. For the majority of positions in the workplace it is impossible to get top performance from the worker by engineering and controlling the job. The worker has to also *want* to perform well, has to exercise discretion and judgement. A body of management knowledge built on the need to get *compliance* from the task worker is precisely what is not needed in order to get *initiative* from a worker whose discretion is essential. "But," one might object, "if management knowledge is simply an accumulation of useful facts, how can we not be fine just adding one then another brick to the edifice we've been building since God spoke to Moses in Leviticus?"

This is where history becomes valuable, even essential. If we take Kuhn (1962) seriously – and we should – we understand that any body of knowledge we could have produced was produced as a result of interests and values. This is not a failing; it is a necessity. Who has had the ability to articulate what problems merit researching? Whose voices have been heard and whose have not? What problems has our accumulated knowledge been developed to solve? What occupational and intellectual predisposition has conditioned the framing of questions in the research community? The perspective that our knowledge just 'evolved' is not only naïve; in this respect it is counterproductive.

Our blind acceptance and adoption of a modernist mode of emplotment in the construction of the history of management thought weds us to an increasingly outdated body of knowledge because we fail to distinguish it from Truth. This has significant consequences for our discipline to which we now shift our attention.

The consequences of a modernist mode of emplotment

> [O]rganization studies [lacks] an awareness of history that is integrated into the process of knowledge generation in a manner that results in constant scrutiny of the social relevance of the problems addressed by the field and the processes through which this is done. This failure stands in the way of developing [new] organizational knowledge ... because the field is harnessed to cumulatively adding to problems that were of concern to early industrialists.
>
> *(Stager Jacques, 2004: 272)*

What are the consequences for creating and ordering knowledge of the past according to a modernist mode of emplotment? Below, we identify what we feel are those consequences and offer these as sufficient justification for moving toward a new way of telling the past of our discipline.

The God trick: A modernist mode of emplotment conceals the ideological forces at play which act to order the past of our disciplinary knowledge. This can be studied as an 'ideology,' although that term is often inflammatory, suggesting an unquestioned commitment to preconceived values that is incompatible with the presumed open-mindedness and value-neutrality of the scientific enterprise. *Au contraire.* Since the late nineteenth century, those who have studied the history and philosophy of science have been forced to become increasingly sanguine about the overly-optimistic modernist belief that with enough effort, the datum will speak unambiguously of its own meaning. To quote one highly influential source:

> Observation and experience can and must drastically restrict the range of admissible scientific belief, else there would be no science. But they cannot alone determine a particular body of such belief. An apparently arbitrary element, compounded of personal and historical accident, is always a formative ingredient of the beliefs espoused.
>
> *(Kuhn, 1962/1970: 1)*

Kuhn concludes that no scientific community can "practice its trade without some set of received beliefs" (Kuhn, 1962/1970: 4). That is, the data will never simply speak for themselves. Their meanings are subject to beliefs about reality, truth, and the structure of the body of knowledge which – inevitably – reflect the values of that scientific community, the time and the society which produced it. Ideology, then, is not a negative thing, but an integral element of knowledge production; *the science which purports to exist without ideology is a science that exists on pretence.*

One may judge this as good, bad, or otherwise, but one must accept it as inevitable. Not only has the Objectivist view of science not been able to demonstrate the existence of a value-free perspective on any subject, the possibility of doing so has been a receding horizon at least since the 1890s. Kuhn is not alone in this conclusion. Philosophers of empiricism such as Quine (1953) and Popper, although they were *defenders* of empirical inquiry, conceded that: "[A]ll observation involves interpretation in the light of our theoretical knowledge … pure, observational knowledge, unadulterated by theory, would, if at all possible, be utterly barren and futile" (Popper, "Knowledge Without Authority", in Miller, 1985: 49). If the physical sciences have not been able to separate values and beliefs from the datum, how much more is this true of the social sciences? If the 'observer effect' noted by Schrödinger and Heisenberg applies even to atomic particles, how much more is this a quality of social systems, where awareness of being observed fundamentally changes the behaviours available to observe?

A blind acceptance of a modernist ideology, which erases itself from the text, in both the content and emplotment of management history leads to what Haraway (1988: 584) has termed the "'god trick' promising vision from everywhere and nowhere equally and fully". She is critical of the god trick as a patriarchal delusion. Jenkins (2003: 11) calls this the "history narrator as nobody effect" or the "omniscient narrator trick" (Jenkins, 1999: 170). Blindly accepting a representation of the field's past as independent of a specific community's deep-rooted belief system, accepting it as Real, *normalizes* this mode of emplotment (Jenkins, 1995, 1999, 2003), prematurely closing down the conditions of possibility of the ways we can or could come to know our history. According to Foucault (1982: 126–7) members of a discipline

> Do not communicate solely by the logical succession of propositions that they advance … [T]hey communicate by … the conditions of possibility of the enunciative function [which] defines the possibilities of a field's ability to deploy identities, thematic continuities, translations of concepts, and polemical interchanges.

These conditions of possibility are not merely the statements taken as true or valid within a field. They determine the rules for any statement which is to be taken as *sensible*. For instance, one may argue within contemporary medical science that diet cholesterol either is or is not related to blood cholesterol. Whichever position is correct, both are sensible. However, to state that a sanguine or phlegmatic humor is related to diet cholesterol goes beyond the conditions of possibility for making a sensible medical statement today because it appeals to a discursive object (the humors) which is "within the true" (Foucault, 1982: 224) of an incompatible discourse.

One cannot simply paste facts onto a neutral field. In order to attain meaning, they must be interpreted through the filter of a discipline's conditions of possibility. All knowledge, without exception, is bounded by socially-produced conditions of possibility. Those who attest otherwise have, after four centuries of philosophical, social, and scientific dominance, been unable to prove their thesis. A premature closing of these conditions of possibility by naturalizing a discipline as inevitable and power-free prevents reflective study and discussion of the effects these conditions have on the body of knowledge

Certain modes of ordering knowledge are more sympathetic to 'imagining otherwise', which is important as an antidote to believing there is only one possible story. An example is counterfactual history, where embedded in the construction of this knowledge is the need to question at every intersection, what could have been as opposed to merely chronicling what was (Booth and Rowlinson, 2006). To choose a cliché, what would modern European history look like if Hitler had never been born? Removing the cult of the man lets us reflect on the role of *Junker* militarism, multinational anti-Semitism, international capitalism, the 1918 Treaty of Versailles, the failings of the Weimar regime … in short, it helps us to better see forces that were powerful in shaping European history 1933–45 with or without Hitler. This helps us to see events from a different and possibly productive new angle.

Linearity, as a condition of possibility of a modernist mode of emplotment, also prematurely closes down the opportunity to discuss the ways in which our presumed knowledge of our past has been constructed (Ermarth, 1992; Jenkins, 1999). A linear chronicling of events creates a strict and definite association between what it treats as 'prior' and 'later' events, associating them to one another so rigidly that it is impossible to imagine that one event could have led to anything other than what is dictated through the historical construction. The outcome is knowledge that is infused with an essence of false necessity (Unger, 1986). As such, the conditions of what could have been, the conditions of possibility of the historical construction are prematurely closed down. One might ask how chronologically separate events can possibly be ordered in more than one way. Jacques (1996) offers innumerable examples of concepts that were known and discussed decades before they were labelled by organizational 'scientists' and ordered into a discourse with different conditions of possibility. Cut off from this history, the student may well believe that the concept was newly discovered at the time the new term was deployed, when this is not necessarily so. Alternatively, ordering can create a false sense of causation. In 'chapter two', one-best-way management is alleged to have been succeeded by contingency models because the latter were more effective. Perhaps this is so, but it may also be that with managerial capitalism firmly established in public common sense by the 1950s, it was no longer necessary to legitimate it as the one best way. The causality is complex and by no means determinate.

Ermarth (1992), Rosenstone (2007), and Jenkins (2003: 3), among others, have adamantly stressed that there is "no way that any historical closure can ever be achieved". Nothing is ever given in the order of things as "complete or stable" or fixed "once and for all" (Jenkins, 2003: 4). Instead, this illusion is created through emplotment configurations such as those of modernist histories. Jenkins (2003: 4) critiques modernist histories by offering that no hegemonic settlement on the configuration is conclusive. Instead, texts should continuously be subjected to the "risk of being transformed; refigured" (Jenkins, 2003: 4). The aim then, is to refigure the historical enterprise in the direction of a "radical, open-ended democracy that grasps the impossibility of enacting a total historical/historicizing closure of the past" (Jenkins, 2003: 5). This type of "open-ended democracy" will breathe emancipatory potential into the historical enterprise and allow us to ask questions that were not otherwise permissible.

'Emancipatory' potential? We cannot be emancipated from history itself and there is no 'right' story of our past that will liberate us. The potential lies in our ability to develop a reflective, critical dialogue about our past because our past is not simply past; it has a huge presence in our present and our future. Actively questioning the canon, what it has incorporated and why, what it has silenced, how it became the canon, how it does and does not serve various interests … these are all massively important questions we cannot ask if we accept as dogma a naturalizing, modernist, empiricism in which facts are assumed to have self-evident meanings.

The questions we can(not?) ask: As noted, prematurely closing down the conditions of possibility denies the occasion to formulate and develop a voice that challenges dominant discourse. Drawing on Rosenstone (2007: 13) we suggest the need to "liberate history from its own history" and develop histories that "surprise and startle us", that "let us see things we haven't seen". This is a call to open our imaginations to other ways of seeing and of telling. It is a call for the development of new modes of emplotment which by their nature demand that we write-in transparently as part of our histories the answer to questions such as:

- What values are embedded in our research?
- What significant events have been written out of our story?
- In what ways does our knowledge play into relationships of power?
- What other research questions might we ask? How else might we ask them?
- Whose voices are and are not being heard?
- What other stories could we tell with the same data?
- Do we accept our dogma on faith or scrutinize it critically as we claim scientists do?
- What interests are most represented in the development (and funding) of questions?

These questions demand reflection from the chroniclers of our discipline's past, but beyond this, they must become part of a thread of reflexivity in the mainstream discussion of meanings within the discipline.

Being reflexive about the content and emplotment of our histories: If we have learned anything from twentieth-century philosophy, as Kuhn, Popper, and many others have noted, the most carefully controlled inquiry can only restrict the interpretations which can be put on the data; there is never only one possible interpretation. We cannot avoid embedding our beliefs about the nature of reality and social life into the constructs we create from the data we study. Since this is necessary, we, the authors, do not – cannot – advocate stopping it. We, the discipline, can, however, become reflective about *how* we are doing this; we can become more aware of the consequences of our choices. Until truly objective data are produced which transcend the need to interpret (and this seems unlikely), we must provisionally accept that our knowledge – all of it – is value- and power-laden.

In crafting any history, the role the historian plays in shaping the narrative must be stressed. She or he first selects certain traces over others to use as 'evidence', followed by a decision concerning which events can be described as history from those traces. In making sense of the traces and events, she or he is active in deciding which mode of emplotment will be used to construct a coherent and recognizable narrative out of otherwise disparate events (White, 1973). If the historian is so central to the activity of doing history, how is his or her ordering hand so easily erased in modernist histories? We need to write "the kind of self-reflective history that places the historian in the moment – or better, process – of creating the historical text" (Kellner, 1997: 402).

No, this does not mean abandoning factual histories for some sort of relativism. We should bear in mind that, in their origins, the terms 'fact' and 'fiction' do not represent an opposition of truth to fantasy. A 'fact', from the Latin *faceo*, represents a deed, something that is done. A 'fiction', from *fingere*, is something moulded, crafted by hand. Both verbs refer to active construction of knowledge and neither refers to truth or falsehood. It would be well to bear in mind that it is both possible and necessary for us to fiction historical fact. Our fictioning cannot be judged by a standard as unattainable as truth-value. More immediate standards must be used, such as usefulness, correspondence with data, and consequences.

Conclusions

The recent, growing call for an historic turn in organization studies (Zald, 1993; Kieser, 1994; Üsdiken and Kieser, 2004; Booth and Rowlinson, 2006; Stager Jacques, 2006) offers hope for more attention to the history of our discipline. It holds the promise of histories of a different kind, and even potential for a "transformation of organization studies" (Rowlinson, Stager Jacques, and Booth, 2009). This call for an historic turn represents a:

> [T]urn against the view that organization studies should constitute a science analogous to the physical sciences ... [P]eople – and society – cannot be reduced to a deterministic, laboratory science ... [It would also] entail a return to debates regarding historiography – the methods and historical theories of interpretation through which historical meaning is created.
>
> *(Rowlinson, Stager Jacques, and Booth, 2009: 289)*

It is questionable what effect this historic turn has had on the dominance of modernist histories. In this chapter, we have attempted to relate the shrinking 'chapter two' to conditions of modernism and its scientistic mode of emplotment. We follow Jenkins (1995: 10) who offers that the historical "moment of modernism has passed". It is time to move on from a modernist condition to something beyond it, perhaps a postmodern condition (Jenkins, 1999)? Postmodern*ism* as an intellectual movement seems to have long since reached its point of exhaustion, but the fundamental changes which led to questioning the passing of the modern as a way of understanding are substantive. Something 'amodern' is slowly emerging (Latour, 1990, 1993; Durepos and Mills, 2012a, 2012b).

> I wonder whether we may not envisage modernity rather as an attitude than as a period of history. And by 'attitude,' I mean a mode of relating to contemporary reality ... And, consequently, rather than seeking to distinguish the 'modern' era from the 'premodern' or 'postmodern', I think it would be more useful to try to find out how the attitude of modernity, ever since its formation, has found itself struggling with attitudes of 'countermodernity'.
>
> *(Foucault, 1984: 39)*

References

Andreano, R. (ed.) (1962) *The Economic Impact of the American Civil War*. Cambridge, MA: Shenkman Publishing.

Argyris, C. (1957) *Personality and Organization*. New York: Harper.

Barnard, C. (1938) *Functions of the Executive*. Cambridge, MA: Harvard University Press.

Bion, W. (1961) *Experiences in Groups*. London: Tavistock.

Blackford, K. M. H. and Newcomb, H. (1914) *The Job, The Man, The Boss*. Garden City, NY: Doubleday, Page & Co.

Booth, C. and Rowlinson, M. (2006) Management and organizational history: Prospects, *Management & Organizational History*, 1(1): 5–30.

Bowditch, J. L. and Buono, A. F. (2005) *A Primer on Organizational Behavior* (6th edn). New York: John Wiley.

Carnegie, A. (1920) *The Autobiography of Andrew Carnegie*. Boston: Houghton-Mifflin.

Cartwright, D. and Zander, A. (1968) *Group Dynamics* (3rd edn). New York: Harper & Row.

Chandler, A. (1977) *The Visible Hand: The Managerial Revolution in American Business*. Cambridge, MA: Harvard University Press.

Cooper, R. and Burrell, G. (1988) Modernism, postmodernism and organizational analysis: An introduction, *Organization Studies*, 9(1): 91–112.

Durepos, G. and Mills, A. (2012a) Actor network theory, ANTi-History, and critical organizational historiography, *Organization*, 19(6): 703–21.

Durepos, G., and Mills, A. (2012b) *ANTi-History: Theorizing the Past, History, and Historiography in Management and Organizational Studies*. Charlotte, NC: Information Age Publishing.

Ermarth, E. D. (1992) *Sequel to History, Postmodernism and the Crisis of Representational Time*. Princeton, NJ: Princeton University Press.

Ermarth, E. D. (2007) The closed space of choice: A manifesto on the future of history, in K. Jenkins, S. Morgan, and A. Munslow (eds), *Manifestos for History* (pp. 50–66). New York: Routledge.

Ford, H. (1922) *My Life and Work*. Garden City, NY: Doubleday, Page & Co.
Foucault, M. (1982) *The Archaeology of Knowledge and the Discourse on Language*. New York: Pantheon Books.
Foucault, M. (1984) What is enlightenment?, in P. Rabinow (ed.), *The Foucault Reader* (pp. 32–50). New York: Pantheon.
Gibson, J. W., Ford, R. C., Greenwood, R., Griffin, R. W., Van Fleet, D. D., and Wren, D. A. (2005) Authors reflect on Chapter 2: Is management history still important?, Symposium presented at the Academy of Management Annual Meeting, Honolulu.
Gillespie, R. (1993) *Manufacturing Knowledge: A History of the Hawthorne Experiments*. Cambridge: Cambridge University Press.
Gillette, J. and McCollom, M. (1990) *Groups in Context: A New Perspective on Group Dynamics*. New York: Addison-Wesley.
Haraway, D. (1988) Situated knowledges: The science question in feminism and the privilege of partial perspective, *Feminist Studies*, 14(3): 575–99.
Hays, S. P. (1957) *The Response to Industrialism, 1885–1914*. Chicago, IL: University of Chicago Press.
Hunt, F. (1857) *Worth and Wealth: Maxims for Merchants and Men of Business*. New York: Stringer & Townshend.
International Correspondence Schools (1901/1904) *The Business Man's Handbook: A Convenient Book of Reference for Business Men*. Scranton, PA: International Textbook Co.
Jacques, R. (1996) *Manufacturing the Employee: Management Knowledge from the 19th to 21st Centuries*. London: Sage.
Jacques, R. (1997) Review of: *Early Management Thought*, D. A. Wren (ed.), *Electronic Journal of Radical Organization Theory*, 3(3): 1–6, http://www.mngt.waikato.ac.nz/ejrot/EJROT(newdesign)Vol3_2_front.asp
Jacques, R. and Hobson, M. (2011) *The Sergeant Major Syndrome: A Book for People Who Want to Advance Their Careers*. San Francisco: Berrett-Kohler, OBE.
Jenkins, K. (1995) *On What is History?: From Carr and Elton to Rorty and White*. London: Routledge.
Jenkins, K. (ed.) (1997) *The Postmodern History Reader*. London: Routledge.
Jenkins, K. (1999) *Why History? Ethics and Postmodernity*. London: Routledge.
Jenkins, K. (2003) *Refiguring History*. New York: Routledge.
Kellner, H. (1997) 'Never again' is now, in K. Jenkins (ed.), *The Postmodern History Reader* (pp. 397–412). London: Routledge.
Kieser, A. (1994) Why organization theory needs historical analyses – and how this should be performed, *Organization Science*, 5(4): 608–20.
Kuhn, T. S. (1970 [1962]) *The Structure of Scientific Revolutions* (2nd edn). Chicago, IL: University of Chicago Press.
Lakin, M. (1979) What's happened to small group research? *Journal of Applied Behavioral Science*, 15(3): 265–70.
Langton, J. (1984) The ecological theory of bureaucracy: The case of Josiah Wedgwood and the British pottery industry, *Administrative Science Quarterly*, 29(2): 330–54.
Latour, B. (1990) Postmodern? No, simply amodern: Steps towards an anthropology of science – An essay review, *Studies in the History and Philosophy of Science*, 21: 145–71.
Latour, B. (1993) *We Have Never Been Modern*. Hemel Hempstead: Harvester Wheatsheaf.
Le Fevre, M., Matheny, J., and Kolt, G. S. (2003) Eustress, distress, and interpretation in occupational stress, *Journal of Managerial Psychology*, 18(7): 726–44.
Likert, R. (1967) *The Human Organization*. New York: McGraw-Hill.
Litterer, J. (1985 [1959]) *The Emergence of Systematic Management as Shown by the Literature of Management From 1870 to 1900*. New York: Garland.
McClelland, D. C. (1961) *The Achieving Society*. Princeton, NJ: Van Nostrand.
McGregor, D. (1960) *The Human Side of Enterprise*. New York: McGraw-Hill.
March, J. G. and Simon H. A. (1958) *Organizations*. New York: John Wiley.
Midgeley, M. (1985) *Evolution as a Religion*. New York: Methuen.
Miller, D. (ed.) (1985) *Popper Selections*. Princeton, NJ: Princeton University Press.
Mintzberg, H. (1968) The manager at work – Determining his [*sic.*] activities, roles and programs by structured observation, doctoral dissertation, Massachusetts Institute of Technology, Cambridge, MA.
Mintzberg, H. (1971) Managerial work: Analysis from observation, *Management Science*, 18(1): B97–B110.
Moore, K. J. and Lewis, D. C. (1998) Keiretsu capitalism and multinational investment in ancient Phoenicia, Academy of Management Annual Meeting, San Diego.
Prude, J. (1983) *The Coming of Industrial Order: Town and Factory Life in Rural Massachusetts 1810–1860*. Cambridge: Cambridge University Press.

Quine, W. V. O. (1953) *From a Logical Point of View*. Cambridge, MA: Harvard University Press.
Rigney, A. (2007) Being an improper historian, in K. Jenkins, S. Morgan, and A. Munslow (eds), *Manifestos for History* (pp. 149–59). New York: Routledge.
Rindova, V. (1994) Theories X, Y and Z BC: Concepts of management in ancient China, Academy of Management Annual Meeting, Dallas.
Robbins, S. P. (1990) *Organization Theory: Structure, Design and Applications* (3rd edn). Englewood Cliffs, NJ: Prentice-Hall.
Roethlisberger, F. J. and Dickson W. F. (1939) *Managment and the Worker*. Cambridge, MA: Harvard University Press.
Rosenstone, R. A. (2007) Space for the bird to fly, in K. Jenkins, S. Morgan, and A. Munslow (eds), *Manifestos for History* (pp. 11–18). New York: Routledge.
Rowlinson, M., Stager Jacques, R., and Booth, C. (2009) Critical management studies and organizational history, in H. Willmott, M. Alvesson, and T. Bridgman (eds), *The Oxford Handbook of Critical Management Studies* (pp. 286–303). Oxford: Oxford Press.
Simon, H. A. (1945) *Administrative Behavior*. New York: Free Press.
Skinner, B. F. (1971) *Beyond Freedom and Dignity*. New York: Bantam.
Sloan, A. E. (1963) *My Years with General Motors*. New York: Doubleday.
Stager Jacques, R. (2004) Laying new foundations: Manufacturing management knowledge in a post-industrial knowledge economy, in P. Jeffcutt (ed.), *The Foundations of Management Knowledge* (pp. 254–77). London: Routledge.
Stager Jacques, R. (2006) History, historiography and organization studies: The challenge and the potential, *Management & Organizational History*, 1(1): 31–49.
Tarbell, I. M. (1902) Ida M. Tarbell on the methods of the Standard Oil Company, in R. Hofstadter (ed.), *The Progressive Movement: 1900–1915* (pp. 20–27). New York: Simon & Schuster.
Taylor, F. W. (1911) *The Principles of Scientific Management*. New York: W. W. Norton.
Thompson, J. D. (1967) *Organizations in Action*. New York: McGraw-Hill.
Unger, R. M. (1986) *False Necessity: Anti-necessitarian Social Theory in the Service of Radical Democracy*. New York: Press Syndicate of the University of Cambridge.
Üsdiken, B. and Kieser, A. (2004) Introduction: History in organization studies, *Business History*, 46(3): 321–30.
White, H. (1973) *Metahistory: The Historical Imagination in Nineteenth-Century Europe*. Baltimore: Johns Hopkins University Press.
White, H. (1985) *The Tropics Discourse: Essays in Cultural Criticism*. Baltimore: Johns Hopkins University Press.
Wiebe, R. H. (1967) *The Search for Order 1877–1920*. New York: Hill & Wang.
Wren, D. A. (1979) *The Evolution of Management Thought* (5th edn). New York: John Wiley.
Wren, D. A. (2004) *The History of Management Thought* (5th edn). New York: John Wiley.
Wren, D. A. and Bedeian A. G. (2008) *The Evolution of Management Thought* (6th edn). New York: John Wiley.
Zald, M. (1993) Organization Studies as a scientific and humanistic enterprise: Towards a reconceptualization of the foundations of the field, *Organization Science*, 4: 513–28.

9

History in management textbooks

Adding, transforming, or more?

Terrance G. Weatherbee

Introduction

In this chapter I foreground how the absence of a robust engagement with history in the literature on management education has contributed in part to the abstraction of the knowledge that we teach to our students in business schools. The manner in which we present management knowledge once history and historical context is written-out of the content means that our textbooks are more likely to serve as an intellectual entry point and values-based framework for managerialism than for management. In response to this condition I suggest that the solution is neither simply adding history back in, as some have recommended (Wren, 2005), nor just the re-historicizing of knowledge as others have encouraged (Cummings & Bridgman, 2011; Stager Jacques, 2006). Instead, I argue that we must also give scholars and students the conceptual tools to allow them to develop an historical consciousness. Awareness of how 'management' knowledge comes to be created and presented in historical terms will enable us to critically assess the knowledge and theory we deliver and which students are exposed to; whether it is located in the texts used in our classrooms or the popular business press.

I lay out my argument in the following manner. First, I describe some of the past conditions which have contributed to the current ahistorical nature of management and organizational studies (MOS) research and relatedly to management education. Second, I situate the scholarship found at the intersection of history and management education in light of the call for an historic turn. In doing this I wish to highlight the different approaches that have been used to argue for more history in management education and to position these arguments against the management textbook as a pedagogic tool. In the final section, I draw upon the most recent work being undertaken in disciplinary history to demonstrate why instilling an historical awareness in ourselves and our students can serve as an important tool for thinking critically about management and for separating management knowledge from managerialist ideology.

MOS and the loss of history

History and historical consideration of past management and business practices was once intended to be the gateway for the development of a theory of business. At the newly created business school at Harvard it was believed that the systematic study of the past experiences of business would allow academics and practitioners to move away from the traditions of 'rule of thumb' (Donham, 1922a, 1922b) and vocationalism towards a proper science of business (Brown, 1938). However, while this project did bear some academic fruit, e.g. the Harvard Case System, the development of a science of business ultimately based upon history would fail as history as a constitutive element was to be overwritten and then edited out by the arrival of a more scientific approach to the study of business itself (Boothman, 2001; Weatherbee, 2012).

The subsuming of this first historical orientation would result from the interplay of three discourses taking place in the broader social context within which we would see the emergence and development of the professionalized and disciplinary form of MOS in the decade after the Second World War (Augier, March & Sullivan, 2005). These discourses included: the rise of the natural sciences, the growth and legitimization of the Business School/MOS within the university, and finally, the social changes to the normative roles expected of science, technology, and management/management education. All three of these discourses would come to constitute and be constituted by the growth and socio-economic changes taking place in the post-war West.

The notion of 'Big Science' arose out of the relationship that had developed between industry and government during the Second World War. This first cooperative impulse was accelerated by the emergence of the Cold War. This period thus saw the intertwining of foreign policy, the economy, and academia on a scale previously unknown in modern times. This relationship would be intensely sustained for several decades as the knowledge-producing capacities in the West, government, industry, and the university, were harnessed for national security purposes (Abella, 2009). This relationship created a new demand-driven approach for research and knowledge production. It shifted national-level resource focus to what was seen as a less risky, more economical, and instrumentally oriented investment model for knowledge production and technological advancement. This new formulation of scientific practice would become the norm within the natural sciences and would eventually spill over into the social sciences as well (Galison & Hevly, 1992; Kinsella, 1999).

While the social sciences had already been moving towards a more functional and quantitative orientation during the first part of the twentieth century (Lasswell, 1951), this shift was accelerated as the social sciences found themselves competing for research funding with the natural sciences in the Cold War context. To compete for attention from government and funding agencies, researchers in the social sciences would increasingly adopt or emulate the methodological practices of experimentation and quantification used in the sciences. These methods would thus grow to become the dominate norm throughout the academy in general (Galison & Hevly, 1992; Kinsella, 1999) and in the social-policy-organization strand of sociology in particular (Wagner, 2001).

As the policy or administrative science branch of sociology was the intellectual conduit through which the study of business would seek to create its disciplinary boundaries (see for example Parsons, 1956a, 1956b) the nascent MOS would follow the methodological pathways carved out by the social sciences. This movement gained significant momentum when business schools reacted to the Ford and Carnegie studies (Carter, 1998; Gordon & Howell, 1959; Pierson, 1959). In order to legitimate their place within the university, business schools rapidly 'scientized' themselves in response to the observations and recommendation contained in these reports (McKenna, Cotton & Van Auken, 1997; Nelson, 1961). The escape hatch used by business schools to avoid accusations of continued vocational or trade-schoolism was to vigorously embrace the latest scientific norms and practices (Khurana, 2007).

Therefore, it was in the very emergence and growth of MOS as a separate field of study that management researchers embraced a positivistic and functionalist approach to theory development and thought (Burrell & Morgan, 1979; Weatherbee, 2012). At a time when the Cold War meant that research, policy, and business were expected to work to protect the free nations of the West, the Cold War would also have significant implications for the professionalization of MOS as an academic field, both in terms of how the management academy would structure itself and how management would become perceived in society at large (Genoe McLaren & Mills, 2008; Grant & Mills, 2006).

The academization and professionalization of MOS was reinforced and supported by a third and powerful discourse arising in the Second World War and accelerated by the Cold War afterwards. This was the growing sense, especially in the West, that the benefits of science and technology would be able to provide the technical and economic solutions necessary to address the problems of society (Hodgson, 2000). This belief, coalesced as a cultural orientation located primarily in the United States, would work to promote a world-scale socio-economic system founded on the concept of progress. Politically specific to the Democratic West, economically enabled by the potentials believed to be inherent in technological and scientific progress, this was to be a system where scientific progress would lead to an imagined future where technology and science had resolved all economic and political challenges. A system economically organized by a growing and professionalized class of managers to be harnessed and serve as the free world's bulwark against the communist threat (Abella, 2009). One consequence amongst many was that the social orientation of the West was now set firmly towards the future (Iggers, 1982); an orientation which rendered cultural and social concerns with history and the past increasingly unimportant.

However, the Janus-faced nature of each discourse was such that while individually providing fertile ground for the explosive growth of business schools and management education, each would also contribute to the exclusion of substantive historical work from MOS research. These would interact to dehistoricize the academy in general (Koselleck, 2002) and MOS specifically (Clark & Rowlinson, 2004).[1] History and historiographic considerations eventually became either ignored, marginalized, or quantized in such a way that historical work in MOS research would be largely restricted to the academic niches of Business Strategy and Business History (Khurana, 2007; Weatherbee, 2012). With the balance of MOS's disciplinary practices having solidified around scientific theoretical and methodological norms and with history and historiographical concerns confined to these two sub-specialties, the marginalization of history from management education would follow a similar devolutionary path.

Management education and history

A century after the formal tenets of history and the study of business first encountered one another at Harvard, we have seen a renewal of interest prompted by a recent call for reengagement between the two disciplines; what has been coined, by those interested, as an historic turn in MOS (Clark & Rowlinson, 2004; Rowlinson this volume). While there is progress being made in the intellectual space(s) where history overlaps with MOS (Weatherbee *et al.*, 2012) much remains still unexamined and underexplored (Stager Jacques, 2006). This is particularly true when observing the limited body of work located at the crossroads where history and management pedagogy intersect.[2]

While the topic of how and what should be taught to students of management in business schools is one which has spawned lively debates for the last half century (see Bennis & O'Toole, 2005; Cheit, 1985; Donaldson, 2002; Gordon & Howell, 1959; Mintzberg, 2004; Porter & McKibbin, 1988) little of this attention has taken an interest in or focused on history as a component part of management education. The arguments made for the inclusion of history in management education, while persistent, have occupied the attention of only a very small set of enthusiastic scholars (see the extensive and detailed arguments in Van Fleet & Wren, 2005; Wren, 1987; Wren & Van Fleet, 1983).

Even as the research and scholarly dialogue on history and management education still remains scanty,[3] what there is may be broadly separated into two different camps. While each camp views history as an important element of management education, indeed they are mutually sympathetic in this respect, they do differ as to what they see as the way to resolve the ahistorical condition. Distinctions between the two may be made along both temporal and intellectual contours. Temporally their origins lay on either side of the historic turn in MOS; intellectually they each take a different stance with regard to their theoretical positioning on the relationship between the past world and the historical representations we make of it. More importantly for my intent herein is one final difference. A difference which pivots on the purposes for which history should be used within management in relation to its project in the world, including both its scholarly and pedagogical deployments. For the purposes of this discussion I have loosely categorized each as being either additive or transformative in their orientation towards the use of history and its relationship with the management project and education.

The adding and/or transforming of history in management education

The additive approach pre-dates the call for an historic turn (for representative examples see Van Fleet & Wren, 2005; Wren, 1987; Wren & Van Fleet, 1983) and is the more established of the two. This approach was developed in concert with the academization of MOS in the business school and hence its intellectual traditions are firmly founded within the orthodoxies of both MOS and historical scholarship. Though it has been an almost marginalized sub-specialty within MOS, for over four decades now this small group has ardently presented a strong set of arguments identifying history as an essential and synergistic component of MOS education. To this end there have been regularly calls and prescriptions for the inclusion of history to be added at the undergraduate and graduate levels (Bedeian, 1976, 1998; Wren, 1987). Their overall intent has been to contribute to the construction of the history of the development of management thought and theory as a tool through which to inform business students of their theoretical and practical heritage, and to demonstrate the progressive and beneficial contributions made by scholars and notable practitioners of management and business (Wren & Bedeian, 2010).

However, despite the longevity of effort and the persistence of argument for the promotion of an historical agenda within MOS education, the survey studies that have been undertaken reveal that there has been a continuous and steady decline of the presence of management history taught within business programs (Madansky, 2008; Van Fleet & Wren, 2005; Wren & Van Fleet, 1983). So, the present ahistorical condition of management education, which they have meaningfully argued against and so eloquently lamented, continues in an unabated state (Stager Jacques, 2006).

While I have not revisited their detailed arguments in any granularity here, I am in agreement with their basic contention concerning the import of history for students of management. I too believe that there are many and significant benefits to having students understand the history and development of management thought, theory, and practice. I do, however, differ in my theoretical approach towards history and how such history should be deployed and employed within management studies and education. These preferences position the siting of my own 'tent' firmly in the bounds of the transformative camp.

Similar to scholars in the additive camp, proponents of the transformative approach are also a relatively small and loosely related group who share a common concern and interest in history, MOS, and management education in combination – to one extent or another. Unlike the former group, however, this project is a very recent and still emerging stream of inquiry (see for example Cummings & Bridgman, 2011; Durepos, Weatherbee & Mills, 2011; Foster, Helms Mills & Mills, 2014; Mills, Weatherbee & Durepos, 2013). While there is a significantly greater degree of heterogeneity in the methods employed here when compared to the additive approach, transformative orientations are all similarly informed by theory of history and most of the scholarship in this camp intellectually cleaves to tenets of the historic turn in either its weaker or stronger forms. Research here has generally been either contemporaneous with recent developments in the field of history; that is, a movement away from a purely Rankean or realist notion (see Green & Troup, 1999 for a review of the various 'schools' of history) of history-work – the stronger form – or has arisen in reaction to the call for the more conventional address of history in MOS – the weaker form. While there are variations in this approach, some is more critical, some more historio-sociological, and some more socio-historical, most are more nuanced in their treatment of the contested nature of the historical representations of management thought and practice.

Thus, the intellectual positioning of the transformative approaches may be seen as trending away from the center where the stronger, more orthodox, and realist formula of history is used to shore the developmental premise of mainstream perspectives of MOS history. In this sense this approach sees a more valuable intersection of history and MOS at the periphery where stronger critique and critical approaches to historical representations of MOS become possible. In this respect the transformative camp shares more common ground with proponents of critical management studies (Alvesson & Wilmot, 1992), critical management education (Grey, 2004), and critical pedagogy (Boje & Al-Arkoubi, 2009) than to the additive approaches.

Though these two approaches diverge in terms of the epistemological and ontological assumptions they each make concerning the nature of the relationship of history to the past world (for a more detailed explanation on the differences between modern realism, postmodern anti-realism, and amodernist approaches to history see Durepos, this volume), they both are endorsing the rehistoricization of MOS. Primarily, by bringing more historical consideration into MOS. As this chapter centers on history at the site of management education, the challenges associated with infusing more history into research published in journals will be set aside in favor of a discussion of the management textbook.

The management textbook, history and ideology

While the textbook has been a key element in the American educational system for over a century it was not until after the Second World War where it would assume the rather hegemonic centrality it now occupies in college and university classrooms (Apple, 1991), a circumstance most especially true for management education in business schools (Cameron *et al.*, 2003a; Stambaugh & Trank, 2010). It was at this time that textbook production became a large-scale industry and a significant actor in post-secondary education as a market formed in response to the sudden and overwhelming growth of enrollment in universities (Whitten, 1975) and business schools (Cheit, 1985). The first two decades after the war was a halcyon period for textbook production; millions of students entered university, business schools curricula blossomed, faculty clamored for teaching materials, and the prospect for profits lured publishers. Such was the rush into the textbook market that the textbook industry, which had but one dominant publisher before the war, had over 50 afterwards (Lichtenberg, 1992).

However, while this growth served to provide the textbooks needed to educate students, it also meant competition for market share became greater and fierce. As the textbook market developed and challenges between publishers heightened, textbook publishers would seek new ways to garner market share and profits. In their search for an advantage they turned to a new mode of textbook production and in the third decade they would begin to use market rather than pedagogic logic to bring new textbooks to students. During the 1970s the 'managed textbook' process would be introduced. This innovation was so successful that it would be very quickly adopted by a majority of the dominant textbook publishers (Geersten, 1977). The managed textbook was a distinctly different approach than the previous author-centric or author-assisted methods. This new process was market-driven rather than subject-driven. It was now a profit-based construct where market forces would determine the content and form of the text and the market would come to supplant the author as the expert. Textbooks became the child of publishers rather than authors.

Using a combination of surveys of competing texts and student focus groups, publishers would seek ever more marketable forms for the presentation of content. Once the publishers had determined the market demand for the features, content, and format of the textbook they would then seek a suitable author or authors to complete the project. Authors would then be contracted to finalize the content, but with publishers retaining oversight and editorial control to ensure that the textbook continued to meet the publisher's evaluation of market demand. This form of production would result in a publishing environment where the content across texts, even between significant competitor publishing houses, had become so similar that their textbooks were often considered clones of one another (Geersten, 1977).

During this same period, in the United States and Canada, university and college textbooks were becoming the authoritative source of disciplinary knowledge (Weatherbee, Dye & Mills, 2008) in undergraduate education where the content of the textbook had by now become the authoritative 'final word' (Graham, 1988). Students in introductory courses were increasingly expected to learn and digest the contents of the textbook and student learning was to be done in a rote fashion as knowledge of the content became the pragmatic gateway to a career after university (Rynes & Trank, 1999). For students the educational experience had now become a serialized pattern. A cycle of: study the textbook – be evaluated on its content – achieve a passing grade – accrue a course credit – repeat as necessary. Finally, accumulate sufficient credits to fulfill the requirements for a certificate, diploma, or degree and then graduate and get a job (Westhues, 1991).

As market logics came to dominate both textbook production and student motivation alike, each served as mimetic pressure for the convergence of the form and content of introductory or popularly adopted textbooks (Cameron *et al.*,2003b). Cumulatively disciplinary history and historical contextualization of fact and theory development was reduced or removed. Textbooks evolved to become compendiums comprised of similar statements of abstracted fact and theory (Baker, 1988; Hewitt, 1988; Stager Jacques, 2006) presented in a 'rhetoric of conclusions' (Schwab, 1962).

Now while history in management texts has yet to completely disappear, what remains has been observed to be truncated in form, prone to error (Wren, 1987), or has been so 'bowdlerized' it is of questionable utility (Stager Jacques, 2006). Interested observers from both camps recognize this deficit as the 'chapter two' problem (see Gibson *et al.*, 2005; Jacques & Durepos, this volume; Stager Jacques, 2006). However, though each camp laments the loss of history and believes that management education must see history reintroduced, I suggest that there are deeper implications beyond the loss of history in its *explicit* form. While it is quite clear that management textbooks have lost history *presented* as history, we also need to attend to the implications of the *implicit* form as represented by the textbook itself.

Textbooks are conventionally presented as academic works comprised of the objective knowledge of a discipline or subject area which has been *accumulated* on a scientific basis. For MOS the textbook presents to a reader our current understanding of what we know of management as a phenomenon in the world. However, as little if any content in university textbooks explains how the knowledge it contains was produced (Schuster, 2013) and with explicit historical considerations removed, textbooks serve as *implicit* histories. An implicit history is a format for knowledge which conceals its historical nature by absenting the choices previously taken within a discipline, past choices about *what* knowledge is to be presented and *which* facts or theories are to be included. Evidence of this may be observed in how knowledge germane to managing has been written in or written out for various socio-political reasons beyond scientific ones (Cooke, 1999, 2003). Thus, as implicit histories management textbooks also represent a distorted form of knowledge. I do not mean distorted in the sense that they may be challenged on the veracity of their rendering of persons and events of a past world nor for containing erroneous, inaccurate, or outdated theory (though some will argue they are that as well). Instead, I use distorted to mean that their implicit form is itself ideological.[4] The textbook is a taken-for-granted set of fact and theory where the beliefs, values, and politics underpinning the text (Goatly, 2007), those of agents and the agential systems responsible for constructing the text, remain hidden behind the objective nature of its form.

While it has been apparent for some time now that business schools are sites of value inculcation (Alvesson, 1984; Seider, 1974) and that textbooks act as carriers of various ideologies (C. W. Mills, 1943), ideology as a function of the implicitness of history has not been well addressed in the pedagogical literature of management studies. Perhaps because the process of textbook production is not well understood by those who teach or learn from them (Apple, 1989)? Yet management texts have not drawn a significant amount of scholarly concern – even when recognized as products of economic markets and being subjected to the political influence of many actors and active agents (see the discussion on this very issue between Cameron *et al.*, 2003a, 2003b; Gilbert, 2003; Mir, 2003)!

So if we are aware that social and cultural determinants contribute to the form and content of a textbook as much as the activities of scientific research (Stambaugh & Trank, 2010) and textbooks promote "*visions* of legitimate knowledge" (Apple, 1989: 282, emphasis added) which disseminate from textbooks into practice (Miner, 1984, 2003; Weatherbee, Dye, and Mills, 2008), then how should this be addressed in relation to the formulation of history in textbooks. Calling for more history to be added addresses the issue only partly. I suggest that this requires a two-part movement. In the first instance we can choose to study textbooks as implicit historical objects over time. In the second we need to inform ourselves as scholars as to how the production of disciplinary history is used and interpreted inside MOS and management pedagogy. Though there is little effort taken in MOS on the latter, fortunately there has been some headway in the former.

The study of textbooks and their formulations in relation to the historical context of their production has seen some scholarly interest in other related disciplines or specialties, for example sociology (Hewitt, 1988), economics (Watts, 1987), and accounting (Ferguson *et al.*, 2009), and there is a similar and slowly growing literature in MOS. Researchers are attempting to illustrate how the content of management knowledge in textbooks is socio-historically determined and subject to change over time and the implications this has for understanding our own disciplinary formation and its canon. These have included studies of the portrayal of workers across the twentieth century (Foster & Mills, in press) and the changing nature of historical representation and dissemination of notable contributors to MOS thought and theory such as Peter Drucker (Genoe McLaren & Mills, 2008), Max Weber (Cummings & Bridgman, 2011), or of the portrayal of the contributions by other historical management figures such as F.W. Taylor (Payne, Youngcourt & Watrous, 2006), and Abraham Maslow (Dye, Mills & Weatherbee, 2005).

Others work to surface how the contemporary socio-political context is often reflected in the textbook yet remains historically unacknowledged – even given the perfect hindsight of time (Foster, Helms Mills, and Mills, 2014). Still others attempt to surface the processes wherein textbook knowledge is first constructed, reinterpreted, and finally transformed in the management practices outside of business schools has been another focus (Weatherbee, Dye, and Mills, 2008). However, there remains much more work to be done to fully explore the dynamics between MOS research, and the production and use of forms of history in and the management text (Stambaugh & Trank, 2010).

In the second case, how scholars and students do history-work, come to produce, learn, interpret, and deploy historical understanding, has yet to become a significant question in either MOS or its pedagogy. This should not be treated as a surprising circumstance for several reasons. As we have seen, historical consideration has been written out of MOS. Scholars of MOS are rarely trained historians so we remain dominated by an understanding of history derived from our common-sense notions of the relationship between the past world and representations of it (Weatherbee *et al.*, 2012). This common-sense notion could be stated thusly: "a history is the outcome produced in the activities which sustain our effort to determine what happened in the past through the uncovering/discovering the facts of the past world and rendering them in as accurate a fashion as possible to discover the truth of the past." This is a culturally specific and modernist view of history derived from and reproduced in the tradition of the Western European Enlightenment (Iggers, 1997, 2002; Munslow, 2000). So for those whose intellectual worldview does not consider alternative ways of knowing the world (e.g. postmodern, post-structural, postcolonial, etc.) this is history. I would offer that work in response to the call for an historic turn which, while making progress on its own terms, has yet to have any overall effect on the problematic of the past–history relationship in MOS. Finally, and relatedly, as theory of history lies outside our disciplinary domain the developments within this discipline, especially outside of North America, have not been adequately plumbed. For example, the emerging area of research undertaken in the pedagogy of history to understand forms of history, how they are created, and how they are learned and used (Rusen, 2004, 2005b; Sexias, 2006). In the section which follows I will briefly draw upon these developments to illustrate the work exploring these various modes of historical awareness.

Becoming historically conscious

The possession of historical knowledge is a necessary but insufficient condition for historical understanding (Rusen, 2005a). Knowledge of the past is, in and of itself, simply a collection of 'facts,' whether these facts are found in a textbook or an archive. Having a *sense* of the past, what Lukács defines as a 'remembered past' (1968), requires that historical information be given purposive meaning (Carr, 1961). Purposive meaning is only possible when facts are given a temporal orientation (Rusen, 2007c). The act of temporal orientation is that which positions facts in time and space and establishes some form of relationship between the past, the present, and the future. A history then, as distinguished from the narrative of individual memory, is produced when meanings are given to facts. Meanings as mediated via the interpretation of facts presented by various agents and for the purposes to which they are put (Minear, 1940).

While the act of making historical sense may be considered a universal phenomenon, *how* the knowledge of the past is made sense of, how and why it is transformed into history, is not! The making of history, like the making of a textbook, is a cultural production and learned practice (Rusen, 2007b). Variations in how collectivities, such as a discipline, process historical knowledge, indeed even how they determine what *is* historical knowledge, depends upon a set of underlying meta-historical assumptions (Megill, 1994; White, 1973). It is these assumptions that determine how a discipline collects, categorizes, organizes, expresses, and uses knowledge of the past to achieve historical understanding in the present. It is a set of organizing concepts, the assumptions and practices which "educate us on how to know, deal and think about the past" (Liakos, 2010). Conceptualized as Historical Consciousness (Lukács, 1968; Rusen, 1984, 2004) it is the means by which an individual understands, gives meaning to, and relates themselves to the past, present, and future (Rusen, 2007a). Normatively, in the Western tradition, this is achieved by emplotting facts with a narrative structure (White, 1987).

Based upon the study of the development of historical consciousness and the variations in temporal orientation in the construction of history, that is, how cultural conceptions of history and historiography have changed over time, there are at least four modes of thinking in the historical consciousness of the West. These may be considered theoretically derived 'ideal types' and each comprises the configurations of meta-historical assumptions and the historical orientations that may be taken towards the past–present–future relationship and the past–history problematic. These configurations manifest as different modes of historical thinking and include the Traditional, Exemplary, Critical, and Genetic types (these descriptions have been synthesized from Megill, 1994; Rusen, 1984, 2007a, 2007b, 2007c, 2007d; Sexias, 2006). While, in the theoretical fashion of ideal types, there are analytically significant differences between these modes, for example they tend to negate each other, in practice it is possible for them to simultaneously coexist in a culture or collectivity. Also, as there are stronger and weaker forms of historical thinking within each individual mode, it is possible for modes to overlap at the borders.

Traditional: In the Traditional Mode, the collective orientation to past–present–future relations is an orientation which is focused upon continuity and conservation of the past in the present. In comparison to other modes, this orientation is essentially conservative and fundamentalist. The significance of history is to be found in the maintenance of traditions and practices associated with the origins of the collective or other significant events of the collective's past. The primary purpose of history is the preservation and maintenance of traditions over time. The past has a direct relevance for those living in the present as the history establishes and preserves collective identity. The production of history is the grounds for its belief and the collective's history is highly resistant to change as it is simply taken-for-granted as learned. Public heritage and commemorative understandings (Lowenthal, 2006) are examples of this mode of thinking and orientation. In MOS, we can see this manifest in Heathrow Organizational Theory (Burrell, 1997; Clark & Rowlinson, 2004) and in the forms of history presented in many of our textbooks (Stager Jacques, 2006; Weatherbee, Dye, and Mills, 2008).

Exemplary: In the Exemplary Mode, the orientation of the past–present–future is one of progression and progress. This is a more modernist and common-sense form and understanding of history. The past informs the present through an understanding of general rules or laws deduced from the events of the past. It reflects the modern notions of progressive change and social progress made over time. Historical knowledge of the past is considered to be cumulative in nature and so the aggregation and increase in knowledge of the past represents progress. In this regard, the past is considered as a prelude to the present and the present in turn establishes the conditions to determine the future. While events of the past are recognized as having a historicity, the notions of change drawn from the study of past events are themselves considered relatively timeless. This mode of thinking has been and continues to be the dominant mode within Western historical consciousness and it has become a globally hegemonic pattern of understanding and representing the past (Burke, 2002). This approach gives rise to atheoretical or ahistorical forms leading to critiques on the basis of universalism, presentisim, or scientism as found in the MOS' canonical history (Weatherbee & Durepos, 2010).

Critical: In the Critical Mode, and here the term critical while similar is not the same employment as, for example, the use of critical in Critical Management Studies, the concepts of historical continuity and the unity of the past become problematized. This is done through the challenge and questioning of the epistemics of meta-theoretical assumptions and the practices associated with the production and understanding of the past–history relationship. This mode calls into question the validity of extant beliefs in historical precedents by historicizing them and is generally reflexive in epistemic and ontological meta-theoretic terms. Much of the history-work in this mode is premised on the relativism of standpoints and the assumptions of the mediation of reality through narrative and text. In MOS, this may be seen to be present in histories which follow the style of Foucauldian archaeo-geneological studies (Rowlinson & Carter, 2002) or those which privilege narrative and story elements in organizations (Boje, 1991).

Genetic: In the Genetic Mode of thinking, the past–present–future relationship is itself problematized and is understood to be a culturally and temporalized perspective. It is a reflexive mode which holds the most potential for epistemic, ontological, and semantic reflexivity in both meta-theoretic and meta-historical terms. It is also the least developed and is an emergent mode. It is a form of meta-reflection which recognizes that there are multiple orientations and multiple ways to understand the past and to construct history and that understanding of the past and the practices of history production are outcomes of patterns of historical thinking. In MOS, a recent example of this form of orientation to the past–history relationship and the practice of history-work would be found in the work on ANTi-History, which itself is very recent (Durepos & Mills, 2012; Durepos, Mills & Weatherbee, 2012).

As "historical conventions function … as basic tools of thought" (Ermarth, 2007: 51) the most immediate benefits of the conceptualization of historical thinking may be found in the new and different questions that it invokes in how history is produced and used (Megill, 1994). These questions are equally applicable for the investigation and consideration of the challenges posed to the extant or intended use of history in MOS and management pedagogy. Indeed, these are questions which need to be answered by proponents of either the additive or transformative camps.

Adding, transforming, or more?

I see historical modes of thinking as ways of presenting "the human effort to understand the present and expect the future by understanding and interpreting the past" (Rusen, 2007b: 4). Therefore, analytically, it is insufficient to look at only the content and the form of a history (White, 1987), regardless of the representational form a 'history' takes, such as in a textbook. To understand the production and use of history in MOS and management pedagogy we need to look closely at the mode(s) of thinking which produce(s) and use(s) it. We need to surface and interrogate the historical assumptions that are used in the production and consumption in order to understand it as knowledge, as history, and as an outcome of historical thinking. This is important as historical understanding changes attitudes and can move both individuals and collectives to take action and change how we do things in the world (Carpenter, 1995).

Since textbooks are "highly stable and institutionalized" forms of knowledge (Stambaugh & Trank, 2010: 663) and the ideologies they contain are continuously 'policed' by the interests of the agents involved in their production, distribution and adoption (Apple, 2000, 2004), adding more of the same form of history potentially only reinforces that ideology by hiding it further behind the rhetoric of scientific conclusions of management. This leads me to conclude that simply adding more history into MOS or management pedagogy will not yield the benefits it is supposed to herald. Adding is an insufficient project in this respect. There is too much evidence in the world which runs contrary to the perceived benefits of managerialism and free-market logics for me to accept otherwise (for one example, see Boje and Saylors, this volume, there are of course numerous others). In order to change how students see management and avoid this we must change how we as scholars see management. This will necessitate some historical awareness on our part.

This is perhaps the greatest potential of historical thinking for MOS. It lies in recognizing that historical thinking, how we organize and understand the past as a discipline, are only situated and historical effects (Foucault, 1979). Therefore, we can also change them in the present or the future. This is an easier project if we are aware that we have changed them in the past. Thus, transforming how we see history is the escape route from taken-for-granted thinking. I see re-historicizing management knowledge as holding the potential for a return to understanding managing as a necessary phenomenon and yet a contested concept. However, to avoid the danger of replacing one ideology with another, we must seek to educate students in reflexive terms (Grey, 2004), first through understanding how we have organized and managed in the past and second through understanding how we have created the historical knowledge of that past understanding.

The activity of organizing is a form of 'wicked problem' (Rittel & Webber, 1973) defined by its very nature: chaotic, complex, and human. Solving wicked problems requires processes of managing – that is "getting things done through people in organizations" (Locke & Spender, 2011: 174). As our perceptions of the past are always at work within organizations and the persons within them (Warren & Tweedale, 2002) understanding how the past is rendered and presented should be a critical element of management education. Exposing students to the historical dimensions of how management knowledge is produced and presented holds the potential to re-contextualize and re-humanize the management project and counter-balance the ideological effects of managerialism when masked as management.

Notes

1 Ultimately, MOS would so fervently embrace a scientific and quantitative orientation that some two decades later it would be assessed as having become overly scientific and analytically oriented as to make the research being conducted within so abstract as to be irrelevant to practitioners (Porter & McKibbin, 1988). The debate which coalesced around the issues of academic rigor versus practical relevance spawned a critique of MOS and its relationship with the business school model which remains ongoing and unresolved (Pfeffer & Fong, 2002; Trank & Rynes, 2003; Tushman *et al.*, 2007).

2 A review of the major educational and history journals in MOS reveals a significant lack of attention to the conjunctions of history and management education. The study of management education rarely includes history and the study of history rarely speaks to management education. In the two primary journals whose intellectual remit is management education – *Academy of Management Education and Learning* and the *Journal of Management Education* – only nine articles which dealt explicitly with the subject of history could be located. Conversely, in the two MOS journals whose specific focus is history – *Management and Organizational History* and the *Journal of Management History* – only five articles which explicitly treated with history in management education could be located.

3 I have chosen to use the same term used by Daniel Wren to describe his assessment of the degree and presence of history in management education over four decades ago in signal of what little has changed (Wren, 1972).

4 I am not focused on the ideological effects of scientism, universalism, or presentism qua history which has been discussed elsewhere (see for example Booth & Rowlinson, 2006; Cooke, 2006; Cooke, Mills & Kelley, 2005). Following Prasad & Cavanaugh (1997) I use the critical rather than the descriptive form of ideology where it is "distorted knowledge" which passes itself off as objective and scientific and "fails to unveil social contradictions" in its creation rather than simply implying a shared set of beliefs and values (Prasad & Cavanaugh, 1997: 313)

References

Abella, A. (2009) *Soldiers of Reason: The RAND Corporation and the Rise of the American Empire*. New York: Mariner Books/Houghton Mifflin Harcourt.

Alvesson, M. (1984) Questioning rationality and ideology: On critical organization theory, *International Studies of Management & Organization*, 14(1): 61–79.

Alvesson, M. and Wilmot, H. (eds) (1992) *Critical Management Studies*. London: Sage.

Apple, M. W. (1989) Textbook publishing: The political and economic infuences, *Theory into Practice*, 28(4): 282–87.

Apple, M.W. (1991) The culture and the commerce of the textbook, in M.W.Apple and L. K. Christian-Smith (eds), *The Politics of the Textbook* (pp. 22–40). New York: Routledge.

Apple, M.W. (2000) *Official Knowledge: Democratic Education in a Conservative Age*. New York: Routledge.

Apple, M.W. (2004) *Ideology and Curriculum* (3rd edn). New York: Routledge Falmer.

Augier, M., March, J., and Sullivan, B. (2005) Notes on the evolution of a research community: Organization studies in anglophone North America, 1945–2000, *Organization Science*, 16(1): 85–95.

Baker, P.T. (1988) Sociology textbooks: Managing clones or writing works of distinction, *Teaching Sociology*, 16(4): 381–83.

Bedeian, A. (1976) Management history thought, *Academy of Management Review*, 1: 96–7.

Bedeian, A. (1998) Exploring the past, *Journal of Management History*, 4(1): 4–15.

Bennis, W. G. and O'Toole, J. (2005) How business schools lost their way, *Harvard Business Review*, 83(5): 96–104.

Boje, D. (1991) The storytelling organization: A study of story performance in an office supply firm, *Administrative Science Quarterly*, 36(1): 106–26.

Boje, D. and Al-Arkoubi, K. (2009) Critical management education beyond the siege, in S. Armstrong and C. Fukami (eds), *The Sage Handbook of Management Learning, Education and Development* (pp. 104–25). London: Sage.

Booth, C. and Rowlinson, M. (2006) Management and organizational history: Prospects, *Management and Organizational History*, 1(1): 5–30.

Boothman, B. (2001) A theme worthy of epic treatment: N. S. B. Gras and the emergence of American business history, *Journal of Macromarketing*, 21(1): 61–73.

Brown, T. (1938) Science, statistics, and business, *Harvard Business Review*, 16(3): 281–89.

Burke, P. (2002) Western historical thinking in a global perspective: 10 theses, in J. Rusen (ed.), *Western Historical Thinking: An Intercultural Debate* (pp. 15–32). New York: Berghahn Books.

Burrell, G. (1997) *Pandemonium: Towards a Retro-Organization Theory*. Thousand Oaks, CA: Sage.

Burrell, G. and Morgan, G. (1979) *Sociological Paradigms and Organizational Analysis: Elements of the Sociology of Corporate Life*. London: Heinemann.

Cameron, K. S., Ireland, R. D., Lussier, R. N., New, J. R., and Robbins, S. P. (2003a) Management textbooks as propaganda, *Journal of Management Education*, 27(6): 711–29.

Cameron, K. S., Ireland, R. D., Lussier, R. N., New, J. R., and Robbins, S. P. (2003b) Replies to commentaries on 'Management textbooks as propaganda', *Journal of Management Education*, 27(6): 739–43.

Carpenter, R. (1995) *History as Rhetoric: Style, Narrative, and Persuasion*. Columbia, SC: University of South Carolina Press.

Carr, E. H. (1961) *What is History? The George Macaulay Trevelyan Lectures Delivered in The University of Cambridge*. London: Macmillan.

Carter, D. (1998) *MBA: The First Century*. Mississauga, ON: Associated University Presses.

Cheit, E. F. (1985) Business schools and their critics, *California Management Review*, 27(3): 43–62.

Clark, P. and Rowlinson, M. (2004) The treatment of history in organization studies: Towards an 'historic turn'? *Business History*, 46(3): 331–52.

Cooke, B. (1999) Writing the left out of management theory: The historiography of the management of change, *Organization*, 6(1): 81–105.

Cooke, B. (2003) The denial of slavery in management studies, *Journal of Management Studies*, 40(8): 1895–918.

Cooke, B. (2006) The Cold War origin of action research as mangerialist cooptation, *Human Relations*, 59(5): 665–93.

Cooke, B., Mills, A. J., and Kelley, E. (2005) Situating Maslow in Cold War America, *Group and Organization Management*, 30(2): 129–52.

Cummings, S. and Bridgman, T. (2011) The relevant past: Why the history of management should be critical for our future, *Academy of Management Learning & Education*, 10(1): 77–93.

Donaldson, L. (2002) Damned by our own theories: Contradictions between theories and management education, *Academy of Management Learning and Education*, 1(1): 96–106.
Donham, W. (1922a) Business teaching by the case system, *American Economic Review*, 12(1): 53–65.
Donham, W. (1922b) Essential groundwork for a broad executive theory, *Harvard Business Review*, 1(1): 1–10.
Durepos, G. and Mills, A. (2012) *ANTi-History: Theorizing the Past, History, and Historiography in Management and Organizational Studies*. Charlotte, NC: Information Age Publishing.
Durepos, G., Mills, A. J., and Weatherbee, T. G. (2012) Theorizing the past: Realism, relativism, relationalism and the reassembly of Weber, *Management & Organizational History*, 7(3): 267–81.
Durepos, G., Weatherbee, T., and Mills, A. (2011) Reassembling Weber: The past-as-history in management and organization studies, Paper presented at the European Group of Organization Studies, Goethenburg, Sweden.
Dye, K., Mills, A. J., and Weatherbee, T. G. (2005) Maslow: Man interrupted – Reading management theory in context, *Management Decision*, 43(10): 1375–95.
Ermarth, E. (2007) The closed space of choice: A manifesto on the future of history, in K. Jenkins, S. Morgan, and A. Munslow (eds), *Manifestos for History* (pp. 50–66). New York: Routledge.
Ferguson, J., Collison, D., Power, D., and Stevenson, L. (2009) Constructing meaning in the service of power: An analysis of the typical modes of ideology in accounting textbooks, *Critical Perspectives on Accounting*, 20(6): 896–909.
Foster, J. and Mills, A. (in press) Construction work: Evolving discourse of the 'worker' in management textbooks, 1920s to the first decade of the 21st century, *Journal of Workplace Rights*.
Foster, J., Helms Mills, J., and Mills, A. (2014) Shades of red: Cold War influences on Canadian and US business textbooks, *Journal of Management Education*, 38(5): 642–71.
Foucault, M. (1979) *Discipline and Punish: The Birth of the Prison*. New York: Vintage Books.
Galison, P. and Hevly, B. (eds) (1992) *Big Science: The Growth of Large-Scale Research*. Stanford, CA: Stanford University Press.
Geersten, R. (1977) The textbook: An ACIDS test, *Teaching Sociology*, 5(1): 101–20.
Genoe McLaren, P. and Mills, A. (2008) A product of 'his' time? Exploring the construct of the ideal manager in the Cold War era, *Journal of Management History*, 14(4): 386–403.
Gibson, J., Ford, R., Greenwood, R., Griffin, D., Van Fleet, D., and Wren, D. (2005) Authors reflect on Chapter 2: Is management history still important? Symposium. Honolulu, Academy of Management Annual Conference.
Gilbert, D. R. (2003) Propaganda, trusteeship, and artifact: Locating a new place for the management textbook, *Journal of Management Education*, 27(6): 730–33.
Goatly, A. (2007) *Washing the Brain: Metaphor and Hidden Ideology*. Philadelphia, PA: John Benjamins.
Gordon, R. A. and Howell, J. E. (1959) *Higher Education for Business*. New York: Garland Publishing.
Graham, F. C. (1988) Some observations on sociology textbooks: An editorial perspective, *Teaching Sociology*, 16(4): 356–65.
Grant, J. and Mills, A. (2006) The quiet Americans: Formative context, the Academy of Management leadership, and the management textbook, 1936–1960, *Management and Organizational History*, 1(2): 201–24.
Green, A. and Troup, K. (eds) (1999) *The Houses of History: A Critical Reader in Twentieth-Century History and Theory*. New York: New York University Press.
Grey, C. (2004) Reinventing business schools: The contribution of critical management education, *Academy of Management Learning and Education*, 3(2): 178–86.
Hewitt, J. P. (1988) The trouble with textbooks: A view from the profession, *Teaching Sociology*, 16(4): 366–69.
Hodgson, G. (2000) *America in Our Time: From World War II to Nixon – What Happened and Why*. Princeton, NJ: Princeton University Press.
Iggers, G. (1982) The idea of progress in historiography and social thought since the enlightenment, in G. Almond, M. Chodorow, and R. Pearce (eds), *Progress and Its Discontents* (pp. 41–66). London: University of California Press.
Iggers, G. (1997) *Historiography in the Twentieth Century: From Scientific Objectivity to the Postmodern Challenge*. Hanover, NH: Wesleyan University Press.
Iggers, G. (2002) The professionalization of historical studies and the guiding assumptions of modern historical thought, in L. Kramer and S. Maza (eds), *A Companion to Western Historical Thought* (pp. 225–42). Oxford: Blackwell.
Khurana, R. (2007) *From Higher Aims to Hired Hands: The Social Transformation of American Business Schools and the Unfulfilled Promise of Management as a Profession*. Princeton, NJ: Princeton University Press.

Kinsella, W. J. (1999) Discourse, power, and knowledge in the management of 'Big Science', *Management Communication Quarterly*, 13(2): 171–208.

Koselleck, R. (2002) *The Practice of Conceptual History*, trans. T. Presner *et al.* Stanford, CA: Stanford University Press.

Lasswell, H. (1951) The policy orientation, in D. Lerner and H. Lasswell (eds), *The Policy Sciences: Recent Developments in Scope and Method* (pp. 3–15). Palo Alto, CA: Stanford University Press.

Liakos, A. (2010) What is historical critique about? *Historein*, 10: 144–52.

Lichtenberg, J. (1992) The new paradox of the college textbook, *Change*, 24(5): 10–17.

Locke, R. and Spender, J. (2011) *Confronting Managerialism: How the Business Elite and Their Schools Threw Our Lives Out of Balance*. New York: Zed Books.

Lowenthal, D. (2006) *The Heritage Crusade and the Spoils of History*. Cambridge: Cambridge University Press.

Lukács, J. (1968) *Historical Conciousness: Or the Remembered Past*. New York: Harper & Row.

McKenna, J. F., Cotton, C. C., and Van Auken, S. (1997) The new AACSB accreditation standards: A prospect of tiering? *Journal of Organizational Change Management*, 10(6): 491–502.

Madansky, A. (2008) Teaching history in business schools: An outsider's view, *Academy of Management Learning & Education*, 7(4): 553–62.

Megill, A. (1994) Jorn Rusen's theory of historiography between modernism and rhetoric of inquiry, *History and Theory*, 33(1): 39–60.

Mills, A., Weatherbee, T., and Durepos, G. (2013) Reassembling Weber to reveal the-past-as-history in management and organization studies, *Organization*, 21(2): 223–41.

Mills, C. W. (1943) The professional ideology of social pathologists, *American Journal of Sociology*, 49(2): 165–80.

Minear, P. (1940) Historical consciousness vs. historical knowledge, *Journal of Bible and Religion*, 8(2): 72–76.

Miner, J. B. (1984) The validity and usefulness of theories in an emerging organizational science, *Academy of Management Review*, 9(2): 296–306.

Miner, J. B. (2003) The rated importance, scientific validity, and practical usefulness of organizational behavior theories: A quantitative review, *Academy of Management Learning and Education*, 2(3): 250–68.

Mintzberg, H. (2004) Third-generation management, *T&D*, 58(3): 28–39.

Mir, A. (2003) The hegemonic discourse of management texts, *Journal of Management Education*, 27(6): 734–38.

Munslow, A. (2000) *The Routledge Companion to Historical Studies*. London: Routledge.

Nelson, H. G. (1961) Impact and validity of the Ford and Carnegie Reports on business education, *The Accounting Review*, 36(2): 179–85.

Parsons, T. (1956a) Suggestions for a sociological approach to the theory of organizations – I, *Administrative Science Quarterly*, 1(1): 63–85.

Parsons, T. (1956b) Suggestions for a sociological approach to the theory of organizations – II, *Administrative Science Quarterly*, 1(2): 225–39.

Payne, S., Youngcourt, S., and Watrous, K. (2006) Portrayals of F. W. Taylor across textbooks, *Journal of Management History*, 12(4): 385–407.

Pfeffer, J. and Fong, C. (2002) The end of business schools? Less success than meets the eye, *Academy of Management Learning and Education*, 1(1): 78–96.

Pierson, F. C. (1959) *The Education of American Businessmen: A Study of University-College Programs in Business Administration*. London: McGraw-Hill.

Porter, L. and McKibbin, L. (1988) *Management Education and Development: Drift or Thrust into the 21st Century?* New York: McGraw-Hill.

Prasad, A. and Cavanaugh, J. M. (1997) Ideology and demystification: Tom Peters and the mangerial (sub-) text: An experiential exploration of critique and empowerment in the management classroom, *Journal of Management Education*, 21(3): 309–24.

Rittel, H. and Webber, M. (1973) Dilemmas in a general thoery of planning, *Policy Sciences*, 4: 155–69.

Rowlinson, M. and Carter, C. (2002) Foucault and history in organization studies, *Organization*, 9(4): 527–47.

Rusen, J. (1984) Theory of history in the development of West German historical studies: A reconstruction and outlook, *German Studies Review*, 7(1): 11–25.

Rusen, J. (2004) Historical consciousness: Narrative structure, moral function, and ontogenetic development, in P. Sexias (ed.), *Theorizing Historical Consciousness* (pp. 63–85). Toronto: University of Toronto Press.

Rusen, J. (2005a) *History: Narration, Interpretation, Orientation*. Toronto: Berghahn Books.

Rusen, J. (2005b) How to compare cultures? The case of historical thinking, *Koers-Bulletin for Christian Scholarship*, 70(2): 265–89.

Rusen, J. (2007a) How to make sense of the past: Salient issues of metahistory, *Journal of Transdisciplinary Research in South Africa*, 3(1): 169–221.

Rusen, J. (2007b) Introduction, in J. Rusen (ed.), *Time and History: The Variety of Cultures* (pp. 1–4). New York: Berghahn Books.

Rusen, J. (2007c) Making sense of time: Toward a universal typology of conceptual foundations of historical consciousness, in J. Rusen (ed.), *Time and History: The Variety of Cultures* (pp. 7–18). New York: Berghahn Books.

Rusen, J. (ed.) (2007d) *Time and History: The Variety of Cultures*. New York: Berghahn Books.

Rynes, S. L. and Trank, C. Q. (1999) Behavioral science in the business school curriculum: Teaching in a changing institutional environment, *Academy of Management Review*, 24(4): 808–24.

Schuster, D. G. (2013) How do we know? Inquiry-based front ends for conventional topic treatments in STEM textbooks, Paper presented at the Advancing the STEM Agenda, Grand Valley State University, Grand Rapids, MI.

Schwab, J. J. (1962) *The Teaching of Science as Enquiry*. Cambridge, MA: Harvard University Press.

Seider, M. S. (1974) American big business ideology: A content analysis of executive speeches, *American Sociological Review*, 39(6): 802–15.

Sexias, P. (ed.) (2006) *Theorizing Historical Consciousness*. Toronto: University of Toronto Press.

Stager Jacques, R. (2006) History, historiography and organization studies: The challenge and the potential, *Management and Organizational History*, 1(1): 31–49.

Stambaugh, J. and Trank, C. Q. (2010) Not so simple: Integrating new research into textbooks, *Academy of Management Learning & Education*, 9(4): 663–81.

Trank, C. Q. and Rynes, S. L. (2003) Who moved our cheese? Reclaiming professionalism in business education, *Academy of Management Learning and Education*, 2(2): 189–205.

Tushman, M., O'Reilly, C., Fenollosa, A., Kleinbaum, A., and McGrath, D. (2007) Relevance and rigour: Executive education as a lever in shaping practice and research, *Academy of Management Learning & Education*, 6(3): 345–62.

Van Fleet, D. and Wren, D. (2005) Teaching history in business schools: 1982–2003, *Academy of Management Learning & Education*, 4(1): 44–56.

Wagner, P. (2001) *A History and Theory of The Social Sciences*. London: Sage.

Warren, R. and Tweedale, G. (2002) Business ethics and business history: Neglected dimensions in management education, *British Journal of Management*, 13(3): 209–19.

Watts, M. (1987) Ideology, textbooks, and the teaching of economics, *Theory into Practice*, 26(3): 190–97.

Weatherbee, T. (2012) Caution! This historiography makes wide turns: Historic turns and breaks in management and organization studies, *Management and Organzational History*, 7(3): 203–18.

Weatherbee, T. and Durepos, G. (2010) Dar'Wren'ian evolution in management: Implications of the ethics of epistemology for the scholar, Paper presented at the Academy of Management, Montreal, Quebec, 8–9 August.

Weatherbee, T., Dye, K., and Mills, A. J. (2008) There's nothing as good as a practical theory: The paradox of management theory, *Management & Organizational History*, 3(2): 147–60.

Weatherbee, T., Durepos, G., Mills, A. J., and Helms Mills, J. (2012) Theorizing the past: Critical engagements, *Management & Organizational History*, 7(3): 193–202.

Westhues, K. (1991) Transcending the textbook world, *Teaching Sociology*, 19(1): 87–92.

White, H. (1973) *Metahistory: The Historical Imagination in Nineteenth-Century Europe*. London: Johns Hopkins University Press.

White, H. (1987) *The Content of the Form: Narrative Discourse and Historical Representation*. London: Johns Hopkins University Press.

Whitten, P. (1975) College textbook publishing in the 1970s, *Annals of the American Academy of Political and Social Science*, 421(1): 56–66.

Wren, D. (1972) The scanty scent of management history: Putting it all together, Paper presented at the Academy of Management Annual Conference, Minneapolis, MN.

Wren, D. (1987) Management history: Issues and ideas for teaching and research, *Journal of Management*, 13(2): 339–50.

Wren, D. (ed.) (2005) *The History of Management Thought* (5th edn). Hoboken, NJ: John Wiley.

Wren, D. and Bedeian, A. (eds) (2010) *The Evolution of Management Thought* (6th edn). New York: John Wiley.

Wren, D. and Van Fleet, D. (1983) History in schools of business, http://www.thebhc.org/publications/BEHprint/toc121983.html

Part III

Methods: doing management and organizational history

10
Managing the past

Alun Munslow

The postmodern (multi-sceptical) incursion with its epistemic doubts about any form of foundationalism in terms of the 'story of the past' has produced but failed to answer what are for most practitioner historians a series of tiresome and irrelevant questions. These questions have been about whether history is *the* fundamental prerequisite to (a) knowing where we came from and (b) becoming the basis for future planning. As is well known, for 'postmodern historians' the utility – indeed the very idea – of 'learning from the past' is unavoidably fraught with epistemological and ontological problems. Not least among these is how to manage 'the-past-*as*-history'. Of course, for some history theorists – one immediately thinks of Keith Jenkins – the question is whether we need 'history' at all (Jenkins, 1991, 2003, 2013). Or at least, do we need history defined in a particular way – that particular kind of history that its advocates and practitioners have self-defined as being practical, realist, empirical, analytical (specifically inferential/colligatory) and representationalist?

The late 1960s and early 1970s have become characterized (shall we say 'narrated'?) as a time of a widespread rethinking of the theory, practice, and functioning of the academic discipline of history. Like all narrative discourses the 'discipline of history' – itself characterized by a series of narrative discourses – was and for many historians still is validated by and through its supposed ability to help shape and explain the 'historical' nature of our society by discovering and offering its most likely narrative. Indeed (as I write in early 2013), the outgoing President of the American Historical Association, William Cronon, defended 'Storytelling' for keeping the past alive. This is done by the historian's self-consciousness about how they narrate the past (Cronon, 2013). For him, it is telling well-founded interpretational stories about the past that makes the past come alive.

According to Cronon the aesthetics of storytelling – narrative techniques – are by professional convention not permitted to professional historians. But, while he laments the failure of historians to acknowledge that they are authors, the constraints of evidence remain. In his analysis historians need to recognize the complementarity nature of history and fiction in creating 'historical reality'. In saying this he seems to be suggesting that historians ought to be aware of how the past can be more open to representational conventions in narrative forms. Historians ought to be more open to the trade-off between fiction and history in trying to make 'living history'. To do this historians need to be more explicit in their storytelling in order to make 'living history'.

But this argument, while it sounds reasonable is fundamentally wrong. The epistemological notion of 'living history' is a contradiction in terms. It is an oxymoron just as much as is 'auto-pilot' and 'an accurate estimate'. The reason is simple but profound. It is that the past is the past and history is a narrative we create about it. They belong to distinct ontological worlds. Thus, how can 'the past' become 'living history'? Indeed, is the notion of a 'historical consciousness' really about the past at all? Perhaps (though I would say 'surely') the ontology of history is that it must be considered a narrative consciousness/creation that is written about the past. That there may be heavy-duty well-attested empirical references makes no difference to its ontology as a form of narrative.

But (possibly to make matters worse?), a 'historical consciousness' is assumed to be essential to understanding our culture and ourselves. But, of course, there are many different practical forms – or kinds – of historical consciousness. So, it is 'naturally' supposed because it seems to be simple common sense that like all cultural discourses the discourse of Management and Organization Studies needs not just a historical consciousness but its own historical consciousness. It must have a sense and understanding of the past not just to comprehend its own development but more widely to allow practitioners to 'learn and remember and apply the lessons' that MOS – in its historical form' – provides. This 'surely' allows sensible and rational decision-making for the present and future? Without 'a sense of the past' or 'a historical perspective', which is defined in terms of acquiring the probable meaning and or explanation of events, we are all (including managers), surely, cut adrift in time? Indeed, we cannot operate at all? But this 'historical consciousness logic' is wrong. Let me explain why I think this.

I was taught as both an undergraduate and early on as a postgraduate, and what remains axiomatic for the substantial majority of 'history practitioners', that 'the historical consciousness' is always and forever to be defined as an empirical, analytical (which as I have already noted is specifically inferential and colligatory), and written representationalist discourse. So, the (narrative of the) past is 'discovered' by historians in their professionalized pursuit of the most likely meaning/explanation of the past. Narrative and meaning are one in the same. Thus, the British historian Arthur Marwick famously defined history as "[t]he bodies of knowledge about the past produced by historians, together with everything that is involved in the production, communication of, and teaching about that knowledge" (Marwick, 2013). He argued that what happens in the present, and probably what will happen in the future, is very much governed by what happened in the past. So, as he said, imagine what it would be like with no organized and empirically accurate knowledge of the past. Surely, we could not make enlightened judgements concerning parallels with the present?

Because of this epistemological belief there is a common understanding among historians and just about everyone else who wishes to 'know what happened in the past' that (a) what the past most probably means will (b) inform sensible decision-making. Now, in 'the pursuit of history' it is claimed that all historians owe a duty of care to be sceptical about what the evidence suggests concerning the most likely meaning and explanation of the past. That is, always be wary of what the most likely story seems to be. It follows historians – and managers – have a responsibility not to 'read into' the data of the past meanings/explanations which have more to do with the historian and the manager than the past. Objectivity (aka impartiality, disinterest, detachment, and/or neutrality) is thus a key element in both collecting data and in their interpretation. Essential to this is unambiguous (if occasionally tediously technical) and well-constructed communication. So, the aim of objective interpretation and clear (re-)presentation – and primarily on the printed/online page – demands rationality and insight so it can be a rampart against self-serving subjectivity?

So, the honest, rational, objectivity seeking/sustaining and representationalist historian (manager) of the past ensures that their prose is always bent to the needs of the data and their reasoned inference. Of course, the past will not – in all (Bayesian?) probability – tell us what its history is (McCullagh, 1984, 1998). However, writing history tends to lean on the probabilities in its pursuit of creating 'historical belief'. That is why it is regularly re-'visioned'. It is revised as new data and smarter inferences come along. So, the common compromise is to believe that history is clearly a form of literature but it is not a work of literature. Now, history is increasingly shaped into a variety of 'popular presentational forms' such as re-enactment, stage plays, films, digital games, museum stands, 'historical sites', and monuments and memorials. However, the scholarly, accurately written, and representationalist 'on the page' (with appropriately detailed footnotes so the reader can cross-check data and authorial inferences) form remains the epistemic gold standard. We 'seek' reflection (the verb with and also without object) 'in' and 'on' history.

So, given the professionalization process of the past 150 years or so there are many trained and practised constraints which have been developed in order to ensure this inferential and representationalist process can be achieved. And these constraints have become the core values for all disciplines that deal with the past. These also include management and organization studies. Indeed, not just for most historians but also for almost everyone else the assumption is that the past dictates its own history which can be 'detected' and then 're-presented/represented' for what it most likely meant. Put at its most basic level – the past must have 'its own discoverable story' that the manager, historian, airline pilot, shopkeeper, surgeon, and anyone at any time doing almost anything can 'learn from'.

Of course, there are 'obvious' constraints on this process which everyone recognizes such as the possibility of flawed data and/or the drawing of inappropriate inferences by the 'manager-historian'. And while there is always a desire to reconstruct the past for what it most likely was/meant, human frailty and intervention in the process of 'telling it like it was' mean the best we hope for is a sensible and rational, judicious, and honest construction of the past on the page or the PowerPoint presentation or in the balance sheet. So, while the past cannot be reconstructed for what it was (doing that would be a form of resurrectionism?) the 'realities of the past' can – as much as the available (re-)sources allow – be honestly and faithfully constructed again through the shrewd inferences drawn by the historian from the primary and secondary sources.

So, the 'desire for its history' (of whatever 'object/person') is directly connected to the historian's responsibility to the established procedures of professional historical scholarship, the central tenet of which is that 'the past' is always explained in its own terms. Consequently, judgements of and on the meaning of 'the past' are controlled by their production process conforming to established procedures that are predicated on practical realist and representationalist epistemic beliefs. There is a relatively simple algorithm at work. It is this. The narrative we call 'History' (as just defined) offers the most likely meaning and explanation of the past by comparing and contrasting the sources. This in turn is likely to be informed by 'appropriate theory'. The conclusions of this (actually quite straightforward process) are presented in the refereed academic text or 'report of findings' which is itself cast in a form of writing which is founded on the epistemological belief in written representationalism. Any problems that may exist in the connection assumed to exist between a history's narrative form and explanatory function will be resolved by the provision of an empirically verified and well-argued explanation given in appropriately accurate language. Interpretations remain interpretations but they can be reasoned and reasonable.

It follows, given (a) the balance that is possible between the past real world and its present representation, which (b) accepts an essentially transparent connection between language and reality, 'a history' is (c) a professional form of language-use that cannot be judged in terms that might be applied to 'more literary' and much less 'figurative' forms of writing. And it is certainly not an exercise in aesthetics (even if the PowerPoint presentation uses 'nice graphics' to get the point across). Hence (and obviously?), we cannot judge a history as we might a fictional narrative. Now, it is fairly well understood that this understanding of 'the pursuit of history' has been confronted by the multi-sceptical epistemological insurgency of the past 60 or more years. While it is difficult to summarize this insurrection in a pithy phrase there has been a wholesale deconstruction the logic of empirical–analytical–representationalist historying.[1]

Most (in)famously (in my list) is Hayden White who defined the 'historical work' as a prose discourse that combines data (empiricism), concepts and inferences (analysis) in a (really quite complex) narrative structure (of representation). This logic applies to all forms of discursive literature because as White insisted a history narrative is not a verbatim listing of past real events. It is a prose discourse and as such, it is not possible to view it as being true or false to the meaning of the data selected. By that he meant (well, I think he meant) that we need to define the ontology of a history as a figurative and interpretational representation of past real events and if we do (as we surely must?) we are committed to asking what is the cognitive import of the ontology of the history narrative? And the 'history narrative' can be located in all sites where a 'review of the past' is required. In all this the 'atomic level data' remain.

For White (and many theorists subsequently) 'history' was and should be viewed for what it most patently is (which is still in opposition to the judgement of most professional historians) as an unprivileged narrative form. What he means (as I read him) is that 'histories' contain a profound 'structural content' that is poetic/linguistic in nature. Like all other coherent narratives that endeavour 'to explain'? So, 'to explain' the most likely meaning of 'events in the past' it is ontologically unavoidable (there is no alternative) that the historian's 'authoring' or 'trans-forming' of the past into *a* story (that explains meaning) is systematized by a combination of tropes (figuration), emplotments, arguments, and a range of ideological choices.

As White suggested, the logic in all this is that no singular set of actions or events possess their own intrinsic or given emplotment. Of course most historians still believe the opposite. So, writing history invariably comes down to the individual historian's arrangement of these components of thought. Briefly then, this logic which is still both defended and disputed, is whether one believes or does not believe that the 'meaning' of an event in the past is not located only in the 'historical writing' about it, but in some kind of figurative and semiotic composition of the event itself. To be as plain as language permits: do you (dear reader) believe human beings live narratives, or impose narratives, or both? So what is the logic to written or otherwise (per) formed history? It seems to me that (a) the past is not prearranged for us in the form of coherent stories and this entails (b) historians (managers?) are required to recreate such (hi-)stories (for any number of reasons), and (c) that we historians (managers?) give them referentiality by choosing to believe that in those stories the past 'speaks to us'. Hence we have the common yet highly suspicious notion '… that the data lead us to believe …'. The upshot then is to direct our attention to how we 'narrate our histories' as opposed to 'discovering the most likely narrative back there'.

So, if there is no certain and thereby 'discoverable for what it was' or 'given narrative' in the past, even if we 'commonsensically' think there must be, we are condemned to create 'the-past-*as*-history'. Hence 'history' is most appropriately defined and designated as an emplotted, figured, and argued (for or against) 'form' of 'narrative explanation'. Accordingly, if we assume that 'writing a history' is an authorial activity (which I think is not an unreasonable assumption) it suggests that thinking about the nature of history is at some important level thinking about writing narratives (Munslow, 2007). So, the past is the past – what once was and is no more – and all we have is *a* narrative we write about the past. The claim that 'the past' is capable of being conflated with 'its history' is only persuasive if we ignore their ontologies. This, of course, is what most people do and that includes most historians. For me – and I am happy to admit that I do not think this is much of an insight – creating narratives is all we can do. So, we ought to understand how we do that.

This is why have I laboured over this argument. Let me explain further by asking a question that has been asked before. What is the nature of the knowledge base for management and administration? Over 20 years ago one commentator defended the way public sector managers obtain and deploy knowledge (Hummel, 1991; cf. Willmott, 1997). It was argued in contrast to those who suggested that public administration needed to generate and use knowledge based on 'objectivity' and 'pure reason' that the way managers interpret their world – their 'story-telling' – was and is a valid means for constructing and accruing knowledge. The specific outcome of that 'story-telling' largely derives from how managers 'figure' their world – how they trope or 'figuratively turn' meanings.

So, management decision(s) making is about figurative synthesis – troping literal meaning – as much as it might be analysis. Managers ought not to be worried about this as it is part of the human creation of (a) narrative(s). Commonly (or so I gather) managers deploy the descriptive 'case study narrative'. Of course, as with all narrative making there is a risk because having alternative narratives to hand in any given decision-making situation may have greater utility than the single 'scientific report of findings', but this might force a collective agreement to a narrative that is not – as it might turn out – the 'best' narrative available. Unfortunate though it may be, it is the nature of our narrative-making existence. Once we doubt there is a 'given story back there' then life becomes extremely problematic. There is, after all no such thing as 'literal meaning'. The correspondence theory of truth does not apply to making narratives.

Now, fairly obviously (nice irony?) what you are reading is my preferred narrative about managerial narratives and while I am offering (in a prose form) my research findings I am unavoidably creating a fictive narrative. In my narrative I am writing about a (my) preferred way to think about the functioning of narrative. So, an important part of my narrative (about narrative) is my claim (my understanding?) that for most managers their narratives (usually about solving management problems) require (a) empirical foundations to their knowledge about what once happened which is an *ontological* issue and (b) what they think they know about the past in terms of meaning/explanation which is delivered via an inferential *epistemological* process, but then (c) they (and I) have to *represent* it in some way. So, the fruits of (a) ontology and (b) epistemology are (c) a performative representation as a lecture, a written report, a PowerPoint presentation, and so forth. To reduce all this to a simple formula (not that that is necessarily a good thing) it is empiricism + inference + representation = meaning. I then assume some sort of action/inaction will ensue.

Now, if I am right (and I do not have to be – this is only my unprivileged narrative after all) I think it is necessary for me to illustrate what I am arguing by offering you my own fictive 'historical narrative'. Let me be clear (as much as language allows) about the meaning of fictive. By fictive I refer to the nature of history which derives directly from the rendezvous of the historian as an author/storyteller with the time before now. So, rather than a re(-)presentation of what once was, history is a narrative intervention that is beyond the formula of empiricism, inference, representationalism and probable meaning acquisition. I am suggesting that every history is a narrative constructed by the historian which is not to say the (hi)story is a fiction. But equally it is beyond touching epistemological simplicities of empirical practical realism and the interpretative report of 'findings'.

In arriving at this understanding I make a number of assumptions. My first is, of course, that there are no observers or observations outside the past–history ontological and epistemological universe. While there are probabilities in meaning/explanation they still have to be narrated. Hence, there is no 'outside narrative' position. Human beings (and yes, that includes managers) have to represent their ideas on 'what was' before they can evaluate 'what it is' much less 'what it means'. Arguably the primary element in 'understanding' is the process of 'narrating the observation'. But we must remember that there are no observations without an observer and no 'findings' outside a narrative. All observations have to be narrated (even if 'the narrative' is 'given the form' of a table of 'results' of statistical inference). It is no great insight to acknowledge that no matter how it may be presented if 'the past reality' is not narrated it does not have any meaning – even probabilities have to be narrated and emplotted to acquire a meaning.

None of what I have just said rules out 'the reality' of being run over by a bus, or being punched on the nose or getting divorced. But 'to understand' the nature or 'meaning' of such ontological events they have 'to be narrated'. What I hope is particularly significant in this argument is that what 'the-past-*as*-history' means is not the product of a straightforward empirical, analytical and representationalist activity. As is well known, in his (in)famous text *Metahistory* Hayden White (1973) described the 'historical imagination' as consisting of a determining deep level of human unconscious which is itself configured by the four major tropes of figurative language: metaphor, metonymy, synecdoche, and irony. These are the tropes through which human beings both 'pre-figure' and then constantly 're-figure' the sequence of historical events 'found' in the evidence.

So, which figurative trope is 'preferred' (and it might be an unconscious or conscious choice between metaphor, metonymy, synecdoche, and/or irony) in order to describe any event or body of data, is also likely to determine the nature of the emplotment of the data (which could be romantic, tragic, comedic, and/or satiric). To make matters worse for the 'tell it like it was' hard-hatted historian or manager the argument they deploy (formist, mechanist, organicist, and contextualist) is also going to be in some way or another determined by their previous tropic and emplotment choice. And if this was not enough narrative-making determinism, there is a constrained range of ideological/political implications (anarchist, radicalism, conservatism, and liberalism). But these are only probable connections (which are attested only by studies of narrative forms). Needless to say this has created 40 years of debate over (a) the White model and its correlative affinities (which are pretty much what I have just described) and (b) whether historians really are just another group of unprivileged authors even as we wade hip-deep in data sources. It also throws substantial doubt over the alternative practical realist (non-narrativist) model of empiricism, analysis, and representation which, if I were being ungenerous, I might call 'a non-narrative/scientificist approach' which, for all I know, are likely to be very close to the hearts of hard hat empirical-analytical-representationalist historians/managers.

Anyway, and like it or not, it is not just White but also other heavy-duty philosophers such as Heidegger and Kant who have raised important issues about the nature of 'knowing' and 'representing'. So, while it can be argued that 'scientific' laws may be universal (in the sense that in general apples fall to the ground from trees) but as to their application in specific circumstances 'it all depends' on the presence of an interventionist and observing subject plus the methodology they deploy in understanding and explaining the meaning of any object or process in the physical world. We are all too familiar with the common problem of the observer affecting the observed. And it gets even worse when the object no longer exists, i.e. 'the past'.

And so we are in a serious predicament when it comes to 'what the past means' or 'what is the most likely story back there?'. After all, is it that unreasonable to suggest that while judicious interpretation is possible how can we possibly know that empirical observation shored up with reasonable inference can bottom out the nature of 'what it (the situation being narrated) really means'? It reduces to the now universally recognized situation that empiricism is blind without conceptualization, argument, ideology, and emplotment. Knowing 'what most probably happened' cannot bottom out 'what it most probably means'. So, managers like everyone else have to create useful or 'fitness for purpose' narratives. But to do that they also need to understand the nature of narratives and, of course, why some are (or seem to be) more convincing than others. Narratives do not merely record reality, they help create it.

Now, as it turns out one of my mid-career interests as a historian was the life and work of the entrepreneur Andrew Carnegie (1835–1919) (Munslow, 1988, 1992). Because I was authoring a brief biography of Carnegie (as part of a larger project on the connections between discourse and culture) I endeavoured to evaluate his thinking and actions by searching through his writing as any historian would (and happily/unhappily he wrote a lot). So (or should it be 'but'?), as an author myself I realized that Carnegie's writings were substances and forms of narrative expression as much as they may be considered as anything else. Consequently, I engaged with my subject at several levels – four to be precise. I was interested in the (1) nature and (2) forms of his written *expression* as much as I was in (3) the nature and (4) forms of their *content*. Why? It was because I was interested in Carnegie's authorial decisions/elements that I felt I had to acknowledge as I too was an author who was well aware of when, what, and why I was writing. Carnegie and I were both authors writing history. And you are reading a history. But what is history? Allow me a brief diversion before I return to Carnegie.

Well, we know what Arthur Marwick thought history was (Marwick, 2013). But his definition will not do. It is naïve in its rejection (or what is worse the non-acknowledgement) that history is a body of writing *about* a subject (the past) that no longer exists. So, history is a narrative form that is ontologically distinct from the past. History is a substitution for the past that is, of course, created in another form. So, to conflate 'the past' with 'history' is to commit the fundamental category error of conflating writing with a non-existent reality. Despite the belief that the presence of the past is demonstrably all around us in old chairs, old buildings, established and apparently enduring cultural traditions, economic structures, balance sheets, and people older (and younger) than us it seems to me that all we have in terms of 'understanding' and 'meaning creation' are the histories *we* author *about* the past. At best all we can say is that we create 'the-past-*as*-history'. Or, to put this slightly differently: past events have no meaning until they are narrated *as* history.

This claim, lest it needs repeating, in no way ignores statements of justified belief about the one-time empirical reality of the past. Much less does it mean that some meanings and explanations about 'what once happened' may be more or less 'reasonable' than others (though it is a mare's nest defining 'reasonable'). Nor does it mean that some historical accounts are more or less 'factual' than others. Of course if we think about it even this claim is fraught with major problems given that 'facts' are – ontologically – events under a description. The point I am labouring to make is – and forgive me – the rather obvious one that historians regularly read and write different stories *into* the same body of causally connected events (i.e. make authorial decisions or offer 'interpretations' if you prefer).

This is not really as tendentious as many historians might suggest (or fear) and does not bear any resemblance to what Marwick called the self-indulgence of 'the auteur theory' whereby historians glory in their own subjectivity. As Hayden White so famously argued, a body of data does not necessarily contain a 'given' meaning, let alone the most probable meaning. All that connecting up the empirical dots suggests is at best a sort of pointillist historying. It is not too crude or reductionist to say the past can only be engaged with when it is narrated whether that narration is to oneself or to other consumers of history as a film, play, book, novel, chat over a beer, or whatever.

So, there is an ontological dissonance between the 'the past' and 'history'. The ramifications of this for all forms of historying including MOS reports – even if salted liberally with statistical analysis and 'really smart' inference – remain substantial. I repeat, some historical interpretations may be more or less likely than others but stretching this to the notion of 'objectively' learning lessons about the past shifts epistemic gears considerably. To be frank, it makes no sense to me.

By that I mean 'the lessons' of 'the past' at the(ir) most basic of ontological levels are entirely 'the lessons' of 'history'. I subscribe to the view that there is no 'given' emplotment and/or 'given' meaning and/or 'given' interpretation in the data of the past. When put this way it seems like a statement of the obvious. The facts do not speak for themselves. All interpretations are based on more than probability in the movement of data. Meanings are fictively construed. There are no lessons in the past. There are only lessons of history.

So to repeat – and before getting back to Andrew Carnegie – the validity of a (hi)story does not lie simply or even primarily in 'the facts of the (hi)story'. It also resides in its narrative structure as provided by the historian even if they believe they are not creating but discovering it ('it' being 'the story that is believed must be back there'). Of course, that most historians are not boot camp trained in the creation of narratives is not surprising because of the nature of the epistemic priorities inculcated *during* their training. Historians are not told that they are authors and so are not trained to think and create as authors. They believe they are detecting the (most likely) story. The historian *as* detective is just another trope and for my money a particularly poor and misleading one.

I would suggest that what I have just described also pertains for managers. Adopting 'a narrative approach' to managing everyday life in an office/factory demands explaining and rationalizing what managers do in terms of creating aims and objectives, calculating progress toward achieving objectives (through organizational structures), motivating colleagues (through what are regarded as 'inspirational narratives'), securing capital (a narrative of striving), measuring (a narrative that compares their own and everyone else's) progress, developing staff abilities, and instituting resource acquisition and managing utilization (a scarcity narrative). And all this is done by creating 'useful' narratives of achievement and purpose.[2] And these narratives, or so it seems to me, are well established in capitalist-inspired management narratives. Actually, for all I know they may be universal and economic politics might have no relevance.

Andrew Carnegie was not only the richest entrepreneur in the world when he retired in 1901, he was also one of the most published. As is well known, in many magazine articles and several books he described his philosophy of life and entrepreneurship. In a narrative of pluck over luck and bootstrapping effort over everything else his 1920 *Autobiography* (published a year after his death) suggests that he believed he had two key narratives: a 'destiny narrative' which was reinforced by his 'learning from the past narrative' (Carnegie, 1920). These narratives are also replete (in my interpretational narrative at least) with his sense that what is required in life is rational moral and/or ethical judgement and that genuine effort can be rewarded. Now, as Hayden White argued, every historical emplotment is structured by the power – or lack of it – of the hero over her/his environment (White, 1973). I assume this is significant when it comes to striving managers. This is, of course, just an assumption on my part.

Anyway, it turned out to be convenient (in my narrative) that Carnegie believed his age was inhabited by entrepreneurial heroes.[3] In 1886 he said "to all those who extol the past and dwell upon its heroes … intimating our own age is less heroic than some age which has preceded it, let us make answer, that for one true hero who existed in any age, a hundred surround us today" (Carnegie, 1886: 442). This was his judgement throughout his life. As he believed, "I can confidently recommend to you the business career as one in which there is abundant room for the exercise of man's highest power, and of every good quality in human nature" (Carnegie, 1912: 224). As is well understood Carnegie's defence for his class was a gospel of success which encouraged and marketed the self-made entrepreneur-hero who could surpass the world of experience (Carnegie, 1886). They were his hero.

On one occasion he addressed a commencement class of Cornell University students suggesting that wealth was achievable if they became masters of their world through their own diligence, industriousness, frugality, and temperance which – he announced – were the benchmarks of his own sense of heroic materialism (Carnegie, 1912). And, he said, American heroes succeed because

> universal self-dependence is manifest everywhere and in everything ... The cause of this self-governing capacity lies in the fact that from his earliest youth the republican feels himself a man ... We can confidently claim for the Democracy that it produces a people self-reliant beyond all others; a people who depend less upon governmental aid and more upon themselves ... than any people hitherto known.
>
> *(Carnegie, 1886: 443)*

This set of beliefs and claims is hardly surprising given that Carnegie was (in my interpretation) his own romantic hero and, like all romantic heroes (as a narrative typology), he located himself as the hero-protagonist at the centre of his own introspected existence and was often misanthropic in equal measure to being philanthropic. So, he began as an immigrant setting out to master the new world and willingly he acknowledged that many new arrivals failed because America is only a favoured land for the most competent and resourceful. As he said, 'drones' have no place 'in her hive' (Carnegie, 1886). Although the entrepreneur-hero may begin 'his' journey as an immigrant Carnegie believed he still must possess the traits of the heroic American. So, in Carnegie's narrative those who succeed do/did so because they self-fulfil(led) their own prophecy. As a hero they have a goal. As a hero they enable progress. And, as a hero, if they are thwarted so is everyone else. And, of course, it was always a hero not a heroine.

So, Carnegie's 'Gospel of Wealth' became his foundational and defining narrative but it was also a jeremiad (Carnegie, 1889a, 1889b). Only by achieving the aims and objectives of the 'Gospel of Wealth' could all the other capitalistic and entrepreneurial narratives become reinforced and valorized. It was a narrative/literary composition in which he bitterly lamented what would happen to the state of society and its moral culture if the entrepreneurial culture was thwarted. But Carnegie's narrative was soon in danger of producing what might be described as a metonymic reduction.

By that I mean that in praising American nationalism Carnegie had to acknowledge the possibility of failure for the entrepreneur and through this reduction (of the heroic entrepreneur to one of failed entrepreneur) had a parallel for the American nation. As he said, "The Republic may not give wealth, or happiness; she has not promised these, it is the freedom to pursue these, not their realization, which the Declaration of Independence claims" (Carnegie, 1886: 32). Of course, being an entrepreneur can be risky business because it might lead to a tragic narrative emplotment – the 'failure of the hero to control their environment'. But to maximize the avoidance of tragedy what the 'Ideal Entrepreneur' does is create a new 'common sense' where their values – and only their values – self-defined as harmony and consensus over making profits (which trickles down of course) become the basis of 'the American narrative'. Heroes succeed when everyone understands and supports their narrative.

Further (or should it be 'so'?), in Carnegie's narrative only the entrepreneur-hero could produce social consensus because of his 'talent for organisation and management' (Carnegie, 1889a: 655). Of course the upshot was that such ability "invariably secures enormous rewards for its possessor" (Carnegie, 1889a: 655). This narrative is ideologically expedient as it implies that opposition to the corporation as a mode of wealth formation must be rejected because "the condition of the race is better" with this heroic entrepreneurial narrative (Carnegie, 1889a: 655). Only 'the trust' could secure social harmony.

So, anyone who found a reason to reject his analysis would be "attacking the foundation upon which civilization itself rests" (Carnegie, 1889a: 655). Perversely then, to attack the new corporate state was to challenge heroic economic individualism. Carnegie's heroism was narrated through the re-troping of the lives of heroic historical figures like Jefferson from a metonymic narrative with its conventional tragic emplotment, to what according to White's model is a comic emplotment within the figurative mode of synecdoche whereby there is reconciliation between men that creates a more harmonized national culture – a triumphant democracy. So, for Carnegie the new industrial order had to be narrated (emplotted) to create a narrative of social harmony. The only thing (hitherto) missing from Carnegie's final creation of the idealized entrepreneur-hero was the ultimate proof of the Gospel of Success. This was provided by his rationale for the 'benefits' of poverty – the well-known narrative of Ragged Dick.

So, in Hayden White's narrative model the four arguments presented as modes of explanation are syllogisms. And, of course, their premises appeal to an authorially presumed causal relationship between events (White, 1973). Given my argument that Carnegie rejected a metonymic reduction favouring instead a synecdochic integration in his conceptualization of what constitutes the concept of difference, the explanatory 'social laws' he favoured were those that he believed denoted a move from a mechanistic to an organicist argument through which he accounted for the nature of American social change. We are all in this together despite the manifest variations in wealth. But he needed an outcome that sustained and valorized his worldview. And so, if you were poor it was (a) more than likely your own fault, and (b) in certain individual cases it could be viewed as a blessing; however, (c) there comes a point when the state needs to intervene. Although Carnegie believed that Charles Darwin and Herbert Spencer were essentially correct (in the struggle for survival and adaptation to environment) he believed his 'social corporatism' could avoid social revolution from the left.

As he said in his book *Triumphant Democracy* 'An aristocracy of wealth is impossible ... Wealth cannot remain permanently in any class if economic laws are allowed free play' (Carnegie, 1886: 366). So, for him Social Darwinism shaped a classless and democratic society. There was no need for class war and the struggle for existence could and should be mitigated. So, Carnegie dismissed the sociologist William Sumner's narrative of a state of economic conflict induced by the unequal biological struggle for survival, and found unacceptable not only the philosopher's biological Darwinism, but also the philosophy of Herbert Spencer favouring instead a shift to a form of social amelioration. So, ultimately the private administration of wealth – if done according to his principles – could create an organic 'we are in this together' society.

So in acknowledging the ruptures and fissures in 'the past' and 'history' connection which exist (because history is not derived from the past but fictively designed for it), this raises questions (a) about the ethical construction – and hence the management – of the past, and (b) how historians can/ought to narrate a responsible 'creative accounting' for the past. But in none of this is the empirical reality of the past injured in terms of justified belief *unless* (and usually only in creative and experimental historying) it furthers the pursuit of the wider understanding of the 'nature of history' as opposed to the empirical reality of 'the past'.

This is, of course the really tricky bit in the exercise of confronting the nature of history given the epistemic (and cultural) priority we place on accurate empirical reporting. This act is done (a) in good faith, and (b) with the (rather odd?) belief that data carry within them their own given meaning, and hence (c) 'experimental history' like 'experimental management narratives' thus becomes not merely a pointless pursuit but probably a culturally dangerous act of folly. But then Hayden White pretty much demolished that argument by pointing to the existence of competing (narrative) explanations for exactly the same body of data. Management narratives are subject to the same 'creative constraints' as are all forms of narrative making.

Here I am not necessarily drawing what may seem to be a rather obvious analogy with 'creative accounting' and its practice(s). As I understand it 'creative accounting practices' stick to the rules and regulations but they deviate from what 'accepted standards' aim to accomplish in terms of an accurate statement of the reality of the meaning of the accounts. The empirical data are narrated in such a way as to deliberately create a meaning which may be different to that which the accountant (one could substitute 'historian' for 'accountant') actually believes is the situation, the meaning, the reality, and/or the true explanation.

So, in a different definition of creative 'accounting' we ought to acknowledge the primary functioning of tropic imagination (metaphor, metonymy, synecdoche, and irony) with its strategies of explanation (emplotment, argument, and ideology). But it follows, as White has long argued, that we can reasonably accept that the attested data will regulate the historical explanation (i.e. the history's narrative emplotment) *only* if the historian accepts that there must be a given story (i.e. emplotment = most likely meaning = most probable explanation) *in* the data sets. However, this belief is illogical (in my view) because that belief requires the historian to approve of (and give effect to) the idea that a specified set of (invariably highly complex and extensive) empirical data has only one (most probable?) explanation/meaning.

As is all too well known, a regression correlation coefficient that can be demonstrated between sets of data moving over time does not demonstrate 'cause and effect'. To think it does requires a further odd multiple belief. This is the belief that (a) meaning inheres in the past, (b) that our only access to it (in terms of meaning) 'as we narrate it', has (c) no epistemic and (d) no ontological impact. Now I think something quite interesting follows if a 'historical story' is presented as a symbolic (metaphoric, metonymic, synecdochic, or ironic) representation of real events. What I think follows is that the question of its truthfulness must be both epistemologically and ontologically constrained by the principles governing our calculation of 'the truth of the *fictive*'.

By *fictive* I refer to the fundamental nature of history. I argue that the ontology of history is that of a narrative created by the historian. So, if I am correct it is of central importance to understand the nature of the historian as an author-storyteller who creates 'the-past-*as*-history' (Munslow, 2012). So, rather than being a re(-)presentation of what once was, history is an authorial intercession that *fictively* represents the 'past' in the form of *a* 'history'. It is entirely correct to claim that the nature of historying takes it beyond any spurious claims to scientificist and objective empirical-analytical-representationalism. While inference and plausible meaning can be divined this is not to be confused with 'the truth of the past' at any level beyond the statement of justified belief. So I argue that a history is a narrative discourse that is the construction of the historian. This is not to say the (hi)story is a made up fiction. The important point is that recognizing history is a *fictive* (not a fictional) cultural discourse takes it once and for all out of the category of practical realism with its epistemological security of history understood as an imitative if still interpretative report of 'findings'.

Regardless of whether it is a management history narrative or any other kind (of history) every reader must try to detect not just the literary devices deployed but where the text escapes the control of the author and has become irrepressibly *fictive*. After reaching the not unreasonable assumption that the narrative has become 'fugitive and *fictive*' the deconstructionist reader must seek out (a) its ascendant trope, (b) the dominant emplotment defined through the power of 'the hero' to succeed/fail, (c) its core arguments (aka through the inference of the precise mechanics of cause and effect), and (d) what is the nature of its ideological/ethical implications. Deconstructing history must always have priority over the reconstruction of the past.

To deconstruct the management narrative necessitates exposing another confederacy. This is the unstated modernist complicity that exists between the 'manager-historian' and 'the reader consumer' whereby the former is presuming to and is presumed by the latter to be 'telling truth about history'. By viewing the historian-manager as an author who is not only the constructor of 'the-management-past-*as*-history', but who is also fashioned by and in language, I hope we can see that it is not the past that speaks through the manager-historian, but only the typescript's fictive nature and the ethic/ideology of the author. Not even managers exist outside (their) discourse. If they could then they would have (a) discovered the basis upon which the knowing subject is constructed and (b) demonstrated beyond any possible doubt the modernist conviction that individual consciousness is the fount of knowledge, meaning, and understanding. However, our (once called postmodern) narratively self-conscious and multi-sceptical condition requires that the manager-as-author must be decentred. This also suggests there is no transcendental signified.

This recognition in no way debilitates managers – or anyone else for that matter – from making decisions. It just makes understanding their nature more complex. For this I make no apology. You will recall that the brief for my chapter was to examine current debates in and on the nature of that narrative we call history that might inform management and organization studies. So, by deploying perhaps the most famous entrepreneur-author Andrew Carnegie I have endeavoured to examine how 'postmodern' or (as I prefer to call them) multi-sceptical arguments have confronted the self-styled practical, realist, common-sense investment in and defence of empiricism, analysis, and representationalism. While this triad remains the basis of 'common sense thinking and practice' it is seriously flawed and should only be used with extreme caution when managing the past or endeavouring to learn from it – as history.

Notes

1 See, for as good a start as any, Russell (1954, 1957). It should be noted – but it still rarely is – that Russell also assumes history is essentially narrative in form. Most (in)famous is, of course, White (1973). Perhaps of equal importance is White's (1966) article. The Keith Jenkins oeuvre of multi-scepticism concerning the utility of history understood in empirical-analytical-representationalist terms is also well illustrated in his (2009) collection. The historians who predated White are referenced in his classic text but obviously include Benedetto Croce and R. G. Collingwood. Unavoidably the literature on the sometimes called 'linguistic turn' that acknowledged the frailty of our access to reality outside language is substantial. See for example Gallie (1964); Mink (1978); Munz (1997); White (2000); Ankersmit (1994, 2001, 2005) and most recently (2012); Jenkins (1991, 1999); Jenkins and Munslow (2004); Ricoeur (1984). More specifically on the universality of the structure of narrative and from which historians could usefully learn much that applies to their own literary endeavours see Chatman (1978); Jakobson (1966, 1985); Propp (1958); Genette (1986, 1990); Greimas (1992); Todorov (1964); Ricoeur (1984).

2 The published work on management narratives and narrative making is extensive. See for example: Kilduff and Mehra (1997); Barry and Elme (1997); Boje, Oswick, and Ford (2004); Klein, Connell, and Meyer (2007); Martens, Jennings, and Jennings (2007); Langenohl (2008); Bartel and Garud (2009).

3 The classic 'figure' is Ragged Dick. See Vlahakis (1979).

References

Ankersmit, F. R. (1994) The dilemma of contemporary Anglo-Saxon philosophy of history, in F. Ankersmit (ed.), *History and Tropology: The Rise and Fall of Metaphor* (pp. 44–74). Berkeley and Los Angeles: University of California Press.

Ankersmit, F. R. (2001) *Historical Representation*. Stanford, CA: Stanford University Press.

Ankersmit, F. R. (2005) *Sublime Historical Experience*. Stanford, CA: Stanford University Press.

Ankersmit, F. R. (2012) *Meaning, Truth and Reference in Historical Representation*. Ithaca: Cornell University Press.

Barry D. and Elme, M. (1997) Strategy retold: Toward a narrative view of strategic discourse, *Academy of Management Review*, 2(2): 429–52.

Bartel, C. A. and Garud, R. (2009) The role of narratives in sustaining organizational innovation, *Organization Science*, 20(1): 107–17.

Boje, D. M. Oswick, C., and Ford, J. D. (2004) Introduction to special topic forum: Language and organization – The doing of discourse, *Academy of Management Review*, 29(4): 571–77.

Carnegie, A. (1886) *Triumphant Democracy: Or Fifty Years March of the Republic*. New York: Doubleday Doran & Co.
Carnegie, A. (1889a) The gospel of wealth, *North American Review*, June: 653–64.
Carnegie, A. (1889b) The gospel of wealth, *North American Review*, December: 682–89.
Carnegie, A. (1912) *The Empire of Business*. New York: Doubleday, Page and Co.
Carnegie, A. (1920) *Autobiography of Andrew Carnegie*. Cambridge: Houghton Mifflin.
Chatman, S. (1978) *Story and Discourse: Narrative Structure in Fiction and Film*. Ithaca: Cornell University Press.
Cronon, W. (2013) Presidential Address 'Storytelling', *American Historical Review*, 118(1): 1–19.
Gallie, W. B. (1964) *Philosophy and the Historical Understanding*. London: Chatto & Windus.
Genette, G. (1986 [1972]) *Narrative Discourse*, trans. J. E. Lewin. Oxford: Basil Blackwell.
Genette, G. (1990 [1983]) *Narrative Discourse Revisited*, trans. J. E. Lewin. Ithaca: Cornell University Press.
Greimas, A. J. (1992) *Of Gods and Men: Studies in Lithuanian Mythology*. Bloomington, IN: Indiana University Press.
Hummel, R. P. (1991) Stories managers tell: Why they are as valid as science, *Public Administration Review*, 51(1): 31–41.
Jakobson, R. (1966) Closing statement: Linguistics and poetics, in T. Sebeok (ed.), *Style in Language*. Cambridge, MA: MIT Press.
Jakobson, R. (1985) *Selected Writings*, ed. S. Rudy. The Hague: Mouton.
Jenkins, K. (1991, 2003, 2013) *Rethinking History*. Abingdon and London: Routledge.
Jenkins, K. (1999) *Why History? Reflections on the Possible End of History and Ethics under the Impact of the Postmodern*. Abingdon and London: Routledge.
Jenkins, K. (2009) *At the Limits of History: Essays on Theory and Practice*. Abingdon and London: Routledge.
Jenkins, K. and Munslow, A. (eds) (2004) *The Nature of History: A Reader*. Abingdon and London: Routledge.
Kilduff, M. and Mehra, A. (1997) Postmodernism and organizational research, *Academy of Management Review*, 22(2): 453–81.
Klein, J. H., Connell N. A. D., and Meyer, E. (2007) Operational research practice as storytelling, *Journal of the Operational Research Society*, 58(12): 1535–42.
Langenohl, A. (2008) 'In the long run we are all dead': Imaginary time in financial market narratives, *Cultural Critique*, 70: 3–31.
McCullagh, C. B. (1984) *Justifying Historical Descriptions*. Cambridge: Cambridge University Press.
McCullagh, C. B. (1998) *The Truth of History*. Abingdon and London: Routledge.
Martens, M. L., Jennings, J. E., and Jennings, P. D. (2007) Do the stories they tell get them the money they need? The role of entrepreneurial narratives in resource acquisition, *Academy of Management Journal*, 50(5): 1107–32.
Marwick, A. (2013) History in focus: What is history? http://www.history.ac.uk/ihr/Focus/Whatishistory/marwick1.html
Mink, L. O. (1978) Narrative form as a cognitive instrument, in R. H. Canary and H. Kozicki (eds), *The Writing of History: Literary Form and Historical Understanding* (pp. 129–49). Madison, WI: University of Wisconsin Press.
Munslow, A. (1988) Andrew Carnegie and the discourse of cultural hegemony, *Journal of American Studies*, 22(2): 213–24.
Munslow, A. (1992) *Discourse and Culture: The Creation of America, 1870–1920*. London: Routledge.
Munslow, A. (2007) *Narrative and History*. Basingstoke: Palgrave Macmillan.
Munslow, A. (2012) *A History of History*. New York: Routledge.
Munz, P. (1997) The historical narrative, in M. Bentley (ed.), *Companion to Historiography* (pp. 851–72). London:Routledge.
Propp, V. (1958) *Morphology of the Folk Tale*. Austin: University of Texas Press.
Ricoeur, P. (1984) *Time and Narrative*, trans. K. McLaughlin and D. Pellauer. Chicago, IL: University of Chicago Press.
Russell, B. (1954) *History as an Art*. Aldington: Hand and Flower Press.
Russell, B. (1957) *Understanding History*. New York: Philosophical Library.
Sebeok, T. (ed.) (1960) *Style in Language*. Cambridge, MA MIT Press.
Todorov, T. (1964) La description de la signification en littérature, *Communications*, 4: 33–39.
Vlahakis, R. (1979) Ragged Dick by Horatio Alger, *The English Journal*, 68: 2.
White, H. (1966) The burden of history, *History and Theory* 5(2): 111–134. Collected in his *Tropics of Discourse: Essays in Cultural Criticism* (pp. 27–50). Baltimore: Johns Hopkins University Press, 1978.

White, H. (1973) *Metahistory: The Historical Imagination in Nineteenth Century Europe*. Baltimore: Johns Hopkins University Press.

White, H. (2000) An old question raised again: Is historiography art or science? (Response to Iggers), *Rethinking History: The Journal of Theory and Practice*, 4(3): 391–406.

Willmott, H. (1997) Management and organization studies as science? *Organization*, 4(3): 309–44.

11

Critical hermeneutics for critical organizational history

Scott Taylor

Introduction: presences and absences

The history of hermeneutics as a term and as a practice is long and fascinating. Few methods, methodologies, or epistemologies can boast longer or more complex roots. The idea first surfaces at the beginnings of institutional intellectual life, in the city states of southern Europe and their philosophical academies. It continues more or less uninterrupted with "many surprising twists and turns" (Porter and Robinson 2011: 1) to its present-day position within academic philosophy departments and in social science or humanities research methodology teaching. Hermeneutics is usually described as a two-level practice: as a way of approaching the 'first order' task of reading for understanding, and as a 'second order' way of thinking about the human interpretation of texts. This can be seen as an implicit hierarchy, in that the first aspect of being a 'hermeneut' is a method, while the second aspect is epistemological and/or ontological. The latter became the dominant meaning associated with the term during the twentieth century when hermeneutics was framed as a central concern of critical and post-philosophies, bringing it into the philosophical mainstream from the theological and historical and considerably expanding its range as a way of thinking.

However, despite this recent academic reincorporation and the popularity of critical and post-epistemologies in business schools, there appear to be very few self-identified hermeneuts writing about management and organizations in English. As an analytical method, hermeneutic methodologies are established as a rarity (Prasad and Mir, 2002); as a means of framing empirical approaches to data collection, they are equally unusual (Phillips and Brown, 1993). The reasons for this are unclear, perhaps unknowable. Practicalities such as slow and piecemeal translation of key texts into English and discomfort with the politics of key German figures in hermeneutics' twentieth-century philosophical development are sometimes cited (Murray, 2008). Academic micro-politics may also be significant; hermeneutics' evident neglect might be related to its adoption by medieval theologians in debates as to the 'true' meaning of (especially) biblical texts, and then its more recent association with the humanities generally, two faculties on campus that organization and management researchers tend to walk around or through without looking up (Gagliardi and Czarniawskwa, 2006; Sørensen et al., 2012) in pursuit of methodological and analytic legitimacy from more 'scientific' disciplines (Bell and Thorpe, 2013). However the lack of hermeneuts and hermeneuticians is even more surprising when we consider that it is "one of the two major philosophical-conceptual underpinnings of interpretive approaches to the study of organizations" (Yanow and Ybema, 2009: 40). These authors also note the conventional focus in hermeneutic approaches on text, broadly understood to include visual texts such as film. This may be another clue to the low profile of the approach, in that collection and analysis of either primary or secondary textual data in this form is relatively unusual in organization and management studies (Stablein, 1996).

When we also consider that hermeneutics is perhaps the historical method *par excellence*, its relatively low profile as method and as epistemology within management and organization history becomes even more baffling. A clue to its absence here may lie in its assumption or incorporation into historical studies – in other words, it may be implicitly present, assumed to such a degree that it can remain unspoken. However, it is also possible that hermeneutics' absence indicates less of an implicit presence, and more of an explicit exclusion. There are certainly few of the methodological discussions that would be expected as indicators of a significant method and methodology in review and summary contributions to journals or edited handbooks, and hermeneutics is rarely held up as the way of working that underpins the analyses produced in the name of management and organizational histories.[1]

These presences and absences are the central concern of and reason for this chapter. I explore hermeneutics as method, as well as hermeneutics as both methodology and epistemology. I do this by considering the presence of hermeneutics in organization studies as a synchronic approach that focuses on one moment in time, but also by examining its potential as a diachronic approach that enables a specific historiography of organization and management, institutions as well as individuals. Throughout, I emphasize that hermeneutics is a term that signifies philosophical commitment, and acts as an indicator of how data collection and analysis were carried out. Each implies the other, but each also carries its own meanings, history, and expectations separately from the other. The purpose of the chapter is to locate hermeneutics in its sense as an interpretivist organization studies perspectival schema (Yanow and Ybema, 2009), with the intention of pointing up its potentials and problematics as a way of writing management and organizational histories.

Contemporary practices: hermeneutics, texts, and communication

Although the volume of hermeneutic analysis is low in management and organization studies generally, its presence often indicates original and insightful analysis. Researchers working with a hermeneutic approach are inevitably closely engaged with fundamental issues of explanation, understanding, and language. In addition, all hermeneuticians are at least aware of the complex dialogues, or dialectics, between and among text, author, reader, and interpreter/analyst.

This reflects hermeneutics' remarkably strong presence in philosophy and philosophically informed discussions of social science research methods. Indeed, there is an argument to support the claim that hermeneutics has framed the development of modern philosophy from the period when Kant was writing in the eighteenth century (Porter and Robinson, 2011). This means the primary literature associated with it is vast, difficult if not impossible to survey unless a lifetime's work is devoted to it. Good secondary overviews to aid selective engagement with primary texts are fortunately plentiful, often with a specific disciplinary perspective built into the exposition.

One such disciplinary overview is provided by Alvesson and Sköldberg (2000, chapter 2). They suggest hermeneutics can be understood as a 'bridge' (2000: 52) between empiricist qualitative research, such as grounded theory or ethnomethodology, and more ideologically led critical perspectives, such as the Critical Theory associated with the Frankfurt School and later the philosophical anthropology of Jürgen Habermas. They sub-divide the community of hermeneuticians into objectivist and 'alethic'. The first, according to Alvesson and Sköldberg, is in pursuit of comprehension of underlying meaning, while the second seeks explanatory theory that may involve causal connections. As these authors also note, there is a significant fault-line between the two groups in their attitude towards subject–object distinctions. Objectivist hermeneuts retain a "studying subject" who stands apart from a "studied object" (2000: 56) in the hope of establishing a transcendental meaning-truth, while alethic analysts seek to provide a provisional, intersubjective, plausible agreement about the meaning of a text and how to understand it.

These approaches are supplemented by a more recent philosophical development which sails under the flag of critical hermeneutics.[2] Contributions to this branch of hermeneutics usually cite the philosophical discussions of both Habermas and Ricoeur as foundational, particularly the latter, especially when considering critical hermeneutics as a method of inquiry and knowledge production (e.g. Thompson, 1981). Perhaps the primary attraction of critical hermeneutics, in the form presented by Thompson in particular, is its clarity of methodological guidance in the approach to data analysis. This may reflect the debt to Ricoeur, whose work often presents extremely complex discussions in very clearly structured ways, with surprisingly practical guidance (see, for example, Ricoeur (2004) on memory, hermeneutics, forgetting, and historiography).

Thompson's arguments and guidance are manifest in the structure and content of a landmark critical hermeneutic study of organizational communication, published in 1993 by Nelson Phillips and John Brown. They make a strong argument for the use of a critical hermeneutic approach to understanding organizational communication. They relate this to the cultural and symbolic turn in management and organization studies, especially the 'management of meaning' as an expression of power relations. Their main interest is in understanding how organizational members' and interested outsiders' understandings of an organization may be conditioned by texts. This also involves interrogating the textual sources – in other words, asking who produced the text and what their motives might be. The analytical methods, they suggest, are varied: structural semiotics, psychoanalytics, discourse analysis, Marxist analysis, and other interpretative methods aimed at understanding organizational cultures.

However, the critical hermeneutic approach outlined in this important contribution also limits its reach by excluding subjective meanings attached or attributed to texts. The texts that Phillips and Brown (1993: 1549, fn. 1) want to subject to critical hermeneutic analysis must be 'objectified' and 'abstracted' from their context. This may be a product of their focus on culture-as-communication, so that the lived experience of the symbolic socially negotiated everyday order of organization is excluded. Culture is limited, perhaps reduced, to a system of texts through which people structure and interpret everyday organizational life. They therefore place their approach firmly within Alvesson and Sköldberg's objectivist hermeneutics, with its focus on understanding rather than explanation and theory building.

The social context of the texts is acknowledged; however, it is present only in its more structured forms as hierarchy, control, micro-political coalitions, domination and resistance (in other words, in abstracted objectified forms). Based on their ontological position on culture, and their reading of Thompson's work (1981, 1990), Phillips and Brown frame critical hermeneutic analysis as a means of engaging with five aspects of text: intentional, referential, contextual, conventional, and structural. Each of these ways of reading and interpreting guides the hermeneut towards specific questions:

- What is the purpose of the text as it was created?
- What do texts refer to outside themselves in order to communicate?

- What is the social and historical context of the text's production?
- What are the social conventions that the text's production and consumption reproduce or challenge?
- What are the structural conventions that the text follows or challenges?

This is then related to a base of critical hermeneutic philosophy that is founded on the work of a key contributor to both hermeneutics and historiography, Paul Ricoeur. A framework of interpretative 'moments' is outlined, to guide the researcher through social-historical analysis of the first three aspects of the text, followed by formal analysis to engage with the latter two, and then interpretation/reinterpretation to bring them together into a new authoritative analytical text.

The most important moment, analytically, is the third, which is an uncertain synthetic process that involves the "creative construction of meaning" (Phillips and Brown, 1993: 1568) to be justified or legitimated through the skill of the interpreter and assessment of how convincing the previous two moments are. This is important to be clear about because it is the key shift in all forms of hermeneutic analysis, from testimony (using Ricoeur's term) to an authoritative representation of events, people, and artefacts, something I return to later.

Prasad and Mir (2002) utilize a similar method and methodology, to explore the same empirical context of the oil industry. Their version of critical hermeneutics as method and methodology is, however, subtly different. First, Prasad and Mir focus much more on reading and interpreting symbols and symbolic meanings in corporate communication. Second, they employ a more ideological critique, in a political sense, of the texts they examine. Third, they devote more energy to conceptual development through their hermeneutic analysis. These differences allow Prasad and Mir to develop a much more rounded understanding of the relationship between text and context which is not entirely dependent on the researcher and her interpretation. The context here can be social and cultural, but it is also highly politicized and (importantly for this chapter) intrinsically historical.

In this sense, Prasad and Mir's work is more implicitly theorized as a hermeneutic approach than Phillips and Brown's. They engage with the idea of representation in the texts they objectify, but also in the objective text they themselves produce through their hermeneutic analysis. To use Ricoeur's (2004) terms again, Prasad and Mir acknowledge the epistemological and aesthetic aspects of hermeneutics to create a dialectic between text and theory, such that their analysis has both narrative intelligibility and explanatory intelligibility. It has, in short, a plot as well as a style.

These two empirical studies are important because they are clear about the hermeneutic imagination involved in reading, interpreting, and theorizing. They are critically reflexive in the sense that they are philosophically and methodologically explicit as to the position and role of the researcher-as-author (Fournier and Grey, 2000). This is both epistemological (especially for Phillips and Brown) and political (especially for Prasad and Mir). Neither would be read as historical in the conventional sense that management and organization history usually works to. However, both give clear indications of the promise of hermeneutic analysis, as epistemology and as explanatory/theoretical. For this promise to be more fully realized, within management and organization history as well as in organization studies more broadly, careful examination of its implications is necessary. I do this in the next section, through a reading of a foundational methodological statement of what a hermeneutic approach looks like and enables, followed by an outline of what it might mean for management and organizational history, particularly a critical version of that way of seeing.

The promises of hermeneutic analysis

As Prasad (2002: 12) observes, there was a "hermeneutic ferment" in organization studies for a brief period in the 1990s when cultural and symbolic perspectives came to prominence. However, as he goes on to argue, the epistemological implications of claiming the label of hermeneut were largely unexamined. His aim is to address that by putting together the most philosophically complete account of hermeneutics we have within management and organization studies.

Prasad structures his review through the binary of 'weak' and 'strong' hermeneutics. The former is rather dismissively described as "somewhat nebulous" (2002: 13) and a rather inaccurate shorthand for qualitative or interpretative research. 'Strong' hermeneutics, on the other hand, engages with philosophical discussions of the term and its implications. The complex historical development of philosophical hermeneutics is described by Prasad as a three-stage process. First, scholars spoke of hermeneutic analysis as a way to frame debate over the contested meanings of 'difficult' texts – in other words, hermeneutics could be brought out of the cupboard as a practice when scholars (especially theologians) needed to establish their legitimacy and authority as interpreters of the true intent or motive of the speaker/writer. This highly specific use and usage was widened both by theological shifts, such as Protestantism's challenge to hierarchies of biblical interpretation, and by closely related developments in the philosophy of language and communication.

Classical hermeneutics then slowly transforms into what Prasad terms "philosophical hermeneutics", mostly through the efforts of German philosophers working in what would become defined as the European period of romanticism and idealism. This is the period in which hermeneutics is extended in two important ways. First, it becomes gradually but steadily disassociated from theology, to take a place at the epistemological table as a secularized way of thinking about reality, humanity, and the world we live in. Second, the 'objects' that hermeneuts can apply their ontology and epistemology to in order to interpret the world, expand beyond written texts to systems and processes of communication.

This second key period of hermeneutics' progress through academic disciplines/disciplining brings it well into the twentieth century (and the problematic politics of Europe in the first half of that time, especially for those working in German universities). According to Prasad (2002), there is both a philosophical and a methodological aspect to the writing on hermeneutics from this period. Philosophically, hermeneutics as understanding is re-categorized from an epistemology to an ontology. In other words, the pursuit of understanding that hermeneutics has always been centrally concerned with is conceptualized as ontological, a basic condition of human experience and therefore of humanity and the world. Methodologically, hermeneutics is also repositioned, as the separation and therefore mutual autonomy of text-as-object and interpretation-as-act are questioned. This in turn breaks down the methodological distinction between understanding and interpretation, a second significant issue that we return to later in the chapter.

The third moment described by Prasad, critical hermeneutics, is that which is claimed by both Phillips and Brown (1993) and Prasad and Mir (2002). It involves a commitment, of some kind, to the possibility of a critical theory of society and therefore organizations and management. This has two key implications: first, it helps the hermeneut to avoid (charges of) relativism; and second, it reintroduces transcendental reason (perhaps in the form of social theory) as a means of resolving the inevitable conflicts produced by competing hermeneutic readings of texts.

It is this debate that brought hermeneutics to the attention of a series of mid- and late twentieth-century philosophers, ensuring its presence in accounts of, for example, critical theory, deconstruction, pragmatism, psychoanalytics, and their various combinations. Most contributors to these debates engaged with the tension created when hermeneutics is discussed as ontology and epistemology (or methodology). This is in part an attempt to resolve, or deflect, the issue of relativism, and therefore also retain the possibility of a progressive politics (of society and therefore also of organization and management).

Following this abbreviated historical overview, Prasad's (2002) methodological account then sets out what he sees as key issues that any aspiring contemporary 'hermeneutician' ought to consider. These are the hermeneutic circle, historicality (including the 'hermeneutic horizon'), dialogical understanding, the role of the author-as-interpreter, and critique. I want to concentrate here on the idea of historicality, especially in its methodological implications, for obvious reasons, but the other issues are worth examining briefly as they can be seen as significant in approaching hermeneutics.

The idea of the hermeneutic circle is relatively easily articulated. It describes the belief that an understanding of textual meaning (the desired outcome of practising hermeneutics) can only be achieved through consideration of 'parts' (individual experiences or interpretations) and 'whole' (a sense of context, perhaps analysed as place, time, or culture). This process should happen as a circle or 'spiral' (Porter and Robinson 2011: 41) rather than an exchange or dialogue, such that understanding increases as the two aspects of hermeneutic practice happen repeatedly over a period of time.

The pursuit of such an understanding raises the possibility that understanding is achieved through a conversation that takes place between interpreter and text. This may be understood as similar to the practice of authorial or researcher reflexivity, in which the preconceptions, prejudices, and situated nature of analysis are acknowledged. As always, however, the hermeneutician is encouraged to aspire to the pursuit and capture of truth – in other words, this is not a post-structural or postmodern reflexivity, but a delimited one that maintains authorial positioning.

The notion of authorial intention inevitably has to be considered alongside the pursuit of understanding through working within the hermeneutic circle. If the text being interpreted is defined as carrying or communicating multiple meanings, then the authorial interpretation, as a text, must also be understood in the same way. Authorial intention may be present, but it does not, cannot, determine readerly understanding or interpretation. The final issue, critique, contains a remarkably complex debate within the philosophical community as to the relationship between understanding and critique. At issue is the status of language, whether it is ontological or epiphenomenal, and therefore liable to alteration and/or degradation through other social practices. From this, the question of whether the status of text and interpretation may be differentiated arises, so that, for example, critique (especially political or ideological) may be possible – or not, as perhaps hermeneutics is limited to interpretation.

This last issue and the debate it generated drew in someone concerned with hermeneutics as a practice and philosophy that inflected various parts of his life. Paul Ricoeur wrote throughout his life across a range of academic disciplines (philosophy, theology, history), and his arguments and hermeneutic frameworks have been taken up in many others. Ricoeur suggested that critique is in fact integral to hermeneutic analysis. However, it is Ricoeur's contribution to the interplay of hermeneutics and historiography that is the subject of the next section of this chapter, especially its implications for the historical or historicizing analysis of management and organization via hermeneutic thinking.

The possibility of hermeneutic histories

A number of biographers provide details of Ricoeur's long and remarkable life (e.g. Reagan, 1996). It is only important in the context of this chapter to note that he wrote as a philosopher, historian, Christian, socialist, and historiographer. In many of his works, he engaged in particular with philosophical considerations of the ontological, and therefore epistemological, status of text and language. This in turn would lead Ricoeur to consider the status of the written text-dominated archive materials that so many management and organization historians rely on. Throughout his philosophical and historiographical writings, Ricoeur maintained a commitment to working with phenomenology and hermeneutics as key to understanding the human condition and the knowledge we seek to produce about it through histories.

Like MacIntyre in subsequent works (e.g. MacIntyre, 1982), Ricoeur's philosophical writings are unusual in that he is always interested in the human subject of the most abstract philosophical and existential issues. He makes this interest material through a 'philosophical anthropology', similar but different to grounding the complexities of key themes such as will, freedom, and evil in the experience of everyday embodied action that anthropologists such as Geertz might practise.[3] However, Ricoeur insisted that the status of language and interpretation was central to his philosophy, thereby inevitably taking a "hermeneutical turn" (Porter and Robinson 2011: 111). In this period of his working life, Ricoeur brought together a number of existing philosophical interests to explore the nature of the human and social sciences as disciplines. This brought him into a long relationship with text and understanding. Ricoeur's work is also marked by an abiding concern with narrative over time – in other words, concerns that are (should be) central to history, historicizing, and considering historiography.

These are exceptionally deep waters, all the more so because while Ricoeur was working in the French philosophical tradition with its particular conventions, he also sought to commentate on (and challenge) German, North American, and English understandings in these fields. However, there is one statement of the implications of Ricoeur's development of hermeneutics on history that summarizes and (to some extent) clarifies in an operational sense helpful for practising history in relation to specific categories of life (such as organization or management). It is his final major work, published in English in 2004 as *Memory, History, Forgetting*.

This book has three stated aims for the author. There is a private purpose, as he comes towards the end of life with a desire to think about the maintenance or degradation of memory as the median level between temporal experience and narrative. Second, Ricoeur wants to contribute to the debate surrounding what he sees as the fundamental methodological and philosophical problematic facing historians in their work – the relationship between memory, remembering/forgetting, and (the production of) history. Finally, he sees the act of writing this book as a civic duty, to encourage us all to think about how and why some events, people, or places are celebrated or forgotten, at the end of what had been a century of unprecedented physical and ideological violence.

Thus the first part of the book explores memory. This may be read as a minor concern, more biological than social scientific, simply laying the foundation for subsequent discussions of history's epistemologies and the hermeneutics of the historical condition. However, in a wonderfully evocative metaphor, Ricoeur suggests that each of his three overarching concerns may be seen as a mast on a ship, and that history needs to maintain all three masts to operate effectively. If we wish to think about the past, to write about it, to research it, or to talk about it, we are inevitably representing it. History, then, is not a discipline, a craft, or a thing – rather, history is understood here as a process of remembering, forgetting, and imaginative construction of the "presence of an absent thing stamped with the seal of the anterior" (Ricoeur, 2004: xvi).

Hence it becomes clear why this particular hermeneutics of historiography has to begin then with an examination of how the building blocks of any history come to be. Memories are examined for what they are, and whose they are. This leads into consideration of a fault-line that is fundamental to historians, the distinction between truth and imagination, or mimesis and imagination. Memories are always dysfunctional in a realist sense; they can never hope to represent what happened completely or entirely reliably. However, if the analyst, or hermeneut, exercises the critical agency available to her, then memories are recognized more for their truthful ambition and insight. Memories become excellent and informative data sources, more or less effective efforts to recall that are analysed through an actively reflexive phenomenology of memory that leads towards a historiography and history.

The exploration of memory is only the first section of this remarkable book. Ricoeur goes on to examine the implications of taking memory seriously for an epistemological understanding of history, and thence a critical and ontological perspective on the historical condition, culminating on reflections on the position of history as a contributor or barrier to human happiness. Here, Ricoeur returns to his ruminative starting point, considering the nature and purpose of (his) life, history, and historiography. His conclusion is clear: history can only contribute to the pursuit of a good life, good lives, if its practitioners and consumers strive for reflexivity in the understanding that 'it' is always provisional, open to reconsideration, and engaged.

These are potentially very abstract arguments and conclusions, especially for a notionally applied field of research such as management and organization studies. The concluding comments bring this discussion of hermeneutics back towards critical organizational history to reconsider that activity in the light of hermeneutics' promises, as method, methodology, epistemology, and ontology.

Concluding comments: bringing hermeneutics into critical historical analysis

As this chapter shows, hermeneutics is not an exclusively historical method, methodology, or way of thinking. It has long had a presence in philosophy and theology, most obviously, but it can also be identified as a strand of thought in linguistic and literary theory. Hermeneutics is, however, intrinsically historicized, in the sense that it is a temporal "hybrid of that which is, that which came before, and that which is becoming" (Porter and Robinson 2011: 303). While we may not all agree that being a hermeneut is unavoidable because all research is based on understanding and interpreting (Porter and Robinson 2011), there is a strong argument for scholars in management and organization history in particular to pay it more attention as ontology, epistemology, methodology, and way of seeing. The characterization of hermeneutics as a narrow discipline oriented towards finding the underlying truth of a text is very misleading. Hermeneutics is much better seen, especially from the early twentieth century on, as a way of asking questions – questions about meaning, interrogating the production and reception of social or cultural texts in a very broad sense, without necessarily finding a truth or resolving disagreements about meaning.

This way of approaching the interpretation of data is obviously both useful and challenging for a historically inclined researcher. Its use lies in the historical sensitivity that practising hermeneutics inevitably encourages, its centrality to the historical conditions that we all occupy as we make both history and histories (see Ricoeur, 2004: part 3, chapter 2). Interpretation, understanding, and argument are all enabled by a hermeneutic approach to the texts that historians build narrative on or around. An understanding of hermeneutics as an ontological position implies an approach to being human, and therefore to research, as inevitably historically conditioned (Ricoeur, 2004). The past is not a place, or even a moment, but an aspect of the temporality of being.

Such an understanding of hermeneutics, however, has implications for the objects of history. If, as Ricoeur has repeatedly argued, history is an ontological presence (in other words, that being historical is a condition rather than an option that can be ignored), then both history-as-data and history-as-product have to be seen in a particular light. To start with Ricoeur's (2004: 448) words: "The idea of an exhaustive narrative is a performatively impossible idea … one can always recount differently, by eliminating, by shifting the emphasis, by recasting the protagonists of the action in a different light along with the outlines of the action … the prime danger … lies in the handling of authorized, imposed, celebrated, commemorated history – or official history." These two issues are especially salient for historians of organization and management. The temptation of adapting the performed historical narrative in the published history to gain access to corporate archives is always present (Evans, 2012).

However, it seems most likely that if hermeneutics is to be accorded a place in critical organizational history, it is as a methodology related to interpretivism. Yanow and Ybema propose, playfully but with serious intent, four "takes on the position of interpretivism in organization studies" (2009: 41). These are pluralists, revolutionaries, warriors, and peacemakers. Each label is described through five characteristics, the first two in relation to 'other' methods and methodologies: how interpretivism's position is understood, its identity position, its methods, its contributions, and its limitations. Through this scheme Yanow and Ybema argue convincingly that interpretative research is more often presented as a set of ideals than honoured in practice, as method or methodology. I conclude by suggesting that hermeneutics, in all of its variety, richness, and inquisitiveness, offers a uniquely generative means of asking more and better questions of management and organization histories in an idealistic sense, that may be translated effectively into practice-based methodologies that underpin convincing historiography and historical narratives. In this respect, its neglect is something that historical researchers should feel contrition about, and begin to redress.

Notes

1 It's worth noting the presence of hermeneutics in two well-regarded management, business, and organization history journals. *Business History* provides five references for 'hermeneut~', two to full papers that mention the term once, in its 56-year publishing history; *Management and Organizational History* shows 13 uses of the term in papers from its nine volumes. The former is surprising; the latter might be read as encouraging.

2 Unusually, Alvesson and Sköldberg (2000) use the terms Critical Theory and critical hermeneutics interchangeably. Although a number of philosophers associated with Critical Theory perspectives engage closely with hermeneutics, I read that as a necessary condition of philosophical work in the twentieth century, not an indication that the two approaches are the same.

3 Geertz's debt to Ricoeur's writing on hermeneutics is noted by Alvesson and Sköldberg (2000: 95–8), as are the differences between Geertz's approach to cultural analysis and Ricoeur's hermeneutic frames.

References

Alvesson, M. and Sköldberg, K. (2000) *Reflexive Methodology: New Vistas for Qualitative Research*. London: Sage.

Bell, E. and Thorpe, R. (2013) *A Very Short, Fairly Interesting, Reasonably Cheap Book About Management Research*. London: Sage.

Evans, R. (2012) Nothing they wouldn't do, *London Review of Books*, 34(12): 21–24.

Fournier, V. and Grey, C. (2000) At the critical moment: Conditions and prospects for Critical Management Studies, *Human Relations*, 53(1): 7–32.

Gagliardi, P. and Czarniawska, B. (eds) (2006) *Management Education and Humanities*. Cheltenham: Edward Elgar.

MacIntyre, A. (1982) *After Virtue*. London: Duckworth.

Murray, A. (2008) Hermeneutics, in R. Thorpe and R. Holt (eds), *The Sage Dictionary of Qualitative Management Research*. London: Sage.

Phillips, N. and Brown, J. (1993) Analyzing communication in and around organizations: A critical hermeneutic approach, *Academy of Management Journal*, 36(6): 1547–76.

Porter, S. and Robinson, J. (2011) *Hermeneutics: An Introduction to Interpretive Theory*. Grand Rapids, MI: Eerdmans.

Prasad, A. (2002) The contest over meaning: Hermeneutics as an interpretive methodology for understanding texts, *Organizational Research Methods*, 5(1): 12–33.
Prasad, A. and Mir, R. (2002) Digging deep for meaning: A critical hermeneutic analysis of CEO letters to shareholders in the oil industry, *Journal of Business Communication*, 39(1): 92–116.
Reagan, C. (1996) *Paul Ricoeur: His Life and Work*. Chicago, IL: University of Chicago Press.
Ricoeur, P. (2004) *Memory, History, Forgetting*. Chicago, IL: University of Chicago Press.
Sørensen, B., Spoelstra, S., Höpfl, H., and Critchley, S. (2012) Theology and organization, *Organization*, 19(3): 267–79.
Stablein, R. (1996) Data in organization studies, in S. Clegg, C., Hardy, and W. Nord (eds), *Handbook of Organization Studies* (pp. 509–25). London: Sage.
Thompson, J. (1981) *Critical Hermeneutics: A Study in the Thought of Paul Ricoeur and Jurgen Habermas*. Cambridge: Cambridge University Press.
Thompson, J. (1990) *Ideology and Modern Culture: Critical Social Theory in the Era of Mass Communication*. Cambridge: Polity Press.
Yanow, D. and Ybema, S. (2009) Interpretivism in organizational research: On elephants and blind researchers, in D. Buchanan and A. Bryman (eds), *The Sage Handbook of Organizational Research Methods* (pp. 39–60). London: Sage.

12

ANTi-History

Toward amodern histories

Gabrielle Durepos

Introduction

Debates concerning epistemological and methodological orientations and their suitability for *doing* history and historiography have been vibrant in the discipline of history over the past three decades (Jenkins, 1991, 1995, 1997, 2003; Gunn, 2006; Ermarth, 1992; White, 1973; Munslow, 2010, 2012; Jenkins & Munslow, 2004). Jenkins' (1997) *Postmodern History Reader*, for example, features the debate between modern and postmodern historians concerning 'how' best to represent the past. The debate contrasts, on the one hand, the modernist position underpinned by realism where relativism is viewed as a much feared danger with, on the other, a postmodern position, where pluralist notions of history are celebrated and where it is argued that relativism is the only hope for stimulating the emancipatory potential of the past as history (Jenkins, 1997, 1999; Brown, 2005).

To a large extent, the modern–postmodern debate in the discipline of history has also shaped the contours of the recent call for more history in management and organization studies (henceforth, M&OS). This is apparent in the oft-quoted and highly influential three positions for doing history developed by Üsdiken and Kieser. These "may be labeled as *supplementarist, integrationist* and *reorientationist*" (Üsdiken & Kieser, 2004: 322). Though the authors caution that the three positions are not fixed, preferring instead to highlight each as subject to variation, the supplementarist (and perhaps even the integrationist) position(s) are arguably still informed by modernist assumptions of realism offering promise of objective knowledge. The reorientationalist position, however, is dedicated to inherently challenging the "social scientistic framing of organisation studies" (Üsdiken & Kieser, 2004: 324; Zald, 1993) and shares many similarities with a postmodern orientation to history.

The perennial pitting of modernism versus postmodernism has arguably also influenced the arguments featured on the agenda calling for, and simultaneously offering direction for, doing more history in M&OS (Booth & Rowlinson, 2006; Jacques, 2006). This influence is most evident in the illustration of the relevance for M&OS of "philosophers of history such as Michel Foucault and Hayden White" (Booth & Rowlinson, 2006: 5). Foucault and White have not only weighed in on but have also shaped the modern versus postmodern debate by contributing to the development of postmodern historiography. Calls for more history in M&OS have also suggested the need for theorizing and problematizing foundational concepts such as our understanding of the 'past' and 'history' (Weatherbee *et al.*, 2012). The latter is seen as one way to benefit what has until now been only the nascent potential of what a historical perspective can bring.

The call for more history in M&OS might come as a surprise to those immersed in the historiography literature. In a 2009 book titled *At the Limits of History*, Jenkins called for an end of the academic discipline of history. This book and its arguments surfaced only two decades after the publication of his influential book *Re-Thinking History*. The latter was said to have shaped the discipline of history by rendering accessible what had previously been impenetrable conceptual arguments of postmodern history and historiography (Munslow, 2009). Jenkins' decree is less astonishing if we consider other positions of this nature. An appeal for the end of history for example, was also evident in Foucault's 'anti-historical' position of nearly three decades earlier in his own notion of archaeology (White, 1985: 234; Burrell, 1988).

Is the academic disciple whose focus of study is the past dead? In this chapter I argue that historical analysis has much potential, though to achieve this the past and history might be in need of some re-assembling. In light of the contrasting calls for the 'end of history' by postmodern historians (Jenkins, 1999, 2009) and the 'call for more history' by M&OS (Zald, 1993, Booth & Rowlinson, 2006), this chapter explores an alternative conceptual space for thinking historically. This conceptual space is outlined by first reviewing both modern and postmodern approaches to the past and history. It is my hope that the latter will serve as a sufficient context in which to thoroughly consider the need for what I will call an amodern approach to doing histories. I offer the following discussion while simultaneously remaining fully cognizant of the danger of imposing rigid categories and categorizations such as the three I provide. But I do so in the hope that these allow for the emergence of points of comparison whereby the differences, absences, and deficiencies between positions are more easily exposed. Thus, the amodern manifesto discussed in this chapter has three parts. I begin by discussing modern followed by postmodern histories. In the third section, I attempt a conceptualization of amodern histories.

Modernist management and organizational history

Modern and postmodern historiographies are positionings inspired by entirely different intellectual movements. Furthermore, each is associated with distinctive temporal periods. There is much convergence on the opinion that the emergence of postmodernism was inspired by a thorough critique of modernism (Prasad, 2005; Jenkins, 1995). Perhaps because postmodern historiography, too, was motivated by a reaction to modernism, a reading of these respective literatures allows for the surfacing of facets or points around which to organize their comparison. For the purpose of ordering the discussion in this chapter, comparisons will include: a discussion on their respective contributors and traditions, their ontological and epistemological orientations, their assumptions concerning the relationship of past with/and history, thoughts on the nature of representations of the past-as-history, a summary of the treatment of *context*, and lastly, a discussion on the assumed role of the historian. I have summarized the positions of each tradition with regard to these facets in Table 12.1.[1]

Modernist contributors and traditions

I follow Jenkins (1995) who uses the socio-temporal condition of modernism as a label to describe a type of historiographical work. As a cultural condition, modernism celebrates "rationality, individualism and progress" (Prasad, 2005: 219). Jenkins (2003: 15) offers that most professional historians today are "stubbornly 'modernist'" and are united in their commitment to

Table 12.1 Modes for doing management and organization history

	Modern	Postmodern	Amodern
Ontology	*Realism* Phenomena and the past exist outside of our mental appreciation of them and await our discovery.	*Emphasis on epistemology* Our view of the world (or the past) is mediated entirely through our knowledge of it (history). Ontology is collapsed into epistemology. The past is an absent present, it does not exist in an ontological real(ist) form. Objects or events of the past are constructed in the minds(s) of the subject-knower. All we have is knowledge of the past which is plural due to the various epistemological choices of representation available to the historian. Postmodernism understands history as knowledge of the past, which is an outcome of the community and mind of the historian.	*Emphasis on ontology* The social past is performed as history in practices today; these performances constitute reality (today). Practices are enactive of the socio-past, history is what actors perform (in practice) as they talk about or do the past. Performances or enactments of the socio-past as history occur at the site of the relations of actors. Performances or enactments of the socio-past as history take different shapes in different sets of relations. Knowledge situated in practices is *enactive*. It creates our view of the object of study, thus the object(s) of study (past as history) are performed in practice(s).
Epistemology	*Positivism* It is possible and desirable to accurately represent the past as it happened as history.		

Table 12.1 (*cont.*)

	Modern	*Postmodern*	*Amodern*
The nature of representations of the *Past as History*	*Singular* The objective is to move toward one complete and uncontested version of the past or history by continually seeking to uncover history through verifying it against the past and its traces.	*Plural* Referred to by Mol (1999, 2002) as perspectivalism. Historians, by virtue of their epistemological or ideological situatedness create different versions, knowledge or provide different perspectives on the past. It is the responsibility of the historian to be reflexive and transparent as to how their ideological grounding influences the tale told. Historians with varying ideological or epistemological positionings will 'gather' around a phenomena or event and create knowledge of the past of that event from their standpoint. The focus is on that phenomena and creating knowledge of that phenomena.	*Multiple* The focus is on practice and the different enactments that one phenomenon may take in varyingly situated practices as well as different sets of relations.
Relationship of *Past* and *History*	*Real* History is an accurate portrayal of the past.	*Relative* We have one past but plural (representations of the past as) histories. There are many somewhat unrelated narratives of the past that coexist or compete and there is little emphasis on evaluating the relationship between them. Representations of the past as history are not grounded in their constitutive practices.	*Relational* Enactments of the past as history occur in the relations of actors (in between actors) at the site of oscillation. The site of oscillation is the place between heterogeneous actors where there is potential for translation, or transformation.

Treatment of Context	*Remove from context to study it* Typically, phenomena of interest are isolated from the practices in which they occur to allow for studying the past free from bias or confounding factors. One advantage that history offers is that it provides a more 'holistic' view.	*Place in context* Place events and phenomena into the context in which it has occurred to explain and understand it. Doing history is a vehicle for placing organizations and their practices in context.	*Any practice creates its own context* It is not possible to put things into *context* or their *container* to understand their functioning, as the *context* is what is created through our efforts to define it. The *context* is what actors produce when they perform the socio-past as history. Any practice creates its own *context*. It is what is created through various sets of relations and performances of actors. We cannot start off by assuming as given (context exists) what we wish for our analysis to show (actors efforts or practices that build *context*, or *social past as history*).
Role of the historian, i.e. who does history?	The historian assumes the responsibility for writing the history in an objective manner, but in doing so removes him/herself from the product of history and the reader. The historian assumes a privileged position as historian and mostly so because s/he is removed from view.	The historian includes him/herself in the narrative, talks about history as an outcome of him/herself. The historian assumes responsibility for writing the history. The historian de-privileges him/herself as an authoritative voice by situating the history as an outcome of his/her situated efforts. In doing so, s/he emphasizes that it could have always been otherwise.	The historian (which does not assume her/his status as such based on his/her institutionalized academic category) is part of the performance. History is performed in multiple sets of practices.

ontological realism (White, 1985). Histories they produce can be described as empiricist, factualist, objectivist and documentarist where the study of the past is undertaken for its own sake, thus purportedly uninhibited by present centered motivations.

Leopold von Ranke is often credited with instituting the study of the modern historical method (Geyl, 1962; Gunn, 2006; Hobsbawm, 1997). His colorless and detached approach to historiography is often assumed as the discipline's common sense, especially so in Anglo-American circles (Gunn, 2006). Though Ranke is credited with the origin of modern historiographical practice, many historians have since shared in the pursuit of similar ideals. British empiricist Geoffrey Elton, for example, pursued a scientistic historiographical approach underpinned by a belief in the possibility of objectively and impartially reconstructing the truth of the past reality as it happened (Elton, 1967; Perry, 2002; Jenkins, 1995; Green & Troup, 1999). Whilst some of these hallmarks are celebrated to varying degrees by positivist, scientific, and business historians (Collingwood, 1956; Chandler, 1962; Phillips, 1935), these modernists are united in their commitment to realism (White, 1973; Jenkins, 1997).

Modernist ontological orientation: realist

Historical realism is the belief that (a) the past (and history) exists outside and unencumbered by our mental interpretation and appreciation of it, and (b) that the past is knowable upon its discovery (White, 1973). Realist apprehensions assume the task of the historical enterprise as one of representing the past reality as it happened (Gunn, 2006; White, 1973). The past reality is assumed as a 'fait accompli' and thus has an unchanging form. The goal is providing a singular, all-encompassing, truthful representation of the past by "providing a precise and accurate reconstruction of the events reported in the documents" (White, 1985: 52). The historical enterprise is dedicated to discovering the traces, evidence, or sources of the past, as behind these lie hidden the historical reality (Ankersmit, 1997). By establishing causal linkages between pieces of evidence, the historian recovers the past and provides neutral explanations rather than interpretation (White, 1985; LaCapra, 2007; Brown, 2005). That historians 'find' or 'uncover' stories is what differentiates them from fiction writers who merely 'invent' theirs (White, 1973). Indeed, the work of modernist history is an assumed "culturally neutral task" (Ermarth, 2007: 52).

Histories of this nature are not estranged from the academic discipline of business and management. From early business histories, such as that which documents the past of Woolworth (Phillips, 1935), to those that speak to history as a useful 'diagnostic tool' to "motivate employees in the present" (Smith & Steadman 1981: 164), to those that describe history as a 'leadership tool' (Seaman & Smith, 2012), to using history to maintain a focus on a firm's essential principles (Roowan, 2010), the notion of history is treated as some 'thing' or 'object' that exists outside our mental appreciation and awaits discovery. What is similar in each of these accounts of the past is the ontological realism that underpins them.

Modernist epistemological orientation

Similarities can be drawn between historians who share in their assumptions on the generation of knowledge of the past, or their epistemological orientation (White, 1985; Jenkins, 1995). Following Jenkins (1995), I label those who believe that it is both possible and desirable to represent the past as it actually happened as history as modernist. For these historians, the past is similar to a jigsaw puzzle whose many pieces must be unearthed, respectfully brought into the present, and assembled into its preconceived composition (Jenkins, 2003). The intent is on

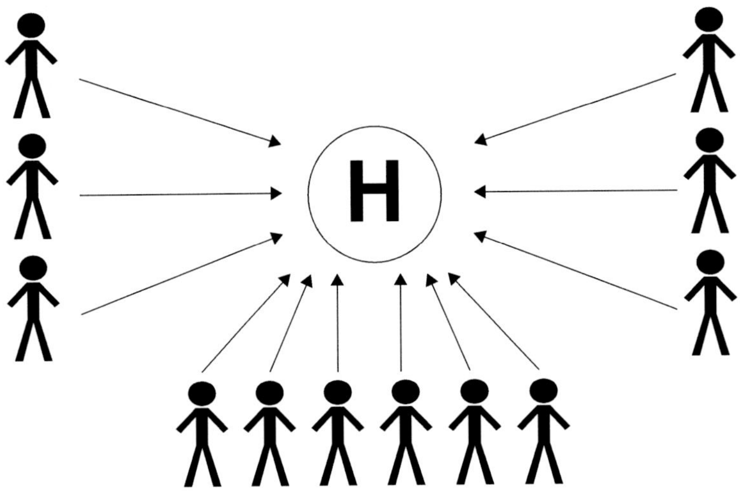

Figure 12.1 Singular history

creating singular, truthful or accurate apprehensions of reality, where different interpretations are understood as due to ideological distortions or inadequate factual data (White, 1985).

Positivist histories are an example of this (in M&OS, positivism is commonly assumed as an epistemological orientation in and of itself; see Burrell & Morgan, 1979). Influenced by Ranke, positivist histories share in the belief that historical processes are "subject to laws or generalizations akin to the natural sciences" (Gunn, 2006: 5; Green & Troup, 1999; Collingwood, 1956). Thus, the first step is to ascertain the facts, the second is to discover the laws, which are then relied upon to order the facts (Collingwood, 1956). Identifying the 'laws of causation governing' historical processes acts as the authority in solving historical disputes. As the methods and concepts of the natural sciences were increasingly used as a guide for 'proper' historical investigation (Hobsbawm, 1997), history began to lay claim to the revered "status of a science" (White, 1985: 54). Those management histories that adopt these facets of positivism are often described as "linear, progressive … and truth-centered" (Jacques, 1996: 14).

Modernist relationship of representations of the past as/to history

Unsurprisingly, modernist historians, characterized by their commitment to ontological realism and epistemological positivism, believe that the ideal relationship of the past as/to history is one where the latter (history) is an accurate, complete, and uncontested representation of the former (past). For modernists, rigorous history is that which is one and the same with the past (Jenkins, 1995; Elton, 1997). The emphasis then, is on discovering the truth of the past (Cousins, 1987; Jenkins, 1995). This is a task to which many historians contribute by adding to the existing stock of knowledge until it is deemed an adequate portrayal of the past. After all, what business historians "are really trying to find out is what was really going on, what really happened" (Kantrow, 1986: 87). Underpinning this quotation lies the assumption that past reality is discoverable and singular, as evidenced in Figure 12.1.

This type of historical enterprise leads to a history that is "ontologically single" (Law, 2008: 137) in that the past has only one form of existence as history (Cousins, 1987). In this scenario, "'other' histories are not really histories at all but fakes" (Jenkins, 1997: 16). Figure 12.1

symbolically places these types of historians grouped in a circle, with their gaze and efforts focused on a singular, upper case 'H'. Thus, there are many historians and (eventually) one agreed upon History. Jenkins (1991, 1995) calls this upper case history.

Modernist treatment of context

What is especially noteworthy about the desire for the emergence of a singular, agreed-upon history is the "nature of the process of convergence" through which historians derive the uniform story. The process occurs over a period of time, as many historians across different time periods add to the existing stock of knowledge to solve a particular "mystery". Perhaps for this reason, historians, following Ranke, have sought to construct history free from the present context and thus "extinguish" themselves from their study of the past (Kalela, 2012: 14). This means that phenomena of interest are studied objectively from the present-centered practices in which historians live (and by which they are surrounded) in an effort to free the study of history from bias or confounding factors. Thus, modernist historians strive to construct histories without influence of present circumstances but nonetheless within the context of the past (Kalela, 2012). It follows then that the past is understood not to illuminate a present societal concern but instead is studied for its own sake and on its "own terms" (Green & Troup, 1999: 2). 'Own sake-ism' refers to "the attempt to understand an earlier human culture or society first and foremost in terms of its own self-conceptions and values rather than in order to serve an immediate practical or political interest of the present" (Zagorin, 2009: 72).

Studying phenomena in a manner free from presumably confounding contextual factors is done by (theoretically) isolating or bracketing it from that context. The tendency to isolate the study of the past from circumstances of the present has led Rankean, traditional empiricist, and positivist historians to caution against any form of interpretation (Geyl, 1962). Modernist historians argue that theory and interpretation are not only present-centered phenomena but, when imposed on historical facts, serve to distort them (Gunn, 2006; Perry, 2002; Jenkins, 1995).

Assumptions concerning the context of historical analysis which modernist historians share are evident, with their importance highlighted in many business histories. For example, Harvard Business School historian Alonzo McDonald emphasizes that what is significant "when looking at a major problem is to try to define the context or environment in which to place that problem. Only then does the problem really begin to take on meaning, make its true severity clear, or point the way toward management actions that might resolve it" (Kantrow, 1986: 81).

When speaking of developing his business history courses for the Harvard Business School, Tedlow notes that it was important to "set up a context within which historians can effectively examine business enterprise and ask questions of it" (Kantrow, 1986: 82). Similarly, Smith and Steadman (1981: 170) note that having a "strong knowledge of contexts" is important in "order to discriminate between good and bad historical data." These studies underline a modernist assumption that the past context not only exists but that it is possible to discover it for the purpose of using it to understand a particular phenomenon.

Role of the modern historian

The discussion above has many consequences for what we assume as the role of the historian in the craft of history. Generally, modernist historians are those who undertake the task of writing history but in doing so, remove any trace of themselves from the text or narrative. In adopting an impartial third-person voice, the historian assumes a god-like view, creating and writing simultaneously from everywhere and nowhere at all (Law, 2008; Green & Troup, 1999).

The historian stands in as "an external, invisible, impersonal, and all-knowing teller of the story" (Zagorin, 2009: 72). In doing so, the historian creates "the illusion of omniscient, neutral narrator" (Zagorin, 2009: 72) and by abolishing himself from the text, the resulting groundless history is assumed to speak for the past, on its behalf, as its neutral transmitter of "what happened" (Jenkins, 1995). History, untouched and uncolored by the historian, becomes a direct representation of the past (Collingwood, 1956). Indeed an illusion is created where "the literary text is a direct record of reality" (Zagorin, 2009: 72).

Postmodern management and organizational history

The condition of postmodernism and postmodern history

The summary of modern historiography above, however brief, provides a fitting frame with which to discuss postmodern contributions to historiography. Postmodernism is often described as a socio-political condition with artistic and scholarly consequences, premised not only on a hard critique of modernism but also on the belief in its utter failure (Jenkins, 1995; Green and Troup, 1999). Central to postmodernism is an outright rejection of realism, the ontological position of modernism (Jenkins, 1997; Jenkins, Morgan & Munslow, 2007; Zagorin, 2009; Jenkins, 2009). What is understood to be particularly problematic is the tendency of modernist theory to produce reductionist, essentialist, and universal accounts.

As Jenkins, Morgan & Munslow (2007: 5) note, postmodernism presents a condition in which "our chosen ways of reading things lack solid, universal foundations." The significance of postmodern thought is signaled by its focus on the conditions of knowledge production as an institutional and cultural activity that is always positioned (Calás and Smircich, 1999). In doing so, postmodern thought challenges the innocence of modernist 'truthful' knowledge claims and threatens the notion that knowledge can ever correspond to a single 'reality.' By virtue of this, knowledge is assumed as always positioned and thus, necessarily plural. Reality then, is pluralized and accessible only through text, language or interpretation. The spread of this idea over the past 30 years represents a central feature of what is commonly called the 'linguistic' or 'textual' turn in the social sciences and history.

Based on a critique of modernism, postmodern historiography concerns the various ways that the past can be written and represented today. It is about destabilizing dominant narratives of the past. It is about the histories that are "not told, retold, untold" and those which have been "forgotten, hidden, invisible, considered unimportant, changed, eradiated" (Jenkins, 1995: 36). Power and emancipation are central to these histories where the weak and subordinate are given a voice to reclaim their past in an effort to deflate imposing meta-narratives (Brown, 2005).

The diversity of postmodern thought is explained in part by the various intellectual traditions from which it has emerged, including Marxism, the liberal center, and the conservative right (Jenkins, 1995; Prasad, 2005). Partially because of this, postmodernism does not represent a coherent and cohesive collective of scholars (Brown, 2005), although they do share a concern for language, representation, subjectivity, and power (Calás & Smircich, 1999). The various traditions and perspectives that are often subsumed within it include poststructuralism, post-Marxism, post-feminism, postcolonialism, and cultural theory (Jenkins, 2009; Gunn, 2006). Contributors who have informed postmodern historiography include Foucault (though he was reluctant to adopt the label), specifically his work on archaeology (1973), discourse (1973), and genealogy (Burrell, 1988). Other contributors include Derrida, Baudrillard, Lyotard (1993), Ankersmit (1997, 2007), Ermarth (1992), Munslow (2010, 2012), White (1973, 1985; Jenkins, 1995; Green & Troup, 1999), Rorty (Jenkins, 1995; Perry, 2002), and Jenkins (1991, 1995). Over the past

25 years management historians working in this vein have included Jacques (1996, 2006), Cooke (2006), Mills (2006), and Booth and Rowlinson (2006), as well as others who have increasingly drawn on the work of the aforementioned postmodern theorists. I briefly summarize some of their points of intersection as a way of fleshing out postmodern historiography.

Postmodern ontological and epistemological orientation

Though far from a homogeneous group, postmodern historians are united in their ontological orientation of post- or anti-realism. The consequences of this for theorizing the notion of the past is that it is said to be an absent present; one that does not exist in an ontological realist form. As Collingwood (1956: 5) explains, the "past has vanished and our ideas about it can never be verified as we verify our scientific hypotheses." This position does not deny that "what happened before now actually happened" (Jenkins, 2003: 35, 2009; Brown, 2005) but instead emphasizes that what happened before now cannot be understood as the one definitive past as would modernist history. Thus, while there is agreement that what 'happened before now' forms part of a past time, it can never stand in for the past or history in and of itself or in its entirety. The past and history then, become absent objects of inquiry, which are signified by remaining traces or artifacts (Jenkins, 1995; Munslow, 2009). Traces and artifacts do not stand in for the past but are what becomes ordered into narrative form in the minds of the knower (Ankersmit, 1997). And, as noted by White (1985: 39), the past as we construct it "enjoys no existence apart from our consciousness of it." In effect, the "past is therefore a permanent dimension of the human consciousness" (Hobsbawm, 1997: 10). Because the past no longer exists, modernist criteria of truth or falsity are not relevant for assessing how the past is re-presented in historical representations (Braun, 1997; Brown, 2005).

Those who do history from a postmodern orientation are also united in their rejection of positivism. The notion that history is subject to general laws and that its discovery follows a natural science model of research is dismissed. History is not understood to follow a single logic or line of development, neither is it assumed to be universal and by virtue of this it is not to be considered singular (Gunn, 2006; Jenkins, 1995). As with the textual or linguistic turn (Lyotard, 1993; Jenkins, 1995; Gunn, 2006; Perry, 2002), the emphasis is on understanding reality of the past as mediated entirely through our knowledge of it, thus through text and language. Because the past is gone and history is understood as its textual representation, it becomes impossible to verify history. History, then, is understood as knowledge of the past (Jenkins, 1991; Munslow, 2010; Kalela, 2012). And history, as the representation of the past, has no referent in 'the world out there' to which we can compare it for accuracy (Jenkins, 2003; Ankersmit, 1997). Historical truth claims, objective history, fixed meanings, and certainty are substituted by a privileging of subjective meaning, fluid interpretations, undecidability, and reinterpretation. The latter has aroused criticism among modernist historians as it undercuts that there is a reality to which the history may correspond (Zagorin, 2009; Braun, 1997).

Because the past is assumed as an absent present and history is knowledge or representation of the past, epistemological questions feature quite prominently in postmodern histories (Gunn, 2006; Jenkins, 1991, 1999). With the textual turn, attention is drawn to the *textual conditions* through which all knowledge of the past is produced and the possibilities and limits it offers for historical understanding (Jenkins, 1995). Postmodernism gives rise to the modernist fear concerning our knowledge of the past: history as fact or fiction debate. Not surprisingly, many postmodernists side with history as fiction (White, 1973; Jenkins, 1995, 2003). Thus all historical representations assume a fictive nature, "the contents of which are as much *invented* as *found* and the forms of which have more in common with their counterparts in literature than they have with those in the sciences" (White, 1985: 82).

In his notion of Metahistory, White (1985) offers that Western academic conventions, which have given shape to the academic enterprise of history, have come with modes of emplotment. Metahistory, in some senses, is a way of taking stock of the existing discourses or modes of emplotment that constitute history. In White's text *Metahistory* (1973: 2) he questions "the epistemological status of historical explanations" or knowledge. He presents a typology of modes of emplotment referring to "the way a sequence of events is fashioned into a narrative that is gradually seen to be of particular kind" (Jenkins, 1995: 159). Emplotment offers advice on the ordering of traces, or the encodation through which the past is narrated or chronicled as history (White, 1985; Jenkins, 1995). Through the historian's mode of emplotment, a "meaningful form" is imposed on a "meaningless past" (Jenkins, 1995: 137). Much to the dismay of modernist historians who profess ideological neutrality, White (1985) argues that all historians, modernists and postmodernists alike, adopt an ideologically positioned mode of emplotment that influences how the past figures as history. After all, to say that one is not ideologically positioned is to make a comment about one's ideological position.

Thus the point is less that historians and novelists are similar because each invents traces or events but their resemblance lies in that each chooses a mode of emplotment, which gives the text meaning beyond the traces themselves. The past offers no inherent mode in which to organize the traces into historical form. Those modes of emplotment are given to us today, as an outcome of our disciplinary endeavors and plural ideological regimes. The fact that there are many ideological regimes, each reflecting particular political interests, leads to the construction of plural histories (Jenkins, 1991, 1995).

Postmodern representations of the past-as-history: plural

The idea of one past and many ways to represent it is what is intended by plural histories (Jenkins, Morgan & Munslow, 2007; Gunn, 2006). Embracing and celebrating this is a central tenet of postmodernism (Jenkins, 2003). To say that histories are plural is not only to comment on the fact that various ideological commitments and modes of emplotment give choices to historians in how to construct history. It is also to suggest that historical interpretations are no longer fixed. Through postmodernism, histories become "contingent, arbitrary and logically unstable" (Jenkins, 2003: 21). Instead of acting as the final authority on the past, histories now have no closure. They are continually at risk of being re-figured or re-interpreted by readers as soon as they are written. The question thus arises, how to deal with "variations on history" (Rigney, 2007: 152)? Whereas modernists solve discrepancies between historical accounts by consulting the traces or archival documents, postmodernists feel that variations on the past should be accepted as an inherent part of history (Jenkins, 1995, 2003).

Plurality is also a result of the postmodern treatment of traces, evidence and facts. Whereas modernist historians assume their facts or traces are 'given' or 'found', postmodernists believe they are created through the kinds of questions historians pose (White, 1985). The subject of the historical investigation causes certain traces to assume relevance over others. What counts as relevant, of course, is the choice of the historian. The historian plays a role in what is read into the trace, as well as the meaning it will contribute to the narrative (Jenkins, 1995, 2003). Instead of assuming that the facts speak for themselves (Kellner, 1997) or that they act as a "magnifying glass" through which we view the past (Ankersmit, 1997: 287), postmodernists emphasize the choice of certain facts over others, the variety of combinations they may take, and the many meanings that can be derived from them as they are fashioned into history (Brown, 2005). Plural

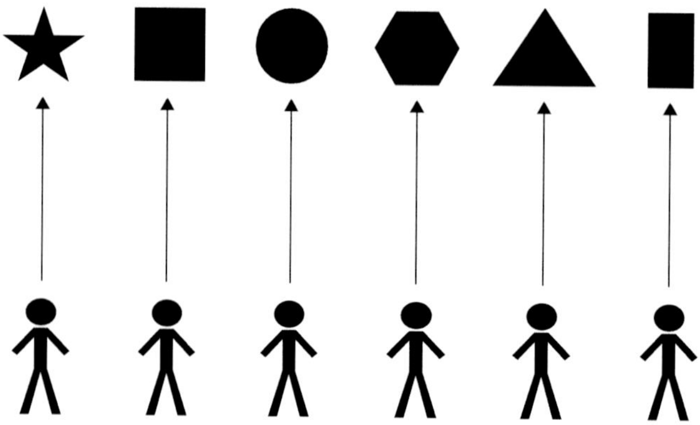

Figure 12.2 Plural histories

histories serve to liberate history from the past, and open the conditions of possibility for the many ways the past can feature as history. Indeed, the emancipatory potential of history lies in its plurality (Jenkins, Morgan & Munslow, 2007; Jenkins, 1995).

While postmoderns have celebrated pluralism, others have instead critiqued it. Modernists for example, have feared plural histories due to the lack of moral ground it offers for the judgment of past events (Brown, 2005). This is a significant point concerning relativism that I take up below. Others, including Mol (1999, 2002), have suggested that in creating plural accounts of the past, postmoderns and moderns actually reveal their similarities. Mol's reasoning is that to construct plural narratives, historians *gather* around a particular phenomenon or event and thus create knowledge from each their own individuated standpoints. The result then, is many historians, each engaged in *their own* crafting of history, each acknowledging that due to their own perspective on the object under study, an independent and different history is likely to emerge, thus a different object (see Figure 12.2). It is, as Jenkins (2009: 5) notes, a condition where "historians can make the past 'historical' any way they like, that is to say, in their *own* image." Each "perspective remains 'absolutely singular' because the subject's gaze is always constitutively in the object gazed at" (Jenkins, 2009: 12). In effect, each historian constructs her own spatially based 'singular' history. Each resulting story is assessed for validity on its own terms, as it is evaluated according to internal criteria and the bounds of its own perspective. Thus, despite the benefits of the textual turn for history, such as acknowledging all history as text as well as the notion of plural histories, some have criticized postmodern history for resembling modernist histories in the construction of their own version of a historical 'singularity' (Mol, 1999).

Before proceeding, three noteworthy points are highlighted in anticipation of the discussion on amodernism that follows. First, not only do postmoderns describe a process where it is 'knowledge' of the object that is being constructed, but, and this is the second point, that knowledge making occurs in the mind of the observer's 'cognition.' Thus, history making is a 'cognitive' and embrained act (Law, 2008). Finally, in focusing their gaze on the object (in this case the past), it is the 'latter and resulting knowledge of it' that assumes a privileged position.

Postmodern relationship of past to history: relative

As noted, plurality in history has been criticized for its potential in leading to moral,[2] political, and epistemological relativism (Brown, 2005). Relativism here refers to a type of knowledge whose value can only be assessed when understood in accordance with the perspective from which it has emerged. The issue, as previously noted, is that because the multitudes of perspectives give rise to many somewhat unrelated narratives, these are assumed to coexist (Jenkins, 2009). When it is the very notion of coexistence that is celebrated, there is no way to judge the good from the bad and claims to historical objectivity are undermined (Green & Troup, 1999). All representations of the past are thus assumed as "equally representative of reality and therefore equally fictitious" (Green & Troup, 1999: 300). Little emphasis is placed on evaluating either their relationship to one another or their legitimacy according to any universally accepted and neutral criteria. This view undercuts any possibility for absolute truth where one history is assumed as unconditionally valid.

Modernists have long feared "the troubling specter of relativism" (Zagorin, 2009: 64) for providing "anything goes" histories where historians "say whatever" they like (Elton, 1997: 179) and there are "no ground(s) even in principle for acknowledging a contradiction between an assertion and a denial" (Lang, 1997: 426). On the other hand, postmoderns have offered that it is the absence of relativism that should be feared (Brown, 2005; Jenkins, 1999; Munslow, 2009). Its absence "allows hegemonies of illiberal culture to blossom, and encourages the training in a History discipline that permits the principle of incontestable Historical certainty" (Brown, 2005: 175). Postmoderns offer that relativism "is not merely unavoidable, but it is valuable precisely because it impairs any historian's commitment to discovering 'the true nature of the past'" (Munslow, 2009: 318).

Whether desired or not, relativism has been suggested as a path leading to perspectivalism. Perspectivalism suggests "each observer sees according to its own point of view" which means that each point of view is irreducible and equally privileged (Latour, 1988: 14). While we construct and read from our own perspective, this plurality of approaches "doesn't lead to subjectivism because we can all agree what we have different perspectives *on*" (Jenkins, 2009: 12). In some senses, a form of consensus emerges. Each is entitled to her own narrative and all agree that there are no grounds for claiming that yours is any better than mine (Law, 2008). What is of interest for our upcoming discussion of amodernism is the following: while it could be claimed that historical representations are grounded by the historian that provide them, I will argue that they otherwise 'float' above the 'practices' that have influenced their construction.

Postmodern treatment of context: put events in context to do history

The potential of history has often been described in terms of the role it can play in placing organizations and their present practices in their context of emergence. For example, Jenkins (2003: 35) notes, "that the past/history really is sort of a containing object which we are somehow *in* ... the past is both all around us and in us." Contexts are used "to frame events" (Jenkins, 2009: 6). For postmodern historians, the past as history acts as the context, or the container in which the present is assumed to take place. Historians are tasked with providing interpretations of the past whose "link with the present" serves to illuminate or explain a present condition (Hobsbawm, 1997: 214). After all, the value of studying the past lies in its explanatory role or its capacity in "providing perspectives on the present that contribute to the solution of problems peculiar to our own time" (White, 1985: 41; Jacques, 1996). Postmodernists prefer present-centered histories (Mannheim, 1985; Jenkins, 1995). These stand in contrast with those of a modernist kind where history is created free from the biases of the present context, with the past studied for its own sake on its own terms.

Whilst moderns have criticized present-centered histories, postmoderns have argued that not only are they desirable but unavoidable. Though many extant reasons may explain this, White

(1985) and Jenkins (1995) have each stressed that it is precisely the methodological tools and modes of emplotment used by historians 'today' that give structure and meaning to past events. Those tools, if only by the fact that they are developed through historians' conventional practice, lead to knowing the past as history – constituted through those very conventional practices. Because the latter is inescapable, postmoderns argue that present-centered histories are our lot.

As the above paragraphs attest, historians' treatment of context is itself contested. For example, though Jenkins (1995) argued for present-centered histories, he also suggests that contexts can be arbitrarily figured. After all, you can always "'produce another context', you can simply add 'more in' and historians can never know if they have constructed the 'right' context and filled it with the 'correct' substance required to yield, say, explanatory meanings of a historical kind" (Jenkins, 2009: 6). Others have critiqued historians' treatment of context due to its assumed continuity, stability and the fact that it is treated as having an uncontested, already established existence (prior to our efforts to define it). After all, might not historians' practices construct the context? Might not the social context actually feature as the past as history? These points are taken up in the section discussing amodernism.

Role of the postmodern historian

Though the role that the postmodern historian plays in the craft of history has been touched upon in previous sections, a few points are worth reinforcing before proceeding further. The first point is that in the craft of postmodern history the historian is assumed as the 'creator' of the knowledge of the past. That history is cognitive, or embrained, is highlighted in Jenkins' (2009: 7) statement that history is "an act of the imagination." Similarly, Hobsbawm (1997: 10) emphasizes the cognitive nature of history when he notes that the "problem for historians is to analyze the nature of this 'sense of the past' in society."

Not only is it worth mentioning that it is the responsibility of the 'historian' to assemble the past as history, but it is the historian, not the past, who dictates what happens in history (Fox-Genovese, 1997; Jenkins, 2003). Collingwood (1956: 236) articulates the point succinctly when he notes that it "is the artist, and not nature, that is responsible for what goes into the picture." Given that the past is assumed as shapeless, it is up to historians to impose a narrative structure on the past according to the various modes of ordering (or emplotment) made available by a community of historians (Jenkins, 1995; White, 1985). Thus instead of focusing on establishing a detached view, as would modernists, postmodern history places emphasis on the individual historian's choices (Kalela, 2012). As noted, the historian faces many choices during the process in which history is constructed from its traces (Jenkins, 1995, 2003; White, 1985; Munslow, 2009; Kellner, 1997). Above all, the craft of history is never a neutral task, as the historian's position on the ideological spectrum influences how s/he tells the tale. The historian's intentions inevitably influence the nature of the tale told, the historian is always involved in the moment of writing (White, 1985; Kellner, 1997).

What is noteworthy in postmodern history is that historians reflexively acknowledge their presence in the moment of writing. Whereas the modernist historian writes from a detached, third-person voice where the ordering hand of the historian is never acknowledged, the postmodern historian situates the history as an outcome of her/his scholarly efforts. In doing so, s/he stresses that it could always be otherwise, thus another historian could configure the facts as history differently. The latter serves to de-privilege the historian as an authoritative voice in the doing of history. This opens the opportunity for reflexivity where it is possible to reflect "critically on the politics of knowledge inherent in any given interpretation or position" (Gunn, 2006: 3). In the quest for reflexivity, postmodern historians, including White (1985), suggest that historians must acknowledge their chosen mode of emplotment as one of many alternatives. Doing so means being transparent about what informed their choice as well as illustrating how it flavors the content of the resulting history.

Past modern history, past postmodern history, the end of history?

As the previous paragraphs have illustrated, postmodern historiography offers a thorough critique of modernism. Based on the issues outlined above, postmodern historiographers have been quick to signal the death of modernist history (Jenkins, 2009). While postmodernism has 'offered' much critique, it has also been its subject. In particular, some have questioned whether it "has become at least partially exhausted" (Calás & Smircich, 1999: 658). These critiques have probed whether the moment of postmodernism has passed and if it is now time to open "up space for other theoretical approaches to appear" (Calás & Smircich, 1999: 649). The critique of postmodernism has spread to postmodern historiography too. The latter has been most intensely pursued by Jenkins (2009: 16) who offers, "we can now live without histories of either a modernist or a postmodernist kind" (Jenkins, 2009: 16). In denouncing modernist and postmodernist histories, Jenkins claims (2009: 17) "without regrets or nostalgia ... we can now wave history goodbye and look forward to a future – which is where we all have to live after all – unburdened and unspoilt by the historicized/historical past."

This drastic signal of the end of history of "any kind" is only somewhat surprising. In many senses, the rationale inherent in Jenkins "end of history thesis" (Munslow, 2009: 315) is similar to that offered by Foucault's (1979) anti-historical stance upon which were premised his notions of archaeology and genealogy (Burrell, 1988). Though Foucault did emphasize the "importance of an historical understanding" it was sought after to foster an understanding and reconstruction of the "present" and not the "past" (Burrell, 1988: 225). Thus, Foucault's histories of the present "traces connections among the arbitrary rather than the intentional, the accidental rather than the planned, in the historical constitution of contemporary practices. These connections denaturalize everyday activities and institutions that we take for granted" (Calás & Smircich, 1999: 655).

It is this very attitude that Jenkins (2009: 18) adopts as he asks whether there is "any reason why we ought to study things under the aspect of their past-ness rather than under the aspect of their present-ness, which is the aspect under which everything offers itself for our contemplation immediately?" Should we follow Foucault (1979) and Jenkins (1999, 2009) in assuming that the study of history is dead? Is it time, as suggested by Latour (1999b: 146), to decide between either rendering the discipline obsolete or rather time for 'reformat(ing) the question' of history? In the sections below, I attempt Latour's (1999b: 169) solution and try to "historicize more, not less."

Amodern management and organizational history

> It would have been better if histories had never been modern.
>
> *(Jenkins, 2009: 15)*

I begin the discussion of amodernism with a quick review of some of the critical arguments made to date, particularly noting that postmodernism developed as a reaction and utter rejection of modernism. To that effect, we can understand the composition of postmodernism as largely influenced, if not limited by, modernism. Amodernism, as a conceptual position, shares in the postmodern critique of modernism but goes further and argues that instead of seeking to move past (or post) the *theoretical damage* imposed by the condition of modernism, and thus also to be limited by it, that "it would have been better if histories had never been modern" (Jenkins, 2009: 15). It is time to consider an alternative historiographical space. One that is neither modern nor postmodern. Following Latour (1990, 1993), we can call it amodern.

Amodernism, drawing on the work of Bruno Latour (1990, 1993), constructs a theoretical position that is 'prior' to that of the condition of the moderns and postmoderns. It proposes a theoretical space that is untouched by the rigid disciplinary categorical apparatus of Kant, unaffected by modernist tendencies to universalize and essentialize, to avoid producing accounts that are reductionist, linear, natural, neutral, or written in the third-person.

Latour's conceptualization of amodernism

Latour's notion of amodernism, as considered in the early 1990s (Latour, 1990, 1993), is an alternative conceptualization developed as part of a broader movement whereby the methods of anthropology were used to problematize the enterprise of the natural sciences (Latour & Woolgar, 1979). Although Latour's notion of amodernism was perhaps not explicitly intended as a comment on history, or an historical category for that matter, contained within it are consequences for history quite distinct from modern or postmodern approaches. These implications are helpful in developing an alternative space for 'doing' history. In the paragraphs that follow, I take the liberty of borrowing Latour's notion of amodernism as a label (though I am conscious of the dangers in doing so) to describe a distinct and hopefully fruitful alternative conceptualization of historiography.

Latour's notion of amodernism stems from a disregard of Kant's rigid disciplinary categories imposed through modernism in which the 'social' world became the object of study of the 'social sciences' and the 'natural' world that of the 'natural sciences'. These categories shaped what each was to study, thus the world of objects or non-humans became the responsibility of the natural sciences while the world of subjects or humans that of the social sciences. Amodernism, for Latour (1993), represents the desire to transcend this human–nonhuman divide by focusing on the relations established between them – 'in practice.' This new constitutive relation re-defined the "divided loyalty between humans and non-humans" (Latour, 1990: 156). Whereas "the old settlement limit(ed) historicity to subjects and ban(ned) it for nonhumans" (Latour, 1999b: 156), the amodern approach looks at the multitude of configurations that human–nonhuman associations take as they engage in practice. Studying the natural and the social from the perspective of distinct categories neglects the fact that in practice we only ever encounter combinations of human–nonhuman actors. In practice, actors are not isolated as the categorical ways we use to study them imply. After all, reserving history for the 'social' denies that "nature shares with society the same historicity" (Latour, 1996: 89). Latour (1993) argues that this relational constitution more appropriately positions the social as composed of human–nonhuman associations and that this was the case prior to the development of modernism – and thus also prior to postmodernism. He offers that any illusion to the contrary was produced by virtue of the convincing categorization of knowledge and knowing imposed by and naturalized through modernism. For Latour *we have never been modern* and by virtue of this, he denies that we could have ever been postmodern, "since this would imply a belief that we have been what we have never been" therefore his (1990: 164) explanation of the social settles on amodernism.

Latour's work has garnered much attention with many scholars from various fields drawing on, and also further developing, his theoretical contributions (Callon, 1986, 1999; Law, 1994, 2008; Law and Hetherington, 1998, 1999; Mol, 1999, 2002; Haraway, 1988, 2004). Recently, some have even extended Latour's work toward theorizing and doing history in M&OS (Durepos, Mills & Helms Mills, 2008; Bruce & Nyland, 2011; Durepos & Mills, 2012a, 2012b; Durepos, Mills &

Weatherbee, 2012; Myrick, Helms Mills & Mills, 2013) as well as information systems (Bonner, 2013). What unites these contributions is the similarity of their ontological and epistemological orientations.

Amodern ontological and epistemological orientation

Amodernism shifts our focus away from the modernist necessity for accurate representations of reality (realism), or the relativist nature of a reality mediated through knowledge and text (the anti-realism of the textual turn) to 'practices.' Focusing on practice means tracing the many shapes that that human–nonhuman associations take when engaged in activity (Mol, 2002). If history "making is an everyday practice" (Kalela, 2012: xi), why not study the various compositions it takes in its situated practices?

To study the various compositions that an object may take in situated practices is to study how it is 'performed' or 'enacted' through those practices (Law, 2008; Mol, 1999, 2002; Latour, 1999b; Law and Hetherington, 1998; Law & Urry, 2004; Tsekeris 2010). Whilst postmoderns have emphasized "representation" through "knowledge" of a phenomenon, the amoderns focus on "enactment" through "performance". Understanding history as but one of many "representations" of the past would imply falling back "on the divide between ontological and epistemological questions that we" can begin to "abandon" through amodernism (Latour, 1999b: 145–46). Abandoning this separation is encouraging if we consider the "ontological character of representation" where "representation not only describes but also works upon the world that it described" (Law & Benschop, 1997: 175). Amodernism considers a "philosophical shift in which knowledge is no longer treated primarily as referential, as a set of statements about reality, but as a practice that interferes with other practices. It therefore participates *in* reality" (Mol, 2002: 153).

We are not simply talking about "knowledge of realities, but also realities themselves, that are generated in the practices of production" (Law, 2008: 36). Thus, it becomes less about acknowledging the historian's gaze or perspective to understand the politics inherent in knowledge production of the past. No longer are we only interested in "different perspectives on a single reality" but in the "enactment of different realities" (Law and Urry, 2004: 397). The focus of study becomes more about how to follow "objects while they are being enacted in practice" (Mol, 2002: 152). And if practice becomes our point of entry for understanding how the past becomes history, epistemology loses its postmodern reverence and questions of epistemology are decentered, if not bypassed. Perhaps it is time to begin to ask ourselves "whether 'knowing' is the metaphor that we need" (Law, 2008: 3). Can we still get away with explanations of the social that reduce everything to text? If, as Mol (2002: vii–viii) suggests, epistemology "is concerned with reference" and "representations" only, how do we account for practices and the multiple enactments that an object may take in these practices? How do we account for the fact that objects have effects? While the latter query invites questions of ontology to assume center stage it is far from resembling the realism of modernism, as "ontology is no longer a monist whole." It becomes "ontology-in-practice" (Mol, 2002: 157).

In the shift of emphasis in the realm of ontology what becomes of interest is how any study of the social both "constitutes and describes its object of interest" (Calás & Smircich, 1999: 663). As Mol (2010: 260) explains, actors "are enacted, enabled, and adapted by their associates while in their turn enacting, enabling and adapting these" (Mol, 2010: 260). For the amoderns, the point of interest is less how a researcher comes to 'know' an object (decentering researchers' perspective), and more about how a particular practice "attunes to, interacts with, and shapes its subjects in its various and varied practices" (Mol, 2002: vii). Of concern is how a practice, institution, or activity "'enacts' the object of its concern and treatment" (Mol, 2002: vii). An amodern historiography then, would focus on practices to understand how history as a nonhuman actor assumes its composition – how it is enacted.

The social sciences, and by virtue of this the historical enterprise itself, play a central role in the composition that history assumes in practice. It is the case where, as Law and Urry (2004: 390–91) suggest, "social inquiry and its methods are productive: they (help to) make social realities and social worlds." Following Law (2008: 5), what is argued is that social science methods "produce the reality they describe" and do so in a "wide range of locations" (Tsekeris 2010: 141). If it is as Law and Urry (2004: 392) suggest, namely that methods "participate in, reflect upon, and enact the social" past, then this has profound implications for undertaking research of any kind (Law, 2008). This includes how we 'do' history. Perhaps a useful starting point for historical reconsideration then is to contemplate considering history an 'actor' (Latour, 1999a).

Before entertaining this challenge it may be useful to describe what is entailed by an actor. Actors are heterogeneous in that they hold intact a combination of humans and nonhumans who come to pursue like interests and thus come to act as one. Their stability as an actor takes effort and depends on the enrollment of whatever actors are deemed necessary to achieve the task. As Latour (1999b: 311) explains, it "is through trials that actors are defined." Thus, actors are never understood as a 'fait accompli',[3] but instead as "a set of associations … made of shifting compromises" (Latour, 1999b: 163). They are actors in the 'doing'.

Because an actor is "in itself the conceptual frame" (Calás & Smircich, 1999: 663), what becomes worthy of interest is a focus on the series of trials of actors. These include "the complex and controversial nature of what it is for an actor to come into existence. The key is to define an 'actor by what it does' or what it has done" (Latour, 1999b: 303). In some senses, the emphasis is on tracing an actor's emergence. The actor assumes its composition as an outcome of itself. Its emergence arises from the chains of translation through which the actor has traveled. It arises from "the work through which actors modify, displace, and translate their various and contradictory interests" (Latour, 1999b: 311). After all, everything that the actor touches along its temporal course of practice alters the composition of the actor and each "change in the series of transformations that composes the reference is going to make a difference" (Latour, 1999b: 150). However, our task is not to document the travel of a single, untouched entity through time but instead to document the "modifications of the ingredients that compose an articulation of entities" over time (Latour, 1999b: 162). It is the aim of amodern history to trace or (re)assemble the composition of an actor and thus, to 'do' history.

The composition of an actor is never accomplished. The various topographical arrangements through which the past can be performed or enacted as history remain open. They are configured in the moment of performance as we 'do' history. In fact, their performance reveals the actors' topographical arrangement. More to the point, it is at the moment of enactment or performance of the past as history that its conditions of possibility reside. As Mol (1999) notes, those conditions of possibility are not given but are in the making – continually – in the possibilities of configurations in which history can be performed. What is of interest then, is "how it is that the representational practices that make up worlds – and so the worlds made up in those practices – co-ordinate themselves" (Law & Benschop, 1997: 175). What is also of critical interest is the specific topographical arrangements that come to assume durability as these help to make certain enactments of history more 'real' than others (Law & Urry, 2004). These travel through time, they enroll some actors, displace others and are performed differently depending on different sets of practices.

An example of an 'academic paper' illustrates this idea. From the point at which its constitutive ideas are developed to the final product, the academic paper travels through various mediums and is touched by a multitude of hands. These include but are not limited to conference reviewers, a patient and concerned author, journal reviewers, and academics in the conference audience where the paper is presented. The point is that the paper travels, and is altered (though also alters those met) at each point in the chain. Thus, it displaces and is displaced. The paper will change because it will be altered based on the reviews. The content will likely change each time it is presented at a conference or research exposition as those who receive the ideas interpret it varyingly. The reviewers are also displaced when they encounter new ideas presented in the paper. Furthermore, the paper will be performed differently based on the set of practices in which it is enacted. The ideas performed in a conference presentation will present a different enactment of the ideas than those inscribed on paper. This example features one academic paper (one actor) and different (more than one) performances of the same academic paper or actor. What we have acknowledged is that the actor is more than one, but less than many. This raises for us the issue of multiplicity.

Amodern nature of representations of the past and/or history: multiple

Whittle and Spicer (2008) have offered that analyses that focus on multiplicity have yet to make their way into M&OS – a circumstance threatening the potential to develop analytical tools that facilitate those very analyses. Amodernism offers a call for tracing multiplicity. Multiplicity stands in contrast to singularity and plurality. It implies "more than one but less than many" (Law, 1999: 11). To say that an object, theory, or history is multiple is to imply that the same object may be performed differently in various practices or relations (Mol, 1999, 2002). Thus we are not talking about one singular history produced by the historians' community as their opinions on 'what happened' converge. This would imply the production of one (dominant, hegemonic) history by many historians (see Figure 12.1). Less so are we talking about the process through which historians create different histories by virtue of viewing them from different perspectives (see Figure 12.2). As noted, the latter leads to what Mol (1999) calls perspectivalism. Perspectivalism is amendable to different eyes on the same object, each constructing 'a different knowledge' of the object by virtue of the choice of perspective. These types of analyses leave the object itself untouched and instead focus on 'knowledge' of the object.

Multiplicity takes us away from the dualism of singularity and plurality (Law, 1999). It moves us away from 'knowledge construction,' from 'singular realities,' and from the desire for 'many unrelated singular' versions of perspectivalism. Instead of merely 'observing' reality, the focus shifts toward 'enactment' and 'performance' of reality (of the past) itself, as it happens in practice (Mol, 1999, 2002; Law, 2008). Instead of merely trying to 'represent' the past as history, the focus is on how it is manipulated in practice. The emphasis is on how historians inevitably interfere with the object of analysis as they partake in its performance (Mol, 1999, 2002). This is multiplicity. What becomes of interest is how one version of the past is enacted as history in different sets of practices. As Law (2008: 55) notes, we are not dealing with different perspectives on one object, but "with different objects produced in *different sets of methods assemblages*." Multiplicity refers to the process through which those very practices give each enactment of the past, each history, a different shape, order, essence or feel (see Figure 12.3). We are talking about the enactment of different versions of the past, and calling these histories. Thus, they are not different histories, but different versions of the same phenomena. Histories are "more than one but less than many," they are "somewhere in between" (Law, 1999: 12).

Figure 12.3 Multiple histories

To speak of multiplicity of history is to foreground the 'practices' in which history 'making' takes place. Instead of "understanding objects as the central points of focus of different people's perspectives" the emphasis centers on understanding histories as "things manipulated in practices" (Mol, 2002: 4). To speak of multiplicity is to make a point about 'enactment' and 'performance' as opposed to mere 'representation.' We are reminded again of the lost reverence of postmodern epistemology in favour of amodern ontology (Mol, 2002). But if reality itself is multiplied, if the past as history is multiplied, then what are we to make of the relationship between 'different versions' that histories may take as they are performed (Mol, 1999, 2002; Law & Urry, 2004; Law, 2008)? What becomes of analytic concern are the relations between different enactments of the past as history, as well as the relations within which one enactment comes into being. This solicits from us new questions, such as what version of an object can be performed by virtue of the set of relations in which it is localized? With this, different enactments of one history can be understood as outcomes of their relations of investigation (Law & Benschop, 1997; Law & Urry, 2004). Histories then come to be considered as relational actors.

Amodern relationship of past and history: relational

To say that histories are relational actors implies a shift of focus on their situatedness, and more specifically, how they assume their composition by virtue of it. Histories as relational actors are not facts with an essence in and of themselves but instead assume their constitution by virtue of the relations in which they reside. As Mol (2002: 54) suggests, "nothing ever 'is' alone. *To be is to be related*." Relationalism gives us an opportunity to bring histories "down to earth" (Law & Mol, 2001: 609–10; Law, 2000: 2) not, however, to its roots or point of origin, nor to its foundation. Instead, relationalism re-associates (or re-lates) histories within the relations of its constitution. Thus, to speak of relationalism is to acknowledge "relations produce effects, including material effects" (Law, 2001: 3). Some of these include inscription devices. Histories, too, are inscription devices that are outcomes of relations. Viewing them as such moves us away from universal histories that are unconditionally true and toward those grounded in their relations of investigation (Law & Mol, 2001; Law & Urry, 2004; Law, 2008). Histories then become localized (Law, 1994).

Relationalism moves us quite far from the realism of modernism and the relativism of postmodernism (Law & Urry, 2004; Tsekeris 2010). Whilst postmodernism introduced the emancipatory potential that could arise from plural knowledge of the past, such analyses were critiqued "for their lack of strong political engagement and for their remoteness from 'the real world'" (Calás & Smircich, 1999: 659). The plurality of postmodern histories foregrounded an emphasis on constructing many 'knowledges of the past,' but lost in the background was the notion that each actor participates in reality itself. Lost was the notion that each assumed its composition by virtue of its inherent relations of production. Also lost were the "complex relations between the different modes of ordering" realities of the past (Law, 2001: 2). The relativism of postmodernism led to many disconnected, independent narratives floating about, thus untied and ungrounded. Relationalism ties analyses "down to earth" (Law & Mol, 2001: 609–10; Law, 2000: 2) and it situates histories as enacted outcomes of their relations, which have 'real' material effects (Law, 2008). To say this is to avoid falling prey to the monolithic realism of modernism. As Law and Urry (2004: 395–96) note, the

> argument is neither relativist nor realist. Instead it is that the real is produced in thoroughly non-arbitrary ways, in dense and extended sets of relations ... In sum, we're saying that the world we know in social science is both real and it is produced.

If reality, or in this case the past as history, assumes an ontological presence with *real* material consequences, then how do we, as co-participants in its production account for its process of enactment? To begin with a shift of focus is necessary. Instead of assuming that it is "entities that come first and relations among them only subsequently" (Emirbayer, 1997: 281), relations enter the foreground (Habers, Mol & Stollmeyer, 2002; Law, 2008; Tsekeris 2010). Instead of focusing on stable states, or on one actor, the emphasis moves to the relations that allow the actor to assume and maintain its composition. To focus on relations implies to look "*in-between*" (Latour, 1988: 35). In the "*betweenness*," "everything is suspended" and "unfinished" (Cooper, 2005: 1691–92). More importantly then, relations need to be seen as "active" (Cooper, 2005: 1704).

Relationalism emphasizes movement and fluidity. Relationalism re-tools analyses to view actors in practice, involved in building, connecting, translating, and associating. It is in this way that histories are produced. After all, as Law (2008: 58) notes, realities and in this case realities of the past "are not explained by practices and beliefs but are instead produced in them. They are produced, and have a life, in relations." Relations are revealed in practice (Mol, 2002), as actors form associations, and are subject to displacement (Law, 2000, 2001). Implied in this is that those associations are a potential site of change for actors. The "*betweenness*" (Cooper, 2005: 1691–92) of actors is a site of oscillation (Law & Benschop, 1997), where one has the potential to become another. But a condition of latency and undecidability precedes the moment where actor 'becomes another,' before one's composition is altered or displaced. Thus, at the site of relations, in the space in-between, resides latency and the possibility of what may become (Cooper, 2005).

Latency implies potential for what can be manifest in the relations of production as to "say that something is latent means that it is unclear, indefinite and even nebulous" (Cooper, 2005: 1693). Latency "suggests something dormant, quiescent, virtual, waiting to be expressed, as well as something malleable, plastic and even formable" (Cooper, 2005: 1693). The site of relations, thus of latency, "exceeds all representation" (Cooper, 2005: 1693), it can "accommodate a multiplicity of mutable forms" (Cooper, 2005: 1701). The space in-between actors, in-between the past and history, or in-between how actors perform history is one of becoming, of potentiality and one whose conditions of possibility are open (Cooper, 2005; Law, 1999). It is in this space that the past performed as history assumes its composition. This space 'in-between' is inherently exciting as it allows us to dream of what may become (Latour, 1999a: 19). For it is at this site where the potential for translation, transformation and displacement resides (Latour, 1999a) and it is at this site where the past is translated as history, or a history is translated and reinterpreted as it is read (Cooper, 2005).

It is in these relations that actors assume their altered composition. An actor's multiple compositions across time, its trials and trajectories, emerge by virtue of the many actors encountered and relations established (Law, 2008; Law & Mol, 1995; Emirbayer, 1997). Indeed it is in "these stories [that] the bits and pieces achieve significance *in relation to others*" (Law & Mol, 1995: 276). As Law (1999: 3) explains, actors "take their form and acquire their attributes as a result of their relations with other entities" (Law, 1999: 3). Their composition is performed in and by virtue of those relations (Cooper, 2005; Latour, 1996, 1999b; Law, 2000; Mol, 2010).

How do we understand the composition of a history as an actor? How do we characterize its constitution? If the composition of the socio-past as history is made of actors, then clues of its composition are formulated through tracing the relations or associations that allow actors to hold a particular shape (Latour, 1986). In short, we must "trace connections" (Law & Mol, 1995: 291). We must re-assemble the associations that hold historical actors intact. We must trace actors' trajectories, their chain of associations, and bring our focus to the many translations that occurred at each link in the chain. Tracing the trail of actors' associations gives us insight into how these actors perform the socio-past as history. Following "the actors themselves" gives us insight into the composition of history (Latour, 2005: 12). Doing history then means taking part in tracing the connections that hold the socio-past together in a given constitution. It means focusing on the ties that glue the elements of the socio-past and looking specifically at which elements are altered through these associations. In doing so, we are not only sketching associations but also unconsciously tracing a 'context' as it is the practices of actors themselves that create their own context.

Amodern treatment of context: practices of actors create the context

If histories are created in relations, then it is those very relations that act as the glue that holds histories intact. Histories come to be viewed as an outcome of relational actors engaged in social practices. The way histories assume their composition is similar to the 'social context' (Latour, 2005). Latour (1986: 273) explains that the social or society "is not the referent of an ostensive definition discovered by social scientist." A negative consequence of this modern notion of the social is that it "designate[s] a stabilized state of affairs" to that which should be understood as an unstable, unfolding performance (Latour, 2005: 1). Latour (1986: 276) explains that the social "is not what holds us together, it is what is held together." What is held together are various heterogeneous actors engaged in practices. Latour's (1986, 2005) conceptualization of the 'social' is therefore critically useful in understanding how the practices of actors, as they are engaged in performing the past as history, create context.

To summarize, the principle idea in its most basic form is that "any practice creates its own context" (Latour, 1990: 169). This notion defiantly disturbs popular modern and post-modern treatment of historical context. Whereas moderns felt it possible to reconstruct the historical context of an event to foster a greater understanding of it, postmoderns celebrated histories for their ability to illuminate phenomena in the present context. In both instances, the context is assumed as a 'container' in which we place phenomena to foster greater understanding of it.

Amodernism refutes the 'putting' of something into the social context or container to understand it because the 'social context' or 'container' is what actors produce when they perform the past as history. Latour (1988: 27) explains that no "matter how sociologists and historians love to put texts, ideas, and events *in* their context, this context is always made up of shifted characters." Since the context is always being assembled before our very eyes, it is not possible to put those actors within it to explain them. In short, the context, either past or present, could never be used to explain phenomena. The context or social "are instead what need explaining" (Latour, 1986: 271). A series of different questions then emerge. For one, what series of associations between actors hold the social, or social past (socio-past) for that matter, together? Another is to ask what is the topographical configuration through which the social past oscillates as history? Or again, how does the socio-past as history keep its form? The socio-past as history, in this sense, is far from the context in which everything is 'framed', it is rather "construed as one of the many connecting elements circulating inside tiny conduits" (Latour, 2005: 4–5). The socio-past as history is what is created through our very efforts to define it (Latour, 2005).

If seen this way the articulation of the socio-past as history becomes the major puzzle. This is what needs to be explained, as opposed to being used to provide or frame the explanation.[4] If the socio-past as history is an outcome of the social context, its composition is what needs questioning, and not what is used to formulate the answer (Latour, 2005). For my amodern argument, the socio-past as history is not only an outcome of the social but at one with it. History making is a 'social' practice.

Role of the amodern historian: co-participant of the practices in which history is produced

If history making is a social practice, then how does this impact the role of the historian? So far, we have assumed that amodern histories are what heterogeneous actors inevitably enact as they speak of the past, or behave in light of a past. The consequence of this for understanding the historians' role is twofold. The first follows from Latour (2005), where it is implied that to talk of histories is to make a comment on the composition of the social as it happens today. Far from being assumed or pre-given, the composition of the social is enacted by heterogeneous actors and not reserved solely for 'human historians.' The second is related to the first in that it offers a comment on who is engaged in history making as well as where it occurs. Assuming an amodern lens with the focus on practices (of all kinds) means history making is said to occur in all types of practices and accordingly, it informs a crucial part of the social. Histories are not only enacted in the classroom, university offices, textbooks, or television documentaries, they are "learned in a multitude of places, and in a variety of ways" (Kalela, 2012: 75).

Actors of any kind have the potential to participate in this practice (Kalela, 2012). As a result, shared histories emerge with no specific author but are what families, communities, neighbors, and friends agree upon to understand and cope in the present (Kalela, 2012). But the enactment of the past as history is not just reserved for people. It is performed by inscription devices by virtue of their relation with humans (and vice versa). It is performed relationally by actors engaged in practices (Law, 2008). Historians are no longer "independent actors standing outside reality, so to speak, who can choose for or against it" (Mol, 2002: 179; Latour, 1986). Historians "become active co-participants rather than arrogant masters of" their "world" (Tsekeris 2010: 146). Far from being the producer of the history, far from producing embrained or cognitive knowledge of the past, historians are active participants in "the never-ending *social process of history making*" (Kalela, 2012: 1). The historian loses her privileged position.

The historian's role, then, becomes one of participating with the actors themselves: learning "from the actors without imposing on them an a priori definition of their world-building capacities" (Latour, 1999a: 20). Thus, the historian no longer decides between various tropes of modes of emplotment while figuring the past as history, they do not "tell anyone the shape that is to be drawn – circles or cubes or lines – but only how to go about systematically recording the world-building abilities of the sites to be documented and registered" (Latour, 1999a: 21). It goes without saying, then, that the historian's work is never finished, never assembled, but constantly being re-figured and reassembled (Kalela, 2012; Latour, 2005).

Conclusions

This chapter has reviewed three conditions in which historiography may be undertaken, namely modern, postmodern, and amodern. As the title of this chapter suggests, it was to feature ANTi-History. In respecting Latour's (2005) advice that we should never start off by assuming as given what we wish for our analyses to show, I have decided not to begin by assuming ANTi-History as a stable, pre-given and uncontested approach. Instead, I wish to end by suggesting it as a name that stands on behalf of the ideas presented in this chapter. As noted in other venues (Durepos & Mills, 2012a, 2012b), ANTi-History is an alternative approach to historiography which draws on actor-network theory, postmodern historiography, as well as the sociology of knowledge. ANTi-History assumes the past is performed as history by following actors and tracing the constitution of their world-building activities in practice. Amodernism, the idea to which this chapter has been dedicated, offers clues about the philosophical grounding and condition through which ANTi-History flourishes as an alternative approach to history.

A historic turn is currently underway in M&OS (Clark & Rowlinson, 2004; Booth & Rowlinson, 2006). Although the amount and nature of scholarly attention that it has attracted has begun to make an important impact in the field, most would agree that its influence has yet to rival the magnitude of, for example, the linguistic turn. In providing a partial explanation for the latter, one might begin by questioning 'for whom' the historic turn has consequences? In other words, are efforts for more historical analysis the sole responsibility of those who have thus far contributed to this debate and as a result might call themselves organizational historians (see for example, the work of Rowlinson, Booth, Hassard, Carter, Jacques, and Mills)? In this chapter, I have sought to show via amodern ANTi-History and its focus on practice that 'history is what all of us do every day.' If there is ever such a thing as an ANTi-Historical historic turn, my hope is that it will show us that adopting an historical perspective is not only the responsibility of historically minded M&OS scholars, but instead our collective enterprise.

Notes

1 I do this conscious of the dangers of oversimplification inherent in organizing complex discussions in a tabular format.
2 Brown (2005: 159) describes moral relativism as "the notion that morality changes with the ages, and that the historian is unable to confer moral blame upon historical figures because they lived under different moral rules."
3 Thus, as objects out there no longer needing consideration.
4 For example, in postmodernism, history was used to illuminate present-centered phenomena, thus it was used to frame a presented-centered phenomena. Could the moderns and postmoderns have confused the questions with the answer?

References

Alcadipani, R. and Hassard, J. (2010) Actor-network theory, organizations and critique: Toward a politics of organizing, *Organization*, 17(4): 419–35.

Ankersmit, F. R. (1997) Historiography and postmodernism, in K. Jenkins (ed.), *The Postmodern History Reader* (pp. 277–97). London: Routledge.

Ankersmit, F. R. (2007) Manifesto for an analytical political history, in K. Jenkins, S. Morgan, and A. Munslow (eds), *Manifestos for History* (pp. 179–96). New York: Routledge.

Bonner, B. (2013) History and IS: Broadening our view and understanding – actor-network theory as a methodology, *Journal of Information Technology*, 28: 111–23.

Booth, C. and Rowlinson, M. (2006) Management and organizational history: Prospects, *Management & Organizational History*, 1(1): 5–30.

Braun, R. (1997) The Holocaust and problems of representation, in K. Jenkins (ed.), *The Postmodern History Reader* (pp. 418–25). London: Routledge.

Brown, C. G. (2005) *Postmodernism for Historians*. London: Pearson.

Bruce, K. and Nyland, C. (2011) Elton Mayo and the deification of human relations, *Organization Studies*, 32(3): 383–405.

Burrell, G. (1988) Modernism, post modernism and organizational analysis 2: The contribution of Michel Foucault, *Organization Studies*, 9(2): 221–325.

Burrell, G. and Morgan, G. (1979) *Sociological Paradigms and Organisational Analysis*. Aldershot: Ashgate.

Calás, M. and Smircich, L. (1999) Past postmodernism? Reflections and tentative directions, *Academy of Management Review*, 24(4): 649–71.

Callon, M. (1986) Some elements of a sociology of translation: Domestification of the scallops and the fisherman of St Brieuc Bay, in J. Law (ed.), *Power, Action and Belief: A New Sociology of Knowledge?* (pp. 196–233). London: Routledge & Kegan Paul.

Callon, M. (1999) Actor-network theory: The market test, in J. Law and J. Hassard (eds), *Actor Network Theory and After* (pp. 181–95). Oxford: Blackwell.

Chandler, A. (1962). *Strategy and Structure: Chapters in the History of the American Industrial Enterprise*. Cambridge, MA: MIT Press.

Clark, P. and Rowlinson, M. (2004) The treatment of history in organisation studies: Towards an 'historic turn?' *Business History*, 46(3): 331–52.

Collingwood, R. G. (1956). *The Idea of History*. London: Oxford University Press.

Cooke, B. (2006) The Cold War origin of action research as managerialist cooptation, *Human Relations*, 59(5): 665–93.

Cooper, R. (2005) Relationality, *Organization Studies*, 26(11): 1689–710.

Cooper, R. and Burrell, G. (1988) Modernism, postmodernism and organizational analysis: An introduction, *Organization Studies*, 9(1): 91–112.

Cousins, M. (1987) The practice of historical investigation, in D. Altridge, G. Bennington, and R. Young (eds), *Post-Structuralism and the Question of History* (pp. 126–36). Cambridge: Cambridge University Press.

Durepos, G. and Mills, A. (2012a). *ANTi-History: Theorizing the Past, History, and Historiography in Management and Organizational Studies*. Charlotte, NC: Information Age.

Durepos, G. and Mills, A. (2012b) Actor network theory, ANTi-history, and critical organizational historiography, *Organization*, 19(6): 703–21.

Durepos, G., Mills, A. J., and Helms Mills, J. (2008) Tales in the manufacture of knowledge: Writing a business history of Pan American Airways, *Management & Organizational History*, 3(1): 63–80.
Durepos, G., Mills, A., and Weatherbee, T. (2012) Theorizing the past: Realism, relativism, relationalism & the reassembly of Weber, *Management & Organizational History*, 7(3): 267–81.
Elton, G. (1967) *The Practice of History*, London: Fontana Press.
Elton, G. (1997) Return to essentials, in K. Jenkins (ed.), *The Postmodern History Reader* (pp. 175–79). London: Routledge.
Emirbayer, M. (1997) Manifesto for a relational sociology, *American Journal of Sociology*, 103(2): 281–317.
Ermarth, E. D. (1992) *Sequel to History: Postmodernism and the crisis of Representational Time*. Princeton, NJ: Princeton University Press.
Ermarth, E. D. (2007) The closed space of choice: A manifesto on the future of history, in K. Jenkins, S. Morgan, and A. Munslow (eds), *Manifestos for History* (pp. 50–66). New York: Routledge.
Foucault, M. (1973) *The Archeology of Knowledge and the Discourse on Language*. New York: Pantheon Books.
Foucault, M. (1979) *The History of Sexuality, Volume I*. Harmondsworth: Penguin.
Fox-Genovese, E. (1997) Literacy criticism and the politics of the New Historicism, in K. Jenkins (ed.), *The Postmodern History Reader* (pp. 84–88). London: Routledge.
Geyl, P. (ed.) (1962) *Debates with Historians*. London: Collins Clear-Type Press.
Green, A. and Troup, K. (eds) (1999) *The Houses of History*. Manchester: Manchester University Press.
Gunn, S. (2006) *History and Cultural Theory*. Harlow: Pearson, Longman.
Habers, H., Mol, A., and Stollmeyer, A. (2002) Food matters: Arguments for an ethnography of daily care, *Theory, Culture and Society*, 19(5–6): 207–26.
Haraway, D. (1988) Situated knowledges: The science question in feminism and the privilege of partial perspective, *Feminist Studies*, 14(3): 575–99.
Haraway, D. (2004) *The Haraway Reader*. New York: Routledge.
Hetherington, K. (1999) From blindness to blindness: Museums, heterogeneity and the subject, in J. Law and J. Hassard (eds), *Actor Network Theory and After* (pp. 51–73). Oxford: Blackwell.
Hobsbawm, E. (1997) *On History*. New York: New Press.
Jacques, R. S. (1996) *Manufacturing the Employee: Management Knowledge from the 19th to 21st Centuries*. London: Sage.
Jacques, R. S. (2006) History, historiography and organization studies: The challenge and the potential, *Management & Organizational History*, 1(1): 31–49.
Jenkins, K. (1991) *Re-Thinking History*. London: Routledge.
Jenkins, K. (1995) *On 'What is History?' From Carr and Elton to Rorty and White*. London: Routledge.
Jenkins, K. (ed.) (1997) *The Postmodern History Reader*. London: Routledge.
Jenkins, K. (1999) *Why History? Ethics and Postmodernity*. London: Routledge.
Jenkins, K. (2003) *Refiguring History*. New York: Routledge.
Jenkins, K. (2009) *At the Limits of History*. London: Routledge.
Jenkins, K. and Munslow, A. (eds) (2004) *The Nature of History Reader*. London: Routledge.
Jenkins, K., Morgan, S., and Munslow, A. (eds) (2007) *Manifestos for History*. New York: Routledge.
Kalela, J. (2012) *Making History: The Historian and Uses of the Past*. Basingstoke: Palgrave Macmillan.
Kantrow, A. M. (1986) Why history matters to managers, *Harvard Business Review*, January/February: 81–88.
Kellner, H. (1997) 'Never again' is now, in K. Jenkins (ed.), *The Postmodern History Reader* (pp. 397–412). London: Routledge.
LaCapra, D. (2007) Resisting apocalypse and rethinking history, in K. Jenkins, S. Morgan, and A. Munslow (eds), *Manifestos for History* (pp. 160–78). New York: Routledge.
Lang, B. (1997) Is it possible to misrepresent the Holocaust? in K. Jenkins (ed.), *The Postmodern History Reader* (pp. 426–33). London: Routledge.
Latour, B. (1986) The powers of association, in J. Law (ed.), *Power, Action and Belief: A New Sociology of Knowledge?* London: Routledge & Kegan Paul.
Latour, B. (1988) A relativistic account of Einstein's relativity, *Social Studies of Science*, 18: 3–44.
Latour, B. (1990) Postmodern? No, simply amodern: Steps towards an anthropology of science, an essay review, *Studies in the History and Philosophy of Science*, 21: 145–71.
Latour, B. (1993) *We Have Never Been Modern*. Hemel Hempstead: Harvester Wheatsheaf.
Latour, B. (1996) Do scientific objects have a history? *Common Knowledge*, 5(1): 76–91.
Latour, B. (1999a) On recalling ANT, in J. Law and J. Hassard (eds), *Actor Network Theory and After* (pp. 15–25). Oxford: Blackwell.

Latour, B. (1999b) *Pandora's Hope: Essays on the Reality of Science Studies*. Cambridge, MA: Harvard University Press.

Latour, B. (2005) *Reassembling the Social: An Introduction to Actor-Network-Theory*. Oxford: Oxford University Press.

Latour, B. and Woolgar, S. (1979) *Laboratory Life: The Construction of Scientific Facts*. Princeton, NJ: Princeton University Press.

Law, J. (1994) *Organizing Modernity*. Oxford: Blackwell.

Law, J. (1999) After ANT: Complexity, naming and topology, in J. Law and J. Hassard (eds), *Actor Network Theory and After* (pp. 1–14). Oxford: Blackwell.

Law, J. (2000) Networks, relations, cyborgs: On the social study of technology, http://www.lancaster.ac.uk/fass/centres/css/ant/ant.htm

Law, J. (2001) Ordering and obduracy, http://www.lancaster.ac.uk/fass/centres/css/ant/ant.htm

Law, J. (2008) *After Method: Mess in Social Science Research*. New York: Routledge.

Law, J. and Benschop, R. (1997) Resisting pictures: Representation, distribution and ontological politics, in K. Hetherington and R. Munro (eds), *Ideas of Difference; Social Spaces and the Labour of Division* (pp. 158–82). Oxford: Blackwell.

Law, J. and Hetherington, K. (1998) Allegory and interference: Representation in sociology, http://www.lancaster.ac.uk/fass/centres/css/ant/ant.htm

Law, J. and Hetherington, K. (1999). Materialities, spatialities, globalities. http://www.lancs.ac.uk/fass/sociology/research/resalph.htm

Law, J. and Mol, A. (1995) Notes on materiality and sociality, *Sociological Review*, 43(2): 274–94.

Law, J. and Mol, A. (2001) Situating technoscience: An inquiry into spacialities, *Society and Space*, 19: 609–21.

Law, J. and Urry, J. (2004) Enacting the social, *Economy and Society*, 33(3): 390–410.

Lawrence, B. S. (1984) Historical perspective: Using the past to study the present, *Academy of Management Review*, 9(2): 307–12.

Lyotard, J.-F. (1993) *The Postmodern Condition: A Report on Knowledge*. Minneapolis: University of Minnesota Press.

Mannheim, K. (1985) *Ideology and Utopia: An Introduction to the Sociology of Knowledge*. New York: Harcourt Brace.

Mills, A. (2006) *Sex, Strategy and the Stratosphere*. New York: Palgrave Macmillan.

Mol, A. (1999) Ontological politics: A word and some questions, in J. Law and J. Hassard (eds), *Actor Network Theory and After* (pp. 74–89). Oxford: Blackwell.

Mol, A. (2002) *The Body Multiple: Ontology in Medical Practice*. Durham, NC: Duke University Press.

Mol, A. (2010) Actor-network theory: Sensitive terms and enduring tensions, *Kölner Zeitschrift für Soziologie und Sozialpsychologie*, 50(1): 253–69.

Munslow, A. (2009) Afterword, in K. Jenkins (ed.), *At the Limits of History* (pp. 315–20). London: Routledge.

Munslow, A. (2010) *The Future of History*. New York: Palgrave Macmillan.

Munslow, A. (2012) *A History of History*. London: Routledge.

Myrick, K., Helms Mills, J., and Mills, A. (2013) History-making and the Academy of Management: An ANTi-History perspective, *Management & Organizational History*, 8(4): 345–70.

Perry, M. (2002) *Marxism and History*. Basingstoke: Palgrave Macmillan.

Prasad, P. (2005) *Crafting Qualitative Research: Working in the Postpositivist Traditions*. Armonk: M. E. Sharpe.

Phillips, C. F. (1935) A history of the F. W. Woolworth Company, *Harvard Business Review*, January: 225–36.

Rigney, A. (2007) Being an improper historian, in K. Jenkins, S. Morgan, and A. Munslow (eds), *Manifestos for History* (pp. 149–59). New York: Routledge.

Roowan, R. (2010) Why Colonel Sanders has his own museum, *Harvard Business Review*, 88(2): 26.

Rowlinson, M. (2002) Public review essay: Cadbury World, *Labour History Review*, 67(1): 101–19.

Seaman, J. T. J. and Smith, G. D. (2012) Your company's history as a leadership tool, *Harvard Business Review*, 90(12): 44–52.

Smith, G. D. and Steadman, L. E. (1981) Present value of corporate history, *Harvard Business Review*, 59(6): 164–73.

Tsekeris, C. (2010) Relationalism in sociology: Theoretical and methodological elaborations, *Philosophy, Sociology, Psychology and History*, 9(1): 139–48.

Üsdiken, B. and Kieser, A. (2004) Introduction: History in organization studies, *Business History*, 46(3): 321–30.

Weatherbee, T., Durepos, G., Mills, A., and Helms Mills, J. (2012) Theorizing the past: Critical engagements, *Management & Organizational History*, 7(3): 193–202.

White, H. (1973) *Metahistory: The Historical Imagination in Nineteenth-Century Europe*. Baltimore, MD: Johns Hopkins University Press.

White, H. (1985) *The Tropics Discourse: Essays in Cultural Criticism*. Baltimore, MD: Johns Hopkins University Press.

Whittle, A. and Spicer, A. (2008) Is actor network theory critique? *Organization Studies*, 29(4): 611–29.

Zagorin, P. (2009) History, the referent and narrative, in K. Jenkins (ed.), *At the Limits of History* (pp. 64–88). London: Routledge.

Zald, M. (1993) Organization studies as a scientific and humanistic enterprise: Towards a reconceptualization of the foundations of the field, *Organization Science*, 4: 513–28.

13

Avec frontières

The discourse of humanitarianism

Adam Rostis

Introduction – humanitarianism

Imagine an organized team of neutral doctors arriving during the Spanish attack on the Aztec city of Tenochtitlan in 1521 pleading with soldiers on both sides to spare civilians. The juxtaposition of what is now the taken-for-granted role of humanitarian physicians within an historical period unfamiliar with such a role indicates the "historical specificity" of humanitarianism and leads to the questions: "[W]hat is it about the present … that casts the care of strangers in such a leading role?" (Bornstein and Redfield 2007: 2) and how have humanitarianism and the humanitarian organization come to be accepted as inevitable, natural, and taken-for-granted?

Humanitarianism can be understood as the "institutionalized patterns of action … oriented meaningfully towards the welfare of distant strangers" (Stamatov 2008: 5). It has become a celebrated, accepted, and taken-for-granted contemporary social force as evidenced by the presence of longstanding formal organizations dedicated to its pursuit. Many of its tenets have become enshrined in laws and policies such as the Geneva Conventions, and the organizations themselves have received formal appreciation and legitimization through awards and recognition such as Nobel Peace Prizes. These organizations are rather unique entities with a global presence and significant impact on human lives. It is difficult to quantify the total value of humanitarian aid, but in 2012 there were 76 million people targeted in United Nations humanitarian assistance programs (Development Initiatives, 2013). The estimated value of humanitarian aid in 2012 was $17.9 billion US dollars (Development Initiatives, 2013).

However, it is my contention that these massive, organized structures of helping are "some of the most powerful pacific weapons of the new world order" Hardt (2000: 136) yet have been largely unexamined by organizational scholars. Perhaps this is because the organization imbued with legal or moral legitimacy and a mission to help, heal, or rescue has seemingly little that can be criticized. As Beck (1999: 44) notes, "[Non-Governmental Organizations – NGOs] have a blank cheque for an almost unlimited store of trust" because of their pure public image. De Waal (1997) argues that crises of war or natural disaster allow humanitarian organizations to intervene into nations in a similar way that financial and debt crises permit international financial institutions to intervene in countries and impose programs of economic and social adjustment. I believe this makes humanitarian organizations worthy of the same attention given to their private sector equivalents.

In this chapter, I am interested in addressing this gap in scholarship through a critical history of humanitarianism and the humanitarian organization. I will show how it has transpired that the present humanitarianism has come to be accepted as inevitable or natural. Concepts (such as humanitarianism) are not isolated, but exist in relation to other concepts and the manner in which they are used (Althusser, 2005). Therefore, one can look at the conditions by which a concept has come into being, or rather the history surrounding a concept in order to understand it (Patton, 1978). As well, a concept exists because of the rules or grammar that must be followed or used in order for it to be understood (Patton, 1978). Reading a text symptomatically can reveal these rules by identifying what is not said; in other words, to identify the absences (Assiter, 1984). This process is a problematization of history and is particularly relevant to humanitarianism because, as Fiering (1976: 196) notes, "of all the great themes of eighteenth-century social thought, humanitarianism has received the least study in intellectual history." Lambert and Lester (2004: 324) argue that a critique of those "who constituted the nexus of globalized philanthropy in the early nineteenth century is long overdue" and Bankoff (2001: 19) suggests that "[i]nadequate attention … has been directed to considering the historical roots of the discursive framework within which hazard is generally presented."

History through genealogy

Genealogy is a method of historical critique that is the product of work done by Michel Foucault, who in turn built on the genealogical critique of morals performed by Nietzsche (1989). Genealogy defamiliarizes taken-for-granted knowledge by rejecting the ahistorical, coherent, systematic production of knowledge. Through an examination of the descent, emergence, and trajectory of events, it attempts to uncover other explanations that have been hidden in the construction of a logical narrative or explanation of how the past occurred. How has popular knowledge been repressed, and how has struggle and conflict resulted in the exclusion of particular parts of history? Genealogy turns the reader's attention away from the importance of the origin stories of institutions towards the discovery of random accidents and rifts in history that give rise to changes in old perceptions and emergences of new orderings of society. These accidents continue always, and it directs us away from supposing that history is on a linear path towards some form of end state (Prasad, 2005). Critique is at the heart of genealogy. The method begins with normal, seemingly inconsequential events or experiences and draws from these narratives the *process* by which they have become inconsequential or normal (Jacques, 1992). In sum, these stories show the contingent nature of practices.

The traces of these practices are contained within the archive. It must be recognized that Foucault uses the term 'archive' to refer to the way in which statements are formed within a society at a given point in time (Prasad, 2005). It is the "general system of the formation and transformation of statements" (Foucault 2002: 146). Doing a genealogy involves re-reading parts of the archive to observe "broadly held cultural assumptions" (Jacques, 1992: 102) and occasions where the relationship changed between a concept's meaning and the specific practices it implied (Jacques, 1992). It implies that there is another way of interpreting and understanding history. But, this re-reading is not an attempt to uncover or correct the true meaning of history. Jacques (1992) has culled from Foucault's genealogical work some guidelines for re-reading, which is, in effect a guideline for conducting a genealogy.

The first is to read between the lines of a document to understand what has made it possible for an author to make a statement. In other words, I must understand the rules of admissibility to a discourse leading to an understanding of what makes something acceptable as knowledge.

Second, contextualize and place the document within a broader historical picture. Third is to look for discontinuities where common sense ceases to be common, or where the nonsensical becomes common sense. This is the dividing line, on either side of which "the structures used to frame what can be known each appear nonsensical when viewed from the other side" (Jacques, 1992: 104). Fourth is to recognize that there could also be changes in other discourses resulting from the discontinuity or rupture; look for these changes. Finally, the discontinuity and emergence of new discourse should also produce new subjects as a result of the rearrangement of social relations; look for the emergence of these subjects. What becomes apparent from Jacques' (1992) approach is that discourse is key.

The term *utterance* is used to refer to speech, writing, dialogue, or a constituted body of knowledge; discourse is the collection of all utterances about a particular idea (Prasad, 2005). Underlying any discourse is a set of assumptions that may overlap with other discourses and change over time (Abercrombie, Hill, and Turner, 2000). At one extreme, discourse is considered not just as a descriptive tool but a mechanism by which a reality is formed (Abercrombie, Hill, and Turner, 2000). Discourse about any particular idea will determine what is and is not admissible, legitimate knowledge about that idea; in other words there are discursive rules that determine what gets admitted to a discourse (Prasad, 2005). It is not so important to understand if a discourse is valid or true. Rather, these concerns are overshadowed in importance by discursive effects; that is, how a discourse manifests itself in practice (Prasad, 2005). Discourse, then, is more than just a collection of statements: it is productive because it has an effect and produces something as a result of its existence (Kendall and Wickham 1999). A discourse is a way "of constituting knowledge, together with the social practices, forms of subjectivity and power relations which inhere in such knowledges and the relations between them" (Weedon 1996: 105).

In my case, humanitarianism is considered a 'good' practice that operates neutrally and opposes war, suffering, and the effects of disaster on human society. People should be rescued, and soldiers should be spared death if injured. This state of affairs, however, was once considered extraordinary (cf. Moorehead, 1999, for the 'creation' of the Geneva Conventions). Genealogy documents how these kinds of changes in society occurred that moved the extraordinary into the mundane (Jacques, 1992). The question that results is that if concepts such as discipline or humanitarianism were once considered remarkable, and are now normal, then is it not equally likely that that which we now take for granted could be replaced by something else?

The archive: the Red Cross and Médecins sans Frontières

In 1859, a Swiss businessman traveling in Italy happened upon the aftermath of a battle between Austrian and French soldiers. Shocked by the terrible conditions of the wounded on both sides of the battle, Henri Dunant marshaled the resources available to him and set about ameliorating their suffering. Soon after, as the story goes, Dunant wrote about his experiences in *A Memory of Solferino*, a book that became widely read throughout Europe and eventually fomented the creation of what is now known as the Red Cross. Nearly 100 years later, a young Red Cross doctor working in the Biafran civil war of 1968 witnessed civilians caught between warring factions, Western nations, and politically neutral aid organizations (Aeberhard, 1996; Redfield, 2005). Bernard Kouchner was frustrated that Red Cross principles dictated that assistance could only be supplied with the consent of a legitimate government. But Biafra was a civil war and the legitimate government refused to allow outside help to be supplied to a rebelling population. Kouchner's frustration motivated him to form Médecins sans Frontières (MSF) in an effort to better match humanitarian assistance with contemporary world politics.

These organizations were formed during the rise and fall respectively of the colonial period. The Red Cross was born on the battlefield in an actively colonizing Europe on the brink of decades of conflict while MSF was also formed on the battlefield, but nearly 100 years later during the heyday of decolonization and African independence struggles. The lineage of the Red Cross is such that it was created with the consent of, and existed alongside, colonial states using state power and sanction to achieve humanitarian goals (Moorehead, 1999). In contrast, MSF was formed as a reaction to a perceived failure of this approach, valuing its independence from state sanctioned humanitarianism above all (Captier, 2005). While seemingly novel at the time, there is now an expectation that the humanitarian organization will act to relieve suffering and assist states that do not have the resources to help their own citizens. How is it that this expectation arose and continues to persist? I believe that genealogy is the most appropriate choice to investigate this question.

The first point of entry into the archive will be the Red Cross. This is an organization, an object of investigation, as well as a research site because it is a visibility that gives rise to statements, but it also houses an archive in the physical sense of the word. This archive forms part of the broader archive of humanitarianism when considered from Foucault's interpretation of the term. A summary of the accounts of the formation and present form of the organization given in Moorehead (1999) and Forsythe (2005, 2007) provides an outline of the organization; this should help to understand it as a research site. In brief, in 1864 it was agreed to establish national Red Cross 'societies' dedicated to caring for battlefield casualties, and to enshrine the principles and conventions of these societies in international law (Moorehead, 1999). The emblem used to identify the neutral volunteers on the battlefield was a red cross on a white background, the reverse colors of the Swiss flag; eventually the organization came to be uniquely known by this symbol, and the committee eventually became today's International Committee of the Red Cross (ICRC) (Moorehead, 1999). The power of the agreement between states gave the Red Cross leave to intervene in conflict, obliged armed forces to respect the neutrality of Red Cross volunteers, and compelled nations to accept the establishment of Red Cross national societies (Forsythe, 2005). Since its creation in 1864 the Red Cross has diversified outside of armed conflict and this causes some degree of confusion for outsiders to the organization as the Red Cross is actually three different organizational forms: the International Committee (ICRC) and the International Federation of Red Cross and Red Crescent Societies (IFRC) are both based in Geneva, and the National Societies are based in each of the 186 member countries (ICRC, 2005). The two 'international' organizations are often referred to as the International Red Cross, and the other organizations as the National Societies. By agreement amongst the International Red Cross, the IFRC focuses its attention on natural disasters and recovery from conflict, while the ICRC has the guardianship of international humanitarian law and concerns itself almost exclusively with conflict and issues surrounding conflict (Forsythe, 2005). The International Red Cross refers often to its network of national societies and a legion of volunteers in disaster relief and recovery.

I chose Médecins sans Frontières as another specific organizational site. The formation story of this organization is that it was a reaction to the inability of established humanitarian organizations (such as the International Red Cross) to help vulnerable people during the Biafran civil war of 1967–70. The expectation was that the parties in that conflict would behave rationally according to principles tested in over 100 years of European wars. However, the Biafran war was fought in the media as well as on the battlefield and in effect both sides utilized civilians to convince the world of the rightness of their cause. In Biafra the template for provision of assistance did not fit with contemporary reality. And so, a new organization was formed with a new approach to humanitarianism. Médecins sans Frontières values its independence from state-sanctioned humanitarianism above all, and it always struggles to maintain vocal opposition without completely isolating itself from state structures that enable it to reach affected populations. Over time, Médecins sans Frontières established principles that would differentiate its humanitarianism from the established order. Its medium for action is Western medicine practiced on individuals, but its method is agitation, disruption and advocacy to change the conditions under which suffering can occur (Jeannerod, 2005; Orbinski, 1999; Vallaeys, 2004).

However, the environment in which Médecins sans Frontières operates reflects an evolving discourse of disasters and a change in the roles of state and non-state actors. Specific principles guiding its work include the right of access to victims, independent assessment of humanitarian situations and monitoring of effectiveness of interventions (Orbinski, 1999). Médecins sans Frontières also seeks to avoid the organizational bureaucracy that its founders believe hampered the humanitarian relief efforts in Biafra. As such, its organizational structure began and remains in a somewhat fractured state with operational cells existing in various so-called developed countries. Each Médecins sans Frontières organization functions somewhat separately, often times at odds with each other, but are held together by the common principles mentioned above. It is a loose federation with each country office operating independently and producing its own annual report. There is an international body, Médecins sans Frontières International, made up of representatives of each of the national organizations but the decision-making components of the organization exist exclusively in the West. The non-Western countries form the theater in which Médecins sans Frontières operates, but they do not seem to form part of the organizational structure. Therefore, the Médecins sans Frontières power structure roughly bisects Western and non-Western countries.

The humanitarian discourse

A discourse of humanitarianism can be found in the conditions by which the concept has come into being and occasions where the relationship changed between its meaning and the specific practices it implied. On these occasions, a discontinuity or dividing line exists. A concept makes no sense if viewed through the rules used on either side of this dividing line and new subjects emerge. People become raw material that can be acted upon by humanitarianism to produce these subjects. A discourse is also signaled by the presence of a relationship *between* subjects as the result of statements. In other words, statements about humanitarianism produce ways of being and acting. Finally, discourse acts through things, foremost of which are the rules embodied in laws, documents, and other texts by which a concept can be understood. These things are found in institutions where these physical objects are limited and authorized and help identify the boundaries of a discourse, which will in turn lead to a discussion of each of the research questions. In summary, then, discourse can be uncovered by examining the conditions by which a concept has come into being together with any discontinuities that signal a change between a concept's meaning and the practices it incurs.

One discontinuity that shaped humanitarian discourse was a change to Christian ontology and its understanding of suffering. This change involved the role of God in determining the lives of humans: on one side of the discontinuity was the belief that conditions of the current world were insignificant in comparison to those of the next world beyond death (Core, 1950). Further, pain and suffering were believed to be natural and imitative of the suffering of Christ and Christianity posited that pain was inevitable and suffering was part of healing (Core, 1950). This is not to deny that benevolence existed, but rather that these actions directed towards others were motivated by self-interest or ego through the belief that such activity contributed towards repenting from sin. In contrast, Core (1950) paints a picture of the other side of a divide where these views of suffering gave way in the face of a more benevolent God. In addition, there emerged a role for the individual in determining his own and others' fates. This was reflected in an overall change in the eighteenth and nineteenth centuries where pain and suffering were viewed as being avoidable and unacceptable. Therefore, the emergence of a benevolent God was key to unlocking the humanitarian impulse of humans: a humane God gave people the authority to be benevolent. It therefore became possible to speak about and act upon a humanitarian impulse.

The humanitarian impulse was hugely evident in the global reaction to the war in Biafra. This was, I believe, another dividing line: humanitarian practice before Biafra would not recognize its counterpart on the other side of the line. The result of Biafra for the International Committee of the Red Cross (ICRC) and for humanitarianism was the creation of a discontinuity: Biafra signaled a divide, on either side of which the meanings attributed to concepts and their practices were no longer interchangeable. After the war, the notions of humanitarianism created and nurtured by the ICRC no longer made sense (Forsythe, 2007; Moorehead, 1999). Why might this be the case? Prior to Biafra, the ICRC followed behind war, visiting prisoners and rendering aid to those affected (Forsythe, 2007). This process was developed following the Battle of Solferino, the formation of the Red Cross, and then refined over decades of European conflicts (Moorehead, 1999). While European conflicts such as the world wars that were attended by the ICRC were vast and complex, the organization could still count on a semblance of order through the so-called laws of war in the Geneva Conventions and through shared cultural and historic linkages amongst combatants, governments, and helpers. However, in Nigeria the organization could not depend upon this common ground and didn't seem to understand why this was the case (Forsythe, 2007). The war was regarded as being confusing, with no real front and with civilians intermixed into sites of conflict (Moorehead, 1999). In addition, the concept of neutrality at the centre of Red Cross humanitarianism was too inflexible to work in the context of Biafra (Forsythe, 2007).

This inflexibility is reflected in the fact that the Red Cross continued to argue for access to victims on the basis of its past performance without taking into account other perceptions of its intentions. These perceptions included claims that Red Cross flights were being used to ferry ammunition and war material, and that the influx of foreign currency for relief work was being used to the benefit of the Biafran government. It seems that these unintended outcomes of humanitarianism together with the non-European context of the conflict created many barriers that confounded the Red Cross. In addition, there was dissent and confusion within the Red Cross organization itself, with France and the Scandinavian countries arguing that the ICRC should do things not officially or legally sanctioned by the Geneva Conventions in order to prevent suffering (Forsythe, 2007).

In summary, then, the presence of discontinuities reveals an intersection of events where social relations should change and new subjects should emerge. In the case of the events cited above, one emergent subject was the humanitarian as a professional worker within an organizational structure: in other words, the professional humanitarian. Another subject created is the citizen transformed into a victim through the action of organizations during a crisis, disaster, or conflict. Yet another is the citizen humanitarian: that is a 'man of feeling' who responds to instances of suffering in another human. Why, though, is the production of the subject of importance to the humanitarian problematic? An example of some recent disasters serves to answer this question.

In her examination of some well-known disasters such as the San Francisco earthquake, Hurricane Katrina, and the 2001 World Trade Center attacks, Rebecca Solnit critiques perceptions of victims as helpless, dazed survivors dependent upon organizations to rescue them from their fate (Solnit, 2009). She joins with other scholars (cf. Drabek and Mcentire, 2003; Furedi, 2007a, 2007b; Rodríguez, Trainor, and Quarantelli, 2006) who try to illustrate that it is the individual citizen rather than state or non-state institutions that serves the key role in responding to a crisis.

In the aftermath of the San Francisco earthquake, Solnit recounts the way in which citizens who survived the disaster established kitchens and shelters for other survivors. She also notes that these efforts met with resistance from the formal organizations such as the military and the fire department. The phenomenon of emergent organizations during disasters is well understood (cf. Drabek and Mcentire, 2003; Rodríguez, Trainor, and Quarantelli, 2006), yet the paradoxical situation remains: formal, organized helping receives the bulk of attention and resources during a crisis. Whether it is a local or distant crisis, the story most often told recounts the role of the professional humanitarian responder working within a defined organizational structure. The object of this professional's practice is the disaster victim. Somewhere in between these two subjects rests Solnit's active citizen helper: the citizen humanitarian.

Discourse can also be found when statements produce subjects and produce a relationship between subjects. Obvious examples of these statements are documents such as the Geneva Conventions. Less obvious, but still figuring large in the archive, is literature and its obsession with humanitarian ideas. Humanitarianism benefited from the way in which literature trained people how to be compassionate. The archive shows that literature and humanitarianism are connected and the one had an influence on the other. Henry Dunant's *Memory of Solferino* is but one example of this kind of humanitarian literature. In its formation story, the Red Cross continually reinforces the impact of this one book on the birth and development of the organization and on humanitarianism. The archive shows, however, that Dunant's book is but one instance in a whole genre of literature that was obsessed with humanitarian ideas. In effect, humanitarianism benefited from the availability and impact of this literature to train people how to be compassionate. The literature provided rules by which humanitarianism could be applied, and it helped created the humanitarian subjects. The questions now are: how are these subjects constituted? How do they interact? We can see this process by examining one of the subjects produced by humanitarianism: the citizen humanitarian.

The citizen humanitarian

One trajectory of the citizen humanitarian is found in the archive through the emergence of a new social type called the "the man of feeling" (Halttunen, 1995: 303) who represented the behaviors that were to be emulated by others. The man of feeling displayed an innate understanding of the difference between good and evil, and this extended to acts of compassion and concern towards suffering individuals. In other words, he displayed a humanitarian sensibility. This sensibility is in stark contrast to earlier feelings of resignation generated from beliefs that current conditions on Earth exist for a reason, suffering is beneficial to heavenly reward, and things will be better in the next life. Replacing the afterlife as a barrier to helping were instead appeals to a transcendent force as a reason for acting in a humanitarian manner. In the eighteenth and nineteenth centuries evil was the universal motivator, the reduction of evil the goal. The transcendent and universal power of humanity and of humanity's ability to change conditions becomes more important. Later, science and evolutionary theory in particular, are implicated in demonstrating the common origins of humans, and thus contribute to claims that there is less difference between people across cultures and borders. Institutions such as churches capitalized upon this belief in commonality and motivated individuals to give gifts such as clothing or food across borders. This enabled the consideration of the poor in another country not as strangers, but as fellow humans deserving of attention.

The existence of associations and groups that considered the suffering of others was also an adaptation in response to the fragmentation of society due to increasing economic and social change attributable to modernization and colonialism. The argument begins to emerge that the state could no longer cope with, or chose not to cope with, the increased demands placed upon it in an industrial society. These demands resulted from the rising expectations of workers, as well as the expectations of citizens that government would also respond in a humanitarian fashion to the suffering of strangers within their own borders. Voluntary associations conveniently filled this gap as part of the so-called natural helping response of humanity. Thus the argument that the state is a weak institution exists in the eighteenth century, well before any contemporary idea of failed states that is so often used as a rationale for a humanitarian response in Africa or elsewhere.

Some examples of these collective efforts included the elimination of slavery, the creation of industrial schools to train the poor, and the creation of legislation that restricted work hours and reduced the use of child labour. The emergence of the Red Cross and its principles of neutrality and impartiality reflect this belief in commonality of human beings through the claim that suffering is something that transcends differences; the Red Cross, however, still respects political differences and the state's power to care for its citizens. A later example comes in the form of MSF and its ethos of working without borders: it also believes in neutrality, but unlike the Red Cross it espouses a sharing in the suffering of strangers. In a paradoxical twist, though, MSF argues that difference between victim and helper is both productive and *necessary* for humanitarianism.

Therefore, the citizen humanitarian emerged from these various trajectories of changing views on suffering, pain, and transcendent rewards versus immediate relief but also from an awareness of distant needs that easily circulated in humanitarian literature and later in broadcast media. In the Biafran conflict, the citizen humanitarian finds a full expression as evidenced through the massive outpouring of individual contributions at the behest of churches, NGOs, and the Red Cross. Today it seems natural and almost expected that the citizen will behave in a humanitarian fashion when non-state organizations call for help on behalf of those suffering. But this was not always the case and it was through the intersection of many different trajectories that the humanitarian discourse has produced various subject positions of the citizen humanitarian. In summary, the citizen humanitarian is the common human with common characteristics and thus able to feel commonly no matter where or who the sufferer might be. This relation between the humanitarian citizen and the distant 'other' needing help is indicative of the emergence of another subject: the humanitarian victim.

The humanitarian victim

The distant suffering stranger is one object of the citizen humanitarian's interest; the stranger at home is another. Victims have been viewed as idle recipients of compassion, but they also emerge in a more complex, often contradictory, relationship with humanitarians. On the one hand there is an expectation that victims should behave in a certain fashion, but on the other there is an acknowledgment that the victims have a part in the creation of their misfortune or in the construction of a situation as a disaster. The victim is now a subject for whom compassion should be felt. However, this compassion is directed such that there is an expectation that help will be provided only if the helper receives something in return. Perhaps what is received in return is not only physical but the victims' implicit participation in being governed, complacent, and unthreatening to existing social order. During the Biafran conflict the struggle for humanitarian control of the war extended to placing war victims at fault for not behaving correctly. This is reflected in the ICRC's desire to avoid creating the mentality of a refugee as a result of the humanitarian intervention; therefore, only well-behaved, well-managed victims of disaster are acceptable.

The Geneva Conventions and International Humanitarian Law are fairly obvious components of the humanitarian discourse. They are rules that are intended to produce ways of being and acting within conflicts. During the Biafra war the ICRC expected that governments and military leaders would instruct citizens and soldiers how to behave in a conflict. It also expected governments to allow it to operate independently and assist victims. The Red Cross expected that victims and combatants should behave in a certain fashion such that the humanitarian discourse produced the well-behaved, managed victim of disaster. However, in Biafra these kinds of subjects simply didn't behave well. These actors were placed at fault for not behaving correctly by the discourse of humanitarianism, namely by not following the Geneva Conventions and International Humanitarian Law. This extended to the Nigerian government for not allowing the free flow of aid, to the combatants for not distinguishing between victims and soldiers, and to victims for becoming accustomed to aid or using it to help fund and prolong the conflict. Therefore, the war was not just over land, it also included a struggle over the meaning of the war and over control of the massive relief operation. This control is, in essence, to dictate the rules of the discourse. Biafra, however, was portrayed as an exceptional event both by the Red Cross and by others. This exceptionality justified the lack of success that the Red Cross and contemporary humanitarian discourse had in making the war behave correctly. Thus, statements about humanitarianism's failure are deemed admissible to the discourse because the war was an exceptional event.

Thus, the humanitarian and the needy are in a hierarchical relationship where the humanitarian occupies a position superior to those needing rescue and knows what is best. On one hand, humanitarianism is under donors' control, and the flow of gifts and resources is only from the giver to the receiver. On the other, the recipients shape this relationship albeit in an unequal fashion through providing legitimacy and status to the event: there can be no disaster or crisis without victims. For example, the Red Cross noted that victims in Biafra began to organize themselves into advocacy groups. This shows that there was a potential for resistance even in the midst of a conflict where the victims were portrayed as helpless.

In further constructing the humanitarian victim MSF contributes its understanding of what constitutes a disaster. MSF devotes considerable time and text to debate around what a disaster looks like and to determining who should be helped. The victim is first of all vulnerable. But a victim exists not because of his or her position in society or because of existing poverty or inequality. The humanitarian victim only exists if there is a crisis or event that causes sufficient *excess* suffering or *excess* mortality. At some point when the disaster is over the subject is no longer a humanitarian victim. This point or dividing line between disaster and non-disaster is an interesting one as it represents a discontinuity within the discourse of the humanitarian victim as a subject. The dividing line is determined by discursive rules governing what is and is not a disaster.

At one end of the spectrum, a disaster is an exceptional event beyond the daily societal background noise of tragedies and avoidable mortality. At the other end of the spectrum, disaster is enmeshed within political and economic systems to the point where it becomes impossible to distinguish disaster from everyday existence. Thus institutions such as the Red Cross and MSF rely upon the former construction to perpetuate the subject of the professional humanitarian. A distinction must be made between the normal and the abnormal to make a space for the helper otherwise his or her task would be largely impossible. The existence of a victim is a necessary condition of the humanitarian act, and thus contributes to the creation of disaster, humanitarianism, and another subject: the humanitarian organization.

Humanitarian organization as a disciplinary institution

People have for a long time expressed their concern over the conditions of victims of disaster or war. In contrast, what we today call 'humanitarianism' is deemed straightforward and taken-for-granted because it is unproblematically associated with *organized* helping, compassion, feeling, and sympathy. Humanitarianism is a word that seems uniquely 'good' because it has only one history. Humanitarian organizations ignore the problematic aspects of its history, and often they make significant efforts to concretize it as a single trajectory. For example, the International Museum of the Red Cross in Geneva is a physical embodiment of 'history.' While it includes the notion that there have been multiple contributors to humanitarianism in its present form, these contributions are sidebars to the main trajectory.

The MSF movement attempts to disavow itself of history through appeals to a transcendent, 'neutral' character of its humanitarianism that implies that humanitarians' actions have no impact on the social construction and meaning of the term. Taken as a whole, this unproblematic view of history justifies specific approaches to helping, to dichotomize people as either 'helpers' or 'victims' and to perpetuate the notion that war and disaster are simply temporary setbacks to forward movement. In other words, I believe it is the case that by working to ensure that only one history is possible, it is easier to have people confuse the origins of the practice of humanitarianism with its meaning. But, in problematizing humanitarianism there are many trajectories of humanitarianism, and its present manifestation is the result of the intersection of these trajectories. There are other, equally believable, manifestations of humanitarianism and other interpretations of its meaning. If the caring face of humanitarianism can be problematized and questioned, and if its taken-for-granted status is called into question, the task now is to try and understand these other purposes that humanitarianism serves.

In a similar fashion, Foucault argues in his genealogical works *History of Madness*, *Security, Territory, and Population*, and *Discipline and Punish* that there has long been an interest in the poor, the insane, and the criminal. We believe that our era and our context are superior to those previous: that ours is more civilized, more humane, more enlightened. Have our present efforts truly evolved from control and punishment of victims into a benign interest in improving their conditions, ameliorating the illness, or reforming their criminality? Taking a longer historical view, Foucault (1997) shows that it is equally as believable that people have also been interested in mitigating the potential impact of the poor or criminals on the exercise of power because of the potential for chaos, resistance, and change. Take, for example, the development of social medicine in France and England in the eighteenth and nineteenth centuries. In this case, the increasing urbanization of the poor meant that rich and poor often shared similar urban spaces. This brought about the potential for, and the actualization of, violent disturbances. Not only this, but these shared urban spaces were characterized as unhealthy because whenever people "came together in closed places their morals and their health deteriorated" (Foucault, 1997: 144).

Thus people can become the object of medical intervention. Foucault (1997) shows how these beliefs about the behavior of the poor, together with medical interventions designed to mitigate these behaviors, resulted in practices that were ostensibly aimed at improving their conditions. However, they also had the effect of quelling the potential for revolution, violence, and resistance. Institutions exist where these mitigative practices are carried out: the prison, the workhouse, and the hospital are examples in this instance. These are ostensibly caring institutions where concern with the fate of others has a point of application.

However, they are also institutions created to see to it that people are governed through the application of discipline. As Foucault saw it, discipline is the application of routine that is sometimes carried out within an enclosed space such as a prison, school, or factory. Skills related to production or certain aptitudes within an individual are a component of discipline. For example, the factory worker is disciplined in the sense that s/he may have a skill necessary for production, but also because s/he works obediently, regularly, and within prescribed times. The individual becomes docile because he can be "subjected, used, transformed, and improved" (Foucault,

1995: 136) through ostensibly caring institutional practices such as funds for workers which, "freely and enthusiastically provided by industrialists for workers with families, are an answer to the need for employers to get men attached to them and to realize their responsibilities and the degree of material and moral interest that these responsibilities entail" (Mauss, 1969: 65). Thus, the notion of the disciplinary institution is that it is a space within which individuals become docile, obedient, and practiced for the specific purpose of applying certain values and regulating behavior.

I believe that humanitarian organizations are an instance of a disciplinary institution directed at a specific subject: that is, the disaster victim. In the aftermath of crisis the victim is constructed as being vulnerable and requiring the attention of formal helping structures. This is despite observations that victims are more often apt to help each other through the formation of temporary emergent organizations, and have in the past been considered resilient rather than vulnerable. But, can the refugee or disaster survivor really be considered equivalent to prisoner, delinquent, patient, or factory worker? That is, are the behaviors of these 'victim' subjects of disaster really subject to the same process applied within disciplinary institutions? I believe that they are. One piece of evidence for this claim comes from the literature and shows a striking intersection between humanitarianism and discipline through the claim that disaster disproportionately affects the poor, those living on marginal lands, and the relatively uneducated. For example, Fothergill and Peek (2004: 103) conduct an extensive review of disasters and poverty in the United States and conclude that the literature shows that "[the] poor are more likely to perceive hazards as risky; less likely to prepare for hazards or buy insurance; less likely to respond to warnings; more likely to die ... have more psychological trauma; and face more obstacles during the phases of response, recovery, and reconstruction."

Taking a more global perspective, one can find poverty and marginality implicated as responsible for individual vulnerability to disaster in the so-called developing regions of the world (Bankoff, Frerks, and Hilhorst, 2004; Bankoff, 2001; Blaikie, 1994). As Bankoff (2001) suggests, these regions have been constructed as being dangerous places not because of the disproportionate frequency of disaster, but because of the vulnerability of the population to the effects of disaster. The regions inhabited by these vulnerable people are therefore dangerous to themselves, but also dangerous to the West: they represent a potential threat to security. On the other hand, the population of the West is not, comparatively speaking, as vulnerable because they have the resilience to be able to withstand disaster. Therefore humanitarianism, at least insofar as it is interested in the suffering of those affected by disaster, considers the poor and especially those in the developing world, to be its main constituency.

It therefore reflects an established belief that the poor are huddled masses: dangerous and potentially threatening. According to Van Leeuwen (1994: 593), this has been a consistent concern about the poor and has motivated philanthropic and compassionate effort, the logic being that "[d]estitution for the many might easily lead to discontent" and "relief was advantageous if its costs were less than those of other means to maintain public order." Poverty itself as not an unfortunate and random situation, but a moral one or rather "a consequence of a seamy way of life" requiring disciplining behavior and so to "give assistance without attaching moral conditions would only reproduce squalor" (Van Leeuwen 1994: 594). In another example, Twohig (1996: 333) notes the manner in which doctors in nineteenth-century Nova Scotia, Canada, "served the needs of a colonial administration actively seeking to settle natives in reserve communities" and that at least part of the reason was the fear of the spread of disease. Relief to the poor through medical intervention, in this case the indigenous Mi'kmaq population of the province, would counter this disease and also provide justification for resettlement in areas away from the colonizers. And it is the poor, and those requiring moral education, who have been precisely the sought-after target of discipline and disciplinary institutions.

Another piece of evidence is that humanitarianism has been removed from the personal and made organizational. That is, the subject of the citizen humanitarian has largely been ignored, except to support the humanitarian professional and to provide ontological status to the humanitarian victim. How did this happen and how does this contribute to the discipline of humanitarianism? Perhaps, as Solnit (2009) writes upon reflecting on the 1906 San Francisco earthquake, Hurricane Katrina, and 9/11, disaster affords people the opportunity to be free: free from institutions, free from laws that assume that society tends to disorder in the absence of rules. This would produce a subject that is or has the potential to become someone "without social moorings" (May, 1993: 17): in short, an undisciplined subject.

Instead, the discourse of humanitarianism produces the victim as subject for the purpose of keeping them where they are physically and psychically, rather than see them migrate away from their borders, agitate for change, suspend productive activity, or form structures in opposition to the state. The persistent view is that disasters are temporary setbacks on the continually moving path of development even though there is considerable evidence to show that this is not the case. The literature suggests that this view arises because disasters are considered to be the result of "natural forces … a departure from a state of normalcy to which a society returns to on recovery" (Bankoff, 2001: 24).

With respect to conflict, one can also see suggestions that war is natural and merely a temporary setback. MSF itself raises the question of whether it would be better to simply allow wars to continue according to some kind of natural path: "is it better to have a brief, decisive war which ignores humanitarian principles, or a conflict prolonged by the respect of humanitarian demands?" (Terry, 1999: 5). However, I believe that when viewed through the lens of disciplinary society, the persistence of this view of the temporary nature of disaster and conflict can instead be understood as the need to make disciplined subjects that quickly return to contribute their part towards production. In other words, the discipline of humanitarianism exists because we cannot allow the disorder of displacement or dislocation: the state won't allow it. It has nothing to do with being kind or compassionate although this may be the stated intention.

The discipline of humanitarianism is borne out in the refugee camp, relocation center, the field hospital, or in more subtle ways outside of institutions or bounded locations. These are humanitarian sites where discipline is applied: they are components of a disciplinary society. This suggestion answers some calls in the literature. Malkki (2002: 353) calls for historicizing humanitarianism to show that "contemporary practices of disciplining movement and segregating people are not newly emergent phenomena, but something much older and established." I am suggesting that viewing these organizations as part of a disciplinary society means that we can no longer accept the Red Cross as a neutral organization, nor can we accept MSF as an activist organization with nothing more than the victims' interests at heart. The problem of humanitarianism is not that it fails through an incorrect application of technology, management practice, or legal principles. It is, instead, the creation of the subject of victim and the subject of professional helper within a disciplinary institution that is the problem. In the refugee camp or disaster site, as one form of state structure withdraws because it is 'weak,' 'failed,' or 'in crisis,' another form of state arises and permeates through discipline. More often than not, it is Third World states that produce these sites while 'developed' world states inject discipline into them.

Further, while physical humanitarian sites are obvious points of application of discipline, it is equally as possible to consider the disciplinary practice of humanitarianism within broader, non-physical spaces. For example, Foucault (1995: 212) observed that "religious groups and charity organizations" have "long played this role of disciplining the population." It is important to note that like the prison or the factory, the disciplinary role of humanitarian organizations is not directed or intentional. Rather, it is the result of "a multiplicity of often minor processes, of different origin and scattered location ... [that] converge and gradually produce the blueprint of a general method" (Foucault, 1995: 138). It is also important to note that while Foucault uses institutions as examples of an 'enclosed space' to explain the function of discipline, discipline "may be identified neither with an institution nor with an approach ... it is a type of power ... it may be taken over ... by specialized institutions" (Foucault, 1995: 215). While discipline can be found to act in enclosed spaces such as "the colleges, or secondary schools ... the military barracks ... great manufacturing spaces" (Foucault, 1995: 141) the principle of enclosure "is neither constant, nor indispensable" (Foucault, 1995: 143) but rather "it was a tactic of anti-desertion, anti-vagabondage, anti-concentration." I suggest, based upon my exploration of the discourse of humanitarianism, that one of these specialized institutions is the humanitarian organization.

Therefore, humanitarianism serves a role in ensuring the separation of populations. The ironic quality of this purpose is noted in relation to the 'without borders' discourse of humanitarianism. Humanitarianism extends the colonization of former colonies by reclaiming these territories through the act of helping. My argument here has raised more questions on borders and their role in framing the humanitarian problematic. In removing borders, humanitarianism seeks territory that is not claimed by others and tries to create its own space. Both the Red Cross and MSF have a complex understanding of borders. While MSF is popularly credited with a humanitarian function that ignores borders, it appears to erect a new and different set of borders related to defining humanitarianism, victims, and professionals. The borderless organization is possessed of many borders. However, the Red Cross was operating in a borderless fashion in Africa well before the arrival of MSF. In its work during the immediate postcolonial period, the Red Cross appealed to universal ideals and attempted to apply them across national borders and cultures. In fact the ideals were not so much universal as they were European. However, this strategy is not unique to humanitarianism as it is similar to the approach taken by colonial powers in appealing to universal tenets of civilization when attempting to justify colonialism. The justification was not so much to convince the colonized population as it was to convince colonizing populations at home that the policies and practices were needed. Humanitarianism extends notions of European culture and intellectual heritage into former colonial countries.

Humanitarianism and organization

I would like to address the notion of the organization in general as a caring or humanitarian institution. To be clear, I am at this point in the discussion *not* talking about humanitarian organizations such as the Red Cross or MSF but rather about applying what I have learned about humanitarianism from these organizations to other situations. In particular, I would like to identify how the humanitarian discourse works within the organization with a caring principle, or caring outlook.

There is evidence in the literature to begin building upon such an examination. In her examination of the role of the American Red Cross in China during the early twentieth century, Brewer (1983) outlines how the organization acted as an agent of productivity and efficiency both at home and abroad in China. She demonstrates that the American Red Cross was a

> progressive agency, its programs developed and managed by the elite to eliminate waste and inefficiency in American society. Its domestic reform programs were developed to prevent or mitigate the effects of accidents in American mining, railroad and lumber industries. Its disaster relief programs existed to provide aid in returning the victims to a productive, self-supporting role in society as soon as possible.
>
> *(Brewer, 1983: 383)*

This philosophy was exported abroad in Red Cross projects in China where "a consistent theme" in the Red Cross efforts in China "was the elimination and prevention of waste and inefficiency through reform of China's leaders, its government and society" (Brewer, 1983: 394). I too have explored this theme of the disciplinary function of humanitarian organizations, but what is important to note here is that in Brewer's (1983) version, the Red Cross could be considered an instrument of a managerialist ethos that values efficiency. As Brewer (1983) explains, the organization represented what then-President Woodrow Wilson called "that spirit ... of absolute disinterestedness, not thinking of ourselves, but thinking of the results we wish to achieve ... spiritual as well as material" (Wilson, 1979). In other words, the *humanitarianism* of the organization was something that others could model their lives upon in order to achieve *material* gain.

Further evidence comes from the 'business and society' field. This area is a normative attempt to look at the relationship between business activities and the social good. This relationship is considered successful if the firm's conduct results in profit maximization within the constraints of socially acceptable behavior and local laws (Swanson, 1999). However, this can only be applicable insofar as the laws exist and are enforceable. For failed states, in situations of conflict, or when the boundary between legal and illegal behavior becomes blurred, the non-profit sector's ostensible reputation of neutrality and morality gives cause for them to play an important role in business: they become stakeholders in the process. The non-profit is considered a neutral, legitimizing partner in a private sector firm's goal of including the excluded.

However, empirical studies (Banerjee, 2000, 2008; Herzlinger and Krasker, 1987) of non-profits cast doubt on this assertion of the inherent goodness of the humanitarian organization as a legitimizing agent and open a theoretical hole in the stakeholder concept into which more nuanced thinking about the role of humanitarianism can be introduced. This is especially important when attempting to view the non-profit as the subject of a stakeholder analysis rather than simply a stakeholder in its own right. This is particularly important as the NGO itself is often used as a legitimizing instrument and not an object of analysis within stakeholder theory. By incorporating the discourse of humanitarianism into stakeholder theory and 'business and society' research, this chapter suggests problematizing what has to this point been an unproblematic conceptualization of the non-profit organization as an unquestionable good.

References

Abercrombie, N., Hill, S., and Turner, B. (eds) (2000) *The Penguin Dictionary of Sociology* (4th edn). New York: Penguin Books.

Aeberhard, P. (1996) A historical survey of humanitarian action, *Health and Human Rights*, 2(1): 30–44.

Althusser, L. (2005) *For Marx*. London: Verso.

Assiter, A. (1984) Althusser and structuralism, *British Journal of Sociology*, 35(2): 272–96.

Banerjee, S. B. (2000) Whose land is it anyway? National interest, indigenous stakeholders, and colonial discourses, *Organization & Environment*, 13(1): 3–39.

Banerjee, S. B. (2008) Corporate social responsibility: The good, the bad and the ugly, *Critical Sociology*, 34(1): 51–79.

Bankoff, G. (2001) Rendering the world unsafe: 'Vulnerability' as Western discourse, *Disasters*, 25(1): 19–35.

Bankoff, G., Frerks, G., and Hilhorst, D. (2004) *Mapping Vulnerability: Disasters, Development, and People*. London: Earthscan.

Beck, U. (1999) *World Risk Society*. Malden, MA: Blackwell.

Blaikie, P.M. (1994) *At Risk: Natural Hazards, People's Vulnerability, and Disasters*. New York: Routledge.

Bornstein, E. and Redfield, P. (2007) *Genealogies of Suffering and the Gift of Care*. Social Sciences Research Council.

Brewer, K. (1983) From philanthropy to reform: The American Red Cross in China, 1906–1930, unpublished thesis, Case Western Reserve University.

Captier, C. (2005) MSF's principles and identity: The challenges ahead. In Médecins sans Frontières International Activity Report.
Core, A. C. (1950) Religion and the rise of humanitarianism in England, unpublished thesis, University of Nebraska.
De Waal, A. (1997) *Famine Crimes: Politics & the Disaster Relief Industry in Africa*. Oxford: James Currey.
Development Initiatives (2013) *Global Humanitarian Assistance Report*, http://www.globalhumanitarianassistance.org/report/gha-report-2013
Drabek, T. and Mcentire, D. (2003) Emergent phenomena and the sociology of disaster: Lessons, trends and opportunities from the research literature, *Disaster Prevention and Management*, 12(2): 97–112.
Fiering, N. (1976) Irresistible compassion: An aspect of eighteenth-century sympathy and humanitarianism, *Journal of the History of Ideas*, 37(2): 195–218.
Forsythe, D. (2005) *The Humanitarians: The International Committee of the Red Cross*. New York: Cambridge University Press.
Forsythe, D. (2007) *International Committee of the Red Cross: A Neutral Humanitarian Actor*. London: Routledge.
Fothergill, A. and Peek, L. A. (2004) Poverty and disasters in the United States: A review of recent sociological findings, *Natural Hazards*, 32(1): 89–110.
Foucault, M. (1995) *Discipline & Punish: The Birth of the Prison*. New York: Vintage Books.
Foucault, M. (1997) *Power*. New York: New Press.
Foucault, M. (2002) *The Archaeology of Knowledge*. New York: Routledge.
Furedi, F. (2007a) Coping with adversity: The turn to the rhetoric of vulnerability, *Security Journal*, 20(3): 171–84.
Furedi, F. (2007b) From the narrative of the blitz to the rhetoric of vulnerability, *Cultural Sociology*, 1(2): 235–54.
Halttunen, K. (1995) Humanitarianism and the pornography of pain in Anglo-American culture, *American Historical Review*, 100(2): 303–34.
Hardt, M. (2000) *Empire*. Cambridge, MA: Harvard University Press.
Herzlinger, R. E. and Krasker, W. S. (1987) Who profits from nonprofits? *Harvard Business Review*, 65(1): 93–106.
ICRC (2005) *Discover the ICRC*. Geneva: International Committee of the Red Cross.
Jacques, R. (1992) Re-presenting the knowledge worker: A poststructuralist analysis of the new employed professional, unpublished thesis, University of Massachusetts, Amherst.
Jeannerod, B. (2005) Taking stances and taking risks. *Messages: MSF France Newsletter*, 135: 14.
Kendall, G. and Wickham, G. (1999) *Using Foucault's Methods*. Thousand Oaks, CA: Sage.
Lambert, D. and Lester, A. (2004) Geographies of colonial philanthropy, *Progress in Human Geography*, 28(3): 320–41.
Malkki, L. H. (2002) News from nowhere: Mass displacement and globalized 'problems of organization', *Ethnography*, 3(3): 351–60.
Mauss, M. (1969) *The Gift: Forms and Functions of Exchange in Archaic Societies*. London: Cohen & West.
May, T. (1993) *Between Genealogy and Epistemology: Psychology, Politics, and Knowledge in the Thought of Michel Foucault*. University Park, PA: Pennsylvania State University Press.
Moorehead, C. (1999) *Dunant's Dream: War, Switzerland, and the History of the Red Cross*. New York: Carroll & Graf.
Nietzsche, F. W. (1989) *On the Genealogy of Morals*. London: Vintage.
Orbinski, J. (1999) Nobel Lecture: Médecins sans frontieres. http://nobelprize.org/nobel_prizes/peace/laureates/1999/msf-lecture.html
Patton, P. (1978) Althusser's epistemology: The limits of the theory of theoretical practice, *Radical Philosophy*, 19: 8–18.
Prasad, P. (2005) *Crafting Qualitative Research: Working in the Postpositivist Traditions*, Armonk, NY: M. E. Sharpe.
Redfield, P. (2005) Doctors, borders, and life in crisis, *Cultural Anthropology*, 20(3): 328–61.
Rodríguez, H., Trainor, J., and Quarantelli, E. L. (2006) Rising to the challenges of a catastrophe: The emergent and prosocial behavior following Hurricane Katrina, *Annals of the American Academy of Political and Social Science*, 604: 82–101.
Solnit, R. (2009) *A Paradise Built in Hell: The Extraordinary Communities that Arise in Disasters*. New York: Viking.
Stamatov, P. (2008) Religious origins of distant humanitarianism, unpublished thesis, University of California, Los Angeles.

Swanson, D. L. (1999) Toward an integrative theory of business and society: a research strategy for corporate social performance, *Academy of Management Review*, 24(3): 506–21.
Terry, F. (1999) Reconstituting whose social order? NGOs in disrupted states, Fondation MSF/CRASH.
Twohig, P. (1996) Colonial care: Medical attendance among the Mikmaq in Nova Scotia, *Canadian Bulletin of Medical History*, 13(2): 333–53.
Vallaeys, A. (2004) *Médecins sans frontières: la biographie*. Paris: Fayard.
Van Leeuwen, K. (1994) Logic of charity: Poor relief in preindustrial Europe, *Journal of Interdisciplinary History*, 24(4): 589–613.
Weedon, C. (1996) *Feminist Practice and Poststructuralist Theory* (2nd edn). Cambridge, MA: Blackwell.
Wilson, W. (1979) *The Papers of Woodrow Wilson, Vol. 31: September 6 – December 31 1914*, ed. A. Link. Princeton, NJ: Princeton University Press.

14

The future of history

Posthumanist entrepreneurial storytelling, global warming, and global capitalism

David M. Boje and Rohny Saylors

It is essential that we rethink the paradigmatic limitations of the field of organizational history (Foster, Mills & Weatherbee, 2014), in particular as related to Management and Organization Studies (cf. White, 2013) and Critical Management Studies (cf. Leca, Gond & Cruz, 2014; Reis, 2014). The purpose of this chapter is to rethink the relationship between history and storytelling by integrating an entrepreneurial posthumanist take on the relation between global warming and global capitalism. The line of logic is as such. Storytelling is an integrative complex relation of posthumanist concerns. Often this is glossed over by simply historicity. If we bring in the polyphonic storytelling of historicity, we see that global warming and global capitalism are fundamental to history. Entrepreneurial posthumanism provides hope for praxis storytelling historicality.

Storytelling is the interplay of grand narratives, webs of living stories, and their interrelationships: antenarratives. A grand narrative is a societal narrative with hegemonic power. That is a big story that pushes down the stories of others. Living stories are just that, stories that live. They are always situated in a particular place, space, and time and intra-act with one another. Antenarratives are before-narratives; they are bets on the future, existing both beneath and between the past and future. As pre-narratives, they well up into what is coming into being. As bets, they represent a multitude of potential futures that an individual may see. As the in-between, they link a story's past and future. Experientially they soon become the past. Beneath they link together non-linear patterns. Antenarrative is a systemicity, a system that is never complete and always ongoing in its creation (Boje, 2006, 2008; Boje & Wakefield, 2011).

There are preliminary distinctions that we feel we should make before moving on. First history is not the same as the past. Instead history is an emergent work of social and/or scholarly creation. This scholarly creation can be historicity, an authenticated past that is in line with other authenticated histories. History also has the potential to be historicality, a step beyond authenticated history that brings in the micro-stories which may be repressed by authenticated pasts. At its core, this chapter relies on what Rosile *et al.* (2013), call a materialist, praxis, antenarrative storytelling paradigm.

History can be historicity, a rather shallow grand narrative that is linear, and overly simplistic (Weatherbee *et al.*, 2012). Historicity creates the sense of a linear, illusory, end that somehow justifies the present means (Agamben, 2000). Modern forms of History have been coopted by grand narratives that pre-construct how we are allowed to make sense of that which is historicized.

Historicality, by contrast, addresses the complexity of history, in a polyphony of entangled contexts. This untangles the concept of history from the naïve conception of it as statements of the past (Mills, Weatherbee & Durepos, 2013). The culturally indeterminate fields around which people interact are always in the middle of a kind of historicality. By taking the stance that historicity is the effluvial storytelling of grand narratives; we set our insights toward moving beyond the hegemony of grand narratives. The use of a storytelling perspective enlivens a potential for historicality that allows for entrepreneurial posthumanism.

Entrepreneurial posthumanism

Entrepreneurship is storytelling (Saylors, Boje & Mueller, 2014). The processes of identification, preparation, creation of resources, and the eventual telling of history that makes the firm a useful fiction are all functions of storytelling (Boje, Cast & Saylors, 2014). There are aspects of grand narratives, living story, and antenarratives integral to each.

The identification process centralizes around grand narratives, living story, and antenarratives. The feeling that there is a need is part of identifying with an opportunity. Without the ability to feel the need, a sense that there is a need worthy of exploitation is mitigated. The felt need comes from the living story of an entrepreneur: be it via vicarious experience, social learning, or personal experience. Once this feeling of need resonates with an opening in the market the entrepreneur makes antenarrative bets on a multitude of future past-narratives. As these bet-antenarratives develop, pre-narrative potentials are squashed by grand narratives (Boje, Helmuth & Saylors, 2014). As potentials for need fulfillment envelop the entrepreneurial storytelling-sensemaking process, the antenarratives move beneath the weight of grand narratives. Eventually, the pre-narrative bets move between potential futures that are not destroyed by grand narratives. Often these hegemonic influences over the entrepreneurial process are worded in terms of 'markets,' 'competition,' and 'profitability'. By entering the word-game of a legitimate, thoughtful entrepreneur, many ideas are destroyed and only those that resonate strongly enough with the living story of the entrepreneur make it past the gauntlet of negativity. Once identification with opportunities occurs the entrepreneurial process moves on to preparation, through the creation of resources, which eventually ends in the telling of a history.

It is in the telling of an entrepreneurial history that the previous weight of a grand narrative's hegemony is integrated into the venture. As the entrepreneur creates a history that is in line with the dominant grand narratives, the legitimacy of being part of that which dominates is integrated into the story. Those antenarratives that were squashed beneath the grand narratives are destroyed. The history of antenarratives between narratives is erased. The bet narratives are called. The pre-narratives are extinguished. This is in service of submission to the grand narrative. But the living story abides. For every one of the antenarrative processes that are shut down, potential for another storytelling emerges (Rosile *et al.*, 2013). It is in understanding the posthumanism-based implications of creating narrative history that we will find praxis implications.

Posthumanism is the recognition of the existence of a phenomenal life-world outside of the individual. From living story, to mother Gaia, to the spirits of entrepreneurship, capitalism, and Marxism, many agential forces exist that are non-human. In short, humans are only one of the many aspects of nature. Bringing entrepreneurial posthumanism into history allows for a historicity that was once lost under the thumb of capitalism. Here we focus on the denial of global warming as an example. The key to entrepreneurial posthumanism in history research is finding those living stories that have been muted by grand narratives. These can be found in the historicity of global capitalist firms. Theirs is the effluvial storytelling of grand narratives. Living stories can be drawn up and re-historicized from the perspective of a post-human agent: nature herself.

Global warming and global capitalism

The future of storytelling integrates an entrepreneurial posthumanist perspective on global warming and global capitalism. We cannot reduce global warming to a grand narrative of global capitalism by erasing webs of living stories of non-human species. Climate change is refracted through global capitalism's grand narratives. The crisis is not a Hegelian dialectic of the movement of human history; rather the human species has become its own geological agent of change, to be found in global capitalism.

One often hears the refrain in open systems thinking that the whole is greater than the sum of the parts. However, in climate change, "we have to admit the Whole is contained by its Part" the human species (Žižek, 2010: 333). The human species is now a geological agent of change. It has an effect not only on other species by hastening their extinction, but on their own species, hastening human extinction (Chakrabarty, 2009; Žižek, 2010; Wainwright & Mann, 2013).

"The discipline of history exists on the assumption that our past, present, and future are connected by a certain continuity of human experience" (Chakrabarty, 2009: 197). The planetary crisis of global warming (aka climate change) elicits a variety of responses, from denial, disconnect, and indifference to activism and engagements in practices of sustainability. With the possible extinction of the human species, the past and present disconnect from the future, as the continuity of human experience ends. This is a radical sense of posthumanism, a planet that continues to exist without humans. Chakrabarty' s point is that our historical understanding is thrown into "deep contradiction and confusion" (Chakrabarty, 2009: 198).

The debate on climate change, therefore, should be of interest to history researchers. The greenhouse gases produced by burning fossil fuel and industrial use of animal stock have a transformative consequence to how we think about human history and globalization. Thus, discussions of global warming, globalization, and posthumanism run parallel to each other. Globalization became a public concern in 1990s, global warming in 2000s, and posthumanism in 2010s.

The melting of the ice caps. Drought in Australia. More frequent cyclones, brush fires, and crop failures in many parts of the world. All are due to the increasing global footprint of the human population which will pass the 9 billion mark by 2050. It is time to say that globalization is affecting climate change and that posthumanism is taking on a new meaning.

Theories of globalization – Marxist analysis, subaltern studies, and postcolonial criticism – are beginning to grapple with the chaos resulting from capitalist economies having reached their ecological limits. Now globalization and global warming have "overlapping processes" (Chakrabarty, 2009: 200). For example, Oreskes' (2007) review of 928 peer-reviewed papers on global warming published between 1993 and 2003 reveals that not a single article refutes the consensus to be found among scientists on the "reality of human-induced climate change" (2007: 201). There is only disagreement on the amount and direction of change. The foundation of our posthumanist perspective regarding history is built on three central theses:

Thesis 1: Collapse of the distinction between natural history and human history serves extant dominant narratives.

Hobbes contended that humans can have only a proper knowledge of the Leviathan of civil and political institutions because nature remains God's work and is inscrutable to humans. Marx's dictum was "men make their own history, but they do not make it just as they please" (cited in Chakrabarty, 2009: 202). Collingwood assumed that nature is just events, rather than nature being agential, and hence "all history properly so called is the history of human affairs" (cited in Chakrabarty, 2009: 203). Nature as events sets up a duality between human history and nature as being non-historical. The duality leaves human animals, their body and its activities and natural appetites, as being outside of human history.

Posthumanism returns humans to nature, not as a social construction but as part of the physical world. In social construction rocks do not exist unless humans think about them and all materialism became subsumed under the central doctrine of human thought, language games, and social construction of reality. Now critical materialist arguments for posthumanism are emerging to problematize humanism's anti-materialism presupposition. Stalin reasoned that the human society changes more rapidly than changes in geographical conditions (Tucker, 1992), so a human relation to the environment was timeless and not a subject for historical materialism at all.

Clearly organization studies, like Stalin, have treated the ecosystem as a silent and passive backdrop to their historical narratives of institutions. Nature's ever-recurring cycles play an active agential role in molding human actions. This role is almost timeless. It is not reaching a tipping point. The environment timelessly transforms itself with a speed that spells disaster for humans. This is a breach of the dualism of natural/human history. The breach of dualism gives rise to environmental history and human history combining into a posthumanist history. Posthumanist history is no longer straightforward in terms of social, economic, political, and cultural history. Humans are no longer the only agents. Further, humans have a newly described "geological agency" (Chakrabarty, 2009: 206). This means deconstructing the time-honored duality between human history and environmental history. This means human beings become much more than simple biological agents, but rather "wield a geological force" that is "changing the most basic physical processes of the earth" (Oreskes, quoted in Chakrabarty, 2009: 206).

We can no longer assume that Earth processes are immune to human chronologies, or that the vastness of geographical time and geological processes are not affected by global capitalism. Humans are geological agents, not just biological agents. Becoming geological agents both historically and collectively, in global capitalism, since burning billions of tons of fossil fuels is changing the chemistry of Earth's atmosphere, melting polar ice caps, and raising sea levels on a scale large enough to result in a mass extinction of species. "Our footprint was not always that large" (Chakrabarty, 2009: 207). Humans have acquired geological agency since the Industrial Revolution, and a tipping point was reached after the Second World War. Organizations are not simply interacting with their environment; rather those organizations are now a force of nature in the geological sense.

Thesis 2: The grand narrative of globalization reveals a voluminous array of living environmental stories based on antenarratives that run before, bet, between, and beneath the linear narrative.

In this postmodern epic, the human production, distribution, and consumption processes of globalization are geological forces. Social, economic, political, and cultural contexts are no longer separate from the realm of nature and its ecological context. Kant, Hegel, and Marx's ideas of human progress, human freedom, and human history to escape injection, inequity, and oppression do not display an awareness of geological agency that humans were acquiring in human-made systems of organizing and consumption rooted in fossil fuel (coal, oil, and gas). Our systemicity of organizations is energy-intensive, and has resulted in "anthropogenic climate change" (Chakrabarty, 2009: 209). Anthropogenic refers to something that originates from humans. Anthropogenic climate change refers to the pollution from burning fossil fuels that emit carbon dioxide, along with other human activities on earth. The anthropogenic effect on climate is now on a global scale and has become so ubiquitous since the 1750s that it deserves its own geological epoch. The Anthropocene is a critique of grand narratives of freedom, because the price of freedom is humanity's increasing geological agency; the grand narrative of humanity's role as planet killer to accomplish short-term survival in the midst of growing food and energy crises.

Thesis 3: By taking a posthumanist perspective on history we can avoid the human–nature dichotomy that presupposes the value of environmental destruction.

Anthropocene thinking requires us to put global histories of the Leviathan into dialogue with the species' history of humans. Global capitalism exists, but its critics do not have a handle on the inseparability of human and planet history. "The problematic of globalization allows us to read climate change only as a crisis of capitalist management" (Chakrabarty, 2009: 212). Making management the focus misses the challenge of the Anthropocene era, where humans' geological agency is "entangled with the now of human history" (Chakrabarty, 2009: 212). Ecosystem problems are emerging on a world scale at a rate unprecedented in the 10,000 years of recorded human history. Going beyond four centuries of textual archives means constructing a deep history of social, economic, political, cultural, and ecological change. This includes working out the consequences of global warming for the history of life on this planet. Posthumanism is becoming a critique of global capitalism along with its "multiplying modernities" in which "there is no universalizing spirit" and "there are, instead, many very specific, very material and pragmatic practices that await critical reflection and historical study" (Chakrabarty, 2009: 214).

Critical Management Studies (CMS) needs to address this world of multiplying modernities and the material and pragmatic practices of global capitalism that are in need of critical reflection. Human 'being' is no longer the only subject standpoint in world history. Humans are one among many species, and humans are dominating other species, in their acquiring of the status of a geological force. Given this condition, the search for Green Capitalism, or some utopian sustainable capitalism, is futile. CMS needs to realize the protagonists of their storytelling, the managers, and other persons, are reductions of the "embodied and whole human being" (Chakrabarty, 2009: 214). The grand narrative of global capitalism is part of a larger story of global domination, written in rather large carbon footprints of rich nations and richer socio-economic classes. Falling into anthropocentric decline is not inevitable. The stories of 'discovery' of oil by the oil tycoons are full of coincidences and historical accidents, rather than any inevitability. The dramatic increase in human population since the Second World War has pushed us into the Anthropocene. Both the capitalist and socialist nations burn fossil fuel to sustain their way of life in global capitalism; a way of life rooted in high-energy-consuming models of society that result in a mass extinction of species; all wrought by organizations.

Thesis 4: By showing in juxtaposition the living stories of species history and human history we can re-historicize in such a manner that the unity of the fate of the human animal is clearly linked to the destruction being wrought by globalization.

Cross-hatching species history with a history of global capitalism moves CMS beyond just human experience to historical consciousness allowing critical reflections on how our pasts connect to the possibility of our species' future survival. Will humans even have a future, that is, a history, given the crisis of global warming and a world without humans? The duality between human and ecosystem history has been breached. Humans are now historical geological agents. Climate change refracted through global capitalism's unintended consequences lets us appreciate that it is not a process of "Hegelian universal" (Chakrabarty, 2009: 222). Our shared sense of catastrophe calls for "a global approach to politics without the myth of a global identity" because unlike the Hegelian universal, our future cannot subsume particularities, and we are served with a rather negative "universal history" (Chakrabarty, 2009: 222).

Wainwright and Mann (2013) argue that we have entered the era of Climate Leviathan. This is an age of hegemonic institutional modes of governance and accumulation that continue to thwart responses to climate warming and unfolds in directions unplotted by Thomas Hobbes or Job (Job 41:1–34). As Walter Benjamin concludes, "the 'state of emergency' in which we live is the rule" (1969: 258).

Our concept of systemicity must keep pace with this insight. It is the task of CMS to bring about a real sense of this state of emergency. A state of emergency is the normal state of organizational systemicity; seeking standards and norms of the regulation and control of the state of emergency: the "neoliberal contagion of financial crisis and market disorders" and "global climate change" that produced the normal condition of "the paradigm of security as the normal technique of government" (Wainwright & Mann, 2013: 2).

CMS can draw attention to how this Leviathan is bringing about the conditions of planetary crisis. This is not some open system theory. Rather it is the very end of open systems. "Our global carbon emissions jumped by 5.9% in 2012" (Wainwright & Mann, 2013: 2). The International Energy Agency, no revolutionary outfit, warns us that "the world is likely to build so many fossil-fuelled power stations, energy-guzzling factories and inefficient buildings in the next five years that it will become impossible to hold global warming to safe levels" (Fiona Harvey, *The Guardian*, November 9, 2011: 3).

CMS can help the Leviathan contemplate the socio-economic-political future in an ongoing war for the world's energy supplies without reduction in global carbon emissions that continues to change the chemical composition of the atmosphere. We may be past the tipping point, and it is no longer possible to tame global capitalism, and avert its deadly consequences. Sustainability is now a relatively weak, frenzied, and marginal reaction to climate change; rather than any change of the material conditions of the world's capitalist nation-states. Green Capitalism is now a grand narrative of great incredulity. The grand narrative of Enlightenment progress is being displaced by a grand narrative of ecological collapse in as in Hobbes' war-of-all-against-all.

Can posthumanism be constituted into planetary sovereignty where management is reconstituted for the purposes of planetary sustainability? This would be a paradigm shift away from Leviathan. This shift is necessary because of the collective action involved in carbon sequestration.

Discussion

The future of storytelling in organizational history holds potential for praxis intervention. These praxis interventions are based on scholars working with history taking entrepreneurial posthumanism seriously. This has four major normative consequences for storytelling history.

First, the service provided to dominant narratives of global capitalism by those who perpetuate an a-environmental historicity should be resisted. We must focus on humans as care-maximizing entities. The basis of faith in economics is that people fundamentally want to do well for themselves. We should attack this faith in homo economics. Instead, we need to work on an alternative paradigm. Instead of being lost in the esoteric weeds of philosophy we must ground our research in a way that resonates with a fundamental ethos of care. We must share our ideas so others can understand how one might act in a caring way in any context. As Asdal (2003) has pointed out this can be achieved by integrating posthumanist thought.

Second, the opportunity to draw entrepreneurial posthumanism into historicality should be exploited. We have the opportunity to be entrepreneurial in our integration of posthumanism into history. By creating new normative influences on how we read history we can subvert existing power structures. Further, by unveiling the falseness of linear historicists we can open readers to the fullness of historicality. This allows us to bring forth the limited lines of thinking that are allowed by those with power. Finally, this opportunity allows a repositioning of anthropocentric thinking. Long ago humanity moved past the idea of the Earth as the center of the universe, but somehow humans themselves remained there. Even on the most fundamental levels we know this dichotomy is false (Ley, Knight & Gordon, 2007).

Third, the implicit impetus to accept the human–nature dichotomy should be deconstructed. As the future of storytelling in history becomes more entrepreneurially posthuman, the implicit raising of humanity as outside of nature is implicitly deconstructed. From this implicit deconstruction, we should move to history that directly deconstructs this disconnect. For example, when we write about institutional history the influence of the physical environment should be incorporated. This sort of critical integration is just on the horizon (Suddaby, 2014).

Fourth, storytelling should unify the fate of the human animal with the destruction wrought by global exploitation. Often this is done in terms of the environment posing some threat to the human condition. Through storytelling cross-hatching between the environment and the human animal becomes possible. We can do research that brings in environmental interactions between organizational history. In its most advanced form a kind of dithering, where bits of the environment appear to provide a greater shade of understanding of human history. The outcomes of our four theses hold the potential to restore history in a way that incorporates posthumanism.

Environmental rehistorying

The point of restorying is to resist existing sensemakings and produce new ones (Cast et al., 2013). In the case of integrating the environment into history, we restory to create a new narrative about an organizational event. Take for example Cemex, the world's third largest cement manufacturer; a firm with monopolistic control of cement production in many countries. The dominant narrative of Cemex may be of producing walkways, hospitals, and the like. But once we find that cement manufacturing is the cause of 5 percent of all CO_2 emissions and that Cemex is controlled by a group of elite oligarchical family groups (Sargent, 2005), we have a much different story. And when the history is written using a posthumanist entrepreneurial perspective a new historicality, a historicality that acknowledges this fact, can emerge.

There are seven basic steps to environmental rehistorying. Each of these must be refracted through the theorization of the past that is guiding the researcher (cf. Durepos, Mills & Weatherbee, 2012):

- Characterization: where environmental impact is brought to light.
- Externalization: where environmental impact is shown as something different from the firm.
- Sympathization: where why the environmental impact exists is accepted.
- Problematize: where despite the sympathy the environmental impact is still functionally troublesome.
- Strategize: where a new idea of what the firm is, now *sans* this environmental impact, is developed.
- Rehistoricize: develop a new historicity out of the strategization.
- Publicize: where the firm takes on both blame and praise for its new structure.

In this way, the future storytelling of organizational history can integrate the four theses of entrepreneurial posthumanism.

The following steps outline the process whereby a theorized rehistorying can be achieved:

1. Characterize – Portray the environmental impact in the history of the firm. This is where a historicality perspective is key. The research must move beyond simply accepting the linear narratives of history to show how there are characterizable environmental impacts.
2. Externalize – Show that this impact is not the total function of the firm. By showing that the firm has positives that are manifest aside from the negatives, the dominant historicity is

not destroyed, but rethought. This research moves into multiple voices, respecting differing perspectives.

3. Sympathize – The environmental impact of the firm is something that was written off as a necessary evil some time ago. Consider the experience of that decision in historical context. Give strong motivations that allow for such a justification.
4. Problematize – Despite the sympathetic motivations the environmental impact is a problem. Look into the historical impacts that run contrary to what was sympathetic previously. For example, if a firm is founded on helping people live better, perhaps there are examples of how the environmental impact mitigates or even negates that intent.
5. Strategize – Create a new story around the firm's interactions between various historicists. This is a detachment of the meaning of the historical context from the now problematized environmental impact. This strategizing can be built on 'little wow moments' in the history of the firm that affirm the firm's disseverance from its previously accepted past.
6. Rehistoricize – Bringing forward all those 'little wow moments' to develop a new kind of historicity. From these historicities, new historicalities can be drawn. The firm can be rehistoricized as though a fundamental part of its ethos is sustainability.
7. Publicize – Engage the network of storytelling processes that uphold the previous history. By working together to integrate a sense of the unified fate of humans and our environment, we can turn away from the economic narrative. As we utilize entrepreneurial posthumanism to change normativity around organizational history, we also disempower those that seek to exploit and destroy for short-term gains. There will be a backlash. Because of this the quality of the historical evidence and storied integration of it into the firm's past is paramount.

Conclusion

If we rethink how history and storytelling relate to each other, our storytelling history research can have a praxis future. In integrating entrepreneurial posthumanism into our storytelling of organizational history, we can draw a stark connection between globalization and global warming. This is because storytelling integrates the complexity of posthuman concerns. Thus, the complexities that are glossed over by historicity can be brought to light. When a polyphony of living stories are expressed the complexity of the link between globalization and global warming becomes paramount. Thus, the entrepreneurial posthumanist re-reading of historical matters advances praxis. Though the thesis of globalism is powerful, we have offered four counter-theses that also have powerful potential. In the end the ability to change the history of the organization is a practical theory (Weatherbee, Dye & Mills, 2008). This method for changing is how we could go about theory in a way that improves the world.

References

Agamben, G. (2000) *Means Without End: Notes on Politics*. Minneapolis: University of Minnesota Press.

Asdal, K. (2003) The problematic nature of nature: The post-constructivist challenge to environmental history, *History and Theory*, 42(4): 60–74.

Benjamin, W. (1969). *Illuminations*. New York: Schocken Books.

Boje, D. M. (2006) Breaking out of narrative's prison: improper story in storytelling organization, *Storytelling, Self, Society*, 2(2): 28–49.

Boje, D. M. (2008) *Storytelling Organizations*. London: Sage.

Boje, D. M. and Wakefield, T. (2011) Storytelling in systemicity and emergence, in D. Boje, B. Burnes, and J. Hassard (eds), *The Routledge Companion to Organizational Change* (pp. 171–80). Abingdon and New York: Routledge.

Boje, D., Cast, M., and Saylors, R. (2014) Liquid times for the entrepreneurial identity non-profit organization, in J. Kociatkiewicz and M. Kostera (eds), *Liquid Organization: Zygmunt Bauman and Organization Theory* (pp. 140–52). Abingdon and New York: Routledge.

Boje, D. M., Helmuth, C., and Saylors, R. (2014) Spinning authentic leadership living stories of the self, in D. Ladkin and C. Spiller (eds), *Authentic Leadership: Concepts, Coalescences, and Clashes* (pp. 271–78). Cheltenham: Edward Elgar.

Cast, M. L., Rosile, G. A., Boje, D. M., and Saylors, R. (2013) Restorying a hard day's work, *Research in Occupational Stress and Well-being*, 11: 257–81.

Chakrabarty, D. (2009) The climate of history: Four theses, *Critical Inquiry* 35(2): 197–222.

Durepos, G., Mills, A. J., and Weatherbee, T. G. (2012) Theorizing the past: Realism, relativism, relationalism and the reassembly of Weber, *Management & Organizational History*, 7(3): 267–81.

Foster, J., Mills, A. J., and Weatherbee, T. (2014) History, field definition and management studies: The case of the New Deal, *Journal of Management History*, 20(2): 179–99.

Leca, B., Gond, J. P., and Cruz, L. B. (2014) Building 'critical performativity engines' for deprived communities: The construction of popular cooperative incubators in Brazil, *Organization*, 21(5): 683–712.

Ley, R. E., Knight, R., and Gordon, J. I. (2007) The human microbiome: Eliminating the biomedical/environmental dichotomy in microbial ecology, *Environmental Microbiology*, 9(1): 3–4.

Mills, A. J., Weatherbee, T. G., and Durepos, G. (2013) Reassembling Weber to reveal the-past-as-history in management and organization studies, *Organization*, 12(2): 225–43.

Oreskes, N. (2007) The scientific consensus on climate change: How do we know we're not wrong? in J. DiMento and P. Doughman (eds), *Climate Change: What It Means For Us, Our Children, and Our Grandchildren* (pp. 65–99). Cambridge, MA: MIT Press.

Reis, C. (2014) Listening to the material life in discursive practices, *Tamara Journal for Critical Organization Inquiry*, 12(2): 9–14.

Rosile, G. A., Boje, D. M., Carlon, D. M., Downs, A., and Saylors, R. (2013) Storytelling diamond: An antenarrative integration of the six facets of storytelling in organization research design, *Organizational Research Methods*, 16(4): 557–80.

Sargent, J. (2005) Large firms and business groups in Latin America: Towards a theory based, contextually relevant research agenda, *Latin American Business Review*, 6(2): 39–66.

Saylors, R., Boje, D. M., and Mueller, T. J. (2014) Entrepreneurial storytelling in moments of friendship: Antenarratives of business plans, risk taking, and venture capital narratives, *Tamara Journal for Critical Organization Inquiry*, 12(4): 557–80.

Suddaby, R. (2014) Can institutional theory be critical? *Journal of Management Inquiry*, http://jmi.sagepub.com/content/early/2014/07/28/1056492614545304

Tucker, R. C. (1992) *Stalin in Power: The Revolution from Above, 1928–1941*. New York: W.W. Norton.

Wainwright, J. and Mann, G. (2013) Climate leviathan, *Antipode*, 45(1): 1–22.

Weatherbee, T., Dye, K., and Mills, A. J. (2008) There's nothing as good as a practical theory: The paradox of management education, *Management & Organizational History*, 3(2): 147–60.

Weatherbee, T. G., Durepos, G., Mills, A., and Mills, J. H. (2012) Theorizing the past: Critical engagements, *Management & Organizational History*, 7(3): 193–202.

White, B. (2013) Coyote and Brother Crow: A little history, *Tamara Journal for Critical Organization Inquiry*, 8(1): 7–28.

Žižek, S. (2010) *Living in the End Times*. London: Verso.

15

Varieties of history in organization studies

Diego M. Coraiola, William M. Foster, and Roy Suddaby

Introduction

A large part of the argument for historicizing management and organizational studies is based on the recognition of the ahistorical character of most research done in management and organizations (Zald, 1990; Kieser, 1994). This can be more clearly seen through the existing divide between the fields of organization studies and business history. This argument usually relies on an assumption about the incommensurability of history and science, which can be traced back to a widely shared practical realist view on the nature of history. We avoid this common argument and advocate for a temporary suspension of the discussion of the incommensurability of science and history to focus on the assumptions about history that guide both 'historical research' (e.g. business history) and 'scientific research' (e.g. organizational theory). As Lorenz (2011) argues, any attempt to define history will raise ontological, epistemological, methodological, and ethical controversies. With this in mind, we embark on an open discussion about the contributions to be gained from an enriched view of history for management and organization studies.

We adopt a critical view of the widely assumed ahistorical character of empirical organizational research. Instead of approaching management and organizational history (MOH) research on the grounds of the incommensurability of scientific and historical modes of knowledge, we start by recognizing that researchers might have different assumptions about the nature of historical knowledge. That these commonly implicit and generalized assumptions contribute to the 'invisibility of historical research' (Rowlinson & Hassard, 2013) is a generally overlooked historical critique of organization studies. The general lack of interest in historical issues is not only a reflex of the inherited ahistorical condition of the scientific project of social sciences (Zald, 1993), but also a consequence of generally overlooked and taken-for-granted ontological and epistemological assumptions of the nature of history in organizational research. The ahistorical character of most organizational research seems to be much less the consequence of a decision taken by an informed scholar interested in developing scientific explanations than the result of an unreflexive espousal of a specific view on history.

We illustrate our argument by discussing the use of history in institutional theory research. Organizational institutionalism is one of the most prominent approaches in organization studies and has already been the focus of researchers interested in the potential benefits of relating institutional theory to historical research (Rowlinson & Hassard, 2013; Suddaby, Foster & Mills, 2014). We analyze some prominent historically-oriented institutional theory papers and identify their manifest or latent views on history. The examination of these papers demonstrates that when history is done 'under cover', or is treated as a variable, it is not necessarily because of a misunderstanding of what history is or what history is intended to accomplish. Instead, the understanding of history is the product of the researcher's ontological beliefs. Identifying these assumptions and bringing these to light will help to clarify how history is used and is presented in organization studies. This clarification will, in our opinion, help produce more historically reflective studies on management and organizational phenomena.

In the following sections we will first outline and synthesize the current debates on the role of history in organization studies. Next, discussion will focus on the existing assumptions about the nature of history and how it can be studied. We use Munslow's (2006a) typology of ontological positions in history as our guide and we classify how history is used in institutional research on the basis of his description of the three main ontological positions on history. Discussion then turns to the implications that arise when assumptions about the nature and access of historical reality are surfaced. Finally, the chapter concludes with suggestions about some possible avenues for future, historically-informed, MOH research.

History and the social sciences

For many social scientists, there is the belief that historical research involves rummaging around in a dusty archive to find evidence of the past so that the historian can paint an accurate picture of the world as it used to be. This common misconception of what history is and what it involves (Clark & Rowlinson, 2004) is grounded in practical realism. The past is seen as a site where scholars can find traces of evidence. Moreover, it is possible to recover the reality of the past in the present and discover the 'truth' through the empirical analysis of historical sources. History, then, is produced through the skilful reconstruction of the past as it actually happened, without bias or prejudice. Thus, to social scientists, studying history means describing how people used to live, what they used to do, what they used to think, and why. It also involves identifying and demarcating distinct historical phases or periods, capturing sequences or chains of events over time, and identifying critical events. This caricature of what history is and how it is produced closely resembles the popular understanding of the work of historians and it can be argued that this is a widely held belief among many scholars in management and organization studies.

Social scientists also tend to accept the historians' accounts of the past. It is characteristic of the academic division of labour that historians are considered 'experts' about the times past and are best suited to discover the 'truth' from the remnants from the past (Weatherbee, 2012). For this reason historical knowledge is not deemed problematic for the study of social science (Zald, 1996). The historian has authority to explain and convey the lessons of the past to others. This authority is grounded in historians' professional training and their adherence to the professional norms of verification, impartiality, and personal detachment.

The historian's authority over the past also clouds the relationship between historical and social sciences research. History and historical research is generally thought of as data that social scientists can use as evidence for historical case studies and/or as illustrations aimed at testing theory (Zald, 1990). However, the role of the historian has been placed under scrutiny and questions have been raised about what it means to be a historian. Some have argued that a historian's ability to produce valid historical knowledge depends on his or her ability to raise questions and develop hypotheses about historical data (Bloch, 1953). Historians in this camp believe that the past can speak for itself and their task goes further than identifying, criticizing, and arranging the sources in a timeline. The research process is emphasized, as is the selection of relevant sources and how these are interpreted. The selection and interpretation of the sources is motivated by a series of questions based on the historian's previous experience and beliefs as well as on shared common social knowledge, which includes scientific knowledge. This pseudo-scientific approach to the work of the historian brings the social scientist and the historian closer than ever before. Thus, there is an unsteady 'agreement' on the set of problems and tools they could use to understand the past.

The same discussion has taken place on the side of 'science', where a debate on social sciences evaluated the possibility of creating a history-as-social-science (Abrams, 1980; Abbott, 1991). During the 1970s and 1980s social scientists engaged with epistemological and methodological issues regarding the historicity of social phenomena and the ways history could inform the practice of research in social sciences. In both cases, the historical search for the contribution of social sciences, and the social sciences analysis of the benefits of a historically-informed discipline, were looking for a synthesis (Abbott, 1991), for a unified historical social science. A series of divergences and incompatibilities prevented this from happening.

A similar divide between social scientists and historians exists in organizational research (Rowlinson, 2001). In fact, a theory-testing function of history has, more than once, been posed as one of the most valuable contributions for more historical analysis in the study of organizations (Kieser, 1994). This supposed divide between organizational theorists and business historians still remains (Greenwood & Bernardi, 2014), although as Zald (1996: 257) pointed out, the meaningful debate that has occurred in history and the social sciences has "somehow … bypassed organizational studies".

Yet, the fact is that both organizational theorists and business historians often share the same ontological and epistemological view on history (Rowlinson & Delahaye, 2009). The 'historic turn' (Clark & Rowlinson, 2004: 336) in organization studies is used to refer to at least three different positions on the role history should play in relation to the theorization about organizations: the supplementarist, the integrationist, and the reorientationist (Üsdiken & Kieser, 2004). But looking closely we find that in each of these three positions history seems to acquire a very precise meaning that is sometimes aligned, and other times conflicts, with the social scientific model.

In summary, we assume that despite claims to the contrary, business history and organization studies are not necessarily at odds nor are they based on incommensurable divisions. We have shown that the apparent divide between history and science in MOH is predominantly ontological and not epistemological. Next we explore how ontological assumptions about history led to particular treatments of historical research in MOH. In the following section we present a more detailed account of Munslow's (2006a) three major ontological orientations over the nature of historical knowledge. This is followed by our illustration of each ontological position with the research developed in institutional theory and our discussion of the implications of an increased awareness of different varieties of history to the development of research in organization studies.

Defining history: three perspectives on the nature of historical reality

The basis for our classification of different varieties of history is Munslow's (2006a, 2006b) ontological positions on the nature of historical reality. We distinguish between the three approaches based on two main dimensions: the extent to which historians consider history to be equivalent to the past, and the extent to which they recognize historical sources as being already a narrative (see Figure 15.1).

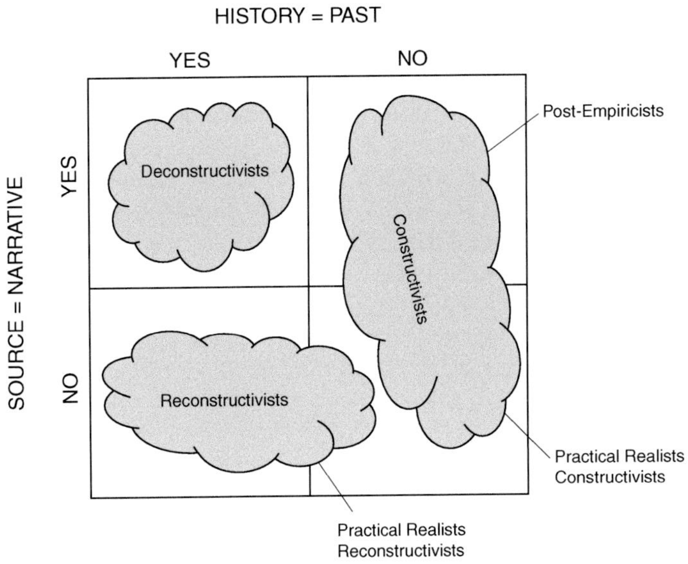

Figure 15.1 Three ontological perspectives on history
Source: Developed by the authors based on Munslow (2006a).

Reconstructivist ontology

The reconstructivist assumption about history can be broadly characterized as a position whereby it is accepted that historians are able to make a truthful assessment of the past in their historical accounts. They do so through "technical and detailed study of the sources through the process of verification, comparison and colligation" (Munslow, 2006a: 181). Also used is the process of the historian empathizing with historical characters to reconstruct the thoughts and decisions taken by the historical agents in a given historical context (Collingwood, 1993). Historians are very careful not to allow their prejudices to get in the way for the writing of the true history. They avoid the interference of their own thoughts about the past reality and focus only on the evidence registered in the sources. They might also expend some effort to block the imposition of presentist agendas of interests. Historians work to let the sources speak for themselves and adopt a referential language that treats events and actions as empirical facts. In other words, reconstructivists believe in their ability to write the past as it has really happened.

Reconstructivists also believe in history as a distinct theory of knowledge, or epistemology. They assume they are able to access and reconstruct the reality of the past in their narrative accounts through an inductive process of impartial selection and critical evaluation of documentary sources. It does not mean that reconstructivists do not recognize the importance of interpretation in historical writing. They concede that history is always an interpretative reconstruction based on some given sources, but they view the historian as an impartial observer whose skill is the ability to access and reproduce the content of the sources objectively. Much like how a forensic scientist approaches physical evidence and attempts to reconstruct a crime scene, a reconstructivist historian pieces together evidence from the past until a picture of some historical event is complete. Throughout this process of discovery, reconstructivist historians sublimate their personal interests, methodological biases, and ideological positions to concentrate on only the data and historical sources which are the final evidence by which the veracity of their historical interpretation must be judged.

In addition to the conservative reconstructivist historians there are some historians who occupy a middle-ground reconstructionist position. The most important difference these researchers exhibit is their refusal to accept the possibility that they can access the past as it once was. These historians accept the central role of interpretation in the production of history. Moderate or practical realist reconstructivists (Munslow, 2006a) diverge from more conservative reconstructionists in that they embrace the process of historical writing that is the result of abduction (Douven, 2011). Their understanding of the historian's use of evidence usually follows Carr's (1961) formulation of the creation of historical facts. Historical facts are not given a priori. Thus, the creation of historical meaning is a product of the interaction between the historian's knowledge and the content of the sources. Accepting that the historians' interpretations intervene in the selection of pertinent evidence to create historical facts brings this group of reconstructivists closer to the constructionist interpretation of the historian's work.

Constructivist ontology

The constructivists, as a group, approach history from a number of perspectives. The most significant departure from a reconstructivist approach is the assumption that it is not possible to revive the totality of the past as it once was. Constructivism is the most complex ontological position put forth by Munslow (2006a). It encompasses a great variety of researchers who accept that historians create evidence through the imposition of historical interpretation on empirical sources. But the application of theoretical frames to the past is not an unbounded project. It is still dependent on the sources and on the professional norms of good historical practice. For constructivists, the past is the past and cannot be retrieved in its entirety. Their knowledge of the past is, then, always partial and bounded by the questions they are able to formulate and the answers the existing sources can provide. Although they recognize the active engagement of the historian and the importance of context to the production of history, they still believe that history is more fact than fiction; to them history is not simply another form of literature and historical knowledge corresponds to the reality of the past.

A characteristic of a constructivist ontology is the belief that historical research is a scientific enterprise. Thus, when history is approached from this position, models and theories of the social sciences are brought to bear on the study of the past. Constructivists eschew the inductive method based on empiricist objectivism and, in contrast, adopt the deductive approach taken from the social sciences. The emphasis on events is replaced by an emphasis on the structures that underlie these events and a focus on a problem-oriented approach to history (Furet, 1984). To the constructivist, history cannot exist without theory and historical knowledge is dependent on the kind of questions the researcher is able to pose to her sources (Bloch, 1953). The production of history is, thus, the result of a "conceptual dialogue between the historian and the past" (Munslow, 2006b: 66). As a detective investigating a crime, constructivists start with a set of assumptions and hypotheses on the historical reality that will be discarded, changed, or reinforced through the progressive analysis of the evidence on the case.

Despite the great diversity in constructivist thought, it is possible to identify two major strands. All constructivists agree that historical sources are the primary way to access the past and validate any historical interpretation. Differences are visible when constructivists are questioned about their beliefs on the nature of the sources. The *practical realist constructivists* (e.g. Marxists), share the reconstructivist notion that the access to the content of the sources is unproblematic and follows directly from the theoretical questions researchers use to address historical problems. The *post-empiricists*, in contrast, embrace a narrative approach and have incorporated the linguistic turn into their reflection on the nature of history. This means that access to the past is always enclosed by narrative emplotment. Furthermore, the sources are not in themselves exempt from ideological biases and from the characteristics of their context of production.

Deconstructivist ontology

Munslow's (2006a) last ontological position, deconstructivism, differs from the other two approaches in the way that postmodernist thought is embraced and espoused. Broadly speaking, deconstructivism can be summarized by the widely-cited statement "'there is nothing outside the text' [il n'y a pas de hors-texte]" (Derrida, 1988: 136). Approaching history from this ontological position means that the narrative itself becomes fundamental for the understanding of history and of the work of the historian. History is understood as a narrative of a narrative and what we know about the past is merely a text that has been created and produced by historians, among other authors. The past is forever lost and cannot be retrieved through analysis or investigation. The historian is bounded to produce *a* historical account, instead of *the* historical account. The irony is, however, that the past only comes into existence when written by the historian. In this strict sense, we can say that the past equals history.

A deconstructivist ontological approach to history does not suggest that there is a finite and ultimate past when historians talk about the past. The past only comes into existence when it comes to be known through the historian's emplotment of it in a narrative. Thus, the past is created though historicizing and can only exist as "the-past-as-history" (Munslow, 2006b).

Deconstructivists do not distinguish between history and literature, subsuming the former under the latter. When history is not distinguished from literature and it is accepted that history is always a narrative representation of the past in the present, then history becomes politicized and ideological. Moreover, history becomes subject to a similar set of issues that affect the production of any kind of narrative, i.e. the emplotment of a story, the use of persuasive and tropological language, and the appeal to the verisimilitude of the story. As clearly stated by Munslow (2006a: 21), "deconstructionist historians tend to view history and the past as a complex series of literary products that derive their chains of meaning(s) or significations from the nature of narrative structure (or forms of representation) as much as from other culturally provided ideological factors."

The rise of deconstructivist thought has shifted the role of the historian away from producing "a truth-finding discourse" to one of producing a "truth-making" discourse (Munslow, 2006b: 11). The task for historians is no longer to discover the truth of the past by inductive or deductive methods, but to disclose possible pasts by applying different lenses to the sources. The sources themselves are seen as "meaningful historical explanations … rather than plain vehicles with which to explain the past as it actually happened" (Munslow, 2006a: 62). The past is not given within the sources but is created by the representative frame chosen by the historian. "The written historical narrative is the formal *re-presentation* of historical content" (Munslow, 2006a: 27). For deconstructivists, all texts (historical, literary, evidence, or interpretation) are but one possible representation of the past, rather than the past itself in a written form. Historical sources and how these are used to tell a story define the possibilities of existence for the past.

A synthesis of Munslow's (2006a) ontologies can be found in Table 15.1. This brief review of each of the three ontological positions demonstrates that history can be approached in different ways by different researchers. Munslow's typology suggests that differences in how history is approached have had a fundamental impact on how history is researched, understood, and presented. This is more clearly seen when we look at the results of empirical research espousing different ontological assumptions on the nature of historical reality. In the following section we

Table 15.1 Synthesis of the ontological perspectives on history

Issue	*Reconstructionism*	*Constructionism*	*Deconstructionism*
History	A theory of knowledge (epistemology)	A form of scientific research (investigation)	A form of literature (narrative)
Historical reality	Objective (given)	Interpreted (culturally constructed)	Represented (discursively produced)
Historical knowledge	Empirical	Theoretical	Literary
Historical truth	Correspondence Theory (primary sources + experienced craftsmanship)	Correspondence Theory (factual knowledge + interpretation)	Coherence Theory (interpretation = knowledge)
Historical sources	Reveal the reality when studied appropriately	Reveal some aspects of the reality if problematized appropriately	Signpost some possible realities and interpretations
Historian	Known but personally unimportant	Known and 'personally' important	Unknown or unimportant
Historian's work	Recover (i.e. discover) the past by being a vehicle for the writing of history	Mediate (i.e. interpret) past reality through social convention and ideological positioning	Represent (i.e. translate) past reality through the production of history
Research metaphor	Forensic reconstruction	Detective investigation	Artistic painting
Explanatory logic	Discovery	Scientific research	Narrative making
Style of reasoning	Inductive	Deductive	Disclosive
Goal of history	Discover	Interpret	Represent
Output of historical work	Truthful History	Propositional History	Meaningful History
Relation to social sciences	Distinct from Social Sciences – the raw material of history precludes the formulation of 'theoretical constructs'	Affiliated with Social Sciences – research methods and hypothesis can help understand the past	Equivalent to Social Sciences – both enterprises develop literary practices that create the historical past

Source: Elaborated by the authors based on Munslow (2006a, 2006b).

illustrate these differences through an analysis of a sample of articles in management and organization studies taken from research in the tradition of organizational institutionalism.

History in neo-institutional research

To illustrate the importance of an increased awareness about the nature of historical knowledge in the development of management and organization studies, we chose to focus in more detail on the research developed under the label of neo-institutional theory. Our choice was informed by three criteria: (1) organizational institutionalism today is a dominant approach in the field of management and organizations; (2) institutional theory possesses a "strong historical component" (Zald, 1996: 257) that, to some, remains largely ignored and unarticulated (Suddaby, Foster & Mills, 2014); and (3) there are a number of recent attempts at specifying the connection between history and institutions (Djelic, 2008; Rowlinson & Hassard, 2013; Suddaby, Foster & Mills, 2014).

Table 15.2 Institutional research understanding of history

Article	*Year*	*Classification*	*Source = Narrative*	*History = Past*	*Interpretation*
Leblebici *et al.*	1991	Reconstructionist	No	Yes	Yes
Hoffman	1999	Reconstructionist	No	Yes	Yes
Hargadon & Douglas	2001	Reconstructionist	No	Yes	No
Rao, Monin & Durand	2003	Reconstructionist	No	Yes	No
Arndt & Bigelow	2005	Constructionist	Yes	No	Yes
Suddaby & Greenwood	2005	Constructionist	Yes	No	Yes
Maguire & Hardy	2009	Deconstructivist	Yes	Yes	Yes
Rojas	2010	Constructionist	No	Yes	Yes
Jones *et al.*	2012	Constructionist	No	No	Yes
Wright & Zammuto	2013	Reconstructionist	No	No	Yes

Our examination is not meant to be comprehensive. We did not intend to identify each institutional article dealing with issues of history and historicity. The goal was to identify specific papers that illustrate the different ontological approaches to historical knowledge. We do so to evaluate what distinguishes one from the other and to comment on possible advantages and disadvantages for the further development of research in organization and management studies. We chose ten articles as our main sample for developing this analysis. The papers were selected on the basis of the knowledge the researchers have about institutional theory and with the guidance of the works of Suddaby, Foster and Mills (2014) and Rowlinson and Hassard (2013). A list of the articles and their classification can be found in Table 15.2.

Interestingly all the articles we selected for further analysis were focused on some kind of institutional change, including major subjects such as institutional logics, institutional work, discourse, categories, identity, legitimacy, and power. Of the ten papers, only two dealt with levels of research other than the organizational field. Eight of the articles stated that they were based on the analysis of historical sources or were developed from some form of archival research. We found a widespread absence of a definition of history and there was little discussion about the possible problems that might occur when using historical sources in most of the papers.

We found that the reconstructivist ontological approach was most common in the papers we selected for our review. However the number of papers we slotted in each category did not vary widely. Nevertheless, a practical realist view of history was the dominant ontological position espoused in the papers analysed in our sample. This was not unexpected since practical realism tends to dominate the way organizational scholars understand and approach history in both business history and organization theory (Rowlinson & Delahaye, 2009; Weatherbee *et al.*, 2012).

Reconstructing history

The research that approaches history as a type of contextual information was classified as reconstructivist. These are the works generally classified as adopting an ahistorical view of organizational phenomena. They present what other scholars have called a "helicopter overview of the past" (Clark & Rowlinson, 2004: 335); this approach is a broad, straightforward and sterile view of the past. As Rowlinson and Hassard (2013) pointed out, there is a great, albeit invisible, problem in this common practice of offering general historical overviews of the phenomena to be studied, usually before the presentation of the methodological procedures used in the research. The exposition of a brief historical account has the role of providing an empirical contextualization of the theoretical problem under study so the reader can have a better understanding and an adequate interpretation of the phenomena and of the contributions generated by the research. The problem implicit in this kind of practice is that it does not do justice to the complexity of historical data and historical reality. History is conceived as an unproblematic and objective domain of reality and "historiography stands outside of methodological discussion … as if they are methodologically self-explanatory" (Rowlinson & Hassard, 2013: 119). The presentation of the 'historical context' is used as a literary device to contextualize the case at hand and create an elegant path to introduce the article's theoretical problem. History in these cases is seen as unproblematic and inconsequential. It is reduced to a set of events that happened in the past that help us understand the actual present (Zald, 1996). If the events are still important today, and thus worthy of being mentioned, it is because their force can still be felt in the actuality of social structures and processes.

Reconstructivist research in institutional theory also uses history as a means of analysing events and things that happened in the past to understand how these events created lasting impressions in social and/or organizational situations. The assumption that is commonly shared in these studies is that significant events are the causes/reasons for present activities and behaviours. As well, these past events only exist in the past and in the traces that live on in the present. The task of institutional researcher is thus to understand how these things happened and to trace their effects on the present. This is the common understanding of the research on path theory and imprinting (Marquis & Tilcsik, 2013; Schneiberg, 2007; Schreyögg, Sydow & Holtmann, 2011).

A good exemplar of this position in our small sample is the work of Rao, Monin, and Durand (2003). The authors developed a longitudinal (1970–97) analysis of the emergence of French nouvelle cuisine and the reconfiguration of institutional logics and role identities in the field of French gastronomy. In the paper, history was used as background to sociological analysis and to introduce the context of transformations to the reader. Their research was based on multiple sources of evidence, however, interestingly, the data and methods section come only after the historical narrative of the changes in French gastronomy. They did not mention having used any kind of 'historical source' other than the memory of the interviewees. Their practice suggests a very objectivist view of history and offers no place for the discussion on the role of the written history in reinforcing or maybe providing the answers to existing theoretical assumptions.

Constructing history

Some institutional research moves beyond a simplistic historical contextualization and a superficial account of the historicity of the phenomenon. In these cases the authors show an interest in using historical data to further develop social and organizational theories. One way this occurs is when the researcher develops a historical analysis based on primary data taken from archives and other sources from the past. Upon completion of the research a reconstructed history is used to test an existing theory. A second possibility is for the researcher to take an already existing historical narrative and use this as the main source of data for a research object. The alternative of generating their own historical account is generally a path not taken by researchers in organization studies, and some of the existing cases (e.g. Chandler Jr, 1984) raise the question about the historical veracity and accuracy of the historical account. The most common alternative is for organizational theorists to base their analysis on second-hand accounts developed by historians (Clark & Rowlinson, 2004; Zald, 1996), or to combine secondary accounts with some form of archival data.

The work of Rojas (2010) is a middle-ground position between the strict empiricism of non-theorized, descriptive reconstructivist history and a constructivist historical approach to organizational research. He analyzes different approaches to institutional work by focusing on the case of the 1968 Third World Strike at San Francisco State College and his analysis shows how the college president was able to convert normative resources at the individual level (e.g. personal reputation and personal ties to political elites, and a personal network of allies sharing worldviews) into coercive resources at the level of the organization, increasing his institutional authority and his ability to counteract the actions of student activists.

Rojas seems to be well aware of the challenges in choosing to develop a historical case study, and he states that he "consulted every known archival collection on the Third World Strike" (Rojas, 2010: 1268). The research used both primary data and secondary data. The secondary accounts were used to triangulate the information found through the research on primary sources from archives, newspaper accounts, and interviews. He took the care to look for multiple accounts or perspectives about the event (outsiders, student and faculty groups, deans and faculty members, and governor's papers) and to attempt to capture the different perspectives of the multiple actors involved. These procedures indicate his preference for first-hand accounts on the strike. Yet, after presenting a detailed description of the data he collected there was no explanation of the methodological procedures used to analyse the data. The historical interpretation of the evidence was enough to reconstruct the story as it happened and to provide an illustration for the author's interest in discovering "how organizational fields affect the way actors transform authority" (Rojas, 2010: 1268).

The work of Wright and Zammuto (2013) provides an illustrative case of a practical realist constructivist position on history. In this article, the authors attempted to understand the role of different actors (marginalized, peripheral, and central) in multilevel institutional change based on a longitudinal archival study of first-class County Cricket in England.[1] The main difference between this work and Rojas (2010) was the development of an in-depth content analysis of the data gathered from the archives, which was interpreted as an attempt to merge historical and social science research. The use of social science methods attached to the authors' interest in providing a truthful account of the past illustrate the espousal of a practical realist constructionist view of history. For example, in two different places in the article the authors make specific reference to 'the veracity' of their interpretation and their criteria to be confirmed independently by the archivist-historian that helped them in selecting the sources for their research.

Another article that adopts a constructivist position is the research by Arndt and Bigelow (2005). Of the papers we analyzed, this paper is furthest removed from a strict empiricist mode of knowledge collection, while still maintaining a constructionist position on history. The authors' central problem was to understand "how a female occupation masculinizes" (Arndt & Bigelow, 2005: 235). They argued that much was known about the feminization of masculine professions, but very little about the opposite situation. To analyze the boundary work developed by male managers and professional associations on the masculinization of hospital administration, they used both primary and secondary data. Their major source of data was a journal called *Modern Hospital*, which, at the time, was considered an accurate representation of "the voice of the American Hospital Association's leadership" (Arndt & Bigelow, 2005: 238). Their analysis of the data followed a qualitative interpretative inductive and deductive process, generating a chronological database of excerpts and the application of boundary work categories to the textual data. Although they did not explore in detail the historical dimension of their case study they conclude their paper by arguing for a need to reclaim a "neglected history of women in hospital administration" (Arndt & Bigelow, 2005: 255), by showing that the debates on the occupation's professionalization have generally overlooked gender implications. Presenting an argument that would place them close to a new cultural history approach (Burke, 2004), they share an interest in recovering stories and perspectives that "have been lost to history" (Arndt & Bigelow, 2005: 255). The notion of losing something to history suggests that it was still there in the past to be recovered but has been forgotten in the present.

Deconstructing history

The deconstructivist ontological position is illustrated by Maguire and Hardy's (2009) research on the deinstitutionalization of DDT. Their paper was the only one classified as a case of historical deconstructivism. The authors argue that the production, distribution, and consumption of texts are major forces behind the maintenance or change of an organizational field. They focus specifically on the role that problematization and translation play in outsider-driven deinstitutionalization processes. Their research was a single exploratory case study on the deinstitutionalization of DDT. They used a multitude of sources to develop their analysis, focusing on sets of texts associated with the cognitive, normative, and regulative dimensions of institutions. They collected data from both primary and secondary sources and created a narrative of the process through which practices of DDT use were deinstitutionalized. They do not provide a definition of history and do not analyze the case from a historical point of view although they are aware of the historical context of the production of the texts as a result of their discourse analysis. They do not discuss the sources as a historian would, but they did select them carefully and are able to expose the rationale behind it. Additionally, they recognize their own act of translation in the analysis when they say "although informed by systematic coding, this analysis was necessarily interpretive. In effect, it represents our translation of Carson's problematizations and a simplification of the complex arguments in her book" (Maguire & Hardy, 2009: 174). At the end, even though they do not talk specifically about history, they recognize they are telling *one* possible history and not *the* history.

Overview

Our analysis has shown that instead of a generalized ahistorical view on management and organizations, the articles we selected for the analysis presented a more explicit or implicit understanding of history. For example, a more objectivist understanding of history was exemplified by Rao, Monin, and Durand's (2003) longitudinal research. In their paper they approached history as a given and did not reference the background sources they used to reconstruct the historical context. In contrast, the deconstructivist view found in Maguire and Hardy's (2009) discourse analysis of the deinstitutionalization of DDT explicitly recognized the interpreted nature of their account among many other possible ways of looking and narrating past events. Regardless, all the authors adopted an ontological view on the nature of the past and history, even though they might not have been completely aware of or would consciously agree with the position they were taking.

The data on our table show an apparent move away from reconstructionist positions in favour of more constructionist orientations of history. Although we cannot generalize from our small sample, this could suggest an increasing awareness of institutional researchers to historical issues and a willingness to incorporate archival research methods and other contributions from the field of history into their research. Even though the authors were generally not very clear about their ontological and epistemological assumptions regarding historical knowledge, we were still able to provide at least one illustration for each ontological position defined by Munslow (2006a). As expected, we found that most of the works we analyzed adopted a reconstructivist or constructionist position.

Our classification of institutional research into one of Munslow's three ontological positions is not meant to be pejorative or didactic. As researchers we have our own ontological and epistemological positions that guide our ability to understand reality, even though we might not be fully aware of our assumptions and their implications. Adopting a reconstructivist, constructionist, or deconstructionist perspective is a choice made by each researcher. To date, we believe that only a handful of scholars would be able to clearly appreciate and justify their ontological position on the nature of historical knowledge. We hope this chapter might provide some guidance for other management and organization scholars to reflect on these matters and more consciously adopt a position best aligned with his or her worldviews.

However, it should be noted that each approach to history implies an existing 'consensus' regarding the relationship between science and history. The reconstructivist approach sees the scientific and historical enterprises as distinct and, at best, complementary. The constructionist approach looks for the development of joint forms of research and hopes for a melding of historical and scientific research. The last perspective, deconstructionism, understands history and science as a narrative construction that is imbued with power, ideology and politics. Regardless of the approach, researchers should be attentive to the coherence of their philosophical assumptions and theoretical arguments.

Discussion

Throughout our chapter we have called for the need for greater ontological clarity in historical research. The superficial dichotomy between business history and organizational research has caused a tension between the members of both areas. We, however, feel that this tension can be minimized and eliminated if greater recognition is placed on the ontological approach of the researcher to problematize and call attention to their treatment of history in their research. As such, we have identified a number of contributions that we have made from our classification of different institutional theory research papers.

First, researchers must recognize that *theoretical choices imply a commitment to a particular worldview and a particular way for it to be investigated.* Our classification of research papers indicates that a possible shortcoming of espousing an empiricist view of history (i.e. of accepting history as an unproblematic set of events capable of being empirically discovered and ordered as they were supposed to have happened in the past), is that it causes an epistemological tension with some versions of institutional research. For example, to believe an objective view of historical reality would thus contradict the phenomenological and structuralist epistemologies that undergird the sociological branch of organizational neo-institutionalism. This inconsistency could undermine the conclusions drawn from research that does not identify and surface these contradictions.

Second, the choice of a historical approach or the development of historical accounts in organization studies needs to be *reflexive*. It will become increasingly difficult to draw on historical accounts when the only grounds of support are the professional status of the historians or the 'official' or 'scholarly' status of a given historical narrative. The choice of one version of the past over the other will have to be based on the conscious espousal of a view on the nature of history associated with a deeper analysis of historical texts and the purposes of its writing. The historical authority of the text or historian can no longer justify the use of history to inform scholarly research in organization studies; it will demand a proper justification by the social and organizational researcher.

Third, there is a need to recognize that *the theoretical work of management and organizational researchers is itself a form of history*. It is not only about 'making' history, but also about 'doing' history and 'using' it for its own purposes. Organizational researchers develop historical accounts about past organizational reality, and also use historical narratives about the past as evidence or as a laboratory for testing their own theories. But, often, their own research is also a valuable record of the past for future historical analysis of the theoretical development of the field and its influence on organizational practices. Also, at the same time, they privilege and endorse a specific version of the past and provide a narrative on the present that could be used in the future to characterize and understand this period of time in the past.

Future directions

Our investigation and classification of existing research has led us to identify a number of ways that a variety of assumptions about the nature of history can be empirically investigated. The first possibility is an investigation of the rhetorical nature of historical accounts used *in* and *by* organizations and other important social actors (e.g. Foster *et al.*, 2011; Suddaby, Foster & Trank, 2010). The current research on rhetorical history is focused on the production of history and the persuasive intent of history. New research in this area can further the current discussion about the content used to construct a persuasive history (e.g. Brunninge, 2009; Schultz & Hernes, 2013; Suddaby & Greenwood, 2005) or how history is structured to be most persuasive and effective (e.g. Anteby & Molnár, 2012; Kroeze & Keulen, 2013; Rowlinson & Hassard, 1993). Rhetorical research can also look at the different ways history is presented (Delahaye et al., 2009; Janssen, 2012) and how a particular medium or presentation of history can affect whether it is more or less persuasive and to whom. Approaching history from a rhetorical position will be a fruitful way to uncover how different ontological positions influence the production and construction of organizational history.

A second area of future investigation would focus on the professional work developed by historians and other history-telling professionals and institutions. This would include archives, museums, and libraries, but also the media, social networks, and websites on history. An approach that could prove useful in this investigation is ANTi-history. ANTi-historians argue that the production of history is the result of a network of multiple actors and their representations and performances of a given history in the present. Thus, the focus of research is on understanding the politics over the representation of the past in organizations (Weatherbee *et al.*, 2012). Applying ANTi-history to the professional production of history in different institutional settings could help uncover and expose the different ontological positions of professional history producers and the implications that this has for the production and consumption of professionally constructed histories.

A third stream of research could look at the process of institutionalizing history, and how some historical accounts tend to be diffused, maintained, reproduced, and changed over time and their relation and implication to social issues and social dynamics. History in this case could be seen both as an important research object for management and organization studies, or as a major site or arena for the study of management and organizational phenomena. The work of Jones et al. (2012) presents a special case for this kind of research. They developed a study connecting institutional logics and categorization in order to understand the emergence of the category of 'modern architecture'. Although they had a strong historical component in their research, they chose to develop a deep semiotic and network analysis of historical texts instead of dealing explicitly with the historical element of their research. The authors have a very interesting component of revisionist history that could be explored in more detail in a further publication. For instance, the article could be reframed as an analysis of the process of social construction of the history of 'modern architecture'. Thus, by being more attentive to the role of history, the authors might be able to bring an even greater contribution to the field.

Conclusion

In this chapter we argued that the lack of debate and problematization of history in management and organization studies is not the result of an informed and conscious choice of researchers or a necessary consequence of producing knowledge inside of a scientific paradigm. The derogation of history in the field can be better understood as a result of taken-for-granted practical realist assumptions about the nature of historical reality generally shared by organizational researchers. Organization scholars tend to see the past as an unproblematic dimension of human inquiry. They generally accept the verisimilitude of historical knowledge as the historical truth. And they usually regard the task of recovering the past as belonging to the domain of an autonomous field of knowledge. History and historians remain responsible for reconstructing the past as it once was through a skilful analysis of the remaining traces of past reality or historical sources. In the end, the narrative on the past produced by the historian would then serve as raw data for the testing of social theories.

As an alternative to this dominant reconstructionist view on the nature of historical reality, we introduced two other approaches to historical knowledge. We argued that history does not need to be seen as the truthful reconstruction of the past through inductive work, but can also be understood as the result of a deductive process that constructs the past based on a set of inquiries directed to the sources. A third possibility relies in an attempt at deconstructing history by exposing the structures of its narrative reality and disclosing a multiplicity of possible existing pasts.

Our discussion of the different possibilities for understanding historical reality is intended to increase the awareness of organizational researchers about different ways of knowing the past. We also wanted to provide researchers with some tools to help create a reflective account and an informed position about history in organizations. By presenting these different varieties of historical understanding we contribute to the enrichment of management and organization studies. Furthermore, we call for the development of research on organizations to be more sensitive to issues of history, historical theory and the epistemology of history.

Note

1 It is also worth noting their use of footnotes in their research. These were exhibited in the Appendix of the article and speak to an old – but always present – criticism on the organization scholars' derogation of historical sources debate (Rowlinson, 2004; Rowlinson & Hassard, 2013).

References

Abbott, A. (1991) History and sociology: The lost synthesis, *Social Science History*, 15(2): 201–38.

Abrams, P. (1980) History, sociology, historical sociology, *Past and Present*, 87(1): 3–16.

Anteby, M. and Molnár, V. (2012) Collective memory meets organizational identity: Remembering to forget in a firm's rhetorical history, *Academy of Management Journal*, 55(3): 515–40.

Arndt, M. and Bigelow, B. (2005) Professionalizing and masculinizing a female occupation: The reconceptualization of hospital administration in the early 1900s, *Administrative Science Quarterly*, 50(2): 233–61.

Bloch, M. (1953) *The Historian's Craft*. New York: Knopf.

Brunninge, O. (2009) Using history in organizations: How managers make purposeful reference to history in strategy processes, *Journal of Organizational Change Management*, 22(1): 8–26.

Burke, P. (2004) *What is Cultural History?* Cambridge: Polity Press.

Carr, E. H. (1961) *What is History?* London: Macmillan.

Chandler Jr, A. D. (1984) *Strategy and Structure: Chapters in the History of the Industrial Enterprise*. Cambridge, MA: MIT Press.

Clark, P. and Rowlinson, M. (2004) The treatment of history in organisation studies: Towards an 'historic turn'? *Business History*, 46(3): 331–52.

Collingwood, R. G. (1993) *The Idea of History* (rev. edn). Oxford: Oxford University Press.

Delahaye, A., Booth, C., Clark, P., Procter, S., and Rowlinson, M. (2009) The genre of corporate history, *Journal of Organizational Change Management*, 22(1): 27–48.

Derrida, J. (1988) *Limited Inc*. Evanston, IL: Northwestern University Press.

Djelic, M.-L. (2008) Sociological studies of diffusion: Is history relevant? *Socio-Economic Review*, 6(3): 538–57.

Douven, I. (2011) Abduction, in E. N. Zalta (ed.), *The Stanford Encyclopedia of Philosophy* (Spring 2011 edition online).

Foster, W. M., Suddaby, R., Minkus, A., and Wiebe, E. (2011) History as social memory assets: The example of Tim Hortons, *Management & Organizational History*, 6(1): 101–20.

Furet, F. O. (1984) *In the Workshop of History*. Chicago, IL: University of Chicago Press.

Greenwood, A. and Bernardi, A. (2014) Understanding the rift, the (still) uneasy bedfellows of History and Organization Studies, *Organization*, 21(6): 907–32.

Hargadon, A. B. and Douglas, Y. (2001) When innovations meet institutions: Edison and the design of the electric light, *Administrative Science Quarterly*, 46(3): 476–501.

Hoffman, A. J. (1999) Institutional evolution and change: Environmentalism and the US chemical industry, *The Academy of Management Journal*, 42(4): 351–71.

Janssen, C. I. (2012) Corporate historical responsibility (CHR): Addressing a corporate past of forced labor at Volkswagen, *Journal of Applied Communication Research*, 41(1): 64–83.

Jones, C., Maoret, M., Massa, F. G., and Svejenova, S. (2012) Rebels with a cause: Formation, contestation, and expansion of the De Novo category 'Modern Architecture,' 1870–1975, *Organization Science*, 23(6): 1523–45.

Kieser, A. (1994) Why organization theory needs historical analyses: And how this should be performed, *Organization Science*, 5(4): 608–20.

Kroeze, R. and Keulen, S. (2013) Leading a multinational is history in practice: The use of invented traditions and narratives at AkzoNobel, Shell, Philips and ABN AMRO, *Business History*, 55(8): 1265–87.

Leblebici, H., Salancik, G. R., Copay, A., and King, T. (1991) Institutional change and the transformation of interorganizational fields: An organizational history of the US radio broadcasting industry, *Administrative Science Quarterly*, 36(3): 333–63.

Lorenz, C. (2011) History and theory, in A. Schneider and D. Woolf (eds), *The Oxford History of Historical Writing* (pp. 13–35). Oxford: Oxford University Press.

Maguire, S. and Hardy, C. (2009) Discourse and deinstitutionalization: The decline of DDT, *Academy of Management Journal*, 52(1): 148–78.

Marquis, C. and Tilcsik, A. (2013) Imprinting: Toward a multilevel theory, *Academy of Management Annals*, 7(1): 195–245.

Munslow, A. (2006a) *Deconstructing History* (2nd edn). New York: Routledge.

Munslow, A. (2006b) *The Routledge Companion to Historical Studies* (2nd edn). London and New York: Routledge.

Rao, H., Monin, P., and Durand, R. (2003) Institutional change in Toque Ville: Nouvelle cuisine as an identity movement in French gastronomy, *American Journal of Sociology*, 108(4): 795–843.

Rojas, F. (2010) Power through institutional work: Acquiring academic authority in the 1968 Third World strike, *Academy of Management Journal*, 53(6): 1263–80.

Rowlinson, M. (2001) Business history and organization theory, *Journal of Industrial History*, 4(1): 1–23.

Rowlinson, M. (2004) Historical analysis of company documents, in C. Cassell and G. Symon (eds), *Essential Guide to Qualitative Methods in Organizational Research* (pp. 301–11), London: Sage.

Rowlinson, M. and Delahaye, A. (2009) The cultural turn in business history, *Entreprises et histoire*, 55(2): 90–110.

Rowlinson, M. and Hassard, J. (1993) The invention of corporate culture: A history of the histories of Cadbury, *Human Relations*, 46(3): 299–326.

Rowlinson, M. and Hassard, J. (2013) Historical neo-institutionalism or neo-institutionalist history? Historical research in management and organization studies, *Management & Organizational History*, 8(2): 111–26.

Schneiberg, M. (2007) What's on the path? Path dependence, organizational diversity and the problem of institutional change in the US economy, 1900–1950, *Socio-Economic Review*, 5(1): 47–80.

Schreyögg, G., Sydow, J., and Holtmann, P. (2011) How history matters in organisations: The case of path dependence, *Management & Organizational History*, 6(1): 81–100.

Schultz, M. and Hernes, T. (2013) A temporal perspective on organizational identity, *Organization Science*, 24(1): 1–21.

Suddaby, R. and Greenwood, R. (2005) Rhetorical strategies of legitimacy, *Administrative Science Quarterly*, 50(1): 35–67.

Suddaby, R., Foster, W. M., and Mills, A. J. (2014) Historical institutionalism, in M. Bucheli and R. D. Wadwhani (eds), *Organizations in Time: History, Theory, Methods* (pp. 100–23). Oxford: Oxford University Press

Suddaby, R., Foster, W. M., and Trank, C. Q. (2010) Rhetorical history as a source of competitive advantage, in J. A. C. Baum and J. Lampel (eds), *Advances in Strategic Management: The Globalization of Strategy Research* (pp. 147–73). Bingley: Emerald.

Üsdiken, B. and Kieser, A. (2004) Introduction: History in Organisation Studies, *Business History*, 46(3): 321–30.

Weatherbee, T. G. (2012) Caution! This historiography makes wide turns: Historic turns and breaks in management and organization studies, *Management & Organizational History*, 7(3): 203–18.

Weatherbee, T. G., Durepos, G., Mills, A., and Helms Mills, J. (2012) Theorizing the past: Critical engagements, *Management & Organizational History*, 7(3): 193–202.

Wright, A. L. and Zammuto, R. F. (2013) Wielding the willow: Processes of institutional change in English county cricket, *Academy of Management Journal*, 56(1): 308–30.

Zald, M. N. (1990) History, sociology and theories of organization, in J. E. Jackson (ed.), *Institutions in American Society: Essays in Market, Political, and Social Organizations* (pp. 81–108). Ann Arbor, MI: University of Michigan Press.

Zald, M. N. (1993) Organization studies as a scientific and humanistic enterprise: Toward a reconceptualization of the foundations of the field, *Organization Science*, 4(4): 513–28.

Zald, M. N. (1996) More fragmentation? Unfinished business in linking the social sciences and the humanities, *Administrative Science Quarterly*, 41(2): 251–61.

16

Mothership reconnection

Microhistory and institutional work compared

Stephanie Decker

Introduction

The marketplace for historical research in business schools is currently split into two camps: business history (BH) and management and organizational history (MOH). This separation shows most clearly in the Routledge Companion series, in which the present volume on MOH is published alongside the one on BH. The ideological and epistemological lines have been most clearly (and combatively) drawn in an exchange in the journal *Management and Organizational History* between Scott Taylor, Emma Bell and Bill Cooke (2009) and the then editors of *Business History*, John Wilson and Steve Toms (2010). Ostensibly a discussion whether the work of Paul Ricoeur, specifically *Memory, History, Forgetting* (2004), should be central for the historiographical practice of business historians, the articles are largely positioning exercises between the constructivist epistemology of the more relativist MOH community, and the objectivist epistemology of the more empiricist business historians. While the lines of this conflict are somewhat overdrawn, as neither camp is entirely as homogeneous as the above implies, it has also been overtaken by new work in recent years. Business historians have begun to heed the call of Taylor *et al.* to reflect more on their practice (Bucheli and Wadhwani, 2014; Decker, 2013; Fellman and Popp, 2013; Hansen, 2012; Schwarzkopf, 2012), while some recent publications suggest that historical approaches might be emerging from their marginal position within management and organization studies (Kipping and Üsdiken, 2014; Rowlinson, Hassard, and Decker, 2014).

In one of the foundational articles in MOH, Clark and Rowlinson (2004: 331) argue that an 'historic turn' in organization studies would imply a greater engagement with historical values of context and process, rather than with the adjacent branch of history. This argument has been reiterated by scholars such as Andrew Popp (2009). By turning towards history as a discipline, historical researchers are seeking a re-connection to the disciplinary 'mothership' as the basis for their work in management studies. Recently, Popp has called for an 'historic turn' in BH specifically, which he argues needs to combine the writing of excellent history with greater reflexivity about historical research practices.[1] I would argue that a 'historiographic turn' is required, by which I mean a consideration of historiography as a repository of historical theory. This is in distinction to Taylor, Bell, and Cooke's reference to the philosophy of history, or Toms and Wilson's suggestion that historians ought to engage with social science theory. Theoretical concerns are embedded in the practice, explanations, and narrativization of historical research, and different historical traditions have differed in how far they make these explicit. Thus when it comes to making a theoretical contribution, historical researchers are faced with a very unequal marketplace for concepts and theories, where little is derived from historiography other than empirics, context, and in the best case some epistemological concerns.

However, if we consider history as a disciplinary body of knowledge (German and other continental European languages usefully distinguish between *Geschichte* and *Geschichtswissenschaft*, i.e. the past and the study of the past) we can draw on a variety of epistemological and theoretical positions, even though these are elaborated differently from the social sciences. These range from the more relativist positions in cultural history, specifically approaches that focus on 'usable pasts' such as those found in gender history (LaRossa, 1997; Lerner, 1994; Jacobitti, 2000), to the enduring base of empiricist history, as defended by Richard Evans (1999), but also contain objectivist yet theory-driven varieties such as economic history. Finally, and most importantly in my opinion, there are varieties of constructivist history that are not relativist in nature, such as aspects of microhistory and postcolonial history. I believe that these harbour opportunities to reassess the role of historical research in organization studies.

In order to illustrate how I think this might be achieved, this chapter will outline a comparison between microhistory and an area of organization theory that appears concerned with similar analytical issues, institutional work (IW). Both the similarities as much as the differences between the interests and methodological statements of the leading Italian microhistorians of the 1980s and 1990s, and the scholarly communities that emerged around issues of institutional entrepreneurship and IW since the mid-2000s, offer potentially interesting avenues for interdisciplinary work for MOH. While it is not unusual for historical research to draw on organization theory (OT), for example Anteby and Molnár (2012), Decker (2010), and Leblebici *et al.* (1991), it is less common to suggest that historical researchers in organization studies actually have recourse to a rich body of conceptual frameworks embedded within historiography, provided that they are prepared to 'overcome the rift' between the two camps (Greenwood and Bernardi, 2014).

Comparing institutional work and microhistory

On the face of it IW and microhistory are scholarly traditions that have emerged at very different times and in very different disciplines, with research subjects that could not be more dissimilar: on the one hand, we find the careful analysis of the practices and political moves of organizational members to create, maintain, or disrupt a theoretical construct known as an institution. An institution here is defined so broadly that it effortlessly contains almost anything that a historian would refer to as structures, culture, discourse, rules, and belief systems. From the perspective of historians, it is important to note that the idea of an institution encompasses phenomena that could be classified as social as well as cultural. Thus while many institutional theorists have become concerned with how individuals can retain the ability to act in the face of cognitively totalizing institutions, they rarely consider their immensely totalizing a priori definition of the concept itself.

On the other hand, we are faced with a diverse body of historical work that has mostly focused on early modern rural communities and individuals living in these communities, who at some point in time became known to the authorities (and were thus recorded for posterity) because they disrupted the status quo by having publicly diverged from acceptable belief systems. Early Italian, and to some extent French, microhistorians have often relied on the records of the Inquisition, an organization in which well-educated members of an intellectual elite adjudicated the misconceptions and deviations from the true faith of more marginal and powerless urban as well as rural artisans, millers and farmers. In terms of the IW literature, this directly addresses issues of disrupting and maintaining institutions, but it does so in settings and with a methodological toolkit which is hardly known in organization studies.

One can easily continue to list the many ways in which these literatures are not only dissimilar, but also at a complete disconnect from each other, but there are also some interesting and largely underappreciated parallels. For the purpose of this chapter, microhistory will make reference to the original Italian *microstoria*, with its strong focus on ethnography (whilst maintaining a critical distance to Clifford Geertz's ideas). There are two reasons why microhistory appears to be a particularly fruitful historical tradition to explore for institutional theorists. Firstly, if one considers the position within their respective disciplines, microhistory and IW make very similar claims, and seek to challenge commonly held assumptions: microhistorians criticized the type of macro-social enquiry in social history that was prominently (though not exclusively) promoted by the French *Annales* school. In one of the earliest programmatic statements, Ginzburg and Poni (1979) suggested that Italy had been subject to a highly unequal exchange in the historiographic marketplace for ideas, but that microhistorical methodology might help to redress the balance. In a similar move, the IW literature has criticized the increasingly restrictive core concepts of institutional isomorphism, organizational fields, and institutional logics that have become central to institutional theory as a macro-theory of organizations.

Secondly, microhistory distinguishes itself from many other historical traditions by discussing its methodology and its theoretical influences and intentions quite clearly, unusual for historians. It shares this more methodological discourse with other historical specializations, such as postcolonial history, which is an important prerequisite for interdisciplinary research as it has the potential to make this type of historical research more accessible. Table 16.1 summarizes some of these similarities in the research programs of IW and microhistory. In fact, as a historian reading the opening paragraph of Lawrence, Suddaby, and Leca (2011), it seemed to almost recall the intense historiographical debates of the 1970s and 1980s in which the dominance of the macro-social model, based on quantitative 'serial history' (Rowlinson, Hassard, and Decker, 2014) was challenged by what became known later as the 'cultural turn', which encompasses a variety of approaches including microhistory as well as poststructural history (Cook, 2012).

> [T]hese core concepts – such as institutionalization, institutional change, and institutional logics – have focused attention on the macrodynamics of fields – the processes through which large-scale social and economic changes occur. Somewhat lost in the development of an institutional perspective has been the lived experience of organizational actors, especially the connection between this lived experience and the institutions that structure and are structured by it.
>
> *(Lawrence, Suddaby, and Leca, 2011: 52)*

Compare this to the following statement by Georg Iggers, a German historiographer, who describes the sensibilities of the leading Italian microhistorians thus:

> [M]icrohistory is an extension and not a repudiation of older social science history, a rediscovery of culture and the individuality of persons and small groups as agents of historical change … Their key argument against social science approaches to history was that such history deprived the past of its qualitative aspects and left it without a human face.… they rejected the preoccupation of the social sciences with anonymous structures and processes.
>
> *(Iggers, 2005: 112, 116)*

Table 16.1 Comparing the research objectives of institutional work and microhistory

	Institutional work	*Microhistory*
Is a response to	– Institutional Theory	– Social science history – Specifically earlier *Annales* school
Challenges commonly held assumptions such as	– Focus on macro-social processes at the expense of the individual lived experience – Specifically concepts such as organizational fields, institutional isomorphism, and institutionalization	– Focus on macro-social processes at the expense of the individual lived experience – Specifically modernization theory and other deterministic conceptions of progress such as in historical materialism
Aims to	– Bring the individual back into analysis and theory – Link action and institution through individuals as well as distributed agency – Investigate complex and equivocal responses to institutional frameworks	– Bring the individual back into historical analysis – Investigate the agency of marginalized individuals vis-à-vis more powerful social actors
Overarching research objective	Show how individuals can act and influence larger structures, or reinterpret them in ways that are personally meaningful	

The similarities between the two research orientations perhaps become even clearer if one considers a programmatic statement by one of the leading microhistorians in the social history tradition, Giovanni Levi:

> Their work has always centred on the search for a more realistic description of human behaviour, employing an *action and conflict model of man's behaviour in the world* [emphasis added] which recognizes his – relative – freedom beyond, though not outside, the constraints of prescriptive and oppressive normative systems. Thus all social action is seen to be the result of an individual's constant negotiation, manipulation, choices and decisions in the face of a normative reality which, though pervasive, nevertheless offers many possibilities for personal interpretations and freedoms. The question is, therefore, how to define the margins – however narrow they may be – of the freedom granted an individual by the interstices and contradictions of the normative systems which govern him.
>
> *(Levi, 1991: 94)*

If one replaced Levi's reference to 'normative systems' with institutions, the contemporary writings on IW appear almost like an echo of the concerns that drove Italian microhistorians:

> Missing from such grand accounts of institutions and agency are the myriad, day-to-day equivocal instances of agency that, although aimed at affecting the institutional order, represent a complex melange of forms of agency – successful and not, simultaneously radical and conservative, strategic and emotional, full of compromise, and rife with unintended consequences. The study of IW takes as its point of departure an interest in work – the efforts of individuals and collective actors to cope with, keep up with, shore up, tear down, tinker with, transform, or create a new the institutional structures within which they live, work, and play, and which give them their roles, relationships, resources, and routines.
>
> *(Lawrence, Suddaby, and Leca, 2011: 52–3)*

Contemporary microhistorians and IW theorists are equally interested in the messy and incomplete comprehension of the social reality that actors face in their attempts to create their own lives within a world that both enables and constricts their freedom of action.

In the next sections I will first discuss the IW literature and its theoretical formalization of the role of actors and agency in creating, maintaining, and disrupting institutions, followed by a brief introduction to microhistory, specifically the original Italian tradition,[2] in its cultural as well as social history orientation, epitomized by Carlo Ginsburg and Giovanni Levi respectively. While Table 16.1 highlights some of the similarities in research objectives between the two research programmes, their research practices are frequently as different as their research settings. Modern microhistory is moreover split between those historians who still believe in answering 'great historical questions', i.e. address issues of conceptual and historiographical importance, and those who want to particularize microhistory in line with poststructural theories and negate the possibility of generalized theory altogether (Magnússon and Szijártó, 2013). It is more difficult to envisage how the latter group could conceivably contribute to the research agenda of IW, and vice versa, thus this introduction to microhistory largely focuses on the former.

Neo-institutional theory in organization studies

As one of the major theoretical approaches to the study of organizations, institutional theory has been described as a "dominant approach", but one that is "creaking under the weight of its own theoretical apparatus" (Lawrence, Suddaby, and Leca, 2011: 52). Its potential relevance to historical enquiry has been pointed out by Suddaby, Foster, and Mills (2014), who advocate a "historical institutionalism" that reflects the importance of historical processes in creating and maintaining enduring institutions, thus emphasizing the constitutive role of individuals and groups in shaping these institutions over time. There have been some examples of research that merges history and institutional theory, even though the way historians employ institutional theory is noticeably different from how institutional theory scholars use history (Rowlinson and Hassard, 2013). Yet none of these examples have addressed an area that Suddaby, Foster, and Mills highlight as potentially relevant for future research: the so-called paradox of embedded agency (Battilana and D'aunno, 2009; Seo and Creed, 2002). This paradox refers to the problem that if institutions are cognitively totalizing structures, how can individuals ever gain sufficient reflexivity to understand, and potentially change, their institutional environment? Suddaby, Foster, and Mills (2014: 117) have argued that historical techniques such as historical materialism or prosopography (the study of the biographical details of social groups) can help institutional theorists in overcoming the paradox in empirical research.

But historians would hardly be the first to tackle this issue, and there has been some substantial work on agency in the context of IW already. IW is a relatively new area of research that addresses theoretical concerns such as the role of actors and agency, which draws on Bourdieu and the wider literature on practice, as well as Giddens' structuration theory and concepts such as organizational fields and boundary work. Most of these attempts to theorize agency would be unfamiliar to historians. There are several good introductions to the area of IW, and the closely related concept of institutional entrepreneurship (Battilana, Leca, and Boxenbaum, 2009; Battilana and D'aunno, 2009; Lawrence, Suddaby, and Leca, 2009, 2011; Lawrence and Suddaby, 2006) and the following will just briefly sketch the main concepts and developments to clarify the main research agendas and the associated terminology.

Institutional entrepreneurship: agency returns to institutional theory

The core issues for the IW literature are based on neo-institutional theory, especially work by DiMaggio (1988) and DiMaggio and Powell (1983). What is termed the 'old' institutional theory, epitomized for example by the work of Selznick (1949) on the Tennessee Valley Authority, was seen as perhaps closer to the humanities and historical research, as it focused more on individual agency and was less concerned with theorizing structural constraints and influences. In its restatements of older positions, neo-institutional theory was largely a reaction against extremely disembedded views of human agency, such as rational choice theory, that in its original format proposed the complete freedom of the individual to maximize in his or her best interest. Later this was mediated by bounded rationality and other ideas from neo-institutional economics, of which neo-institutional theory is the sociological counterpart. Important foundational concepts were Scott's (2013) pillars of institutions, which categorized institutions beyond being formal or informal into regulatory (such as the law), normative (social conventions), and cognitive (largely informal and cultural, referring to proper and taken for granted ways of doing things). DiMaggio and Powell's (1983) work established the idea that within organizational fields (groups of organizations that are structurally equivalent, i.e. occupy comparable positions within a field) organizations will be subject to isomorphic change (small ongoing changes that make all organizations more similar) under certain conditions (technological uncertainty, resource dependence, and high levels of professionalization of organizational members).

While neo-institutional theory was largely a reaction against the disregard for the embeddedness of human agency (or what historians would refer to as context), research focused increasingly on structural embeddedness and cognitive schemas at a high level of abstraction at the expense of agency and interests, which were central to old institutionalism (Seo and Creed, 2002: 223). As a result institutional theory tended to explain stability better than change, and DiMaggio and Powell (1991) criticized these developments by suggesting that research ought to address the role of 'institutional entrepreneurs', by which they referred to individuals who used their agency to change existing institutions. But as Holm (1995), and Seo and Creed (2002) have highlighted, these attempts to reintroduce agency into neo-institutionalism gave rise to what is known as the paradox of embedded agency. It is in effect a restatement of one of the central problems in sociological theory: how to account for both structure and agency at the same time. Here neo-institutionalists draw on the work of Giddens (1984) and Bourdieu (1977), which has given rise to new conceptualizations of institutional change.

On the one hand, the concept of institutional entrepreneurship has been elaborated further. Institutional entrepreneurs are actors "who leverage resources to create new institutions or to transform existing ones" (Maguire, Hardy, and Lawrence, 2004: 657). This has been, however, criticized as an overly muscular and heroic conception of agency (Lawrence, Suddaby, and Leca, 2009), even though there have been attempts to link institutional entrepreneurship more closely to its alternative, the IW literature (Battilana, Leca, and Boxenbaum, 2009). IW, on the other hand, draws more heavily on Bourdieu's concept of habitus and Giddens' structuration theory, focusing on practice as a micro-foundation for institutional research (DiMaggio and Powell, 1991: 15–29). This literature is of great interest to historians, as it reflects the main developments in the historical discipline of the 1980s and 1990s, when research returned to the experience of individuals without seeking to resuscitate the so-called 'history of great men' (the equivalent of the heroic institutional entrepreneur). It is here that the analogies between microhistory and IW become clearest, even though the way these problems are approached differs markedly.

Institutional work: an expanded concept of agency

The definition of IW is more comprehensive than for institutional entrepreneurship, especially in terms of the type of actors, and the type of agency, that are considered relevant, as it refers to "the purposive action of individuals and organizations aimed at creating, maintaining and disrupting institutions" (Lawrence and Suddaby, 2006: 215). This definition shifts the focus away from heroic individuals towards organizations and groups, and also considers any form of agency that engages with institutions as relevant, including the maintenance of institutions, which is usually not considered in agency terms because institutional theory assumes that institutions are self-replicating and require no agency to be maintained. Thus while IW focuses on how agency affects institutions (Lawrence, Suddaby, and Leca, 2009), it views agency as a multi-level phenomenon, in which the societal, organizational, and individual levels are nested within each other (Friedland and Alford, 1991). Again, this underscores the similarities to historical research, which emphasizes the (multiple) contexts and temporalities of the events or phenomena under consideration (Wadhwani and Bucheli, 2014: 10).

Of these three levels, IW is mostly concerned with the individual one, which has remained under-theorized. Battilana and D'aunno (2009) have combined Emirbayer and Miesche's (1998) work on different types of agency (habitual, practical, projective) with the different types of institutional agency (creating, maintaining, disruptive). They particularly highlight the temporal features of different types of agency: habitual or iterative agency is oriented towards the past, practical-evaluative agency is based in the present, while projective agency is envisioning possible futures. Thus even though Battilana and D'aunno (2009: 57) show that all types of agency can be at play when it comes to creating, maintaining, or disrupting institutions, they propose that iterative agency, due to its orientation towards the past, might be more likely to be relevant for the maintenance of institutions, and less likely to either create or disrupt institutions: "For example, it may be the case that iterative agency, because it is oriented to the past, is less likely than practical-evaluative or projective agency to promote action that creates or disrupts institutions" (Battilana and D'aunno, 2009: 50). This inertial view of the past is at odds with the more emancipatory conception of the past prevalent in history, and suggests that despite some common concerns, temporality is still conceptualized differently in institutional theory and historiography.

Similarly what historians would consider contextualization is subject to strict formalization in institutional theory: the organizational and societal levels of analysis are defined by field-level characteristics such as the degree of heterogeneity, or the degree of institutionalization. This theorizes how 'context' influences agency, either as an enabling or a constraining factor on specific types of agency (Battilana, Leca, and Boxenbaum, 2009). Heterogeneity refers to multiple, alternative, and conflicting institutional orders that are more likely to give rise to institutional entrepreneurship (the changing of institutions). The effects attributed to institutionalization are less clear, as low levels of institutionalization are linked to higher levels of uncertainty, and thus might both enable or constrain individual agency.

Moreover, the individual's social position within these fields is significant in enabling them to mobilize allies and resources, as well as allowing them to articulate a vision for change as their status grants them legitimacy to promote new ideas. Whether these are central or marginal figures within their respective fields may depend on the field characteristics, as empirical work has come to contradictory conclusions in this regard (Greenwood and Suddaby, 2006: Leblebici *et al.*, 1991). Research on institutional change has also highlighted that both at the organizational and individual level, agency might be distributed, suggesting that change might be "a collective phenomenon that involves actors with access to varying kinds and levels of resources who act in either a coordinated or uncoordinated way" (Battilana, Leca, and Boxenbaum, 2009: 89).

Distributed agency has been the subject of several studies (Ross, 2007; Quack, 2007) and might be of greater interest to historians because multi-level research on distributed agency is likely to encounter what historians have traditionally referred to as contingency (O'Sullivan and Graham, 2010).

Of even greater relevance to historians is research on the temporal or evolutionary aspects of IW, such as Zietsma and Lawrence's (2010) study of the interplay of boundary work and practice work. Boundaries refer to the limits of organizational fields, the demarcation lines between people and groups, whereas practices are defined as activities that are typical for and acceptable within social groups. In their study they highlight that agency of different varieties is always evident, but changes depending on the state of the organizational field. When boundaries were intact, agency was habitual; when they were challenged, actors reacted in a practical manner to ongoing issues, whereas projective agency dominated when new, temporary boundaries shielded their activities until they could become established or were again successfully challenged. Hence Zietsma and Lawrence (2010: 213) conclude that "embedded agency may only be paradoxical if viewed at a distance" and is resolved by closer attention to actors' boundary and practice work. Somewhat under-theorized is the role of time and sequence, as they describe the transformation of the organizational field as a cyclical phenomenon.

While hardly an exhaustive review, this suggests some limitations in the current literature on IW: with few exceptions, practice-focused studies are limited to investigating short timespans due to their intense research methods that are based on participant observation, interviewing, or (video) ethnography. Yet most significant transformations of institutional frameworks are likely to occur in the medium term, which raises the question whether a practice-oriented approach can adequately connect individual agency with institutional structures (Lawrence, Suddaby, and Leca, 2009: 6). Historical research, for example, largely ascribes a far greater degree of agency to individuals than most IW scholars would, which raises the question of whether a theory of individual agency can be embedded within the organizational and societal level at all, a point of some debate for microhistorians (Ginzburg, 1989).

Microhistory as a distinctive historiographical tradition

Research in microhistory has been far less coherent than the converging research agendas of IW and institutional entrepreneurship, which can be attributed in part to the more individualized nature of research in history and other humanities. Here, research agendas frequently lack the social movement-style dynamics of the social sciences. Over the years microhistory came to refer to a variety of research designs and methodologies, largely united by their focus on the smaller scale, even though the conceptualization of scale and its function within the methodological innovations of microhistory were frequently misunderstood (Levi, 1991). Magnússon and Szijártó (2013) have defined microhistory by three elements: firstly, the reduction of scale and the use of a focal point for the investigation; secondly, the attempt to answer 'great historical questions'; thirdly, the emphasis on human agency in the analysis.

In terms of content, microhistory has become largely associated with medieval or early modern studies of belief systems in rural, or at least marginalized, communities, and as such has not had any great impact on BH. There have been some attempts, however, to highlight the historiographical opportunities of engaging with microhistory for economic, business and social historians, such as in the edited volume by Susanna Fellman and Marjatta Rahikainen (2012) or Anna Linda Musacchio Adorisio's (2014) recent exploration of using microhistory for narrative analysis. Magnússon and Szijártó (2013: 7) similarly argue that microhistory's particular blend of focusing on 'great historical questions', i.e. theoretical concepts, while also being concerned with the discovery of the 'meaning' of the lived experience of historical actors "makes possible a harmonious blend of social historical and cultural historical approaches". Yet even on this point, the two authors disagree, and the above reflects the position of István Szijártó, while his coauthor, Sigurður Gylfi Magnússon, is more influenced by cultural history and thus does not espouse micoanalysis to elucidate more general issues, but rather values the approach for its potential to break with metanarratives.

This, however, is at odds with Italian microhistory, which has, despite some internal diversity between social and cultural history approaches, consistently disputed postmodernist claims (Magnússon and Szijártó, 2013: 19). Instead, leading Italian microhistorians have emphasized their claim to augment social science history through their own, more particularizing, methodologies, and thus explicitly accepted that this would not please either the supporters or detractors of the "integration of history in the social sciences" (Ginzburg and Poni, 1991: 8–9). Thus while this partial commitment to the concerns of traditional social science history, especially its focus on generalization and making contributions to theory, may appear backward to modern cultural history, Szijártó argues that this is precisely its potential advantage as it allows a merging of cultural and social history approaches, which is currently at the forefront of historical practice (Cook, 2012; Magnússon and Szijártó, 2013: 6). That this makes it even more significant as a theoretical approach and methodological practice that would offer great insights to contemporary MOH, as it has the potential to substantially augment its programme of inserting historical approaches into organization studies. This chapter can only serve as a preliminary exploration of these issues, and seeks to sketch some of the insights from microhistory that have potential relevance or bear resemblance to the research agenda of IW.

The issue of scale: history under the microscope

Microhistorians have disagreed with definitions that reduce microhistory either to the small scale, or to specific subject matter. Giovanni Levi described the latter as belonging to a "rather traditional theory of history" (Levi, 2012: 122) in opposition to which microhistory stresses methodology and the cognitive dimension of historical research. Ginzburg has similarly argued against postmodern relativism as depriving history precisely of its cognitive value, even though this also necessitates opposition to the empiricist approach. He espouses an epistemological constructivism, defined as "the definite awareness that all phases through which research unfolds are constructed and not given: the identificaton of the object and its importance; the elaboration of the categories through which it is analyzed; the criteria of proof; the stylistic and narrative forms by which the results are transmitted to the reader" (Ginzburg, 1993: 32).

The primary construct through which microhistorians define their research site is scale. Levi, however, argues that scale as an inherent characteristic of reality is largely tangential, emphasizing instead the importance of the reduction of scale as an analytical procedure, a form of experimentation that assumes that "microscopic observation will reveal factors previously unobserved" (Levi, 1991: 95, 97). Thus scale, in combination with a focal point, permits microhistorians to ask different questions, to follow individuals by virtue of their names through the sources (Ginzburg and Poni, 1991), with an ambition amounting to writing 'total histories' of individuals. This can lead to unpacking, indeed deconstructing, researchers' assumptions about how to interpret the sources. A good example are claims about the functioning of early modern markets, which looked liked they were already exhibiting forms of impersonal exchange due to the large number of monetized exchanges of land titles. However, a reduction of scale allowed researchers to appreciate that the price of land varied according to the kinship relations between the contractual parties, undermining claims about precocious capitalism (Levi, 1991: 97; for a similar point see Martí and Mair, 2009). Thus the analytic approach to scale is constitutive of microhistory, but the 'micro' here refers not to size per se but to the metaphor of the microscope (Levi, 2012: 126).

The paradox of microhistory: balancing the particular with the general

Hand-in-hand with the focused reduction of scale goes the issue of generalization and the status of the particular and the non-reducible. Microhistory adopted a very particular, and on the face of it paradoxical, attitude towards researching the particular, in its rich context. This implied to not reduce individuals and their relationships to abstract constructs, without abandoning the attempt to generalize from unique and by definition non-repeatable events. This is most clearly epitomized in Edoardo Grendi's (1977: 512) notion of the "exceptional normal". Microhistorians self-consciously refused the selection criteria of the *Annales* school, which considered cases relevant only if they were typical and suitable for serialization, in favour of the anomalous, described within its multiple contexts (Ginzburg, 1993: 33). Changing scales towards a micro-social approach is thus not a simple adjustment, which would be based on the assumption that different levels are nested within in each other and thus exist objectively in an outside reality, as argued by Battilana and D'aunno (2009). Indeed, Ginzburg (1993: 27) emphasizes that

> certain phenomena can only be grasped by means of a macroscopic perspective. This suggests that the reconciliation between macro- and microhistory is not at all taken for granted ... This methodological prescription led to an affirmation of a decisively ontological nature: reality is fundamentally discontinuous and heterogeneous. Consequently, no conclusion attained apropos a determinate sphere can be transferred automatically to a more general sphere.

Within a microhistorical ontology, the small-scale is not embedded within its larger contexts, or in terms of institutional theory, institutions are not considered cognitively totalizing and socially all-encompassing structures that affect multiple levels of analysis. Instead, microhistorians seek to demonstrate that the social norms that rule human behaviour are always multiple, inconsistent, conflicting; not homogeneous and easy to navigate (Levi, 1991, 2012; Revel 1995). In IW terms, all organizational fields thus feature a higher than expected degree of heterogeneity at close range (Battilana, Leca, and Boxenbaum, 2009); a point also made by Zietsma and Lawrence (2010). Nevertheless, the original Italian proponents of microhistory, especially Ginzburg and Levi, have always maintained the need for generalization, in order to answer 'great historical questions', and emphatically rejected a postmodern relativist position. But any analogicality of cases on which generalization can be constructed must either be based on a reductionist rendition of the particular case, which, by stripping it of its uniqueness, might render it less valuable, or on generalization at a theoretical level. This distinction between the particular as the empirical, and the general as theoretical, is perhaps one of the most important insights that MOH scholars can derive from microhistory, as it illustrates how concepts and theories can be developed while retaining their historical cognisance (Kipping and Üsdiken, 2014).

How exactly this tension between the particular and the general is resolved in microhistory is perhaps most clearly explained by Ginzburg (2012) with reference to the emic–etic distinction from ethnography, which broadly maps onto historical debates about the role of the present in the past (Lorenz, 2011). While emic refers to an insider's perspective, etic is a more comparative perspective, that of a more distant observer (the terminology is borrowed from the work of

Kenneth L. Pike, an American linguist). Ginzburg equates any attempts to write history from a purely emic perspective with antiquarianism, while an overemphasis on an etic angle will lead to anachronism. Thus it is the dynamic tension between the etic, present-focused questions, and the emic evidence from the past that exemplifies good historical research: we invariably start from etic questions, to be confronted with emic answers, that in turn modify our questions towards becoming more closely aligned to the concerns of the past that is being studied, without ever entirely abandoning the etic dimension, because the historian, by definition, lives and writes in the present (Ginzburg, 2012: 107–11). Different historical traditions shift the emphasis towards one or the other extreme: understanding of the past on its own terms, in contrast to 'presentist' history in the service of a political agenda or theory. At its extremes, both positions are unacceptable to the historical profession today, and can be equated with determinism, relativism, or antiquarianism.

What this discussion of the emic–etic divide thus clarifies is how microhistorians can simultaneously embrace the unique and unrepeatable character of the past, without abandoning the pursuit of 'great historical questions' (which are, ultimately, theoretical). Thus simple juxtapositions that follow Windelband's (Windelband and Oakes, 1980; Lamiell, 1998) dichotomy between idiographic and nomothetic approaches, such as Lippmann and Aldrich's (2014) distinction between sociological approaches as 'all alike' and historical research as 'all unique' do not do justice to specific research agendas in both organization studies and history, which are in fact mutually commensurable. On the one hand, the IW literature seeks to rediscover agency without abandoning the core ideas of institutional theory, while on the other hand microhistory's conception of the 'exceptional normal' highlights that some branches of historiography offer the opportunity for what I would call 'generalizing from the unique'. Levi (2012: 128) summarized this attitude by emphasizing the "absolutely unrepeatable nature of an event while at the same time retaining the possibility of generalizing from particular cases". Thus microhistory does not recognize the paradox of embedded agency, but instead replaces it with a methodology that has paradoxical aims (elucidating the particular and the general concurrently) and a paradigmatic approach that has human agency at its core.

Discussion and conclusion

Even though IW and microhistory share some of the core concerns about the constitutive role of individual agency within organizations and society, there are some disciplinary differences in their respective approaches. Thus while IW seeks to bring agency back into institutional theory, this is fundamentally an attempt to add agency at the micro level to the structural conceptions of the organizational and societal level. Here IW sees different levels as nested, an idea that microhistory has refuted as too objectivist. The microhistorical challenge to the older *Annales* school was more radical in that it rejected structuralist ontologies in favour of a complex and contingent view of agency that is at the core of both individual experience and social interactions. As already indicated above, microhistory does not recognize any paradox of embedded agency, and instead reframes it as the inherent tension within a research methodology focused on analyzing evidence as a form of 'clues'. Indeed such a paradox only makes sense considering the basic premise of institutional theory, that of cognitively totalizing institutions. Microhistory, however, emphasizes the overlapping and conflicting nature of social structures, which permit individuals to maximize their freedom to act independently. In fact, Ginzburg viewed culture (the microhistorical equivalent of institutions) as more enabling than constraining, "a flexible and invisible cage in which he can exercise his own conditional liberty" (Ginzburg, 1992: xxi), thus echoing the image of the 'iron cage' that has been so influential in institutional theory (DiMaggio and Powell, 1983).

IW continues to conceive of institutions as self-replicating structures that require only minimal maintenance work, and thus naturalizes their existence. Thus the role of the individual cannot be central to theorizing, because it is incidental to the creation, maintenance, and disruption of institutions. Microhistory on the other hand is more interpretative and constructivist in origin, and argues, in line with Tsoukas and Chia (2002) that change is not exceptional, but normal. The implications for research in IW is to focus on the practice of maintenance over long periods of time as truly remarkable. This would permit a reconnection with the original drive behind institutionalism, which was the investigation of the (surprising) continuity of certain structures (North, 1990).

As a result of this structuralist focus, not only is the individual level of action undertheorized in institutional theory, the same holds true for time. Any past-oriented activities are classed as iterative, which promotes an inertial view of the past. Yet not only is maintenance work more complex, the same is true for past-oriented action which might well create new institutions, as argued by influential historians such as Hobsbawm and Ranger (1983) or Anderson (1991). Microhistorians, for example, have demonstrated how challenges to the status quo emerged from alternative readings of tradition and entitlements (Ginzburg, 1992; Levi, 1988) and thus focus on the emancipatory potential of action informed by the reinterpretation of history.

Finally, the engagement with temporally embedded action has been limited in IW because of the intense research methods that focus on short timespans (Suddaby, Foster, and Mills, 2014). Thus while microhistory has also used focal events in their research, their methods were based on historical methodology which is retrospective and largely indirect and documentary. Making these as yet underspecified methods such as archival research (Decker, 2013, 2014; Mills and Helms Mills, 2011), oral history (Haynes, 2010; Vansina, 1985), visual history, or critical source analysis (Kipping, Wadhwani, and Bucheli, 2014; Rowlinson, 2004) more available to organizational researchers would permit a more grounded approach to IW from the perspective of actors both contemporary and historically. By drawing on microhistory, the research agenda of IW could develop alternative ways to resolve the paradox of embedded agency. While at an aggregate scale institutions may appear cognitively totalizing structures, at the level of the individual this invisible cage can be surprisingly flexible – a point made by Ginzburg in 1976, and echoed in Zietsma and Lawrence's work in 2010.

When comparing the historiographic tradition of microhistory with the insights from institutional theory, it should become clear that MOH can draw on much more than just management theories or the philosophy of history, without taking an empiricist stance. A 'historiographic turn' would mean to reconnect with the 'mothership' of history as a disciplinary body of knowledge. This is rarely done because theoretical debates in history are usually embedded in empirical issues, unlike the social science practice that keeps both separate. That does not, however, mean that no theoretical insights are available; just that they require a different, a historiographic, sensibility that focuses on the concepts employed and transfers them into an appropriately social scientific language. This may entail engaging with topics that appear far removed from organizational concerns such as the Inquisition in early modern Italy, as the relevance may not lie in the subject per se, but in its conceptualization as a precursor to relevant theory.

As someone who was trained in the more implicit, at times craft-oriented, environment of history departments in both Germany and the UK, I was not equipped on joining the field of management studies to articulate my epistemological, theoretical, or methodological position, which in history are merged at a conceptual level. Yet even though historiography (in the sense of historical theory) did not feature very strongly in my training, my readings were broadly influenced by what might be considered the second generation of cultural historians (Cook, 2012). Microhistory, or philosophers of history like R. G. Collingwood or David Carr, were not familiar to me before I started reading their work in 2013, only to find that here were other historians who put into words what I was struggling to make explicit. Thus I had an experience similar to Ginzburg (1993: 34), who, reflecting on Levi's (1991) description of microhistory, concluded that "[t]o my surprise I discovered how important to me were, unknowingly, books I had never read, events and persons I did not know had existed … the 'I' is porous".

Notes

1 At the Association of Business Historians' conference in Newcastle, UK, in 2014.
2 Microhistory has come to mean different things in different national historiographies, and its relationship with historical anthropology also differs. For a brief introduction see Iggers, *Historiography in the Twentieth Century* and Magnússon and Szijártó, *What is Microhistory?*

References

Anderson, B. (1991) *Imagined Communities: Reflections on the Origin and Spread of Nationalism*. London and New York: Verso.

Anteby, M. and Molnár, V. (2012) Collective memory meets organizational identity: Remembering to forget in a firm's rhetorical history, *Academy of Management Journal*, 55(3): 515–40.

Battilana, J. and D'aunno, T. (2009) Institutional work and the paradox of embedded agency, in T. B. Lawrence, R. Suddaby, and B. Leca (eds), *Institutional Work: Actors and Agency in Institutional Studies of Organizations* (pp. 31–58). Cambridge: Cambridge University Press.

Battilana, J., Leca, B., and Boxenbaum, E. (2009) How actors change institutions: Towards a theory of institutional entrepeneurship, *Academy of Management Annals*, 3(1): 65–107.

Bourdieu, P. (1977) *Outline of a Theory of Practice*. Cambridge: Cambridge University Press.

Bucheli, M. and Wadhwani, D. (eds) (2014) *Organizations in Time: History, Theory, Methods*. Oxford: Oxford University Press.

Clark, P. and Rowlinson, M. (2004) The treatment of history in organisation studies: Towards an 'historic turn'?, *Business History*, 46(3): 331–52.

Collingwood, R. (1994 [1928]) Outlines of a philoshopy of history, in Collingwood, *The Idea of History* (rev edn), ed. J. van der Dussen (pp. 437–96). Oxford: Oxford Oxford University Press.

Cook, J. W. (2012) The kids are all right: On the 'turning' of cultural history, *American Historical Review*, 117(3): 746–71.

Decker, S. (2010) Postcolonial transitions in Africa: Decolonization in West Africa and present day South Africa, *Journal of Management Studies*, 47(5): 791–813.

Decker, S. (2013) The silence of the archives: Business history, post-colonialism and archival ethnography, *Management & Organizational History*, 8(2): 155–73.

Decker, S. (2014), Solid intentions: An archival ethnography of corporate architecture and organizational remembering, *Organization*, 21(4): 514–42.

DiMaggio, P. J. (1988) Interest and agency in institutional theory, in L. Zucker (ed.), *Institutional Patterns and Organizations* (pp. 3–22). Cambridge, MA: Ballinger.

DiMaggio, P. J. and Powell, W. W. (1983) The iron cage revisited: Institutional isomorphism and collective rationality in organizational fields, *American Sociological Review*, 48(2): 147–60.

DiMaggio, P. J. and Powell, W. W. (1991) Introduction, in P. J. DiMaggio and W. W. Powell (eds), *The New Institutionalism in Organizational Analysis* (pp. 1–40). Chicago: University of Chicago Press.

Emirbayer, M. and Mische, A. (1998) What is agency?, *American Journal of Sociology*, 103(4): 962–1023.

Evans, R. (1999 [1997]) *In Defense of History*. New York: W. W. Norton.

Fellman, S. and Popp, A. (2013) Lost in the archive: The business historian in distress, in B. Czarniawska and O. Löfgren (eds), *Coping with Excess: How Organizations, Communities and Individuals Manage Overflows* (pp. 216–43). Cheltenham: Edward Elgar.

Fellman, S. and Rahikainen, M. (eds) (2012) *Historical Knowledge: In Quest of Theory, Method and Evidence*. Newcastle upon Tyne: Cambridge Scholars Publishing.

Friedland, R. and Alford, R. R. (1991) Bringing society back in: Symbols, practice, and institutional contradictions, in P. J. DiMaggio, and W. W. Powell (eds), *The New Institutionalism in Organizational Analysis* (pp. 232–63). Chicago, IL: University of Chicago Press.

Giddens, A. (1984) *The Constitution of Society: Outline of the Theory of Structuration*. Cambridge: Polity Press.

Ginzburg, C. (1989 [1986]) Clues: Roots of an evidential paradigm, in *Clues, Myths and the Historical Method* (pp. 96–125). Baltimore, MD: Johns Hopkins University Press.

Ginzburg, C. (1992 [1976]) *The Cheese and the Worms: The Cosmos of a Sixteenth Century Miller.* Baltimore, MD: Johns Hopkins University Press.

Ginzburg, C. (1993) Microhistory: Two or three things that I know about it, *Critical Inquiry*, 20: 10–35.

Ginzburg, C. (2012) Our words, and theirs: A reflection on the historian's craft, today, in S. Fellman and M. Rahikainen (eds), *Historical Knowledge: In Quest of Theory, Method and Evidence* (pp. 97–120). Newcastle upon Tyne: Cambridge Scholars Publishing.

Ginzburg, C. and Poni, C. (1979) Il nome e il come: Scambio ineguale e mercato storiografico, *Quaderni storici*, 40(1): 181–90.

Ginzburg, C. and Poni, C. (1991) The name and the game: Unequal exchange and the historiographic marketplace, in E. Muir and G. Ruggiero (eds), *Microhistory and the Lost Peoples of Europe* (pp. 1–10). Baltimore, MD: Johns Hopkins University Press.

Greenwood, A. and Bernardi, A. (2014) Understanding the rift, the (still) uneasy bedfellows of History and Organization Studies, *Organization*, 21(6): 907–32.

Greenwood, R. and Suddaby, R. (2006) Institutional entrepreneurship in mature fields: The big five accounting firms, *Academy of Management Journal*, 49(1): 27–48.

Grendi, E. (1977) Micro-analisi e storia sociale, *Quaderni storici*, 35(2): 506–20.

Hansen, P. H. (2012) Business history: A cultural and narrative approach, *Business History Review*, 86(4): 693–717.

Haynes, K. (2010) Other lives in accounting: Critical reflections on oral history methodology in action, *Critical Perspectives on Accounting*, 21(3): 221–31.

Hobsbawm, E. and Ranger, T. (1983) *The Invention of Tradition.* Cambridge: Cambridge University Press.

Holm, P. (1995) The dynamics of institutionalization: Transformation processes in Norwegian fisheries, *Administrative Science Quarterly*, 40(3): 398–422.

Iggers, G. G. (2005) *Historiography in the Twentieth Century: From Scientific Objectivity to the Postmodern Challenge* (2nd edn). Middletown, CT: Wesleyan.

Jacobitti, E. E. (2000) *Composing Useful Pasts: History as Contemporary Politics.* New York: State University of New York Press.

Kipping, M. and Üsdiken, B. (2014) History in organization and management theory: More than meets the eye, *Academy of Management Annals*, 8(1): 535–88.

Kipping, M., Wadhwani, R. D., and Bucheli, M. (2014) Analyzing and interpreting historical sources: A basic methodology, in M. Bucheli and R. D. Wadhwani (eds), *Organizations in Time: History, Theory, Methods* (pp. 305–30). Oxford: Oxford University Press.

Lamiell, J. T. (1998) Nomothetic and idiographic: Contrasting Windelband's understanding with contemporary usage, *Theory & Psychology*, 8(1): 23–38.

LaRossa, R. (1997) *The Modernization of Fatherhood: A Social and Political History.* Chicago, IL: University of Chicago Press.

Lawrence, T. B. and Suddaby, R. (2006) Institutions and institutional work, in S. R. Clegg, C. Hardy, and T. Lawrence (eds), *The Sage Handbook of Organization Studies* (pp. 215–55). Beverly Hills, CA: Sage.

Lawrence, T. B., Suddaby, R., and Leca, B. (2009) Introduction: Theorizing and studying institutional work, in T. B. Lawrence, R. Suddaby, and B. Leca (eds), *Institutional Work: Actors and Agency in Institutional Studies of Organizations* (pp. 1–27). Cambridge: Cambridge University Press.

Lawrence, T. B., Suddaby, R., and Leca, B. (2011) Institutional work: Refocusing institutional studies of organization, *Journal of Management Inquiry*, 20(1): 52–58.

Leblebici, H., Salancik, G. R., Copay, A., and King, T. (1991) Institutional change and the transformation of interorganizational fields: An organizational history of the US radio broadcasting industry, *Administrative Science Quarterly*, 36(3): 333–63.

Lerner, G. (1994) *The Creation of Feminist Consciousness: From the Middle Ages to Eighteen-Seventy.* Oxford: Oxford University Press.

Levi, G. (1988) *Inheriting Power: The Story of an Exorcist*, trans. L. G. Cochrane. Chicago, IL: University of Chicago Press.

Levi, G. (1991) On microhistory, in P. Burke (ed.), *New Perspectives on Historical Writing* (pp. 93–113). Cambridge: Polity Press.

Levi, G. (2012) Microhistory and the recovery of complexity, in S. Fellman and M. Rahikainen (eds), *Historical Knowledge: In Quest of Theory, Method and Evidence* (pp. 121–32). Newcastle upon Tyne: Cambridge Scholars Publishing.

Lippmann, S. and Aldrich, H. E. (2014) History and evolutionary theory, in M. Bucheli and R.D. Wadhwani (eds), *Organizations in Time: History, Theory, Methods* (pp. 124–46). Oxford: Oxford University Press.

Lorenz, C. (2011) History and theory, in A. Schneider and D. Woolf (eds), *The Oxford History of Historical Writing* (pp. 13–35). Oxford: Oxford University Press.

Magnússon, S. G. and Szijártó, I. M. (2013) *What is Microhistory? Theory and Methods*. London and New York: Routledge.

Maguire, S., Hardy, C., and Lawrence, T. B. (2004) Institutional entrepreneurship in emerging fields: HIV/AIDS treatment advocacy in Canada, *Academy of Management Journal*, 47(5): 657–79.

Mantere, S. and Ketokivi, M. (2013) Reasoning in organization science, *Academy of Management Review*, 38(1): 70–89.

Martì, I. and Mair, J. (2009) Bringing change into the lives of the poor: Entrepreneurship outside traditional boundaries, in T. B. Lawrence, R. Suddaby, and B. Leca (eds), *Institutional Work: Actors and Agency in Institutional Studies of Organizations* (pp. 92–119). Cambridge: Cambridge University Press.

Mills, A. J. and Helms Mills, J. (2011) Digging archaeology: Postpositivist theory and archival research in case study development, in R. Piekkari and C. Welch (eds), *Rethinking the Case Study in International Business and Management Research* (pp. 342–60). London: Edward Elgar.

Musacchio Adorisio, A. L. (2014) Organizational remembering as narrative: 'Storying' the past in banking, *Organization*, 21(4): 463–76.

North, D. C. (1990) *Institutions, Institutional Change and Economic Performance*. Cambridge: Cambridge University Press.

O'Sullivan, M. and Graham, M. B. W. (2010) Guest editors' introduction: Moving forward by looking backward – Business history and management studies, *Journal of Management Studies*, 47(5): 775–90.

Popp, A. (2009) History, a useful 'science' for management? A response, *Enterprise and Society*, 10(4): 831–36.

Quack, S. (2007) Legal professionals and transnational law-making: A case of distributed agency, *Organization*, 14(5): 643–66.

Revel, J. (1995) Microanalysis and the construction of the social, in J. Revel and L. Hunt (eds), *Histories: French Constructions of the Past* (pp. 492–502). New York: New Press.

Ricoeur, P. (2004) *Memory, History, Forgetting*. Chicago, IL: University of Chicago Press.

Ross, D. A. (2007) Backstage with the knowledge boys and girls: Goffman and distributed agency in an organic online community, *Organization Studies*, 28(3): 307–25.

Rowlinson, M. (2004) Historical analysis of company documents, in C. Cassell and G. Symon (eds), *Essential Guide to Qualitative Methods in Organizational Research* (pp. 301–11). Beverley Hills, CA: Sage.

Rowlinson, M. and Hassard, J. (2013) Historical neo-institutionalism or neo-institutionalist history? Historical research in management and organization studies, *Management & Organizational History*, 8(2): 111–26.

Rowlinson, M., Hassard, J., and Decker, S. (2014) Research strategies for organizational history: A dialogue between historical theory and organization theory, *Academy of Management Review*, 39(3): 250–74.

Schwarzkopf, S. (2012) What is an archive – and where is it? Why business historians need a constructive theory of the archive, *Business Archives: Sources and History*, 105: 1–9.

Scott, W. W. R. (2013 [1995]) *Institutions and Organizations: Ideas, Interests, and Identities*. Beverley Hills, CA: Sage.

Selznick, P. (1949) *TVA and the Grass Roots*. Berkeley, CA: University of California Press.

Seo, M.-G. and Creed, W. E. D. (2002) Institutional contradictions, praxis, and institutional change: A dialectical perspective, *Academy of Management Review*, 27(2): 222–47.

Suddaby, R., Foster, W. M., and Mills, A. J. (2014) Historical institutionalism, in M. Bucheli and R. D. Wadhwani (eds), *Organizations in Time: History, Theory, Methods* (pp. 100–23). Oxford: Oxford University Press.

Taylor, S., Bell, E., and Cooke, B. (2009) Business history and the historiographical operation, *Management & Organizational History*, 4(2): 151–66.

Toms, S. and Wilson, J. (2010) In defence of business history: A reply to Taylor, Bell and Cooke, *Management & Organizational History*, 5(1): 109–20.

Tsoukas, H. and Chia, R. (2002) On organizational becoming: Rethinking organizational change, *Organization Science*, 13(5): 567–82.

Vansina, J. (1985) *Oral Tradition as History*. Madison, WI: University of Wisconsin Press.

Wadhwani, R. D. and Bucheli, M. (2014) The future of the past in management and organization studies, in M. Bucheli and R. D. Wadhwani (eds), *Organizations in Time: History, Theory, Methods* (pp. 3–32). Oxford: Oxford University Press.

Windelband, W. and Oakes, G. (1980) History and natural science, *History and Theory*, 19(2): 165–68.

Zietsma, C. and Lawrence, T. B. (2010) Institutional work in the transformation of an organizational field: The interplay of boundary work and practice work, *Administrative Science Quarterly*, 55(2): 189–221.

Part IV

Rewriting management and organizational history

17

History of management thought in context

The case of Elton Mayo in Australia

Tuomo Peltonen

Introduction

George Elton Mayo is generally considered one of the most influential theorists in the history of management thought. His name appears regularly in lists of the most important texts on the theory and practice of management (e.g. Wren & Bedeian, 2009; Wren & Hay, 1977). Even more notable is his legacy in the field of organizational behavior, where he is often considered to have laid the theoretical foundations for this emerging discipline (O'Connor, 1999b: 223; Roethlisberger, 1977; Whyte, 1987). Part of that heritage has been transmitted through the vast impact (Gillespie, 1991) of the legendary Hawthorne studies for the practice and theory of organizational management (Mayo, 1933; Roethlisberger & Dickson, 1939). Yet Mayo has not only been cherished as a key scholar in the history of organization theory, but his work has also been the target of extensive historical review and criticism (Wood & Wood, 2004).

Despite the burgeoning literature on Mayo, there is a fundamental problem in most of the reviews and historical analyses conducted so far. The main bulk of these studies tend to evaluate Mayo from the perspective of the intellectual and discursive conventions of the present environment. According to Skinner (1969), this is a common mistake in the history of ideas, where a historian – consciously or unconsciously – interprets a particular author as an 'early advocate' of a theoretical program or doctrine that in reality emerged after the historical writing in question. To say that Mayo was the father of the human relations approach to management theory fails to appreciate the fact that no such school or field existed at the time when he was working within industrial and social studies. Instead of inserting Mayo into the prevailing narratives of the unfolding of management thought over time (e.g. Barley & Kunda, 1992; Wren & Bedeian, 2009), or even into the institutionalized disciplines of sociology or psychology (e.g. Dingley, 1997; Moore, 1948), a more historically specific inquiry would try to locate Mayo in the particular temporal and spatial context within which his concepts and arguments took shape.

Many evaluations in the history of management thought miss the fact that Mayo came to America in 1922 as a well-formed political philosopher already in his early forties. He was well acquainted with the contemporary currents in British political thinking and already had a long career as an adult educator behind him (Trahair, 1984). Most important, he had been a member of an influential circle of scholar-activists promoting an Idealist form of social liberalism in

Australian society (Bourke, 1981; Sawer, 2003; Walter & Moore, 2002). Despite recent historical analyses (e.g. Griffin, Landy & Mayocchi, 2002), this aspect of Mayo has so far been treated as a marginal curiosity in his overall contribution to organizational and workplace studies. When Mayo is treated as a social philosopher, his work is typically assessed with the implicit assumption that he worked in a dialogue with particular texts from social theory (e.g. Bendix & Fisher, 1949; Moore, 1948; O'Connor, 1999b) or psychology (e.g. Dingley, 1997; Hsueh, 2002), without a systematic inquiry into the actual contexts influencing his thinking and writing during the formative years (Sawer, 2003; Walter & Moore, 2002).

In order to remedy these shortcomings in the historical appraisal of Mayo, this chapter undertakes a reading of Mayo as a scholar embedded in the intellectual and societal contexts of his historical time. Following broadly the contextualist 'intellectual history' approach as advocated by Quentin Skinner (1969, 1978), its purpose is to reposition Mayo in the discursive and conceptual milieu of early twentieth-century British Commonwealth political philosophy, taking into consideration the intellectual movements within his local surroundings in Australia. The material used in this historical re-reading of Mayo's work includes secondary literature explicating the scholarly discourse of the British Idealists and their political counterparts, New or Social Liberals (Armour, 2006; Brink, 2003; Tyler, 2006), and reviews of the activities of the Australian group of Idealist Liberals (Bourke, 1981, 1982; Sawer, 2003; Walter & Moore, 2002). Mayo's main publication from the Australian period, the book *Democracy and Freedom* (Mayo, 1919), is closely scrutinized to reveal its debt to Idealist Liberalist concepts, accompanied by other relevant theoretical texts from different periods (e.g. Mayo, 1920, 1949). Some of the Australian period publications obtained from the archives of the Baker Library Mayo collection at Harvard Business School have served as background material in the conceptual and philosophical analysis.

The chapter is structured as follows: the next section takes a brief look at the typical reception of Mayo in the theory and history of management studies. This is followed by an analysis of elements of the intellectual context in Australia, firstly focusing on the philosophical and political program of the Idealist Liberals in Britain and in Australia, then proceeding to a reading of Mayo's 1919 *Democracy and Freedom* as conceptually embedded in the Idealist vocabulary, and finally assessing the more concrete societal situation of the later 1910s as an ideological and political challenge to the Idealist Liberalist cause. The chapter concludes with a discussion of the lessons of the contextual analysis of the 'Australian Mayo' for a revised description and assessment of Mayo's overall project in the theory and practice of social and organizational issues.

A brief overview of the role and reception of Elton Mayo in management studies

Over the years, Mayo has been interpreted and integrated into the evolving canon of management theory in many ways. The initial and most obvious positioning has been to see his work as intimately connected to the Hawthorne Studies and to the articulation of the theoretical implications of the findings from the experiments and fieldwork at the Hawthorne plant (e.g. Moore, 1948). A second convention is to assign Mayo the role of the leader of the Human Relations movement and the founder of the discipline of organizational behavior (O'Connor, 1999b; Whyte, 1987). Thirdly, in a more general history of science, various historical commentators link Mayo to the intellectual context of Harvard University in the late 1920s and 1930s, especially to the activities of the Pareto circle and associated attempts to develop a systems perspective on the study of social organization (Heyl, 1968; Keller, 1984).

While there are sympathetic assessments of his legacy (Smith, 1975, 1998), critical interrogations seem to dominate the evolving corpus of Mayo studies. Bendix and Fisher (1949) opened the critical stream of reviews in an article that became a landmark appraisal. Bendix and Fisher try to reconstruct the core argument of Mayo's thinking by visiting his social theory publications from 1919 to 1947. They find that "there is a consistency in the writings of Mayo" (Bendix & Fisher, 1949: 312), which is found throughout his career. Bendix and Fisher list well-known themes, such as Mayo's emphasis on spontaneous cooperation and dislike of state intervention and trade unions, as well as his focus on the role of enlightened leaders in the building of workplace harmony, to summarize Mayo's philosophy. Criticism of this assumed view of Mayo is based on the observation that "it is evident that [Mayo] prefers cooperation to conflict" (Bendix & Fisher, 1949: 318). That this is problematic is related to the idea that:

> most people in modern society express their sense of social responsibility by their participation in such associations as the National Association of Manufacturers, the Chamber of Commerce, or the Congress of Industrial Organizations. These and other associations will conflict.
>
> *(Bendix & Fisher, 1949: 318)*

Mayo is thus seen as restricting the emergence of natural conflicts that are necessary for the resolving of tensions in the workplace. Mayo's apparent avoidance of conflict implies for Bendix and Fisher that Mayo fails to define "the ethical presuppositions of his scientific work" (Bendix & Fisher, 1949: 319), but instead, passes as "a technical prophet" (Bendix & Fisher, 1949: 319) whose moral values are not laid out in an explicit manner in his articulations of the role of civilized social communities.

To what extent this kind of critique is grounded in Mayo's intentions within the intellectual and conceptual environment where he was articulating his views is open to debate. Bendix and Fisher (1949) make a relatively just assessment of Mayo's main themes, but at the same time it can be argued that they fall short of trying to understand in more depth the philosophical, discursive, and local context into which Mayo was originally embedded as an emerging Australian academic. Instead, they consider Mayo as a student of industrial relations conflict whose sociological theory remains alarmingly vague about its ontological presuppositions. Mayo's contribution is represented as a case of integrationist social science within a frame that identifies only two main categories of paradigm: conflict and cooperation.

The analysis of Bendix and Fisher (1949) is somewhat anachronistic (Skinner, 1969). Mayo was not originally writing as an industrial relations specialist, because neither industrial relations nor industrial sociology had yet been established as separate disciplines during his formative years at the beginning of the twentieth century. Mayo bore the title of Professor of Philosophy in Australia. At that time, psychology was still included in the philosophical subjects and was only gradually establishing itself as a separate scholarly discipline (Griffin, Landy & Mayocchi, 2002). Sociology was also in its infancy. The first sociology professor was appointed to the London School of Economics in 1907, with Australia receiving its first sociology chair in 1917 (Bourke, 1981). Mayo was working in the middle of the transformations that led to the development of the academic fields of psychology and sociology (anthropology, economics, etc.); hence he could not, at the time, have employed the types of disciplinary concepts that later commentators have used in their subsequent assessments of his project.

Bendix and Fisher (1949) operate with the nascent sociological vocabulary that takes inspiration from sociological classics such as those of Weber and Marx. Mayo, instead, was primarily operating with terminology influenced by contemporary political philosophy of the turn of the century (e.g. Mayo, 1919). Sociological schools of thought were not yet clearly formed as scientific paradigms during his Australian years. For Mayo then, the concept of moral responsibility echoed the concepts of the Idealist philosophical discourse, where morality has a specific ontological meaning, as the level of being at which citizens develop self-control and mastery over nature (Brink, 2003). For Bendix and Fisher (1949), in contrast, 'social responsibility' equates to participation in political organizations and other associations that express the interests of various societal groups and classes. Bendix and Fisher articulate responsibility in a fashion that emphasizes the primacy of the organization of political activity into institutions that then control the staging and resolving of societal contradictions and conflicts. Their vocabulary is closer to those of the Marxist political economy and Weberian class analysis than to the classical Idealist repertoire characteristic of Mayo's social theory discourse.

Let us next analyze in more detail the intellectual, conceptual and societal context of Mayo's theoretical work in Australia in the first decades of the twentieth century.

The context of Mayo's work in Australia

Elton Mayo was active as a student, adult educator, clinician, and university faculty member in Australia between 1907 and 1922 (Trahair, 1984). During that time, he was part of a group of academic intellectuals influenced by the Idealist philosophy of Social Liberalist political thought, and a commitment to the social scientific and political agenda of the activities of the Workers' Educational Association in Australia. Concurrently, this was the time of the First World War and the rise of the trade unions and the Australian Labour Party into the Australian political scene. All of these can be seen as playing a role in the way Mayo's theoretical and political-practical thinking took shape.

The influence of British Idealism and Social Liberalism

Mayo's university training immersed him in a philosophical scene dominated by the British Idealists. Trahair (1984: 53–54) details the influence of scholars such as Green, Bosanquet, and Sedgwick on Mayo's education and early teaching. The Idealist school in Britain emerged from a particular interpretation of Greek and German Idealism that de-emphasized the idea of the state as the embodiment of an Absolute Spirit and focused more on the conditions of freedom of individual citizens. It was an amalgam of the Idealist writings of Hegel and the more agent-centered approach of classical Liberalism.

Perhaps the most important scholar in the Idealist movement was T. H. Green, an Oxford philosopher, Idealist, moralist and political reformist (Brink, 2003). Green based his ethical and political theories on a distinct metaphysical view. As Armour (2006) argues, reality, for him, "consists of an eternal consciousness and a number of finite consciousnesses, which develop over time, while participating in and being individuated from the eternal consciousness" (Armour, 2006: 173). The proper purpose of finite selves is to realize their potential by cooperating with other finite selves and to take responsibility for global self-development. A good society is one in which everyone is free, "in the sense of being able to participate optimally in this process" (Armour, 2006: 173). For Green, our very nature depends on a successful understanding of the process of moral co-evolution.

Yet as Tyler (2006: 59) notes, although Green was an Absolute Idealist believing in the existence of a spirit that seeks its self-realization in the world:

> Green differed from Hegel, however, in that … he held that his version of the absolute, which he called 'the eternal consciousness', was individuated as a potential of each particular human consciousness rather than as a single spirit that realized itself in some sense through communities of particular consciousnesses.

Green's Idealism sees the state and its individual human subjects in a more reciprocal relationship, in which the state empowers and supports individuals in their pursuit of higher faculties, but in which, on the other hand, individuals with their moral sensibilities constitute the state as the ethical finality. The powers of the state are limited in the sense that they are restricted to maintaining favorable external conditions for citizens to be able to realize their moral potential through aiming at the higher states of being. The state philosophy has license to intervene in public action whenever external conditions for the pursuit of moral citizenship are in jeopardy, but it does not have permission to participate in the inner processes of the individuals following the higher principles for moral standing. Thus, the political role of the state is, for Green, that of a moral authority whose task is to intervene whenever external conditions are not favorable to the pursuit of moral citizenship in various domains of action (Brink, 2003). The state may use negative force, but only in order to offer citizens the possibility of practicing the kind of moral life that leads to true social harmony (Green, 1895/1999).

One of Green's most well-known contributions to political philosophy is his concept of 'positive freedom' (Wempe, 2004). The classical liberalist tradition of Hobbes, Locke, Mills, and others entails a broadly negative view of freedom, in which liberty is equated with the absence of various political, social and economic obstacles (Berlin, 1969). Political liberty then, is "simply the area within which a man can act unobstructed by others," while "if I am prevented by others from doing what I could otherwise do, I am to that degree unfree" (Berlin, 1969: 120). In his reformulation, Green looks at the concept of freedom from the Idealist perspective as the pursuit of self-realization and mastery over nature. Green (1906: 370) emphasizes that liberty is not taken to "mean merely freedom from restraint or compulsion." Instead:

> When we speak of freedom as something to be so highly prized, we mean a positive power or capacity of doing or enjoying something worth doing or enjoying, and that, too, something that we do or enjoy in common with others.
>
> *(Green, 1906: 370)*

Freedom for Green is the consequence of realizing the higher potential in individuals and transforming actors into moral subjects freed from the shackles of self-interest and material desires.

The Idealist legacy is visible in the central concepts advocated by Mayo in his main philosophical writings. At a general level, Mayo used Idealist concepts in several contexts during his academic career. His two major Harvard-period books include in their titles the word 'civilization' (Mayo, 1933, 1949). The choice of the word 'civilization' resonates with ideas about advanced social forms and the importance of higher purpose, morality and culture within the Idealist discourse. The concept of civilization can be seen as the English equivalent of the German term 'Kultur,' which denotes culture not only in its conventional sense of the norms, values and meanings of a particular community, but also in the more specific sense of enlightened civilization (e.g. Markus, 1986).

A related concept in Mayo's vocabulary is 'education.' Education equals simultaneously the processes of knowledge acquisition, character development and the building of a moral community. 'Education' in Mayo's sense comes closer to the German concept of 'Bildung,' which has traditionally referred to the formative nature of educational processes in the holistic maturing of the human person (Geuss, 1996). In its broadest sense, education is seen as a process whereby an individual becomes a civilized moral being, or a fully human person. Education here covers the totality of one's developmental experiences and passages, and is not limited to formal learning contexts. To put this in another way, formal education or expertise does not guarantee true progress towards the ideal of a morally civilized person. Civilization and education are closely related in that to achieve a high level of civilization individuals need to embark on a journey of educating themselves, while at the same time, education in its German Idealist sense becomes understandable when viewed as the process whereby concrete individuals develop fully realized human personhood or citizenship.

The conceptual context of Democracy and Freedom

Mayo's *Democracy and Freedom* (1919) is a commentary on the contemporary political and industrial changes in the advanced Western societies. It is fundamentally a critical treatise on the phenomenon of parliamentary politics and the rise of the organized labor movement. As the title suggests, Mayo wishes to juxtapose democracy and freedom in the book. However, on closer reading, it becomes obvious that the two concepts are not at the same level in the way they are semiotically framed. 'Freedom' is the meta-concept that refers to the type of community where human moral properties are being put to the best possible use. Achieving this state of freedom requires that there is a 'civilized' community whose members are continuously 'educating' themselves toward higher purposes and moral values.

Mayo does not explain his usage of 'freedom' in an explicit manner. The synonyms he uses for freedom, however, reveal an underlying slant toward Idealist vocabulary, where liberty is a project of civilization and moral betterment. Recurring phrases used by Mayo include 'social growth' and 'traditions.' The concept of social growth refers to evolution toward a distinct goal in the development of a human community, broadly in the Hegelian sense of striving in the direction of a synthesis in the form of 'the end of history.' On this journey, the accumulated cultural knowledge of previous generations operates as a pool of experiential wisdom, embedded in the habits and beliefs of the prevailing social traditions. The accumulated wisdom, as stored in social traditions, is the actualized manifestation of the more abstract form of civilizing wisdom, or, as Mayo puts it, "civilization makes itself concrete and actual in social traditions" (Mayo, 1919: 7).

Another key concept is 'social will,' which denotes not so much the historical journey of the community from the past toward perfection, but more the collective political mood of civil society. This is the liberalist side of the Social Liberalist thinking inherited from British Idealism. The concept of 'the will of the people' as used by Mayo refers to the notion that the legitimacy of any government is always, in the last instance, dependent on the popular consent of civic society. This is where Social Liberalism differs from the more state-centered political philosophy of the German Idealists (Brink, 2003). The 'social will' of Mayo is, however, treated as a less abstract notion than in the classical liberalist depiction of the political subject. *Social* will is the popular pursuit of political and moral ideals, embedded in the context of the existing traditions. It is an expression of the desire for the development and ultimate realization of the human potential in any given community. The role of the state and its public institutions is to support this endeavor by enabling individuals and groups to use their human potential in the best possible way and also to participate in the quest for moral growth, the state setting itself as an example of ethical conduct.

In sum, Mayo's concept of 'freedom' can be interpreted against the Idealist notion of a moral community, with emphasis on the uninhibited pursuit of human perfection, and the enabling and supporting role of the state in that process. Freedom is possible only when a community has progressed toward human perfection in the form of the cherishing of higher moral purposes. Central to this is the readiness of the actors to leave the material empirical world behind and to turn instead to the perfection of the innate human-ethical qualities of the social person.

'Democracy,' on the other hand, is a secondary concept in Mayo's (1919) vocabulary. It has a narrower meaning, of the activities of the political parties and the societal outcomes of party tactics in electoral campaigns. Democracy is treated here primarily as a form of government that has its place alongside other modes of governing (autocracy, monarchy, etc.). Mayo is particularly concerned here with the unintended consequences of the new representative democracy associated with the introduction of general voting rights and the emergence of organized political parties. Politics within this system tends to be reduced to the manipulative maneuvers of political parties and their leaders. Parties are organized around class identities and assumed material interests and are prone to sustaining and affirming various societal divides instead of promoting the development of moral perfection and social harmony. Democratic politics tends to lead to adversarial methods in order to ensure the greatest popular support in an electoral situation.

In this context, the state cannot fulfill its role of promoting the moral growth of its citizens. The divisive politics of party-oriented tactics hinders the civilizing development of the body social. Mayo uses the notion of 'positive freedom' (Berlin, 1969) as the background against which the success of democracy as a form of political culture is to be evaluated: "'Government' ... is only one aspect of a wider social cooperation" (Mayo, 1919: 66). The conclusion is that democracy in its current form severely limits the civilizing process. Democracy is based on a "misunderstanding of the facts of human nature and social organization" (Mayo, 1919: 13), and thus is not a guarantee of the possibility of pursuing human freedom.

Industrial democracy

The secondary argument of *Democracy and Freedom*, often observed with more interest in management and organization history (e.g. O'Connor, 1999a, 1999b), concerns the question of industrial or organizational democracy. Mayo attacks the operation of the recently formed trade unions and their political counterparts, socialist labour parties. Given the Idealist striving toward social harmony and the centrality of overcoming materially based divisions, this exclusive focus on the failures of workers to follow the perfection program seems at first contradictory. Mayo does try to balance his treatment by making passing notes about the limited visions of employers at the beginning of his evaluation of the industrial situation. He argues that the prevailing "class consciousness" of employers obscures the "social responsibility" of owners and managers (Mayo, 1919: 41).

The discussion that follows, however, centers entirely on the harmful effects of trade union collectives on the civic enlightenment of the commercial world. The utilitarian and egoistic ideology of the capitalist class is not analyzed with the same philosophical rigor as the situation of the politically mobilized workers. This selective attention within the analysis of industrial relations reflects the broader trend in the Australian adoption of British Idealism in regard to the social and industrial problems of the day. The Australian Social Liberal intellectuals took a more empirical or sociological approach to the question of human perfection in the promotion of the human moral community (Bourke, 1981; Walter & Moore, 2002).

Similarly, the journey toward social harmony is seen by Mayo as being implemented in the pursuit of cooperative efforts between discrete groups of skilled professionals. A moral community is to be achieved by recognizing the distinct specialisms of various occupational groups in a way that leads to respectful dialogue and the fusion of sectional interests in the name of the common good. Mayo blends here the actual degree of professional skill with the potential to participate in the shaping of organizational power structures. He is concerned about the consequences of industrial democracy in cases where an unskilled but politically empowered worker is capable of controlling the conduct of a skilled craftsman. At the root of the problem is the incapability of the unskilled worker-activist to enable moral growth in the form of a civilizing dialogue between enlightened professionals. The argument emerging from the discussion is that occupational knowledge and skill enable an inherently 'social' input for the promotion of industrial harmony, and that, conversely, the unskilled worker cannot contribute in the same fashion to the process of moral community building (Mayo, 1919: 50–51).

Workers' Educational Association as the practical realm of Idealist policies

Apart from the particularistic interpretation given to the application of British Idealist metaphysics in the realm of industrial relations, the Australian promoters of Social Liberalism were intensively engaged with the adult education initiative called the Workers' Educational Association (WEA). Originally English, the WEA was a direct offshoot from the Idealist program of civic development. Its roots lie in the Settlement movement that was inspired by the charity work of T. H. Green (Sawer, 2003). The WEA was designed as a platform for the meeting of university teachers and industrial workers. The idea was to build a moral community where both groups would learn from each other and embark on a social process of self-development. The teaching method of tutorial discussions reflected the underlying philosophy of mutually affecting interaction in an open environment.

The WEA's role in Australia went beyond that of a tool for societal reform. It became the prime institutional context through which the academic activities of the Idealists spread to society in general and the universities. The WEA introduced the scholarly field of sociology to the Australian university scene (Bourke, 1981). At a time when social sciences were just starting to take shape as independent scholarly fields, WEA intellectuals tried to define sociology as the theory and practice of coping with the social and political problems of the day. This was a more holistic and speculative form of sociological practice than the contemporary research-based activities of empirical social research.

The advancement of the new fields of sociology, psychology, and economics took place in the 1910s and 1920s in Australia via the publication of a series of books analyzing the current situation of the local society and culture from the vantage point of the Liberalist Idealist program developed within WEA intellectual circles (e.g. Atkinson, 1920). The books were intended as reading materials for the tutorial classes and had, hence, a primarily educational function as commissioned adult textbooks. On the other hand, they were also targeted at a wider audience consisting of Australian and international political actors and academic commentators.

Mayo's *Democracy and Freedom* was the first pamphlet-textbook published in the Australian WEA series. It was written for the adult audience that was assumed to be hesitating between the new political mobilizations of the trade unions and the Australian Labour Party on the one hand, and the WEA message of gradual reform through personal and communal enlightenment on the other. Mayo can be pictured in *Democracy and Freedom* as talking to his tutorial attendees, trying to persuade them to see the human shortcomings of the materialist class-based struggle and the associated confrontational party politics of the day.

There were several imminent threats to the WEA-Idealist project at the time of writing *Democracy and Freedom*. In 1919, the First World War had severely affected the popularity of German nationalist thinking and its cultural legacy in the British Commonwealth. For example, the British royal family changed its name from Hanover to Windsor in order to downplay the German background of its ancestors. Hegelian philosophy was not a particularly suitable candidate to become a leading political theory in the country in the aftermath of the disappointments of the war, since it was interpreted as supporting a nationalist and aggressive political doctrine that had been one of the primary ideological causes for a devastating international war (Skidelsky, 2007).

Secondly, the British Liberal Party was in decline in the face of the ascent of the Labour Party and the associated class-based political landscape. Trade unions had emerged as a new actor in the industrial realm, and were uncomfortable with the WEA tradition of middle-class academics having a direct educational and ideological channel for molding the identity of the workers. In Australia, Labour had formed the first left-wing government in the world in 1904, and was consolidating its power position in the emerging national structures (Griffin, Landy & Mayocchi, 2002).

Thirdly, sociology as espoused by WEA academics had not been successfully incorporated into the university mainstream. There was just one designated sociology chair in the whole of Australia, meaning that academic career opportunities were relatively thin. When the leader of the WEA group, Meredith Atkinson, resigned from his University of Melbourne post in 1922, there were a total of 40 applicants for the vacancy, including Mayo (Bourke, 1981). Not long after that time, sociology began to develop into a more rigorous empirical science, pushing the interdisciplinary and action-oriented project of the WEA intellectuals further into the academic margins. Other social science fields also took rapid leaps toward professional and scientific autonomy. Taken together, the wider shifts in the political situation and climate, as well as the advancement of scientific disciplines, were responsible for several cracks in the cohesion of the WEA–Idealist controlled assemblage of metaphysics, politics, and industrial and social development (Sawer, 2003).

It becomes apparent, then, why one can sense a slight degree of desperation in the voices of the WEA intellectuals, evident in the relatively demagogic style of *Democracy and Freedom* as well as other WEA publications of the time (e.g. Atkinson, 1920). Within a couple of years, the Idealist Liberalist project had largely dissolved in Australia. Several of the leading figures had resigned from their university posts and left the country (Bourke, 1982). Mayo famously embarked on a round trip to the USA from which he never returned. Another major figure, Clarence Northcott, emigrated to the UK, eventually becoming the father of British personnel management theory (Northcott, 1950). In the ensuing years, elements of the Social Liberalist program were carried forward in various ways in economic and social policy, as well as in the social sciences, albeit without their unifying links to the philosophical and moral-educational activities of the core Idealist Liberalist group (Sawer, 2003).

Discussion

The starting point for this chapter was the relative absence of studies explicating the role of the formative Australian years in the work of Elton Mayo. Mayo's contribution to management theory has so far been historically assessed mainly through the prism of his activities and publications in the USA, where he lived from 1922 to 1945. These reviews have highlighted his role in the theoretical interpretation of the Hawthorne Studies and in laying the ground for the Human Relations School and the subsequent field of organizational behavior (e.g. Bruce & Nylund, 2011; Gillespie, 1991; O'Connor, 1999a, 1999b). This chapter has taken a different perspective and approached Mayo's thinking from the influences and circumstances that surrounded and shaped his academic work in the Australian context, broadly following the contextualist school of the study of the history of ideas (Skinner, 1969, 1978).

Apart from occupying a chair in philosophy and psychology, Mayo was integrally linked with a local circle of intellectuals who shared a commitment to the metaphysical and political views inherent in British Idealism. These New Liberals or WEA intellectuals were responsible for introducing an early form of sociology to the Australian academy, as well as contributing to the wider efforts of political and industrial nation-building. Mayo's main publication in his Australian period, *Democracy and Freedom* (Mayo, 1919), was written for a WEA series as a tutorial textbook that also carried a wider message regarding the nature of the current problems of national and industrial development.

As the analysis above has demonstrated, *Democracy and Freedom* is conceptually aligned to the program of Idealist Liberalism. The question of liberty is framed in the book from the viewpoint of 'positive freedom' originating from the work of T. H. Green and the Idealists (Berlin, 1969). Following Hegel, freedom is pictured as the state of individuals and groups who have raised themselves above immediate material conditions and interests through self-realization and moral growth. Throughout the text, Mayo uses words such as 'civilization,' 'harmony,' 'education,' and 'higher purpose,' which are all part of the political-philosophical vocabulary of the Idealist Liberals of the early twentieth century.

The Australian version of Idealist Liberalism directed its political attention to the industrial realm, and especially to the morally questionable trends inherent in trade union mobilization and the associated ascent of the Labour Party. While the Social Liberals of the 1910s and 1920s generally advocated the stance of Green, where the aim was to overcome material and empirical divisions by way of human perfection and the emergence of moral communitarian subjectivity (Brink, 2003), in practice they pointed their critique exclusively toward the failure of the workers in pursuing the ideal of ethical citizenship. Managers and capitalists were seen as "less sinful" in this respect (Mayo, 1919: 59). With the rise of the trade unions, workers became more powerful in their material demands, but started at the same time to neglect the need for occupational and civic education. Workers had become morally lazy (Walter & Moore, 2002).

It is this formative context in Australia that largely defines the broader philosophical vocabulary to which Mayo returns in his later works. The psychological part of *Democracy and Freedom* is primarily concerned with the way in which new trade union agitators are engaged in the manipulation of the minds of the workers. Mayo animates the ideas of Freud, Jung, and Janet to demonstrate how the political activists of the labor movement succeed in firing up fears and prejudices among the proletariat. The new political leaders do not want their followers to seek reasoned dialogue or education of their human faculties, but instead arouse primitive emotions that reinforce, rather than smoothen, the disharmony brought about by diverging material interests and class-based identities (Mayo, 1919: 12–30).

This unusual interpretation of the role of psychological and unconscious processes in contemporary industrial life became the trademark feature of the commentaries retrospectively constructing Mayo's Human Relations paradigm (Griffin et al., 2002; O'Connor, 1999a, 1999b; Wood & Wood, 2004). In this interpretation, Mayo is considered to have argued that unrest in working life is a consequence of the psychological maladjustment and neurotic pathology of the employees (Bourke, 1982). Mayo continues the psychological theme in his early organizational writings in North America (Mayo, 1923a, 1923b, 1923c, 1924), leading to his participation in the Hawthorne Studies and, subsequently, to public notoriety as the pioneer of a new line of thinking in the theory and practice of management.

The psychological approach to work organization dynamics has more or less come to dominate the evaluation of Mayo's work. The generalized image of Elton Mayo in the current historical consciousness within organization studies tends to picture him as the 'psychoanalyst' or 'psychiatrist' of early management thought (e.g. Dingley, 1997; O'Connor, 2011; Sarachek, 1968). Yet there are grounds to challenge this type of description of his profile. Mayo developed his views at a time when the social sciences were not yet institutionalized into the disciplines recognized today as sociology, anthropology, psychology, and so on. His project was inherently interdisciplinary, and may appear undefined or fragmented to a contemporary analyst accustomed to clearly identifiable scientific disciplines with a linear historical narrative.

Mayo's activities also spanned academia and adult education, and later spread to practical workplace experiments in a fashion that may be difficult to grasp, given today's separated realms of empirical research and normative practice. Yet in the early twentieth century, university intellectuals were often active in other domains of public activity, participating in national political life and inaugurating institutions in various social and economic domains (Sawer, 2003).

To better understand the particular context in which Mayo was embedded, and where he developed his social and organizational theories, it is necessary to consider the intellectual and political environment of his Australian years. Mayo emerged from a group of Idealist Liberals who worked across academia, economy, and politics with a philosophical program borrowed from the conventions of the British Idealists. The New Liberal intellectuals integrated selected insights from early sociological, anthropological, and psychological writings into their overarching Idealist vision of the role of human perfection for social and human harmony. In this connection, Mayo's interest in psychoanalysis and the psychology of the worker can be seen as a particular extension of the general program of the Idealist Liberalists, rather than as a separate stream of inquiry. He also returns to the broader social theoretical questions of the relationship between human growth and the advance of industrial society in his later writings (Mayo, 1949). By locating Mayo in the conceptual and practical context of the Australian movement in Idealist Liberalism, it is possible to uncover a general theme in his writings and activities across the decades and also perhaps to do justice to the possibilities and limits of the dream of moral humanity that was implicit in much of Mayo's work.

References

Armour, L. (2006) Green's idealism and the metaphysics of ethics, in M. Dimorova-Cookson and W. J. Mander (eds), *T. H. Green: Ethics, Metaphysics and Political Philosophy*. Oxford: Oxford Scholarship Online.

Atkinson, M. (ed.) (1920) *Australia: Economic and Political Studies*. Melbourne: Macmillan.

Barley, S. and Kunda, G. (1992) Design and devotion: Surges of rational and normative ideologies of control in managerial discourse, *Administrative Science Quarterly*, 37(3): 363–99.

Bendix, R. and Fisher, L. H. (1949) The perspectives of Elton Mayo, *Review of Economics and Statistics*, 31(4): 312–19.

Berlin, I. (1969) Two concepts of liberty, in *Four Essays on Liberty* (pp. 118–72). Oxford: Oxford University Press.

Bourke, H. (1981) Sociology and the social sciences in Australia, 1912–1928, *Journal of Sociology*, 17(1): 26–35.

Bourke, H. (1982) Industrial unrest as social pathology: The Australian writings of Elton Mayo, *Historical Studies*, 20(79): 217–33.

Brink, D. O. (2003) *Perfectionism and the Common Good: Themes in the Philosophy of T. H. Green*. Oxford: Oxford University Press.

Bruce, K. and Nylund (2011) Elton Mayo and the deification of Human Relations, *Organization Studies*, 32(3): 383–405.

Dingley, J. C. (1997) Durkheim, Mayo, morality and management, *Journal of Business Ethics*, 16(11): 1117–29.

Geuss, R. (1996) Kultur, bildung, geis, *History and Theory*, 35(2): 151–64.

Gillespie, R. (1991) *Manufacturing Knowledge: A History of Hawthorne Experiments*. Cambridge: Cambridge University Press.

Green, T. H. (1906) Lecture on liberal legislation and freedom of contract, in R. L. Nettleship (ed.), *Works of Thomas Hill Green* (pp. 365–86). London: Longmans, Green, and Co.

Green, T. H. (1999 [1895]) *Lectures on the Principles of Political Obligation*. Kitchener, ON: Batoche Books.

Griffin, M. A., Landy, F. J., and Mayocchi, L. (2002) Australian influences on Elton Mayo: The construct of revery in industrial society, *History of Psychology*, 5(4): 356–75.

Heyl, B. (1968) The Harvard 'Pareto' circle, *Journal of the History of the Behavioral Sciences*, 4(4): 316–34.

Hsueh, Y. (2002) The Hawthorne experiments and the introduction of Jean Piaget in American industrial psychology, 1929–1932, *History of Psychology*, 5(2): 163–89.

Keller, R. T. (1984) The Harvard 'Pareto circle' and the historical development of organization theory, *Journal of Management*, 10: 193–204.

Markus, G. (1986) The Hegelian concept of culture, *PRAXIS International*, 2: 113–23.

Mayo, E. (1919) *Democracy and Freedom: An Essay in Social Logic*. Melbourne: Macmillan.

Mayo, E. (1920) The Australian political consciousness, in M. Atkinson (ed.), *Australia: Economic and Political Studies* (pp. 127–41). Melbourne: Macmillan.
Mayo, E. (1923a) The irrational factor in society, *Journal of Personnel Research*, 1(10): 419–26.
Mayo, E. (1923b) Irrationality and revery, *Journal of Personnel Research*, 1(11): 477–83.
Mayo, E. (1923c) The irrational factor in human behavior: The 'night-mind' in industry, *Annals of the American Academy of Political and Social Science*, 110: 117–30.
Mayo, E. (1924) Revery and industrial fatigue, *Journal of Personnel Research*, 3(8): 273–81.
Mayo, E. (1933/2003) *The Human Problems of an Industrial Civilization. Early Sociology of Management and Organizations*, London: Routledge.
Mayo, E. (1949/1975/1998) *The Social Problems of an Industrial Civilization*. London: Routledge.
Moore, W. E. (1948) Industrial sociology: Status and prospects, *American Sociological Review*, 13(4): 382–91.
Northcott, C. (1950) *Personnel Management: Principles and Practice*. London: Pitman.
O'Connor, E. (1999a) Politics of management thought, *Academy of Management Review*, 24(1): 117–31.
O'Connor, E. (1999b) Minding the workers, *Organization*, 6(2): 223–46.
O'Connor, E. (2011) *Creating New Knowledge in Management: Appropriating the Field's Lost Foundations*. Stanford, CA: Stanford University Press.
Roethlisberger, F. J. (1977). *The Elusive Phenomena: An Autobiographical Account of My Work in the Field of Organizational Behavior at the Harvard Business School*. Boston, MA: Harvard University Press.
Roethlisberger, F. J. and Dixon, W. J. (1939). *Management and the Worker*. Boston, MA: Harvard University Press.
Sarachek, B. (1968) Elton Mayo's social psychology and human relations, *Academy of Management Journal*, 11(2): 189–97
Sawer, M. (2003) *The Ethical State? Social Liberalism in Australia*. Melbourne: Melbourne University Press.
Skidelsky, E. (2007) The strange death of British Idealism, *Philosophy and Literature*, 31(1): 41–51.
Skinner, Q. (1969) Meaning and understanding in the history of ideas, *History and Theory*, 8(1): 3–53.
Skinner, Q. (1978) *The Foundations of Modern Political Thought*, 2 vols. Cambridge: Cambridge University Press.
Smith, J. H. (1975) Elton Mayo revisited, *British Journal of Industrial Relations*, 12(2): 282–91.
Smith, J. H. (1998) The enduring legacy of Elton Mayo, *Human Relations*, 51(3): 221–49.
Trahair, R. (1984) *Humanist Temper: The Life and Work of Elton Mayo*. New Brunswick, NJ: Transaction Books.
Tyler, C. (2006) *Idealist Political Philosophy: Pluralism and Conflict in the Absolute Idealist Tradition*. London and New York: Continuum.
Walter, J. and Moore, T. (2002) The new social order? Australia's contribution to 'new liberal' thinking in the interwar period, Paper presented to the Jubilee conference of the Australasian Political Studies Association, Australian National University, Canberra, October.
Wempe, B. (2004) *T. H. Green's Theory of Positive Freedom*. Exeter: Imprint Academic.
Whyte, W. F. (1987) From human relations to organizational behavior: Reflections on the changing scene, *Industrial and Labor Relations Review*, 40(4): 487–500.
Wood, J. C and Wood, M. C. (eds) (2004) *George Elton Mayo: Critical Evaluations in Business and Management*. London: Routledge
Wren, D. A. and Bedeian, A. G. (2009) *The Evolution of Management Thought*. Hoboken, NJ: John Wiley.
Wren, D. A, and Hay, R. D. (1977) Management historians and business historians: Differing perceptions of pioneer contributors, *Academy of Management Journal*, 20(3): 470–76.

18

Re-examining 'flexibility'

Ali Mir and Raza Mir

The financial crisis of 2008, widely heralded as the biggest since the Great Depression, can be – and has been – read in multiple ways. The dominant understanding is that the crisis came about as a consequence of "a broad national breakdown in personal responsibility, government regulation and financial ethics" (Friedman, 2008). The explanations for the so-called Great Recession have pointed towards, *inter alia*, the absence of regulatory oversight (Varoufakis, 2011), the Wall Street culture of risk-taking (Lewis, 2008), the widespread adoption of toxic economic theories that assumed away risks (Smith, 2010), the cyclical tendencies of capital to move through expansions and recessions (see National Bureau of Economic Research, 2014), and the inevitability of periodic and/or endless crises under the reign of monopoly-finance capitalism (Foster and McChesney, 2012). Some, such as the philosopher du jour, Slavoj Žižek (2009), have argued that this moment represents nothing less than a moral failure of the modern world.

Organizational scholars, though a little late to the party, did eventually focus on the fallout of the crisis, and the Academy of Management even held the 2013 edition of its annual meeting – ironically in the flourishing Disney World theme park – under the theme 'Capitalism in Question?' The discussions among management academics have, however, tended to focus on the *proximate* causes of the financial meltdown, and with some exceptions, haven't paid much attention to the role of their own discipline in creating the conditions for the disaster. In this chapter, we seek to bring a historical perspective to the analysis of the financial crisis by revisiting the arguments of Fordism–Keynesianism and post-Fordism that emerged in the 1970s, in order to question the role of managerial practices in the period that led towards the crisis. Based on these arguments, we examine the contention that the financial crisis can be read as a particular variant of the crisis of overaccumulation, and place it in the historical context of the post-Fordist debate in organizational theory and industrial geography. Specifically, we intend to scrutinize the link between the crisis and the management practices enacted in the 1980s and the 1990s in search of 'flexibility' – exemplified by the idealization of concepts such as the lean corporation, core competencies, outsourcing, subcontracting, offshoring, just-in-time – and as a response to the crisis of 'rigidity' that characterized the end of the age of Fordism. By doing so, we hope to persuade scholars of management and organizing history to – in the words of the Management History division of the Academy of Management – conduct a "historical assessment of the social consequences of management."

The crisis of Fordism

The ultimate purpose of modern capitalism is the generation of profit through the process of circulation (Marx 1867/1976). In the event that there is an 'over-production of capital' or a lack of opportunity for its fruitful circulation, the system experiences a crisis that some economists refer to as the crisis of overaccumulation (see Bello, 2006). Over-accumulation, a defining feature of the early 1970s, is characterized by a glut of commodities, excessive inventories, idle capacity, surplus money capital, underemployment, and falling rates of return. There are a number of meta-narratives that have been offered in an attempt to understand the change in the trajectory of capitalism following the stagflation of the early 1970s and the end of the post-Second World War period referred to as the 'Golden Age of Capitalism'. Labels such as post-industrialism (Bell, 1973), post-bureaucracy (Heydebrand, 1989), postmodernism (Harvey, 1989), social structures of accumulation (Bowles & Gintis, 1986; Gordon, 1988), and disorganized capitalism (Lash & Urry, 1987) have been used to describe theoretical formulations that seek to outline the broad sweep of transformations within the system of capitalist enterprise in the latter part of the twentieth century. We use the discourse of Fordism, not as any final word on the subject, but as a complex, historically grounded template that offers a useful framework for mapping the trends that became increasingly visible in the industrial societies of the time.

While there are many different versions of Fordism and its alleged successor – post-Fordism – the following description by Hall (1988: 24) articulates a blend of the markers of this change:

> A shift to the new 'information technologies'; more flexible, decentralized forms of labor process and work organizations; decline of the old manufacturing base and the growth of the 'sunrise,' computer-based industries; the hiving off or the contracting out of functions and services; a greater emphasis on choice and product differentiation, on marketing, packaging and design, on the 'targetting' of consumers by lifestyle, taste, and culture rather than by categories of social class; a decline in the proportion of the skilled, male, manual working class, the rise of the service and white-collar classes and the 'feminization' of the work force; an economy dominated by multinationals, with their new international division of labor and their greater autonomy from nation state control; and the 'globalization' of the new financial markets, linked by the communication revolution.

Fordism is grounded in a set of mass production practices that were pioneered by Henry Ford and are now widely seen as the dominant form of production for most of the twentieth century. These practices were founded on the principles of standardization, mechanization, scientific management, and the rationalization of work through the use of an assembly line that fixed the worker in both space and time (Murray, 1989; Taylor, 1911). The resulting system cut manufacturing costs greatly and the system's dependence on economies of scale created a compelling need for high volume production. Despite Ford's attempts, Fordism as a system evolved over a long period of time stretching over nearly half a century and depended upon "myriad individual, corporate, institutional, and state decisions, many of them unwitting political choices or knee-jerk responses to the crisis tendencies of capitalism, particularly as manifest in the great depression of the 1930s" (Harvey, 1989: 127). Several developments permitted the emergence of Fordism as a full-fledged regime of accumulation. The depression of the 1930s led to the adoption of Keynesian economics and the emergence of a form of the welfare state. The Second World War saw the rise and rationalization of industries such as steel, petrochemicals, automobiles, electric goods, and construction. Radical working-class movements lost ground and the Taft-Hartley Act of 1947 trimmed the sails of the labour movement;

power in collective bargaining by unions was largely won at the expense of conceding collaboration to the Fordist systems of production. State fiscal policies organized investment in sectors like transportation and public utilities in order to try and promote full employment and to stabilize mass production *and* mass consumption. Fordism spread internationally too as a consequence of the post-war rebuilding efforts. The United States became the world's banker under the Bretton Woods agreement and GATT helped stabilize international currency and commodity markets. Under this regime, the economies of capitalist nations, and in particular that of the United States, prospered for the 25-year period following the Second World War during which "mass production was coupled with mass consumption in a virtuous circle of growth" (Graham, 1992: 394).

By the late 1960s, Fordism had begun to unravel. Many factors contributed to the beginning of Fordism's demise as a coherent regime. The recoveries of the Japanese and West European markets resulted in the beginnings of true international competition led by the desire of these nations to find markets for their surplus production. The Bretton Woods agreement collapsed and the international monetary system experienced highly volatile exchange rates. Labour resistance to the increasing Taylorization of work intensified (Edwards, 1979), consumption patterns failed to keep up with the capacities of the mass production system, niche markets for specialized and luxury products grew faster than the markets for standardized products, and the social safety system started to wither (Graham, 1992).

While the general analyses of the resulting crisis tend to point at the changing pattern of demand resulting from international competition and the saturation of the durable-goods market (the so-called underconsumption crisis; see Piore & Sabel, 1984), many argue that the latent crisis of over-accumulation inherent in the Fordist paradigm led to a decline in the growth of productivity in the 1960s resulting in a corresponding decline in profitability (Leborgne & Lipietz, 1988). Management reacted to this decline through policies of internationalization and the state through practices of austerity. This, in turn, was responsible for the crisis in employment and in the working of the welfare state; the dual onslaught of stagnation and internationalization precipitated the demand crisis of the 1970s.

The broad consensus on the crisis of Fordism pointed accusingly at the *rigidities* of the system that prevented, or at least delayed, its ability to respond to the changing times. These rigidities could be seen at several different levels. First, capital was locked into investments that were based on large-scale and long-term mass production systems which in turn depended upon the sustenance of growing demands of the market. Second, the model of labour relations followed in the United States and elsewhere and the corresponding nature of labour power created rigidities in labour allocation and utilization. Third, the state's commitments to entitlement programmes such as social security and pension rights (along with its war spending in Vietnam) limited its ability to launch a serious fiscal plan to counter the threat of the emerging crisis leading eventually to a monetary policy that resulted in the stagflation that heralded the end of the post-war prosperity (Aglietta, 1979; Arrighi, 2010; Harvey, 1989).

The system worked well as a stable mode of macroeconomic growth as long as undifferentiated mass production could be sustained by mass consumption. Mass production led to rising productivity based on economies of scale. Incomes, linked to productivity, rose correspondingly leading to an increased mass demand based on rising wages. As a greater amount of investment was directed towards the improvement of mass production equipment and techniques and as the capacity utilization increased, profits grew, leading to the virtuous cycle of Fordist growth (Jessop, 1994). The limits reached by the growth potential of mass production, the saturation of mass markets, and the disruption of Fordist accumulation due to internationalization brought the problems of Fordist rigidities into sharp focus and demanded resolution.

Post-Fordist response: the age of flexibility

Since the crisis of Fordism was perceived as a crisis of rigidity, the institutional and *managerial* response to this crisis therefore, had to address this 'problem'. Gradually at first, but with increasing intensity, organizations embraced the notion of *flexibility*. The new system that took root came to be characterized by flexible manufacturing systems that allowed firms to cater to niche – as opposed to mass – markets, flexible work practices combined with flexible labour processes, and flexible consumption patterns, while a new mode of macroeconomic growth, characterized by flexible accumulation, replaced the old regime. Some of the prominent features of this system included dual labour markets, accelerated deunionization, erosion of the social contract between management and labour, a shift towards a service economy domestically with the concomitant globalization of manufacturing, financial deregulation, and an increasing use of computers and information technologies which contributed to a growing space–time compression.

The concept of flexibility is difficult to pin down if only for the reason that it is used in so many different ways. This multi-dimensional idea extends in a variety of directions (see Sayer & Walker, 1992; Schoenberger, 1989) and finds its way in terms such as flexible machinery (Kaplinsky, 1984), flexible employment (Standing, 1992), flexible technologies and manufacturing systems (Zammuto & O'Connor, 1992), flexible specialization (Piore & Sabel, 1984), flexible product types (Storper & Scott, 1988), flexible labour skills (Atkinson & Meager, 1986), flexible employment (Atkinson, 1984), flexible organizational forms (Scott, 1988; Sabel, 1989), and flexible accumulation (Harvey, 1989). In addition, flexibility is used in conjunction with labour–management relationships, size of the firm, scale of output, and locational tendencies (Gertler, 1988; Piore & Sabel, 1984; Storper & Scott, 1988). Flexibility is also seen to operate at various levels from the production process (flexible manufacturing systems) to issues of labour processes and labour markets (functional and numerical flexibilities) to competitive firm strategies (flexible specialization and integration) to the broad bases upon which organizational economies are founded (flexible accumulation).

The concept of flexible accumulation, which is based upon the work of scholars known to English-speaking audiences as the French regulation school (e.g. Aglietta, 1979; Boyer, 1988; Lipietz, 1987) attempts to theorize the relationships between the sphere of production and consumption and the role of the state in these domains. According to the regulationists, it is inadequate to examine regimes of production as being based on a single set of unchanging laws. Rather, history needs to be seen as "a succession of phases, each distinguished by certain historically developed, socio-institutionally defined structural forms that give rise, so long as they are maintained, to distinctive economic trends and patterns" (Brenner & Glick, 1991: 46). The claim the regulationists make is that historically different solutions (or modes of development) have been employed to tackle the problems arising due to the wage-relations in society and the commodity-producing nature of capitalism. Each mode of development involves a macroeconomic pattern (a regime of accumulation) which allocates social output between consumption and accumulation, and a collection of widely accepted, institutionalized rules that unite the decentralized decisions taken by individual economic units into a coherent system of economic relationships (a mode of regulation).

A regime of accumulation is concerned with the allocation of the net product between consumption and accumulation. In order to stabilize this allocation, all political-economic agents – capitalists, managers, workers, financial institutions, state agencies – need to work in a relatively coherent manner. The role of the state and other social-political-economic decision-makers is to use a mode of regulation that persuades, influences, and regulates laws and norms in order to ensure the unity of the regime of accumulation. The regulationists argue that the transition to a flexible regime of accumulation commenced in the early 1970s after the first oil crisis followed by the period of stagflation – a sign that the post-Second World War boom had ended. It was characterized by a restructuring of the labour market (the division of the labour market into a core group of full-time employees with employment benefits and reskilling prospects and a peripheral group of part-time or casual workers, short-term contract staffs, temporary employees, and sub-contractors), patterns of uneven development (both domestically and globally), a space–time compression (accomplished through fast means of communication and transport leading to easier geographical, often global, dispersion of production activity), the replacement in some sectors of economies of scale by economies of scope, the increasing importance of timely access to new technologies and products, and the reorganization of the global and national financial systems (deregulation of the financial system in the United States, the replacement of the Bretton Woods agreement with a flexible exchange rate, the formation of global financial conglomerates, and the creation of new financial markets and instruments). This regime of accumulation thus attempted to respond to "the crises of flagging productivity gains, increasing international competition, market saturation, and excessively rigid fixed capital and labour". Competition was thought to be "based increasingly upon firms' flexibility, and hence it [fell] to the state to help overcome rigidities through exhortation and legislation which deregulates key markets such as finance and labor" (Gertler, 1988: 422).

In contrast to the neo-Schumpeterian (Freeman & Perez, 1988, for instance) and the neo-Smithian perspectives (Piore & Sabel, 1984, for instance), the regulation school was concerned not so much with the capitalist forces of production but with the reproduction of capitalism itself. It seriously asked the questions of how capitalism weathers the chaos and conflict inherent in the phases of creative destruction and of what permits the advent of new paradigms that replace existing systems with other cohesive and stable ones.

The argument of the regulationists was that the Golden Age of capitalism represented by Fordism depended not only on the sectors of production goods but also on the sector of consumption goods. It drew sustenance from "a new wage-labor nexus which recognized wages not only as a cost but also an outlet for expanding capitalist production" (Elam, 1994: 63) leading to a "mutually advantageous compromise" between the capitalist and the labour class (De Vroey, 1984: 56). The crisis of Fordism led to the breakdown of this compromise due to (1), limits reached by the division of labour; (2), the expansion of mass production, the intensification of economies of scale, the globalization of production and sales, the increased competition between countries, and the massive penetration of domestic markets; (3), the increase in social expenditure through collective consumption activities such as education and health, and the consequent inflationary pressures; and (4), the changing consumption patterns of the affluent worker and the corresponding demand for non-standardized goods.

The regulationists, unlike the neo-Schumpeterians and the neo-Smithians, rejected both technological and market determinism, and did not offer a definite view of the future. For them, the future was a contested terrain and "the new rule book of capitalism" had "room for many more co-authors" (Elam, 1994: 66). The period of flexible accumulation propelled capitalism decisively into a new configuration, in which both supply and demand were significantly restructured (Scott, 2001). An interplay of globalization and technological development along with the loosening of a variety of regulations and the new porosity of nation-state borders unleashed financial and production capital resulting in a phase of dramatic economic expansion in world capitalism. The result of the search for flexibility had a remarkable impact on labour in the United States.

The flexible firm

The notion of the flexible firm drew a lot of attention in the mid-1980s (see Atkinson and Meager, 1986; Brown, 1986; Pollert, 1988; Shutt & Whittington, 1987). Drawing upon the managerialist literature, the flexible firm model made the claim that the shift in managerial practices was fuelled by the increasing demand for labour flexibility. Atkinson and Meager (1986) suggested that the search for functional flexibility and numerical flexibility resulted in the separation of the work force into core and peripheral groups. The 'core' was comprised of workers, managers, and other professionals who were essential to the basic structure of the firm. This group had full-time permanent status, relatively strong job security, prospects for promotion, and better compensation benefits. In return, the members of this group offered adaptability, flexibility, and mobility. Functional flexibility, which was closely linked to multiskilling, was primarily associated with this core group of workers. By taking on multiple roles and thus crossing rigid occupational boundaries, the core provided the organization with not only functional flexibility in the labor process but also flexibility in time "in terms of adjusting more closely to production demands" (Pollert, 1988: 47).

Other groups of workers were submitted to different strategies of peripheralization (Penn, 1992), thus offering the organization a degree of numerical flexibility. This 'periphery' consisted of workers who were either irregularly employed or who were not directly employed by the firm. The flexible firm model separated the periphery into two groups. The first peripheral group was drawn from the secondary labour market and offered full-time employment to clerical, secretarial, and lesser skilled workers who performed routine jobs and had very limited career opportunities. Since this group typically exhibited a high turnover, workforce reductions were relatively easy. The second peripheral group offered organizations the strategic opportunity to enhance numerical flexibility in the firm through the use of part-time and casual labour, fixed-term contract employees, temporary workers, and sub-contractors. This casualization of a large part of the labour force was reflected in the brutal downsizing and relentless layoffs that were seen through much of the 1980s and 1990s.

The globalization of the economy was accompanied by a shift from manufacturing to services in the US economy, driven in large part by cheaper labour costs abroad (see Bluestone & Harrison, 1982 for a discussion on the deindustrialization of America). Since manufacturing industries tended to be heavily unionized with even non-union jobs benefiting from union-scale pays, the dismantling of a sector that employed nearly a third of US workers had a significant effect on the wages of the workforce. The service jobs that came to dominate the economy ranged from highly-skilled, well-paid professions such as surgeons, financial analysts, and IT engineers to low-skilled, poorly paid occupations such as health aides, data-entry operators, and restaurant workers. This huge disparity resulted in a widening of the income gap among American workers. Bluestone (1995: 21) contends that "between 1963 and 1987, the earnings ratio between college graduates and high school dropouts working in the goods-producing sector (mining, construction, and manufacturing) widened from 2.11 to 2.42 – an increase of 15 percent. In services, however, the school-related earnings ratio mushroomed from 2.20 to 3.52 – a 60 percent increase."

A significant feature of the knowledge economy was the advent of new information technologies, which played a vital role in the reconfiguring of global labour, and were pivotal to the project of flexibility that defines the new organizational paradigm. The IT revolution changed the landscape of organizations in a fundamental fashion with significant implications for US labour. First, it facilitated mass production through programmed production, flexible specialization, flexible manufacturing, and mass customization. Production of undifferentiated goods and services could now be replaced by customized small batch production for niche markets. Second, it broke down the traditional nature of the division of labour resulting in newer forms of job classifications, mergers between blue- and white-collar work, and the production of newer forms of workers (Zuboff, 1988). Third, it allowed integration across organizational boundaries, creating the possibilities of linkages between and among firms, suppliers, and customers. In Williamson's (1975) terms, it encouraged the use of markets over hierarchies as coordinating mechanisms, extending the geographical reach of organizations, and assisting the process of decentralization. Information technologies were seen as having the potential to create a frictionless market economy, and a 'virtual corporation' – an entrepreneurial firm with low fixed costs and a tiny core of permanent workers, whose work was predominantly performed by contract labour (Davidow & Malone, 1992; Kuttner, 1997). The deployment of information technologies, the shift towards a service economy, and the transformation to a knowledge economy brought about a set of profound changes in the macroeconomic environment, especially in terms of labour–management relations and the regulatory framework.

The globalized flexible firm had a huge impact on the organized labour movement in the United States and elsewhere. In their book *The Transformation of American Industrial Relations*, Kochan, Katz, and McKersie (1986: 6) outlined the issues at stake for the future of industrial relations and argued for a strategic choice perspective to deal with the fundamental transformation in the nature of organizing in general and the industrial relations system in particular:

> Once again, American society in general, and American unions in particular, face fundamental choices with respect to the most basic questions concerning the structure of employment relationships. Is there still a 'need' for unions? ... Should collective bargaining be promoted, or are new forms of employee participation and representation needed to supplement or substitute for this process? ... How can the basic clash between a democratic society's need for a free labor movement be reconciled with the deep-seated opposition to unions embedded in American managerial ideology?

Ever since the 1930s, the institution of collective bargaining had been the predominant mode of workplace governance in large organizations, thanks to the organizing drives of the AFL and the CIO in the 1930s and the 1940s, and the passage of the Wagner Act in 1935. Membership of non-agricultural organized labour had soared to around 9 million in 1940, and to over 14 million in 1945 – a representation equalling 35.5 per cent of the workforce. Unions never saw this peak again. The challenge to unionism which began around the mid-1950s involved unions in a losing battle for membership which has now turned into a battle for survival. The decline of the institution of collective bargaining was clearly reflected in the figures: union representation in the private workforce had slid down to 19 per cent by the mid-1980s and to 12 per cent by the mid-1990s.

As Harvey (1989) argues, the defeat of the radical union movement in order to ensure worker participation in the drudgery of the assembly line was a vital element in the Fordist mix. Strong anti-union measures, helped by the passage of the Taft-Hartley Act, were adopted by management, and workers were routinely fired for signing union cards (Weiler, 1990). As globalization proceeded through the 1990s, the threat of layoffs and plant closures was used effectively to reduce the power and the presence of unions. Collective bargaining negotiations were mostly focused on management demands for 'givebacks' by labour (Kuttner, 1997) and union-busting management strategies met with little resistance from the already weak unions.

All this was facilitated through a climate of deregulation which intensified in the early 1980s. It was spurred by the demand for flexibility made by a corporate sector that felt hobbled by the constraints placed upon it, and which saw regulation as a needless intervention by the state in the arena of commerce. Experts, scholars, and consultants argued that the changing paradigm, particularly in the context of increasing global competition, required firms to be lean and nimble in order to enable them to react quickly to the dynamic environment (Kanter, 1989; Peters, 1992). Regulations were seen as holding corporations back and as an impediment that had helped generate the Fordist crisis. Deregulation, aided by the rise of laissez-faire economics, took several forms, two of which are immediately relevant for our argument. First, the deregulation of industrial sectors such as telecommunications, airlines, trucking, healthcare, and utilities created conditions that forced corporations into competitive price cutting, most of which was accomplished by lowering labour costs. Second, the reluctance of the state to continue its role of reducing inequality through wage regulation resulted in the stagnation of minimum wages and the absence of regulatory oversight, which allowed companies to super-exploit workers in modern-day sweatshops and many forms of service work. Immigrant labour was increasingly used to perform tough tasks for very poor pay, while the state agencies looked the other way or were too strapped for resources to be able to conduct effective enforcement (see Bowe, 2007 for an account of what he calls "modern American slave labor," and Mathew, 2005 for a detailed story of the transformation of the New York City taxi industry). Along with the decline of organized labour, wage deregulation took away "two of the principal countervailing forces offsetting the market's tendency to create extreme earnings-inequality" (Kuttner, 1997: 96).

A significant consequence of these forms of flexibility was the growth of inequality, by now a very well-documented economic trend (Piketty, 2013). Data from the US Census Bureau shows the upward trend of the Gini coefficient of US households from the late 1960s to the present, while the growing inequalities in both wealth and income and the increasing concentration of both among a handful of people (the 'one percent' made emblematic by the Occupy Wall Street movement) has been underlined by a variety of observers and researchers (Graeber, 2011). The causes of this inequality can be found to a very large extent in the erosion of a long-held social contract between capital and labour, the emergence of the dual labour market, the shift to the service economy and the loss of well-paying manufacturing jobs, the erosion of union power and their ability to collectively bargain for better wages, the diminishing value of minimum wage along with the withering of the welfare state, the lack of regulatory oversight on wages and work practices, turbulences in the labour market and the insecurities caused by layoffs and plant closings, relatively high unemployment (with the exception of the late 1990s), trade policies and the pressures of cheap imports that forced labour to take pay cuts, and the increasing size of a low-wage immigrant workforce.

Flexibility revisited

'Flexibility', as outlined above, is clearly more than a descriptor of managerial practices. It is a trope that stands in for a broader paradigmatic position, characterized by a faith in new forms of employment, new inter-firm relationships, new technologies, and new organizational forms. It claims to represent a socio-technological paradigm which values skills, innovation, and participation, and liberates organizations from the yoke of wage regulation, place restrictions, and demanding unions.

However, some questions need to be addressed in order to engage more satisfactorily with this concept. To begin with, we need to ask whether 'flexibility' is a novel concept, one that was an innovative response to the Fordist rigidities that became a problem for the economy from the late 1960s onwards, or whether it is part of a longer pattern of capitalist development (Arrighi,

2007, 2010). Some scholars have contended that flexibility is a mere ahistoric 'discovery' of labour market uncertainty, thus drawing our attention to its ideological dimension, which seeks to legitimize an array of managerial practices and allow the "discussion of restructuring to veer away from the global issues of capital structure, investment, exchange rates, trade relations, to the homely and apparently more manageable 'problem' of labour" (Pollert, 1988: 43). Flexibility of commodified labour has long been used within the capitalist enterprise; for example, the presence of a 'reserve army of labour' has always provided the necessary basis for the competitiveness of the labour market and the consequent control on wages and the recalcitrant worker. Seen from this perspective, the notion of flexibility might be considered an ideological attempt to legitimize the secondary economy, casualization of labour, unemployment and insecurity, and to position the new forms of labour market segmentation as an imperative for the new post-Fordist times. Further, as Fernand Braudel (1982) pointed out in his magnum opus, *Civilization and Capitalism, 15th–18th Centuries*, flexibility has always been a central feature of historical capitalism right from its thirteenth-century manifestations in the Italian city states of Venice and Genoa. What Braudel convincingly argues is that notwithstanding the concrete forms that capital took over time, its essential characteristic was (and remains) its capacity to transform and adapt itself in the pursuit of converting money capital into an increased amount of money capital. In Marx's (1887/1976) general formula of capital (M-C-M′), the expanded liquidity afforded to the capitalist in the form of M′ is the true objective of the capitalist enterprise. The conversion of the initial capital (M) into commodity capital (C) is merely the means towards M′. When expedient, for instance under the conditions of falling rates of profit, the capitalist is perfectly willing to shorten this circuit and turn M directly into M′ (Marx's abridged formula). This is the dominant form of capitalist accumulation during periods of financialization.

World systems theorists such as Fernand Braudel (1982), Immanuel Wallerstein (1984), Andre Gunder Frank (1998), and Giovanni Arrighi (2010) assert that the turn to financialization which marks the era of flexible accumulation is not a new phenomenon but part of a recurrent tendency of historical capitalism. In their formulation, financialization is a marker of the maturity of a phase of capitalist development and represents a fundamental reorganization of the regime of accumulation. The argument runs as follows (see Arrighi, 2010 for a detailed analysis): Periods of material expansion lead to over-accumulation of capital, resulting in a sharp increase in inter-capitalist competition. Capitalists, hitherto operating in their own spheres, begin to poach on the territory of others. In the presence of such competition, earlier cooperative arrangements fall by the wayside. As profit margins fall, capitalist agencies seek to keep money in a liquid form (the share of US corporate profits accounted for by financial firms surpassed that of manufacturing by the 1990s, as demonstrated with some clarity by Krippner, 2005), thus producing the supply conditions for liquid capital. The demand for this capital is generated by states, which faced with budgetary constraints as a result of the slowdown of material expansion, compete with one another for mobile capital. It is useful to note here that Max Weber (1961, 1978) had argued that inter-state competition for capital was a major feature of the modern period, calling it "the world-historical distinctiveness of the era" (Weber, 1978: 354). The economic slowdown of such periods exacerbates the competition for capital, leading to a period of financial expansion. The high demand for capital accumulated in the financial markets results in the so-called *belle époques* of financial capitalism, which are characterized by a vast redistribution of income and wealth from different segments of the society to the individuals, institutions, and agencies that control the financial markets. Such periods are marked by increasing inequalities in societies. As Braudel details, this was seen during periods of the financial expansions in sixteenth-century Italy, eighteenth-century Holland, and twentieth-century England. Arrighi (2010) adds that the financial expansion of the 1980s onwards in the United States echoes the same pattern. In *Capital*, Marx (1867) had briefly pointed towards these tendencies in the following paragraph:

> With the national debt arose an international credit system, which often conceals one of the sources of primitive accumulation in this or that people. Thus the villainies of the Venetian thieving system formed one of the secret bases of the capital-wealth of Holland to whom Venice in her decadence lent large sums of money. So also was it with Holland and England. By the beginning of the 18th century the Dutch manufactures were far outstripped. Holland had ceased to be the nation preponderant in commerce and industry. One of its main lines of business, therefore, from 1701–1776, is the lending out of enormous amounts of capital, especially to its great rival England. The same thing is going on today between England and the United States. A great deal of capital, which appears today in the United States without any certificate of birth, was yesterday, in England, the capitalised blood of children.

Flexibility, seen through the lens of these arguments serves as a shorthand for a particular set of practices at a specific stage in the cycle of capitalist development. In that sense, it is not a novel feature of this era, but an indicator that a period of material expansion has ended and that the turn to financialization has commenced. The financial crisis of 2008 can be seen as the culmination of that turn, a stage of 'terminal crisis' for a particular regime of accumulation, and a possible move to a different kind of regime, one that remains to be negotiated.

The 'post' in post-Fordism announced a cleavage from the past and signalled a departure from the world of Fordism. But as the arguments above demonstrate, the contention of a departure itself must be seriously questioned. While the 'new' organizational paradigm is characterized by newer permutations of the rules of capitalist enterprises, the transformation points not so much to a radical departure from Fordism but to the construction of a new structure that relies significantly on the foundation of Fordism for its sustenance. In that sense, post-Fordism needs to be read as post-*Fordism* as much as it is read as *post*-Fordism, marked both by its continuities with the older regime and by its differences.

The history of organizational theory and managerial practice during this period must be understood within the framework of not merely the system of production but also the systems of power and signification (Escobar, 2005). While the systems of production and power work towards the transformation of human beings into productive subjects that can be subjected to managerial control, they are naturalized through the use of a dominant discourse. Organizational theory has played a huge part in that discourse: the stability of a regime of accumulation demands the creation of the individual as a labouring body subject to disciplinary mechanisms as well as the production of 'subjecthood' that allows the reification and the hegemony of the concepts of production, consumption, competitiveness, and efficiency. Fordism and the regimes that replace it should thus be read as systems of production and control but also as systems of legitimation. The crisis of a regime of accumulation, therefore, is not just an economic crisis, but also a crisis of legitimation.

These two spheres are intricately intertwined since the implementation of any policies of reform in response to a crisis – including the ongoing one – requires not just a set of solutions to the problem, but also their acceptance by the stakeholders, whose influence is directly proportional to their power. The crisis of Fordism produced a set of responses that limited worker power, weakened regulatory oversight, enabled price competition that spurred wage-cutting, greatly expanded the dual labour market converting large segments of the primary labour-market into casual labour, and moved manufacturing to low-wage countries. This reflected not merely a shift in economic and policy priorities, but also a shift in political power. As we negotiate a tumultuous economic period, where the organizational landscape is being redefined, organizational scholarship has an obligation to intervene in the discourse, and to revisit the debates from the earlier crises, especially in order to unpack its ideological underpinnings. As always, the resolution of the contradictions served up by the changing times will form part of a contested terrain.

References

Aglietta, M. (1979) *A Theory of Capitalist Regulation*. London: New Left Books.

Arrighi, G. (2007) *Adam Smith in Beijing: Lineages of the Twenty-First Century*. London: Verso.

Arrighi, G. (2010) *The Long Twentieth Century: Money, Power and the Origins of our Times*. London: Verso.

Atkinson, J. (1984) *Flexibility, Uncertainty and Manpower Management*. Institute of Manpower Studies, University of Sussex, Report No. 89.

Atkinson, J. and Meager, N. (1986) Is flexibility just a flash in the pan? *Personnel Management*, August: 28–31.

Bell, D. (1973) *The Coming of Post-Industrial Society*. New York: Basic Books.

Bello, W. (2006) The capitalist conjuncture: Over-accumulation, financial crises, and the retreat from globalization, *Third World Quarterly*, 27(8): 1345–67.

Bluestone, B. (1995) *The Polarization of American Society: Victims, Suspects, and Mysteries to Unravel*. New York: Twentieth Century Fund Press.

Bluestone, B. and Harrison, B. (1982) *The Deindustrialization of America*. New York: Basic Books.

Bowe, J. (2007) *Nobodies: Modern American Slave Labor and the Dark Side of the New Global Economy*. New York: Random House.

Bowles, S. and Gintis, H. (1986) *Democracy and Capitalism*. New York: Basic Books.

Boyer, R. (1988) *The Search for Labour Market Flexibility*. Oxford: Clarendon Press.

Braudel, F. (1982) *The Wheels of Commerce*. New York: Harper & Row.

Brenner, R. and Glick, M. (1991) The regulation approach: theory and history, *New Left Review*, 188: 45–120.

Brown, W. (1986) The changing role of trade unions in the management of labour, *British Journal of Industrial Relations*, 24(2): 161–66.

Davidow, W. and Malone, M. S. (1992) *The Virtual Corporation*. New York: Harper Business Press.

DeVroey, M. (1984) A regulation approach interpretation of contemporary crisis, *Capital and Class*, 23: 45–66.

Edwards, R. (1979) *Contested Terrains*. New York: Basic Books.

Elam, M. (1994) Puzzling out the post-Fordist debate, in A. Amin (ed.), *Post-Fordism: A Reader* (pp. 43–71). Oxford: Blackwell.

Escobar, A. (2005) Economics and the space of modernity: The tales of the market, production and labor, *Cultural Studies*, 19(2): 139–75.

Foster, J. B. and McChesney, R. W. (2012) *The Endless Crisis: How Monopoly-Finance Capital Produces Stagnation and Upheaval from the USA to China*. New York: Monthly Review Press.

Freeman, C. and Perez, C. (1988) Structural crises of adjustment, business cycles and investment behavior, in G. Dosi, C. Freeman, R. Nelson, G. Silverberg, and L. Soete (eds), *Technical Change and Economical Theory* (pp. 38–66). London: Frances Pinter.

Friedman, T. (2008) All fall down, *The New York Times*, 25 November, 2008, http://www.nytimes.com/2008/11/26/opinion/26friedman.html

Gertler, M. (1988) The limits to flexibility: Comments on the post-Fordist vision of production and its geography, *Transactions of the Institute of British Geographers*, 13: 419–32.

Gordon, D. (1988) The global economy: New edifice or crumbling foundation?, *New Left Review*, 168: 24–65.

Graeber, D. (2011) *Debt: The First 5,000 Years*. New York: Melville House Publishing.

Graham, J. (1992) Post-Fordism as politics: The political consequences of narratives on the left, *Society and Space*, 10(4): 393–410.

Gunder Frank, A. (1998) *ReORIENT: Global Economy in the Asian Age*. Berkeley, CA: University of California Press.

Hall, S. (1988) Brave new world, *Marxism Today*, October: 24–29.

Harvey, D. (1989) *The Condition of Postmodernity*. Cambridge, MA: Blackwell.

Henwood, D. (2008) Crisis of a gilded age, *The Nation*, October 13: 3–4.

Heydebrand, W. F. (1989) New organizational forms, *Work and Occupations*, 16(3): 323–57.

Jessop, B. (1994) Post-Fordism and the state, in A. Amin (ed.), *Post-Fordism: A Reader* (pp. 251–79). Oxford: Blackwell.

Kanter, R. M. (1989) *When Giants Learn to Dance*. New York: Touchstone.

Kaplinsky, R. (1984) *Automation*. London: Longmans.

Kochan, T. A., Katz, H. C., and McKersie, R. B. (1986) *The Transformation of American Industrial Relations*. New York: Basic Books.

Krippner, G. R. (2005) The financialization of the American economy, *Socio-Economic Review*, 3(2): 173–208.

Kuttner, R. (1997) *Everything for Sale: The Virtues and Limits of Markets*. New York: Alfred A. Knopf.

Lash, S. and Urry, J. (1987) *The End of Organized Capitalism*. Madison, WI: University of Wisconsin Press.

Leborgne, D. and Lipietz, A. (1988) New technologies, new modes of regulation: Some spatial implications, *Environment and Social Planning D: Society and Space*, 6: 263–80.

Lewis, M. (ed.) (2008) *Panic: The Story of Modern Financial Insanity*. New York: W. W. Norton.

Lipietz, A. (1987) *Mirages and Miracles: The Global Crisis of Fordism*. London: Verso.

Mathew, B. (2005) *Taxi!: Cabs and Capitalism in New York City*. New York: New Press.

Marx, K. (1976 [1867]) *Capital, Volume 1*. London: Penguin Books.

Murray, R. (1989) Fordism and post-Fordism, in S. Hall and M. Jacques (eds), *New Times: The Changing Face of Politics in the 1990s* (pp. 54–64). London: Verso.

National Bureau of Economic Research (2014) US business cycle expansions and contractions, http://www.nber.org/cycles.html

Penn, R. (1992) Flexibility in Britain during the 1980s: Recent empirical evidence, in N. Gilbert, R. Burrows, and A. Pollert (eds), *Fordism and Flexibility: Divisions and Change* (pp. 66–86). New York: St. Martin's Press.

Peters, T. (1992) *Liberation Management: Necessary Disorganization for the Nanosecond Nineties*. New York: Fawcett Columbine.

Piketty, T. (2013) *Capital in the Twenty-First Century*. Cambridge, MA: Harvard University Press.

Piore, M. J., and Sabel, C. F. (1984) *The Second Industrial Divide: Possibilities for Prosperity*. New York: Basic Books.

Pollert, A. (1988) Dismantling flexibility, *Capital and Class*, 34: 42–75.

Sabel, C. (1989) Flexible specialization and the reemergence of regional economies, in P. Hirst and J. Zeitlin (eds), *Reversing Industrial Decline?* (pp. 17–70). New York: St. Martin's Press.

Sayer, A. and Walker, R. (1992) *The New Social Economy*. Cambridge, MA: Blackwell.

Schoenberger, E. (1989) Thinking about flexibility: A response to Gertler, *Transactions of the Institute of British Geographers*, 14: 98–108.

Scott, A. (1988) *New Industrial Spaces*. London: Pion.

Scott, A. J. (2001) Capitalism, cities and the production of symbolic forms, *Transactions of the Institute of British Geographers*, 26(1): 11–23.

Shutt, J. and Whittington, R. (1987) Fragmentation strategies and the rise of small units, *Regional Studies*, 21(1): 13–23.

Smith, Y. (2010) *Econned: How Unenlightened Self Interest Undermined Democracy and Corrupted Capitalism*. New York: Palgrave Macmillan.

Standing, G. (1992) Alternative routes to labor flexibility, in M. Storper and A. Scott (eds), *Pathways to Industrial and Regional Development* (pp. 255–75). London: Routledge.

Storper, M. and Scott, A. (1989) The geographical foundations and social regulation of flexible production complexes, in J. Wolch and M. Dear (eds), *The Power of Geography* (pp. 21–40). Boston: Allen & Unwin.

Taylor, F. W. (1911) *The Principles of Scientific Management*. New York: Harper.

US Census Bureau. The changing shape of the nation's income distribution, http://www.census.gov/prod/2000pubs/p60-204.pdf

Varoufakis, Y. (2011) *The Global Minotaur: America, the True Origins of the Financial Crisis and the Future of the World Economy*. New York: Zed Books.

Wallerstein, I. (1984) The three instances of hegemony in the history of the capitalist world-economy, *International Journal of Comparative Sociology*, 24(1–2): 100–8.

Weber, M. (1961) *General Economic History*. New York: Collier.

Weber, M. (1978) *Economy and Society*. Berkeley, CA: University of California Press.

Weiler, P. C. (1990) *Governing the Workplace: The Future of Labor and Employment Law*. Cambridge, MA: Harvard University Press.

Williamson, O. E. (1975) *Markets and Hierarchies: Analysis and Antitrust Implications*. New York: Free Press.

Zammuto, R. F. and O'Connor, E. J. (1992) Gaining advanced manufacturing technologies' benefits: the roles of organization design and culture, *Academy of Management Review*, 17(4): 701–28.

Žižek, S. (2009) *First as Tragedy, Then as Farce*. London: Verso.

Zuboff, S. (1988) *In the Age of the Smart Machine: The Future of Work and Power*. New York: Basic Books.

19

The New Deal for management and organizational studies

Lessons, insights, and reflections

Albert J. Mills, Terrance G. Weatherbee, Jason Foster, and Jean Helms Mills

Introduction

> Recreating an accurate and objective picture of the New Deal may be more important today than at any other time in the last eight decades. To study the period is to be struck by the parallels between the economic and political conditions of the 1930s and those of the opening years of this century.
>
> (Hiltzik, 2011: 426)

The New Deal refers to a set of sweeping legislative reforms that characterized much of the early stages of President Franklin Delano Roosevelt's administration, from 1933 to 1945. In particular it refers to a series of progressive enactments that saw millions of unemployed workers engaged in public works to improve the infrastructure and cultural life of the United States; the institution of trade union rights to organize; and the institution of social welfare (Genoe McLaren, 2011).

This chapter builds on earlier work (Foster, Mills, and Weatherbee, 2014) that examines the implications of our neglect of the New Deal era in Management and Organization Studies (MOS). In that work we argued that the sheer magnitude of the Roosevelt administration's 'New Deal' activities make it hard to imagine how and why it was subsequently ignored by the emergent field of MOS. Drawing upon various sources that explain the development of the field in the Cold War context (Cooke, 1999; Tadajewski, 2006; Kelley, Mills, and Cooke, 2006; Landau, 2006) as a time in which MOS emerged as an 'historical' field of study (George, 1972; Wren, 1972),[1] we agreed with Burrell and Morgan's (1979) characterization of the field as having become ahistorical, managerial, and overly focused on private sector organizations.

Drawing on these two foci – the socio-political context of the Cold War and the role of history in field definition – we go on to argue that the exclusion of the New Deal from MOS study was part of a paradigmatic process (Burrell & Morgan, 1979) that was bounded by networked politics (Latour, 2005) and a particular formative context (Unger, 2004). It was a process that saw certain actors, theories, studies, and areas of interest included within the MOS domain while others were excluded.

We argued that as MOS developed as a field of enquiry in the United States it was heavily influenced by the context of the Cold War and related activities, such as the rise of McCarthyism (Foster, Mills, and Weatherbee, 2014), an era that encouraged the intellectual avoidance of issues and topics that may be viewed as challenging the social, political, and economic status quo (Kelley, Mills, and Cooke, 2006; Schrecker, 1986; Robin, 2001). Over time, as the field was entering a more mature stage of paradigm development (Kuhn, 1962), creating boundaries of inclusion and exclusion (Khurana, 2007), it went through a period of narrowing focus, in part through the development of retrospective histories (George, 1968, 1972; Wren, 1972, 1979), that helped to shape who was and who was not considered a significant contributor to the emerging field of MOS.

For example, Fredrick Taylor and Max Weber were deemed the fathers of Scientific Management and Organization Theory respectively (Mills, Weatherbee, and Durepos, 2014). It would not be until decades later before any 'mothers' would be added to the histories of the field, in particular Mary Parker Follett (Graham, 1996; Schilling, 2000; Phipps, 2011; Tancred-Sheriff and Campbell, 1992). Individuals who were considered 'radicals' or 'liberals' were left out of historical accounts while those considered pro-business theorists were privileged in their inclusion (Cooke, 1999). Frank Gilbreth found his place as an extender and contributor to scientific management while the 'leftist' Mary van Kleeck was all but exorcized out of any account (Nyland and Heenan, 2005). As Scientific Management was designated as the founding school of MOS with Frederick Taylor as its founder, other pioneers, including Harrington Emerson, all but disappear behind Taylor's historical shadow (Urwick, 1956; Urwick and Brech, 1957). Histories of the emergent Human Relations School, seen as spanning the late 1920s to the early post-war years (Koontz, 1962; Wren, 1972), refer, for the most part, solely to the Hawthorne Studies and Lewin, Lippitt, and White's (1939) leadership studies. The New Deal simply happened elsewhere, i.e. outside of the realm of management studies. At the same time that Elton Mayo (1933), Fritz Roethlisberger and William Dickson (1939) are credited as leading members of the new Human Relations School, Whiting Williams "was all but forgotten" (Muldoon, 2012: 107) as were others. The names of the men and women at the forefront of the progressive philosophy of the New Deal were, with few exceptions.[2] completely ignored. This notable group includes Frances Perkins, Harry Hopkins, Harold Ickes, Henry Wallace, David Lilienthal, Adolf Berle, and several others.

In this chapter, we first set out to recover the New Deal and some of its leading figures and bring them into MOS. We do not simply seek to add them into the existing histories of MOS but rather to show how MOS histories have served to not only define the field but also to constrain what is considered a valid area of study. Second, we argue MOS as a discipline is too narrow and needs, going forward, to be more imaginative in its choice of stories and exemplars when dealing with the broad range of economic, behavioural, social and political factors that confront humankind's ability to organize and manage its affairs.

While we share Hiltzik's (2011) contention about the need to study the New Deal for lessons relevant for today, it is not our intention to create a more 'objective' or more 'accurate' historical picture of the New Deal. Our purpose is to explore several aspects of the New Deal with the aim of developing insights for management theory, practice, and history. We remain aware of the criticisms levelled at the New Deal, including issues such as segregated work practices and the failure to adequately deal with questions of fair or equal treatment of employment opportunities regardless of race and gender (Taylor, 2008; Katznelson, 2013; Rowbotham, 1999; Josephson, 1967). We certainly agree with most, if not all of these criticisms, but we would also argue they cannot be levelled at the New Deal alone. Scientific Management, Human Relations, and MOS in general have all been subject to these same criticisms (Acker and van Houten, 1974; Nyland and Heenan, 2005; Hearn and Parkin, 1983). Valid criticisms are not a reason to exclude the New

Deal from consideration in MOS, but rather a tempering factor to be taken into account when evaluating its contributions.

Before beginning our analysis of the New Deal and its adherents, it is important to clarify our approach to history in order to avoid the impression that we view the task as one of revealing the facts of the case and of adding to existing histories. As has been contended elsewhere, 'history' and 'the past' need to be viewed as outcomes of a series of socio-political activities rather than an act of the uncovering of facts (Durepos and Mills, 2012b). We are arguing for a new way of conceptualizing history and the importance of allowing our imagination to be open to new and different social constructions of the boundaries of MOS. We employ ANTi-History (Durepos and Mills, 2012a, 2012b; Foster, Mills, and Weatherbee, 2014), an approach which sets out to deconstruct the notion of history as a meta-discourse (Jenkins, 1995) while simultaneously celebrating the importance of storytelling about the past to social life. This approach leads us to view history as the outcome of socio-political relations rather than factual accounts of the past (White, 1973; Jenkins, 1991).

Methodological approach

In this section, we outline our approach to the study of history and the past that draws upon poststructuralist historiography (Jenkins, 1991; Munslow, 2010), cultural theory (Green and Troup, 1999), Actor-Network Theory (Latour, 2005), and the sociology of knowledge (Mannheim, 1985) to constitute what Durepos and Mills (2012b) call ANTi-History. In brief, it is an approach that views history as a social construction of the past; one that is rooted in the knowledge-producing activities of actor-networks (Latour, 2005). The approach has been outlined (Durepos and Mills, 2012a, 2012b; Weatherbee *et al.*, 2012) and applied (Myrick, Helms Mills, and Mills, 2013; Durepos, Helms Mills, and Mills, 2008) in depth elsewhere. Here we will make five key arguments of particular relevance for understanding our focus upon the New Deal and its importance for MOS.

History as narrative (White, 1965): According to White, facts do not simply 'speak for themselves' but are selected and produced through narratives. A plausible history is a result of the historian's ability to select and assemble 'facts' (persons, events, places, and times) into a particular narrative form, rather than being a reflection of the past based on 'facts'. In histories of MOS, therefore, it can be argued that the people (e.g. Weber) and events (e.g. the Hawthorne Studies) which characterize the origins of the field are the outcome of selective choices made by various actors in MOS such as historians (e.g. George, 1968; Wren, 1972), well-known textbook authors (e.g. Robbins, 1989) and other researchers, theorists, and educators. Further, the process of selection is also a process of non-selection. The exclusion of certain events, we contend, is a function of narratives that are grounded in and built out of the extant philosophies of managerialism and the capitalist enterprise. Heeding Witzel's (2012: 103) call for "more managerial biodiversity [through] the circulation of as many management models and paradigms as possible", we hope to offer MOS an alternative narrative to the dominant viewpoint through our focus on the New Deal.

The "past-as-history" (Munslow, 2010 – see also Chapter 10 this volume): So far we have talked as if narratives build on the facts of the past and somewhere in those narratives (or histories) can be found elements or factual traces of the past that are somehow selected over others. However, Munslow (2010) argues the past and history is largely conflated in studies of history, where what happened before now (namely the past) becomes represented as history (i.e., seemingly more or less accurate accounts of the past). In the process, history is seen as a legitimate account of the past and the past becomes viewed as history ready for the telling. However, as Munslow (2010) further contends, the past and history are arguably "ontologically dissonant"; the past is ontologically unavailable to the historian. Applying this logic to the New Deal, we contend the people and events associated with MOS through its various histories (Wren, 1972; George, 1968), and other accounts (Robbins, 1988) are the results of specifically selected actors that serve a particular paradigmatic worldview. In the process the New Deal and its architects have been excluded from MOS past-as-history. Through our own selection and social construction of an historical narrative we set out to challenge the narrow paradigmatic character of MOS and to open debate about the multitude of organization and management stakeholders whose voices, as of yet, have been marginalized by the field's restrictive for-profit focus.

History as meta-discourse (Durepos and Mills, 2012b; Jenkins, 1995): In terms of power/knowledge (Foucault, 1980) it can be argued that the conflation of history with the past reinforces the idea of history as knowledge of the past (i.e. reproduction of the past is underwritten by the understanding that the past has a real character whose truth can ultimately be revealed). This understanding of history is produced through the practices of History (particularly at the disciplinary level but also through public and popular histories – Kalela, 2012), which have a powerful impact on what people accept as truth.

History and the socio-politics of relations (Durepos and Mills, 2012a; Durepos, Helms Mills, and Mills, 2008; Law, 1994; Latour, 2005): To understand the relationship between knowledge and the past we turn to Actor-Network Theory (ANT). Here we seek to understand how particular forms of knowledge arise out of the interactions of a series of human and non-human actors working in concert. This exploration raises questions of how history is made and how its influence is felt. As Witzel (2012: 5) expresses it, "the study of management history is important [because of] the light it can shed on why some ideas and concepts in management survive and are widely adopted, while others disappear". Witzel suggests the answer lies in the socio-economic contexts in which ideas arise, technological advancement, and the simplicity and practicality of the ideas presented. We largely agree but would also add there is a need to study the role of networks of actors (human and non-human) in the spread or failure of ideas (Latour, 1988). Recent accounts by Shenhav and Weitz (2000) and Bruce and Nyland (2011) have usefully attempted to reveal the effect of actor networks on the respective development of Scientific Management and the Human Relations School.[3] While these accounts sometimes reinforce and sometimes contradict the broader links to technology and socio-economic context in mainstream historical accounts, they don't fully explain how the New Deal and its architects came to be almost wholly ignored by MOS (Foster, Mills, and Weatherbee, 2014).[4]

History as a non-corporeal actant (Weatherbee *et al.*, 2012; Mills and Durepos, 2010; Durepos and Mills, 2012a; Hartt, 2013): Here we ask how does history as knowledge come to be developed? The process is iterative and double-looped in that not only must we seek to 'follow the actors' in the development of knowledge but we must also simultaneously seek to understand history as an actor in the process. Hartt (2013) refers to history in this sense as a "non-corporeal actant" – something that profoundly influences the pursuit and understanding of knowledge that is itself embedded in flows of ideas. As a consequence, in attempting to recover a sense of the New Deal we need to be mindful that our sense is highly filtered through various extant histories, histories which are themselves outcomes of the socio-politics of relations (Durepos, Helms Mills, and Mills, 2008). This reminder alerts us to the fact we are not setting out to replace one truth (e.g. dominant notions of the development of management theory) with another (i.e. a New Deal focus). Rather we are encouraging a greater multiplicity of thought within MOS.

In the following section of the chapter we make a case for the importance of New Deal studies based on the sheer magnitude of the New Deal undertaking and relevance for MOS. To do this we explore selected theorists, philosophies, and action before examining some of the key themes and issues raised by the New Deal undertaking as a whole.

The magnitude

In contemporaneous accounts[5] and histories of MOS (George, 1968; Rose, 1978; Wren and Bedeian, 2009), two companies stand out in the strength of their associations with the theoretical contributions of management theorists – Bethlehem Steel and Taylor (e.g. 1911), and Western Electric's Hawthorne Works and the works of Mayo (1933) and Roethlisberger and Dickson (1939). There can be no doubt these two companies occupied an important role in the US economy of the day and employed large numbers of workers. Bethlehem Steel at its peak was the second largest steel producer in the United States and Western Electric played a pivotal role in the telephone equipment industry as the supplier of almost "90 percent of all the telephone equipment used in the United States."[6] Arguably then, the sheer size and importance of these organizations in economic and social terms were factors in the legitimation of management theorizing by Taylor, Mayo, Roethlisberger and Dickson. While a focus on these companies and associated management research is understandable, less understandable is the neglect by MOS researchers of the agencies of the New Deal, whose magnitude dwarfs that of Bethlehem Steel and Western Electric combined.

Even at the time the when the initial concept of the 'New Deal' was being developed it was, for the most part, ill-defined (Taylor, 2008; Morgan, 2003; Schlesinger, 1959; Kennedy, 2005). Nonetheless, it became most closely associated with a number of agencies and laws (see Table 19.1) that were far-reaching in their impact upon the socio-economic and cultural lives of the people of the United States through much of the 1930s and 1940s and beyond.[7]

In terms of work and employment alone, New Deal agencies collectively, at one time or another, employed almost 10 million people. For example, the Civil Works Administration (CWA) was employing around 4.25 million people by the start of 1934. By late 1935 the Civilian Conservation Corps (CCC) was employing 500,000 young men, with more than 2.5 million moving through its ranks over its brief tenure. By its peak in late 1938 the Works Projects Administration (WPA) alone was employing 3.3 million workers (Taylor, 2008; Schlesinger, 1959; Hiltzik, 2011). Over its duration, Roosevelt's New Deal agencies built 85 per cent of all airports in the United States; 650,000 miles of roads; 125,000 civilian and military buildings, and 78,000 bridges (Taylor, 2008).

The impact was not just economic but was also profoundly social. For example, the WPA is credited with serving "900 million hot lunches to schoolchildren"; operating 1,500 nursery schools; presenting 225,000 concerts to audiences and performing "plays, vaudeville acts, puppet shows, and circuses before 30 million people"; and producing around 475,000 works of art, 276 full-length books and 701 pamphlets (Taylor, 2008: 523–24). Finally, the welfare philosophy behind the WPA's approach to work relief programs would also "dictate welfare policy, for better or worse, for the next sixty years" (Taylor, 2008: 111). As Hiltzik (2011: 421) contends, "the New Deal physically reshaped the country. To this day, Americans still rely on its works for transportation, electricity, flood control, housing, and community amenities."

In developing and operating these various agencies, those involved were forced to confront a range of organizational, management, social, and political problems in a very short space of time. While managerial and organizational decisions sometimes came from progressive impulses, at times they were conservative ones, and in others even reactionary (Josephson, 1967). More often than not they arose out of necessity and were pragmatic, political, and the outcome of negotiated compromise. New Deal activities were not unified nor homogeneous, and have been described as "the product of varying circumstances, impulses, beliefs that often stood in flagrant contradictions with one another" (Robert Moley, quoted in Hiltzik, 2011: 427). In other words, the New Deal should not be seen or characterized as either a progressive or a conservative panacea for

Table 19.1 Selected New Deal agencies and organizational contribution

Agency	*Years*	*Purpose*	*Potential contribution to organizational studies*
Public Works Administration	1933–1943	Financed 35,000 public works projects	Methods for ensuring accountability in projects with tight timelines; navigating conflicting organizational goals and cultures
Civil Conservation Corps	1933–1942	Work projects for 500,000 young men conserving natural resources	Case study of inter-organizational cooperation/partnerships
Rural Electrification Administration (now Rural Utilities Service)	1935– Present	Electrification of rural areas	Dynamics in development of alternative organizational structures (cooperatives)
Securities and Exchange Commission	1934– Present	Regulation and policing of financial exchanges	Goal-achieving in hostile environments; regulator–regulated relationships
National Labor Relations Board	1935– Present	Regulation and enforcement of union–employer relations	Labour–management relations; organizational institutionalization (e.g. trade unions)
Works Progress Administration	1935–1943	Multi-faceted work projects through direct employment	Decentralized financing models; managing complex, multi-layered organization structures; elimination of patronage
Tennessee Valley Authority	1933– Present	Conservation and development of natural resources in Tennessee River Valley	First publicly-owned corporation in USA; decentralization; power in organizations; hybrid public–private organization

organizational and management issues but rather a complex phenomenon that challenges our understanding of what should appropriately compose the field of MOS.

A brief examination of some of the major issues to confront 'New Dealers' yields a sense of the types of concerns and problems relevant to MOS today – specifically the interrelations of capitalism, government, and business, and the place of social responsibility, social and industrial welfare, and the role of labour unions.

Capitalism and the role of government

Perhaps the most critical issue that New Dealers faced was the role of government and its relationship to capitalism. That Roosevelt's administrations (1933–45) were often torn between progressive and conservative forces is beyond the scope of this chapter (Leuchtenburg, 2009; Schlesinger, 1959; Taylor, 2008). What is of interest, however, is that the associated debates and policy decisions raised widespread questions about private ownership and its relationship to social welfare. To some extent these debates had been taking place for some time among scientific management adherents and the members of the Taylor Society (Nyland and Heenan, 2005) but the New Deal provided a greater, more widespread, platform for dissemination, awareness, and discussion of these issues.

When Roosevelt was elected in 1932 it was the tail end of the so-called New Era in which successive administrations, including that of Coolidge and Hoover, had been notably friendly to business interests.[8] The era can be characterized by "weak central government" (Witzel, 2012: 104) that "was dictated by a revered American political philosophy that denied central government a role in addressing social problems" (Taylor, 2008: 8). Much of this philosophy can be found embedded in the business textbooks of the time. The textbooks either expressed opposition to government intervention in the affairs of business (Koontz, 1941) or were absent of any discussion of the role of government in business (e.g. Barnes, 1940). With the onset of the Second World War much of this debate subsided and did not resurface during the Cold War era (Kelley, Mills, and Cooke, 2006), an absence which defaulted to a pro-business worldview (Burrell and Morgan, 1979).

In the face of mass unemployment and rising social unrest Roosevelt had little time to find a way forward and, if nothing else, was open to new ideas and experimentation. Although initially drawing on both conservative and progressive forces, Roosevelt found himself increasingly drawn to the latter in his first term of office (Schlesinger, 1959). These included persons such as Adolf Berle, Rex Tugwell, Henry Wallace, Robert Wagner, David Lilienthal, Frances Perkins, Harold Ickes, and Harry Hopkins.

Berle, a noted liberal economist, argued against the concentration of corporate power (Berle and Means, 1932), contending that "the domination of the US economy by a shrinking cadre of industrial barons had stifled opportunity for the average American" (Hiltzik, 2011: 9), and at one point argued for the nationalization of "great blocks of industry" (Leuchtenburg, 2009: 265) to deal with the economic crisis. According to Schlesinger (1959: 183), "Berle's deeper interest was in developing a new moral climate. Business could no longer be primarily an affair of making profits, its object must now be to provide goods and services to allow people to live full lives." Rex Tugwell came to the New Deal with a distrust of business (Leuchtenburg, 2009: 35) and an interest in economic planning (Tugwell, 1933) that would see industries coordinated through an Industrial Integration Board and then each board's planning would be reconciled "with the basic plan laid down by the government" (Schlesinger, 1959: 93). As Assistant Secretary of Agriculture, Tugwell sought "national regulation of production through democratic planning" (Schlesinger, 1959: 183), and argued for a widespread commitment to public works, large-scale expenditures on relief and curbs on profiteers (Leuchtenburg, 2009: 84). What Berle and Tugwell urged for industry, Henry Wallace, the Secretary of Agriculture, planned for farming.

Meanwhile, New York Senator Robert Wagner constantly raised the issue of labour rights, contending that "labor must have a guarantee of collective bargaining" (Leuchtenburg, 2009: 57). Wagner's efforts led, in 1935, to the National Labor Relations Act (NRLA – or Wagner Act) and the establishment of the National Labor Relations Board (NLRB). The Wagner Act was far-reaching in giving employees the right to collective bargaining and in compelling employers to allow unionization of their workplaces when a majority of workers were in favour of so doing (Foner, 2012). David Lilienthal brought forth calls for "grass roots democracy" and the "decentralized administration of centralized authority" (Schlesinger, 1959: 332) into the debates about the future of work and large-scale organizations. These principles were then applied to the Tennessee Valley Authority (TVA) that Lilienthal himself helped to conceive and lead.

While some were questioning managerial rights in industry, others, including Perkins, Ickes, and Hopkins, were more concerned with social welfare and citizens' rights. Between them they managed to oversee the employment of tens of millions of people through the WPA, the CCC, and the Public Works Administration (PWA) and the advent of the Social Security Act. All of which had a tremendous impact on work, organization, and employment in the United States.

Theorists, philosophies and action

> As a movement human relations was diffuse, and Mayo never led it except in a symbolic sense – and largely from the grave.
>
> *(Rose, 1978: 113)*

In his account of the first 100 days of the Roosevelt administration Cohen (2009) singles out five of Roosevelt's advisers – Lewis Douglas, Raymond Moley, Henry Wallace, Harry Hopkins, and Frances Perkins – as having the greatest impact. For reasons of space we focus on the three advisers who had the longest impact on New Deal workplace programmes. Douglas and Moley became disillusioned and left the administration and Wallace had a huge impact on agriculture. Ickes' influence is underplayed during the first 100 days but in any event had probably the longest lasting influence as public works began to materialize. Indeed, according to the columnist Walter Lippmann, "Ickes (along with Perkins) were the 'advanced guard' of the struggle to constrain predatory wealth and to oppose social control and social standards upon corporate property" (quoted in Hiltzik, 2011: 37).

Harold Ickes and the new democracy

> It is the old struggle between the power of money and the power of the democratic instinct. In the last few months this irreconcilable conflict … has come into the open as never before, has taken on a form and an intensity which makes it clear that it must be fought through to a finish – until plutocracy or democracy – until America's sixty families or America's 120,000,000 people – win … The fight in this country today is one between the great mass of the people and wealth.
>
> *(Harold Ickes, Radio Speech, December 1937 – quoted in Hiltzik, 2011: 386–87)*

Harold Ickes wrote several books, including *The New Democracy* (1934) and *Back to Work: The Story of the PWA* (1935), which along with his Secret Diaries published posthumously in 1953 and 1954 (see Ickes, 1953, 1954), provide considerable insights into his philosophy of management.

Ickes was a progressive Republican, appointed as Roosevelt's Secretary of the Interior in 1933. Along with Frances Perkins, he was the only cabinet member to serve the entire twelve years of the Roosevelt administrations (Hiltzik, 2011). Following passage of the National Industrial Recovery Act (NIRA), with an appropriation of $33 billion, Ickes found himself in charge of the Public Works Administration (Foner, 2012). The PWA was established to develop a series of public works that would pump funds into the ailing economy. Yet, despite the urgency, Ickes moved cautiously (Kennedy, 2005: 176); his approach dubbed "obsessively prudent management", he only managed to spend $110 million in 1933 (Kennedy, 2005: 178). Ickes' main concern was to avoid corruption, fraud, and the misuse of public monies through haste (Kennedy, 2005; Hiltzik, 2011).

Nonetheless, despite his caution, Ickes oversaw the building of roads, schools, courthouses, hospitals, and infrastructure that included the Triborough Bridge, the Lincoln Tunnel, La Guardia

Table 19.2 Timelines of the New Deal, selected MOS events, socio-political and cultural contexts

Year	*Unemployment No. (% workforce)*	*New Deal administrations*	*Selected MOS Events*	*Popular culture*
1924	2.4 million (5.5%)[a]	Calvin Coolidge elected President[b]	Hawthorne Studies – 1st phase (Human factor industrial psychology)[c]	
1928	2 million (4.4%)	Herbert Hoover elected President	Hawthorne Studies – 2nd phase (Clinical)	
1929	1.5 million (3.2%)		Wall Street Crash	
1930	4.3 million (8.9%)		Translation of Max Weber by Talcott Parsons[d]	
1931	8 million (15.9%)	FDR[e] as NY Governor establishes the Temporary Emergency Relief Administration – headed by Harry Hopkins	Hawthorne Studies – 3rd phase (Anthropological)	
1932	12 million (23.6%)	FDR elected President FDR Inaugurated (March 4)	Hawthorne Studies terminated during slump	Movie *American Madness*[f]
1933	12.8 million (24.75%)	National Recovery Administration (NRA) (Glass-Steagall) Banking Act Civil Conservation Corps (CCC) Public Works Administration (PWA) Agricultural Adjustment Act (AAA) Tennessee Valley Authority (TVA) National Industrial Recovery Act (NIRA) Civil Works Administration (CWA) – 2.6 million employed	Mayo's *The Human Problems of an Industrial Civilization* published Mary Parker Follett dies Mary van Kleeck joins the Federal Advisory Council but resigns in protest at New Deal failure to workers	Movie *A Farewell to Arms* Sinclair Lewis' *Ann Vickers* published

Table 19.2 (cont.)

Year	*Unemployment No. (% workforce)*	*New Deal administrations*	*Selected MOS Events*	*Popular culture*
1934	11.3 million (21.7%)	Ickes' *New Democracy* published CWA employs 4.3 million	Business corporation leaders (including Alfred P. Sloan) set up American Liberty League to oppose New Deal FDR invites W. B. Donham, Dean of Harvard Business School to White House. Finds Donham has "no concrete answers"[g] Josephson's *Robber Barons* published	Movie *It Happened One Night*
1935	10.6 million (20.1%)	Works Progress Administration (WPA) Social Security Act (Wagner) National Labor Relations Act NRA and AAA struck down by Supreme Court Federal Program Number One CCC employing ½ million	Ickes' *Back to Work: The Story of the PWA* published	Movie *Les Miserables* Sinclair Lewis' *It Can't Happen Here* published
1936	9 million (17%)	FDR Re-elected (second administration) WPA employing 2.8 million	Hawthorne Studies – 4th Phase (Counselling) Initial Academy of Management meeting[h] Van Kleeck's *Creative America* published Hopkins' *Spending to Save* published	Movie *Mr. Deeds Goes to Town* Publication of Dos Pasos' *Big Money* (Negro Theatre's) *Macbeth* opens in Harlem Sinclair Lewis' play *It Can't Happen Here* opens in 16 cities

1937	7.7 million (14.3%)		2nd AoM meeting held	*The Cradle Will Rock* opens Movie *The Good Earth*
1938	10.4 million (19%)	Second Agricultural Adjustment Act HUAC investigates Federal One WPA employs 3.3 million Hopkins becomes Secretary of Commerce	3rd AoM meeting held Barnard's *The Functions of the Executive* published	Movie *You Can't Take It With You*
1939	9.4 million (17.2%)		Roethlisberger & Dickson's *Management and the Worker* published 4th AoM meeting held Drucker's *The End of Economic Man* published	Publication of Steinbeck's *The Grapes of Wrath* Movie *Mr. Smith Goes to Washington*
1940	8.1 million (14.6%)	FDR Re-elected (third administration)	5th AoM meeting – 1st formally constituted	Movie *The Grapes of Wrath*
1941	5.5 million (9.9%)			Japanese Attack on Pearl Harbor US Enters Second World War Movie *Meet John Doe*
1944	0.67 million (1.2%)	FDR Re-elected		
1945	1 million (1.9%)	Death of FDR		

[a] Estimates vary widely. These figure are illustrative of the magnitude of the problem of unemployment if nothing else – see Lebergott (1957).

[b] Coolidge and Hoover are both noted for their pro-business sentiments, stating, respectively, "The business of Government is business" and "The sole function of Government is to bring about a condition of affairs favorable to the beneficial development of private enterprise."

[c] Based on Rose (1978).

[d] Weber's work would not make any impact on MOS for two more decades Mills, Weatherbee, and Durepos (2014).

[e] FDR refers to Franklin Delano Roosevelt.

[f] The selected movies are by Oscar winning directors and have New Deal (and other progressive) themes.

[g] Quoted in Schlesinger (1959).

[h] It is debatable whether the meeting constituted the first meeting of what is today's Academy of Management (AoM). For analysis of the problems of constructing a history of the Academy of Management see Myrick, Helms Mills, and Mills (2013) and Grant and Mills (2006).

Airport, and numerous projects that are still at the heart of US infrastructure to this day (Kennedy, 2005: 252). Along the way, Ickes, a former President of the Chicago Chapter of the National Association for the Advancement of Colored People (NAACP), did what he could to reverse discriminatory practices (Katznelson, 2013: 176), and spoke out against "segregation, disenfranchisement, and lynching" (Foner, 2012: 825). He also established quotas for African-Americans on PWA projects (http://www.spartacus.schoolnet.co.uk/USARickes.htm). For his various 'progressive' stands, he was accused (along with Perkins and Hopkins) of being a communist sympathizer by Martin Dies, Chairman of the House Committee on Un-American Activities (Caute, 1979: Goldstein, 1978 – see Table 19.2).

Organizations, work, and the new democracy

Ickes suggests the "determination of problems" in regard to management and the organization of work need to take into account the "particular political and social background" in which they are being posed (1934: vii). The particular problem, as he saw it, was that big business and the capitalist system of production had been responsible for ushering in an "era of overproduction, underconsumption, and high structural unemployment" (Golay, 2013: 15). Along the way, an "industrial and commercial empire" had been built out of the "exploitation … of native Indians" and the institution of slavery (Ickes, 1934: 17). Business had thrived on the "unchecked and ruthless exploitation" not only of blacks and indigenous peoples but also women and children of all races (Ickes, 1934: 19). Ickes found fault with current practices of "inadequate pay", inequitable pay, "long hours", technological developments designed to benefit the few at the expense of the many, and little regard for the "impairment and destruction" of society's aesthetic and spiritual treasures (Ickes, 1934: 18, 21, 26, 38).

Ickes' viewpoint is a philosophy that sees business organizations and their management as part of an organic whole of various social, economic, and political influences. It is a philosophy of management arguing for the treatment of people at work in a manner that values the human mind over physical tools and plant (Ickes, 1934: 68); ensures that work is "ennobling" rather than disheartening; "guarantees self-respect"; provides a right to "adequate" and equitable wages; equal opportunities, regardless of race and gender; and keeps to the fore the principle of "the greatest good for the greatest number" (Ickes, 1934: 70, 64, 65, 72, 32).

At the very least, Ickes' philosophy prefaces the later post-war developments in Human Relations thinking in terms of theory 'Y' types of management – less the more overt managerial aspects of McGregor (1957) but more towards the wide-reaching socio-political context that Maslow (1954) attempted to incorporate in theories of motivation. But it goes much further. It sees senior management, rather than employees, as the problem of business. Thus, Ickes goes far beyond theory 'X' in his characterization of the inefficient management style. He cites the extant philosophy of "rugged individualism" that served as a clarion call to those who saw anything less as an attack on Americanism and all it stood for (Ickes, 1934: 31). For Ickes, there is a clear distinction between individualism and rugged individualism:

> [There is that individualism] that is the natural result of the self-sufficiency and forthrightness which have been distinguishing traits of the average American, the insistence upon the right to live and let live, and the acquisitive, exploiting, lawless qualities of a ruthless minority who would achieve wealth and power regardless of the rights of others. The latter qualities are characteristic of rugged individualism.
>
> *(Ickes, 1934: 31)*

Here we can see a view of management and the workplace that is placed clearly in the arena of political philosophy. Ickes contends those business leaders who evoke "rugged individualism" to argue against the intrusion of politics and government in business are not slow in attempting to influence and control government for their own ends (Ickes, 1934: 22). Nor are they slow to come running to government when they are financially in trouble (Ickes, 1934: 23). It was perhaps Ickes' deep-rooted suspicion of business leadership that encouraged him to be extra cautious when spending PWA monies.

Ickes' argument makes a case for the political character of the management process and the need for government planning and intervention in the realm of business (Ickes, 1934: 76–96) to ensure that the vast majority benefits. And those gains are not only in terms of wages and working conditions but also the possibility of human development (Ickes, 1934: 97). His vision of the 'new democracy' was not a Marxist vision of a workers' state or one dominated by the large corporations, rather it was one where 'the people' as a whole have a democratic say over business affairs that affected them through strong government: "at last the Government is doing its job in the spirit of Jefferson and Lincoln. And the job in question is the management of the affairs of the United States for the greatest good for the greatest number of its people" (Ickes, 1934: 156).

Harry Hopkins – social evangelist

> We are beginning to wonder if it is not presumptuous to take for granted that some people should have much, and some people should have nothing; that some people are less important than others and should die earlier; that the children of the comfortable should be taller and fatter, as a matter of right, than the children of the poor.
>
> *(Hopkins, 1936: 184)*

At the end of May 1932, Roosevelt hired Harry Hopkins to head up the newly established Federal Emergency Relief Administration (FERA).[9] In a sharp contrast to Ickes, Hopkins moved into action straight away, authorizing $5 million in relief in his first two hours on the job (Golay, 2013: 33). In June he hired a journalist, Lorena Hickok, to travel the length and breadth of the country and take stock of the experiences of the people. He told Hickok, "to look things over. I don't want statistics from you. I don't want the social worker angle. I just want your reaction, as an ordinary citizen" (quoted in Golay, 2013: 39). Hickok's role was to send Hopkins regular reports so that he could keep on top of the experiences of the American people. Many of her reports were shared with FDR. Although formerly a social worker himself, Hopkins did not share the then dominant idea held by the profession that people should be treated either as victims (given charity) or as mistrusted shirkers (have their finances controlled). Hopkins felt those on relief should be provided with jobs to earn money and given their wages in cash rather than the more restrictive vouchers.

By November Hopkins was heading up the newly established Civil Works Administration (CWA) and then, in 1935 he took over the Works Progress Administration (WPA). In the first year of the CWA, Hopkins placed 2.6 million people in CWA jobs, and the number rose to 4.3 million the following year. Over an eight-year period, Hopkins oversaw the placement of 8.5 million people in 1.4 million projects at a cost of $11 billion (Taylor, 2008). The majority of the work involved a series of construction projects, but in a dramatic and controversial move[10] in 1935 Hopkins introduced Federal Project Number One (or Federal One) that saw the employment of over 40,000 artists, writers, actors, and musicians. For Hopkins, people's unique skills and talents should not go to waste but should be preserved, but artists also had to eat. Federal One saw payments to artists of all kinds to support them and enable them to pursue their art. This, arguably, benefited not only the artists themselves but also the American people as a whole. It created a society of citizens who were increasingly exposed to affordable and accessible artistic performances and works of art.

Thus, for Hopkins, the federal work programmes were not only about material but also about social and spiritual benefit. Federal One in particular not only led to creative developments in the arts (e.g. the work of Jackson Pollock) and theatre (e.g. the Black Theatre's version of *Macbeth*) but also came to imprint itself upon American history (e.g. state guidebooks and the establishment of Oral History archives on slavery).

While Ickes focused on the structuring of work in line with a new form of economic democracy, Hopkins focused on the social outcomes of work in terms of spirit, morale, creativity, and the development of a new society based on community values; issues rarely studied in management and organizational thinking.

Frances Perkins: the state and social welfare

> I first saw Franklin Roosevelt in 1910 at a tea dance … I was studying for a Master's degree and working in a settlement house on a survey of the social conditions in the neighborhood … I already had a conviction, a 'concern,' … about social justice; and it was clear in my own mind that the promotion of social justice could be made to work practically. As a student and professional social worker, I was taking an active part in proposals to use the legislative authority of the state to correct social abuses – long hours, low wages, bad housing, child labor, and unsanitary conditions.
>
> *(Perkins, 1947: 9–10)*

In March 1933 Frances Perkins was appointed Secretary of Labor in Roosevelt's administration – the first female cabinet member in US history. Before accepting the appointment "she laid before Roosevelt an extensive agenda, including unemployment and old-age insurance, minimum wages and maximum hours; and he told her to go ahead" (Schlesinger, 1959: 300). According to one commentator, Perkins' conditions "became the most lasting contributions of the New Deal … [and much] of the modern-day American social welfare system" (Alter, 2007: 166). Under Perkins' leadership and commitment the Social Security Act was passed into law on 15 August 1935. For many commentators this was the start and the hallmark of the Second New Deal (Alter, 2007; Kennedy, 2005).

Perkins' attitude towards social welfare was decidedly different from that of Hopkins. She viewed social welfare as a middle-class calling, something that one does for labour, and she was less interested in "enabling labor to do things for itself" (Kennedy, 2005: 146). It has been claimed "she was more interested in improvement of standards than on development of labor self-organization" (Kennedy, 2005: 146). Distrustful of corporate as well as union leaders, Perkins felt, like Ickes and Hopkins, that the state needed to take a hand in regulating business and looking after the social welfare of the great majority of people. By all accounts, Perkins had the greatest influence on the development of social welfare and public works programs (Cohen, 2009).

It is interesting to note that, alongside Mary Parker Follet and Mary van Kleeck,[11] several of the leading New Dealers shared a background in social welfare and social reform. Perkins and Hopkins (along with Berle) had come out of the social reform movement, which in turn was influenced by the Social Gospel tradition[12] (Kennedy, 2005; Hiltzik, 2011; Leuchtenburg, 2009). Many involved in social welfare reform were also involved in the industrial welfare movement through the early part of the twentieth century (Adler, 2003). This is an area of influence that has also been neglected by MOS.

The critics of the pro-business approach were not all avowed anti-capitalists. A few were socialists. Even fewer were communists. Most were liberal reformers (Hiltzik, 2011; Taylor, 2008; Morgan, 2003) seeking to temper the excesses of capitalism through various mechanisms of control (e.g. the Securities and Exchange Commission), standards (e.g. the NRA), and social welfare legislation (e.g. the Social Security Act). This latter group included a number of people, whose interest in politics and change developed out of experiences in a variety of social welfare agencies.

Discussion and conclusion

In arguing for introducing New Deal studies in MOS our aim has been twofold and paradoxical. On the one hand, we have attempted to surface the problematics of management and organizational history through (a) the neglect of the New Deal, and (b) the way that histories develop in the service of selected networks of actors. On the other hand, following Witzel's (2012: 103) call for "the circulation of as many management models and paradigms as possible," we have also tried to show the value of New Deal stories for MOS.

As to the first major point, we have argued that much of what counts as modern management thought was developed during the Cold War era, a context that shaped what was written, selected, or ignored. Subsequent histories served to further define and refine the boundaries of the emerging, but narrow, paradigm that would become MOS. As Morgan (2003) has contended, much of the struggles in the early post-Second World War/Cold War era were a continuation of 'battles' around New Deal legacies (see also Katznelson, 2013; Josephson, 1967), particularly those that favoured the bargaining rights of union leaders over those of ownership or management. Pre-war anti-communist attacks on the New Deal came from two powerful forces that were strengthened in the Cold War era – the House Un-American Activities Committee and the growing influence of the corporate business communities.[13] Ickes, Hopkins, and Perkins, among others, were accused during their time in office of being communists and, in the post-war era, rumours circulated about Hopkins being a Soviet spy (Andrew and Mitrokhin, 1999).[14] Senator Joseph McCarthy went one further in a 1954 speech in Charleston, West Virginia when, referring to the Democratic Party, he spoke of "[t]wenty years of treason" and their "historic betrayal" (McCarthy, 1954). Little wonder the New Deal became neglected in emerging MOS thought, theory, and history.[15]

Beyond the political dimensions we can also perceive various other reasons why the emergent field neglected the New Deal. One of the primary reasons, we would suggest, may lie in the fact that MOS tended, at first, to hone in on organizations as closed systems. But as the field progressed beyond this focus, even 'open systems' thinking had little or nothing to say about the socio-political environment in which work, management, and organizations existed. The New Deal, on the other hand, was based upon and offered philosophies and practices that focused on the interrelationships between business and the socio-political environment. It might also be argued the focus of New Deal policies was more about government than organizations; work rather than organization; politics rather than management; and philosophy rather than research.

Thus, it could be argued, New Deal studies are more appropriately assigned, respectively, to the disciplines of public administration, sociology of work, political science, and philosophy. While we understand these concerns we would argue this compounds the problem of disciplinary boundaries by referring the limits of MOS to the limits of other disciplines. Assigning New Deal studies to a specific discipline thus is arbitrary and the result of socio-political and historical contingency rather than anything inherent in management, organization, or research studies.

Current boundaries do not deal with the growing case for understanding business in context. Nor are the philosophizing aspects of New Deal practices grounds for disqualifying them. They are no less 'philosophical' than the works of Peter Drucker, Mary Parker Follett, Elton Mayo, the founding members of the Academy of Management, or Roethlisberger and Dickson (Rose, 1978; Grant and Mills, 2006; Graham, 1996) – all of whom are held up as key management thinkers.

With regard to our second major point, New Deal accounts raise numerous issues that challenge the dominant foci in MOS. Specifically these accounts raise issues about government owned, not-for-profit, and other, alternative, forms of organization; social welfarism and the notion of work as part of an organic concern with social as well as economic outcomes; and the idea of the atomized worker (Hoover's 'rugged individual') versus the 'social man' theories that surface in some aspects of MOS. It also raises issues of experimentation versus planning in management and organization; the role of government in business (e.g. the United States versus Canada); the continuing neglect of race, gender, and issues of power in MOS; the challenges of the divorce of culture and aesthetics from MOS; and finally, the lessons from the New Dealers' deliberations on the role of labour unions and relations with owners and managers in MOS. It strikes us that stories and tales of the New Deal offer new imaginings and new frontiers for MOS study into the twenty-first century, particularly in light of the ongoing period of worldwide economic downturn.

Finally, we would reiterate that we accept that New Deal programmes were not one-sidedly progressive nor without their faults in terms of the fate of working people, trade unions, people of colour, and women or support for some of the more 'seamier' sides of capitalism (Zinn, 1999; Katznelson, 2013), but to exclude New Deal studies on those grounds would also exclude study of much of what has been taken as management theory both in that era and beyond (Rose, 1978; Acker and van Houten, 1974; Benschop and Doorewaard, 1998; Nkomo, 1992). Before we can develop critiques of New Deal thinking we first need to open up historical dialogues around it and the implications it has for MOS today.

Combining poststructural notions of the differences between history and the past reveals how history is constructed by groups of actors who, through the selection and narration of facts, construct the domain boundaries of a field – in this case MOS. We also hope we have shown how the socio-political processes of knowledge production of actors and networks in MOS have served to deem certain facts as domain relevant (i.e. the delimiting effects of MOS histories as represented by our canonical understanding) through the exclusion of other facts considered domain irrelevant (i.e. the writing-out of the New Deal amongst others). Given that all of these facts are drawn from the very same socio-political context within which MOS activities, and its histories, developed, understanding the relationship of history and the past and the processes of history-making in MOS may help us bypass the constricting, artificial, and arbitrary nature of what we take as our domain of research and objects of study.

Notes

1 In making this assertion we distinguish between research into management, which clearly predates the Second World War, and the origins of the 'modern' form of Management and Organizational Studies as currently found in North American academia.
2 Lilienthal's (1944) study of the Tennessee Valley Authority is the one exception.
3 Both, however, fall into the trap of accepting the broader historical narrative of a field of study that began with scientific management, specifically the work of Taylor, and progressed through the Hawthorne Studies and the development of the Human Relations School. Nonetheless, each account offers useful insights into how knowledge is shaped through networks of human and non-human actors.

4 An interesting exception can be found in Urwick and Brech (1957) who discuss President Franklin Roosevelt's Committee on Administrative Management as proof of the extent of scientific management's impact on society. In a rare mention of the New Deal Ellen O'Connor's (1999) wonderful piece on the development of the Human Relations School, focuses on "the period between World War I and the New Deal", with no discussion of the latter.

5 A review of 26 management textbooks published between 1933 and 1949 were analysed for their treatment of the New Deal. Of the 26 textbooks only one, Koontz (1941), has anything to say about the New Deal and its relationship to management and organization. Fourteen make no reference to the New Deal and its agencies, while 10 others reference the NLR (or Wagner) Act but primarily to communicate new employer responsibilities under these regulatory regimes. The NLRB system is framed as being a problem and a complication for management. The final book focuses on leadership (Tead, 1935) and uses Roosevelt as an example of strong leadership, but contains no substantial discussion of the content of New Deal policies or of their impact on management or organization. The texts are part of the Sobey Management Textbook Collection of over 500 management textbooks, published between 1926 and 2013.

6 See <http://www.encyclopedia.chicagohistory.org/ pages/2900.html>.

7 Katznelson (2013) argues that the influence of New Deal thinking can be traced through to the onset of the 1960s.

8 For Coolidge "the chief business of the American people is business", and for Hoover "the sole function of government is to bring about a condition of affairs to the beneficial development of private enterprise" (Taylor, 2008).

9 Hopkins was no stranger to Roosevelt. Eighteen months earlier, as Governor of New York, Roosevelt had hired Hopkins to head up the State's Temporary Emergency Relief Administration.

10 Federal One – especially the Federal Theatre Program – became an early target of the House Un-American Activities Committee, under the leadership of Martin Dies, formerly established in 1938 (Flanagan 1965; Taylor, 2008).

11 Mary Parker Follett died in the United Kingdom in 1933 during the first year of the Roosevelt administration. Mary van Kleeck was offered a position on the Federal Advisory Council of the US Employment Service. She promptly resigned the position, protesting the NRA's "insufficient support for collective bargaining and the labor movement" (Alchon, 1992). She apparently feared that the New Deal proffered a new form of corporatism that was a harbinger of fascism rather than democracy (Nyland and Heenan, 2005).

12 The Social Gospel movement was influenced by the writings of New York Baptist minister Walter Rauschenbusch and emerged in the United States towards the end of the nineteenth century. Its basic tenets included the idea that unbridled competition was against the Christian faith and that "freedom and spiritual self-development required an equalization of wealth and power" (Foner, 2012). The various activities of Social Gospel adherents included the establishment of welfare missions and relief programmes and working with labour unions on issues of health and safety.

13 Established by Congress in 1938 to fight Nazism in the United States, the House Un-American Activities Committee (led by Texas Democrat Martin Dies) quickly turned on progressive forces (Taylor, 2008). One important corporate body at this time was the American Liberty League that included Alfred P. Sloan and other corporate leaders.

14 See also <http://www.frontpagemag.com/2013/john-earl-haynes-and-harvey-klehr/was-harry-hopkins-a-soviet-spy/>.

15 See, for example, the respective accounts by Schrecker (1986) and Summers (2011) on the influence of McCarthyism and the Federal Bureau of Investigations (FBI) on US campuses during the Cold War.

References

Acker, J. and van Houten, D. R. (1974) Differential recruitment and control: The sex structuring of organizations, *Administrative Science Quarterly*, 9(2): 152–63.

Adler, P. S. (2003) Towards collaborative independence: A century of change in the organization of work, in B. E. Kauffman, R. E. Beaumont, and R. B. Helfgott (eds), *Industrial Relations to Human Resources and Beyond: The Evolving Process of Employee Relations Management* (pp. 353–400). Armonk, NY: M. E. Sharpe.

Alchon, G. (1992) Mary Van Kleeck and scientific management, in D. Nelson (ed.), *Mental Revolution: Scientific Management since Taylor* (pp. 102–29). Chicago, IL: Ohio State University Press.

Alter, J. (2007) *The Defining Moment. FDR's Hundred Days and the Triumph of Hope*. New York: Simon & Schuster.

Andrew, C. and Mitrokhin, V. (1999) *The Mitrokhin Archive: The KGB in Europe and the West*. Harmondsworth: Penguin.

Barnes, R. M. (1940) *Motion and Time Study*. New York: John Wiley.

Benschop, Y. and Doorewaard, H. (1998) Six of one and half a dozen of the other: The gender subtext of Taylorism and team-based work, *Gender, Work and Organization*, 5(1): 5–18.

Berle, A. A. and Means, G. C. (1932) *Modern Corporation and Private Property*. New York and Chicago, IL: Commerce Clearing House.

Bruce, K. and Nyland, C. (2011) Elton Mayo and the deification of Human Relations, *Organization Studies*, 32(3): 383–405.

Burrell, G. and Morgan, G. (1979) *Sociological Paradigms and Organisational Analysis*. Burlington, VT: Ashgate.

Caute, D. (1979) *The Great Fear: The Anti-Communist Purge Under Truman and Eisenhower*. New York: Touchstone.

Cohen, A. (2009) *Nothing to Fear*. New York: Penguin.

Cooke, B. (1999) Writing the left out of management theory: The historiography of the management of change, *Organization*, 6(1): 81–105.

Durepos, G. and Mills, A. J. (2012a) Actor network theory, ANTi-history, and critical organizational historiography, *Organization*, 19(6): 703–21.

Durepos, G. and Mills, A. J. (2012b) *ANTi-History: Theorizing the Past, History, and Historiography in Management and Organizational Studies*. Charlotte, NC: Information Age Publishing.

Durepos, G., Helms Mills, J., and Mills, A. J. (2008) Tales in the manufacture of knowledge: Writing a company history of Pan American World Airways, *Management & Organizational History*, 3(1): 63–80.

Flanagan, H. (1965) *Arena: The History of the Federal Theatre*. New York: Benjamin Blom.

Foner, E. (2012) *Give Me Liberty! An American History*. New York: W.W. Norton.

Foster, J., Mills, A. J., and Weatherbee, T. G. (2014) The New Deal, history, and management & organization studies: Constructing disciplinary actors and theories, *Journal of Management History*.

Foucault, M. (1980) *Power/Knowledge*. New York: Pantheon.

Genoe McLaren, P. (2011) James Burnham, the managerial revolution, and the development of management theory in post-war America, *Management & Organizational History*, 6(4): 411–23.

George, C. S. (1968) *The History of Management Thought*. Englewood Cliffs, NJ: Prentice-Hall.

George, C. S. (1972) *The History of Management Thought* (2nd edn). Englewood Cliffs, NJ: Prentice-Hall.

Golay, M. (2013) *America 1933*. New York: Free Press.

Goldstein, R. J. (1978) *Political Repression in Modern America: 1870 to the Present*. Cambridge, MA: Schenkman Publishing.

Graham, P. (ed.) (1996) *Mary Parker Follett: Prophet of Management*. Cambridge, MA: Harvard Business School Press.

Grant, J. D. and Mills, A. (2006) The quiet Americans: Formative context, the Academy of Management leadership, and the management textbook, 1936–1960, *Management & Organizational History*, 1: 201–24.

Green, A. and Troup, K. (1999) *The Houses of History: A Critical Reader in Twentieth-Century History and Theory*. New York: New York University Press.

Hartt, C. M. (2013) The non-corporeal actant as a link between actor-network theory and critical sensemaking: A case study of Air Canada, PhD Thesis, Saint Mary's University, Halifax, Nova Scotia.

Hearn, J. and Parkin, P. W. (1983) Gender and organizations: A selective review and a critique of a neglected area, *Organization Studies*, 4(3): 219–42.

Hiltzik, M. (2011) *The New Deal: A Modern History*. New York: Free Press.

Hopkins, H. L. (1936) *Spending to Save: The Complete Story of Relief*. New York: W.W. Norton.

Ickes, H. L. (1934) *The New Democracy*. New York: W.W. Norton.

Ickes, H. L. (1935) *Back to Work: The Story of PWA*. New York: Macmillan.

Ickes, H. L. (1953) *The Secret Diary of Harold L. Ickes: The First Thousand Days, 1933–1936*. New York: Simon & Schuster.

Ickes, H. L. (1954) *The Secret Diary of Harold L. Ickes: The Inside Struggle, 1936–1939*. New York: Simon & Schuster.

Jenkins, K. (1991) *Re-thinking History*. London and New York: Routledge.

Jenkins, K. (1995) *On 'What is history?' From Carr and Elton to Rorty and White*. London: Routledge.

Josephson, M. (1967) *Infidel in the Temple: A Memoir of the Nineteen-Thirties*. New York: Alfred A. Knopf.

Kalela, J. (2012) *Making History: The Historian and Uses of the Past*. Basingstoke: Palgrave Macmillan.

Katznelson, I. (2013) *Fear Itself: The New Deal and the Origins of Our Time*. New York: W.W. Norton.

Kelley, E. S., Mills, A. J., and Cooke, B. (2006) Management as a Cold War phenomenon?, *Human Relations*, 59(5): 603–10.

Kennedy, D. M. (2005) *Freedom From Fear*. Oxford: Oxford University Press.

Khurana, R. (2007) *From Higher Aims to Hired Hands: The Social Transformation of American Business Schools and the Unfulfilled Promise of Management as a Profession*. Princeton, NJ: Princeton University Press.

Koontz, H. (1941) *Government Control of Business*. Boston: Houghton Mifflin/Riverside Press.

Koontz, H. (ed.) (1962) *Toward a Unified Theory of Management*. New York: McGraw-Hill.

Kuhn, T. S. (1962) *The Structure of Scientific Revolutions*. Chicago, IL: University of Chicago Press.

Landau, O. (2006) Cold War political culture and the return of systems rationality, *Human Relations*, 59(5): 637–63.

Latour, B. (1988) *The Pasteurization of France*. Cambridge, MA: Harvard University Press.

Latour, B. (2005) *Reassembling the Social: An Introduction to Actor-Network-Theory*. Oxford: Oxford University Press.

Law, J. (1994) *Organizing Modernity*. Oxford: Blackwell.

Lebergott, S. (1957) Annual estimates of unemployment in the United States, 1900–1954, in Universities-National Bureau (ed.), *The Measurement and Behavior of Unemployment* (pp. 211–42). National Bureau of Economic Research.

Leuchtenburg, W. E. (2009) *Frankilin D. Roosevelt and the New Deal*. New York: Harper.

Lewin, K., Lippitt, R., and White, R. K. (1939) Patterns of aggressive behavior in experimentally created 'social climates', *Journal of Social Psychology*, 10: 271–99.

Lilienthal, D. E. (1944) *TVA Tennessee Valley Authority: Democracy on the March*. Harmondsworth: Penguin.

McCarthy, J. (1954) Speech in Charleston, West Virginia, February 4, http://www.youtube.com/watch?v=e4LZsDqSSfk

McGregor, D. (1957) The human side of enterprise, *Management Review*, 46(11): 22–28.

Mannheim, K. (1985) *Ideology and Utopia: An Introduction to the Sociology of Knowledge*. New York: Harcourt Brace.

Maslow, A. H. (1954) *Motivation and Personality*. New York: Harper.

Mayo, E. (1933) *The Human Problems of an Industrial Civilization*. New York: Macmillan.

Mills, A. J. and Durepos, G. (2010) ANTi-History, in A. J. Mills, G. Durepos, and E. Wiebe (eds), *Sage Encyclopedia of Case Study Research* (pp. 26–29). Thousand Oaks, CA: Sage.

Mills, A. J., Weatherbee, T. G., and Durepos, G. (2014) Reassembling Weber: The-past-as-history in management and organization studies, *Organization*, 21(2): 225–43.

Morgan, T. (2003) *Reds: McCarthyism in Twentieth-Century America*. New York: Random House.

Muldoon, J. (2012) The Hawthorne legacy: A reassessment of the impact of the Hawthorne Studies on management scholarship, 1930–1958, *Journal of Management History*, 18(1): 105–19.

Munslow, A. (2010) *The Future of History*. Basingstoke: Palgrave Macmillan.

Myrick, K., Helms Mills, J., and Mills, A. J. (2013) History-making and the Academy of Management: An ANTi-history perspective, *Management & Organizational History*, 8(4): 345–70.

Nkomo, S. (1992) The emperor has no clothes: Rewriting 'race in organizations', *Academy of Management Review*, 17(3): 487–513.

Nyland, C. and Heenan, T. (2005) Mary van Kleeck, Taylorism and the control of management knowledge, *Management Decision*, 43(10): 1358–74.

O'Connor, E. S. (1999) The politics of management thought: A case study of the Harvard Business School and the Human Relations School, *Academy of Management Review*, 24(1): 117–31.

Perkins, F. (1947) *The Roosevelt I Knew*. New York: Viking Press.

Phipps, S. T. A. (2011) Mary, Mary, quite contrary, *Journal of Management History*, 17(3): 270–81.

Robbins, S. P. (1988) *Essentials of Organizational Behavior* (2nd edn). Englewood Cliffs, NJ: Prentice-Hall.

Robbins, S. P. (1989) *Organizational Behavior: Concepts, Controversies, and Applications* (4th edn). Englewood Cliffs, NJ: Prentice-Hall.

Robin, R. (2001) *The Making of the Cold War Enemy*. Princeton, NJ: Princeton University Press.

Roethlisberger, F. J. and Dickson, W. J. (1939) *Management and the Worker*. Cambridge, MA: Harvard University Press.

Rose, M. (1978) *Industrial Behaviour*. Harmondsworth: Penguin.

Rowbotham, S. (1999) *A Century of Women: A History of Women in Britain and the United States*. London: Penguin.

Schilling, M. A. (2000) Decades ahead of her time: Advancing stakeholder theory through the ideas of Mary Parker Follett, *Journal of Management History*, 6(5): 224–42.

Schlesinger, A. M. (ed.) (1959) *The Age of Roosevelt: The Coming of the New Deal*. Boston, MA: Houghton Mifflin.

Schrecker, E. (1986) *No Ivory Tower: McCarthyism & the Universities*. New York: Oxford University Press.

Shenhav, Y. and Weitz, E. (2000) The roots of uncertainty in organization theory: A historical constructivist analysis, *Organization*, 7(3): 373–401.

Summers, A. (2011) *Official and Confidential: The Secret Life of J. Edgar Hoover*. New York: Ebury Press.

Tadajewski, M. (2006) The ordering of marketing theory: The influence of McCarthyism and the Cold War, *Marketing Theory*, 6(2): 163–200.

Tancred-Sheriff, P. and Campbell, E. J. (1992) Room for women: A case study in the sociology of organizations, in A. J. Mills and P. Tancred (eds), *Gendering Organizational Analysis* (pp. 315). Newbury Park, CA: Sage.

Taylor, F. W. (1911) *Principles of Scientific Management*. New York: Harper & Row.

Taylor, N. (2008) *American-Made: The Enduring Legacy of the WPA*. New York: Bantam Dell.

Tead, O. (1935) *The Art of Leadership*. New York: McGraw-Hill.

Tugwell, R. G. (1933) *The Industrial Discipline and the Governmental Arts*. New York: Columbia University Press.

Unger, R. M. (2004) *False Necessity: Anti-Necessitarian Social Theory in the Service of Radical Democracy*. London and New York: Verso.

Urwick, L. (ed.) (1956) *The Golden Book of Management: A Historical Record of the Life and Work of Seventy Pioneers*. London: Newman Neame.

Urwick, L. and Brech, E. F. L. (1957) *The Making of Scientific Management: Thirteen Pioneers*, 3 vols. London: Sir Isaac Pitman & Sons.

Weatherbee, T. G., Durepos, G., Mills, A. J., and Helms Mills, J. (2012) Theorizing the past: Critical engagements, *Management & Organizational History*, 7(3): 193–202.

White, H. (1965) The burden of history, *History and Theory*, 5(2): 111–34.

White, H. (1973) *Metahistory: The Historical Imagination in Nineteenth-Century Europe*. Balitimore, MD: Johns Hopkins University Press.

Witzel, M. (2012) *A History of Management Thought*. London: Routledge.

Wren, D. A. (1972) *The Evolution of Management Thought*. New York: Ronald Press.

Wren, D. A. (1979) *The Evolution of Management Thought* (2nd edn). New York: Ronald Press.

Wren, D. A. and Bedeian, A. G. (2009) *The Evolution of Management Thought* (6th edn). Hoboken, NJ: John Wiley.

Zinn, H. (1999) *A People's History of the United States, 1492–Present*. New York: HarperCollins.

20

Capitalist ideologues and the Cold War "struggle for men's minds"

Bert Spector

Writing in a 1957 *Harvard Business Review* article, securities lawyer J. Anthony Panuch expressed his disdain for ideology; not a particular ideology, but the very idea of ideology. Ideologies "may be primarily altruistic or they may be simply dressed up in moral clothing to make them successful." Whatever their nature, ideologies "get in the way of sound, rational … policy planning and execution" (Panuch, 1957: 42). Here, Panuch was expressing a common theme among both business practitioners and observers. Participants in management discourse typically profess to be blind to, even antagonistic toward, the use of ideology. Twenty years after Panuch's piece, Harvard Business School Professor George Lodge suggested that reluctance to acknowledge ideology was a particularly *American* phenomenon (Lodge, 1977). In the United States, ideologies were viewed as alien constructs, essentially European in origin. Communism, fascism, totalitarianism – these and other 'isms' – denoted non-American or even un-American activities.

That insistence on denying the essentially ideological nature of American business values was, in Lodge's view, "nonsense" (Lodge, 1977: 9).

Ideology refers to a widely shared and internally consistent belief system. It provides a value-based lens through which adherents view, understand, and react to external events. Ideologues believe their arguments to be rational, and aspire to have their arguments accepted as factual (Walsby, 1946; Bendix, 1956; Althusser, 1961; Anthony, 1977; Shrivastava, 1986; Burke, 1999; Mayer, 2001; Foley, 2004). In recent years, a number of scholars have worked to recognize and analyze the ideological foundation of management discourse, focusing on specific management practices: industrial relations, human relations, employee motivation, strategic planning, organizational change, executive compensation, corporate social responsibility, and shareholder value among them (Harris, 1982; Guillen, 1994; Shrivastava, 1986; Kleiner, 1996; Dye, Mills, and Weatherbee, 2005; Gantman, 2005; Diefenbach, 2007; Spector, 2008a; Spector & Spital, 2011; Stout, 2012).

In this chapter,[1] I look at the ideology not of a specific management practice but at the ideology of capitalism itself. In the immediate post-Second World War years, American executives and academics willingly, even enthusiastically, embraced ideology, expressing a need to articulate an ideology of capitalism. Although the arguments took many forms and occasionally divergent positions, they amounted to a coherent and consistent belief system based on four core tenets:

- That the overall well-being of a society is best judged by the *per capita income* of individual citizens.
- That business, insulated from government *interference* but aided by government *promotion*, could and would solve the problems of the nation.
- That expansive capitalism would *eliminate poverty* and obliterate *class distinctions*.
- That liberal market capitalism represented the *natural order of things*, an order ordained by God and embedded in the most fundamental beliefs of Christianity.

This set of beliefs was held to be well suited not just for the United States but for the rest of the world, particularly the underdeveloped world.

I have adopted the term liberal market capitalism from the "varieties of capitalism" argument first put forth by Hall and Soskice (2001). They identified two primary capitalist paradigms. A Liberal Market Economy (LME) relied on market relations to insure unfettered competition and access to markets and capital. LME endorsed an essentially passive role for the state, calling on voluntary actions of business executives to protect competition, labor, consumers, and the environment. In contrast, a Coordinated Market Economy (CME) addressed fundamental coordination problems through collaboration and strategic interaction among multiple stakeholders, most especially business and the government.

Subsequent to the publication of Hall and Soskice's 2001 book, there have been occasional critiques of their bifurcation of capitalism into just two varieties (see, for example, Coates, 2005). Regardless of those challenges, the general premises of the varieties of capitalism thesis generated a robust stream of research (for a review of the literature, see Wilkins, 2010), the conclusions of which can be captured in three generalizations. First, no single variety can lay claim to being the one, legitimate mode of capitalism. Second, all varieties have demonstrated a capacity for creating dynamic economic growth. And third, no variety can be strongly correlated with the presence of democratic institutions in the host society.

During the Cold War, economist Kenneth Boulding (1959) proposed a framework with some apparent similarities. Like Hall and Soskice would do over four decades later, Boulding posited two systems: a market-justified system "in which the individual obtains his livelihood by selling his services or products to anyone who will buy them" (Boulding, 1959: 43), and a budget-justified system that emphasized plans, budgets, and other centralized controlling mechanisms. Although that argument appears, at first glance, to be consistent with the Hall–Soskice thesis, there was a vital distinction. Boulding did not articulate two varieties of *capitalism*. Rather, he equated capitalism with the market-justified system. The budget-justified system, however, amounted not to a variety of capitalism but to communism.

That distinction is vital. Budget-justified systems were not legitimate alternatives to capitalism. Rather, they represented a "crudely manipulative society," explained Boulding, that "rightly fills us with disgust and fear" (Boulding, 1952: 40). Boulding was doing more than analyzing. He was advocating for a particular variety of capitalism to be taken as the sole alternative to a disgusting, fearful, and manipulative budget-justified system.

The ideology of liberal market capitalism fit the dynamics of the age. The Cold War era was shaped by three key challenges, one external to the United Stated and the other two internal.

- Externally, American capitalism faced a major competitor, often depicted as a 'threat': Soviet Communism. The Soviet Union was seen as a hearty economic power. Sure, individual freedoms were sacrificed – and *individual* freedoms remained a cornerstone of the capitalist ideology – but Soviet economic growth was real and potentially threatening to US hegemony (Flanders, 1945; Copland, 1945; Prince, 1946; Abbott, 1953; Butler, 1956).

- Internally, domestic forces were openly challenging the assumptions of liberal market capitalism. In order to avoid a return to Great Depression levels of unemployment, New Deal liberals who controlled the White House through 1952 endorsed a strong role for government as a way to ensure economic growth, full employment, and equitable distribution of income. In the view of capitalist ideologues, that advocacy for a coordinated market economy amounted to a threat to not just capitalism but to something they frequently referred to – as if it were a unitary and commonly understood concept – as the American way of life (Wright, 1945; Gras, 1949; Donald, 1950; Miller, 1951).
- A second internal challenge, rarely acknowledged explicitly, was the evolution of giant conglomerates (Sobel, 1984, 1993). Conglomerates grew not through traditional methods but by amassing portfolios of unrelated investments. Their rise was fueled by pent-up demand created during the Second World War, huge infusions of federal spending on Cold War weaponry, and federal antitrust enforcement that unwittingly encouraged large-scale circular or non-related diversification.[2] Suspicion of big business and the motives of the men who directed large corporations ran deep throughout the country's history (Pollack, 1962; Thelen, 1972; Goodwyn, 1978; Thelen, 1986; Kazin, 1998; McGerr, 2003). The collapse of capitalism during the Great Depression reinforced a general notion, widely shared among the American public, that "a few rich men and large corporations" wielded a disproportionate and unhealthy amount of power (Gallup, 1972: 277). And there was evidence from popular culture that the American public remained uncertain of – if not alienated from – these giant conglomerates (see, for example, Spector, 2008b).

It was in this socio-historical context that a theory of liberal market capitalism emerged.[3]

The Cold War era in the United States offers an especially rich opportunity for analyzing the intersection of management and ideology (e.g. Cooke, Mills, and Kelley, 2005; Cooke, 2006; Kelley, Mills, and Cooke, 2006; Landau, 2006; Runté & Mills, 2006; Spector, 2006, 2008a, 2008b). The period was characterized by a strong, consistent, and widely shared ideology that shaped views of foreign threats and domestic anxieties (Spector, 2006). Difficult global dynamics were blurred by what historian Paul Boyer called a "starkly bipolar analytic framework," one that oversimplified the complexities of a fragmented post-war world and denied many disconfirming realities (Boyer, 1999: 92).

The years 1945 through 1960 do not encompass the entirety of what is generally identified as the Cold War era: the epoch spanning the 1945 collapse of the Second World War allied coalition (Dobbs, 2012) and the 1991 implosion of the Soviet Union (McCauley, 2004). The focus of this chapter ends at 1960, a year that represents not so much an end to the Cold War as a significant alteration in tone and content. Fear of domestic espionage largely evaporated despite the ongoing insistence of the increasingly out-of-touch FBI director J. Edgar Hoover. The anti-communist blacklist that held such powerful sway over Hollywood crumbled, symbolized by the willingness of Hollywood studios to entrust large-budget projects to formerly blacklisted writers and directors. Even the President-elect, John F. Kennedy, viewed *Spartacus*, one of the first Hollywood films to openly employ a blacklisted writer, despite the picketing of the American Legion. Unconscionably, the television networks maintained this Red Scare legacy through much of the 1960s, but even that unwillingness to embrace a new cultural moment attracted widespread comment and protest (Spector, 2008a).

The chapter adopts intellectual history as its broad framework for analysis. That framework is broad because 'intellectual history' is a far from specified field of inquiry (Gordon, 2007). The point of reference for my approach is Higham's (1961) classic definition of intellectual history as the history of thought. Specifically, intellectual historians ask how and why ideas occur when they do. The sociohistorical context of the focal idea – in this case, the articulation of a liberal market capitalist ideology – must be appreciated by the intellectual historian (Gordon, 2007). An appreciation of the context in which an idea is expressed, however, does *not* divest the historian of a responsibility to offer a critical weighing of its tenability.

Locating management discourse in the *Harvard Business Review*

In order to analyze Cold War management discourse, the chapter focuses on one particular forum: the *Harvard Business Review* (hereafter, the *Review*). My choice of focus is based on the particular importance and influence of that publication, as well as its university owner/sponsor, the Harvard Business School (HBS). Founded in 1908, HBS was among a small number of university-affiliated business schools at the time seeking to professionalize the education of managers in America. The goal of HBS, along with the University of Pennsylvania's Wharton School (founded in 1881) and Dartmouth's Amos Tuck School of Business Administration (1900), was to increase executives' awareness "of themselves as constituting as distinct occupational group, separate from labor and capital" (Khurana, 2007: 93).

HBS graduates soon dominated the ranks of MBA-educated executives in corporate America (Newcomer, 1965; Mayo, Nohria, and Singleton, 2006). HBS expanded its influence further by virtue of its becoming the primary training ground of case-based teaching among business school professors. Large supporting grants from the Carnegie and Ford Foundations recognized and reinforced HBS's leadership role in developing the MBA curriculum that would help shape the thought processes of future industry leaders. HBS gained specific prominence during the post-war years due to the broad influence of its Dean, Donald K. David, who served on federal commissions and corporate boards and as a member of the Ford Foundation's board of trustees, eventually sitting as chairman of its executive committee. He became, according to Khurana (2007), a prototypical member of America's new power elite.

HBS's founding dean Wallace B. Donham launched the *Review* in 1922 with the goal for the *Review* as providing executives with the "breadth of view so urgently demanded of business administrators in this century" (quoted in Bates, 1942: 3). The *Review*'s ambition extended beyond publishing helpful how-to articles on management techniques. From its inception, the *Review* proclaimed its intention to create what Donham referred to as a "broad executive theory" that would allow readers to learn effectively from the experience of others in order to move business beyond an "unsystematic, haphazard, and for many men, a pathetic gamble" (Donham, 1922: 1). Harvard University President A. Lawrence Lowell expanded on Donham's desire to codify knowledge by extolling the formation of a "business administration" profession, one in which practitioners seek not just to "raise the level of the profession" but to "increase its usefulness to mankind" (Lowell, 1923: 129).

During the Cold War, the *Review* was not the nation's most popular business-oriented publication. That distinction belonged to *Fortune*, a magazine owned and managed by Henry Luce, who maintained an explicit political agenda promoting Cold War ideology (Brinkley, 2010). The *Review*, however, was unique at the time in its affiliation with a university. It attracted major management theorists from the worlds of academics, consulting, and practice who mingled with economists and other intellectuals on its pages.

The post-Second World War years saw readership for business-oriented publications, including *Fortune* and *Business Week*, explode (see Yarrow, 2006 for a history of financial coverage in the popular press). General interest magazines such as *Life* and daily newspapers including the *New York Times* featured business news more prominently than ever. With the emergence of post-war prosperity and economic growth – GNP increased from $221 billion in 1945 to $284 billion in 1950 (Sobel, 1993) – as well as a fierce economic competition with the Soviet Union, business became a story of national interest and significance. The *Review* experienced explosive growth, its circulation expanding from 6,000 in 1946 to 35,000 by 1953 (Landry, 2005).

I have reviewed the approximately 500 articles that appeared in the *Review* between 1945 and 1960. The vast majority of these articles focus on technical aspects of the business enterprise – finance and accounting, marketing, and so forth – as well as regular industry analysis: housing, automobiles, steel, and the like. I have devoted special attention to articles in which the authors reflected explicitly on the nature of American capitalism and the role of America in the world's economy, along with the technical articles that occasionally contained statements of ideology. No attempt has been made to determine the political views of the *Review*'s editors at the time except as expressed explicitly in the *Review* itself. Likewise, I have not tried to ascertain the degree to which authors were expressing their 'real' views or purposefully using obfuscation and misdirection to advance hidden agendas. This is a work of intellectual history based on a qualitative analysis of the explicitly stated thoughts of the authors.

The Cold War as an ideological construct

The Cold War opened with an American President, Harry Truman (who had been Vice President for just three months when President Franklin Roosevelt died in April 1945), confronting a world devastated by war and sharply divided by tension among former allies. The European conflict came to an end a month later, and the Pacific war ended in August with Truman's deployment of two atomic bombs. Joseph Stalin, USSR leader from 1929 to his death in 1953, had already made known his intention of leading the worldwide struggle against what Marxists typically referred to as "capitalist imperialists" (Dobbs, 2012). Soviet leadership continued its iron-fisted rule over Eastern Europe as well as its hyper-aggressive rhetoric following Stalin's death, most famously with the 1956 crushing of the Hungarian Revolt and Khrushchev's provocative 1956 "We will bury you" speech.

Cold War ideology refracted empirical judgments through often-distorted perceptions. By the time the President announced the Truman Doctrine in March 1947 – the commitment of the United States to "support free peoples who are resisting attempted subjugation by armed minorities or by outside pressures" – the two basic tenets of the Cold War ideology were in place. The first was the belief that post-war tensions should be viewed through a starkly bipolar framework (Boyer, 1999). In the President's 1947 speech to Congress, he divided the world into two: a way of life "based on the will of the majority … distinguished by free institutions, representative government, [and] free elections," and the other way of life based on the "will of a minority, forcibly imposed upon a majority" (quoted in McCauley, 2004: 83). That bipolar view became officially embedded in US foreign policy in 1950 in the top-secret and highly influential National Security Document, NSC-68 (McCauley, 2004).

Implicit in that bipolar framework was a blurring of distinctions and divisions on *both* sides of the divide. Truman's "free world" included any number of governments – from Greece, Spain, Iran, and Nationalist China to military dictatorships in Latin America – that manifestly failed to meet his own specifications for free institutions, representative government, and open elections. On the other side, the Communist monolith was, in reality, an uneasy, often acrimonious blend of national distinctions, ideological variation, and local political realities (Gaddis, 2005).

The second key element of Cold War ideology was a belief that Soviet intentions went beyond the realpolitik demands of sovereignty, national interest, and control, however ruthlessly pursued. Communism, it was held, represented "a massive, ideologically-based assault upon everything Americans valued" (Freeland, 1972: 9). Totalitarianism would replace democracy everywhere, including in the United States, should the Communist victory be complete. Godlessness would supplant the Judeo-Christian tradition, and the world would be transported "back into the dark ages and beyond" (David, 1949: 2).

Defining capitalism as a Cold War ideology

The term 'capitalism,' like other labels used to define economic systems, is a highly generalized concept, typically referring to the web of institutions and organizations in which property is owned and production and distribution occur. Frederick Pryor offered greater specificity when he defined capitalism as "an economic system in which goods, labor, land, and financial services are transferred through relatively competitive markets and in which the means of production are primarily owned privately or by groups of individuals, rather than by governments." Prices fluctuate largely based on the law of supply and demand, and government regulations are called upon mainly to enforce contracts and protect private property (Pryor, 2010: 8–9).

Even that definition, as Pryor conceded, offered much room for variation. Terms like 'relatively,' 'primarily,' 'largely,' and 'mainly' present expansive opportunities for interpretation. The opportunity to replace generality with specificity was taken up by capitalist ideologues in the Cold War years. Because the Communist challenge of that era was interpreted and understood largely in ideological terms, it is not surprising that an effort was made to offer a contrary ideology that, it was hoped, would appeal to the American public and the world, while simultaneously advancing the interests of corporate America. That felt need to articulate an ideology also grew from regular expressions of defensiveness by *Review* authors.

A sense of siege

In the immediate aftermath of the Second World War, Peter Drucker's unexpectedly popular study of General Motors, *Concept of the Corporation*, asserted that the war had made large corporations "the representative institution of American society." The public, claimed Drucker, embraced "the privately-owned, independently managed corporation" which "sets the standards for the way of life and the mode of living of our citizens" (Drucker, 1946: 3, 6, 7). Undoubtedly, America's experience in the war helped refurbish the reputation of business that had been so damaged during the Depression. Through the application of sophisticated public relations techniques, corporations "incessantly proclaimed their patriotism and the indispensability of their huge productive capacity," writes Ronald Merchand. Even companies focused on consumer goods "found ways of touting their own sacrifices as they preached wartime sacrifices to the public" (Merchand, 1998: 119, 320). The reputation of big business now took on a "fresh luster" as corporations pointed to their "Can Do" contribution to America's victory (Boyer, 1999: 68).

Public attitudes reflected much more unease than might be inferred from Drucker's sweeping claim. A 1949 public opinion poll with results published in the *Review* revealed that there existed a large body of opinion "which is convinced that business is at best amoral and at worst greedy" (Roper, 1949: 171). Before the Second World War had even ended, *Review* writers were warning that underlying public unease was both more widespread and more dangerous than many readers realized. It was not just the Communist challenge mounted by the Soviet Union, although that was deemed to be potent. There were also internal enemies. "During the past 50 years," wrote University of Virginia economics professor David McCord Wright in 1945, "the trend in economic thought has been increasingly in the anti-capitalist direction." That attack on capitalism was so widespread that "now there is virtually no line of conduct which the businessman can follow without inviting condemnation" (Wright, 1945: 393).

And who were these domestic anti-capitalists? "Social idealists" (Flanders, 1945: 439), an uninformed public (Bursk, 1948 – the *Review*'s editor at the time), unions (Rowe, 1949), fiction writers (Gras, 1949), welfare state advocates (David, 1950 – HBS Dean at the time), workers (Stevenson, 1951), liberals (Miller, 1951), conformists (Levitt, 1956 – a future *Review* editor), intellectuals (Hoover, 1959[4]), and even foreign agents who had allegedly penetrated the domestic economy (Abbott, 1948a, 1948b). David McCord Wright (1945) identified the anti-capitalist ideology as consisting of three tenets: the use of taxation to redistribute wealth, the encouragement of greater participation of labor in the management of business, and the demand for greater business–industry–government cooperation. The pressing question facing the United States, wrote Studebaker CEO and Chairman of the Committee for Economic Development Paul Hoffman in 1946, "is not whether capitalism, with its emphasis on individual freedom and opportunity will sweep the world, but whether ... we can maintain it here in our own country" (Hoffman, 1946: 21). Both Wright and Hoffman conflated capitalism with a single variety: liberal market capitalism. Capitalism of the collective market type was condemned as a threat to the American way of life, and critics of liberal market capitalism denounced as a clear and present danger.

Articulating an ideology

Review authors rallied to defend and promote a set of concepts that were variously labeled "the private enterprise economy" (Sumberg, 1945: 167), the "American way of life" (Copland, 1945), "a free economy with free enterprise" (Hoffman, 1946: 21), and the "free business enterprise" (Johnson, 1957). "If the system is to endure," David McCord Wright warned, "an ideological reconstruction is imperative" (Wright, 1945: 393). *Review* editor Edward Bursk agreed, writing, "Actually, what management wants to sell is its own philosophy rather than an economic system as such" (Bursk, 1948: 374). So, what exactly was the system under siege and in need of an ideological defense? To answer that, *Review* authors coalesced on four key themes.

Minimum government interference combined with optimum government promotion

The call for "minimum government interference" in order to protect "the private enterprise society" (Sumberg, 1945: 157, 167) was a constant theme expressed by *Review* authors. In a liberal market economy, it was enterprise owners (presumably represented by manager-agents, although 'agency theory' had yet to be articulated) who took all the risks. It was therefore owners who, according to the 'Golden Rule,' should have the unfettered and unregulated ability to make decisions (Dale, 1960). Lincoln Gordon added that "the 'divine right to fail'" marked "the hallmark of private enterprise" (Gordon, 1960: 136).

It is not surprising that the role of the government represented a particular challenge in the immediate post-war years. The New Deal and the war effort had invited the government into the affairs of commerce to a degree not experienced previously. With the 1935 formation of the Congress of Industrial Organizations and passage of the Wagner Act, organized labor gained new strength and militancy (Galenson, 1960). That invitation to the government's participation, in turn, invited spirited and at times ferocious opposition from business voices represented by the Liberty League, the National Association of Manufacturers, and the US Chamber of Commerce (Fones-Wolf, 1994).

In the immediate post-war years, with the federal government led by New Dealer Harry Truman, the role of the state in economic affairs was still up for debate. Public option polls indicated that support for an active government role in the economy was strong and *growing* (Tedlow, 1979). In particular, a proposed Full Employment Bill would have embedded Keynesian economics in the quest to avoid massive unemployment through government spending. The lobbying efforts of the Business Advisory Council and the Committee for Economic Development succeeded in altering the bill to assert the role of private enterprise rather than the involvement of the federal government in achieving full employment (Fones-Wolf, 1994). Although business interests seemed on the ascendancy with the adoption of a much-enfeebled Full Employment Act and the weakening of the Wagner Act with Taft-Hartley, the 1948 presidential election sent a shock wave through the business community. Truman, the candidate advocating a stronger Full Employment bill and the repeal of Taft-Hartley won unexpectedly. Now what?

Truman's New Deal/Keynesian agenda ground to a halt with the 1948 mid-term elections and the 1952 Republican victory led by the ostensibly business-friendly Dwight Eisenhower. It was in the years leading up to the Eisenhower election that *Review* writers warned against the dire consequences of a resurgent central government. "Nothing would be more hostile to 'the American way of life'," wrote economist Douglas Copland, than "the intrusion of government into industry" (Copland, 1945: 418–19). HBS professor N. S. B. Gras went even further in warning of the "threat" of a coordinated market economy, suggesting that the New Deal fostered "fascism" in the United States by establishing "control over business from Washington" (Gras, 1949: 435).[5] A return to New Deal policies would firmly establish fascism in the United States.

Condemnation of government "interference" as a concept should not be equated with "wise action" (Knorr, 1946: 394) on the part of government. Indeed, a number of writers suggested that the interest of business would be best served not through a laissez-faire approach by government, but rather through selective government protection and promotion. The call for government protection typically focused on foreign trade: the promotion of "a sustained high demand for the export of American goods and services" combined with high tariffs and import duties to protect American industry (Korican, 1946: 499; Knorr, 1946; Hoffman, 1946).

Writing in the *Journal of Politics*, James Prothro suggested that the real objection of the capitalist ideologues was not directed at government intervention per se but rather to government intervention in response to the "voice of the people" (Prothro, 1953: 80). Governmental protections and promotions sponsored by businessmen were fine; governmental interventions on behalf of the public represented a drift toward socialism (David, 1950). "Speaking generally," Paul Hoffman added to his call for government "promotion" of international private trade, "the most vital function of the Federal Government is to create conditions under which free business [i.e., *unregulated* business] and free labor [i.e., *non-unionized* labor] can function more effectively in the general public interest" (Hoffman, 1946: 24).

The preordained order of things

In the context of the Cold War, liberal market capitalism was seen to have God on its side. Cold War ideology emphasized the perceived Soviet threat not just to US hegemony, but also as a challenge to the Western institutions of religion. Karl Marx had famously denounced religion as the "opiate of the masses," and, according to historian Richard Ellis, "in the early years of the Cold War, religious language infused political rhetoric and national identity in new and significant ways" (Ellis, 2005: 127). Congress created National Prayer Day in 1952, inserted "one Nation under God" into the Pledge of Allegiance in 1954, and added "In God We Trust" to paper money the next year.

Review writers during the 1950s frequently conflated religious values with capitalism, publishing a number of religiously-oriented pieces: "Business and Religion," "Religious Foundations of Economic Progress," "Capitalism and Christianity," and "Can the Businessman Apply Christianity?" (Culliton, 1949; Boulding, 1952; Campbell, 1957; Johnson, 1957). Even discussions of the newly emergent field of human relations contained references to spiritual values, as when consultants Elizabeth and Francis Jennings defined among basic human needs being "loyal to whatever is within ourselves which makes us keep our agreement with God" (Jennings & Jennings, 1951: 55).

If Communism represented Godlessness, then capitalism – in the dichotomous thinking of the Cold War – stood at the opposite end of the spectrum. West Virginia University Professor Thomas Campbell drew the connection explicitly. "Because the free-enterprise system produces greater economic progress than would be possible under any other economic system known at the present," he wrote, "it is doing more to advance the broader goals of Christianity than could any other existing arrangement" (Campbell, 1957: 43).

Review writers did not view the alignment between capitalism and Christianity uncritically. Modern-day capitalism, wrote Kenneth Boulding, tends to reward speculation rather than hard work and savings, thus negating some of the basic premises of the Protestant work ethic. The general sense of the articles, however, was that business and Christianity were co-dependent and able to bring out the best in each other. Adherence to Christian values on the part of executives would make them "less likely to commit the idolatry of worshipping the business enterprise, the economic system, or career as the ultimate of existence," wrote Emory Professor Harold Johnson (1957: 76). By proclaiming a synergistic alignment between business values and Christianity, he placed capitalism on the spiritual side of the Cold War. Liberal market capitalism represented the preordained future.

Per capita individualism

"Individualism," wrote Harvard philosophy professor Raphael Demos, lay at the heart of the American way of life, separating us from "authoritarianism" and "fixed dogma" (Demos, 1955: 33). To *Review* writers, individualism was an undisputed and foundational tenet of American capitalism (Hoffman, 1946). The basic point of a free society, wrote University of Pennsylvania Professor Thomas Cochran, was to permit and encourage "each individual to fulfill and develop his own talents and his own personality" (Campbell, 1957: 43). Individualism was not a mere artifact of Western culture or America's historical experience, but rather a "natural tendency" of man (Stevenson, 1951: 76).

If individualism stood at the heart of the capitalist ideology, then collectivism represented the straw-man enemy. William Stevenson defined collectivism as "more and more people accepting the idea that they are entitled to security [and] look to the government as the greatest generator of security" (Stevenson, 1951: 76). Collectivism, he was convinced, was the force that could spell "the eventual doom of all freedoms – including free enterprise" (Stevenson, 1951: 76). The "danger" – and HBS Dean David referred explicitly to the "danger of drifting" (David, 1950) – was a "revolutionary trend" not just around the world but also domestically.

Review writers placed the individual rather than the group, community, or society, at the center of the economic universe. "Economic well-being," wrote Kenneth Boulding, "must rise on a per capita basis" (Boulding, 1952: 34). Per capita income is, of course, a calculation of averages. It does nothing to reveal possible inequities in income distribution.

Per capita individualism was a key ingredient in spreading the appeal of liberal market capitalism abroad. Citizens of underdeveloped nations must feel that their individual income was rising lest they succumb to the appeal of collectivist Communists. "The improvement of society," Boulding concluded, "is nothing more than the sum of improvements of individuals" (Boulding, 1952: 36). The notion that individualism was the "natural tendency" of man around the world and not just in the United States has been contradicted by Geert Hofstede's findings on the collectivist nature of non-Western cultures (Hofstede, 1980, 2005). The thought that non-US cultures may have held values different from our own simply did not occur to *Review* writers during the Cold War.

Individualism had consequences in real-world actions. One of these consequences was to offer a value-based condemnation of unions. The central argument made against unionization was that it interfered with *individual* contributions (Rowe, 1949). People were not masses, wrote William Stevenson, and needed to be treated one at a time (Stevenson, 1951). Organized labor sought protection, Robert Rowe insisted, without regard to how the individual employee contributed to the individual organization. Thus could unionization be denounced not so much as a threat to the unilateral imposition of management prerogatives but as the enemy of man's 'natural tendency' toward individuality.

The irrelevance of class and the elimination of poverty

"I believe with all my heart that a nation of capitalists – and certainly anyone who owns one share of stock or one thousand is a capitalist – is an effective answer to communism's false doctrines," insisted New York Stock Exchange president Keith Funston (quoted in Traflet, 2013: 11). The promotion of stock ownership for every American citizen became a central aspect of a campaign sponsored by the Stock Exchange and the Advertising Council to promote what was referred to as People's Capitalism and was heralded by *Time* magazine in a cover story entitled "Every Man a Capitalist." The popular press was rife with stories of how "classes, or at least the old-style 'working class,' had given way to one all-American middle class that shared the same objectives and putatively consumed the same things" (Yarrow, 2006: 69).

Central to the we-are-*all*-capitalist-owners theme was the belief that employees could, should, and would shed any separate class identification and cast their fates instead with their employers. In one of the rare times that the *Review* gave over its pages to a truly dissenting voice, Solomon Barkin, Director of Research of the Textile Workers Union of America, dismissed the notion of an overlap of interests, at least between the *individual* employee and the employer. "The trade unionist knows that the individual worker is helpless in the face of the economic and social power of the employer" (Barkin, 1950: 60). If there was any possibility of mutuality – and Barkin gave no indication that he was optimistic on that score – it must be negotiated with the union.[6]

Barkin was a lone voice among *Review* authors. Johnson & Johnson CEO Robert Wood Johnson, who placed the establishment of "sound, cooperative relations between workers and management" as the central challenge facing US industry, suggested that "there is no basic conflict between workers' loyalty to their company and their allegiance to their union" (Johnson, 1949: 521, 533). Other writers dismissed the notion that loyalty to a union was compatible with the advance of the business. Elizabeth and Francis Jennings suggested that workers "in the real world" found it difficult to divide their loyalties (Jennings & Jennings, 1951). Robert Rowe argued that, even if workers *could* divide their loyalty, the results would be disastrous. Union loyalty promoted waste, lowered productivity, and increased wages and "other costly benefits" (Rowe, 1949: 559).[7]

Rather than negotiate common interests with a union, many executives preferred an approach that involved "educating" workers that "their economic, social, and political well-being" lie with "their specific employer and more broadly with the free enterprise system" (Fones-Wolf,

1994: 6). "Practically every prominent leader of business in the United States today," wrote William Stevenson in 1951, "is talking about teaching economics to employees" (Stevenson, 1951: 75). Stevenson made no pretense about viewing economics education as anything other than ideological advocacy. Courses were designed explicitly to help alert workers to "the revolutionary trend toward collectivism." Business leaders are "tired of standing by," Stevenson insisted. "More and more of them feel that if the collectivist trend is to be stopped, they had better do the stopping." Economic education could be used to "reconcile" any mistaken impression that the interests of employees and those of owners might be in conflict (Stevenson, 1951: 75–76).

The beyond-class argument was built on the assertion that ascendant American capitalism was creating a vast and undifferentiated middle class. "We have seen the income of the average family [again relying on averages] more than double," wrote Paul Hoffman in 1946, "with the result that our standard of living is the highest in the world" (Hoffman, 1946: 21). That growth had, according to consultant Lewis Galantiere, "removed class warfare" in the United States. "There is no rejection of fundamental American institutions" (Hoffman, 1951: 58). In addition to economic plenty, educational opportunities have created a "fluid society," according to philosophy professor Rafael Demos, that allowed the United States to avoid a "rigid class structure" (Demos, 1955: 35). Even the elites in America, in contrast to other societies, were drawn from many economic groups, thus reinforcing our fundamentally classless nature (Hoffman, 1952). Writers acknowledged the challenge of interfacing with nations in which "class- and caste-societies" still existed (Fayerweather, 1957: 128). But the hope, indeed the belief, was that the inculcation of American values would promote classlessness in underdeveloped countries and thus offer an attractive counterpart to Communist claims of a 'people's socialism' or a 'people's republic.'

These assumptions were supported by claims that American capitalism had eliminated, or possessed the capacity to eliminate, poverty. Economic development and growth would raise Americans out of the sea of poverty, promised *Review* writers, using pro capita income as the gauge. And the method of that growth was vital. "We now see that, in practice, the abolition of poverty can come only from development," wrote Kenneth Boulding, "not from redistribution, not from taking from the rich to give to the poor, but from making everybody [on average] richer" (Boulding, 1952: 35). By decade's end, Boulding was willing to predict in the near-term future that "poverty ceases to be a serious problem, except in isolated pockets" and that "equality no longer becomes a matter of major society concern (Boulding, 1959: 41).

The argument had some appeal. As GNP rose through the decade of the 1950s, *average* income followed. Americans increasingly moved to the suburbs, which supposedly provided a classless melting pot. The 'good life' seemed equally available to virtually all. A *Review* reader would encounter no recognition on its pages that the actual picture of America, even during these boom times, was not nearly so seamless. Stock ownership may have spread somewhat, but real control of corporate affairs increasingly moved toward large investors and institutions (Perlo, 1958; Traflet, 2013). Suburbs were far from melting pots, maintaining instead strict class and racial lines (Berger, 1960, 1961). Consumption – including the purchase of suburban homes – was increasingly fueled by debt, and borrowing was far from race blind (Hyman, 2011). Some of these cracks were apparent at the time, others became obvious in retrospect. All were ignored.

The elimination of poverty argument relied exclusively on denial. Poverty was certainly reduced, particularly in contrast to the Great Depression years. Still, the prosperity of the middle class eluded large populations, most especially the elderly and children, living in increasingly segregated inner cities and the rural south. The revelation made in 1962 in Michael Harrington's *The Other Americans* that fully one-quarter of the country's citizens were living in poverty demolished the "end of poverty" mirage (Harrington, 1962). Now, the 'war' on poverty (an unfortunate term) moved the issue from the apparently less than capable hands of free enterprise to the center of the federal government's agenda through the Kennedy, Johnson, and Nixon years (Gillette, 2010).

Exporting capitalism

"Since World War II," wrote oil executive W. Jack Butler, the United States had "been offering goods and services to foreign countries in order to keep them off the Communist band wagon" (Butler, 1952: 63). Butler was only partially right. Certainly, foreign trade was seen as part of the Cold War battle with the Soviets. However, there were also pragmatic reasons to increase trade. *Review* commentators recognized that "no country is a self-contained economic unit" (Martin, 1955: 25). The emphasis on overseas markets was fueled in part by an economic concern that the production capacity built up during the war would overwhelm domestic demand.

Expanding world trade became the route to maintaining the domestic economy (Copland, 1945). The Bretton Woods Agreement of 1944 sought to create a global economic system based on free trade, convertible currencies, and fixed exchange rates through the International Monetary Fund (IMF) and the International Bank for Reconstruction and Development (the World Bank). The US dollar replaced gold as the anchor of the international monetary system, and the Marshall Plan built demand for US goods and expertise in war-torn Europe (Bruder, 2009).

It was the underdeveloped world – the term was used to identify "less-privileged countries by their relative national productive power and the economic well-being of their people … generally (1) Southeast Asia, (2) Africa and the Near East, and (3) Central and South America" (Emlen, 1958: 70) – that offered the greatest opportunities for market expansion. This was, after all, "three-quarters of the world's population" (Boulding, 1952: 39). It was also the new battleground in the Cold War confrontation with the Soviet Union. "American-Russian relations, for instance, would not constitute the apparently insoluble problem which they now pose," added Boulding, "if the relationship were simply one of America and Russia; in that event they could perfectly well leave each other alone!"

The news from the underdeveloped world was disheartening, at least in the Cold War interpretation offered in the *Review* by UN consultant Raymond Miller. "As things now stand, the free world has been losing Asia at the rate of over 250,000 persons a day for the last four years, considering the hundreds of millions of people in China and other territories who have come under 'Communist' domination since 1946" (Miller, 1951: 52). The "losing Asia" argument was a frequent trope of Republican anti-Communists, with Joseph McCarthy and others blaming Communist sympathizers and spies among Democrats for "losing China" (Morgan, 2003). This was a trend, Miller insisted, that needed to be altered.

The struggle in the view of *Review* writers was primarily a "struggle for men's minds abroad" (Davis *et al.*, 1952). David McCord Wright warned that the struggle could not be won by a "shoot-'em-up" approach emphasizing military might. The United States needed to "implant in the minds of people of the undeveloped countries a set of ideas and beliefs which will lead them to agree to the changes, incentives, and inequalities needed for economic growth" (Wright, 1959: 28). Oil executive Butler agreed, writing that the spread of the American way of life overseas (without, he added, creating a "mirror image" of the American system) was possible (Butler, 1956). It would be only a few short years before leftist foreign policy critics would accuse the United States of adhering to precisely the "shoot-'em-up" approach condemned by Wright as a way of influencing hearts and minds in both Latin America and Southeast Asia. In the 1950s, America's largely ideological approach was seen by *Review* authors as a key advantage over Communist militancy.

The Cold War and ideology in management discourse

Despite the confidence of Cold War era capitalist ideologues, *all* of their basic beliefs – that poverty had been eliminated, that large corporate conglomerates spoke for the best interests of America, that individuals rather than communities stood at the center of the good life, and that the world, especially the underdeveloped world, could and should follow liberal market capitalism into the future – came under assault by the mid-1960s. *Review* authors had believed that their views represented not just a *desired* 'solution' but the inevitable endgame of historical evolution. That belief was questionable and aggressively questioned.

By the 1980s, liberal market capitalism emerged as the dominant economic paradigm in the United States (Reaganism) and the United Kingdom (Thatcherism). What came to be viewed, according to Brick (2006), as the "natural order of things," would, through its capacity for endless growth, end poverty, obliterate class distinctions, marginalize cultural differences under a single, homogenous national culture, and subdue the inherently jingoistic, backward-looking, and conspiracy-minded voice of the populace (Gilman, 2003). The "end of history" argument articulated by Fukuyama (1992) suggested that liberal market capitalism had achieved, with the death of Soviet Communism, an unabashed victory. The root causes of social and economic inequities had essentially been solved.

The assumptions of liberal market capitalism faced another set of challenges in the aftermath of the 2009 global economic collapse. The "too big to fail" phenomenon overtook laissez-faire assumptions concerning the "divine right" of capitalists to succeed or fail on their own (Gordon, 1960: 136). The intense interconnectedness of the global economy led to a resurgent advocacy for a more coordinated market economy. Global climate change and other insults to the environment as well as the disastrous results of offshoring to 'cheap labor countries' in emerging economies led to calls on the state to take an active role in protecting competition, labor, consumers, and the environment. 'History' – that is, the struggle to control the ideological story of unfolding events – has a way of not ending.

Management studies typically present themselves in non-ideological terms. Managers, after all, are purely pragmatic, concerned with what works and does not work. Scholars are fundamentally empirical, following evidence wherever it might lead. These assertions are fictive. The *Review* specifically and management dialogue generally is deeply ideological. Not that there is anything necessarily wrong with that. The danger occurs when proponents of an ideology present their views as "universal and exclusively correct" (Kinloch & Mohan, 2000: 2).

The capitalist ideologies of the 1950s engaged in simplification (liberal market capitalism vs. communism), contradiction (against government *interference* but for government *protection*), misdirection (*People's* Capitalism) and denial (poverty). When ideologues present the subjective as objective, advocacy as observation, and self-interest as mutuality, the result is denial, distortion, false consciousness, and the concealment of real interests.

Notes

1 The phrase "struggle for men's minds" in the chapter title is taken from the title of a 1952 *Harvard Business Review* article (Davis *et al.*, 1952). In order to reflect the era under analysis in this chapter and the primary sources upon which the analysis draws, I will purposefully utilize gendered language. The gendered nature of the language of management discourse generally and of Cold War dialogue in particular, has been analyzed in Mills, 1992; Cuordileone, 2000; Runté & Mills, 2006; Dye & Mills, 2011.

2 It was, according to Sobel (1993), defense contractors that led the way in circular diversification in order to avoid dependence on a single customer: the federal government.

3 Fones-Wolf (1994) has analyzed the antecedents of that ideology in the 1920s.

4 This reference is to economist Calvin B. Hoover rather than FBI Director J. Edgar Hoover. The *Review* did print a single article by *that* Hoover, a 1964 piece warning businessmen that "the United States is today Soviet Spy Target No. 1. Never in history has a nation been under such highly organized and competent spy attack" (Hoover, 1964: 143). Morgan (2003) has demonstrated that Soviet espionage efforts in the United States reached their peak during World War II and decline steadily thereafter.
5 Gras is identified as the founder of business history at HBS.
6 *Review* editors opened the article with an unusual disclaimer: "Whether or not we agree with Mr. Barkin's interpretation, we feel that all businessmen may gain in having a clearer understanding of the thinking of this well-known union leader" (Barkin, 1950: 59).
7 Rowe expressed special disdain for "Communist dominated unions which have so repeatedly demonstrated a complete dissatisfaction with any system of private enterprise" (Rowe, 1949: 560). Explicit Red-baiting like this was an exception in *Review* articles.

References

Abbott, C. C. (1948a) Economic defense of the United States, *Harvard Business Review*, 26(5): 613–26.
Abbott, C. C. (1948b) Economic penetration and power politics, *Harvard Business Review*, 26(4): 410–24.
Abbott, C. C. (1953) Thinking ahead, *Harvard Business Review*, 31(6): 21–22.
Althusser, L. (1961) *For Marx*. London: Verso.
Anthony, P. D. (1977) *The Ideology of Work*. London: Tavistock Press.
Barkin, S. (1950) A trade unionist appraises management personnel philosophy, *Harvard Business Review*, 28(5): 59–64.
Bates, G. E. (1942) Twenty years, *Harvard Business Review*, 21(1): 1–4.
Bendix, R. (1956) *Work and Authority in Industry: Managerial Ideologies in the Course of Industrialization*. San Francisco: John Wiley.
Berger, B. M. (1960) *Working-Class Suburb*. Berkeley, CA: University of California Press.
Berger, B. M. (1961) The myth of suburbia, *Journal of Social Issues*, 17(1): 38–49.
Boulding, K. E. (1952) Religious foundations of economic progress, *Harvard Business Review*, 30(3): 33–40.
Boulding, K. E. (1959) Symbols for capitalism, *Harvard Business Review*, 37(1): 41–48.
Boyer, P. E. (1999) *Promises to Keep: The United States since World War II*. Boston: Houghton Mifflin.
Brick, H. (2006) The postcapitalist vision in twentieth-century American social thought, in N. Lichtenstein (ed.), *American Capitalism: Social Thought and Political Economy in the Twentieth Century* (pp. 21–46). Philadelphia: University of Pennsylvania Press.
Brinkley, A. (2010) *The Publisher: Henry Luce and His American Century*. New York: Knopf.
Bruder, S. (2009) *Capitalizing on Change: A Social History of American Business*. Chapel Hill, NC: University of North Carolina Press.
Burke, H. (1999) *Meaning and Ideology in Historical Anthropology*. New York: Kluwer Academic.
Bursk, E. C. (1948) Selling the idea of free enterprise, *Harvard Business Review*, 26(3): 372–84.
Butler, W. J. (1956) Business fights communism overseas, *Harvard Business Review*, 34(4): 96–104.
Butler, W. J. (1952) Public relations for industry in underdeveloped countries, *Harvard Business Review*, 30(5): 63–71.
Campbell, T. C. (1957) Capitalism and Christianity, *Harvard Business Review*, 35(4): 37–44.
Coates, D. (ed.) (2005) *Varieties of Capitalism, Varieties of Approaches*. Basingstoke: Palgrave Macmillan.
Cooke, B. (2006) The Cold War origin of action research as managerialist cooptation, *Human Relations*, 59(5): 665–93.
Cooke, B., Mills, A. J., and Kelley, E. S. (2005) Situating Maslow in Cold War America: A reconceptualization of management theory, *Group & Organizational Management*, 30: 129–52.
Copland, D. B. (1945) America's economic leadership, *Harvard Business Review*, 23(4): 415–19.
Culliton, J. W. (1949) Business and religion, *Harvard Business Review*, 27(3): 265–71.
Cuordileone, K. A. (2000) Politics in an age of anxiety: Cold War political culture and the crisis in American masculinity, 1949–1960, *Journal of American History*, 87(2): 515–45.
Dale, E. (1960) Management must be made accountable, *Harvard Business Review*, 38(2): 49–59.
David, D. K. (1949) Business responsibilities in an uncertain world, *Harvard Business Review*, 29(supplement): 1–9.
David, D. K. (1950) The danger of drifting, *Harvard Business Review*, 28(1): 25–32.
Davis, S., Miller, R. W., Jayanty, S. M., Lwin, M. K. M., Maegli, J. U., Ojo, S. O., Takeno, Y., and Vassiliadis, A. S. (1952) Struggle for men's minds abroad, *Harvard Business Review*, 30(4): 121–32.

Demos, R. (1955) Business and the good society, *Harvard Business Review*, 33(4): 33–44.

Diefenbach, T. (2007) The managerialistic ideology of organizational change management, *Journal of Organizational Change Management*, 20(1): 126–44.

Dobbs, M. (2012) *Six Months in 1945: FDR, Stalin, Churchill, and Truman – From World War to Cold War*. New York: Knopf.

Donald, D. K. (1950) The danger of drifting, *Harvard Business Review*, 28(1): 25–32.

Donham, W. B. (1922) Essential groundwork for a broad executive theory, *Harvard Business Review*, 1(1): 1–10.

Drucker, P. F. (1946) *Concept of the Corporation*. New York: John Day.

Dye, K. and Mills, A. J. (2011) Dueling discourses at work: Upsetting the gender order, *Canadian Journal of Administrative Sciences*, 28(4): 427–39.

Dye, K., Mills, A. J., and Weatherbee, T. (2005) Maslow – Man interrupted: Reading management theory in context, *Management Decisions*, 43(10): 1375–95.

Ellis, R. J. (2005) *To Our Flag: The Unlikely History of the Pledge of Allegiance*. Lawrence, KS: University of Kansas Press.

Emlan, W. J. (1958) Let's export marketing know-how, *Harvard Business Review*, 36(6): 70–76.

Fayerweather, J. (1957) Foreign operations: A guide for top management, *Harvard Business Review*, 35(1): 127–35.

Flanders, R. E. (1945) The moral dilemma of an industrialist, *Harvard Business Review*, 23(4): 433–41.

Foley, D. K. (2004) Rationality and ideology in economics, *Social Research*, 71(2): 329–42.

Fones-Wolf, E. A. (1994) *Selling Free Enterprise: The Business Assault on Labor and Liberalism, 1945–60*. Urbana, IL: University of Illinois Press.

Freeland, R. M. (1972) *The Truman Doctrine and the Origins of McCarthyism: Foreign Policy, Domestic Politics, and Internal Security, 1946–1948*. New York: Knopf.

Fukuyama, F. (1992) *The End of History and the Last Man*. New York: Free Press.

Gaddis, J. L. (2005) *The Cold War: A New History*. New York: Penguin Books.

Galenson, W. (1960) *The CIO Challenge to the AFL: A History of the American Labor Movement, 1935–1941*. Cambridge, MA: Harvard University Press.

Gallup, G. (1972) *The Gallup Poll: Public Opinion, 1935–1971*, Vol. 2: *1949–1958*. New York: Random House.

Gantman, E. R. (2005) *Capitalism, Social Privilege and Managerial Ideologies*. Aldershot: Ashgate.

Gillette, M. L. (2010) *Launching the War on Poverty: An Oral History*. New York: Oxford University Press.

Gilman, N. (2003) *Mandarins of the Future: Modernization Theory in Cold War America*. Baltimore, MD: Johns Hopkins University Press.

Goodwyn, L. (1978) *The Populist Movement: A Short History of the Agrarian Revolt in America*. New York: Oxford University Press.

Gordon, L. (1960) Private enterprise and international development, *Harvard Business Review*, 38(4): 134–38.

Gordon, P.E. (2007) *What is Intellectual History? A Frankly Partisan Introduction to a Frequently Misunderstood Field*, http://history.fas.harvard.edu/people/faculty/documents/pgordon-whatisintellhist.pdf

Gras, N. S. B. (1949) Leadership, past and present, *Harvard Business Review*, 27(4): 419–37.

Guillen, M. F. (1994) *Models of Management: Work, Authority, and Organization in a Comparative Perspective*. Chicago, IL: University of Chicago Press.

Hall, P. A. and Soskice, D. W. (2001) *Varieties of Capitalism: The Institutional Foundations of Comparative Advantage*. New York: Oxford University Press.

Harrington, M. (1962) *The Other America: Poverty in the United States*. New York: Macmillan.

Harris, H. J. (1982) *The Right to Manage: Industrial Relations Policies in American Business in the 1940s*. Madison, WI: University of Wisconsin Press.

Higham, J. (1961) American intellectual history: A critical appraisal, *American Quarterly*, 13(2): 219–33.

Hoffman, P. G. (1946) The survival of free enterprise, *Harvard Business Review*, 25(1): 21–27.

Hoffman, P. G. (1951) Basic elements of a free, dynamic society – Part I, *Harvard Business Review*, 29(6): 55–68.

Hoffman, P. G. (1952) Basic elements of a free, dynamic society – Part II, *Harvard Business Review*, 30(1): 87–104.

Hofstede, G. (1980) *Culture's Consequence: International Differences in Work-Related Values*. Thousand Oaks, CA: Sage.

Hofstede, G. (2005) *Culture and Organizations: Software of the Mind*. New York: McGraw-Hill.

Hoover, C. B. (1959) Can capitalism win the intellectuals? *Harvard Business Review*, 37(5): 47–54.

Hoover, J. E. (1964) The US businessman faces the Soviet spy, *Harvard Business Review*, 42(1): 140–58.

Hyman, L. (2011) *Debtor Nation: The History of American Red Ink*. Princeton, NJ: Princeton University Press.

Jennings, E. and Jennings, F. (1951) Making human relations work, *Harvard Business Review*, 29(1): 29–55.

Johnson, H. J. (1957) Can the businessman apply Christianity? *Harvard Business Review*, 35(5): 68–76.
Johnson, R. W. (1949) Human relations in modern business, *Harvard Business Review*, 27(5): 521–41.
Kazin, M. (1998) *The Populist Persuasion in American History*. Ithaca: Cornell University Press.
Kelley, E. S., Mills, A. J., and Cooke, B. (2006) Management as a Cold War phenomenon?, *Human Relations*, 59(5): 603–10.
Khurana, R. (2007) *From Higher Aims to Hired Hands: The Social Transformation of American Business Schools and the Unfulfilled Promise of Management as a Profession*. Princeton, NJ: Princeton University Press.
Kinloch, G. C. and Mohan, R. P. (eds) (2000) *Ideology and the Social Sciences*. Westport, CT: Greenwood Press.
Kleiner, A. (1996) *The Age of Heretics: Heroes, Outlaws, and the Forerunners of Corporate Change*. New York: Currency/Doubleday.
Knorr, K. E. (1946) World rubber problems, *Harvard Business Review*, 24(2): 394–404.
Korican, O. H. (1946) Aims of our foreign investment policy, *Harvard Business Review*, 24(4): 498–511.
Landau, O. (2006) Cold war political culture and the return of systems rationality, *Human Relations*, 59(5): 637–63.
Landry, J. (2005). A Brief History of the *Harvard Business Review*, Unpublished manuscript [copy held at the Backer Library Archives, Harvard Business School].
Levitt, T. (1956) The changing character of capitalism, *Harvard Business Review*, 34(4): 37–47.
Levitt, T. (1958) The dangers of social responsibility, *Harvard Business Review*, 36(5): 41–50.
Lodge, G. D. (1977) *The New American Ideology*. New York: Knopf.
Lowell, A. L. (1923) The profession of business, *Harvard Business Review*, 1(2): 129–31.
McCauley, M. (2004) *America and the Cold War, 1949–1991*. London: Pearson.
McGerr, M. E. (2003) *A Fierce Discontent: The Rise and Fall of the Progressive Movement in America*. New York: Free Press.
Martin, H. D. (1955) Thinking ahead, *Harvard Business Review*, 33(2): 25–28.
Mayer, T. (2001) The role of ideology in disagreements among economists: A quantitative analysis, *Journal of Economic Methodology*, 8(2): 253–73.
Mayo, A. J., Nohria, N., and Singleton, L. G. (2006) *Paths to Power: How Insiders and Outsiders Shaped American Business Leadership*. Boston, MA: Harvard Business School Press.
Merchand, R. (1998) *Creating the Corporate Soul: The Rise of Public Relations and Corporate Imagery in American Big Business*. Berkeley, CA: University of California Press.
Miller, R. W. (1951) Our economic policy in Asia, *Harvard Business Review*, 29(4): 52–70.
Mills, A. J. (1992) *Gendering Organizational Analysis*. Newbury Park, CA: Sage.
Morgan, T. (2003) *Reds: McCarthyism in Twentieth-Century America*. New York: Random House.
Newcomer, M. (1965) *American Business Executives, 1964: A Study of His Social and Educational Background*. New York: Scientific American.
Panuch, J. A. (1957) A businessman's philosophy of foreign affairs, *Harvard Business Review*, 35(2): 41–53.
Perlo, V. (1958) 'People's capitalism' and stock ownership, *American Economic Review*, 48(3): 333–47.
Pollack, N. (1962) *The Populist Response to Industrial America*. Cambridge, MA: Harvard University Press.
Prince, C. (1946) The USSR's role in international finance, *Harvard Business Review*, 25(1): 111–28.
Prothro, J. W. (1953) Business ideas and the American tradition, *Journal of Politics*, 15(1): 67–87.
Pryor, F. L. (2010) *Capitalism Reassessed*. Cambridge: Cambridge University Press.
Roper, E. (1949) The public looks at business, *Harvard Business Review*, 27(2): 165–75.
Rowe, R. L. (1949) Profit-sharing in industry, *Harvard Business Review*, 27(5): 559–84.
Runté, M. and Mills, A. J. (2006) Cold War, chilly climate: Exploring the roots of gendered discourse in organization and management theory, *Human Relations*, 59(5): 695–720.
Shrivastava, P. (1986) Is strategic management ideological?, *Journal of Management*, 12(3): 363–77.
Sobel, R. (1984) *The Rise and Fall of the Conglomerate Kings*. New York: Stein & Day.
Sobel, R. (1993) *The Age of Giant Corporations: A Microeconomic History of American Business, 1914–1994*. Westport, CT: Greenwood Press.
Spector, B. (2006) The *Harvard Business Review* goes to war, *Management & Organizational History*, 1(3): 273–95.
Spector, B. (2008a) 'Business responsibilities in a divided world': The Cold War roots of the corporate social responsibility movement, *Enterprise and Society*, 14(2): 314–36.
Spector, B. (2008b) 'The Man in the Gray Flannel Suit' in the 'Executive Suite': American corporate movies in the 1950s, *Journal of Management History*, 14(1): 87–104.
Spector, B. and Spital, F. (2011) The ideology of executive bonuses: An historical perspective, *Journal of Management History*, 17(3): 315–31.

Stevenson, W. H. (1951) Economic education for employees, *Harvard Business Review*, 29(1): 75–85.
Stout, L. (2012) *The Shareholder Value Myth: How Putting Shareholders First Harms Investors, Corporations, and the Public*. San Francisco: Berrett-Koehler Publishers.
Sumberg, T. A. (1945) The government's role in export trade, *Harvard Business Review*, 23(3): 157–73.
Tedlow, R. S. (1979) *Keeping the Corporate Image: Public Relations and Business, 1900–1950*. Greenwich, CT: JAI Press.
Thelen, D. P. (1972) *New Citizenship: Origins of Progressivism in Wisconsin, 1885–1900*. Columbia: University of Missouri Press.
Thelen, D. P. (1986) *Paths of Resistance: Tradition and Dignity in Industrializing Missouri*. New York: Oxford University Press.
Traflet, J. M. (2013) *A Nation of Small Shareholders: Marketing Wall Street after World War II*. Baltimore, MD: Johns Hopkins University Press.
Walsby, H. (1946) *The Domain of Ideologies: A Study in the Development and Structure of Ideologies*. Glasgow: Social Science Association.
Wilkins, M. (2010) Multinational enterprises and the varieties of capitalism, *Business History Review*, 84(4): 638–48.
Wright, D. M. (1945) Business and the radical indictment, *Harvard Business Review*, 23(4): 393–414.
Wright, D. M. (1959) Thinking ahead, *Harvard Business Review*, 37(3): 23–28.
Yarrow, A. L. (2006) The big postwar story, *Journalism History*, 32(2): 58–76.

21

A critical historiography of public relations in Canada

Rethinking an ahistorical symmetry

Amy Thurlow

Introduction

Public relations as an emerging profession (Lages & Simkin, 2003) has been criticized as atheoretical in its approach (Brown, 2006; Grunig & White, 1992). Critics contend that public relations is a discipline currently lacking "paradigmatic and topic diversity and strongly influenced by practice" (Lages & Simkin, 2003: 298). Over the past three decades, public relations scholars have endeavoured to develop discipline-specific theories that represent a theoretically based body of knowledge representative of a scholarly profession. This process has been defined by excellence theory, introduced by Grunig and Hunt (1984). Excellence theory is a normative theory that prescribes how to do public relations in an ideal situation (Pompper, 2004). This theory articulates an evolution of public relations from asymmetrical (focused on organizational goals and one-way communication) to symmetrical (respecting both organizational goals and those of other stakeholders) two-way communication. Since its inception, excellence theory has dominated the public relations landscape, embedding with it a corresponding historical narrative which moves public relations from asymmetrical to symmetrical over a period of the past 100 years or so. The historical narrative which supports this theory attempts to construct a linear history which is singularly American, corporate, and characterized by the experiences of high-profile (mostly male) practitioners of the twentieth century (Miller, 2000). Lamme and Russell (2010) describe the approach of excellence theory as a 'periodization approach' which sets up a linear progression from 'worst' to 'best' practices. This chapter calls, in broad terms, for increased research outside this dominant paradigm.

A perspective of critical historiography (Jarzombek, 1999; Durepos & Mills, 2012) suggests that our knowledge of public relations has been defined by a dominant theoretical/historical narrative which is at once self-producing and isolationist in its approach. Although much of the current research on public relations is concerned with either excellence theory or the lack of alternative theoretical work, the attention to the impact of a lack of historical scholarship in this area is a more recent and less fully explored area. Brown (2006: 206) asserts that the "idea of public relations, once regarded as a-theoretical, is actually more a-historical." He illustrates that what has been critiqued as a lack of diversity in theory and history is actually reflective of a "writing out" (Cooke, 1999) of historically relevant material in deference to the dominant narrative. Although Cooke's analysis focused largely on the field of change management, his contention was that managerialist and organizational histories have produced a "historiographical shaping effect" (Cooke, 1999: 81) which has led to the construction of organizational theory as a political process.

It is important for public relations scholars to understand our knowing of the history of Canadian public relations as a historiographic process which privileges some events as significant, and by definition, writes others out. As Jenkins (1991: 17) tells us, 'history is never for itself. It is always for someone." In this sense, the ways in which understandings of public relations, or any historical understandings, are assembled through the writing of a history reveal elements of power, privilege, and the shaping of knowledge (Cooke, 1999: 83).

From a perspective of critical historiography it is the lack of awareness of this process and the resulting power effects on theorizing and understandings of the profession which require further study. The historical narrative which currently defines the evolution of public relations in Canada, and arguably around the globe, has had a significant impact on processes of theorizing and theory development within the profession. "The withdrawal from historical scholarship has not only diminished our consciousness of public relations. Leaving history out of public relations research weakens our confidence in theory. Public relations is a social institution, and for historical sociology, it is axiomatic that sociological explanation is necessarily historical" (Borgatta & Borgatta, 1992: 838).

This necessary relationship between theory and history has not been widely acknowledged within public relations scholarship. The epistemological and ontological frames which are constructed through a history shape our ways of theorizing within the field. As Somers (1998: 722) asserts, "theory cannot escape history and both misunderstands itself and introduces potential distortions into its work if it tries to do so". Essentially, all theory must be grounded in history (Brown, 2006).

Beyond the field of public relations, there has been a growing call across management and organization studies for an historically informed approach to critical management studies in broader terms (Booth & Rowlinson, 2006). As management and organization scholars continue to call for an historic turn, public relations researchers may be able to apply this approach and understanding of the importance of knowledge production within and about this field.

The overreliance on excellence theory and symmetry has not only limited the possibilities of theorizing from other perspectives within the profession, it has also "caused and resulted in historical distortions … and ethical oversimplifications like the dissociation of public relations from propaganda" (Brown, 2006: 206). Although excellence theory and the history of public relations which supports it provide one way of knowing the field of public relations, the dominant nature of this knowledge has eclipsed other histories to the extent that a very narrow understanding of the field prevails. This history is almost exclusively concerned with an American corporate orientation (Miller, 2000). Histories of the study and practice of public relations in Canada, for example, have not been well documented or understood. Thus, the Canadian experience of public relations and opportunities for theoretical development as a result of this, have been very limited.

Responding to the limited scope of public relations history in the mainstream literature, Lamme and Russell (2010) call for a new theory of public relations history. Their work outlines some of the limitations imposed on dominant narratives of public relations history by American domination of the field, the influence of the role of propaganda in the emergence of public communication disciplines, and the role of business interests in the establishment of models of PR. Their study of public relations practice prior to the traditional starting point of the dominant narrative "removed the imprint of the traditional timeline" (Lamme & Russell,

2010: 357) within this narrative and introduced possibilities of pluralized histories illuminating the emergence of public relations.

The dominant narrative

The prevailing historical narrative offers an Americanized, twentieth-century model of corporate public relations (Miller, 2000). This narrative is developed around a construct of the progressive evolution of the profession from unethical to ethical practice, represented in a move away from propaganda towards strategic, socially responsible communication. The origins of this narrative are not definitively known, but Hoy, Raaz & Wehmeier (2007) speculate that the author may have been Edward Bernays (a 'father' of American public relations) who began writing on the history of the field as early as the 1930s. By now, however, the narrative has been so widely used and reproduced so frequently that it is virtually undisputed and established within the public relations literature.

The dominant theoretical perspective in public relations is excellence theory (Grunig & Hunt, 1984). Grunig and Hunt define excellent public relations as "part of the management of communication between an organisation and its publics" (1984: 7). This definition is consistent with the managerialist approach reflected in excellence theory and its corresponding models of public relations practice. Drawing on systems theory, excellence theory was developed out of a study of best practices in public relations funded by the International Association of Business Communicators (IABC) and led by James Grunig. This study established benchmarks for excellence in public relations practice and presented an understanding of public relations as moving through four models of public relations: press agentry/publicist; public information; two-way asymmetric and two-way symmetric (Grunig & Hunt, 1984: 22). This evolution of symmetry as a term that represents a more sophisticated and enlightened form of public relations where interests of both organizations and other stakeholders are considered equally remains the gold standard for excellence within the profession. Deatherage and Hazleton (1998: 71) point out that "[t]he assumption that asymmetrical and symmetrical worldviews influence the selection of models and consequently the effectiveness of public relations is central to Grunig's (1992) theory of public relations excellence." However, they further contend that there has been no empirical research in the literature that confirms the existence of such worldviews, or links them to public relations practices.

Excellence theory presents an evolution to symmetrical communication as an historical process, moving current public relations practice away from its ethically questionable origins in the early 1900s. This dominant history follows the development of PR through the First and Second World Wars where propaganda was a prominent aspect of the discipline. Post-Second World War the symmetry model reflects an approach of cleansing the public relations from its propaganda past and moving towards strategic communication management, a term which is used within excellence theory to reflect strategic communication resulting in mutually beneficial relationships between organizations and publics.

Brown (2006) disputes this history, asserting that this theoretical/historical narrative was constructed in the absence of scholarship about the history of public relations. The history which supports the symmetry model, he contends, is a distortion of history and theorizing within the field.

> These distortions have advantages in the classroom: they offer undergraduates a historically linear, ethically justified, technologically oriented explanation of public relations. The cost, however, has been the marginalization of the actual history, art and culture of the subject at hand.
>
> *(Brown, 2006: 210)*

As post-secondary institutions set out to teach the history of PR in their introductory courses, a narrative of the profession began to emerge. This process began to unfold, for the most part, in the post-Second World War era, and with the growth of university courses came a demand for textbooks on the subject. Although textbooks did serve to solidify disciplinary knowledge, particularly around accepted practices, through their structure they also served to shape and normalize existing knowledge and present it as truth (Smyth, 2001).

The public relations histories developed in academic textbooks offer consistent accounts as they maintain an ethically and technically progressive progress of PR development in history, a development from manipulative beginnings to symmetric communication (Hoy, Raaz & Wehmeier, 2007: 198). Also worth noting, public relations education which occurred at this time took place almost exclusively in the United States. Although some courses were available in other countries, the United States was the source of virtually all textbooks and documentation on the evolution of public relations, and remains so today. Recent scholarship now indicates that although leading textbooks in the field of public relations let us assume that the practice of public relations was invented in the USA (Hoy, Raaz & Wehmeier, 2007), there is much evidence that indicates the presence of other stories (L'Etang, 2006). These histories have been largely eclipsed by a narrative defined within an American timeline.

For the most part, distinctly Canadian histories have not been established for public relations. In their place, the Americanized history of public relations, widely exported around the world, has been adopted and reproduced in concert with the establishment of excellence theory. This hegemonic effect on knowledge of public relations is described by Rodriguez Salcedo (2012: 332):

> Until very recently, the prevalence of US-based and published monograph studies and research articles on the history of PR has required scholars to teach such works as standard, and has framed PR as a profession from a similarly American perspective.

The immediate challenge for researchers attempting to analyse Canadian histories of PR from within textbooks is that there are no Canadian foundational PR textbooks in circulation. Although much discussion has percolated on this topic among Canadian academics and publishers there are no Canadian textbooks available that document any histories of public relations in Canada. As a result, Canadian public relations students are most often exposed to American histories of the industry, supplemented at times by Canadian articles or accounts of the discipline. Thus, the dominant figures who characterize historical public relations practice in Canada are Ivy Lee and Edward Bernays, American "fathers of public relations" (Colf, 2007; Hiebert, 1966).

A Canadian narrative

Although not widely available, preliminary scholarship on the historical Canadian experience indicates public relations had its origins in efforts of public policy and government administration, largely aimed at immigration and settlement campaigns.

Emms' (1995) research on the history of Canadian public relations traces the first full-time publicity activities to the general immigration campaign of the late 1800s. After Confederation in 1867, the growth and development of Canada became a priority for the new government. Incentives of land grants and free passage across the Atlantic were widely advertised in an effort to convince European farmers to seek a new life in the Canadian West. In 1896, Wilfrid Laurier became Prime Minister of Canada and brought with him a renewed commitment to improving the communications strategies employed to recruit settlers and sell the West. To lead this strategic communication campaign, Laurier appointed Cliford Sifton as Minister of the Interior, the portfolio responsible for immigration and western settlement. Norman David of the Canadian Encyclopedia identifies Sifton's work in promotion "as a model in communications, targeted to specific audiences, and it probably represents the greatest and most successful public relations campaign in Canadian history" (David, 2011).

To further his efforts at recruitment, Sifton incorporated a number of public relations tactics and strategies into his campaign. These included familiar tools of modern public relations practice such as media tours, lectures, advertising, and special events. However, he was employed primarily as a government official and it is quite likely that Sifton did not consider himself a public relations practitioner. That being said, the term public relations itself was not well used at this time. The term public relations counsellor was coined in 1923 by Edward Bernays in the United States and represents the first incidence of individuals practicing public relations being 'named'. Throughout the early 1900s and up until the mid-1920s in Canada, government communication and publicity campaigns were by far the most significant and most common of what would become identified as public relations practice. During this era, Canadian railways began to emerge as important corporate actors within the expansion of the Canadian west. The railways also adopted public relations strategies to promote travel, and along with a small number of other private companies began to introduce full-time corporate publicity programs by the early 1900s (Johansen, 2001: 59).

Although public relations practice was growing, it was not until about 40 years later that the Canadian experience included formalized public relations education. In 1948, Leonard Knott introduced a course in public relations at McGill University, Montreal. Knott was a founding member of the Canadian Public Relations Society (CPRS) in Montreal, and the author of *The PR in Profit*, published in 1955. The University of Toronto's public relations course soon followed in 1949. Mount Saint Vincent University in Halifax became the first university in Canada to offer a Bachelor of Public Relations degree programme in 1977. These educational programmes were supported by the establishment of professional associations in Canada, namely the CPRS and the International Association of Business Communicators (IABC). While little is available in the literature in terms of documenting this educational experience, Wright (2011) has highlighted differences between the Canadian and American experiences of public relations education. These include such differences as where post-secondary programmes were located, i.e. university versus community college programmes, the time-frame of expansion of public relations education, and the location of the programmes within faculties. For example, whereas the American programmes were often located within schools of journalism, this was not the case in Canada where programmes tended to be located within schools of business or as a stand-alone unit. Wright (2011: 236) also points to a number of "factual inaccuracies" that frequently surface in mainstream accounts of the evolution of PR education, calling for further research into the evolution of PR education in North America.

Through an examination of a PR history from a Canadian perspective, the impact of geography, public policy, and the early settlement patterns of Canadians can be seen to influence both the evolution and the practices of PR. As the field developed over the following decades, differences in focus and professional development are also evident. By moving away from the dominant focus of a corporate model of public relations, the Canadian experience of public policy development and related communication initiatives offers a new lens through which to view histories of theory and practice.

Theoretical perspective

As a theoretical framework, the approach of critical historiography offers a retrospective and critical approach, responding in part to what McKie and Munshi (2007) define as a need for a plurality of epistemological perspectives within our knowledge of public relations.

A critical historiography is not history, "but rather a critique that simulates history in order to expose the imperative of closure" (Jarzombek, 1999: 203). As Durepos and Mills (2012) explain, this type of analysis does not contest that events occurred in the past, or advocate that the past is to be denied. The focus of the analysis is to critique "depictions of the past as stable, already assembled, unchanging, closed, and done, prior to our efforts to assemble it (and after our efforts in assembling it for that matter)" (Durepos & Mills, 2012: 710).

Problematizing symmetry as both a model of public relations and a historical timeline of PR development is central to the analysis of how histories are written, produced, reproduced, and understood within a Canadian context. This perspective also facilitates an investigation of the relationship between history and theory within public relations and the ways in which these elements exist in tension with each other as they define the field.

Consistent with what Booth and Rowlinson (2006) describe as a reorientationalist agenda, this study contributes to a call for a critique of both the ahistorical nature of existing theories and the atheoretical character of much of historical analysis. Within this theoretical framework, the written histories of the pioneers represent a way of writing history that is mediated by powerful ontological and epistemological influences (Munslow, 2010). The shaping effects of language, voice, ideology, perspective, and context in the broadest sense all contribute to and influence the retrospective writing of these historical accounts (Mills, Weatherbee & Durepos, 2013). From that perspective, these written histories are not presented to contest the 'truth' of a dominant narrative, but more so to establish alternative histories and create space for pluralized ways of knowing public relations as a profession, a practice, and a scholarly discipline.

Method

Using an historiographically-informed approach of critical discourse analysis, the written histories of Canadian public relations pioneers are analysed to surface emergent themes. These themes are further investigated to explore the construction of narratives which reflect a Canadian history of public relations.

Critical discourse analysis has been employed as a method compatible with a theoretical approach of critical historiography in organizational studies (e.g. Flowerdew, 2012) and provides a natural tool through which to engage ideas of power, pluralized histories, and discourse in a retrospective analysis of an emerging profession. Arens (1998), in her work on sémanalyse, an "analysis that critiques the social space and subjectivity produced by the language shared within a community," (1998: 23) introduces critical discourse analysis as a tool of analysis in an historical investigation of feminist texts. She advocates critical discourse analysis as an appropriate method "based on the premise that language and consciousness are intertwined in social practice, and must be subject to a general historical critique of subjectivity" (Arens, 1998: 23).

In this study, critical discourse analysis offers a method uniquely suited to the analysis of issues of power and language in the crafting of histories of public relations. The texts analysed in this study comprise the *Jack Yocom Public Relations Profile Collection*, named for one of the pioneers. This collection is produced by the Communication and Public Relations Foundation, a recognized, not-for-profit, charitable organization committed to increasing public knowledge and awareness of the role of public relations which was established in 1979. The CPRS, Canada's only professional association dedicated specifically to the public relations profession, contributes to the funding of the collection. These 17 profiles of Canadian public relations pioneers are presented as a collection on the Foundation page of the CPRS website (www.CPRS.ca). This series reflects interviews with the featured individuals and comments from their colleagues and peers within the PR industry.

A close reading of the texts provided the foundation for coding of the data and the identification of emergent themes from within the text. The specific approach to critical discourse analysis employed in this research incorporates the work of van Dijk (1993) and Phillips and Hardy (2002) to apply a critical focus in the investigation of language and discourse present in the text. From this perspective, signposts were established to facilitate coding within the text and to surface language that most explicitly reflected issues of power, theoretical perspectives, and historical frames. In the first phase of analysis, the text was coded with particular attention to the interplay between text and context, most notably the ways in which elements of language and power were privileged in the context of their production. The second phase of the analysis was a coding of text which reflected the use of power, privilege, and access to discourse which informed broader knowledge/power relationships. The text was further interrogated to surface inconsistencies, ironies, or contradictions, and to highlight language that silenced other perspectives, knowledge, or histories.

The themes which emerged through this process were further analysed to investigate the historical frames, or the connections made to histories, used by the pioneers to construct their own histories of public relations in Canada. The signposts described above assisted the research process by ensuring that analysis of the text would be conducted within an historically sensitive and critically informed manner.

Analysis

The profiles featured in the Jack Yocum Collection are introduced on the CPRS website and described in the following way:

> Currently, there are no recorded profiles of Canadian public relations practitioners. Some are listed in the Canadian Who's Who. Others can be found on the Order of Canada web site. Some may have been the subject of a magazine or periodical article but, generally, there is no systematic collection of the lives and accomplishments of Canadian public relations practitioners who have made significant and extended contributions to the practice.
>
> This collection of profiles, that will include several phases, will provide a consistent method of recording the history of public relations in Canada through the personalities who have developed and influenced the practice. The collection is named in memory of John H. "Jack" Yocom who died in February, 2003.
>
> In the case of those practitioners who have died, colleagues have been interviewed to discuss the individual's impact on the profession. Other practitioners who have been profiled have been interviewed using a standard set of pre-determined questions prepared by the College of Fellows, Canadian Public Relations Society.
>
> *(http://www.cprs.ca/foundation/yocom.aspx)*

The introductory text which sets up the collection does not problematize the process of "writing" histories. As such, the histories are presented as 'the' history of public relations in Canada as told by those who produced it. This collection of profiles is said to "provide a consistent method of recording the history of public relations in Canada through the personalities who have developed and influenced the practice." This articulation of history implies one linear historical path that is 'done' and documented through this series. Again, the method of writing is described as a "standard set of pre-determined questions" almost as if to preserve the consistent, scientific assembly of this "history of public relations in Canada". In this introduction the text serves to at once legitimize the construct of a fixed and factual history, while inviting individuals to contribute their personal experiences within that narrow historical context.

Notwithstanding the approach described above, a critical reading of the histories themselves reveals narratives that are not consistent in that they reflect some aspects of a common, historical experience or their contradiction of dominant historical and theoretical knowledge. Although excellence theory and the American corporate narrative are certainly present in the stories of the pioneers, there is diversity in the ways in which this influence is represented. In addition to themes of symmetry and excellence, themes of ethical practice, Americanization and encroachment were also present.

Excellence theory/symmetry

One of the most prominent themes that emerged from the text was that of excellence theory and the symmetry model. The language reflected in this theme was represented in terminology such as strategic communication, objectives, and mutually beneficial relationships. Consistent with the dominant narrative, the pioneers referred to elements of Grunig and Hunt's (1984) models of public relations practice as a linear historical frame, describing early public relations as propaganda, or at least one-way and not strategic, and contemporary practice as enlightened and symmetrical.

Within this theme, language emerged to support a theoretical/historical relationship which came to define "excellent public relations." At the same time, contradictions were present in the text which indicated that although practitioners were aware of what excellence should look like, that model was not always what was valued in their practice. As a result, a sub-theme of asymmetry was identified.

Two-way symmetrical communication was described by most pioneers in language that reflected either strategy (strategic communication which incorporated goals and objectives of organizations and stakeholders) or mutually beneficial relationships. As strategy, pioneers referenced an evolution from "seat of the pants" to "more strategic and thought out" public relations practice. In the early stages of their careers, pioneers, describe an environment defined by "putting out fires."

The evolutionary process pioneers describe as they move along the path to symmetrical, strategic communication, emphasizes that they become more involved in the organizational decision-making process and therefore able to influence senior decision-makers to adopt a more symmetrical approach. The location within the organizational structure is an important indicator of the evolution of the profession. As one pioneer describes:

> In the job interview, I was told I would report directly to the CEO which is the right reporting relationship for PR, but when I started, I was assigned to someone else whose only interest seemed to be making me speak French. I came home from that first day and said to my wife, 'Don't unpack; we won't be here long.'

Nevertheless, in contrast to this narrative of evolution from asymmetry to symmetry, organizational interests do emerge as paramount when pioneers describe their greatest career accomplishments. The following quote highlights the disconnect between the description of public relations as evolved into a symmetrical model, while the practitioners themselves continued to value the organizational objectives over those of other stakeholder groups. One pioneer describes a career highlight as "defeating the Innu and about 100 plus engaged supporters they'd aligned over some years, from the major faiths to unions and foreign activist groups". This 'defeat' of activists organized against organizational (in this case government) interests was offered as proof of effective and excellent communication management.

Another pioneer employs language of a battle or conflict in describing his reaction to "losing" in a disagreement on how to proceed between management and board members, "I had/have never 'lost' a crisis/issues battle/assignment. It's like being a lawyer with a lot of court experience losing a case for the first time." This polarization in the narrative, defining a win-lose situation is the antithesis of symmetry, which is defined in the literature as establishing "mutually beneficial relationships" (Cutlip, 1994) for organizations and their stakeholders.

In another contradiction to the theoretical narrative, the texts here reflected at least some resistance to incorporating theory too fully into practice:

> In the immediate post-war era, the subject was taught from American textbooks, with more emphasis on the theoretical than the practical. We persuaded the academics to see the value in teaching the profession with case studies that are recent and relevant to public relations. I enlisted the support of veteran practitioners to give guest lectures to students, and to give practical examples of case assignments they had managed.

This tension between theory and relevance is evidenced throughout the pioneer histories as individuals make sense of their own experiences in context of the more 'sophisticated' symmetrical communication.

Ethical practice

The struggle to be seen as, and actually be, an ethical public relations practitioner emerges as an important theme in every pioneer history in this study. As demonstrated in the dominant narrative, pioneers frame an historical progression from unethical to ethical practice as a defining characteristic of the evolution of Canadian public relations. Nevertheless, contradictions are present in the text around this point. One pioneer describes an event that stands out in his career where he had to "smooth over" an incident that would have damaged relationships in an international partnership. When two Canadian air force pilots flew into restricted Italian airspace, "we concocted a story about their instrument panel not working properly and apologized. They bought it, or pretended to, but it always bothered me. I think it's important for PR people to be honest and accurate; otherwise your credibility comes into question." Although the pioneer reflects on the actions as unethical, and troubling, the situation was not resolved in a manner consistent with a two-way symmetrical approach.

As well, several pioneers reflected with a kind of nostalgia about the old days where ethics were not at the forefront of practice.

> When I started, PR was seen as the 'pay for play' field, the fun thing to do: wine and dine journalists and plant stories; trade on goodwill and good relationships to get good stories placed in print, on radio or TV and wire services, and in major magazines. That was our universe. For most, strategic communications planning in the deepest sense was not understood or used; our goal used to be to figure out what we should do to spend the budget we're asking for that looks most productive and helpful.

Professionalism

In contrast, other pioneers reflected on the need for professionalism in public relations. As one pioneer states, "When I talk to new people entering the profession I tell them, your reputation is all you have. Public relations is about trust and professionalism." This professionalism was most often described in connection with education or licensing from an association. When asked to speculate on the future of PR, one pioneer stated, "the most important change for those in PR will be the demand for higher and higher degrees of professionalism." Another commented, "We are not a profession and won't be until there is some form of licensing and accountability, which we don't yet have."

Distinct from this position of requiring education or licensing, there was a parallel story of what 'really matters' in public relations practice. As noteworthy as the statements in support of professionalism was a lack of acknowledgement of the role of theory in informing scholarship and practice. Theory was not identified as central to the profession; it was seen as something 'done' at universities, not relevant to practice. And within this perspective is embedded a message that the basic practice of PR has not actually changed over time.

As one pioneer described:

> The development of a structured training program has brought with it over the years a practice based on new themes. This training is now steeped in university vocabulary. But while people may not have talked about 'communications orientations' in the old days, every project they undertook was based on the famous RACE (Research, Analysis, Communication, Evaluation) formula. It's no less relevant today.

This scepticism of "university vocabulary" echoes the previous theme, where the pioneers both recognized the importance of theory and education in the narrative, but struggled to reconcile their own preference for "seat of the pants" on the job training.

Americanization

The power of the dominant American corporate narrative of public relations was evidenced in the histories of the pioneers. Most often, the references invoked language which set up a relationship where the American model represented the standard to be achieved, and Canadians were in a "catch up" mode. This language was very specifically defined by some pioneers, even to the point of attaching an historical timeframe.

This perspective is illustrated in the comments of one pioneer who says "[i]n the 1950s and 1960s in Canada, the public relations function was about 25 years behind the United States." In another reference it is stated "[b]ut during the Second World War, we made great progress … (towards catching up to the US)." The progress was defined by a boom in employment of public relations practitioners during the war as the government hired communicators to develop public information programs and "they informed the public about what was happening by developing, for instance, Victory Loan campaigns."

As one history indicates, this work gave public relations a higher profile. "In addition to daily wartime newspaper coverage by reporters and editors, numerous well known newspapermen worked for the armed forces public relations units, and other government departments."

This definition of public relations as 'catching-up' during the war parallels the American narrative presented in most commonly used textbooks. During the Second World War employment in the PR field exploded, and the profession gained a higher profile. At the same time, the relationships between public relations and propaganda became more central and increasingly problematic to understandings of public relations theory and practice.

Differentiation

Carving out a space for public relations within other management disciplines has been a central theme in the literature. As Smith (2012: 838) points out, "Public relations scholarship has long been weighed down by a singular challenge: to differentiate the discipline from related areas – marketing, advertising, and organizational communication, to name a few."

Consistent with this perspective, concern with both defining themselves as public relations practitioners and earning respect from other disciplines emerged as an important narrative within the pioneer histories. All but one of the pioneers had entered the profession through journalism and media. As one pioneer stated:

> Back then most PR people were former journalists. Their strengths were that they knew everyone in the media business in terms of getting placement of a story or an article. Today, that doesn't hold true ... There is a need to differentiate public relations scholarship from other related communication disciplines like marketing, advertising, and communication studies.

Many of the pioneers assert that they "learned the ropes in sales, marketing and advertising" before moving into a PR role. But at the same time there is a strong feeling that they "always had been doing PR back then but it wasn't called that then".

The concern with encroachment expressed in the narratives focused most often on frustration in the reporting structures for public relations within organizations.

> Many of today's public relations departments are reporting through marketing. Having public relations departments or agencies reporting to marketing is not ideal. There is an immediate bias to present only good or sales oriented news. The public relations department is most effective in its role when it is a standalone department and not associated with marketing, or sales or legal, though the latter should be consulted as their input can be vital in many situations.

At the same time, when itemizing accomplishments of a public relations career for one pioneer, recognition within a marketing journal was considered a highlight. "In an August 2008 issue of *Marketing*, she was proclaimed as one of the 10 most influential pioneers in Canadian marketing history." The respect and acknowledgement of the related disciplines was featured as an important aspect of a process of public relations establishing its own credibility as a profession.

Within the dominant narratives of public relations history, the evolution of public relations from an un-named or differently-named profession to a distinctly public relations discipline is identified as occurring in the 1920s and 1930s. The pioneer histories analysed in this study appear to indicate that although the term public relations is recognized by other disciplines, there still exists a struggle to define the field itself as distinct and separate from related fields. Likewise, the pressure to ensure that public relations is respected within the process of organizational decision-making remains.

Discussion

The written histories of the pioneers reflect the influence of a dominant theory and a corresponding history which have served to define understandings of public relations. Equally important, these texts reveal examples of dissonance between the histories crafted by Canadian practitioners and the dominant theoretical/historical narrative. These spaces contrasting the Canadian and dominant narratives have yet to be fully explored, and may offer valuable insights into how practitioners and scholars come to see themselves and their discipline. As the dominant theoretical/historical narrative of public relations remains largely uncontested within the field, limited space exists for the exploration of alternative understandings of what public relations is, or has been, or can be.

The language of symmetry present in these histories indicates that there are some terms or figures of speech that hold a great deal of influence in the sensemaking processes of practitioners and educators. The terminology around the symmetry model appears as a filter in this process, lending plausibility to those accounts that most closely followed the model. As the pioneers reflect on their experiences, language around an evolutionary process and an acknowledgement of the need for strategy and mutually beneficial relationships emerged. On a broader scale, McLaren, Mills, and Durepos (2009: 399) suggest that "we need to examine more closely the development of tropes that serve as dominant filters for management knowledge or, more accurately, what is to count as management 'knowledge'." This study suggests that the trope of symmetry, constituted within excellence theory, in the construction of public relations knowledge represents one such dominant filter. In this role as gatekeeper, symmetry serves to limit diverse understandings of both histories and identities of public relations.

In the texts analysed above, the language of strategic communication was enacted frequently to convey a progression from a "seat-of-the-pants" past to a strategic present. Strategic communication is identified in the use of the RACE model, an approach of two-way symmetrical communication, and the organizational requirement to report to a CEO or senior decision-maker. This language and the narrative it constructs runs in contrast to examples provided by individual practitioners of their career highlights and greatest achievements. In several examples practitioners cited career highlights marked by events that were successful, yet not strategic.

The language of ethics was also prevalent in the histories, and conveyed a progression from an unethical practice to an ethical practice as an historical evolution. In contrast, several pioneers provided examples of career highlights including actions or events that were decidedly unethical. In one case, these actions were reflected upon as troubling and acknowledged as unethical. In others, they were celebrated as successful or, at least, unavoidable. There was certainly a sense that public relations practitioners ought to act ethically; at the same time there was evidence and discussion in the text that indicated unethical practice is still condoned within the profession if it is enacted to protect organizational interests.

Conclusion

This tension between understandings of the profession, what is known and what is valued, and the dominant theoretical/historical narrative has contributed to inconsistency in understandings of what constitutes 'excellent' public relations. Perhaps contributing to a fragmentation within the public relations identity which exists today (Thurlow, 2009), a lack of acknowledgement of different histories has resulted in dissonance between the dominant narrative and the lived experiences of the pioneers.

There remains much work to be done in unravelling the relationship between public relations practitioners' understandings of who they are and the historiography that contributes to the production of this identity. As Lamme and Russell (2010: 356) point out "simply put, no area of public relations history has been adequately researched". Equally important, the ways in which this historical research is written will influence, constrain, or enable alternative representations of historical experiences and meanings. Future research is essential to expand understandings of the origins and development of the field of public relations, and to enable possibilities of theorizing that have so far been constrained within a dominant frame.

This chapter contributes to the development of more pluralized and diverse histories of public relations, working towards a more complete understanding of theorizing within the discipline. Constrained by a lack of scholarship on the relationship between theory and history within public relations, alternative narratives of the evolution of public relations have been written out of the mainstream literature. Further study is required to surface these alternative narratives and give voice to different ways of knowing public relations. In this way, scholars may challenge the Americanized, twentieth-century corporate orientation (Miller, 2000) which dominates the field's history (Lamme & Russell, 2010: 357).

This historiographical work is essential to expanding and supporting theorizing and theory development within the discipline. Further research in this area will contribute to the call for more historicized research within public relations, including the need for acknowledgement of pluralized histories and diverse approaches to documenting these. Within the Canadian context alternative histories must be identified, explored, and 'written in' to create space for a more robust understanding of how public relations scholars and practitioners come to know themselves and their profession; past, present, and future.

References

Arens, K. (1998) Discourse analysis as critical historiography: A sémanalyse of mystic speech, *Rethinking History*, 2: 23–50.

Booth, C. and Rowlinson, M. (2006) Management and organizational history: Prospects, *Organization Studies*, 16(6): 1021–46.

Borgatta, E. F. and Borgatta, M. L. (1992) *Encyclopedia of Sociology: Volume 2*. New York: Macmillan.

Brown, R. E. (2006) Myth of symmetry: Public relations as cultural styles, *Public Relations Review*, 32(3): 206–12.

Colf, R. T. (2007) Who's the father of public relations?, *Public Relations Strategist*, 13(4): 24–27.

Cooke, B. (1999) Writing the left out of management theory: The historiography of the management of change, *Organization*, 6(1): 81–106.

Cutlip, S. (1994) *The Unseen Power: Public Relations: A History*. Mahwah, NJ: Lawrence Erlbaum.

David, N. (2011) Public relations, in *The Canadian Encyclopedia*. Historica-Dominion.

Deatherage, C. P. and Hazleton, V. (1998) Effects of organizational worldviews on the practice of public relations: A test of the theory of public relations excellence, *Journal of Public Relations Research*, 10(1): 57–71.

Durepos, G. and Mills, A. J. (2012) Actor-network theory, ANTi-History and critical organizational historiography, *Organization*, 19(6): 703–21.

Emms, M. (1995) The origins of public relations as an occupation in Canada, MA Thesis, Concordia University.

Flowerdew, J. (2012) *Critical Discourse Analysis in Historiography: The Case of Hong Kong's Evolving Political Identity*. New York: Palgrave Macmillan.

Grunig, J. E. and Hunt, T. (1984) *Managing Public Relations*. New York: Holt, Rinehart & Winston.

Grunig, J. E. and White, J. (1992) The effect of worldviews on public relations theory and practice, in J. Grunig, D. Dozier, W. Ehling, L. Grunig, F. Repper, and J. White (eds), *Excellence in Public Relations and Communication Management* (pp. 31–64). Mahwah, NJ: Lawrence Erlbaum.

Hiebert, R. (1966) Ivy Lee: Father of modern public relations, *Princeton University Library Chronicle*, 27(2): 113–20.

Hoy, P., Raaz, O., and Wehmeier, S. (2007) From facts to stories or from stories to facts? Analyzing public relations history in public relations textbooks, *Public Relations Review*, 33(2): 191–200.

Jarzombek, M. (1999) A prolegomena to critical historiography, *Journal of Architectural Education*, 52(4): 197–206.

Jenkins, K. (1991) *Re-Thinking History*. London: Routledge.

Johansen, P. (2001) Professionalisation, building respectability, and the birth of the Canadian Public Relations Society, *Journalism Studies*, 2(1): 50–62.

Knott, L. (1955) *The PR in Profit*. Toronto: McClelland and Stewart.
Lages, C. and Simkin, L. (2003) The dynamics of public relations: Key constructs and the drive for professionalism at the practitioner, consultancy and industry levels, *European Journal of Marketing*, 37(1/2): 298–328.
Lamme, M. O. and Russell, K. M. (2010) Removing the spin: Towards a new theory of public relations history, *Journalism & Communication Monographs*, 11(4): 280–362.
L'Etang, J. (2006) Public relations and propaganda: Conceptual issues, methodological problems, and public relations discourse, in J. L'Etang and M. Pieczka (eds), *Public Relations: Critical Debates and Contemporary Practice* (pp. 23–40). Mahwah, NJ: Lawrence Erlbaum.
McKie, D. and Munshi, D. (2007) *Reconfiguring Public Relations: Ecology, Equity and Enterprise*. New York: Routledge.
McLaren, P. G., Mills, A. J., and Durepos, G. (2009) Disseminating Drucker: Knowledge, tropes and the North American management textbook, *Journal of Management History*, 15(4): 388–403.
Miller, K. S. (2000) US public relations history: Knowledge and limitations, *Communication Yearbook*, 23: 381–420.
Mills, A., Weatherbee, T., and Durepos, G. (2013) Reassembling Weber to reveal the-past-as-history in management and organization studies, *Organization*, 21(2): 225–43.
Munslow, A. (2010) *The Future of History*. Basingstoke: Palgrave Macmillan.
Phillips, N. and Hardy, C. (2002) *Discourse Analysis: Investigating Processes of Social Construction*. Thousand Oaks, CA: Sage.
Pompper, D. (2004) Linking ethnic diversity and two-way symmetry: Modeling female African American practitioners' roles, *Journal of Public Relations Research*, 16(3): 269–99.
Rodriguez Salcedo, N. (2012). Mapping public relations in Europe: Writing national histories against the US paradigm, *Comunicación y Sociedad*, 25(2), 331–73.
Smith, B. (2012). Public relations identity and the stakeholder-organization, *Public Relations Review*, 38: 838–45.
Smyth, M. (2001) Certainty and uncertainty sciences: Marking the boundaries of psychology in introductory textbooks, *Social Studies of Science*, 31(3): 389–416.
Somers, M. R. (1998) 'We're no angels': Realism, rational choice, and relationality in social science, *American Journal of Sociology*, 104(3): 722–84.
Thurlow, A. (2009) I just say I'm in advertising: A public relations identity crisis, *Canadian Journal of Communication*, 34(2): 245.
van Dijk, T. (1993) Principles of critical discourse analysis, *Discourse and Society*, 4(2): 249–83.
Wright, D. K. (2011) History and development of public relations education in North America: A critical analysis, *Journal of Communication Management*, 15(3): 236–55.

Part V

Management and organizational history at the margins

22

History and the absence of Canadian management theory

Patricia Genoe McLaren and Albert J. Mills

As we follow the historic turn (Booth and Rowlinson, 2006; Kieser, 1994) within management and organizational studies (MOS), we can explore not only what has happened and why (or what we can know of it), but also what has not happened and why. In particular, we are interested in the fact that historical accounts of MOS tend to largely focus on American (i.e. US-born and/or based scholars) contributions (Wren & Bedeian, 2009), with occasional references to European (largely UK) contributions (Urwick, 1963).

In this chapter we present the case of Canada and the lack of a distinct body of management theory that acknowledges and considers the country's differences from the dominant force in MOS – the United States of America. We argue that while ostensibly developing a scientific, rational management science, MOS researchers have developed a body of knowledge that is unconsciously informed and constrained by its context, a context in which the United States dominates. A management theory that has inherent consideration for contextual differences at a societal level has never developed because management science was being developed in such a way that context was never taken into consideration. The theories being formulated applied to all organizations alike, so why would Canadian, or any non-American, organizations be studied separately? Likewise, a management theory, or body of knowledge, specific to Canada has never developed. We specifically posit in this chapter that Canada is distinct enough from the United States that management theory as developed does not fit, and we more generally posit that management theory is so US-centric as to be inapplicable for most other societal contexts.

Problematizing a 'Canadian' history

As we set about making our case for a Canadian management theory, we delve into Canada's past for an understanding of both why a Canadian management theory does not exist, and why we need one. We proceed with the understanding that history is a social construction. We do not question that there is a past in which Canada has developed as a country, but we acknowledge that the past is not ontologically available to us (Munslow, 2010). We do not, and cannot, know that past except through powerful traces of networked, or relational, behaviours (Latour, 2005) upon which we impose a sense of the history. Thus, as we explore the idea of a Canadian management theory through our understanding of the past, we are socially constructing a history that comes together based on the 'information' available to us through the works published by historians and other networked traces (e.g. archival materials, newspapers, artefacts, etc.). As our focus in this chapter is to convince management researchers of the differences between Canadian and American business contexts, our history accentuates the differences between the countries and glosses over the similarities. Rather than being 'the history' of Canada, this is our history. It has validity in that it is drawn from accepted works, but it is not, and does not claim to be, the whole picture.

As has been argued elsewhere, histories of the development of MOS have played an important role in the construction of the development of the field, creating retrospective accounts of who and what came to constitute the field (Cooke, 2006; Kelley, Mills & Cooke, 2006). In the process, the field of MOS has largely been constructed as an American project, dominated by American theorists (e.g. Taylor, Maslow), schools of thought (e.g. Scientific Management, Human Relations), and key studies (e.g. Mayo and the Hawthorne Studies, Lewin, Lippitt and White's leadership studies). The most widely known of these histories are themselves authored by US scholars, including George (1968, 1972) and the work of Wren and Bedeian (Wren, 1972; Wren & Bedeian, 2009) whose editions have spanned the 1970s until the present.

It is our intention, both in this chapter and as part of a broader research collective, to develop histories of Canadian management theory. We are interested in both developing (some might argue recovering) a history and also in explaining how and why such a history has been 'written out' (Cooke, 1999). In the process we also want to contribute to the deconstruction of (MOS) history in general (Durepos & Mills, 2012), and US management history in particular (Foster, Mills & Weatherbee, 2014b). However, we recognize the tendency that existing histories of management theory have toward declaring themselves representations of the past as it actually happened, and of accepting this reality as the inevitable outcome of the development of management theory (Weatherbee and Durepos, 2010). We differ from this realist perspective in that we acknowledge that we present here only one of many possible histories, that in going forward with the development of a Canadian management theory we recognize it will be relational to our own context (Durepos, Mills & Weatherbee, 2012), and that where existing accounts of management theory present a history, we intend to use history to both make a case for developing a Canadian management theory and to play an important role in establishing what that theory is.

Canadian management theory – or the lack thereof

The lack of Canadian management theory is evident in Canadian business schools from both curriculum and research perspectives. Canadian business students are generally assigned either American textbooks, or 'Canadianized' editions of American textbooks. The textbooks and the models within, developed to teach students how to manage in American corporations, are adopted uncritically in Canada (Boothman, 2000). The use of American or Canadianized textbooks perpetuates the belief that management theory as developed in the United States is universal and can be applied in any context. While the textbook is ostensibly universal, studies have shown the influence of context on the development of management education curricula and textbooks, and that the textbook is very much a product of its geographic and temporal context (Foster, Helms Mills & Mills, 2014a; Grant and Mills, 2006; McLaren, 2011; McLaren and Helms Mills, 2010; McLaren and Mills, 2008; McLaren, Mills & Durepos, 2009; Mills and Helms Hatfield, 1998).

Canadian business school faculty are exhorted to publish in 'top tier' academic journals to earn tenure and promotion for themselves, and prestige and funding dollars for their university. Those so-called 'leading' management journals are strongly positivist and decontextualized,

English-language, and mainly American. Management journals publish research that adds to the extant literature, incrementally filling in gaps, rather than research that questions dominant assumptions (Alvesson and Sandberg, 2012). The paucity of research focused on Canadians and Canadian organizations suggests that it is not valued by the leading management journals, and Canada's only MOS journal, the *Canadian Journal of Administrative Sciences*, struggles to gain legitimacy as a high-quality academic journal (McLaren and Mills, 2013). This results in Canadian academics feeling that they need to conduct 'context-free' (meaning American) research to be successful in their careers in Canadian universities. Similarly, the Administrative Sciences Association of Canada (ASAC), was created to provide a home for Canadian business scholars and research, but has struggled over the years with maintaining a Canadian identity and attracting senior and expert scholars to its membership and conferences (McLaren and Mills, 2013). Canadian business schools themselves are based on the structure of American business schools, and are becoming more American under increasing pressure to earn AACSB (Association to Advance Collegiate Business Schools) accreditation for both legitimacy and financial reasons (McKee, Mills & Weatherbee, 2005).

Management theory in Canada

The impetus for the development of management theory as a formal body of knowledge and an academic discipline came from the United States and was provided, in part, by the influx of Second World War veterans into business schools on the GI bill (Cheit, 1985), the push for professionalization and specialized training of managers by industry (Khurana, 2007), and the perspective of academics that the existing vocational schools of business (based in the universities through University Extension) were unscholarly and a threat to academic legitimacy (O'Connor, 2012).

Both the Second World War and the increasing separation of ownership and control of corporations led to a push for specialized training of managers, as the realization that good managers, who were no longer the owners, were made, not born (Bendix, 1974). The massive managerial effort required to support the Second World War and the subsequent Marshall Plan, also known as the European Recovery Plan, showed that effective management required specific management processes that needed to be learned (Drucker, 1973). As US Second World War veterans flooded into the business schools, which made themselves the most open of the professional and academic schools (O'Connor, 2012), a curriculum needed to be developed and faculty needed to be found. The organizational and efficiency principles developed by the military during the Second World War formed the foundation of the business school curriculum (McFarland, 1964), with the ensuing Cold War years having a strong, and until recently ignored, influence on the research undertaken and the curriculum taught (Grant and Mills, 2006; McLaren and Mills, 2008; Mills and Helms Hatfield, 1998). The faculty were first pulled from related disciplines, such as economics, psychology, and sociology (Khurana, 2007).

Along with the need for individuals in managerial roles to have specialized training, US industry was seeking professionalization for the management profession, to elevate managerial status to the same levels as doctors and lawyers (Khurana, 2007). At the same time, business schools were seeking legitimacy within the academy, and the academy was likewise concerned about increasing the legitimacy of business schools to protect its own reputation (O'Connor, 2012). The search for legitimacy, as both a profession and an academic discipline, led to a concerted effort to develop management theory as a science. In a backlash against the classics-based university that came before, the research-based university was founded on the basis of science, positivism, and empiricism. Rather than being an institution for passing existing knowledge along to the next generation, the research-based university was a place for knowledge to be created. First the social sciences, and then the business school, adopted the scientific method of inquiry to achieve legitimacy within the research-based university (Kieser, 1994; O'Connor, 2012). The concept of history was written out of management theory as nomothetic, abstract principles were favoured, context was ignored, and teleology and determinism were assumed (Weatherbee, 2012; Zald, 1993).

The immediate post-war years saw the rise of behaviourism in American business schools and an associated influence on the fields of psychology and sociology (Robin, 2001). This was led and exemplified by the RAND Corporation, which for many years was to play an influential role in the development of business theory and the social sciences in the United States (Abella, 2008). In the process the US military played an important role in the funding of behavioural research (Abella, 2008; Deitchman, 1976; Witzel, 2012), as did the large funding bodies such as the Ford and Carnegie Foundations (Abella, 2008; Macdonald, 1956).

Canadian business schools saw similar pressures as those in the United States, with growth through Second World War veterans, pressure for managers to become professionalized, and pressure for the business discipline to achieve legitimacy within the Canadian academy. While American business schools had been developing since the late 1800s, with rapid growth following the Second World War, Canadian business schools were in their early growth stages following the war. The backlash against vocational and professional programmes within the Canadian academy was greater than that in the United States, and Canadian businessmen were sceptical of the value of a post-secondary business education (Boothman, 2000), and of the techniques college-educated managers were bringing to the shop floor (Taylor, 2009). Canadian business schools based their structures on their American counterparts (Austin, 2000), and by the time they were actively recruiting faculty for undergraduate and MBA programmes, US business schools were graduating PhDs in business. The first Canadian business PhD degree was not approved until 1961 (Yavas, Kaynak & Dilber, 1985), so business school faculty consisted of American PhDs, Canadian PhDs from other disciplines, and part-time instructors; deans were either American, or educated in the United States (Boothman, 2000).

With American structures, deans, and faculty came American curriculum and textbooks. The Canadian business degree curriculum was based on textbooks written and published by Americans, and for the most part remains that way today. The small size of the Canadian textbook market means that the publication of distinctly Canadian texts, readings, or cases is not economically viable (Boothman, 2000). Some publishers produce Canadianized editions of American management textbooks (i.e. texts that were originally written for the US market that are subsequently altered to sell in Canada) but differences are generally restricted to simple substitutions of legal requirements of employers, employment rights (McLaren and Helms Mills, 2010), or terminology, such as substituting 'municipal council' for 'county board' (Fitzgerald and Mills, 2012). The sheer volume of US texts continues to this day to greatly outweigh the number of Canadian texts on offer – although the existing publishers have increasingly produced Canadian and Canadianized texts over the past two decades. While it appears that a call for Canadian content is being answered by publishers, further analysis will be needed to determine how Canadian the content actually is. We view as 'Canadian' those texts that are written specifically for Canadian-based university students and faculty by setting out to relate theories of management to the political, economic, and legal systems in place in Canada.

Over time, in continued attempts to legitimize the business school within the academy, business faculty, both American and Canadian, were placed under increased pressure to publish their research in social science-based journals. Tenure and promotion became increasingly dependent on publication in 'top tier' journals. The top tier journals for business schools are mainly

American, and strongly favour positivist, quantitative, decontextualized research (Alvesson and Sandberg, 2012). The publishing environment lays strict boundaries on what is acceptable research. Consequently, challenges to the existing bases of management theory – let alone with the assertion that it does not work for Canadians – is unlikely to get published. Top tier journals are far more likely to publish gap-spotting work, rather than work that challenges the status quo (Alvesson and Sandberg, 2012).

Among many obvious reasons as to why a Canadian management theory has never emerged, including the development and dominance of the business school in the United States (Boothman, 2000), and the influence of the Cold War (Hewitt, 2002; Horn, 1999), there lies a more subtle reason. As management theory came to be treated as a science, a perspective that was engaged explicitly to provide legitimization for the discipline and over time became the unquestioned and accepted reality, nomothetic, deterministic, and teleological principles became the expectation (Weatherbee, 2012). Management researchers were seeking the overarching theories that applied to every organization, and every person in that organization, in the same way. Differences in social, political, and economic contexts were either considered only as variables to be controlled or, more often, not considered at all. Researchers were seeking to develop not an American management theory, but a management theory that could be applied everywhere (Rowlinson, Jacques & Booth, 2009). US-based management theory had become universalist management theory.

Context, however, cannot be removed from research into, or the practice of, management. In our situation context applies in two ways – the context in which the researcher is working that is guiding what s/he studies, and the context of the population under study in terms of location, culture, diversity, etc. Canadian business academics work in a context that marginalizes the study of management in Canada as distinct from management in the United States. For hiring, tenure, and promotion, they are expected to publish in American 'context-free' journals. In the classroom, they are expected to teach curriculum developed largely in the United States. Research focused on Canadian issues can find a home with ASAC and CJAS, which exist to support Canadian research, but the research published by those outlets is deemed of second or third-tier quality by Canadian business school faculty (McLaren and Mills, 2013). Underlying all of this is the belief that management theory is a science, and therefore existing research applies to both Canadians and Americans equally.

Making the case for Canadian management theory

Setting aside, for the moment, discussion of the nomothetic nature of management theory, and accepting that current management theory is mainly American, one might question if Canada is different from the United States in ways that are relevant to management theory. Canada is often seen as the economically smaller, more polite neighbour to the north and beyond the stereotypical differences (the Great White North) is viewed as essentially American. Is there a need for Canadian management theory?

We present a set of fundamental ways in which Canada differs from the United States to make our case that Canada does need its own management theory, but we are not the first to make this call. In 1957, deans of Canadian business schools met as a formal group for the first time, a meeting which led to the creation of what is now known as the Administrative Sciences Association of Canada (ASAC). In existence, in various incarnations and with a variety of names, for over 60 years, one of the fundamental elements of ASAC's mission has been to provide a home for Canadian business researchers and to solve the problems distinct to Canada (McLaren and Mills, 2013). A recent study of Cold War influences on Canadian and American business textbooks (Foster, Helms Mills & Mills, 2014a) found calls from the 1960s for textbooks geared to the Canadian context, and a recognition that the contexts differ:

> One consideration prompting this book was that many good texts in this field are written by Americans for the American scene, with consequently no allowance for the fact that our constitutional structure, trade and balance of payments picture, banking system, government regulations, system of taxation, degree of foreign ownership, size of market, and business laws are very different.
>
> *(Pugsley, 1965, as quoted in Foster, Helms Mills & Mills, 2013: 654)*

In Boothman's end of the twentieth century analysis of Canadian management education he raises the complaints of students and practitioners that "business faculty give grossly inadequate attention to the actual organizational traits and environmental framework of 'Canadian' capitalism" (2000: 304).

At a broader Canadian level, from 1972 to 1976 Thomas H. B. Symons chaired the Commission on Canadian Studies, whose mandate was to study and to make recommendations on the state of teaching and research in various fields of study relating to Canada at Canadian universities. The resulting report, *To Know Ourselves*, found that "[i]t would be a betrayal of their social and intellectual functions if Canadian universities failed to contribute substantially to an understanding and amelioration of Canada's distinctive problems" (Symons, 1978: 19). Across disciplines throughout Canadian universities many felt that Canadian problems were "almost by definition of only second-rate importance" (Symons, 1978: 26) and were failing to study Canadian problems. Scientists viewed publishing in Canadian journals "as an act of charity" (Symons, 1978: 108). Specific to business, Symons found that while there is no country in the world in which business has occupied a more central role in national development, Canadian business and management have received far too little detailed study (Symons, 1978).

Looking back

Canada differs from the United States in fundamental ways: the country developed as a resource-based economy with significant amounts of foreign investment; while geographically large in size it has a small population spread across its southern border, divided regionally by cultural, linguistic, political, and economic differences; and it is a welfare state with a history of strong activist governments and an electorally-viable social democratic political party. This political, economic, and cultural context has a strong influence on how organizations operate and people are managed, and there needs to be management theory that fits the context, explains the behaviours, and helps Canadian organizations be successful. At the same time, some aspects of the context have contributed to the dominance of American management theory in Canadian business schools and organizations.

We briefly introduce some aspects of Canada's history and context here, to begin to illustrate how fundamentally management in Canada is impacted by its context. The history of Canada and its relationship to the United States is obviously far more detailed, complex, and nuanced than we can present in this chapter, and we recognize that in selecting a few differences on which to focus, and in simplifying them, we are creating our own history.

Economic protectionism

Geographic size notwithstanding, Canada's population has been consistently about one-tenth the size of the United States, with the majority of Canadians dwelling within 100 miles of the

US border (Thompson and Randall, 2008). The significantly larger population of the United States, and the position of the United States on the world stage, has created an ongoing power imbalance between the two countries, economically, politically, and culturally. Canada's economic growth and development since the 1500s has been based on its natural resources, with wealth coming from fisheries, furs, forests, agriculture, minerals, oil, and hydro-electricity (Martin and Milway, 2012). Rather than developing secondary industries to manufacture products from the resources, early Canadian business leaders were more interested in extracting and trading the raw materials (Craib, 1986). Canada's resources have been developed primarily through foreign investment, in the beginning British and French, in the post-First World War years mainly American (Taylor, 2009), and now still mainly American, with China playing an increasingly greater role in the past two decades.

The Canadian government has enacted a long history of activist and interventionist measures to protect Canada from dominance by the United States and to bring other foreign investment into the country. The National Policy, brought into effect in 1878 (Granatstein, 1983), created protective tariffs for domestic manufactured goods and a national railway for market development (Taylor, 2009). As the tariff system protected products, rather than producers, it encouraged American companies to set up branch plants in Canada, injecting foreign capital and employing Canadians. At the same time, however, Canadian manufacturers struggled to compete with the branch plants that could draw on the financial resources and experience of American-owned companies. Canadian entrepreneurship, innovation, and risk-taking was discouraged by the National Policy through both the foreign-owned branch plants (Craib, 1986) and the protection of Canadian business from foreign competition (Granatstein, 1983), the impacts of which we are still seeing today (Martin and Milway, 2012). Branch plants also had implications for research and development (R&D) and innovation in Canada. The responsibility of a branch plant was to penetrate the local market with a product that had been developed by the parent company (Craib, 1986), and as such subsidiaries were rarely equipped with R&D capabilities (Taylor, 2009). At the same time, the best and brightest Canadians were being recruited to US and multinational firms, not Canadian.

Social welfare

Along with being an activist state in terms of protectionism, Canada has also developed a strong ideological foundation as a socialist welfare state. Canada's move toward socialism actually followed the Americans, as Canadians and Canadian governments followed both the American Populist era and the implementation of the New Deal (Boyko, 2010; Taylor, 2009). Where the post-Second World War era in the United States saw a turning away from socialism and the rise of big business, in part in response to the Cold War, the fear of a return to the Great Depression led Canadians to demand jobs, security, and a good standard of living. Canada's first socialist-democratic party, the Co-operative Commonwealth Federation (CCF), promised Canadians social security, and indeed was the party that introduced socialized healthcare to Canada during the time that they held the provincial government in Saskatchewan. Recognizing the importance of the welfare state to Canadians, it was the Liberal government of Mackenzie King that responded (Granatstein, 1983). Canada's welfare state now includes a national healthcare system, a national pension plan, unemployment insurance, a welfare system, and provincially-run and subsidized post-secondary education.

We see again how the context in which Canadian versus American organizations exist differs drastically. At an explicit level, the influence of national healthcare to Canadian organizations, relative to the expectation that American organizations provide medical insurance to employees, must have had, and is still having, a huge impact on management theory areas of research such as, to name only a few, employee motivation, organizational culture, and productivity. At an ideological level, employees who believe in the value of the welfare state are a different group of people than those who believe in individual rights over the collective. These differences must be taken into consideration when understanding how to manage.

Diversity

Canada is a country composed of distinct regions which are reflected politically, culturally, and economically. Economically and politically businesses deal with multiple levels of government, with some regulatory structures provincial, some federal, and some both. As regulations differ between levels, business owners struggle to understand their implications, but can also choose which jurisdiction is most favourable to their operations (Taylor, 2009). The National Policy, put in place to protect Canada from American dominance, was also purposively crafted to bring the disparate regions of Canada together (Thompson and Randall, 2008), through the construction of trans-Canadian railway systems and strong support for immigration to western Canada.

Alongside the cultural differences between Atlantic Canada, Ontario, the prairies, and western Canada, lie the official legislation of Canada as a French-English bilingual country and its pursuit of a policy of multiculturalism. Multiculturalism in Canada refers to "the presence and persistence of diverse racial and ethnic minorities who define themselves as different and who wish to remain so" (Dewing, 2009: 1). In the 2006 Canadian census, more than 200 different ethnic origins were reported, 19.8 per cent of the population had been born outside of Canada, the visible minority population was 16.2 per cent, and allophones (having a mother tongue other than English, French, or an Aboriginal language) were at 20.1 per cent of the population (Dewing, 2009). Canada is known as a cultural mosaic relative to the American melting pot, and strives to integrate immigrants into Canada without asking them to give up their cultural distinctiveness. While it is acknowledged that maintaining cultural diversity has not translated into integration of races and ethnicities throughout all levels of Canadian society (Porter, 1965), the diversity is still a factor that needs to be understood within organizations.

As workplace diversity is becoming a matter of concern for both academics and practitioners within the new global marketplace, Canada has a long history of dealing with diversity issues as a result of cultural differences between regions, official national bilingualism, and strong immigration rates into a country that ideologically espouses ethnic integration rather than ethnic suppression. What can we, as management theorists, learn from how Canadian organizations handle diversity and what value could we bring to Canadian organizations by understanding their specific diversity needs?

Looking forward

Understanding how and why the Canadian context differs from the United States, and therefore why a Canadian management theory would have had value for Canadian organizations, is the first step in moving from a purely scientific, context-free model of management theory. Using this understanding, and our understanding of Canada, we can look forward and assess the Canadian context with an eye to exploring how the current context may be influencing the business world and what direction our research should take to provide value to Canadian business practitioners.

Traces of a body of work that can be termed Canadian management theory can be found. Canadian management textbooks published in the 1960s reflect Canada's slightly more moderate stance on the Cold War through acknowledgement of communism as an alternative to capitalism, and Canada's welfare capitalism through the acknowledgement of legitimate forms of organization other than the free enterprise, such as cooperatives and Crown corporations. This is in comparison to American textbooks of the same decade, in which neither communism nor organizational forms other than free enterprise were discussed (Foster, Helms Mills & Mills, 2014a). We see here empirical evidence of the influence of ideological differences on management practice and theory.

Management practice, while yet to be studied specifically, must differ in many ways between the two countries as Canadian organizations work within different regulatory environments, with a different population demographic embedded within different ideological frameworks, and within a different economic reality. A Crown corporation does not function in exactly the same way as a for-profit corporation, and as Crown corporations play a large role in the Canadian economy there must be different management practices in use than are currently accounted for in the American management theory that we have adopted as our own.

Based on their work with the Institute for Competitiveness & Prosperity, Roger Martin and James Milway published the book *Canada: What It Is, What It Can Be* (2012), an assessment of Canada's past economic performance, the three drivers of productivity and innovation, and how to take Canada's economy to a higher level of sophistication. The book alone provides a strong argument for a need for Canadian management theory. Let's look at some specifics. Martin and Milway (2012) contend that, for a variety of historical reasons, Canada is currently a strong country, both economically and in terms of happiness. They contend, though, that also for a variety of historical reasons, over the past few decades Canada has begun falling farther and farther behind countries such as the United States, Belgium, France, Germany, and the Netherlands in terms of economic prosperity, competitiveness, and innovation. They posit that Canadians trail in innovation measures, that we are slow in adopting new technologies, that fewer Canadians live in metropolitan areas as compared to Americans, that Canadians lack competitive intensity, that we have significant amounts of regulation protecting us from intense foreign and domestic competition, that we under-invest in both technology and education, and that we do not adequately recognize the importance of management for innovation.

If any of their conclusions have a basis in fact (which we think they do), why would Canadian management academics ever assume that research done in an American context, with American participants, embedded in American ideologies, develop theory that is valuable for solving problems in Canadian industry? If Canadians are falling behind in innovation we need to understand why it is happening and how to fix it. Or, maybe a greater understanding of Canadians would lead us to the conclusion that there is nothing to fix. Martin and Milway (2012) assert that Canadian workers are less productive because those with higher education and higher incomes choose to work fewer hours over the course of a year than American workers of similar education and income levels. They think that there is greater financial return for highly-skilled Americans to work more hours than for Canadians, so Canadians choose to work fewer hours because they will not be financially rewarded at a high enough level. Their explanation of the productivity gap treats Canadians and Americans as having the same underlying goals – earning as much money as possible, as efficiently as possible. Maybe, though, highly-skilled Canadians choose to work fewer hours than Americans because the hours that they do work earn them enough money to meet their desired standard of living, and that they value life outside of work more than they value higher financial standing; significant sociological reasons for the difference. We have no way of knowing which explanation is correct, or, most likely, what combination of the two reasons, without studying Canadian workers in their Canadian context.

The introduction to Canada that we have presented in this chapter raises questions around, to name but a few, issues such as the National Policy and its impact on Canadian entrepreneurship, risk-taking, and innovation; Canada's welfare state ideology and organizational culture, motivation, and form; Canada's response to the Cold War and organizational form and labour relations; Canada's economy and population size and organizational form, risk-taking, and innovation; Canada's federal and provincial governments and organizational form and innovation; Canada's regional and ethnic diversity and workplace diversity, creativity, and innovation; and the impact of all of these factors on the integral management issue of power.

Conclusion

While management theory is espoused as scientific, deterministic, and teleological (Burrell and Morgan, 1979), the growing body of work incorporating history into both the analysis of existing theory and the development of new theory is showing the contextual and relational nature of the body of knowledge, and changing our understanding of what it means to develop management theory (Witzel, 2012). In this chapter we have presented a history of the development of management theory that illustrates the influence of the political, social, and economic situation during which the main body of knowledge was being developed, and we have drawn specific attention to the lack of a distinct Canadian management theory. We then briefly presented some fundamental elements of Canada's past that have created a distinct context from that of the United States, and explored how those differences have created a context in which business and management is done differently. Finally, we look forward at Canada's economic future and posit a few areas, out of many possibilities, in which studying the Canadian business and organizational context as distinct from the United States would be of great benefit to Canada. All of this is undertaken while maintaining awareness that in 'creating' a Canadian history we do so as actors embedded within our own networks, needs, and goals.

Moving forward we see many avenues of study for individuals interested in taking up the call to develop a Canadian management theory. One of the current concerns being raised by Canadian industry and government is the lack of innovation in Canada, an issue that can be directly tied to the National Policy and Canada's history of protectionism. We are confident that many more of the concerns in Canadian industry today can be traced back, in part, to Canada's historical context. In understanding why we are in our current situation, we can begin looking forward to how to develop theory that works for Canadian organizations. We also believe that there are many elements of management practice in Canada that differ from that in the United States, and from commonly-accepted management theory. Determining what those differences are, and why, forms the basis of our new Canadian management theory project.

The American influence on management education and dominance of management theory is not restricted to Canada. A 2004 symposium on the Americanization of European management education published in the *Journal of Management Inquiry* presents historical and comparative perspectives on the Americanization of form and content in management education (Üsdiken, 2004) in four distinct European regions: the Nordic countries (Engwall, 2004), Britain (Tiratsoo, 2004), Germany (Kieser, 2004), and Mediterranean Europe (Kipping, Üsdiken & Puig, 2004). One of the ways in which the European situation differs from the Canadian is that each of the regions had developed its own business, or economic, education systems prior to the dominance of the United States, and each has slowly, to varying extents and in varying ways, been adopting American form, content, and research. Wanderley and Faria (2012) have recently published an analysis of the suppression of management theory from South America due to epistemic coloniality. Their specific argument is that if Americans considered all knowledge legitimate, rather than unilaterally imposing their own knowledge on everyone else, the crisis of legitimacy in strategic management could have been avoided through the acknowledgement and use of the work of Celso Furtado in response to, and conjunction with, that of Alfred Chandler.

We, as Canadians, will undertake empirical work to move forward into a deeper and more detailed understanding of Canadian history and its influence on a Canadian management theory, as well as the development of a Canadian management theory. At the same time we put forth a call for management scholars from other regions, including the United States, to understand how and why their management theory has developed as it has, and to begin the process of developing a body of knowledge that takes into consideration, at all levels, our contextual differences. As theories are interesting and influential when they challenge dominant assumptions in significant ways (Alvesson and Sandberg, 2012), we believe that in calling for a body of literature that develops a Canadian management theory, and in extending that call beyond Canada to all contexts, we are calling for management scholars to undertake interesting and influential work.

References

Abella, A. (2008) *Soldiers of Reason: The Rand Corporation and the Rise of the American empire*. New York: Harcourt.

Alvesson, M. and Sandberg, J. (2012) Has management studies lost its way? Ideas for more imaginative and innovative research, *Journal of Management Studies*, 50: 128–52.

Austin, B. (2000) The Administrative Sciences Association of Canada, 1957–1999, in B. Austin (ed.), *Capitalizing Knowledge: Essays on the History of Business Education in Canada* (pp. 266–94). Toronto: University of Toronto Press.

Bendix, R. (1974) *Work and Authority in Industry*. Berkeley, CA: University of California Press.

Booth, C. and Rowlinson, M. (2006) Management and organizational history: Prospects, *Management & Organizational History*, 1(1): 5–30.

Boothman, B. (2000) Culture of utility: The development of business education in Canada, in B. Austin (ed.), *Capitalizing Knowledge: Essays on the History of Business Education in Canada* (pp. 11–86). Toronto: University of Toronto Press.

Boyko, J. (2010) *Bennett*. Toronto: Key Porter Books.

Burrell, G. and Morgan, G. (1979) *Sociological Paradigms and Organizational Analysis*. London: Heinemann.

Cheit, E. (1985) Business schools and their critics, *California Management Review*, 27: 43–62.

Cooke, B. (1999) Writing the left out of management theory: The historiography of the management of change, *Organization* 6: 81–105.

Cooke, B. (2006) The Cold War origin of action research as managerialist cooptation, *Human Relations*, 59: 665–93.

Craib, P.W. (1986) Canadian-based research and development: Why so little? in K. L. P. Lundy and B. Warme (eds), *Work in the Canadian Context: Continuity Despite Change* (pp. 6–21). Toronto: Butterworths.

Deitchman, S. J. (1976) *The Best-Laid Schemes: A Tale of Social Research and Bureaucracy*. Cambridge, MA: MIT Press.

Dewing, M. (2009) *Canadian Multiculturalism*. Ottawa: Library of Parliament.

Drucker, P. F. (1973) *Management: Tasks, Responsibilities, Practices*. New York: Harper & Row.

Durepos, G. and Mills, A. J. (2012) *ANTi-History: Theorizing the Past, History, and Historiography in Management and Organizational Studies*. Charlotte, NC: Information Age Publishing.

Durepos, G., Mills, A. J., and Weatherbee, T. G. (2012) Theorizing the past: Realism, relativism, relationalism, and the reassembly of Weber, *Management & Organizational History*, 7: 267–81.

Engwall, L. (2004) The Americanization of Nordic management education, *Journal of Management Inquiry* 13: 109–17.

Fitzgerald, C. and Mills, A. J. (2012) Human resource management a function of the past: A content analysis of the first edition Canadian introductory human resource management textbooks, *Research and Practice in Human Resource Management*, 20: 13–27.

Foster, J., Helms Mills, J., and Mills, A. J. (2014a) Shades of red: Cold War influences on Canadian and US business textbooks, *Journal of Management Education*, 38: 642–71.

Foster, J., Mills, A. J., and Weatherbee, T. G. (2014b) History, field definition and management studies: The case of the New Deal, *Journal of Management History*, 20: 179–89.

George, C. S. (1968) *The History of Management Thought*. Englewood Cliffs, NJ: Prentice-Hall.

George, C. S. (1972) *The History of Management Thought* (2nd edn). Englewood Cliffs, NJ: Prentice-Hall.

Granatstein, J. L. (1983) *Twentieth Century Canada*. Toronto: McGraw-Hill Ryerson.

Grant, J. D. and Mills, A. J. (2006) The quiet Americans: Formative context, the Academy of Management leadership, and the management textbook, 1936–1960, *Management & Organizational History*, 1: 201–24.

Hewitt, S. (2002) *Spying 101: The RCMP's Secret Activities at Canadian Universities, 1917–1997*. Toronto: University of Toronto Press.

Horn, M. (1999) *Academic Freedom in Canada: A History*. Toronto: Univerity of Toronto Press.

Kelley, E., Mills, A., and Cooke, B. (2006) Management as a Cold War phenomenon? *Human Relations*, 59: 603–10

Khurana, R. (2007) *From Higher Aims to Hired Hands: The Social Transformation of American Business Schools and the Unfulfilled Promise of Management as a Profession*. Princeton, NJ: Princeton University Press.

Kieser, A. (1994) Why organization theory needs historical analyses: And how this should be performed, *Organization Science*, 5: 608–20.

Kieser, A. (2004) The Americanization of academic management education in Germany, *Journal of Management Inquiry*, 13: 90–97.

Kipping, M., Üsdiken, B., and Puig, N. (2004) Imitation, tension, and hydridization: Multiple 'Americanizations' of management education in Mediterranean Europe, *Journal of Management Inquiry*, 13: 98–108.

Latour, B. (2005) *Reassembling the Social*. Oxford: Oxford University Press.

Macdonald, D. (1956) *The Ford Foundation: The Men and the Millions*. New York: Reynal & Company.

McFarland, D. E. (1964) *Management: Principles and Practices*. New York: Macmillan.

McKee, M. C., Mills, A. J., and Weatherbee, T. G. (2005) Institutional field of dreams: Exploring the AACSB and the new legitimacy of Canadian business schools, *Canadian Journal of Administrative Sciences*, 22: 288–301.

McLaren, P. G. (2011) James Burnham, the managerial revolution, and the development of management theory in post-war America, *Management & Organizational History*, 6: 411–23.

McLaren, P. G. and Helms Mills, J. (2010) Appropriation, manipulation, and silence: A critical hermeneutic analysis of the management textbook as a tool of the corporate discourse, *Management & Organizational History*, 5: 408–27.

McLaren, P. G. and Mills, A. J. (2008) A product of 'his' time? Exploring the construct of the ideal manager in the Cold War era, *Journal of Management History*, 14: 386–403.

McLaren, P. G. and Mills, A. J. (2013) Internal cohesion in response to institutional plurality: The Administrative Sciences Association of Canada, *Canadian Journal of Administrative Sciences*, 30: 40–55.

McLaren, P. G., Mills, A. J., and Durepos, G. (2009) Disseminating Drucker: Analysis of the work of Peter F. Drucker in the North American management textbook, *Journal of Management History*, 15: 388–403.

Martin, R. and Milway, J. (2012) *Canada: What It Is, What It Can Be*. Toronto: University of Toronto Press.

Mills, A. J. and Helms Hatfield, J. (1998) From imperialism to globalization: Internationalization and the management text, in S. Clegg, E., Ibarra and L. Bueno (eds), *Theories of the Management Process: Making Sense Through Difference* (pp. 37–67). Thousand Oaks, CA: Sage.

Munslow, A. (2010) *The Future of History*. Basingstoke: Palgrave Macmillan.

O'Connor, E. S. (2012) *Creating New Knowledge in Management: Appropriating the Field's Lost Foundations*. Stanford, CA: Stanford Business Books.

Porter, J. (1965) *The Vertical Mosaic: An Analysis of Social Class and Power in Canada*. Toronto: University of Toronto Press.

Pugsley, W. H. (1965) *Canadian Business Organization and Management*. Toronto: McGraw-Hill.

Robin, R. (2001) *The Making of the Cold War Enemy*. Princeton, NJ: Princeton University Press.

Rowlinson, M., Jacques, R., and Booth, C. (2009) Critical management and organizational history, in M. Alvesson, T. Bridgman, and H. Willmott (eds), *The Oxford Handbook of Critical Management Studies* (pp. 286–303). Oxford: Oxford University Press.

Symons, T. H. B. (1978) *The Symons Report: An abridged version of volumes 1 and 2. To Know Ourselves: The Report of the Commission on Canadian Studies*. Toronto: The Book and Periodical Development Council.

Taylor, G. D. (2009) *The Rise of Canadian Business*. Toronto: Oxford University Press.

Thompson, J. H. and Randall, S. J. (2008) *Canada and the United States: Ambivalent Allies*. Athens, GA: University of Georgia Press.

Tiratsoo, N. (2004) The 'Americanization' of management education in Britain. *Journal of Management Inquiry*, 13: 118–26.

Urwick, L. (1963) *The Golden Book of Management*. London: Newman Neame.

Üsdiken, B. (2004) Americanization of European management education in historical and comparative perspective, *Journal of Management Inquiry*, 13: 87–89.

Wanderley, S. and Faria, A. (2012) The Chandler-Furtado case: A de-colonial re-framing of a North/South (dis)encounter, *Management & Organizational History*, 7: 219–36.
Weatherbee, T. G. (2012) Caution! This historiography makes wide turns: Historic turns and breaks in management and organization studies, *Management & Organizational History*, 7: 203–18.
Weatherbee, T. G. and Durepos, G. (2010) Dar'Wren'ian evolution in management: Implications of the ethics of epistemology for the scholar, Academy of Management Annual Meeting, Montreal.
Witzel, M. (2012) *A History of Management Thought*. London: Routledge.
Wren, D. A. (1972) *The Evolution of Management Thought*. New York: Ronald Press.
Wren, D. A. and Bedeian, A. G. (2009) *The Evolution of Management Thought* (6th edn). Hoboken, NJ: John Wiley.
Yavas, U., Kaynak, E., and Dilber, M. (1985) The managerial climate in less-developed countries, *Management Decision* 23: 29–40.
Zald, M. N. (1993) Organization studies as a scientific and humanistic enterprise: Toward a reconceptualization of the foundations of the field, *Organization Science*, 4: 513–28.

23

Is there any future for critical management studies in Latin America?

Moving from epistemic coloniality to 'trans-discipline'

Eduardo Ibarra-Colado

To discuss properly the situation of Critical Management Studies in Latin America, it is necessary to recognize the colonial condition under which the region has developed since the 'discovery/(invasion)' of America five centuries ago. Generally, the discussion over coloniality emphasizes its political dimension, but not its epistemic one.

When we consider Management Studies and how they have been developed in Latin America, it is essential to discuss the function of knowledge as a mechanism of colonization.

Coloniality must be understood in its institutional dimensions, as a deliberate action of power to dominate and subjugate the other. It is the hidden face of Modernity, always considered the stage made possible by the development of reason, instead of the process of invasion/destruction/invention based on the power of weapons, ideas and symbols to impose a unique civilizing process. From this point of view, power instead of reason explains the splendour of Europe and America and the prevalence of some kind of knowledge over others.

At least three institutions have been essential in the operation of colonization: the Church and evangelism to produce silence and colonize the soul; the *Hacienda* and mills to produce discipline and obedience at work and to colonize the body; and the University and science to produce truth and colonize the understanding of the world. The organization of knowledge and their associated practices in the modern *Universitas* has guaranteed the reproduction of disciplines as we know them and, at the same time, has obstructed different ways to live and imagine academic work, discouraging or forbidding alternative practices.

This institutional conformation is essential when debating the current situation of Management Studies in Latin America, because it has facilitated the transfer of knowledge from the centre. Until now and dominantly, most of the Latin American researchers have been copying and pasting syllabus, theories, methodologies and other management fads and fashions manufactured in the Anglo-Saxon countries, it doesn't matter if the appropriation is on mainstream theories or in those produced by critters or pomos.

In a preliminary exercise of intuition, we can recognize some mechanisms that stimulate these copy-paste practices. For example, most of the Latin American scholars in the field do not recognize the colonial condition of the region and, consequently, they systematically deny the structural differences and asymmetries with the centre. The problem is seen as one of development and the solution is reduced to the appropriate application of those management and organizational knowledge produced in the most developed countries. This uncritical acceptance of the Anglo-Saxon theories conditions the type of explanation of the problems of the region and the type of solutions to confront them, producing in this way a certain kind of self-imposed coloniality.

Other mechanisms operate when the Latin American governments support young scholars to study overseas. By obtaining the status of 'foreign students', they can be 'educated properly' before returning to their countries and teach all the secrets obtained in the modern temples of knowledge. They will be trained in those 'proper academic practices' to become first-class scholars and to be able to follow the rules of the discipline to produce 'good science'. We are thinking, for example, in the argumentative and expository logic of a paper or presentation, usually governed by the internalized sequence of beginning with an introduction, establishing the main questions, developing the arguments to prove them with some sort of 'legitimate' data, and closing with a conclusion. Gaining this discipline implies also the adoption of a specific written style, the use of some expressions instead of others, the avoidance of some metaphors or symbolic constructions that seem to have no meaning for 'the modern self' and the scrupulous observation of schedules and deadlines.

Aside from this expertise about proper academic practices, language also plays a central role, operating in different ways. For example, when Latin American scholars speak or write in English, they adopt a strange way of expressing themselves, losing in their communicative action some degree of elaboration, complexity and specific meanings associated with some ways of saying or writing that can be expressed only in their native language. We must recall and emphasize that language is more than a neutral or innocent tool. It is a cultural device historically and locally constructed, that mediates the relationships between concrete individuals that live and operate in specific spaces and times. It entails the ways in which people learn and imagine who they are, what the world is, and to what community they belong.

Under these sorts of adopted rules, practices and language, 'the other' disappears and is silenced. Thus, when a Latin American scholar speaks and writes, their voice and words usually pronounce the learned ideas and arguments of 'the modern self' reinforcing the epistemic coloniality through transference and translation.

Despite this dominant situation, Latin America retains the vitality of its history and culture. There has been an important production of original ideas related to management and organization problems in the region. To give only some examples, there are relevant contributions made by Guillermo Bonfil-Batalla, Enrique Dussel, Enrique Florescano, Nestor García-Canclini, Alberto Guerreiro-Ramos and Leopoldo Zea to refer to only a few of a broader list. Scholars in Management Studies have usually ignored these contributions because they were produced in fields like philosophy, history, anthropology or sociology, and because they only read management literature! However, these contributions are important insights to develop CMS in the region to the extent they help us to recognize the organizational conformation of Latin American countries and of the specific experiences of management associated with some traditional, communitarian or non-modern ways of organization and government. Consider, for example, the experiences of communities that have learned how to survive in the worst conditions and how to create something with nothing, a real art of management and organization. By working in this direction, Latin American scholars will be able to recognize themselves in their differences and specificities, producing original knowledge about other ways of organizing and managing, and breaking the mechanical application of current approaches and recipes developed in the context of the centre.

The future of CMS in Latin America rests in the capacity to recognize and transcend the colonial condition, and to move from a stage of copying and pasting to a stage of self-recognition sustained in the production of knowledge locally referred. In addition, the future of CMS entails an encounter with a '*trans-discipline*', understood as a corpus of knowledge that 'transcend the discipline' because their knowledge is transversally built from one locale to another, considering different problems, experiences and solutions all over the world. In addition, the future of CMS must be imagined as a set of multiple dialogues and conversations between scholars and people of different regions and cultures to learn from each other, in the permanent re-construction of diverse management and organizational devices to improve and protect local styles of life respecting the differences.

24

Remembering Eduardo Ibarra-Colado

Nidhi Srinivas, Ana Guedes, and Alex Faria

Introduction

This chapter is written by three friends and colleagues of Eduardo Ibarra-Colado. It is our reflection on his scholarship and ideas, and how working with him shaped our perspectives on organizations and organization studies. We have divided this chapter into three parts: we begin first with a chronological overview of Eduardo's career and scholarship including his publications in Spanish; second we discuss some of the ideas and philosophies that animated Eduardo's engagement with the field of management; and finally we each share an anecdote of our encounter with Eduardo and what they demonstrated of his values and particular personality.

Eduardo's career: an overview

Eduardo's career from a distance can appear similar to that of many other successful academics in Latin America, completing their doctoral education, establishing a publication record in dual languages, serving on editorial boards, and working with doctoral students. From a closer gaze it was also a career of bold critique and resistance.

Eduardo was Professor of Management and Organization Studies at the Department of Economic Production at the Autonomous Metropolitan University, Campus Xochimilco, and founder of the *Laboratorio de Análisis Institucional del Sistema Universitario Mexicano* (Laboratory for Institutional Analysis of the Mexican University System) (LAISUM) which produced and maintained the website for the most complete and detailed analysis of the development and growth of public universities in Mexico.

He held academic positions at three campuses of the Autonomous Metropolitan University, as, from 1981, Professor of Management and Organization Theory, Coordinator of the BA on Management, and Head of the Organization Studies Research Group at the Department of Economics; and Coordinator of the MA and PhD in Labor Studies at the Department of Sociology, in Campus Iztapalapa. He was the Founder and First Head of the Department of Institutional Studies (2005–2009) and Professor of Management and Organization Theory,

Department of Institutional Studies, Campus Cuajimalpa. In 2010 he was Visiting Fellow at the Graduate School of Arts and Sciences Harvard University.

Eduardo obtained his PhD in Sociology with Honours at the Universidad Nacional Autónoma de México (1999) and received an award for the Best PhD Thesis in the Social Sciences and the Humanities, Universidad Nacional Autónoma de México, 2000. He was a National Researcher of the Mexican National System of Researchers, and regular member of the Mexican Academy of Sciences. His intellectual contributions are spread among numerous books, articles, editorial boards, research grants, conferences and associations, teaching, supervision and consultancies.

He published in the fields of Organization Studies and Higher Education Studies in México and abroad. Particularly notable are his contributions on power (*Mito y poder en las organizaciones* in 1984) and the Mexican higher education system (*La universidad en Mèxico hoy: gubernamentalidad y modernizacion* in 2001, for which he received the Research Award in Social Sciences and Humanities in 2003), and global management (*Global Management: Universal Theories, Local Realities*, with Steward Clegg and Luis Bueno in 1999). In 2006 his influential article 'Organization Studies and Epistemic Coloniality in Latin America: Thinking Otherness from the Margins', was published in *Organization*. The same issue of the journal also contained his important collaboration with the noted philosopher Enrique Dussel, 'Globalization, Organization and the Ethics of Liberation'. This text was originally the address delivered by Dussel to the Asia-Pacific Researchers of Organizations (APROS) conference in 2003, in San Cristóbal de las Casas, Mexico. Dussel worked with Ibarra-Colado in presenting the implication of his own philosophy of liberation for scholars of organizations.

These two articles, published in an internationally recognized journal, while reminding a generation of South American scholars of the hegemonic role of epistemic coloniality, also introduced Eduardo to many of us. It may seem superficial to observe that scholars in countries not so far apart from each other, functioning in sister languages such as Spanish and Portuguese, needed the global presence of an English-language journal such as *Organization* to acknowledge each other. Yet it is a reminder of the historical pattern of perceived superiority and recognition offered by knowledge published in English, a pattern we scholars continue to perpetuate in this region and outside it. Ironically enough Eduardo's journal articles argued precisely that such linguistic hegemony prevailed.

In 2007, he received the Best Critical Management Studies (CMS) Paper Nominee for his paper '"Entrepreneurialization" of the University: Shadows of the US History on the Ongoing Mexican Reform'. The same year, Walter Mignolo, coordinator of the *Worlds & Knowledges Otherwise Project*, stated that

> Ibarra-Colado makes a signal contribution as he unveils the logic of coloniality underneath current celebration of management; management as the key that opens all the doors toward a bright neo-liberal future. He sees, correctly in my view, 'management' as the new face of the logic of coloniality.
>
> *(Mignolo, 2007)*

From 2008 onward, there were a variety of significant contributions by Eduardo in critical management studies and more specifically critical international management, as convenor, guest editor, author, and co-author. But one particular moment has special meaning to us, the article 'Internationalization of management, neoliberalism and the Latin America challenge'[1] (Faria, Ibarro-Colado & Guedes, 2010) which marked the start of joint initiatives and projects at the

CMS and the Latin American and European Meeting on Organization Studies (LAEMOS). During this period as ties among the three of us with Eduardo grew, we particularly delighted in sharing and exploring the historic meaning of the concept of Latin America and the parochialism of the so-called 'international' domains within management. These ties also remind us of the poignancy in the title of one of his final publications, 'Cómo comprender y transformar los Estudios Organizacionales desde América Latina y no morir en el intento' (Ibarra-Colado, 2012) ('How to understand and transform Organization Studies within Latin America and not die while trying').

Across these projects as must be apparent by now, we see a thematic pattern, an argument on the need to struggle against, to bring forth, a set of ideas that offered an alternative view of organization studies, with a sensitivity to the history of Latin America and with an eye on social inequality, including that created by contemporary capitalism and the ideologies of business schools. The next section turns to this thematic pattern and fleshes out the guiding ideas in Eduardo's work.

Guiding ideas

A particular set of ideas and philosophies appeared to characterize Eduardo's research to the three of us. In this section we discuss four of them.

Firstly, the process of colonization and decolonization remains a vital influence on management theorizing. To Eduardo it was hardly coincidental that the directionality of management theorizing was oriented to the West, specifically towards the United States and Europe, such that production of theory occurred in their metropolitan centers and consumption of such theories dispersed outward to the peripheries of Latin America, South Asia, China, and elsewhere. The historical expansion of European societies, first towards the Americas, and then towards other continents, had transformed not only these societies, but also the way in which they were studied, assessed, and planned. The expansion had led to a differentiated and unequal configuration of the knowledge of societies, where the concepts, language, and evaluative standards, especially in the field of organization studies, rested in the historical centers of global capitalism, and were then applied as universal context-neutral tools to classify the societies that had been colonized by these very same centers.

Secondly, this process of colonialism had been elided and obscured within management studies. Few management scholars problematized colonization or discussed its influence on management theories and on the societies and organizations that such theories sought to explain. As a result of this silence, the trajectory of management knowledge appeared natural and inevitable, moving from Western Europe and the United States to Eastern Europe with the fall of communism and of the Soviet bloc in the 1990s, and then to the Global South as the pace of economic globalization quickened. This sense of historical inevitability strengthened a view of the South being somehow barren of management expertise and theories, requiring such specialized knowledge from the West. Crucially it was also taken for granted and deemed to be natural and inevitable that the language in which the knowledge would be offered was that of English.

Thirdly, this elision was part of a larger historical process. Eduardo's particular contribution was to situate this elision within a regional historical trajectory, that of the creole colonization of South America by Spanish and Portuguese through the sixteenth and seventeenth centuries. His collaboration with Enrique Dussel was particularly influential in this regard. Following Dussel, Eduardo argued that the creole colonization of South America brought with it an emphasis on a particular set of views of what individuals, nature, and society should be. These were views that became symptomatic of European modernity and displaced existing indigenous beliefs and values. What were these views? The primacy of agency was placed in the individual. Following René Descartes, European thinkers during the Enlightenment saw human beings as divinely gifted with intelligence, with an ability to reason. Such ability separated into two parts, that of the corporeal entity that housed the individual and the brain that offered cognition and identity. Thus I think therefore I am. Such a view of the individual displaced local ways of imagining agency that did not emphasize individuality alone, nor a separation of corporeality from cognition, and instead sought forms of relationality and empathy.

Similarly the onrush of the conquistadors and settlers into South America brought with it a view of the natural world as directly available for human exploitation. Nature was understood as being present for conquest and use, a resource to be exploited for human ends. Another alternative view of nature was displaced in this colonial process, one sensitive to the interdependence of human beings with the natural world that sought to find meaning through nature and not solely by dominating it. Finally, European settler society was stratified in a particular way. Power rested with colonizers and an expectation of market society, of economically distinct ideas of work productivity, employment and wages. This in turn displaced other forms of stratifications apparent in indigenous South American society, based on kinship, personal charisma, or divinity.

Creole colonization therefore created a dual pull within these countries. There was a pull away from the locality itself, where the indigenous people were violently moved out of their homes, dispossessed, resettled, exterminated, and converted to Western modes of thinking and being. And there was also the pull towards a metropole, where cultural resonance and legitimacy rested in these centers, and not in the peripheries of the colonies themselves. To Eduardo, it was this dual pull that shaped profoundly the dissemination of management ideas and the manner in which they were incorporated in South America. In these ways colonialism and its aftermath remained a potent influence on the discipline of management.

Fourthly, engaging with this history was a critical move. Such engagement was in effect a critical project, where the effort of challenging existing disciplinary investments and theoretical positions, was to mark, even re-imagine alternative epistemes and ontologies for managers, as well as for those studying them. There was in effect a possibility of reconstructing the trajectory of management knowledge, so that this dual pull now became instead a dual push, of indigenes asserting their identity and needs, and therefore pushing against urban creole constructions, and of former colonies redefining their professional identities away from metropolitan pressures. It was this dual push, we believe, that marked the aspirations and bounds of Eduardo's theoretical project.

Reflecting on Eduardo Ibarra-Colado

From 2008, Eduardo, Ana, and Alexandre worked together on the proposal of a CMS stream for the 2009 conference at Warwick University (although Eduardo could not be present due to institutional problems at his university). During this time, other South American scholars were being subject to hostile pressure at their institutions, at business schools in Chile and in Brazil, due to their research interests in critical studies. Critical management, depending on the particular university setting, was seen as irrelevant, marginal, or threatening the prevailing manner in which management education was to be conducted. Eduardo was always sympathetic to these many struggles and consistently argued for the idea that universities should be a locus of shared knowledge and experiences, with a tolerance for multiple and different theoretical perspectives.

Eduardo's ideas, concepts, and narrative style, especially in Spanish, always reminded his interlocutors that epistemic coloniality remained present and that a huge effort was required to overcome it, to credibly respect local realities and knowledge, in any effort of engagement, critique, or transformation. Each of us has vivid memories of Eduardo that remind us of his commitment to respecting local histories and realities. Ana and Alex recall first encountering Eduardo in Rio de Janeiro (II LAEMOS, 2008) and Buenos Aires (III LAEMOS, 2009). Through their encounters they were able to understand better the paradox that Latin America, usually represented as a cohesive whole, is in actuality incommunicable fragments whose scholarly representatives typically know of each other only through the intermediation of European and North American academics and journals. Ana recognizes especially that this sort of mutual solitude meant it took even longer for her to realize Eduardo's contributions.

At the same time Ana and Alex recall his ability to be a powerful catalyst, to explain what was needed for us to think otherwise. As the keynote speaker at the Brazilian Academy of Management conference held in Rio de Janeiro in 2008, he was able to personally experience the distance and the depth of the epistemic coloniality embodied in the scholars present in that room (Ibarra-Colado, 2008). Despite a powerful address, the audience reacted quite critically to it. What was at issue to them was not the content of what Eduardo said, nor what could be accomplished together, it was rather the fact that he chose to speak in Spanish! The questioning that followed reflected confusion and discomfort concerning his choice of language. He accepted it all with tranquillity, integrity, and politeness. In the following year, at the Third LAEMOS in Buenos Aires he appeared unsurprised during a fierce debate among Brazilian scholars on whether they were or were not Latin Americans. Naturally this was a debate conducted in English in front of a broader audience. (The irony would not have escaped Eduardo.) Consensus could not be reached that day, and we remain far from an accommodation since. But the informal conversations that followed in the humdrum and soulless lobby of the conference venue were vital and exciting ones, on the implications and possibilities for overcoming epistemic coloniality. The effort to smother linguistic differences and to render research in a global register in such conferences seemed nonsensical and a waste of time to Eduardo, though it did provide for encounters that encouraged many of us to take his views seriously. And indeed though the LAEMOS sessions were to be conducted, in English, some conveners did subvert this as a group, usually when the room comprised Spanish and/or Portuguese-speaking students and scholars.

Nidhi met Eduardo at the Third LAEMOS conference in Buenos Aires. Eduardo was co-convenor of the stream and had communicated with him, before the conference, in English. They had not met before, and their email exchanges had been in English. However just as the stream was about to begin, Eduardo turned to Nidhi and explained that with one exception (Nidhi) all the stream presenters were native Spanish and Portuguese speakers. It made sense therefore, to allow presenters to speak in their local language rather than compel them to speak in English. Would this be alright? Eduardo explained that LAEMOS guidelines stated quite clearly that all sessions should be in English, and that he did not agree with these guidelines. In this way Nidhi received an invaluable insight into epistemic coloniality, and thanks to Eduardo's intervention, also increased his sensitivity to the two reigning European languages of South America.

When the news of Eduardo's passing reached the wide circle of his readers, collaborators, admirers, colleagues, and students, many offered tributes to his memory. "Much more than his achievements in print were his great accomplishments as a person: a man of great integrity … he was a scholar *par excellence*" (Clegg, 2013). Others expressed their shock at the news: 'Con gran pesar nos enteramos de la temprana muerte de nuestro amigo y colaborador' ('With great sadness we have learned of the sudden death of our friend and collaborator', Rodríguez Gómez, 2013). There were commemorations: "Eduardo was a dear friend, a kind man, and is much missed, and we dedicate this special issue to him" (Cooke and Faria, 2013). There was a reflection on his legacy for organization studies at the LAISUM, for an alternative epistemic community. LAISUM was, in Eduardo's vision, to be an open, free access laboratory to share knowledge, experiences, media, and other resources as a public good (Buendía Espinosa, 2013), and its tribute titled '*Continuación y legado* Eduardo Ibarra Colado (2013 – ∞)' commemorates his visionary nature or, in his own words, '*cosmovisión*' (Ibarra-Colado, 2013).

In Cuba, the Caribbean, and in parts of South America, a quote is recalled from Brecht's play, *The Mother*, a quote that has smuggled into a variety of other media, including popular songs. The quote is that "there are those who struggle for a day and they are good … But there are those who struggle all their lives: these are the indispensable ones" (quoted in Reynolds, 1997: v). The quote reminds us of the importance of struggle, of the necessity to embed a life in a process of exploration, questioning, and resistance. Eduardo made great contributions to organizational studies, to critical management, and to critical international management as a scholar and as a practitioner. To the three of us he will remain *uno de los imprescindibles*, one of the indispensable ones, willing to commit to a lifetime of questioning, conflict, and struggle.

Notes

1 This paper was the Outstanding Paper Award Winner at the Emerald Literati Network Awards for Excellence 2011, co-authored with Alex Faria and Ana Guedes.

References

Buendía Espinosa, A. (2013) Continuación y legado Eduardo Ibarra Colado (2013 – ∞), 8 July, http://laisumedu.org/showNota.php?idNota=231195&cates=&idSubCat=&subcates=&ssc=&m=mail1&p=mail1

Clegg, S. (2013) APROS, 21 May, http://www.apros.org/?s=Ibarra+colado&x=0&y=0

Clegg, S. R., Ibarra-Colado, E., and Bueno, L. (eds) (1999) *Global Management: Universal Theories, Local Realities*. Thousand Oaks, CA: Sage.

Cooke, B. and Faria, A. (2013) Development, management and North Atlantic imperialism: For Eduardo Ibarra Colado, *Cad.EBAPE.BR*, Editorial, 11(2), Rio de Janeiro: FGV, http://bibliotecadigital.fgv.br/ojs/index.php/cadernosebape/issue/view/915

Dussel, E. and Ibarra-Colado, E. (2006) Globalization, organization and the ethics of liberation, *Organization*, 13(4): 489–508.

Faria, A., Ibarra-Colado, E., and Guedes, A. (2010) Internationalization of management, neoliberalism and the Latin America challenge, *Critical Perspectives on International Business*, 6(2–3): 97–115.

Ibarra-Colado, E. (2001) *La Universidad en Mèxico Hoy: Gubernamentalidad y Modernizacion*. Mexico: UNAM/UAM-I/ANUIES, Col. Posgrado, No. 26.

Ibarra-Colado, E. (2006) Organization studies and epistemic coloniality in Latin America: Thinking otherness from the margins, *Organization*, 13(4): 463–88.

Ibarra-Colado, E. (2008) Cómo comprender y transformar los Estudios Organizacionales desde América Latina y no morir en el intento, Painel Internacional de Estudos Organizacionais. Associação Nacional de Pós-Graduação e Pesquisa em Administração, Rio de Janeiro, 6–10 de setembro.

Ibarra-Colado, E. (2012) Cómo comprender y transformar los Estudios Organizacionales desde América Latina y no morir en el intento, in A. Martínez, R. G. Rabiela, H. Vessuri, and A. V. Corona (eds), *Apropiación Social del Conocimiento y Aprendizaje: Una Mirada Crítica Desde Diferentes âmbitos*. Madrid: Plaza e Valdez Editores.

Ibarra-Colado, E. (2013) Los zarzales y las flores. Carta póstuma, Mayo 17, 2013, 6 July, http://laisumedu.org/showNota.php?idNota=231195&cates=&idSubCat=&subcates=&ssc=&m=mail1&p=mail1

Ibarra-Colado, E. and Montaño, L. (1984) *Mito y Poder en las Organizaciones: Análysis Críticos de la Teoría de la Organización*. Mexico: UNAM-Iztapalapa, Col. Cuadernos Universitarios, No. 10.

Mignolo, W. (coord.) (2007) *Worlds & Knowledges Otherwise Project: On Decoloniality*, 2(1), 1 October, https://globalstudies.trinity.duke.edu/wko-v2d1

Reynolds, D. (1997) *Democracy Unbound: Progressive Challenges to the Two Party System*. Boston: South End Press.

Rodríguez Gómez, R. (2013) Campus Milenio, 23 May, http://www.campusmilenio.com.mx/

25

The inner circle: towards a 'Canadian' management history – key Canadian contributors to new institution theory

Kristene E. Coller, Corinne McNally, and Albert. J. Mills

Introduction

> In the passage I have just read from Tolstoy, the young second lieutenant Boris Bubretskow discovers that there exists in the army two different systems or hierarchies. The one is printed in some little red book and anyone can easily read it up. It also remains constant. A general is always superior to a colonel, and a colonel to a captain. The other is not printed anywhere. Nor is it even a formally organised secret society with officers and rules which you would be told after you had been admitted. You are never formally and explicitly admitted by anyone. You discover gradually, in almost indefinable ways, that it exists and that you are outside it; and then later, perhaps, that you are inside it.
>
> *(Lewis, 1944)*

This passage by C. S. Lewis, from his memorial speech at London University, reflects the complexity of social networks and the powerful role they can play in socially constructing knowledge. Nonetheless, despite the passage of years, the dominant positivist perspective from which a large proportion of knowledge creation in the management discipline flows (Burrell and Morgan, 1979) still tends to privilege the objective, methodical discovery of facts and truth over knowledge production as a socially influenced process.

In recent years two important trends within management and organization studies (MOS) have served to focus attention on the socially constructed nature of knowledge and its relationship to social networks. The first trend has developed with, and out of, the call for an 'historic turn' in MOS (Booth and Rowlinson, 2006). A number of scholars have sought to draw attention to historical context in shaping how extant studies of management and organization are influenced by the context in which they are developed. Acker and van Houten (1974), for example, showed how the socio-economic conditions of Chicago in the 1920s influenced gendered attitudes to the study of female employees in the Hawthorne Studies. Similarly Bill Cooke

(1999) contended that the Cold War context in which management theory developed in the United States led to a marginalization of radical approaches to managing and organizing. The second trend is the increasing use of Actor-Network Theory (ANT), which, drawing on the sociology of knowledge, sets out to reveal how knowledge is an outcome of sets of relationships between human and non-human (e.g. computers, written histories, textbooks) actors involved in complex networks (Latour, 2005a).

More recently there have been several moves to draw these two trends together in the development of studies that examine the role of history and the past in network formation and persistence (Durepos and Mills, 2012a), including the development of organizational histories (Durepos, Helms Mills, and Mills, 2008). These studies critically draw on ANT to argue for an account – 'ANTi-History' (Durepos and Mills, 2012b) – that problematizes history and the past as socially constructed outcomes of actor networks.

Drawing on ANTi-History, we set out to study the contribution of Canadian scholars to the development of the field of MOS, with a specific focus on New Institution Theory (NIT). Our aim is twofold. First, and foremost, our study is part of a broader project to raise questions about the largely absent history of management thought in Canada (Austin, 2000b; Boothman, 2000). Second, the case study is designed to contribute to a (hopefully) emergent study of the history of management thought in Canada.

Towards the study of management theory and the Canadian context

More than a decade ago Austin (2000c: 3) contended that while there has been considerable growth in management education in Canada since the Second World War Canadian historians "have displayed scant interest in management as an academic subject". Similarly, Boothman (2000: 12) argues that, in Canada "the content, pedagogy, and academic status of [the nature of management] ... have received limited analysis." Despite Austin's (2000) edited collection of "essays on the history of business education in Canada" (book subtitle) there has been little or no attempt since to grapple with the issue of a history or histories of management thought in Canada. There has, however, been a number of studies of the Administrative Sciences Association of Canada (ASAC – Austin, 1994, 1995, 1998, 2000a; McLaren and Mills, 2013) and the regional Atlantic Schools of Business (ASB – Barragan and Mills, 2008; MacNeil and Mills, 2012; Genoe McLaren and Mills, 2008). These studies of ASAC and ASB have, arguably, provided useful traces of contributions to management thought in Canada, but have not centrally addressed the issue of a Canadian contribution to the development of management thought: the foci have been on the scholarly organizations themselves rather than on the development of management thought that may have been evidenced at those conferences.

Using ANTi-History to explore the development of New Institution Theory (NIT) research in Canada, this chapter serves as a starting point to unearthing and recognizing Canadian contributions to management knowledge (see also Chapter 22 in this volume).

Towards a Canadian history of management thought

In North America in particular, but also to some extent in parts of Northern Europe, the history of management thought is a well-established history and is generally accepted as a straightforward account of the development of management theory through the years. It is accepted as if it is the inevitable outcome of over a century of management thinkers (Durepos and Mills, 2012b), starting with Taylor and Scientific Management, followed by other well-known schools of thought including: Human Relations, Systems Approach, Contingency Approach, and so on (Wren and Bedeian, 2009; Wren, 2005). Nonetheless, there have been challenges to this dominant strain of thought. It has, for example, been argued that many important contributions appear to have been left out of the dominant history (or histories). Cooke (1999), for example, points to the exclusion of leftist-thinking scholars, while Tonn (1996) focuses on the exclusion of women writers, particularly Mary Parker Follett. While Cooke (1999) uses his critique to reveal the problematic of existing histories, Tonn (1996) focuses on 'writing in' selected female researchers into existing histories.

Recently this conventional wisdom about the history of management thought has been challenged, with a growing number of management history scholars arguing that extant histories of management thought reflect certain historiographical processes (Booth and Rowlinson, 2006; Cooke, 1999), rooted initially in Cold War influences (Kelley, Mills, and Cooke, 2006). Grant and Mills (2006), for example, argue that what has come to stand as the history of management thought today was heavily influenced during the Cold War period by dominant social and cultural themes such as anti-communism, military-based hierarchy, behaviouralism, and positivism. Written during the era of the Cold War, management histories were a form of retrospective thinking that was influenced by the context of the authors of the time. Arguably, this discourse continues to determine what knowledge is privileged and marginalized in management thought today. As Cooke (1999) points out, while Kurt Lewin is well recognized for his three phases of change model (unfreeze/change/refreeze) his contributions from the left have been written out, just as other leftist theorists have been. Their contributions are not accepted by the dominant managerialist ideology, and are therefore not recognized in the history of management thought.

From a Canadian perspective, the lack of representation of Canadian management thought should be an obvious omission yet it appears to go unnoticed, even by Canadian scholars (as evidenced in Boothman's 2000 account). In the absence of Canadian management history Canadian scholars often rely on American content for both history and management thought.

In the meantime, for various reasons, we have chosen to begin our exploration at a point much closer in time to the present. Our primary aim was to focus on an area where we are aware that Canadian scholars have/are making a contribution and then to 'follow the actors' to make sense of how that work was developed and disseminated. To that end, we adopted a historiographical approach to the study of actor networks; specifically ANTi-History (Durepos and Mills, 2012b), which focuses on understanding how knowledge of the past is produced as an effect of actor networks.

ANTi-History

ANTi-History has been detailed at great length elsewhere (Durepos and Mills, 2012b; Mills and Durepos, 2010, Durepos, Mills, and Weatherbee, 2012). Its central focus is drawn from the sociology of knowledge literature, including Marx (Marx and Engels, 1940) and Mannheim (1968), and particularly the work of Latour (1987, 2005a, 2005b), Law (1986, 1992, 1994) and Callon (1986) in the development of Actor-Network Theory. While ANT sets out to 're-assemble' knowledge by following the actors as they engage in the socio-politics of enrolment (i.e. drawing other actors into a joint set of activities and beliefs), translation (i.e. the process of making sense of joint activities and beliefs), and black-boxing (i.e. fixing a set of activities and beliefs as a form of truth or knowledge), it has failed up to now to problematize history and the past – vaguely seeing them as given, contextual factors (Durepos and Mills, 2012b). ANTi-History draws on

ANT to reassemble knowledge but goes beyond ANT in simultaneously setting out to reassemble history and the past and their relationship to knowledge effects (i.e. how we come to believe in something as knowledge).

ANT

ANT can be applied as a methodology that offers insight into the construction of knowledge.[1] ANT assumes that knowledge is a result of social ordering; it presents knowledge creation as an effect of heterogeneous actor-networks. Heterogeneous actor-networks involve both humans and objects as actors (Law, 1992).

In fact, ANT originates from work in laboratories (Latour, 1983) where many materials such as chemicals, equipment, papers, and pencils come together with people to be transformed into reports, which contain accepted truth and facts (Godfrey-Smith, 2003). Such reports appear to hide human participation altogether. The purpose of the ANT lab studies was to expose the subjectivity of scientific knowledge by illustrating its socially created nature. In this sense, ANT aims to demonstrate scientific knowledge as a socio-cultural product (Pickering, 1992).

Instead of seeking the contributions of a single actor, we will view knowledge as socially constructed. We will take ANT's relational approach to focus on what has happened between actors to understand how one is altered by interacting with another and, as a result, what their contribution has been. As such ANT does not take a realist approach. It does not aim to seek truth and falsity. Its epistemological assumptions are anti-positivist and influenced by social constructivism (Latour, 2005a).

Analyses in ANT treat actors symmetrically, meaning that one actor is not privileged over another. Actors considered 'important', socially or culturally, are not included to the neglect of other 'less important' actors (Law, 1991). Rather than basing their analyses on assumptions, ANT theorists begin their analysis with a blank slate, allowing actors to emerge and speak for themselves (Latour, 2005a).

We do not begin our analysis with the assumption that there is an important contribution in NIT waiting to be uncovered. Instead, we investigate NIT's actor network, recognizing the socially constructed nature of knowledge. We are seeking to understand what, if any, contribution has been made by NIT's actor network and the social processes by which it has evolved and been constructed.

Our approach

To a certain extent, this endeavour reflects our own interests as Canadian management scholars with a curiosity in understanding the identity and contribution of Canadian management research to the discipline as a whole. The first author's research background is focused on radical organizational change, which is heavily influenced and informed by NIT. This connection, along with NIT being a strongly established theoretical perspective which is popular and relevant today, influenced our decision to deploy the NIT actor network as a starting point to unearthing Canada's contribution to management thought. We also noted that the University of Alberta and the University of Toronto appear to be producing significant work in this area.

Our relational involvement in the analysis inevitably influences the outcome. As researchers we are not separate from the social processes of NIT that we are studying. In our involvement we are not neutral but instead we are actors seeking to expose the social processes which we are simultaneously influencing (Law, 1994).

Methodology

Our investigation of NIT begins in 1980 and continues into the present. Limiting our investigation to this time period is particularly interesting as a renewed interest in Institutional Theory began in the 1980s (Greenwood, Oliver, and Suddaby, 2008)[2] and business schools and research in Canada were well established by this time (Austin, 1998). While a 30-year period ensures a sufficient amount of work was produced for the purpose of this analysis, it is in no way an exhaustive timeframe. As Kieser (1994) notes, selection is unavoidable and in limiting our analysis to a certain time period we are choosing to exclude certain contributions and include others based on their years of publication. Of course, exploring the origins of NIT and its evolution from Institutional Theory could have provided insight into the micro processes involved in the emergence of new theories, their development and application to the mainstream discourse. However, this is beyond the scope of our analysis.

We will limit our analysis to include only Canadian scholars. For the purpose of clarity only (i.e. what or who it is we are talking about) we consider Canadian scholars to be individuals who were living and working in Canada during the period in which his or her formative works were published. This establishes their 'solid connection to Canada' (Mandelbaum and Hlynka, 2009). Babe (2000) makes a similar distinction in his book *Canadian Communication Thought: Ten Foundational Writers*, where he indicates that while the ten authors identified may not necessarily have been born in Canada, they did live and work in Canada during the time that their formative works were published.

Locating Canadian scholars and their contributions is much like that of a private investigator. It requires in-depth knowledge of the individual and his/her affiliations, publications, co-workers, and detailed elements of their career. As a starting point, Google Scholar was used to uncover individuals who have identified themselves as having an interest in NIT.

Google Scholar was chosen because of its widespread accessibility worldwide and inclusion of journal articles, theses, books, and institutional repositories (2013). It provided an effective means of identifying relevant work produced by actors by identifying citation counts for articles. This allowed us to avoid searching multiple databases. Although Google Scholar proved to be an efficient way of identifying and evaluating actors in the network, the use of Google Scholar has inherent flaws. Not all academics subscribe to Google Scholar and as such it can be challenging to identify the number of citations an author has received over the course of his/her career. This limited our ability to accurately assess the impact an individual has had on the field. The publication process takes time, as does citation by other authors. As a result, significant contributions to the field may not be fully recognized for decades. As we shall show below, our focus on self-identification (as an NIT scholar) proved to be highly problematic and we had to use other search tools to overcome this.

We started off our Google search with four criteria – *self-identification* (i.e. the author views their work as being in the field of NIT), *timespan* (we limited the search to those publishing in NIT since 1980 – see above), being based at a Canadian university (see above), and the *number of citations* per article. In the latter case we took an arbitrary figure of 500 citations or more per article. The figure was arrived at as an outcome of our search, which revealed a large number of papers had greatly less than 500 citations and a number also had substantially more than 500. As we wanted to identify 'key contributors' (based on citation counts) we tried to find a number that would be sizeable (e.g. indicative of academic interest and attention) for the contributors in a given field, namely NIT.

Our initial Google Scholar search generated a list of 35 scholars worldwide who self-identified themselves as having an interest in NIT, five of whom were associated with Canadian universities. However, only one of these scholars, namely Joel A. C. Baum, had citation counts over 500.

Table 25.1 Key Canadian actors and their formative works

	Author	*Article*	*Co-authors*	*Year published*	*Number of citations*
University of Alberta	**C. R. (Bob) Hinings** PhD	Understanding radical organizational change: Bringing together the old and the new institutionalism	R. Greenwood	1996	1,691
		Theorizing change: The role of professional associations in the transformation of institutionalized fields	R. Greenwood R. Suddaby[a]	2002	1,070
		Configurational approaches to organizational analysis	A. D. Meyer A. S. Tsui	1993	882
		The structuring of organizational structures	S. Ranson R. Greenwood	1980	855
		Understanding strategic change: the contribution of archetypes	R. Greenwood	1993	564
	Royston Greenwood PhD, University of Birmingham, 1976	Understanding radical organizational change: Bringing together the old and the new institutionalism	C. R. Hinings	1996	1,691
		Theorizing change: The role of professional associations in the transformation of institutionalized fields	C. R. Hinings R. Suddaby	2002	1,070
		The structuring of organizational structures	S. Ranson C. R. Hinings	1980	855
		Rhetorical strategies of legitimacy	R. Suddaby	2005	612
		Understanding strategic change: The contribution of archetypes	C. R. Hinings	1993	564
	Roy Suddaby PhD, University of Alberta, 2001	Rhetorical strategies of legitimacy	R. Greenwood	2005	612
		From the editors: What grounded theory is not		2006	634

Table 25.1 (cont.)

	Author	Article	Co-authors	Year published	Number of citations
University of Toronto	**Joel A. C. Baum** PhD, University of Toronto	Don't go it alone: Alliance network composition and startups' performance in Canadian biotechnology	T. Calabrese B. S. Silverman	2000	1,455
		Institutional linkages and organizational mortality	C. Oliver	1991	1,037
		Organizational ecology		1999	721
		Localized competition and organizational failure in the Manhattan hotel industry, 1898–1990	S. J. Mezias	1992	536
		Survival-enhancing learning in the Manhattan hotel industry, 1898–1980	P. Ingram	1998	513
		Institutional embeddedness and the dynamics of organizational populations	C. Oliver	1992	521
	Brian S. Silverman PhD, University of California at Berkeley	Strategic alliances and interfirm knowledge transfer	D. C. Mowery J. E. Oxley	1996	2,282
Simon Fraser	**Thomas B. Lawrence** PhD, University of Alberta	Discourse and institutions	N. Phillips C. Hardy	2004	621
		Institutional entrepreneurship in emerging fields: HIV/AIDS treatment advocacy in Canada	S. Maguire C. Hardy	2004	620
York University	**Christine Oliver** PhD, University of Toronto, 1988	Strategic responses to institutional processes		1991	3,811
		Determinants of interorganizational relationships: Integration and future directions		1990	1,839
		Sustainable competitive advantage: Combining institutional and resource-based views		1997	1,475
		Institutional linkages and organizational mortality	J. A. C. Baum	1991	1,035
		The antecedents of deinstitutionalization		1992	887
		Institutional embeddedness and the dynamics of organizational populations	J. A. C. Baum	1992	521

[a] Was affiliated with the University of Iowa at the time of publication.

We could have stuck with this outcome and focused on the work of Baum but we knew that other NIT scholars in a Canadian context existed, in particular Christine Oliver at York University. So we decided to use Google Scholar to 'follow' both Oliver and Baum through their work and co-authors to uncover additional Canadian NIT scholars who did not self-identify with NIT on our initial search.[3]

The next step involved searching for each of Oliver and Baum's co-authors to determine their institutional affiliations and research interests. Using our selection criteria of the 30-year time period starting in 1980, authors writing their formative works in Canada, and citation counts greater than 500, additional individuals were identified and included in the final analysis (Table 25.1).

To ensure other scholars were not overlooked for their contribution to NIT, faculty members at the institutions of each of the identified actors were reviewed to determine if they had published on NIT. Interest in NIT was determined by taking a cursory review of publications on their faculty home page and by searching for their name on Google Scholar. When this process uncovered no new names we felt satisfied that key contributors to NIT within Canada had been identified. See Table 25.1 for a summary of these results.

Once key contributors had been identified, it was important to establish any connections that may or may not exist between actors in our network. Résumés or curriculum vitaes (CVs) were downloaded and used to determine detailed work history, affiliations, editorial positions, publications, positions held, research chairs, etc. Although many of the CVs were detailed and provided vital information about our 'key contributors', it is important to recognize that they do not necessarily provide a complete picture of an individual and his or her personal relationships. However, they did provide useful information for our analysis. For example, while article citations were useful in identifying NIT scholars for the present analysis, a closer look at other publications such as edited books and book chapters, editorial appointments and other service responsibilities (i.e. student supervision) were all essential in determining the connectivity between actors that were identified in Table 25.1.

As Lawrence and Suddaby (2006) suggest, it is particularly important to address actors' work within organizations to determine how the field and/or institutions have been influenced through implicit and explicit activities. Given institutional requirements to meet specific publishing, service and teaching requirements, CVs are a useful repository where scholars are able to document participation in each of these areas.

Analysis

Seven key actors were identified in our NIT network; three affiliated with the University of Alberta, two with the University of Toronto, and one each at Simon Fraser, and York University. Our analysis focuses on the relationships between the seven key actors identified in Table 25.1. While our analysis below will progress in a linear fashion, outlining accomplishments, roles, and contributions, we are not denoting an order of importance among our key actors. We have arbitrarily selected an order in which to present the actors.

Although the order of actors listed is arbitrary, it became apparent that some of the actors were connected more or less strongly to one another as the analysis progressed. Co-editing books, editorial appointments, and even PhD student committees appear to have fostered relationships between specific actors of the network and led to the creation of what we have called the inner, bridging, and outer circles. The inner circle is comprised of individuals who have co-authored journal articles together, sat on the same editorial boards, and may even have sat on PhD student committees with one another. Members of the inner circle also appear to have enacted other members into the Canadian NIT network differentiating them from the other actors and making them powerful influencers of the NIT network. The bridging circle, comprised of one individual, has involvement with some of the actors in the inner circle and sat on similar editorial boards but also appears to be enacting members of the outer circle into the Canadian NIT field. The bridging circle therefore connects the two groups to each other; however, despite academic success and contributions to Canadian NIT, lacks the same level of connectivity to other members of the Canadian NIT field in a comparable way.

Finally, the outer circle, comprised of accomplished academics, has in most cases been enacted into the network by members of the inner and bridging circles. While they have co-authored informative articles with other influential NIT scholars, many of whom reside outside of Canada, this group did not work with the highly connected Canadian scholars that comprise the inner circle. Given that the primary interest of the present chapter was to identify Canadian contributors to NIT, we differentiated between the groups and their levels of connectivity; however, we wanted to retain the members of the network in an effort to build on Canadians contributing to the field of NIT and management thought.

These connections reflect the capacity of actors to act upon one another (Law, 1986) and demonstrate the continuous participation in political work by engaging other actors' interests to eventually enrol them in a cause such as research in NIT, thus strengthening the cause (Law, 1992). This process is demonstrated in our analysis.

The inner circle

Our analysis reveals the University of Alberta and the University of Toronto as the apparent centres of NIT; however, the strongest relationships appear to be between C. R. (Bob) Hinings (University of Alberta), Royston Greenwood (University of Alberta), Roy Suddaby (University of Alberta), and Christine Oliver (York University). Given the strength of the relationships between these four actors (Tables 25.1 and 25.2) and their strong ties to Canada, they define our inner circle.

C. R. Hinings and R. Greenwood are the most strongly connected of our actors. Greenwood and Hinings began their relationship in the United Kingdom and came to the University of Alberta at similar times in 1979. As a result, Greenwood and Hinings have worked and published together for more than 30 years and have both been active members of developing and contributing to NIT in Canada. Greenwood and Hinings continue to work together with two books forthcoming, numerous journal articles, and have written 11 book chapters between 1980 and 2012 with one another (Greenwood, 2011). Much of their early work focused on the structure and characteristics of organizations and the processes involved in shifting between archetypes (Greenwood and Hinings, 1993, 1996; Ranson, Hinings, and Greenwood, 1980). Although this continues to be of interest based on recent publications, later work has shifted to focus on radical change in organizations and building theory (Greenwood, Miller, and Hinings, in preparation) and has included contributions by other members of the inner circle, other established and emergent scholars, and PhD students interested in NIT – most notably Roy Suddaby, another member of the inner circle. The remainder of this section will highlight the connections between each of the actors in the inner circle.

C. R. Hinings. A founding member of the Aston School (Clegg, Ibarra-Colado, and Bueno-Rodriquez, 1999), Hinings has spent the bulk of his career at the University of Alberta, continuing to be a leader in NIT. Although Hinings' publication record speaks for itself, the University of Alberta website reinforces Hinings' scholarly prominence:

Table 25.2 Editorial appointments of key actors[a]

Name	*Editorial appointments*	*Editorial board*
R. Greenwood	*Academy of Management Annals* (current) *Strategic Organization* **Co-editor** (2002–2011) *Journal of Management Inquiry* (1998, 2002)	*Academy of Management Journal* *Canadian Accounting Perspectives* *Canadian Journal of Administrative Studies* *Handbook of Organizational Research* *Journal of Management Studies* *Organization Science* *Organization Studies* *Research in the Sociology of Organizations*
R. Suddaby	*Academy of Management Review* (current)	*Academy of Management Journal* *Academy of Management Review* *Business Research* *Journal of Management Studies* *Organization Studies* *Scandinavian Journal of Management* *Strategic Organization*
Joel A. C. Baum	*Strategic Organization* **Founding editor** (current)	*Academy of Management Journal* *Administrative Sciences Quarterly* *Advances in Strategic Management* *Strategic Management Journal*
B. S. Silverman	*Advances in Strategic Management* (current)	*Administrative Sciences Quarterly* *Academy of Management Review* *Business and Politics* *Organization Science* *Strategic Organization*
C. Oliver	*Strategic Management Journal* (current) *Administrative Science Quarterly*	*Academy of Management Review* *Administrative Science Quarterly* *Canadian Journal of Administrative Sciences* *Journal of Management Studies*

[a] Information relating to editorial appointments and positions on editorial boards was not available for Hinings or Lawrence through their CVs or academic web pages.

> The contributions of Professor Bob Hinings were recognized when he became the first faculty member from the Alberta School of Business to be elected to the Royal Society of Canada. He also was named a Distinguished Scholar of the Academy of Management, the world's largest association of management academics.
>
> *(20 September 2012)*

In addition to his publication record, or perhaps because of it, Hinings has supervised ten PhD students at the University of Alberta (Document search, 29 September 2012) and has sat on the committees of other PhD students including Roy Suddaby who will be discussed below. Much like their journal and book publication record, Greenwood appears on five of the PhD committees supervised by Hinings and sits on a number of boards including the college of reviews for the Canada research chair (Hinings, 2011).

Royston Greenwood. With an established career at the University of Alberta, Greenwood has been an active member of academia, publishing extensively, sitting on a number of editorial boards (Table 25.2), and doing professional service in positions such as chair designate at the Academy of Management and professor of strategic management (Greenwood, 2011).

In addition to working extensively with Hinings, Greenwood has worked with the two other members of our inner circle, Christine Oliver and Roy Suddaby. Having sat on a number of editorial boards together (Table 25.2), Greenwood and Oliver have co-edited two books and authored one book chapter together and continue to work together with one book forthcoming (Greenwood, Oliver, and Sahlin, forthcoming; Greenwood *et al.*, 2008) thereby enacting Oliver into the growing Canadian NIT network.

Greenwood has also been active in attracting emerging academics with an interest in institution theory. He has supervised two PhD students (ProQuest, 29 September 2012), the most notable being Roy Suddaby (Suddaby, 2001), another member of our inner circle. Following their supervisor–student relationship, Greenwood and Suddaby went on to write a number of articles together on organizational change and institutional entrepreneurship and have sat on similar editorial boards (Table 25.2).

Roy Suddaby. Although Suddaby is in the comparatively earlier stages of his academic career he has made significant contributions to the field of NIT, thus solidifying his position in the inner circle. Suddaby has strong ties to the University of Alberta, having received his PhD (2001) there under the supervision of Greenwood[4] and with Hinings as a committee member (Suddaby, 2001). Suddaby maintained the relationship with Greenwood following the completion of his PhD and they co-authored a paper (Suddaby and Greenwood, 2005) while Suddaby was working at the University of Iowa. Suddaby and Greenwood have since co-authored a total of nine journal articles, one book, two book chapters, and edited for three of the same journals (Greenwood, 2011). Suddaby has maintained his relationship with Greenwood, and established a working relationship with Oliver and Lawrence, a member of our outer circle.

Suddaby and Oliver, in addition to both sitting on the editorial board for the *Academy of Management Review* and *Journal of Management Studies*, have co-edited at least one book together. Suddaby has also established a working relationship with Lawrence, a member of the outer circle who also obtained his PhD at the University of Alberta. The relationship between the two scholars has resulted in at least two journal articles together and according to Dobbin (2010: 673): "Lawrence and Suddaby (2006) coined the term 'institutional work' to describe the range of ways that people build, sustain and change institutions." The relationship between the two scholars could become more prominent as Suddaby has recently accepted a new position at the University of Victoria.

Aside from Suddaby's apparent ability to build and maintain relationships, he is a notable academic in his own right. Eight years after receiving his PhD, Suddaby was promoted to full professor status and was appointed as Director of the Canadian Centre of Corporate Social Responsibility and Social Entrepreneurship in 2010 and has been the recipient of numerous awards (Suddaby, 2011). Suddaby is also the outgoing editor of the *Academy of Management Review* and sits on a number of editorial boards (Table 25.2) (Suddaby, 2011).

Christine Oliver. Christine Oliver is the face of Institution Theory in Canada with more citations on a single article than any other Canadian scholar and five articles with more than 800 citations (Table 25.1). While many of Oliver's formative journal articles have been written independently, this could be a reflection of the publication guidelines and standards established by the University of Toronto, where she was formerly affiliated. Although many of her formative works were written independently, she has established relationships with the other members of the inner circle as well as members of the outer circle. Oliver has co-edited two books and journal articles with both Greenwood and Suddaby and has co-authored four journal articles with Baum, the sole contributor to the bridging circle.

Co-editing books and appointments on editorial boards with members of our inner and outer circle have made Oliver an influential NIT scholar in Canada. Oliver's position on the editorial board at the Academy of Management, alongside Greenwood and Suddaby also give them international acclaim for their contributions to NIT. Oliver's contributions specifically have been recognized at international venues including the Academy of Management where she was named as a distinguished speaker for the Management Organization Theory and Management Division (Oliver, 2011).

Oliver has written extensively on Institution Theory and the dynamics of institutionalism (Oliver, 2011) and has been referenced widely throughout NIT literature. From the articles on our list alone (Table 25.1), Oliver's work has been cited more than 8,500 times. In addition to her extensive publication record, which includes one book and more than 25 journal articles and book chapters, Oliver has been the recipient of numerous academic awards, sat on a number of editorial boards (Table 25.2), and has sat on various university committees (Oliver, 2011).

Her contributions don't stop at the number of publications to her name. Accolades and service on university and academic based committees (2011) have also been prominent. Oliver has supervised 16 PhD Students (Oliver, 2011) and sat on the committee of 20 other students throughout her career. Three of the committees Oliver has sat on were for students at the University of Alberta, an institutional actor that appears to be influential in developing scholars with an interest in NIT. An additional two students from the University of Toronto, another institutional actor identified in the network, had Oliver as a committee member.

Bridging circle

An accomplished academic, Baum has published a number of journal articles on NIT and has more than 11,436 citations to his name (Google Scholar, 29 September 2012) when all of his published work is considered. He has co-authored three articles with B. S. Silverman, one of which makes our list of formative works (Baum, Calabrese, and Silverman, 2000).[5] Baum received his PhD at the University of Toronto, continues to build on his relationship with Silverman and has since developed ties with Oliver and other scholars now at the University of Toronto with interests in NIT (i.e. Joanne Oxley and Bill McEvily).

In addition to a strong research background and affiliations with organizations such as the Academy of Management and the Administrative Sciences Association of Canada, Baum was the founding editor of *Strategic Organization* where he continues to sit on the editorial board. Baum enacted Greenwood as a co-editor as well as Suddaby and Silverman who have both sat on the editorial board of *Strategic Organization* (Table 25.2). Although it is clear that Baum has affiliations with members of the inner circle, he resides in between the inner and outer circles since he doesn't have the same level of connectivity through the co-authorship of journal articles, book chapters, and editorial appointments as Greenwood, Hinings, Suddaby, and Oliver.

Although he doesn't have the same level of connectivity that members of the inner circle have, Baum has demonstrated strong skills in academia and is developing relationships with other individuals now at the University of Toronto (i.e. B. S. Silverman) with NIT interests as well as with other established and emergent scholars.

Outer circle

The outer circle consists of two key actors: Thomas B. Lawrence and B. S. Silverman who were both brought into the NIT network through members identified in the inner and bridging circles. These individuals, proven academics with an established track record in NIT reside in the outer circle because, despite their connections and affiliations, they have not been fully enacted into the NIT network.

Thomas B. Lawrence. Although Thomas B. Lawrence currently works at Simon Fraser University, he has strong ties to the University of Alberta. Having received his PhD there, he has contributed a chapter in a book edited by two members of our inner circle (Lawrence, 2011); despite his strong ties to the University of Alberta, Lawrence has not co-authored any journal articles with members of our inner circle and does not list any editorial appointments on his CV (Lawrence, 2011). As a result, his connections to the members of the inner circle are in part attributed to where he obtained his PhD and not as a result of continued and active enrolment into the network. Despite the lack of explicit connectivity to other members of the NIT network, Lawrence has co-authored numerous journal articles with other established NIT scholars as well as one book and two book chapters and is therefore establishing a presence in the field of NIT.

B. S. Silverman. Silverman received his PhD at the University of California at Berkeley (Silverman, 2011). Although he has two articles with more than one thousand citations, only one was written while in Canada (Table 25.1). Although Silverman has a single article on our list, he has been included in the outer circle given his affiliations with individuals that have since been recruited by the University of Toronto. Silverman, in addition to working with individuals who appear to have been recruited to the University of Toronto because of their interest in NIT, has worked with Baum publishing least four journal articles and book chapters with one another (Silverman, 2011). Baum and Silverman have also sat on at least one editorial board together (Table 25.2). Silverman has also sat on the editorial board for the *Academy of Management Review*; however, despite this connection with members of the inner circle, he has not co-authored or developed this connection further thus residing in the outer circle despite his academic success.

The academic institution as an actor

If a network is capable of sustaining extreme alignment of its actors, and if it is capable of acting as 'one', it comes to be viewed as a single actor rather than a network (Latour, 2005b). It becomes punctuated as a black box (Akrich, 1992). In this way actors can be understood as networks and networks can be understood as actors. A given actor comes to represent the complex mode of ordering which initially made up the network (Durepos and Mills, 2012b). In this sense, the academic institutions have come to be represented as actors, and represent their entire actor network. For example, we are not exploring the University of Toronto actor network, instead the University of Toronto is treated as a non-human actor in the NIT actor network. From an ANT perspective both human and non-human actors have the capacity to alter each other's courses of action. ANT's focus lies in understanding the relationships established between both types of actors to understand the nature of their connectedness (Durepos and Mills, 2012b). The University of Toronto and the University of Alberta are two notable non-human actors in the NIT network and we cannot overlook the role that they have played.

While the University of Alberta is the home to many strong NIT scholars, its emphasis on excellence in research and publications suggests that the university as an actor may play an important role in its development as a hub of excellence in NIT. The University of Alberta website states: "[r]ecently, our department was ranked 10th internationally with respect to the number of articles per department member placed in the *Academy of Management Journal*" (University of Alberta, 20 September 2012) and "[o]ur department is one of the most highly ranked in Canada with respect to publications in top tier journals" (University of Alberta, 20 September 2012). The University of Toronto boasts similar accomplishments such as their "stellar reputation for groundbreaking research … and insight into a wide range of management issues" (Rotman, September 22, 2012).

Our analysis revealed that both institutions are host to multiple NIT actors with publications having over 500 citations. The institutions (or perhaps individuals within the institutions) appear to play a role in actively enrolling individuals with research interests in NIT. For example, the University of Alberta has two additional actors who have already made significant contributions to NIT – Michael Lounsbury and David Deephouse. However, since their papers were published while affiliated with American institutions, they were not included in our analysis. The University of Alberta also appears to be recruiting promising PhD graduates with an interest in NIT. As we have seen from Suddaby and Lawrence, former University of Alberta graduates, the University of Alberta has produced at least two graduates with an emphasis on NIT.

We identified a similar pattern at the University of Toronto, which has recruited established or emerging NIT researchers. Joanne Oxley, currently affiliated with the University of Toronto, wrote her formative works while at the University of Michigan, and had co-authored a paper with Silverman. The same phenomenon appears to have occurred with Silverman, who co-authored a paper with Baum while affiliated with Harvard University prior to writing later works at the University of Toronto. Bill McEvily, at the University of Toronto, is another example of an exemplary scholar recruited from another institution with NIT interests.

Given the promising and established NIT scholars at both of these institutions, conducting this analysis again in five years would further enhance our understanding of how the network has developed and enrolled new actors.

Discussion

Our analysis brought to light several types of relationships and actors in the NIT actor network. They include actors such as editors and the institutions and relationships such as that of students and supervisors, and of co-authors.

As demonstrated by Greenwood and Suddaby, the PhD student and supervisor relationship has the potential for great influence. These mentorship relationships can facilitate the publishing process, guide the development of original research, and pave the road to future tenure track positions with target institutions (Chao, Walz, and Gardner, 1992). The role of this relationship in influencing an individual's future professional development should not be underestimated (Ortiz-Walters, 2009; Zipp, Cahill, and Clark, 2009). Through our analysis we understand the relationship only as we can see it on CVs and the creation of publications; however, this is a very complex relationship, which can influence a student's role and contribution to the network for many years to come.

The relationship between Greenwood and Suddaby is perhaps the most evident example in our analysis of how a student/supervisor relationship can develop into a long-lasting, collaborative relationship. Over time, their relationship has evolved to be one of continued collaboration through publications, sitting on editorial boards together, and even a colleague relationship at the University of Alberta. Greenwood and Suddaby have been identified as members of our inner circle. They have worked together frequently over the past decade and have produced several publications, as have the other members of the inner circle. These types of long-term co-authorship and collaborative relationships have proven important in this network as they appear to have had great influence over the field of NIT.

It could be suggested that the development of these collaborative relationships is encouraged by the requirement for scholars to publish. Our analysis relied heavily on publications and CVs as we used them to track relationships. Therefore, we cannot overlook the essential role of editors in the publication process. They have a great amount of influence on which contributions are made to the field. While many editors come in contact with the network, although not identified in our analysis, they act as gatekeepers accepting some content while rejecting others (Fogarty and Liao, 2009). These choices made by editors are not only reflected in our analysis (as we are only able to track publications accepted at some point by editors) but they also influence the direction of the field as a whole and the way it is and will be understood historically (Dye, Mills, and Weatherbee, 2005). As noted in our analysis, many of our identified actors including members of the inner circle, act as editors for various scholarly journals (Table 25.2). It could be argued that these individuals have an added level of influence in the NIT actor network. Not only do they influence the network through their own work but as editors they determine what comes to be considered knowledge in NIT by selecting certain contributions while rejecting others.

Our approach using sources such as CVs, publication records, and faculty websites provides only so much insight into the relationships within the network; particularly between the human actors and institutions as actors. We identified the University of Alberta and University of Toronto as centres of NIT excellence and they appear to be doing something different than other institutions with regard to attracting NIT scholars. While they make it clear that they prioritize top tier publications, it is not clear if they take an active role in recruiting NIT scholars, or if this process is more informal with NIT scholars being recruited by other NIT scholars within the institution. Perhaps NIT scholars are attracted to these institutions for their known excellence in NIT research. While the links of human actors to the institutions are clear, the actual level of influence of the institutions on the network is unclear. The nature of our analysis does not allow us to gain in-depth insight into this issue. To have a better understanding of it, we would need to deploy the University of Alberta and Toronto actor networks.

Conclusion

Supervision of doctoral students, publications and their selection by editors, and the hiring of faculty by institutions are part of the formalized practices or 'written rules' of academia. However, as evidenced by the strength of the actors and their relationships in our inner circle, informal and collaborative relationships play an important role in shaping the network and the field of NIT. These influential actors are truly constructing our understanding of NIT through their roles as supervisors, editors, authors, and collaborators. As C.S. Lewis highlighted in his speech, there appear to be two systems at work in the NIT network. One involves the formalized aspects of academia. The other, the inner circle, while more influential, is also more elusive.

In an attempt to identify the inner circle we began by identifying known Canadian scholars who have contributed to NIT. Our exploration of the social processes involved in the creation of the Canadian NIT actor network identifies an impressive body of work and recognizable contributions that have been made by individuals (often in collaboration) working and trained in Canada. Both Suddaby and Oliver, from the inner circle, and Lawrence and Baum are all Canadians – born, raised, and trained in Canada. Accounting for these Canadian contributions is important for emerging scholars that are looking for successful mentors close to 'home' to learn, grow, and cultivate expertise in NIT (and other developments in MOS).

Our analysis provides an indication that Canadians are making an impactful contribution and suggests the potential in continuing to identify distinctly Canadian content as we have done. The intent of this chapter was to deploy the NIT actor network as but one example to act as a starting point. We urge scholars interested in continuing along this line of investigation to further unearth Canadian contributions. These seemingly important insights should not, however, blind potential authors to the fact that what they are helping to create is socially constructed knowledge. Nonetheless, a possible outcome may be the unearthing of an otherwise hidden and hopefully valuable body of work that has hitherto gone unnoticed or neglected. More importantly the study of management thought in Canada may reveal the social processes through which it has been rendered absent from histories of the field and, to the contrary, how it might be developed.

Notes

1 There is some debate around whether ANT is a theory, a method, a methodology, or an approach (Law and Hassard, 1999). We have chosen to view it as *a way* (i.e. methodology) of reassembling social phenomena.
2 Interest in NIT was solidified with the publication of DiMaggio and Powell's (1983).
3 The issue of self-identification, although beyond the scope of this chapter, raises a highly interesting phenomenon when considering how certain work gets disseminated – we are thankful to Trish McLaren for this observation.
4 Other members of Suddaby's PhD thesis committee included P. D. Jennings, H. Krahn, C. R. Hinings, D. Cooper, and L. Steir.
5 Silverman wrote this article while affiliated with Harvard University.

References

Acker, J. and Van Houten, D. R. (1974) Differential recruitment and control: The sex structuring of organizations, *Administrative Science Quarterly*, 9: 152–63.

Akrich, M. (1992) The de-scription of technical objects, in W. Bijker and J. Law (eds), *Shaping Technology/Building Society: Studies in Sociotechnical Change* (pp. 205–24). Cambridge, MA: MIT Press.

Austin, B. (1994) ASAC: The early years of the association, 1957–1972, *Proceedings of the 1994 Administrative Sciences Association of Canada, Business History Interest Group*, Halifax, 25–28 June, 15: 1–11.

Austin, B. (1995) ASAC and the crisis in management education, 1973–1985, *Proceedings of the 1995 Administrative Sciences Association of Canada, Business History Interest Division*, Windsor, 3–6 June, 16.

Austin, B. (1998) The role of the Administrative Sciences Association in institutionalizing management education in Canada, *Canadian Journal of Administrative Sciences*, 15: 255–66.

Austin, B. (2000a) The Administrative Sciences Association of Canada, 1957–1999, in B. Austin (ed.), *Capitalizing Knowledge: Essays on the History of Business Education in Canada* (pp. 266–94). Toronto: University of Toronto Press.

Austin, B. (ed.) (2000b) *Capitalizing Knowledge: Essays on the History of Business Education in Canada*. Toronto: University of Toronto Press.

Austin, B. (2000c) Introduction, in B. Austin (ed.), *Capitalizing Knowledge: Essays on the History of Business Education in Canada* (pp. 3–10). Toronto: University of Toronto Press.

Babe, R. E. (2000) *Canadian Communication Thought: Ten Foundational Writers*. Toronto: University of Toronto Press.

Barragan, S. and Mills, A. J. (2008) Narrating the ASB Conference: How the conference is socially constructed through the time, *Proceedings of the 38th Atlantic Schools of Business Conference. St. John's, Newfoundland & Labrador, 17–19 October.*

Baum, J. A. C., Calabrese, T., and Silverman, B. S. (2000) Don't go it alone: Alliance network composition and startups' performance in Canadian biotechnology, *Strategic Management Journal*, 21: 267–94.

Booth, C. and Rowlinson, M. (2006) Management and organizational history: Prospects, *Management and Organizational History*, 1(1): 5–30.

Boothman, B. (2000) The development of business education in Canada, in B. Austin (ed.), *Capitalizing Knowledge: Essays on the History of Business Education in Canada* (pp. 11–86). Toronto: University of Toronto Press.

Burrell, G. and Morgan, G. (1979) *Sociological Paradigms and Organisational Analysis*. Aldershot: Ashgate.

Callon, M. (1986) The sociology of an actor-network: The case of the electric vehicle, in M. Callon, J. Law, and A. Rip (eds), *Mapping the Dynamics of Science and Technology: Sociology of Science in the Real World* (pp. 19–34). London: Macmillan.

Chao, G. T., Walz, P. M., and Gardner, P. D. (1992) Formal and informal mentorships: A comparison on mentoring functions and contrast with nonmentored counterparts, *Personnel Psychology*, 45(3): 619–36.

Clegg, S. R., Ibarra-Colado, E., and Bueno-Rodriquez, L. (1999) *Global Management: Universal Theories and Local Realities*. Thousand Oaks, CA: Sage.
Cooke, B. (1999) Writing the left out of management theory: The historiography of the management of change, *Organization*, 6: 81–105.
DiMaggio, P. J. and Powell, W. W. (1983) The iron cage revisited: Institutional isomorphism and collective rationality in organizational fields, *American Sociological Review*, 48(2): 147–60.
Dobbin, F. (2010) Review of Thomas B. Lawrence, Roy Suddaby, and Bernard Leca (eds), Institutional Work: Actors and Agency in Institutional Studies of Organizations, *Administrative Science Quarterly*, 55: 673–76.
Durepos, G., Helms Mills, J., and Mills, A. J. (2008) Tales in the manufacture of knowledge: Writing a company history of Pan American World Airways, *Management & Organizational History*, 3: 63–80.
Durepos, G. and Mills, A. J. (2012a) Actor network theory, ANTi-history, and critical organizational historiography, *Organization*, 19: 703–21.
Durepos, G. and Mills, A. J. (2012b) *ANTi-History: Theorizing the Past, History, and Historiography in Management and Organizational Studies*. Charlotte, NC: Information Age.
Durepos, G., Mills, A. J., and Weatherbee, T. G. (2012) Theorizing the past: Realism, relativism, relationalism and the reassembly of Weber, *Management & Organizational History*, 7: 267–81.
Dye, K., Mills, A. J., and Weatherbee, T. (2005) Maslow: Man interrupted – Reading management theory in context, *Management Decision*, 43(10): 1375–95.
Fogarty, T. J. and Liao, C.-H. (2009) Blessed are the gatekeepers: A longitudinal study of editorial boards of *The Accounting Review*, *Issues in Accounting Education*, 24(3): 299–318.
Genoe McLaren, P. and Mills, A. J. (2008) 'I'd like to thank the academy': An analysis of the awards discourse at the Atlantic Schools of Business Conference, *Canadian Journal of Administrative Sciences*, 25: 307–16.
Godfrey-Smith, P. (2003) *An Introduction to the Philosophy of Science*. Chicago, IL: University of Chicago Press.
Google (2013) *Google Scholar* [Online], http://scholar.google.ca/
Grant, J. D. and Mills, A. J. (2006) The quiet Americans: Formative context, the Academy of Management leadership, and the management textbook, 1936–1960, *Management & Organizational History*, 1: 201–24.
Greenwood, R. (2011) Curriculum Vitae. University of Alberta.
Greenwood, R. and Hinings, C. R. (1993) Understanding strategic change: The contributions of archetypes, *Academy of Management Journal*, 36: 1052–81.
Greenwood, R. and Hinings, C. R. (1996) Understanding radical organizational change: Bringing together the old and the new institutionalism, *Academy of Management Review*, 21: 1022–54.
Greenwood, R., Hinings, C. R., and Suddaby, R. (2002) Theorizing change: The role of professional associations in the transformation of institutionalized fields, *Academy of Management Journal*, 45: 58–80.
Greenwood, R., Miller, D., and Hinings, C. R. (in preparation) *Radical Organizational Change*. Thousand Oaks, CA: Sage.
Greenwood, R., Oliver, C., and Sahlin, K. (forthcoming) *Institutional Theory in Organization Studies*. Thousand Oaks, CA: Sage.
Greenwood, R., Oliver, C., Suddaby, R., and Sahlin, K. (2008) *The Sage Handbook of Organizational Institutionalism*. Thousand Oaks, CA: Sage.
Hinings, R. (2011) Curiculum Vitae [Online], http://www.business.ualberta.ca/BobHinings/Research
Kelley, E., Mills, A., and Cooke, B. (2006) Management as a cold war phenomenon?, *Human Relations*, 59: 603–10.
Kieser, A. (1994) Why organization theory needs historical analyses: And how this should be performed, *Organization Science*, 5: 608–20.
Latour, B. (1983) Give me a laboratory and I will raise you the world, in K. Knorr-Cetina and M. Mulkay (eds), *Science Observed* (pp. 141–70). London: Sage.
Latour, B. (1987) *Science in Action: How to Follow Scientists and Engineers through Society*. Cambridge, MA: Harvard University Press.
Latour, B. (2005a) On recalling ANT, in J. Law and J. Hassard (eds), *Actor Network Theory and After* (pp. 15–24). Oxford: Blackwell.
Latour, B. (2005b) *Reassembling the Social: An Introduction to Actor-Network Theory*. Oxford: Oxford University Press.
Law, J. (1986) Editor's introduction: Power, knowledge and the dissolution of the sociology of knowledge, in J. Law (ed.), *Power, Action and Belief: A New Sociology of Knowledge?* (pp. 1–19). London: Routledge & Kegan Paul.

Law, J. (1991) Introduction: Monsters, machines and sociotechnical relations, in J. Law (ed.), *A Sociology of Monsters* (pp. 1–23). London: Routledge.
Law, J. (1992) Notes on the theory of the Actor-Network: Ordering, strategy and heterogeneity, *Systems Practice*, 5: 379–93.
Law, J. (1994) *Organizing Modernity*. Oxford: Blackwell.
Law, J. and Hassard, J. (1999) *Actor Network Theory and After*. Malden, MA: Blackwell/Sociological Review.
Lawrence, T. (2011) Curiculum Vitae [Online]. http://beedie.sfu.ca/profiles/TomLawrence
Lawrence, T. B. and Suddaby, R. (2006) Institutions and institutional work, in S. R. Clegg, C. Hardy, and T. Lawrence (eds) *The Sage Handbook of Organization Studies* (pp. 215–55). Beverly Hills, CA: Sage.
Lewis, C. S. (1944) The inner ring, C. S. Lewis Society of California.
McLaren, P. G. and Mills, A. J. (2013) Internal cohesion in response to institutional plurality: The Administrative Sciences Association of Canada, *Canadian Journal of Administrative Sciences*, 30(1): 40–55.
MacNeil, R. and Mills, A. J. (2012) Visualizing the ASB actor-network: A management scholar training camp, *Proceedings of the annual meeting of the Atlantic Schools of Business, Dalhousie University*, 28–30 September, Halifax.
Maguire, S., Hardy, C., and Lawrence, T. B. (2004) Institutional entrepreneurship in emerging fields: HIV/AIDS treatment advocacy in Canada, *Academy of Management Journal*, 47: 657–79.
Mandelbaum, M. and Hlynka, M. (2009) History of queueing theory in Canada prior to 1980, *INFOR*, 47: 335–53.
Mannheim, K. (1968) *Ideology and Utopia*. London: Routledge.
Marx, K. and Engels, F. (1940) *The German Ideology*. London: Lawrence & Wishart.
Meyer, A. D., Tsui, A. S., and Hinings, C. R. (1993) Configuational approaches to organizational analysis, *Academy of Management Journal*, 36: 1175–95.
Mills, A. J. and Durepos, G. (2010) ANTi-History, in A. J. Mills, G. Durepos, and E. Wiebe (eds), *Sage Encyclopedia of Case Study Research* (pp. 26–29). Thousand Oaks, CA: Sage.
Oliver, C. (2011) Curiculum Vitae.
Ortiz-Walters, R. (2009) Mentorship collaborations: A longitudinal examination of the association with job performance and gender, *Journal of Business and Economic Studies*, 15(1): 26–47.
Phillips, N., Lawrence, T. B., and Hardy, C. (2004) Discourse and institutions, *Academy of Management Review*, 29: 635–52.
Pickering, A. (1992) *From Science as Knowledge to Science as Practice*. Chicago, IL: University of Chicago Press.
Ranson, S., Hinings, B., and Greenwood, R. (1980) The structuring of organizational structures, *Administrative Science Quarterly*, 25: 1–17.
Silverman, B. S. (2011) Curiculum Vitae [Online], http://www.rotman.utoronto.ca/FacultyAndResearch/Faculty/FacultyBios/Silverman.aspx
Suddaby, R. (2001) Field-level governance and the emergence of new organizational forms: The case of multidisciplinary practices in law, DPhil Thesis, University of Alberta.
Suddaby, R. (2011) Curriculum Vitae. University of Alberta.
Suddaby, R. and Greenwood, R. (2005) Rhetorical strategies of legitimacy, *Administrative Science Quarterly*, 50: 35–67.
Tonn, J. C. (1996) Follett's challenge for us all, *Organization*, 3: 167–74.
Wren, D. (2005) *The History of Management Thought*. Hoboken, NJ: John Wiley.
Wren, D. A. and Bedeian, A. G. (2009) *The Evolution of Management Thought* (6th edn). Hoboken, NJ: John Wiley.
Zipp, G. P., Cahill, T., and Clark, M. (2009) The role of collaborative scholarship in the mentorship of doctoral students, *Journal of College Teaching and Learning*, 6(8): 29–35.

Part VI

Commentaries on the future of management and organizational history: does it have a past?

26

Processing history

Bringing process-oriented research to management and organizational history

William M. Foster and Roy Suddaby

Introduction

Management and organizational history (MOH) is a growing area of research. This is evidenced by the growing number of new outlets for historical research on organizations. One example is the development of *Management & Organizational History* as a leading journal for research about history in organizational studies. Another has been growth in the number of meetings and conferences (e.g. the Standing Working Group at the European Group for Organizational Studies, the Business History stream at the Atlantic Schools of Business) for research that straddles the boundary of history and organization theory. There is a growing awareness that MOH research has a reach and influence that cuts across the paradigmatic boundaries and silos of traditional management theory. The Special Topics Forum for the *Academy of Management Review* is but one of a number of examples of how MOH is reaching a level of recognition as a growing and influential part of management research.

That said, there are still unexplored opportunities and possibilities for MOH research. Recent work on organizational memory (Rowlinson *et al.*, 2010; Schultz and Hernes, 2013), rhetorical history (Anteby and Molnar, 2012; Foster *et al.*, 2011; McGaughey, 2012; Suddaby, Foster and Trank, 2010), and ANTi-History (Durepos and Mills, 2012) demonstrate the breadth and creativity of research that integrates history and institutional theory, critical theory, identity theory, and related organizational disciplines. There is increasing cross-fertilization of ideas from other scholarly areas such as historical sociology (Schneiberg, 2007), literary and narrative research (Delahaye *et al.* 2009; Kroeze and Keulen, 2012; Wertsch, 2004), and gender studies (Aaltio-Marjosola and Mills, 2002). This offers a clear indication that MOH is poised to produce emerging and interesting ideas about management and organizations.

So where do we go from here? The growth of the field and the creative impetus of the branches of MOH that combine disciplinary interests suggests that there is much more intellectual terrain to be explored using a historical lens. One of the most promising of these is process research (Langley, 1999). It is somewhat surprising that historically trained management researchers, as attentive as they are to historical processes, do not explicitly recognize process as an explicit theoretical lens within which we can analyze organizations.

We see two ways that process can be brought to the MOH discussion. One is to investigate process management in historical settings. *Historical process research* addresses how the processes of management and in organizations have changed over time. The second is to look at the processes involved in constructing and presenting a coherent organizational history. *Research of historical processes* would be directed at understanding how the different elements of the organization work together to produce a specific version of its history. We feel that this focus on process in MOH will open new avenues of research for inclusion into the current discussions of MOH.

What follows is our argument for why MOH researchers should be more attentive to process as an explicit variable in historical research. We begin by mapping the intellectual terrain of MOH research. We use this as a springboard for a discussion of where we think the field can and should go. Next, we discuss how process research can be used to enhance the descriptive and explanatory power of MOH research while limiting some of its major points of contention. In closing, we identify and elaborate areas of research where we see new and exciting opportunities. These include organizational work, identity and identification, entrepreneurs and entrepreneurship, and memory and remembering. In this penultimate section we will posit new questions and explore how a focus on historical process research and research of historical processes can lead to new and different understandings of management and organizational research.

Mapping the field – where have we been?

Management and organizational history lacks a unified and coherent voice (Booth and Rowlinson, 2006; Üsdiken and Kieser, 2004). The diversity of approaches makes MOH a vibrant and lively area for study. Yet, at the same time, it creates tension and conflict about what history is and the place it has in organizations. To understand where the field can go, we must understand where it has come from. So we start with a brief overview of the evolution of fragmented voices in organizational history. This brief and broad review is not meant to be exhaustive but merely illustrative of the variety of ways that history is approached in management and organizations.

History as fact

Perhaps the dominant perspective understands history in organizations as objective and factual. Research in this vein explores what happened in the organization and explains how and why this happened. The events from the past offer lessons that can be learned. The idea is that we can understand present management and organization situations by looking backward. Thus, managerial decisions about policy, strategy, staffing, and other organizational actions are to be viewed in the light of the past and past experiences. Historical case studies (Chandler, 1962), oral histories, and the stories of great business leaders of the past (Barnard, 1938) are representative of history done in this way.

With the call for a historical turn in MOH, most research has moved beyond a simple, factual account of an organization's past. Yet the historical baby shouldn't be thrown out with the bathwater of the past. We see an important place for historical case studies and research grounded in strong archival and empirical historical work.

History as data

In many cases, history in organizational and management research is equated with longitudinal research and some scholars have deemed the collection of data over significant periods of time as history. In some ways this is the most accepted and acceptable form of historical research for organizational scholars and journals. The best examples of this are studies of population ecology (Hannan and Freeman, 1977, 1984, 1989), path dependence (Arthur, 1994; David, 1986; Stinchcombe, 1965; Sydow, Schreyogg and Koch, 2009), and neo-institutional theory (Baum and Haveman, 1997; DiMaggio and Powell, 1991 [1983]). In these studies the past is a variable that affects the organization and what the firm can or cannot do. The history of the organization is something that is to be controlled for and measured.

Furthermore, history is also explained as a factor that constrains or enables the organization (Oliver, 1997). Some organizations are rich in history while others are saddled with an unfortunate past (Barney, 1986). A rich history is to be valued and embraced, while an unfortunate history can be limiting and, often, destructive. When history is equated with data, managers are limited in their actions and the choices they can make. The organization and the management of it is the product of circumstances and these are unchanging.

History as a tool

A third way that MOH scholars have looked at history is as a tool. This approach is different from the two above approaches in that history, when looked at as a tool, is not conceived of as a variable or as a fact. History is a malleable construct that is to be built and employed in the service of achieving organizational goals (Brunninge, 2009; Ericson, 2006; Foster et al., 2011; Gioia, Corley, and Fabbri, 2002; Ooi, 2002). History is developed and discussed to accomplish things in organizations. The facts of history are irrelevant and are inconsequential in the hands of a skillful manager who can identify the meaningful elements of history when connected to an organization. This approach to history is grounded in the idea that history is a rhetorical device that can be used strategically to persuade organizational stakeholders (Suddaby, Foster, and Trank, 2010). When it is recognized that history is not the actual set of events that once occurred but a reconstruction of the past for present use and present goals, it becomes another strategic tool that managers can use to lead a company into the future.

This area of research is still developing and new ways of understanding history as a tool are still to be developed. Yet, there are limits to seeing history as a tool. In particular, it is still unclear how organizations construct a particular version of history that conveys the same message to different groups at different times. The assumption is that history can be constructed, presented, and interpreted in the way that the manager chooses. Often this can and does happen; however, there are times where the organization's version of events is not accepted. There are numerous cases where an organization presents their history only to find it has been reinterpreted and, in some cases, hijacked. Moreover, a history as tool perspective is open to criticism as being overly managerial and focused too much on what the manager can control versus what the employees and other stakeholders think of the company's history. History may be used as a tool, but it is not always the case that it will be appropriate for the specific job at hand.

History as power

Closely related to the history as tool perspective is the view that history is the product of power relations (Clegg, 1989; Foucault, 1972, 1979; Hardy and Clegg, 1996; Hobsbawm and Ranger, 1983; Rowlinson and Hassard, 1993). MOH research from this perspective investigates how history is presented and is constructed to advantage those who are in power. Also of concern is the issue of who makes the rules, how they create the organizational values, and how this helps these groups retain power. Drawing on neo-historical studies and critical management, history is viewed not as fact or data but as a site of contestation and control.

It is in and through history that managers can construct particular images of their organization, which are then taken for granted. The role of the researcher is to understand how power has been used to create a particular image or view of the organization's past and how this reinforces and allows for the continuation of existing power arrangements. Managers have control over the artifacts of the past and how these are understood. What is important is that power relations, their unequal distribution and how these have been hidden in historical arrangements, are uncovered and identified.

Bringing process research to MOH

Research of historical processes

One way to bring process research to MOH is to investigate the way that history develops in organizations and through management actions. The emphasis is not on the facts of history or on how history is used or who is using it. The focus is on the processes involved with creating and using organizational history. This shift is away from the past or history as a thing or as an arrangement of power structures, although research of historical processes does not preclude or exclude these discussions. The study of the historical processes is concerned with the different *interactions and mechanisms* that occur at the different stages in the development of a specific historical conception of an organization.

One way this research can be manifested is by researching how managers influence historical processes. Because organizational history is a social construction it is important to recognize the influence that managers have on its production. Yet, what is not known is when and where managers have influence over the construction and presentation of an organization's history. The common debate is the degree of influence that managers have on producing the organization's history. What is missing from the MOH literature is a study of how managers influence historical processes and whether there are specific places or times that make their influence more salient and consequential.

A process approach to history also avoids talking about whether events happened and if they were 'right.' The investigation of how history is developed and managed in organizations addresses how organizational actions and decisions conspire, deliberately or unintentionally, to produce the organization's history in the present. This type of historical research also analyzes how and why some histories have greater impact and persuasiveness than do others. The ties to national symbols and collective memories tend to become more influential and effective than histories that are specific and local. Research about how these histories develop and how they are constructed can possibly uncover what makes these 'national' histories more important and useful than other histories.

Historical process research

Another way for process to be brought to MOH is to look to the past with an eye toward how processes have changed over time. The focus for this type of research is on how organizations operated or managed in the past and how this compares to what occurs today. Unlike research that explores past organizational and management practices to glean lessons about how to manage in the present, historical process research is interested in comparing practices and determining what processes have changed (if any) and why these processes have been altered. In other words, the unit of analysis of historical process research is the change in processes over time and what this tells us about management and organizations.

An area where this research has particular applicability is in the study of rituals and how these have changed. Rituals, traditions, ceremonies, and other forms of memorializing are taken-for-granted processes in organizations. However, little research has questioned how these change or stay the same (Dacin, Munir, and Tracey, 2010 being a notable exception). A common expectation is that many of these historically grounded activities remain static and rigid which can be problematic to an organization. Yet, there are also other examples where historical processes evolve and are changed to accommodate the needs and aspirations of the current organization. What we currently do not know is the degree of change that is acceptable to make to these rituals within organizations. We also are not clear about how changes to longstanding traditions and celebrations are initiated and maintained. Further research of historical organizational processes will help expand how we understand historically ground processes and how these processes change over time.

Applying process research to MOH

Our call for more process-oriented research in MOH is relevant to a number of different areas of organizational research. Below we offer a brief examination of where and how historical process research and the research of the historical process can be studied.

Organizational work

Organizational work explores micro-processual actions that actors take within their organizations. This area of investigation is common in institutional theory (Lawrence, Suddaby, and Leca, 2009; Lawrence and Suddaby, 2006; Zietsma and Lawrence, 2010) and identity theory (Beech, MacIntosh, and McInnes, 2008; Bruijn and Whiteman, 2010; Creed, Dejordy, and Lok, 2011). From a MOH perspective, there is a great opportunity to explore the different ways that organizational members and managers create, maintain, and disrupt the various presentations and understandings of an organization's history. For example, an interesting question revolves around questions of maintaining (Balmer, 2011; Trank and Washington, 2009) and enduring (Anteby and Molnar, 2012). How do certain conceptions of an organization (e.g. values, traditions) persist throughout the existence of the organization while others are forgotten and cast asunder? Many organizations point to their history as a defining or unifying feature of their organization. Nevertheless, how does this history continue and persist?

To investigate these questions one could look at the historical 'work' that individuals have to do to ensure that one version of the organization's history continues. Thus, questions that could be asked include: What different steps occurred in order for the organization to endure? What were the mechanisms that were involved in constructing a particular version of the organization and its history? What actions and factors interact or impact the maintaining or the dissolution of an organization and its history? Bringing history to organizational work explores the micro-foundations of history and how these contribute to the continuation and persistence of specific historical narratives within an organization.

Similarly, we can ask whether work changes over time. A tacit assumption in the work literature is that the practices of creating, maintaining, and disrupting are invariant. In other words, are organizations, institutions, and identities maintained using similar processes as they were in the past? We are not clear if work has evolved or stayed the same over time. Moreover, what does this tell us about the nature of creating, maintaining, and disrupting if these aspects of work have/have not changed? An exploration and study of past conceptions of work might lead to new insight about creating, maintaining, and disrupting in various organizational contexts.

Identification and identifying

Organizational identity has close ties to organizational history (Kieser, 1994; Ravasi and Schultz, 2006). A firm's history and how it is presented is an important factor in strengthening an organization's identity. What is less investigated is the connection between an organization's history and the process of identifying with an organization. Questions can be asked about how a particular organizational history attracts individuals to an organization and how a specific history facilitates identifying. For example, are there particular aspects of an organization's history that make it more or less likely that members will identify with the organization? As well, Elsbach (1999) has categorized different types of organizational identification. What also could be investigated is how these different types of identification are related to a firm's history and how historical processes can lead to one of the types of identification.

Questions can also be asked about how a firm's history is complicit in the process of building and enhancing identification of existing organizational members. Are there particular historical events that when drawn upon or emphasized create highly identified members? We can also ask if the way members identify with the organization has changed and whether strong bonds amongst individuals and organizations persist and continue. Finally, what are the different processes that both organizations and individuals have to engage in to continue identifying with an organization and how does the managerial presentation of history impact this process?

Entrepreneurs and entrepreneurship

Another area that could benefit from a historical process-oriented approach is entrepreneurship. A great many historical studies have attended to the actions and backgrounds of the individual entrepreneurs. These studies paint an interesting picture of who it is that becomes an entrepreneur. Nevertheless, what isn't as clear is how these individuals identified and cultivated the different opportunities that they then turned into successful ventures. A historical process study of entrepreneurs would lead to new insight about the ways that entrepreneurs identified their opportunities and the different steps that pushed them to make certain decisions about their organizations (e.g. Hargadon, and Douglas 2001). Moreover, comparing how early entrepreneurs identified their opportunities to how it is done by entrepreneurs today could provide more insight into how entrepreneurs identify and capitalize on new ventures.

Similarly, a historical focus on entrepreneurship could also be a fruitful avenue for research. Instead of addressing the traits or characteristics of the person who created the venture and the processes involved with the development of the business, historical process research could explore the discipline of entrepreneurship and how it operates as a whole. It is entirely possible that entrepreneurship has remained relatively static and that entrepreneurial processes from the early 1900s are the same as they are today. A comparison of how different processes involved in creating a business have changed could also offer new insights into what is considered entrepreneurship and the mechanisms involved with business creation.

Finally, the role of history in new ventures is an important and understudied aspect of entrepreneurship. A strong culture is an important part of building cohesive and highly productive organization and the history of an organization is one component of a strong culture. Yet, new ventures are devoid of history and it is not clear how new organizations manage this history deficit. There are anecdotal stories about how high tech companies deliberately worked in garages to supplement their history and to create historical events from which to base future organizational narratives. It is less clear if all new companies and new ventures need to create histories and what needs to be done to ensure that these are credible and authentic renditions of past events.

Studying the processes of building a history for and in new ventures could be an interesting opportunity to examine and debate what qualifies as an organizational history and how these new histories are managed.

Memory and remembering

The study of organizational history and organizational memory are two established streams of thought. However, there is very little cross-fertilization of these ideas in the MOH literature. Most organizational memory studies, with some notable exceptions (Anteby and Molnar, 2012; Rowlinson *et al.*, 2010; Schultz and Hernes, 2013), focus on the storage and retrieval of facts. Management and organizational history is interested in the appearance of the past in organizations and the impact this has on organizational stakeholders. What is missing is a conversation of how memory, and what is remembered, informs MOH and how organizational history works to focus memory and organizational remembering (e.g. Nora, 1989). Memory is grounded in the past and remembering is an historical process. The exploration of how historical processes interact with organizational memory and remembering could lead to new insight about how organizations remember and what it is that is being remembered and by whom. As well, an exploration of how events and people are remembered differently could also expand our understanding of what it means to remember and how it is related to MOH.

Conclusion

In our discussion we have identified a number of ways that history appears in management and organizational discussions. Each of these different perspectives contributes to our understanding about what role history has for organizations and managers. A history as fact view emphasizes the importance of learning from past lessons and engaging in empirical work to help answer difficult questions. A history as data approach suggests that history is an important variable that can and does significantly impact organizational actions and decisions. Approaching history as a tool suggests that managers can control and shape their histories to create optimal strategic outcomes. Finally, history as power emphasizes that history and the presentation of history is not neutral and is the product of different power relations.

Our suggestion, a stronger emphasis on process research, is meant to augment and not supplant other approaches to MOH. In fact, we hope that our suggestion will help to stimulate more research in all the areas we have identified. A process-oriented approach to MOH will, in our view, enhance and expand how history is studied and understood by management and in organizations. We have identified four specific sites where we anticipate historical process research could be of great value. However, we anticipate that there are other areas of research that are equally ripe for investigation from a historical process approach.

In closing, our goal has been to encourage new conversations and to advocate for another approach to MOH studies. We hope that our commentary has piqued the interest of the MOH community and others because we see historical process research and the research of historical processes as a journey and not just a destination or foreign land.

References

Aaltio-Marjosola, I. and Mills, A. J. (2002) *Gender, Identity and the Culture of Organizations*. London and New York: Routledge.

Anteby, M. and Molnar, V. (2012) Collective memory meets organizational identity: Remembering to forget in a firm's rhetorical history, *Academy of Management Journal*, 55(3): 515–40.

Arthur, W. B. (1994) *Increasing Returns and Path Dependence in the Economy*. Ann Arbor, MI: University of Michigan Press.

Balmer, J. M. T. (2011) Corporate heritage brands and the precepts of corporate heritage brand management: Insights from the British Monarchy on the eve of the royal wedding of Prince William (April 2011) and Queen Elizabeth II's Diamond Jubilee (1952–2012), *Journal of Brand Management*, 18: 517–44.

Barnard, C. I. (1938) The functions of the executive, reprinted in J. S. Ott (ed.), *Classic Readings in Organizational Behavior*. Belmont: Wadsworth, 1996.

Barney, J. B. (1986) Organizational culture: Can it be a source of sustained competitive advantage?, *Academy of Management Review*, 11(3): 656–65.

Baum, J. A. C. and Haveman, H. A. (1997) Love thy neighbor? Differentiation and agglomeration in the Manhattan hotel industry, 1898–1990, *Administrative Science Quarterly*, 42: 304–38.

Beech, N., MacIntosh, R., and McInnes, P. (2008) Identity work: Processes and dynamics of identity formations, *International Journal of Public Administration*, 31(9): 957–70.

Booth, C. and Rowlinson, M. (2006) Management and organizational history: Prospects, *Management and Organizational History*, 1(1): 5–30.

Bruijn, E. and Whiteman, G. (2010) That which doesn't break us: Identity work by local indigenous 'stakeholders', *Journal of Business Ethics*, 3: 479–95.

Brunninge, O. (2009) Using history in organizations: How managers make purposeful reference to history in strategy processes, *Journal of Organizational Change Management*, 22(1): 8–26.

Chandler, A. D. (1962) *Strategy and Structure: Chapters in the History of the Industrial Enterprise*. Cambridge, MA: MIT Press.

Clegg, S. R. (1989) *Frameworks of Power*. London: Sage.

Creed, W. E. D., Dejordy, R., and Lok, J. (2011) Being the change: Resolving institutional contradiction through identity work, *Academy of Management Journal*, 53(6): 1336–64.

Dacin, M. T., Munir, K., and Tracey, P. (2010) Formal dining at Cambridge colleges: Linking ritual performance and institutional maintenance, *Academy of Management Journal*, 53(6): 1393–418.

David, P. A. (1986) Understanding the economics of Qwerty: The necessity of history, in W. N. Parker (ed.), *Economic History and the Modern Economist* (pp. 30–49). Oxford: Blackwell.

Delahaye, A., Booth, B., Clark, P., Procter, S., and Rowlinson, M. (2009) The genre of corporate history, *Journal of Organizational Change Management*, 22(1): 27–48.

DiMaggio, P. J. and Powell, W. W. (1991 [1983]) The iron cage revisited: Institutional isomorphism and collective rationality in organizational fields, in W. W. Powell and P. J. DiMaggio (eds), *The New Institutionalism in Organizational Analysis* (pp. 1–40). Chicago, IL: University of Chicago Press.

Durepos, G. and Mills, A. J. (2012) *ANTi-History: Theorizing the Past, History, and Historiography in Management and Organization Studies*. Charlotte, NC: Information Age.

Elsbach, K. D. (1999) An expanded model of organizational identification, *Research in Organizational Behavior*, 21: 163–200.

Ericson, M. (2006) Exploring the future, exploiting the past, *Journal of Management History*, 12(2): 121–36.

Foster, W. M., Suddaby, R., Minkus, A., and Wiebe, E. (2011) History as social memory assets: The example of Tim Hortons, *Management & Organizational History*, 6(1): 101–20.

Foucault, M. (1972) *The Archaeology of Knowledge*. London: Routledge.

Foucault, M. (1979) *Discipline and Punish: The Birth of the Prison*. New York: Random House.

Gioia, D. A., Corley, K. G., and Fabbri, T. (2002) Revising the past (while thinking in the future perfect tense), *Journal of Organizational Change Management*, 15(6): 622–34.

Hannan, M. T. and Freeman, J. (1977) The population ecology of organizations, *American Journal of Sociology*, 82(5): 929–64.

Hannan, M. T. and Freeman, J. (1984) Structural inertia and organizational change, *American Sociological Review*, 49(2): 149–64.

Hannan, M. T. and Freeman, J. (1989) *Organizational Ecology*. Cambridge, MA.: Harvard University Press.

Hardy, C. and Clegg, S. (1996) Some dare call it power, in S. R. Clegg, C. Hardy, and W. R. Nord (eds), *Handbook of Organization Studies* (pp. 622–41). London: Sage.

Hargadon, A. B. and Douglas, Y. (2001) When innovations meet institutions: Edison and the design of the electric light, *Administrative Science Quarterly*, 46: 476–501.

Hobsbawm, E. J. and Ranger, H. O. (1983) *The Invention of Tradition*. Cambridge: Cambridge University Press.

Kieser, A. (1994) Why organization theory needs historical analyses: And how this should be performed, *Organization Science*, 5(4): 608–20.

Kroeze, R. and Keulen, S. (2012) Leading a multinational is history in practice: The use of invented traditions and narratives at AkzoNobel, Shell, Phillips and ABN AMRO, *Business History*, 55(8): 1265–87.

Langley, A. (1999) Strategies for theorizing from process data, *Academy of Management Review*, 24(4): 691–710.

Lawrence, T. and Suddaby, R. (2006) Institutions and institutional work, in S. Clegg, C. Hardy, T. Lawrence, and W. R. Nord (eds), *Handbook of Organization Studies* (pp. 215–54). London: Sage.

Lawrence, T. B., Suddaby, R., and Leca, B. (eds) (2009) *Institutional Work: Actors and Agency in Institutional Studies of Organizations*. Cambridge: Cambridge University Press.

McGaughey, S. L. (2012) Institutional entrepreneurship in North American lightning protection standards: Rhetorical history and unintended consequences of failure, *Business History*, 55(1): 73–97.

Nora, P. (1989) Between memory and history: Les lieux de Mémoire, *Representations*, 26 (Spring): 7–24.

Oliver, C. (1997) Sustainable competitive advantage: Combining institutional and resource-based views, *Strategic Management Journal*, 18: 697–714.

Ooi, C.-S. (2002) Persuasive histories: Decentering, recentering and the emotional crafting of the past, *Journal of Organizational Change Management*, 15(6): 606–21.

Ravasi, D. and Schultz, M. (2006) Responding to organizational identity threats: Exploring the role of organizational culture, *Academy of Management Journal*, 49(3): 433–58.

Rowlinson, M. and Hassard, J. (1993) The invention of corporate culture: A history of the histories of Cadbury, *Human Relations*, 46(3): 299–326.

Rowlinson, M., Booth, C., Clark, P., Delahaye, A., and Procter, S. (2010) Social remembering and organizational memory, *Organization Studies*, 31(1): 69–87.

Schneiberg, M. (2007) What's on the path? Path dependence, organizational diversity and the problem of institutional change in the US economy, 1900–1950, *Socio-Economic Review*, 5(1): 47–80.

Schultz, M. and Hernes, T. (2013) A temporal perspective on organizational identity, *Organization Science*, 24(1): 1–21.

Stinchcombe, A. L. (1965) Social structure and organizations, in J. G. March (ed.), *Handbook of Organizations* (pp. 153–93). Chicago: Rand McNally.

Suddaby, R., Foster, W. M., and Trank, C. Q. (2010) Rhetorical history as a source of competitive advantage, in J. A. C. Baum and J. Lampel (eds), *Advances in Strategic Management: The Globalization of Strategy Research* (pp. 147–73). Bingley: Emerald.

Sydow, J., Schreyogg, G., and Koch, J. (2009) Organizational path dependence: Opening the black box, *Academy of Management Review*, 34(4): 689–709.

Trank, C. Q. and Washington, M. (2009) Maintaining an institution in a contested organizational field: The work of the AACSB and its constituents, in T. Lawrence, R. Suddaby, and B. Leca (eds), *Institutional Work: Actors and Agency in Institutional Studies of Organizations* (pp. 236–51). Cambridge: Cambridge University Press.

Üsdiken, B. and Kieser, A. (2004) Introduction: History in organisation studies, *Business History*, 46(3): 321–30.

Wertsch, J. V. (2004) Specific narratives and schematic narrative templates, in P. Seixas (ed.), *Theorizing Historical Consciousness*. Toronto: University of Toronto Press.

Zietsma, C. and Lawrence, T. B. (2010) Institutional work in the transformation of an organizational field: The interplay of boundary work and practice work, *Administrative Science Quarterly*, 55(2): 189–221.

27

Turning how and where?

The potential for history in management and organizational studies

Matthias Kipping and Behlül Üsdiken

Both in our own writing and in our institutional efforts, namely through a standing working group at the European Group for Organizational Studies (EGOS), jointly organized with Lars Engwall, we have tried to help promote a larger role for history in management and organization studies. And we welcome and support all efforts in the same direction, including this *Companion*. Indeed, a lot has been said and done since the early calls for linking management and organization studies and history, namely Zald's (1990, 1993) and Kieser's (1994) essays. At the same time, among those advocating more history or even an 'historic turn', there is still not much consensus on how this should be done – and where such a turn should lead us or, put differently, what exactly the contribution of history might be (Üsdiken and Kieser, 2004). And while plurality is generally positive and should be welcomed, we argue that the multiplicity – and sometimes vagueness – of aims and approaches also hampers debate and a possible movement towards broader consensus. Moreover, we also believe that the juxtaposition between management and organization 'science' and (business) history, which underpins much of the calls for more of the latter, might be counterproductive and block some possible directions for history finding a larger and at the same time useful place in research on management and organizations.

In the remainder of this commentary, we will briefly discuss each of the following: (i) the origins and the nature of the early calls for more history in management and organization studies, which we suggest were a reaction to the increasingly dominant timeless and universalist theorizing on management and organizations since the 1960s; (ii) the divergence that became apparent in the ways to engage with history in the 2000s, which, in our view, has somewhat obscured the explicit or latent anti-scientistic/anti-positivist position of most recent supporters of management and organizational history; (iii) finally, moving beyond recent suggestions on how to bridge the now taken-for-granted gap between history and management and organization studies, we argue that there is promising and largely unexplored potential in accommodating, though not fully embracing, the dominant (social) science paradigm.

Discontent with ahistorical theorizing

As mentioned above, Zald's and Kieser's essays from the early 1990s are often credited with providing the initial impetus for the revival of interest in connecting management and organization studies with history. It was not that there was no prior reference to history or use of historical research, even after management and organization studies took the scientistic route (see Üsdiken and Kipping, 2014). There was, of course, Chandler (1962) as well as ensuing research of the same genre (e.g. Fligstein, 1990); and there were the sporadic journal articles in the US-based literature, which pointed to the value that might be derived from taking a historical perspective or doing historical research (e.g. Goodman and Kruger, 1988; Lawrence, 1984). There was management history too, which had been around for quite some time as a recognized sub-specialty within the American business school environment, though pushed to the margins already by the 1980s (Üsdiken and Kipping, 2014; see also Marens, Chapter 7, this volume).

What distinguished Zald and Kieser was their explicit call for a greater engagement with history. Zald had a broader agenda though. His plea involved developing closer links not only with history, but with humanities at large, including literature and philosophy. In his view, such links would help to shift management and organization studies as an 'applied discipline', from an 'engineering' to an 'enlightenment' model. With this distinction, he was pointing to the predominant 'engineering' conception of the discipline, whereby the main aim was defined as developing solutions to managerial problems. What Zald (1993: 514) sought with the 'enlightenment' model was a re-definition, where the "goal is education for public and civic participation, not necessarily for specific problem solving". For Zald strengthening the humanities base of the discipline was geared towards this particular purpose. Part of his emphasis on the humanities also had to do with pointing to what he saw as the 'limits' of using the natural sciences model not only in studying organizations but also in other social sciences, such as sociology (see also Zald, 1991). It is important to stress here, however, that Zald did *not* advocate abandoning the science orientation. For him the question was how to "combine a positivistic program of theoretical and empirical cumulation with the enriching possibilities of the humanities" (Zald, 1993: 516). His stance was mainly against timeless general models. In this vein, the roadmap that he charted included four possibilities for "combining history, theory, and the study of organizations": (i) a "history-for-itself" approach with some concern for generalization; (ii) history used as a basis for testing "nomothetic propositions"; (iii) developing "historical theories of organizations" where outcomes are explained by prior events or processes and finally, as his preferred way, (iv) using historical and comparative analyses to account for the historically specific features of organizations (Zald, 1990: 102–4).

Although developed independently of Zald's writings (as indicated by the absence of references to his work), Kieser's (1994) appeal for returning to Weberian roots and re-engaging with history was in many ways similar. For him too, recourse to history was not intended as a replacement for organization theory, but rather as a way of enriching organizational analyses. The latter could be achieved, Kieser (1994) thought, by bringing history into internationally comparative research, studying past developments to account for present-day organizational arrangements, and putting current theories to the test in historical contexts.

Zald's and Kieser's calls came at a time when two disparate sets of currents had developed within management and organizational research, though with a differential hold on the two sides of the Atlantic (see Üsdiken, 2010 for a review). On the US side, research was becoming longitudinal with the advent and consolidation of organizational ecology and neo-institutionalism. The former was at the forefront as the focus was on histories of organizational populations, though coupled with strong universalist and scientistic aims. Institutionalist research became more oriented towards process and history only when the interest began to shift towards studying institutional formation and change (see Kipping and Üsdiken, 2014 as well as Üsdiken and Kipping, 2014 for reviews; also Zald, 1996). In parts of Europe, particularly in the UK, management and organization studies had developed along totally different tracks. The reaction to the scientistic/positivist approach dominant in the USA initially took the form of labour process theory and an interpretivist orientation, the former having closer links to history (Kieser, 1994). A shift from labour process theory towards critical management studies was then to follow coupled with the rise of postmodernism (Rowlinson, Stager Jacques, and Booth 2009; Üsdiken and Kipping, 2014; Weatherbee, 2012). However, none of these so-called 'alternative' perspectives, namely, the interpretivist, critical, and postmodern, were particularly attentive to history at that stage, perhaps with the exception of the postmodernists who sometimes followed Foucault's archaeo-genealogy – an approach considered problematic in its view of history though (see Rowlinson and Carter, 2002).

Nonetheless, the divergence of developments on the two sides of the Atlantic in the 1980s and the 1990s did provide the background for more pronounced calls for greater emphasis on history as well as the different ways in which history and historical evidence were actually employed in empirical research. They also set the foundations, however, for the emergence and persistence of divisions as to how management and organization studies should engage with history.

Juxtaposing history and social science

The quest for greater engagement with history after the turn of the century developed along three main lines. These originated in part from the ontological, epistemological, and methodological divisions mentioned above, which had already taken shape within the management and organizational literature (see also Üsdiken and Kieser, 2004) as well as within history itself (Durepos, Chapter 12, this volume). These approaches all stressed the fundamental differences between 'history' and the dominant social scientistic paradigm in management and organization studies – even if they differed in the degree to which they proposed moving away from the latter.

Thus, largely remaining loyal to Zald's and Kieser's aspirations, some have been searching for ways in which history could be *integrated* into management and organization studies without necessarily abandoning the social scientistic aims of the latter. There were suggestions, for example, for a 'historical organization theory' that would allow addressing the temporal nature of organizations (Leblebici and Shah, 2004). Likewise, evolutionary theory has been proposed as a framework that could combine scientistic generalization with the narrative orientation in history (Lippmann and Aldrich, 2014). But these have been exceptions in what has been a fairly widespread attempt to use history to move away from the dominant (social) science paradigm. A second approach, and most radical in this respect has been the call for an 'historic turn', which seeks to transform management and organization studies by turning away from social science and turning instead to history (but not to business history) and to theories of history (Clark and Rowlinson, 2004). This quest for reorientation came not only as a reaction to the scientization in management and organizational studies but also called for a 'deconstructionist' approach to history (Rowlinson and Hassard, 2014; Rowlinson, Stager Jacques, and Booth, 2009; see also Coraiola, Foster, and Suddaby, Chapter 15, this volume). In the third approach, the main concern has not been to seek integration or a full-scale rejection. Here, authors have pointed to the benefits that could be derived from employing history as an empirical method, positioning history as one of the alternative methodologies that could be used within a particular domain or theoretical perspective in management and organization studies (see, for example, Ingram, Rao, and Silverman, 2012). Typically, history is classified as one of the qualitative methodologies, which can be utilized as a narrative or analytical narrative. It thus enables the adoption of a social constructionist and subjectivist approach to the phenomena under study (Suddaby and Greenwood, 2009; Suddaby, Foster, and Mills, 2014).

Despite their differences, all three of these approaches have juxtaposed history and organization studies, often portraying them as ultimately incommensurable. Even Zald (1990: 102), the early protagonist of the integrationist approach, saw the combination of history and the theoretical study of organizations as a "large methodological issue". More recently, Rowlinson and Hassard (2013), for instance, compare what they called 'historical neoinstitutionalism' and 'neo-institutionalist history', highlighting in particular the differences in terms of the more formal methods applied by historical neo-institutionalists and the recourse to primary (rather than secondary) sources by neo-institutional historians. More broadly, Leblebici (2014: esp. 74) contrasts 'organizational theory' and 'business history' in terms of their 'cultures of inquiry' and their 'types of understanding' showing, based on Runciman's (1983) categories, how they differ significantly in terms of reportage, description, explanation, and evaluation, stressing namely the historians' insistence on the uniqueness of events and their causes as well as the subjective nature of meaning (attributed to the phenomena by both historical actors and current observers). Rowlinson, Hassard, and Decker (2014) are even more explicit about the differences between history and organization theory, identifying three 'epistemological dualisms' in terms of explanation, evidence, and temporality. This leads to a distinction between 'narrative organizational history' based on periodization and verifiable documentary sources and 'historical organization theory', which involves the analysis of constructed data with a constant chronology. Others have developed similar dichotomies – though perhaps not quite as categorically (see, for example, Ingram, Rao, and Silverman, 2012; Wadhwani and Bucheli, 2014).

How much this usually implicit consensus regarding the opposition if not incommensurability between the historical and the social scientific approaches has taken hold in the literature (despite the variation in the opinions about what role history could and should have in research on management and organizations) can be seen in the recent suggestions about how to bridge this gap. Greenwood and Bernardi (2014), for instance, have explicitly argued against trying to combine the two disciplines. Although they attempt to show that the epistemological and methodological boundaries may not be as rigid as they are often made to be, they still believe that the barriers are not easily surmountable. In their opinion therefore, the aim should not be to seek integration but rather to search for avenues of cooperation among historians and management and organizational researchers. Likewise, Leblebici (2014), in the essay we referred to above, has proposed improving the relationship between (business) history and management and organization studies not through an 'interdisciplinary' but a 'transdisciplinary' approach. This, he argues, will (i) not be privileging any one of the two disciplines, (ii) allow each of them to maintain its distinctive identity, and (iii) create opportunities for building on the strengths of each. In his view, the benefits of such a transdisciplinary approach will be obtained if both sides are willing to accept their dissimilarities, if debate is moved from methodological differences to mutually interesting research questions, and if publication outlets can be created that would be open to problem- rather than discipline-driven research. For Leblebici (2014) such an approach would not only add to both disciplines but also enhance 'relevance' by addressing changes in managerial problems over time.

This apparently now taken-for-granted juxtaposition is understandable, given the origins of the call for more history in an environment dominated by the, as Zald called it, 'engineering' or science paradigm. But management and organization studies have evolved (Üsdiken and Kipping, 2014) and there is now more history than 'meets the eye', as we have shown in detail elsewhere (Kipping and Üsdiken, 2014). We would therefore suggest that management and organizational history do the same and look for ways to reconcile with social science – while maintaining its own plurality and without fully espousing all of the latter's assumptions or methods.

Moving forward: time for reconciliations?

Thus, to repeat, we do not believe that the juxtaposition of history versus social science is helpful at this stage of development and neither do we think that history should be confined as one particular method within the social sciences. There are actually many different ontological, epistemological, and methodological positions within the history discipline itself (Decker, Kipping, and Wadhwani, forthcoming) – a fact that those referring to it within management and organization studies at times ignore, as has been pointed out by Coraiola, Foster, and Suddaby (Chapter 15, this volume). Thus, we agree with Rowlinson, Hassard, and Decker (2014: 268) when they say that "it makes no sense to try to find a unified ontological or epistemological foundation, let alone a unitary 'historical method' for organizational history".

Yet, we should also stress that a corollary of this position, for us, is acknowledging the legitimacy and potential contributions of the (now) many different ways of engaging with history and making use of historical research. The position that we take accords with the plurality (fragmentation if you like) that has come to characterize the field of management and organization studies at large, emanating from the divergent orientations that, as we mentioned above, appeared in the 1980s. Indeed, the heterogeneity that we observe in historically orientated research is a reflection and extension of the diversity of ontological, epistemological, and methodological orientations already existing within the field of management and organization studies (see, for examples of these alternative perspectives, Coraiola, Foster, and Suddaby, Chapter 15; Durepos, Chapter 12; Novecivic, Jones, and Carraher, Chapter 2; Taylor, Chapter 11, this volume).

One route that responds to calls for more history, for example, has been the carving of a space for what now comes under the label 'management and organizational history', as exemplified by this very *Companion*. The move in this direction has been very much along the lines of the appeal for an 'historic' turn. It has involved both a closer link with critical management studies and a deconstructionist orientation towards history (Rowlinson and Hassard, 2014; Rowlinson, Stager Jacques, and Booth, 2009; Weatherbee, 2012). Thus, the 'new' management and organizational history stands as an alternative to evolutionary 'management history' (or the 'history of management thought') that has developed but then become increasingly marginalized within the American business school environment. Indeed, research and commentary constituting the alternative orientation has developed mainly around a deconstructionist critique of the content and the historiography of traditional management history (e.g. Novecivic, Jones, and Carraher, Chapter 2, this volume; see also Bruce and Nyland, 2011 and Hassard, 2012 as other recent examples).

At the same time, not all engagements with history should be about writing organizational, or for that matter, management history. Other domains connecting to history are equally important and legitimate in our view. Some will be at the level of populations or fields (Coraiola, Foster, and Suddaby, Chapter 15, this volume; Kipping and Üsdiken, 2014; Rowlinson, Hassard, and Decker, 2014). Likewise, although welcome, not all research should or might involve collaboration between historians and organizational researchers. Neither can it or need to always be transdisciplinary. There have been and will be attempts towards integration where history is made an integral part of the theory (Kipping and Üsdiken, 2014). Again, in methodological terms, not all historical management and organizational research does or should rely on primary sources, as Rowlinson, Hassard, and Decker (2014) also acknowledge. Neither will historical research within organization studies necessarily be deconstructionist or subjectivist (cf. Coraiola, Foster, and Suddaby, Chapter 15, this volume).

What is important to stress – and here we beg to differ from many of those making the case for history or an 'historic turn' – is the need to also include among the variety of legitimate approaches the historical research and theorizing emanating from scholars firmly based within the (social) science paradigm. As we have shown in detail elsewhere (Kipping and Üsdiken, 2014), there has been much more history than 'meets the eye' in the field of management and organization studies at large. In our survey (Kipping and Üsdiken, 2014) we have proposed to subdivide these efforts by distinguishing what we refer to as 'history *to* theory' and 'history *in* theory'. The former involves the use of history as data or evidence, akin to what Rowlinson, Hassard, and Decker (2014) have labelled 'serial history'. History *in* theory, on the other hand, refers to approaches, where history is an explanatory or a moderating element of theorizing at the organizational or inter-organizational levels, in particular, imprinting, path dependence, structural inertia, co-evolution, and dynamic capabilities. Probably our most important finding in terms of providing more space for history within mainstream management and organization studies was a growing type of research that we identified as displaying what we called 'historical cognizance'. It meant that their authors were conscious of the idiosyncrasies of the historical context they dealt with and made explicit the 'limits to generalizability' – resulting from the use of history as evidence or as a driver in their theoretical model – with 'limits' rather than impossibility being the key term here. This, we believe, is a way of 'taking history seriously' without having to move too far from or fully rejecting the social scientistic foundations of management and organization studies.

Personally, against the background of this deepening engagement with history *within* mainstream management and organization studies, we would even go one step further in suggesting that those wishing to find a larger place for history should take on board some of the basic precepts of (social) science (see also Kipping, 2014). It bears repeating that this does not mean we believe in or suggest a single –purportedly the 'best' – way of connecting history with management and organization studies or would want management and organizational historians to espouse its dominant hypothesis-testing methodology as recently suggested to business historians by de Jong, Higgins, and van Driel (forthcoming) for instance. But we do believe that the legitimacy – and publishability – of the wide range of historical approaches discussed above and partially exhibited in more detail in this *Companion* would benefit from: (i) contributing to debates in the social sciences that have a relatively broad relevance and appeal – or starting new ones for that matter; (ii) explicating as much as possible their sources and the methodology used to analyze them, in order to substantiate their claims and their narratives and to make them replicable for others; and (iii) engaging in some form of generalization – naturally a limited one given historical contingencies – and attempting, if possible, some mid-level theorizing. This, we believe, transcends the artificial and increasingly unhelpful dichotomy between history and social science and would also ultimately allow history to be taken more seriously within (mainstream) management and organization studies.

References

Bruce, K. and Nyland, C. (2011) Elton Mayo and the deification of human relations, *Organization Studies*, 32(3): 383–405.

Chandler, A. D. Jr. (1962) *Strategy and Structure: Chapters in the History of the Industrial Enterprise*. Cambridge, MA: MIT Press.

Clark, P. and Rowlinson, M. (2004) The treatment of history in organization studies: Towards a 'historic turn'?, *Business History*, 46(3): 331–52.

de Jong, A., Higgins, D., and van Driel, H. (forthcoming) New business history? An invitation to discuss, *Business History*.

Decker, S., Kipping, M., and Wadhwani, R. D. (forthcoming) New business histories! Plurality in business history research methods, *Business History*.

Fligstein, N. (1990) *The Transformation of Corporate Control*. Cambridge, MA: Harvard University Press.

Goodman, R. S. and Kruger, E.V. (1988) Data dredging or legitimate research method? Historiography and its potential for management research, *Academy of Management Review*, 13(2): 315–25.

Greenwood, A. and Bernardi, A. (2014) Understanding the rift, the (still) uneasy bedfellows of history and organization studies, *Organization*, 21(6): 907–32.

Hassard, J. S. (2012) Rethinking the Hawthorne Studies: The Western Electric research in its social, political and historical context, *Human Relations*, 65(11): 1431–61.

Ingram, P., Rao, H., and Silverman, B. S. (2012) History in strategy research: What, why and how?, in S. J. Kahl, B. S. Silverman, and M. A. Cusumano (eds), *History and Strategy* (pp. 241–73). Bingley: Emerald.

Kieser, A. (1994) Why organization theory needs historical analysis: And how this should be performed, *Organization Science*, 5(4): 608–20.

Kipping, M. (2014) Open up business historians! Be more explicit about methods and less afraid of theorizing, Discussion paper prepared for a plenary round table at the annual meeting of the European Business History Association, Utrecht, 21–23 August.

Kipping, M. and Üsdiken, B. (2014) History in organization and management theory: More than meets the eye, *Academy of Management Annals*, 8(1): 535–88.

Lawrence, B. S. (1984) Historical perspective: Using the past to study the present, *Academy of Management Review*, 9(2): 307–12.

Leblebici, H. (2014) History and organization theory: Potential for a transdisciplinary convergence, in M. Bucheli and R. D. Wadhwani (eds), *Organizations in Time: History, Theory, Methods* (pp. 56–99). Oxford: Oxford University Press.

Leblebici, H. and Shah, N. (2004) The birth, transformation and regeneration of business incubators as new organisational forms: Understanding the interplay between organisational history and organisational theory, *Business History*, 46(3): 353–80.

Lippmann, S. and Aldrich, H. (2014) History and evolutionary theory, in M. Bucheli and R. D. Wadhwani (eds), *Organizations in Time: History, Theory, Methods* (pp. 124–46). Oxford: Oxford University Press.

Rowlinson, M. and Carter, C. (2002) Foucault and history in organization studies, *Organization*, 9(4): 527–47.

Rowlinson, M. and Hassard, J. (2013) Historical neo-institutionalism or neo-institutionalist history? Historical research in management and organization studies, *Management and Organizational History*, 8(2): 111–26.

Rowlinson, M. and Hassard, J. (2014) History and the cultural turn in organization studies, in M. Bucheli and R. D. Wadhwani (eds), *Organizations in Time: History, Theory, Methods* (pp. 147–65). Oxford: Oxford University Press.

Rowlinson, M., Hassard, J., and Decker, S. (2014) Research strategies for organizational history: A dialogue between historical theory and organization theory, *Academy of Management Review*, 39(3): 250–74.

Rowlinson, M., Jacques, R. S., and Booth, C. (2009) Critical management and organizational history, in M. Alvesson, T. Bridgman, and H. Willmott (eds), *The Oxford Handbook of Critical Management Studies* (pp. 286–303). Oxford: Oxford University Press.

Runciman, W. C. (1983) *A Treatise on Social Theory*, vol. 1, Cambridge: Cambridge University Press.

Suddaby, R. and Greenwood, R. (2009) Methodological issues in researching institutional change, in D. A. Buchanan and A. Bryman (eds), *The Sage Handbook of Organizational Research Methods* (pp. 176–95). London: Sage.

Suddaby, R., Foster, W. M., and Mills, A. J. (2014) Historical institutionalism, in M. Bucheli and R. D. Wadhwani (eds), *Organizations in Time: History, Theory, Methods* (pp. 100–23). Oxford: Oxford University Press.

Üsdiken, B. (2010) Between contending perspectives and logics: Organizational studies in Europe, *Organization Studies*, 31(6): 715–35.

Üsdiken, B. and Kieser, A. (2004) Introduction: History in organisation studies, *Business History*, 46(3): 321–30.

Üsdiken. B. and Kipping, M. (2014) History and organization studies: A long-term view, in M. Bucheli and R. D. Wadhwani (eds), *Organizations in Time: History, Theory, Methods* (pp. 34–55). Oxford: Oxford University Press.

Wadhwani, R. D. and Bucheli, M. (2014) The future of the past in management and organization studies, in M. Bucheli and R. D. Wadhwani (eds), *Organizations in Time: History, Theory, Methods* (pp. 3–30). Oxford: Oxford University Press.

Weatherbee, T. G. (2012) Caution! This historiography makes wide turns: Historic turns and breaks in management and organization studies, *Management and Organization History*, 7(3): 203–18.

Zald, M. N. (1990) History, sociology, and theories of organization, in J. E. Jackson (ed.), *Institutions in American Society: Essays in Market, Political and Social Organizations* (pp. 81–108). Ann Arbor, MI: University of Michigan Press.

Zald, M. N. (1991) Sociology as a discipline: Quasi-science and quasi-humanities, *The American Sociologist*, 22(3): 165–87.

Zald, M. N. (1993) Organization studies as a scientific and humanistic enterprise: Toward a reconceptualization of the foundations of the field, *Organization Science*, 4(4): 513–28.

Zald, M. N. (1996) More fragmentation? Unfinished business in linking the social sciences and the humanities, *Administrative Science Quarterly*, 41(2): 251–61.

28

Actors, networks, theory, and history – what are we producing?

Albert J. Mills, Terrance G. Weatherbee, and Patricia Genoe McLaren

Those who fail to learn from history are doomed to repeat it.

(Winston Churchill, 1935)

Those who fail to learn from the ontological status of history are doomed to reproduce it.

(Weatherbee et al., *2012).*

In this commentary we reflect on history as an actor-network effect. In particular we explore how our (shift in) thinking on history positions us in a supposed actor-network.

A good place to start is at the beginning, that is, a place that we designate as the starting point – a socially constructed point which allows us to 'follow the actors' (Latour, 2005). To that end, we pose a question about *what we think we have produced*. This will allow us to 'reassemble' (Latour, 2005) the various interactions – enrollment, translation, punctuation, etc. – that have played a part in the construction of our actor-network connectedness. When we say "think we have produced" that is not to say that we are confused or uncertain about what we are doing but, rather, we are acknowledging that actor-network effects are always ongoing and often depend on the various interactions involved as to what the perceived outcome (namely 'knowledge') is. Karl Weick (1995) captures this process well when he says that "we don't know what we think until we have said it." By the end of this chapter we may know more.

At the time of this writing, what we set out to produce is a different approach to the study and understanding of history. The ingredients of that approach – which we call ANTi-History (Durepos & Mills, 2012; Durepos, Chapter 12, this volume; Mills & Durepos, 2010) – center on a fusion of the sociology of knowledge literature (Mannheim, 1968; Marx & Engels, 1996), post-structuralist historiography (Jenkins, 1994; Munslow, 2012a), and actor-network theory (Callon, 1986; Latour, 1988; Law, 1994) – especially the 'ANT and After' (Law & Hassard, 1999) literature. Not surprisingly, many of these elements are dotted throughout various chapters in this edited collection and so we will only provide a brief overview here.

Essentially, we view history as an effect of actor-networks. As such history is not to be viewed as real or verifiable – it is, as Alun Munslow would say, ontologically unobtainable (see Chapter 10). This, and a multitude of other reasons, has driven historian Keith Jenkins (2009) to reject history as a useful pursuit. Nonetheless, for the very reasons that Jenkins rejects history we see it as a vitally important aspect of socio-political life that needs to be explored, especially if we are to mitigate its powerful effects. We argue that history, what people come to accept as knowledge of the past (or, what Munslow, Chapter 10, succinctly calls "the-past-as-history"), is both powerful and meaningful. Its very meaningfulness is what makes it powerful, in a Foucauldian (1980) sense of dispersed positive and negative effects. As such, history is arguably a meta-discourse (Jenkins, 1995) or meta-narrative (Munslow, 2012b) that serves to provide meaning to people's lives.

Given this, we contend that it is worth preserving 'history' as a way of making sense of and valuing social life: it is for us a useful fiction (White, 1985). However, the very properties of history (the story) are subject to socio-political pressures, not the least of which includes the inherent power of History (the discipline) and those who influence the construction and dissemination of its historical accounts (Kalela, 2012; Lemisch, 1975; Zinn, 1990). Thus, if we can shed light on the processes of history production, what becomes viewed as received knowledge of the past, we can help to liberate people from the dead hand of history. That, at least, is the aim of ANTi-History, which we view as critical organizational historiography. Therefore ANTi-History is, as we presently understand it, part critique (of the problematic nature of history); part methodology (in encouraging and producing multiple histories); part ontological (in revealing the ontological oscillation between the material effects of actor-networks and the fictive outcome(s) of history production); and part socio-political (as we attempt to enroll others to this or that way of viewing history).

In the process of laying out our notion(s) of how history comes to be produced we are learning our craft and doing so within the context of actor-network effects (at least that is our supposition). This means that we have, as yet, only partly practiced aspects of our declared approach. Some of our earlier attempts preceded a more fully developed theory of history, let alone ANTi-History, and focused on the importance of history for understanding management and organizational phenomena – very much in the vein of Alfred Kieser's (1994; see Chapter 3, this volume) call for a greater understanding of history (see, for example, Genoe McLaren, 2011; Mills, 1996). Other attempts have involved the production of alternative accounts of the past in an attempt to produce multiple histories of management and organizational studies (MOS) – see Chapters 22 (McLaren and Mills) and 25 (Coller, McNally, and Mills) of this book. Other work has focused on critique of the field – to open up space for more diversity of accounts and ways of understanding history (Mills, Weatherbee, & Durepos, 2014; Weatherbee, 2012). There have also been some preliminary attempts to apply ANTi-History to the understanding of how histories themselves are produced. An early version involved a following of the actors involved in the development and publication of a history of Pan American Airways (Durepos, Helms Mills & Mills, 2008) and a more recent version focused on the construction of a history of the Academy of Management (Myrick, Helms Mills & Mills, 2013). In this last regard further research is underway on a wide range of projects.

All this is by way of suggesting that what we *think* we are producing is defined by the publications we have produced to date and how these non-human actants (namely publications) tend to take on a life of their own (become actors) and influence what we are attempting to produce (ANTi-History and ANTi-histories). For example, recently two colleagues were advised to revise their article on management and history through greater theorization. They were seemingly advised to seek out our ANTi-History work. They did so and the article was eventually published, with some credit to our work. However, the article, although highly interesting and well written, bore little relationship to what we think is our suggested approach. It is as if ANTi-History serves as what Hartt (2013) terms a "non-corporeal actant," namely, a set of disparate ideas whose influence owes more to the parts that are cobbled together through various publications than the overall intent of the authors themselves. But then who are the authors?

This question takes us to another actor-network effect – the production of an actor-network itself.

ANTi-History, we argue, is an effect of a network of actors that has steadily formed over the years through its various relationships with the Sobey School of Business' PhD in Management and the work on Anti-History arising from it. All the actors are linked through association with the PhD program as either students/graduates/faculty and non-human actors (Latour, 2005), such as program elements (courses, stories, myths, etc.). In the latter case it can be argued that elements of the PhD program helped to shape the idea of ANTi-History. These elements include a strong emphasis on postpositivist thinking (Prasad, 2005) with its focus on social constructionism, critical management philosophies (Burrell & Morgan, 1979), and the role of history in MOS. Nor can we ignore the strong elements of positivism in the program, which serve as a contrasting mode or modes of thinking, serving to provide a context of multi-paradigmatic choice, which may be linked to enrollment and translation processes and the inhibition of early black-boxed thinking.

Some sense of an actor-network at play was captured quite early on by two or three Sobey PhD students, at different points when they spoke about what came to be called 'the Halifax School.' What would constitute such a school was never really specified. For some it was a generalized sense that the program combined some unique features; for others it was more narrowly focused on management and organizational history (see Corrigan, 2015). The point here is not to argue any claim for the existence of a 'Halifax School' so much as to identify a feeling among some of the actors involved that there is a specific effect of combinations of exposure to the Sobey PhD. At the very least it may serve as an enrollment and translation element as actors are drawn to self-identify with something.

Outside of the Sobey PhD program itself there has been some identification of the "Sobey School of Business at [Saint] Mary's University in Canada" as an "important research cluster for MOH" (management and organizational history) (Decker, Rowlinson & Hassard, 2014). The description is part of a successful grant proposal to the Economic and Social Research Council (of the United Kingdom) for the development of a seminar series on MOH that includes 'Actor-Network Theory and ANTi-History' as one of its six proposed seminars. In describing the purpose of the seminar, the authors go on to attribute the Sobey research cluster as having developed "a new critical approach to history based on Latour's Actor-Network Theory (ANT)," citing "Gabrielle [Durepos] … a graduate of Sobey … [as] instrumental in developing the ANTi-History concept together with [Albert] Mills. Their contribution will be discussed by leading UK and US scholars such as John Hassard, Bill Cooke and R. Daniel Wadwhani" (Decker, Rowlinson & Hassard, 2014).

Here we catch a glimpse of another, larger and linked actor-network – those scholars interested in encouraging a greater interest in, and emphasizing the importance of, the role of history in MOH (see for example Booth and Rowlinson, Chapter 5, this volume). To that end, the Sobey actor-network may be described as a node of this broader network, namely an "important research cluster *for* MOH" (Decker, Rowlinson & Hassard, 2014, our emphasis).

Summary and conclusion

It is to this last point that we want to return. It strikes us as a very fair and welcoming comment to cast 'us' as part of a wider actor-network. We can be considered enrolled. Any sense of a 'Halifax School' has tended, at the very least, to include reference to MOH. So, we have no concerns about being included in a fairly broad actor-network that embraces a number of actors (human and non-human) who are interested in (re)developing an interest in history in management and organizational theory. Like other actor-networks this broad network contains a series of smaller nodes that have the potential to engender tensions – tensions that may lead to de-enrollments. One of those nodes is likely a fairly sizeable group of actors who view the process of history as the discovery or uncovering of factual truths about the past, who view the past-as-history (Munslow, Chapter 10, this volume). Another node likely consists of those actors involved in the development of critical approaches to organizational history – we see ourselves within this node.

Despite the potential for tension and conflict amongst actors and actor-networks, the field *appears* to be going through a period of growth and discussion as scholars from different nodes meet and discuss various issues. Perhaps a good example of this is the joint Critical Management Studies (CMS) and Management History (MH) divisions' joint seminars and sessions at the 2014 Academy of Management annual conference. The situation may be helped by perceived frustrations with management and organization theory and continued evidence of ahistorical work, which creates a common goal in uniting the efforts of all management and organizational history scholars. See Kipping and Üsdiken, Chapter 27, this volume, for their take on the common goals of, and increasing tensions between, various proponents of the importance of history to management and organizational studies.

Enrollment triumphs over translation. But there are cracks as evidenced by scholars "from the South" who view the current debate as an argument about the production of newer or different Western histories of MOH (see Ibarra-Colado, Chapter 23, this volume). We see our own position as, if not in the cracks, standing on a precipice of them. While the broader networks of which we are a part focus *on* history (e.g. Wren & Bedeian, 2009), historical *context* (Kieser, Chapter 3, this volume), or the writing *of* history (Booth and Rowlinson, Chapter 5, this volume), ANTi-History focuses on how the past is (re)produced *as* history. In other words, there is an inherent tension in our work that helps to place us within the realm of those interested in history while simultaneously having the potential to pit us against those who see history as more than just an effect. In the former pursuit we seem to fit squarely in MOH, while in the latter we may be more akin to Cultural Theory. It is arguably the oscillation between contributing to multiple histories while focusing on the production of something called a 'history' that allows us to be simultaneously enrolled yet apart from MOH. It's all in the translation.

References

Burrell, G. and Morgan, G. (1979) *Sociological Paradigms and Organisational Analysis*. Burlington, VT: Ashgate.

Callon, M. (1986) Some elements of a sociology of translation: Domestification of the scallops and the fishermen of St Brieuc Bay, in J. Law (ed.), *Power, Action and Belief: A New Sociology of Knowledge?* (pp. 196–223). London: Routledge & Kegan Paul.

Corrigan, L. T. (2015) Budget theatre: A postdramaturgical account of municipal budget making, PhD Thesis, Saint Mary's, Halifax, Nova Scotia.

Decker, S., Rowlinson, M., and Hassard, J. (2014) *Seminar Series in Management and Organizational History*. UK and Denmark: Economic and Social Research Council Grant.

Durepos, G. and Mills, A. J. (2012) *ANTi-History: Theorizing the Past, History, and Historiography in Management and Organizational Studies*. Charlotte, NC: Information Age.

Durepos, G., Helms Mills, J., and Mills, A. J. (2008) Tales in the manufacture of knowledge: Writing a company history of Pan American World Airways, *Management & Organizational History*, 3(1): 63–80.

Foucault, M. (1980) *Power/Knowledge: Selected Interviews and Other Writings 1972–1977*. London: Tavistock.

Genoe McLaren, P. (2011) James Burnham, the managerial revolution, and the development of management theory in post-war America, *Management & Organizational History*, 6(4): 411–23.

Hartt, C. M. (2013) Actants without actors: Polydimensional discussion of a regional conference, *Tamara: Journal for Critical Organization Inquiry*, 11(3): 15–25.

Jenkins, K. (1994) *Re-Thinking History*. London: Routledge.

Jenkins, K. (1995) *On 'What is history?' From Carr and Elton to Rorty and White*. London: Routledge.
Jenkins, K. (2009) *At the Limits of History: Essays on Theory and Practice*. London and New York: Routledge.
Kalela, J. (2012) *Making History: The Historian and Uses of the Past*. Basingstoke: Palgrave Macmillan.
Kieser, A. (1994) Why organizational theory needs historical analyses: And how this should be performed, *Organization Science*, 5(4): 608–20.
Latour, B. (1988) *The Pasteurization of France*. Cambridge, MA: Harvard University Press.
Latour, B. (2005) *Reassembling the Social: An Introduction to Actor-Network Theory*. Oxford: Oxford University Press.
Law, J. (1994) *Organizing Modernity*. Oxford: Blackwell.
Law, J. and Hassard, J. (1999) *Actor Network Theory and After*. Oxford: Blackwell.
Lemisch, J. (1975) *On Active Service in War and Peace. Politics and Ideology in the American Historical Profession*. Toronto: New Hogtown Press.
Mannheim, K. (1968) *Ideology and Utopia*. London: Routledge.
Marx, K. and Engels, F. (1996) *The German Ideology*. New York: International Publishers.
Mills, A. J. (1996) Corporate image, gendered subjects and the company newsletter: The changing faces of British Airways, in G. Palmer and S. Clegg (eds), *Constituting Management: Markets, Meanings And Identities* (pp. 191–211). Berlin: de Gruyter.
Mills, A. J. and Durepos, G. (2010) ANTi-History, in A. J. Mills, G. Durepos, and E. Wiebe (eds), *The Sage Encyclopedia of Case Study Research*, vol. 1 (pp. 26–29). Thousand Oaks, CA: Sage.
Mills, A. J., Weatherbee, T. G., and Durepos, G. (2014) Reassembling Weber: The-past-as-history in management and organization studies, *Organization*, 21(2): 225–43.
Munslow, A. (2012a) History in the discursive condition: Reconsidering the tools of thought, *Rethinking History*, 16(1): 147–54.
Munslow, A. (2012b) *A History of History*. London: Routledge.
Myrick, K., Helms Mills, J., and Mills, A. J. (2013) History-making and the Academy of Management: An ANTi-history perspective, *Management & Organizational History*, 8(4): 345–70.
Prasad, P. (2005) *Crafting Qualitative Research: Working in the Postpositivist Traditions*. Armonk, NY: M. E. Sharpe.
Weatherbee, T. G. (2012) Caution! This historiography makes wide turns: Historic turns and breaks in management and organization studies, *Management & Organizational History*, 7(3): 203–18
Weatherbee, T., Durepos, G., Mills, A. J., and Helms Mills, J. (2012) Theorizing the past: Critical engagements, *Management & Organizational History*, 7(3): 193–202.
Weick, K. E. (1995) *Sensemaking in Organizations*. London: Sage.
White, H. (1985) *Tropics of Discourse: Essays in Cultural Criticism*. Baltimore: Johns Hopkins University Press.
Wren, D. A. and Bedeian, A. G. (2009) *The Evolution of Management Thought* (6th edn). Hoboken, NJ: John Wiley.
Zinn, H. (1990) *The Politics of History* (2nd edn). Urbana and Chicago, IL: University of Illinois Press.

Part VII
Endnote

29

Essaying history and management

Stewart Clegg

Introduction

Students new to management might assume that it has a brief but glorious history, one in which the initial ideas of foundational thinkers such as F. W. Taylor, were slowly amended and corrected, in which ideas evolved in a Whiggish way, mounting up to the truths of today – or at least those embraced in the last few years' issues of the key journals that impact factors dictate.

In terms of the caricature, which accentuates elements of an all too pervasive reality, history, where it enters the textbook frame, usually consists of chronological studies in an evolutionary mode; a scientistic parceling out of history's errors; the occasional retrieval of forgotten voices from the past, such as Follett or Deming; studies uncovering examples from the past to serve as benchmarks for the future along with studies aimed at distinguishing the eternal hard core of knowledge from the flotsam and jetsam of the moment. It should be evident from the outset that the present volume sets itself against such caricatures and is to be regarded as a contribution to the emerging turn to history in management and organization studies. I shall concentrate in what follows on the historiographical element of the various contributions that make up this *Companion to Management and Organizational History.*

The historic turn in management and organizational studies

The rather mundane ideas of Taylor, popularizer of popular mechanics, have played a disproportional and dismal role in management history, as Novecivic, Jones, and Carraher's critical analysis of Wren's foundational history discusses. Whatever the canon of management history it is a safe bet that Taylor will play a celebrated role in it – either as hero, or less often, as in Braverman (1974), villain. This celebratory individuation dismisses the extent to which figures such as Taylor were more or less emblematic of deep-seated currents of social thought and functioned in the role of a public intellectual in advocating them. The constitution of canonical texts always privileges the individual and the text to such an extent that the wider structural factors at play are written out of the history at worst, or, at best marginalized (Clegg and Dunkerley 1980).

These factors were not neglected in the 1970s renaissance of Marx's labor process theory occasioned by the success of Braverman's (1974) book and the many labor process studies that ensued. However, as Kieser notes, the enthusiasm for labor process theory had very little impact outside of the converted – by and large, mainstream organization theory simply ignored its existence. Its Marxist auspices did not fit well in the Business School frame nor, perversely, despite its avowed historical perspective, did its historical lack of specificity endear it to non-Marxist historically inclined scholars. General histories make abstract patterns into which many diverse histories have to be molded, doing violence to specific forms of variation and local patterning, industrially, regionally, nationally and cross-nationally, a point that Kieser makes clearly. He also makes the point that the very notion of a national culture or an organizational culture, in the singular, must always be an ideological gambit because its construction depends on suppression of difference. Hence, in looking at the development of management practices across nations it is far better to focus on some middle range empirical indicators, he suggests.

Historical analysis is antithetical to parodies of covering law-like explanations whether these derive from Marxist or positivist ambitions. Such 'explanations' cover more than they reveal and must always downplay the circumstances in which people make choices, albeit not often those of their choosing, in order to make those elegant patterns that straddle and shape specific histories. Of course, this does not mean that there can be no history other than the infinitesimal compilation of narratives; these must always be arranged in patterns if understanding is to flourish. But the patterns are neither invariant nor eternal: as Kieser writes, there is evolution of evolutionary mechanisms. Several of these are put to the test in explaining the development of the German putting-out system and all are found wanting when confronted with the specificities of the historical record. As Kieser states "it is probably always possible to select historical facts that fit any general model, but one can never be sure that the researcher is not leaving out important facts that contradict it.". Following an inductive strategy in regard to the known historical data is, he suggests, the best way to increase, if never complete, surety. Twenty years after writing the article that is reproduced as a chapter, Kieser has little to add, except irony.

Manifestos of historical purpose are not unknown amongst those who would write (and sometimes make) history and Booth and Rowlinson offer us a ten-point example of the genre, styled as an agenda. The agenda is wide ranging: it traverses orientations to history and organization studies stretching from perspectives that would supplement the latter with the former; integrate them or reorient them through a reformation of the basis for inquiry as is called for by critical management studies. The latter, however, seems particularly susceptible to the ideology critique that was made by Kieser twenty years ago: critique demands a viewpoint and that viewpoint is necessarily transcendental and a priori, wherever it seeks to articulate a specific interest as the basis of its critique. Such questions overlap with the practice of writing history: is the interest in seamless narrative or in its interruption? While the latter has become increasingly popular under the influence of Foucault's histories of ideas the latter constitute the more mainstream approach. Historians are not the only practitioners to register history; organizations also do so in terms of their branding, promotions, symbolic posturing, and collective representations of memory and a moot point is the politics of their representation, the genealogical principles followed and repressed, the symbols valorized and glossed over. How they do these things is grist for the historical grind, which, in future, the authors hope to see being fashioned by instruments other than those purely of economic history. Ethics, as they note, are clearly one important compass through which to view the past but whether the past can be studied in terms of contemporary insights and dilemmas or whether it should be judged by the standards that were acknowledged to have prevailed then is a moot point. On the basis of the latter, considerable contemporary calumny can be avoided, whether rightfully or not; on the basis of the former many a fortune and the organizations on which such wealth was based would be de-legitimated by association with past misdemeanors and crimes such as slavery, plunder, conquest, and extermination.

Rowlinson also contributes a personal history of the history turn in which the significant and under-appreciated role of Peter Clarke as a crucible for fostering historical thinking is nicely made. Clarke was one of the very few people in 1970s business schools who read history seriously – very much a Braudel man in those days – and a figure whose contributions have been significant.

Debates in management and organizational history

There are pertinent questions to be addressed about the relation between business history and overarching history. For instance, it is difficult to inscribe the history of a firm and industry without making connections to the changing fortunes of national economics, politics, culture, and society, as well as the supranational events and institutions in which these are embedded. Likewise, without an understanding of how approaches such as structural contingency theory grew out of systematic accounts of management ideas at a particular moment in the evolution of modern organizations one could easily mistake their dimensions as eternal rather than historically contingent. Size, for instance, the most important explanatory variable in the Aston School's contingency theory, relies on the tacit assumption that organizations only grow or shrink through extending or diminishing the number of contracts of employment that they have with individual persons. In the early 1960s this was a reasonable assumption to make; in the twenty-first century, after a decade or more of outsourcing, external subcontracting, and complex supply chains, we now know that employment contracts are not necessarily the most important and that their scope does not necessarily delimit capabilities and size. Also, counterfactually, if this history had been read after Foucault, would not Weber's stress on discipline have been accorded a conceptual significance that the Aston scholars failed to see? Perhaps not, for the stress was already evidently there in Weber and was not amplified, conceptually.

Discipline, in its changing modes, did enter into the canon through Braverman's (1974) rounding out of Baran and Sweezy's (1966) theses concerning *Monopoly Capitalism*. Baran and Sweezy are an example of one field in which, as Marens argues, Marxist historiography has been fluent, fluid, and open to historical evidence and that is economic history. While business schools still typically tend to teach economic history in either an institutional or great men mode there has developed a robust and highly respected set of approaches to economic history that have built on core elements of the agenda that Marx sketched in *Capital*. The roll call of honor is formidable: Baran and Sweezy but also Hobsbawm, Arrighi, and Brenner amongst historians but also a considerable number of sociologists who have done fine work, such as Useem, Roy, Lash and Urry, and Fligstein, to name a few. These are remarkably insightful and empirically rich resources for management and organization theorists but are rarely drawn on.

It is not only that they are not drawn on; they are, as Jacques and Durepos argue, unacknowledged in those canonical textbooks that introduce students to the field. Indeed, it is worse than that: there is not only an absence of decent historiography in most textbooks, whether influenced by Marxian analysis or not; there is also an absence of much in the way of historical consciousness at all, which the authors see as a result of modernist emplotment. As a narrative device this systematically downplays discontinuous change in favor of continuous evolution that is linear and progressive. The narrative style assumed is that of value neutrality and disinterest, blind to power relations in all their complexity, paying homage to physics envy that produces a bizarre scientism in which social relations, such as those of gender and other forms of identity, seem absent. The effects are all too evident: a history emptied of perspective, made to read as if it were news from nowhere in particular; a history resolutely unreflexive about its assumptions and practices; historians whose lack of reflexivity is assured.

Terrance Weatherbee nails it: "The manner in which we present management knowledge once history and historical context is written-out of the content means that our textbooks are more likely to serve as an intellectual entry point and values-based framework for managerialism than for management." Effectively, once the trade school approaches that existed prior to the Carnegie and Ford reforms that were shaping US Business Schools in the 1960s had been suspended in favor of the behavioral sciences, the new forms of knowledge eschewed historical causality in favor of cross-sectional causality between variables modeled on a presumption of experimental science, albeit in open systems impossible to close so that standing conditions could be controlled. Cold War, Big Science, and fear of failure in the wake of Sputnik drove the fetishization of these 'physics envy' (Flyvbjerg, 2001) models in US Business Schools.

Historical approaches continued in the margins. As Weatherbee notes there were a small number of researchers that persisted with historical research; some writers of monographs/ textbooks such as Clegg and Dunkerley (1980) also conceived of the field in historical terms but these were to prove less popular than approaches that raised Platonic forms to the level of mutually incomprehensible paradigms or metaphors (Burrell and Morgan, 1979; Morgan, 1985). The historical turn of recent times, suggests Weatherbee, can be consigned to one or other camp of either an additive or transformative use of history in relationship with management.

The additive program, calling for more history to be incorporated in management education, is a failing project in terms of the numbers of those enrolled to it, suggests Weatherbee. By contrast, the transformative approach is emergent and its wave may still be cresting or merging with other undercurrents such as 'critical' management studies. At this point the text takes an abrupt turn into textbooks as the bearers of 'normal' science – normally bereft of history, infused with managerialist values, stuffed with solutions, and blissfully unproblematic as their production is increasingly market focused. What the market doesn't want are history, ideology critique, and theoretical problematics.

There is an emerging problematization of specific histories in newer contributions, both of major figures and of textbook knowledge; however, this is not Weatherbee's major concern – that turns out to be a guide to theories of history as forms of cultural production. Given that it has already been established that there is insufficient history in MOS the diverse approaches have little resonance. At this point the chapter concludes, inconclusively.

Methods and madness: doing management and organizational history

Does recourse to the postmodern effect a way out of the modernist impasse? In Munslow's terms a postmodern account of historical method would see it as a narrative constructed by the historian. Such construction depends on past normative framings of observers and observations in terms of past–history ontological and epistemological underpinnings. Narratives from nowhere are simply impossible; there are no findings without narration. Inasmuch as the objects of analysis are documents created in the past then any subsequent narration is necessarily dependent on the narrations that created that past documentation; not only the subjectivities of the historian-narrator but also the recorder-narrators enter the frame. Adapting Hayden White's terms 'historical imagination' consists of already constituted narrative fragments of evidence of various kinds, arranged in part by design and often more by accident, that are configured by the four major tropes of figurative language: metaphor, metonymy, synecdoche, and irony, each of which is as likely to be chosen through habit as reflexive awareness. Empiricism is blind without conceptualization, argument, ideology, and emplotment; which is to say that there is no such thing as a purely empirical history because past events have no historical meaning until they are narrated as history, albeit that they might have many other meanings in various non-historical imaginations. History is what it is written to be and it can be written in as many genres as there are available. Historians are Weickian sensemakers (Weick, 1995): they are engaged in the ongoing retrospective development of plausible narratives that rationalize what people were doing at some time documented and otherwise indexed as being in the past. The fundamental nature of history consists of producing likely stories that can be legitimated according to genre requirements.

One major genre of historical understanding remains hermeneutics, which Scott Taylor addresses. Hermeneutics has many precursors but it is the work of Ricouer that is most often chosen as foundational by contemporary scholars such as Phillips and Brown (1993) and Prasad and Mir (2002). The latter analyze both the mode of representation in the texts they address as well as in the objective text their hermeneutic analysis produces. They acknowledge the dialectical epistemological and aesthetic aspects of hermeneutics to create a relation between text and theory, producing both narrative and explanatory intelligibility and plot as well as style.

Key ideas in hermeneutics are the hermeneutic circle, historicality (including the 'hermeneutic horizon'), dialogical understanding, the role of the author-as-interpreter, and critique.

The hermeneutic circle entails that any understanding of textual meaning requires consideration of 'parts' in the 'context' of the 'whole' and a process of interplay between the two. The interpreter engages the text in reflexive inquiry in which the possibility of the text as that text is deconstructed. Part of that possibility might be constituted by authorial intention, although this can only ever be assumed and never known for sure, nor can authorial intention be seen as authorizing whatever interpretation is made: legitimate interpretation does not kowtow to the presumed intentions of the author in authoring some text. As a stricture on interpretative understanding this is particularly important in the field of management and organization history, in which many of the historical traces that are left for the analysts to consider have been carefully chosen, designed, and fabricated by organizational elites with a very definite interpretation of events and other phenomena that they seek to advance. We must never forget that the subjects who produced the texts and contexts that we, as analysts, attend to, are themselves practical hermeneuticians with a range of interests in play in their social construction of the traces to which subsequent generations might attend.

Once the hermeneutic researcher begins to question the presumed or expressed intentional auspices of the texts under analysis then modernist stipulations that entail assumptions about the representation in an historical account of the true nature of events in and phenomena from the past become precarious. Such ontological realism is naïve and usually fulfills an ideological function of legitimating a particular historical gloss. More often than not it will do so through the assumptions of a linear narrative that recovers the facts and arranges them without adornment in a causal sequence. In this kind of history an accurate, complete, and uncontested representation of the past is presumed to be possible, at least in principle: more or new data may revise the picture slightly but the essential contours of the past, once uncovered, remain as they are, undisturbed by the authorial voice of the narrator whose sole concern is with the facts. Postmodern scholarship reverses each modernist assumption as we have seen in Munslow: it licenses histories rather than a singular history. Different historians will ask different questions, with different interests, and focus on different aspects of the possible historical traces that they make evident in text and context.

Durepos argues for neither a modern nor a postmodern history but one that is amodern, derived from the French sociologist, Latour (1993), in his attempt to overcome the binaries of the modern and the postmodern through his argument that *We Have Never Been Modern*. Key to overcoming the representational and relativist dualism cleaving the modern and the postmodern conceptions of what is knowledge is a turn to conceiving of it as a practice. Historians inevitably interfere with the object of analysis if only because in their doing of history they constitute it on each occasion of its invocation. Different versions of the past are enacted through different histories, each of which inscribes that which it attends to – and differences will be evident in the phenomena attended to – differently, specifically in terms of differing relevancies. What is of significance are the relations between different enactments of the past as history, as well as the relations within which any enactment comes into being. What is significant is not the status of any particular history compared to another but the relations between these histories: how are they constituted, how are they possible?

These views are all well and good but they do presume a rather crowded interpretative landscape; in those areas of the field more sparsely populated than yet another Taylor interpretation or account of what Hawthorne really meant, in say the ranks of business histories, the plurality presumed is most unlikely to exist. Hence, the advice given is of limited value to the researcher who wants to try and get their one-shot at history 'right.' If, as Rostis suggests, it is through "an examination of the descent, emergence, and trajectory of events" that genealogically influenced histories attempt "to uncover other explanations that have been hidden in the construction of a logical narrative or explanation of how the past occurred," then there is a reliance on other accounts as a foil.

Genealogical histories are, of course, influenced by Foucault's work. What is entailed in this particular form of amodern history, to use Durepos' phrase, is to first question the possibility of what is in the archive under inspection: why this knowledge, these facts, that interpretation? What role does context play in framing the text in question? What continuities and discontinuities are embedded in the sense being made in that context? How is this sense related to other discourses implicit in and around that context? What are the subjects and objects that are specified in and through these discourses? Using these sorts of questions as a guide Rostis provides a compelling analysis of the emergence of the Red Cross and Médecins sans Frontières as responses to seemingly quite similar but actually dissimilar political contexts. The assumed meaning of humanitarian NGOs is questioned and new insights generated.

In a characteristically Bojean piece Boje, together with Saylors, brings history down to the philosophically posthumanist salon where entrepreneurial storytelling reigns supreme. The story this time concerns climate change. What follows is a posthumanist manifesto, albeit modeled in part on earlier famous 'Theses.' If the point of the famous thesis eleven is to change the world, not philosophize it, then the future, if we are to have one in the long term, from the perspective of the posthumanist manifesto entails seven basic steps to environmental rehistorying. Entrepreneurial storytelling indeed: follow these steps and the "firm can be re-historicized as though a fundamental part of its ethos is sustainability."

Coraiola, Foster, and Suddaby begin by reiterating Munslow's (2006a, 2006b) distinctions between three perspectives on the nature of historical reality: these are generated by the extent to which historians consider history to be equivalent to the past, and the extent to which they recognize historical sources as being already a narrative. The three approaches are differing versions of ontology: the reconstructivist, constructivist, and deconstructivist. Reconstructivist historians seek to arrive at a truth about history based on correspondence theory that stresses verification, comparison, and colligation. Historical processes of interpretative understanding, which in the German tradition we know as *Verstehende*, from Weber (1978), are central devices. Faithfulness to sources, commitment to value freedom in their interpretation, and a dedication to getting the facts right, characterize this approach. The reality of the past can be captured in narrative accounts based on inductive processes of impartial selection and critical evaluation of documentary sources. The approach is essentially one of using fragments of data from the past to create a plausible evolutionary history as faithful to sources as possible. The more adventurous reconstructivists would admit that the creation of historical meaning is a product of the interaction between the historian's knowledge and the content of the sources; the facts do not simply speak for themselves.

Constructivists do not accept that the past can be retrieved in its entirety. They are not witness to history as it happens but as fragments, themselves socially constructed at another time and place, according to interests and prejudices that are not wholly intelligible to the contemporary historian, but which can be imaginatively divined. Knowledge of the past is always bounded by the questions they are able to formulate and the answers available sources can provide. History cannot exist without theory – it is this that frames what is relevant and interesting for the researcher.

Deconstructivism, influenced by French scholars such as Derrida and Foucault, is highly inter-textual. There are texts from the past that the historian consults; there are the texts that the historian produces in the present; there are other texts that other people, including historians, may have produced in the past. History is what one makes of it through the narrative accounts that historians produce. What are central are the forms of representation that constitute these texts, both historical (as having been produced in the past), and as histories produced in the present. In a sense, one can thus only ever write histories of the present if only because the relevancies that one brings to bear on the past, and its archaeology of relevancies, are necessarily and irredeemably those of the present, as the authors demonstrate in their analysis of recent institutional theory influenced by historical methods or focused on history topics.

Decker also discusses institutional theory, joining it to recent Italian microhistory, as a way of warding off the overly deterministic currents of institutional isomorphism, organizational fields, and institutional logics. There are evident similarities in focus as her tabulation makes clear but also some significant differences. Mostly, institutional work approaches are focused on very short timespans compared to the typical periodicity of historical research. The focus is driven by methods that require presentism, such as audio and video recording, or participant observation and interviewing. As Decker points out, most significant transformations of institutional frameworks are likely to occur in the medium-term not a relatively brief timespan. Moreover, some of the structural mechanisms deployed by institutional theories, such as 'institutional logics,' would seem overly structural to most microhistorians.

Magnússon and Szijártó (2013) define microhistory in terms of an approach that is precise and small in scale, using a focal point for investigation while still trying to address what have been formulated as major historical questions in extant scholarship. Doing this enables them to maintain a central role for human agency in their analysis, such as being able to see how seemingly early market transactions were in fact systematically skewed by whether or not they were with kin or non-kin (Levi, 1991). In terms of case selection the microhistorians favor the exemplary anomaly, perhaps best seen in Ginsburg's (1980) classic *The Cheese and the Worms: The Cosmos of a Sixteenth Century Miller.* Indeed, this work is prototypical in demonstrating that social norms guiding human behavior are always multiple, inconsistent, conflicting; not homogeneous and easy to navigate, not handed down by institutional isomorphism or embedded in an institutional logic. Microhistory seeks to integrate and elucidate the particular and the general concurrently through its scaled-down focus on particular events and agencies, emphasizing the overlapping and conflicting nature of social structures, within the interstices of which individuals have freedom to act as other than the ciphers of institutions.

Rewriting management history

Peltonen provides an account of Mayo in his early Australian context – but it is a context that is quite partial inasmuch as the focus is on the history of ideas context for Mayo's early thought.

Much is made of Mayo's fidelity to ideas derived from British Liberal Idealism; however, there is no reference to the context in which he developed these ideas. Brisbane in the immediate post-First World War was a contested city. The Workers' Educational Association in Brisbane, with which Mayo was associated, saw a split after the First World War. The more militant members founded the Workers' School of Social Science in Brisbane. They were characterized by a distinct lack of neutrality on the educational front of the class war (unlike the Workers' Educational Association, from whom they had broken away) by standing for industrial democracy. What they meant, however, as can be seen in their series of lectures on job control, was direct action by revolutionary unions (*Syllabus of the Workers' School of Social Science*, 1919).

For the radicals, industrial democracy meant the same as socialism and the revolutionary method for attaining it. As Irving (no date) says, "[i]t was a usage that responded to the growing democratic mood while at the same time rejecting the initiatives by governments and employers to open up new avenues for dialogue with workers." In Queensland, unions in the railways and meatworks were militant and increasingly 'industrial,' as can be seen in a pamphlet called *Who Shall Control Industry?* The pamphlet was written by T. C. Witherby, who was Director of Tutorial Classes at the University of Queensland, where Mayo held the first chair of philosophy between 1919 and 1923:

> Here in Queensland, because we are in Australia, and because we are under a Labor government, the wage-earners' position has elements of strength not known in Europe. And this for three reasons. These reasons I owe to a pamphlet by Mr Childe. They are that the politician is more under the control of the industrialist [i.e. the radical unionist] than in other countries; the permanent official is not so far apart from the ordinary man as in the bureaucracy of Europe; and more consumers in this country are producers. However autocratic therefore State enterprises may appear to the worker in Queensland, there is here the possibility scarcely existing in Europe of a large share of workers' control. It is only because of the indifference of the wage-earners on this matter that no advances have yet been made.
>
> *(Witherby 1919)*

These were anathema to Mayo's ideas.

> Observing the disturbing level of industrial strife and political conflict in Australia, Mayo formulated an analogy between war neurosis and the psychological causes of industrial unrest. Drawing on social anthropology, he argued that the worker's morale, or mental health, depended on his perception of the social function of his work. He saw the solution to industrial unrest in sociological research and industrial management rather than in radical politics.
>
> *(Bourke 1986)*

It should be evident that we cannot recover the context in which ideas developed simply by looking at the history of ideas. We need also to see, as an important part of the context, what gave these ideas life, vitality, which is to say how and in what ways were these ideas contesting other ideas? When we do this we can recover a more enveloping set of dynamics. The war legacy is crucial as it was the returning soldiers and sailors, especially, who had been most radicalized by the appalling experiences and who were well aware of what was happening in Russia. As Clegg, Courpasson, and Phillips (2006: 79) stated:

> The interpretations that Mayo (1933) made of the Hawthorne Studies were in large part already well rehearsed and accorded with views that he had formed in Brisbane in the

> aftermath of the First World War, in his work with 'shell-shocked' soldiers returning to sunny Queensland from the dark horrors of trench warfare in the European theater. It was Mayo's early and incomplete training as a doctor, and his collaboration with a Brisbane specialist, which provided the occasion for the formation of his ideas about the importance of psychological subjectivity. From the treatment of maladjustment on the part of veterans, it was a small step to the treatment of industrial malaises: 'Industrial unrest is not caused by mere dissatisfaction with wages and working conditions but by the fact that a conscious dissatisfaction serves to "light up" as it were the hidden fires of mental uncontrol' (Mayo 1922: 64; cited in Bourke 1982: 226). Elton Mayo prescribed several short rest breaks per shift, to relieve physiological strain and to disrupt the negative feelings that led to industrial unrest. These ideas were subsequently to develop much further, as a result of his research involvements during the Second World War.

Idealist liberalism did not exist in a void: it was a part of class struggle and Mayo was a keen protagonist in these struggles, waged against Guild Socialism:

> Guild socialists were centrally concerned with democracy, differentiating themselves from the Fabians who failed to appreciate the aspirations of ordinary people for empowerment, and from the syndicalists who ignored the potential for selfishness and conflict in their schemes for industries to be owned by the workers in them. Guild socialists wanted to rise above the conflict in the movement between Fabian 'political action' and syndicalist 'industrial action' by drawing on pluralist and distributivist philosophies that recognised differences (local and occupational, for example) but assumed a common interest of all citizens as consumers. They were not Marxists, for although they recognised the class struggle, they did not, on theoretical as well as empirical grounds, see it as resolving itself in favour of the working-class. Although they disagreed on details, guild socialists in general accepted that the state would continue [–] it was needed to act as trustee for the community and provide representation in parliament for citizens as consumers – but insisted that effective control would be vested in the industrial guilds, set up by the state and consisting of representatives of the relevant industrial union, the experts, and the state managers. It was therefore a scheme to unite citizen democracy with worker democracy.
>
> *(Irving, no date)*

It is against this backdrop that the formation of Mayo's early ideas and their consistency throughout his American career should be seen. A turn to history should enable attention to wider discursive contexts than just the history of ideas a key figure draws on; it should also explore the context in which they were contested.

Mir and Mir chart a narrative familiar to all scholars au fait with Marxist accounts of recent economic history in detailing the rise and contradictions of Fordism. Seeing the problem of Fordism from the late 1960s onwards as a crisis of rigidity, the institutional and managerial solution was to call for enhanced flexibility: in manufacturing systems; work practices; consumption patterns; and new patterns of flexible accumulation based on increasing financialization, diminished unionization, increased globalization of manufacturing, and increasing digitalization enhancing space–time compression. Mir and Mir elaborate these themes at length. The historical component of their essay is to point out that flexibility did not spring on the world, fully formed, as a relatively recent phenomenon but that, from a world systems perspective, there are far deeper roots to the present tendencies. Financialization is not a new phenomenon but a pattern that can be seen in the cyclical and evolutionary phases of historical capitalism from the thirteenth century onwards. Clearly, in terms of historiographical method, Mir and Mir are interpreting the historical record through an essentially deterministic pattern, cast by the marriage of Braudel and Marx that produced the progeny of world systems theory (Wallerstein, 1974).

The focus of the chapter by Mills, Weatherbee, Foster, and Helms Mills is the New Deal era in US political economy. In this period some similar political currents that flowed through Mayo's Brisbane politics also animated the US scene. The New Deal was a large-scale national attempt to reorder relations of production and consumption on lines that were influenced by debates concerning democracy that were rooted in socialism of various kinds. Key figures are singled out for discussion. These figures, and the New Deal philosophy they embraced and exemplified, have been written out of Management and Organization Studies history: the authors seek to write them in.

The New Dealers embraced various forms of ideology in putting their programs together, not always coherently or consistently. By contrast, Spector argues, in the immediate post-Second World War era, the capitalist opponents of the New Deal were much more coherent ideologically, despite professing an antipathy to the very idea of ideology. The emergence of ideological coherence was nurtured by the Cold War, corporate opposition to the New Deal, and an uneasy and equivocal relation on the part of Americans with the new conglomerates that were shaping the business scene.

It would be surprising if there were a coherent ideology of business if it did not find systematic expression in one of the key organs of business. Hence, the frame for analysis is the *Harvard Business Review*, in which four dominant and intertwined themes are identified. First, there was an expectation of minimum government interference combined with optimum government promotion, an ideological thrust directly aimed against the New Deal. Second, there was an explicit equation of Christianity and capitalism in terms of values ranged against ungodly communism. Third, individualism was constitutive of the American psyche and, as such, an expression of a natural state that the collectivist ideals of communism abroad and unionism at home ground down. Hence, fourth, at home business should do all it could to educate the broader public that it was not unions that could improve the prosperity of workers but unfettered free enterprise in which the interest of owners of capital and those who were merely employed in it were fused on an ever-improving trajectory that rendered class warfare redundant. The best cure for global poverty was the export of this free enterprise system to the more benighted parts of the globe that did not enjoy America's benefits; as national liberation movements adopted socialist colors in countries such as Korea and Vietnam the force of words subsequently had to be joined by the force of arms.

In the 1950s and 1960s, Spector concludes, the foundations of the "end of history" argument articulated by Fukuyama (1992), which suggested that liberal market capitalism had achieved vindication and victory with the death of Soviet Communism, were laid. Yet, history has a way of not ending and ideology a way of refolding: the global financial crisis and the escalating crisis of climate change being the folds in question.

> The capitalist ideologies of the 1950s engaged in simplification (liberal market capitalism vs. communism), contradiction (against government *interference* but for government *protection*), misdirection (*People's* Capitalism) and denial (poverty). When ideologues present the subjective as objective, advocacy as observation, and self-interest as mutuality, the result is denial, distortion, false consciousness, and the concealment of real interests.
>
> *(Spektor, this volume)*

Well, I would not disagree with the verdict although I would question the terms in which it is expressed. The identification of distortion, false consciousness, and real interests presumes a position of theoretical sovereignty as an a priori that is every bit as ideological as the positions opposed (Clegg, 1989).

Scale is reduced greatly in the other essay in this section: the focus is on public relations (PR) in Canada, a field characterized by a broadly North American (read US) narrative of the progressive evolution of more ethical practice, represented in a move away from propaganda towards strategic, socially responsible communication. The development of textbooks as paradigms of ideological normalcy was central to the process.

Canadian experience belies ideological normalcy. In Canada it was the nineteenth-century desire to populate the vast tracts of open land with settlers from Europe that occasioned the development of a particular form of propaganda that might subsequently be recognized as PR. "Throughout the early 1900s and up until the mid-1920s in Canada, government communication and publicity campaigns were by far the most significant and most common of what would become identified as public relations practice," Thurlow argues. As the railways opened up the frontier they developed rhetoric for communication that drew on the same skills. By the early 1900s a few private enterprises were developing a PR profile.

The explicit recognition of PR dates back to the foundation of a course at McGill University in 1948, from which incipient professionalization other courses and professional bodies developed. These are represented, discursively, in an archive that the author subjects to Critical Discourse Analysis (CDA), demonstrating the centrality of the theory of excellence, the model of symmetry for professional practice via mutually beneficial relationships between organizations and publics, an increasing representational concern with ethics, as well as an increasing Americanization of the field and the necessity of securing a privileged space for the nascent profession. In terms of historiography, the use of CDA to explore a specific focal object through analysis of an archive is the major contribution.

Management history at the margins

Management theory was born in the USA yet it has colonized the world. Why and how? McLaren and Mills seek to answer this question through researching a determinate absence – non-existent Canadian management theory. Their argument seeks to construct a history of Canadian difference that conventional accounts gloss over. These conventional arguments are usually first encountered by those entering into a career in management in Candianized US textbooks – often where the place names and little else is changed to Canadian – a practice that Australian (and, one suspects, many other nations) management inductees would also be familiar with. Canadian scholars, they argue, further this Americanization by seeking publication in US rather than Canadian journals because of their greater 'legitimacy' globally, especially as Canadian Business Schools become more aligned with their US models through factors such as AACSB accreditation. These business schools were largely post Second World War creations forged on US models, often hiring those Americans who did not find or want US employment or recruiting from cognate social science disciplines. Professionally, the demand grew for a universal management theory for all countries based on positivist assumptions, empiricist methods, and functionalist theories – all strongly ensconced as US orthodoxy. An unfortunate paradox occurred: if management science was universal there was no need for specifically Canadian contexts; moreover, specifically Canadian contexts were of less universal value in a domain that defined the universe as principally that of the United States.

Canada is different, note the authors. It is not the US nor is it similar to the US in important ways:

> the country developed as a resource-based economy with significant amounts of foreign investment; while large in size it has a small population spread across its southern border, divided regionally by cultural, linguistic, political, and economic differences; and it is a welfare state with a history of strong activist governments and an electorally-viable social democratic political party.
>
> *(McLaren and Mills, this volume)*

As a settler dominion Canada has far more in common with societies such as Australia and New Zealand, than it does with the United States. The history of economic protectionism and the development of social welfare have far more parallels with these dominions than the United States. Indeed, although the essay does not mention it, a distinctive Canadian political economy centered on the staples thesis and the work of Harold Innis as an explanation for how the pattern of settlement and economic development of Canada was influenced by the exploitation and export of natural resources. Unfortunately, Innis' (1930; 1940) theory seems to have had negligible influence in Canadian business schools; had it done so there would be a far better basis for understanding the specificity of Canadian experience in its foundations than is offered by the Americanized texts, something that the authors recognize as only just beginning.

The legacy of Innis has been built on by researchers such as Wallace Clement (1997; Clement and Vosko, 2002) but seems not to be recognized in the business schools. Another aspect absent from consideration must also be the question of the distinct bicultural context of Canada's predominant multiculturalism split between Quebec and other French-speaking provinces and the dominant Anglo sphere. There is a distinctive and different account, albeit still subaltern, of management in the Francophone world that does not have such a strong US character.

There are many Americas. Canada to the north is a different reality to the United States to the south. Further south still, there are the more complex realities of Latin America. Across the US border in Mexico, one of the most significant voices in Latin and world management and organization studies, Eduardo Ibarra-Colado, was recently and sadly stilled. Before his death he left a significant legacy, informed by an acute understanding of the history of Mexico, an example of which is collected in the volume.

Central to Ibarra-Colado's concerns was the condition of coloniality:

> Coloniality must be understood in its institutional dimensions, as a deliberate action of power to dominate and subjugate the other. It is the hidden face of Modernity, always considered the stage made possible by the development of reason, instead of the process of invasion/destruction/invention based of the power of weapons, ideas and symbols to impose a unique civilizing process. From this point of view, power instead of reason explains the splendour of Europe and America and the prevalence of some kind of knowledge over others.
>
> At least three institutions have been essential in the operation of colonization: the Church and evangelism to produce silence and colonize the soul; the Hacienda and mills to produce discipline and obedience at work and to colonize the body; and the University and science to produce truth and colonize the understanding of the world. The organization of knowledge and their associated practices in the modern *Universitas* has guaranteed the reproduction of disciplines as we know them and, at the same time, has obstructed different ways to live and imagine academic work, discouraging or forbidding alternative practices.

The door to a whole world of potential differences is opened that, instead of being buried by putative universalism, might be explored for innovation and productive tensions. As noted, the vast majority of Latin American intellectual production in the field of management and organization studies is mimicry: it copies Anglo-Saxon norms in all areas of intellectual reproduction. Government funding of students to do doctoral work in these centers of excellence elsewhere inducts and indoctrinates the emerging generation of scholars to learn to think, speak, and write with inauthenticity. Elsewhere, in the broader fields of history and social sciences there are more authentic voices to be found but these are both neglected by indigenous management and organization scholars and are unknown to those from the hegemonic discourse. Fusion of these authentic and indigenous sources in a 'trans-discipline' corpus of knowledge builds knowledge 'transversally' in a set of multiple dialogues and conversations. These must not be dominated by the hegemons of language and orthodoxy and they must include both scholars and the people of different regions and cultures. In this way they might learn from each other and reconstruct management and organizational knowledge that recognizes, improves, and protects local styles of life through respecting the differences that are embedded therein.

Following the contribution from Eduardo there is a remembrance and homage from three colleagues, Srinivas, Guedes, and Faria. It is moving and fitting. Eduardo was one of my best friends. I came to know him during the period when I was editor of *Organization Studies*. He sent a paper that was not, for a variety of reasons, publishable as it was. I wrote back to him as editor explaining how and why this was the case and suggested some ways that it might be revised. The resit is history, as we say. Eduardo invited me to Mexico, there followed many collaborations around APROS, EGOS, and LAEMOS, and much correspondence between meetings. He was the best organization theorist; my first point of reference when writing my Foucauldian inspired history contributions to *Power and Organizations* with my colleagues David Courpasson and Nelson Phillips. As I wrote in the acknowledgments to that book he "made incisive, extended scholarly comments on a great deal of the manuscript." In the words of Brecht that open the colleagues' homage "there are those who struggle all their lives; those are the indispensable ones." Eduardo's legacy is indispensable.

Coller, McNally, and Mills explore some of the mechanism by which hegemonic forms of privileged discourse are constituted theoretically. Using the fusion of Actor Network Theory (ANT) and reconstructive history that has featured in several other chapters in the book that these authors have contributed to, the authors provide an ANTi-history of the Canadian networks of new institutional theory (NIT). A number of scholars central to these networks are stipulated using citation statistics as the basis. An inner circle, comprised, not surprisingly to scholars familiar with the field, of Hinings, Greenwood, Suddaby, and Oliver is identified, as well as an outer circle of still well-known but lesser figures. The chapter analyzes the mechanism of reproduction of these centers of excellence, stressing in particular recruitment and training of PhDs and institutional promotion. Historiographically, the authors use quite conventional network analysis and ranking methods to identify their circles, demonstrating, perhaps, that historical work need not be equipped with any specific method but can borrow freely from the broader social sciences.

Conclusion

The history turn is well represented in the volume and an eclectic range of approaches to the doing of a historical management and organization studies is well prepared. The time is certainly ripe for more such work as the recent call for papers that focus on the history turn in major journals, such as the *Academy of Management Review* and *Management and Organizational History* suggests. Doubtless, some of the perspectives highlighted herein will find their way into these special issues. Should they do so what one might wish for would be both a more grounded and a more rounded management and organization theory, one able to appreciate the specific contours of the contexts in which inquiry is conducted, both in terms of the intellectual context of those conducting it and the contexts that are attended to empirically. It would make a change from much standard fare.

References

Baran, P. A. and Sweezy, P. M. (1966) *Monopoly Capital: An Essay on the American Economic and Social Order.* New York: Monthly Review Press.

Bourke, H. (1982) Industrial unrest as social pathology: The Australian writings of Elton Mayo, *Historical Studies*, 20(79): 217–33.

Bourke, H. (1986) Mayo, George Elton (1880–1949), *Australian Dictionary of Biography*, National Centre of Biography, Australian National University, http://adb.anu.edu.au/biography/mayo-george-elton-7541/text13155

Braverman, H. (1974) *Labor and Monopoly Capitalism.* New York: Monthly Review Press.

Burrell G. and Morgan G. (1979) *Sociological Paradigms and Organizational Analysis.* London: Heinemann.

Clegg, S. R. (1989) *Frameworks of Power.* London: Sage.

Clegg, S. R. and Dunkerley D. (1980) *Organization, Class and Control.* London: Routledge & Kegan Paul.

Clegg, S. R., Courpasson, D., and Phillips, N. (2006) *Power and Organizations.* Thousand Oaks, CA: Sage.

Clement, W. (1997) *Understanding Canada: Building on the New Canadian Political Economy.* Montreal: McGill-Queen's University Press.

Clement, W. and Vosko, L. (2002) *Changing Canada: Political Economy as Transformation*, (edited with Leah Vosko). Montreal: McGill-Queens University Press.

Flyvbjerg, B. (2001) *Making Social Science Matter.* Cambridge: Cambridge University Press.

Fukuyama, F. (1992) *The End of History and the Last Man.* London: Hamish Hamilton.

Ginsburg, C. (1980) *The Cheese and the Worms: The Cosmos of a Sixteenth Century Miller.* Baltimore: Johns Hopkins University Press.

Innis, H. A. (1956 [1930]) *The Fur Trade in Canada: An Introduction to Canadian Economic History.* Toronto: University of Toronto Press.

Innis, H. A. (1954 [1940]) *The Cod Fisheries: The History of an International Economy.* Toronto: University of Toronto Press.

Innis, H. A. (1971) *A History of the Canadian Pacific Railway*, Toronto: McClelland & Stewart. Toronto: University of Toronto Press.

Irving, T. (n.d.) Early views of industrial democracy: Australia, 1914–1921. Worksite: Issues in Workplace Relations, http://worksite.econ.usyd.edu.au/early_views.html

Latour, B. (1993) *We Have Never Been Modern.* Cambridge, MA: Harvard University Press.

Levi, G. (1991) On microhistory, in P. Burke (ed.), *New Perspectives on Historical Writing* (pp. 93–113). Cambridge: Polity Press.

Magnússon S. G. and Szijártó, I. M. (2013) *What is Microhistory? Theory and Methods.* London: Routledge.

Mayo, E. (1922) Industrial unrest and nervous breakdowns, *Industrial Australian and Mining Standard*, 67: 63–64.

Mayo, E. (1933) *The Human Problems of an Industrial Civilization.* Cambridge, MA: Harvard University Press.

Morgan, G. (1985) *Images of Organizations.* Thousand Oaks, CA: Sage.

Munslow, A. (2006a) *Deconstructing History.* London: Routledge.

Munslow, A. (2006b). *The Routledge Companion to Historical Studies* (2nd edn). London and New York: Routledge.

Phillips, N. and Brown, J. (1993) Analyzing communication in and around organizations: A critical hermeneutic approach, *Academy of Management Journal*, 36(6): 1547–76.

Prasad, A. and Mir, R. (2002) Digging deep for meaning: A critical hermeneutic analysis of CEO letters to shareholders in the oil industry, *Journal of Business Communication*, 39(1): 92–116.

Syllabus of the Workers' School of Social Science, Brisbane Trades Hall, August 1919, in Merrifield Collection, State Library of Victoria, box 65; *Daily Standard*, 18 September 1919.

Wallerstein, I. (1974) *The Modern World-System, vol. I: Capitalist Agriculture and the Origins of the European World-Economy in the Sixteenth Century*. New York: Atlantic Press.
Weber, M. (1978) *Economy and Society*. Berkeley, CA: University of California Press.
Weick, K. E. (1995) *Sensemaking*. Thousand Oaks, CA: Sage.
Witherby, T. C. (1919) *Who Shall Control Industry?* Workers' Educational Association, Queensland.

Index